THE ECONOMICS OF GROWTH

THE ECONOMICS OF GROWTH

Philippe Aghion and Peter Howitt

with the collaboration of Leonardo Bursztyn

The MIT Press
Cambridge, Massachusetts
London, England

This book was set in Times Roman by SNP Best-set Typesetter Ltd., Hong Kong.

Library of Congress Cataloging-in-Publication Data

Aghion, Philippe.
The economics of growth / Philippe Aghion and Peter W. Howitt.
    p. cm.
Includes bibliographical references and index.
ISBN 978-0-262-01263-8 (hardcover : alk. paper), 978-0-262-55310-0 (pb)
1. Economic development.   I. Howitt, Peter.   II. Title.
HD82.A5452 2009
338.9—dc22
                                            2008029818

A Mikhaela et Edouard
        —Philippe Aghion

To Suzanne, Paul, and Katherine
        —Peter Howitt

Contents

Preface

Why This Book?

To learn about economic growth you need formal theory, for organizing the facts, clarifying causal relationships, and drawing out hidden implications. In growth economics, as in other areas of economics, an argument that is not disciplined by a clear theoretical framework is rarely enlightening.

Our experience with graduates and undergraduates at Brown and Harvard has taught us, however, that the theory needed to understand the substantive issues of economic growth is much simpler than what is found in most modern textbooks. You do not need to master all the subtleties of dynamic programming and stochastic processes in order to learn what is essential about such issues as cross-country convergence, the effects of financial development on growth, and the consequences of globalization. The required tools can be acquired quickly by anyone equipped with elementary calculus and probability theory.

These considerations are what motivated us to write *The Economics of Growth*. We believe that what is going on at the frontiers of research on economic growth can also be made accessible to undergraduates, as well as to policy makers who have not been to graduate school for many years, even though gaining this access requires learning some basic tools and models. Although there are many other excellent books on growth economics,[1] those that focus on theory are either too removed from policy and empirical applications or too involved with formal technicalities to be useful or interesting to the uninitiated reader wanting to learn about the substantive issues, while other books that focus on substantive issues are not as concerned with formal models as is necessary. None of them present the main facts and puzzles, propose simple tools and models to explain these facts, acquaint the reader with frontier material on growth—both theoretical and empirical— or initiate the reader into thinking about growth policy. What follows is our attempt to fill this gap.

To bring the reader up to date on the frontiers of the subject, we have had to write a comprehensive book. In the first part we introduce all the major growth paradigms (neoclassical, AK, product-variety, and Schumpeterian), and then in subsequent chapters we show how these paradigms can be used to analyze various aspects of the growth process and to think about the design of growth policy. The

---

1. For example, Weil (2008), C. Jones (1998), Barro and Sala-i-Martin (1995a), Helpman (2004), and Acemoglu (2008a, forthcoming). Modesty does not prevent us from also including Aghion and Howitt (1998a).

book is also comprehensive in its account of the most recent contributions and debates on growth: in particular, we acquaint the reader with the literature on directed technical change and its applications to wage inequality; we provide simple presentations of recent models of industrialization and the transition to modern economic growth; we show simple models of trade, competition, and growth with firm heterogeneity; we analyze the relationships between growth and finance, between growth, volatility and risk, between growth and the environment, and between growth and education; we reflect on the recent debates on institutions versus human capital as determinants of growth; and we introduce the reader to the nascent literature on growth and culture.

Although comprehensive, the book does not provide an unbiased survey of all points of view. On the contrary, it is opinionated in at least two respects. First, in order to keep the book from getting too big, we had to be selective in the material covered on each topic. At the end of each chapter, however, we include literature notes that provide the reader with extensive references on the subject and, in particular, direct her to the corresponding chapter(s) in the *Handbook of Economic Growth* (Aghion and Durlauf 2005), the most recent compendium of research on economic growth. Second, even though we repeatedly use the AK or product-variety models in the text or in problem sets, we do not hide our preference for the Schumpeterian model, which we use more systematically than the others when analyzing the growth process and when discussing the design of growth policy.

For Whom?

The book is aimed at three main audiences. The first is graduate students. The book can be taught in its entirety in a one-semester graduate growth course. It can also be used as part of a growth and development sequence, in which case one can start with the first four chapters, then move on to the chapters on finance (and wealth inequality), convergence, directed technical change (and appropriate technologies), stages of growth, institutions, democracy, and education, and the concluding chapter (on culture and development). The book can also be used for topics courses—for example, in trade or in industrial organization (with the general-purpose technologies, competition, and trade chapters) or in labor economics (with the chapters on directed technical change and general-purpose technologies that analyze the issue of wage inequality, and of course the chapter on education). In each case, the book provides the graduate student with easy access to frontier material, and hopefully it should spur many new research ideas.

The second target group is intermediate or advanced undergraduate students. In particular, the first four chapters of the book have been conceived so as to make the basic growth paradigms fully accessible to students who have no more background than elementary notions of calculus (derivatives, maximization) and a very basic knowledge of economic principles. One can then complete the undergraduate course or sequence by using some of the other chapters of the book—for example, the chapters on stages of growth, finance, convergence, institutions, education, and volatility. The more advanced material, which can be skipped at the undergraduate level, is put in starred sections and problems. (Problems with two stars are the most difficult.)

The third audience is that of professional economists in government or in international financial institutions who are involved in advising governments on growth and development policies. With parsimonious use of models and equations, the book provides them with the basic paradigms (part I), and also with the tools (chapters 11–18), to think about the design of growth policy.

More generally, this book can be used by any reader with a basic mathematical background who is interested in learning about the mechanics of growth and development.

Outline of the Book

The book comprises three parts. Part I presents the main growth paradigms: the neoclassical model (chapter 1), the AK model (chapter 2), Romer's product-variety model (chapter 3), and the Schumpeterian model (chapter 4). Chapter 5 concludes part I by introducing physical capital into a growth model with endogenous innovation, in order to provide a theoretical framework for interpreting the results of growth accounting.

Part II builds on the main paradigms to shed light on the dynamic process of growth and development. Chapter 6 analyzes the relationship between financial constraints, innovation, and growth, and then the relationship between financial constraints, wealth inequality, and growth. Chapter 7 analyzes the phenomenon of "club convergence," in other words, why some countries manage to converge to growth rates of the most advanced countries whereas other countries continue to fall further behind. Chapter 8 introduces the notion of directed technical change and uses it to analyze wage inequality or to explain persistent productivity differences across countries. Chapter 9 introduces the notion of general-purpose technology and explains why new technological revolutions can produce both temporary slowdowns and accelerating wage inequality. Chapter 10 analyzes how an economy can evolve from a stagnant Malthusian agricultural economy into a persistently growing industrial economy, or from an economy that accumulates capital to an innovating economy, or from a manufacturing to a service economy. Chapter 11 discusses the role of institutions in the growth process, and introduces the notion of appropriate growth institutions to understand why different institutions or policies can be growth enhancing in countries at different levels of development.

Part III focuses on growth policies. Chapter 12 analyzes the growth effects of liberalizing product market competition and entry. Chapter 13 analyzes the growth effects of education policy. Chapter 14 focuses on the relationship between risk, financial development, and growth. Chapter 15 discusses the effects of trade liberalization. Chapter 16 analyzes how growth can be sustained in an economy with environmental or resource constraints. And Chapter 17 investigates the relationship between democracy and growth.

Chapter 18 concludes the book by summarizing the main conclusions from previous chapters and then by linking growth to culture and to modern development economics.

Finally, the appendix acquaints the reader with basic notions of econometrics, so that without any prior knowledge this chapter should allow her to read and understand all the empirical sections and tables in the book.

Acknowledgments

We are primarily indebted to all the students and colleagues on whom we tested the material of this book until we felt we had achieved our goal of making it broadly accessible. Our students at Brown and Harvard, especially Quamrul Ashraf, Leonardo Bursztyn, Filipe Campante, Alberto Cavallo, Azam Chaudhry, Quo-Hanh Do, Georgy Egorov, Jim Feyrer, Phil Garner, David Hemous, Michal Jerzmanowski, Takuma Kunieda, Kalina Manova, Daniel Mejia, Erik Meyersson, Stelios Michalopoulos, Petros Milionis, Malhar Nabar, Manabu Nose, Omer Ozak, and Isabel Tecu, have taught us at least as much as we have taught them.

We are also grateful for feedback from those individuals who attended our lectures at University College London, the Stockholm School of Economics, the University of Zurich, the University of Bonn, the University of Munich, the University of Kiel, the Paris School of Economics, the New Economic School in Moscow, the Di Tella University in Buenos Aires, the CEPII in Paris, Javeriana University in Bogota, the 2001 NAKE Workshop at the Vrije Universiteit Amsterdam and the 2005 NAKE School at the University of Maastricht, Wuhan University, and the IMF Institute.

Our simple reformulations of the main growth paradigms owe a lot to joint modeling efforts with Daron Acemoglu, Marios Angeletos, Philippe Bacchetta, Abhijit Banerjee, David Mayer-Foulkes, Gianluca Violante and Fabrizio Zilibotti. Our concern for matching growth theories with data and empirics grew out of a long-standing collaboration with our colleagues Richard Blundell and Rachel Griffith from the London Institute of Fiscal Studies, and also from joint work with Alberto Alesina, Yann Algan, Nick Bloom, Robin Burgess, Pierre Cahuc, Diego Comin, Gilbert Cette, Thibault Fally, Johannes Fedderke, Joonkyung Ha, Caroline Hoxby, Enisse Kharroubi, Kalina Manova, Ioana Marinescu, Costas Meghir, Susanne Prantl, Romain Ranciere, Steven Redding, Stefano Scarpetta, Andrei Shleifer, Francesco Trebbi, Jerome Vandenbussche, and John Van Reenen. We have benefited over the years from numerous discussions on various aspects of growth theory with our colleagues Pol Antras, Costas Azariadis, Robert Barro, Flora Bellone, Roland Benabou, Francesco Caselli, Guido Cozzi, Elias Dinopoulos, Esther Duflo, Steve Durlauf, Oded Galor, Gene Grossman, Elhanan Helpman, Wolfgang Keller, Tom Krebs, Chris Laincz, Ross Levine, Robert Lipsey, Greg Mankiw, Borghan Narajabad, Pietro Peretto, Thomas Piketty, Francesco Ricci, Paul Segerstrom, Andrei Shleifer, Enrico Spolaore, David Weil, Martin Weitzman, Jeff Williamson, Marios Zachariadis, and Luigi Zingales. Finally, our views on growth policy design have been greatly influenced over the past years by discussions and collaborations with Erik Berglof, Elie Cohen, Mathias Dewatripont,

Steven Durlauf, William Easterly, Ricardo Hausmann, Martin Hellwig, Andreu Mas-Colell, Jean Pisani-Ferry, Ken Rogoff, Dani Rodrik, Andre Sapir, Nicholas Stern, and Federico Sturzenegger.

We have greatly benefited from our association with the Institutions, Organization and Growth (IOG) Group at the Canadian Institute for Advanced Research. There, we particularly benefited from continuous feedback from Elhanan Helpman, George Akerlof, Tim Besley, Daniel Diermayer, James Fearon, Patrick Francois, Joel Mokyr, Roger Myerson, Torsten Persson, Joanne Roberts, Jim Robinson, Ken Shepsle, Guido Tabellini, and Dan Trefler.

The encouragement and support of Daron Acemoglu, Kenneth Arrow, Robert Barro, Olivier Blanchard, Oliver Hart, Martin Hellwig, Edmund Phelps, Mark Schankerman, Robert Solow, Jean Tirole, and Fabrizio Zilibotti over the years have been invaluable to us.

The book would never have been completed on time without the active collaboration of graduate students at Harvard. Here our biggest debt is to Leonardo Bursztyn, who worked with us on the literature reviews, provided the background notes for the econometric appendix, collaborated with us on the environment chapter, produced all the figures, proofread the material, and coordinated the team that produced the problem sets and solutions. In this endeavor, Leonardo worked with David Hemous, Dorothée Rouzet, Thomas Sampson, and Ruchir Agarwal.

We owe special thanks to John Covell from MIT Press, who managed the tour de force of getting the book to be ready on time in spite of initial delays in delivering the manuscript, and provided us with all the support we needed along the way to completion. In particular, Nancy Lombardi did an outstanding job in supervising the copyediting of the manuscript and then handling the page proofs until the book was ready to print.

Sarah Chaillet did us an immeasurable favor by offering one of her paintings for the book cover.

Philippe Aghion is infinitely thankful to Benedicte Berner whose sense of humor, "joie de vivre," and continuous faith in this project have been so essential for its completion.

Peter Howitt's biggest debt is to Pat Howitt for the loving support, lively spirit, and uncommonly good sense that contributed more than words can describe.

Introduction

I.1   Why Study Economic Growth?

Economic growth is commonly measured as the annual rate of increase in a country's gross domestic product (GDP). Why should anyone care about this dry statistic instead of focusing on more specific welfare, consumption, or happiness indicators? Perhaps the most compelling reason is that economic growth is what mainly determines the material well-being of billions of people. In economically advanced countries, economic growth since the Industrial Revolution has allowed almost the entire population to live in a style that only a privileged handful could have afforded a hundred years ago, when per capita GDP was a small fraction of what it is today. Indeed, growth in some sectors of the economy, especially the medical and pharmaceutical sectors, has allowed almost everyone to live a longer and healthier life than could have been expected by anyone in the 19th century, no matter what position a person held on the economic ladder. In contrast, the lack of economic growth in the poorest countries of the world has meant that living conditions for hundreds of millions of people are appalling by the standards of rich countries; per capita income levels in many 21st-century countries are much lower than they were in 19th-century Europe. To understand why the human race has become so much wealthier and why our wealth is shared so inequitably among the inhabitants of the world, we need to understand what drives economic growth.

I.2   Some Facts and Puzzles

Our first goal is to provide the reader with analytical tools to understand the growth process. The basic theoretical paradigms are laid out in part I. Then part II analyzes various facts and puzzles raised by world growth history. The following subsections present some examples of these facts and puzzles.

I.2.1   Growth and Poverty Reduction

A number of economists argue that growth is the best way to achieve massive reduction in poverty. For example, table I.1 summarizes a study by Deaton and Dreze (2002), showing a substantial reduction in the fraction of Indian population below the poverty line. The reduction is particularly important for urban areas (from 39.1% in 1987–88 to 24.1% in 1999–2000).

At the same time, table I.2 from Rodrik and Subramanian (2004) shows a marked acceleration in GDP growth between the 1970s and the 20 years that

Table I.1
Poverty Reduction in India Headcount Ratios (Percentage)

	Official Methodology			Adjusted Estimates		
	1987–88	1993–94	1999–2000	1987–88	1993–94	1999–2000
Rural	39.4	37.1	26.9	39	33	26.3
Urban	39.1	32.9	24.1	22.5	17.8	12

Official: Consumption data from Planning Commission Sample Survey
Adjusted: Consumption data from improved comparability and price indices

Table I.2
India in Cross Section: Mean of Growth Rate of Output per Worker, 1970–2000

	1970–80	1980–90	1990–2000
Mean of growth rate	0.77	3.91	3.22

followed. What caused growth to accelerate in India in the 1980s? Was the cause a favorable external environment, fiscal stimulus, trade liberalization, internal liberalization, the Green Revolution, public investment, or, as Rodrik and Subramanian argue, an attitudinal shift on the part of the national government toward a probusiness approach? A definitive answer to this question would be invaluable to many other countries desperate to grow their way out of poverty.

I.2.2   Convergence

Figure I.1 shows how the average growth rate of countries over the period 1960–2000 (on the vertical axis) varies with the country's proximity to the world productivity frontier (on the horizontal axis). The measure of proximity is simply the country's productivity at the beginning of the period (in 1960) divided by U.S. productivity also in 1960. We see that more advanced countries tend to grow more slowly. What explains this "convergence" phenomenon? Is it the fact that rich countries have high levels of physical and human capital per person and hence are running into diminishing returns to the accumulation of more capital? Is it the fact that poor countries can catch up to rich ones technologically by making use of inventions that have taken place in the rest of the world?

Another interesting fact about convergence is that although there is a general tendency for countries to grow faster when they are further below the world productivity frontier, the very poorest of countries tend to grow more slowly than

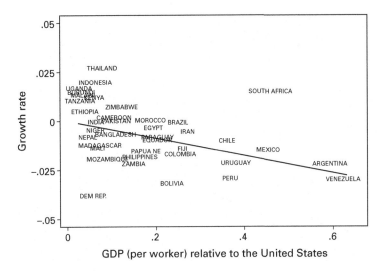

Figure I.1
Cross-country convergence

the rest. So, instead of converging, these very poor countries as a group seem to be diverging. In other words, it seems that economic growth is characterized by "club convergence." The rich and middle income countries in the "club" tend to grow faster the further behind they fall, while the poor countries that are not members just keep falling further behind. Quah (1996, 1997) has shown that the world distribution of per capita income is becoming more and more "twin peaked," with most countries lying at the top and the bottom levels of income. What explains this pattern?

In particular, one of the most dramatic changes of the 20th century was the revival of economic growth in many formerly poor Asian countries, which appear to have joined the convergence club during the final decades of the century. From the 1960s until now, countries like South Korea, China, and India have grown much faster than the rest of the world, and they are continuing to close the gap in per capita income that separates them from the richest countries of the world. What accounts for their success?

Why have other poor countries not also joined the convergence club? Is this due to poor geographical conditions? Or to the absence of institutions to protect private investments and entrepreneurship? Or to the inability of poor countries to attract credit, diversify risk, or finance infrastructure? Or to insufficient human capital?

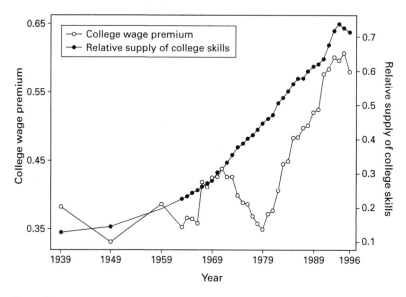

Figure I.2
Relative supply of college skills and college premium

I.2.3   Growth and Inequality

What is the relationship between growth and inequality? The fact that per capita income is growing more rapidly in very rich countries than in very poor countries implies that inequality at the national level is increasing as growth takes place. But Sala-i-Martin (2006) argues that the last decades of the 20th century actually witnessed a reduction in world income inequality at the individual level, because there are so many individuals in countries like India and China whose incomes are catching up to the world average. Does this mean that growth necessarily reduces inequality? Or does reduced inequality reduce growth? Or does the relationship between growth and inequality change over time, as suggested by the famous "Kuznets curve"? (Kuznets argued that as countries begin to industrialize, inequality tends to rise, but that during a later phase of growth the income distribution begins to compress.)

In fact the Kuznets curve remained the common wisdom on growth and inequality up until the closing decades of the 20th century. But then the economic profession changed its mind, based on the fact that in many advanced countries, especially the United States and the United Kingdom, wages of skilled workers rose much more rapidly than less skilled wages. More specifically, figure I.2 shows that the college wage premium, equal to the ratio of the average wage of college graduates to the average wage of high school graduates, and depicted by the curve with fewer dots, has been sharply increasing since 1980.

Surprisingly, figure I.2 also shows that the relative supply of skilled labor, equal to the ratio between the number of college graduates and the total labor force, and depicted by the curve connecting the dark dots, was also increasing, more rapidly so since 1970. What is surprising is that, at first sight, an increase in the relative supply of skilled labor should lead to a reduction in the wage premium as skilled labor becomes relatively less scarce. How can we reconcile these two facts? How can we explain that during that period, there was also an increase in "residual" wage inequality—that is, inequality within groups of people having the same measurable characteristics (education, experience, gender, occupation, etc.)? Was this a by-product of globalization, with wages of low-skilled people being depressed by competition from low-wage countries that were beginning to export to the rich countries? Was it the result of changing labor-market laws and regulations? Or did it result from skill-biased technical change, which enhances the productivity of highly skilled workers while automating the jobs of the less skilled? And if it was skill-biased technical change, where does the bias come from?

I.2.4   The Transition from Stagnation to Growth

Growth is a recent phenomenon: it took off very rapidly in the United Kingdom and then in France toward the mid-1800s. During most of human history, economic growth took place at a glacial pace. According to Maddison's (2001) estimates, per capita GDP in the world economy was no higher in 1000 than in year 1, and only 53 percent higher in 1820 than in 1000, implying an average growth rate of only 1/19th percent over those 820 years. But then growth increased up to 0.5 percent from 1820 to 1870, and it kept increasing to achieve a peak rate of nearly 3 percent from 1950 to 1973. Was the earlier period of stagnation the result of Malthusian pressure of population on limited natural resources, or was it something else? And why did growth suddenly take off in the 19th century? More generally, how can we explain other transitions such as the transition from agriculture to manufacturing, and then from manufacturing to services, or from industrial economies that accumulate capital to economies in which growth relies primarily on innovation?

I.2.5   Finance and Growth

Figure I.3, based on Rajan and Zingales (1998), uses cross-country comparisons to show that industry growth is positively correlated with financial development (for example, measured by the ratio between the total flow of credit to the private

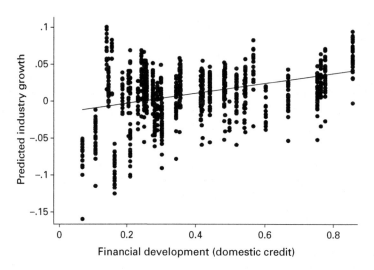

Figure I.3
Industry growth and financial development

sector in a country in a given year, divided by the country's GDP that year). Is finance a cause of growth or just a symptom? That is, does financial development allow a country to grow faster, or is it just that countries that grow fast also happen to use a lot of finance? Of course this question matters a lot because if finance causes growth, then a country wanting to grow faster should maybe reform its financial institutions, whereas if finance is just a symptom, then financial reform will provide the trappings of growth without the growth. At the same time, if finance does cause growth, then just how does that relationship work? Is finance an important determinant of cross-country convergence or divergence? How does finance interact with other policies, in particular macroeconomic policies aimed at stabilizing the business cycle? How can we explain that capital does not flow from rich to poor countries, as stressed by Lucas (1990)?

I.3   Growth Policies

The second purpose of this book is to equip the reader with paradigms and empirical methods to think about growth policy design, which we do in part III. Various countries and regions have recently tried to come up with adequate "growth diagnostics," that is, with analyses of the most binding constraints to growth and of how to define the appropriate set and sequence of growth-enhancing reforms.

I.3.1   Competition and Entry

Innovation is a vital source of long-run growth, and the reward for innovation is monopoly profit, which comes from being able to do something that your rivals haven't yet been able to match. Economists since Schumpeter have argued that this analysis implies a trade-off between growth and competition. Tighter anti-trust legislation would reduce the scope for earning monopoly profits, which would lower the reward to innovation, which should reduce the flow of innovation and hence reduce the long-run growth rate.

It is not easy, however, to find convincing evidence of this Schum-peterian trade-off. Indeed, historians and econometricians have produced evidence to the contrary—evidence that more competitive societies and industries tend to grow faster than their less competitive counterparts. More recent evidence points to an inverted-U-shaped relationship between growth and competition, as shown in figure I.4. Figure I.4 shows how innovation

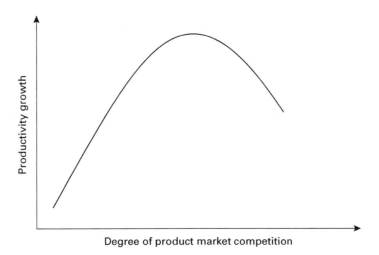

Figure I.4
Innovation and product market competition

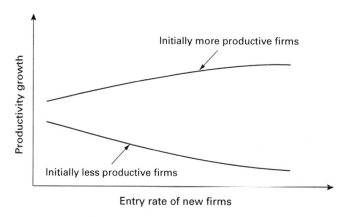

Figure I.5
Entry and total-factor-productivity growth

(measured by the flow of new patents) or productivity growth on the vertical axis varies with the degree of product market competition on the horizontal axis (where competition is inversely measured by the ratio of firm rents to value added or to the asset value of the firm). How can we explain this inverted-U pattern? Why does the Schumpeterian trade-off appear only at high levels of competition?

Figure I.5 depicts how firm-level productivity growth (on the vertical axis) reacts to an increase in the rate of new firm entry in the firm's sector (horizontal axis). The upper line depicts the average reaction of firms that are initially more productive than the median firm in the sector. The lower line represents the reaction of firms that are less productive than the median. How can we explain that the more advanced firms react positively to a more intense competition by new entrants, whereas less advanced firms react negatively? What policy implications can we derive from this observation?

I.3.2 Education and Distance to Frontier

Figure I.6 shows how growth depends upon a country's proximity to the world frontier productivity, respectively, for countries that invest mostly in primary and secondary education (upper graph) and for countries that invest more in tertiary

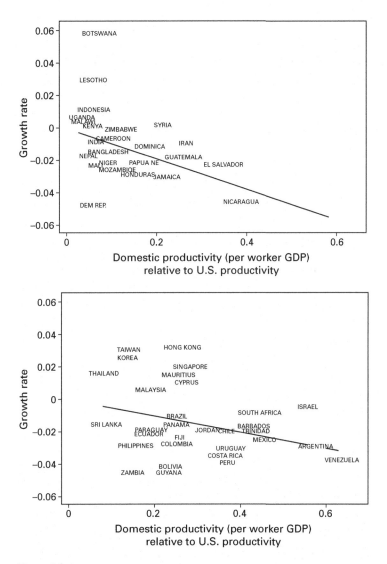

Figure I.6
Growth and level of development for low and high education countries. Upper graph, low education countries; lower graph, high education countries

education (lower graph). Comparing the two graphs, we see that countries that are close to frontier productivity and invest more in tertiary education (these are the countries to the right of the lower graph) do significantly better than countries that are close to the frontier and invest less in tertiary education (these are the countries to the right of the upper graph). However, investing in tertiary education does not make much of a difference for countries that are far from the world productivity frontier (growth rates are comparable for countries to the left of the upper graph, and for countries to the left of the lower graph).

Why is higher education more growth enhancing for countries (or regions) that are more developed? More generally, is education so important for growth, and how should countries organize their education systems in order to maximize growth?

I.3.3   Macroeconomic Policy and Growth

Figure I.7 shows how macro policies in the United States and the euro area react to booms and recessions. Short-term interest rates are depicted on the vertical axes, whereas the structural deficit is depicted on the horizontal axes. We see that the United States reduces its interest rates and increases budget deficits a lot during recessions, whereas the euro area barely changes these two variables over the business cycle. Macroeconomic textbooks usually disconnect the analysis of budgetary and monetary policy from the analysis of growth. Are they justified in doing so, and if not why not? More generally, what underpins the relationship between macroeconomic volatility and risk on the one hand, and innovation and growth on the other hand?

I.3.4   Trade and Growth

All the Asian countries that joined the convergence club in the last decades of the 20th century followed export-oriented trade policies, while many of the Latin American countries that experienced a collapse of economic growth in the middle of the century promoted restrictive trade policies favoring import substitution. We also mentioned the example of India where growth accelerated since the 1990s following trade liberalization reforms. Does this mean that trade liberalization is always good for growth?

Recent studies also show that growth benefits less from openness in bigger countries than in smaller ones. How can we explain this fact? Other studies suggest that growth in more advanced countries or sectors benefits unambiguously from more trade openness, in a way that parallels the effect of entry. Can trade liberalization ever be detrimental to growth in laggard countries or sectors?

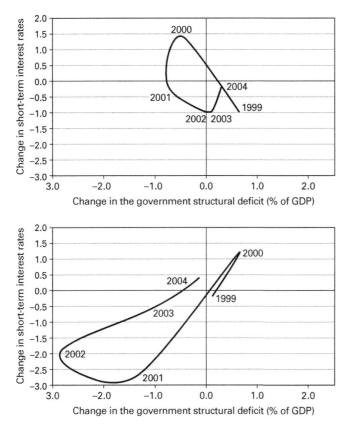

Figure I.7
Macropolicy reactions to booms and recessions in the Euro area and the United States

What are the main channels whereby trade may enhance growth and innovation? What do data tell us about the relative importance of these channels? How should trade reforms be implemented in countries that differ in size or in their levels of development?

I.3.5   Democracy and Growth

Figure I.8 considers the period 1960–2000 subdivided in five-year subperiods. It then depicts, for each subperiod, industry growth (measured on the vertical axis by the five-year average growth rate) as a function of the country's proximity to the world frontier (measured on the horizontal axis by the ratio of the country's level of per capita GDP to U.S. per capita GDP at the beginning of the five-year

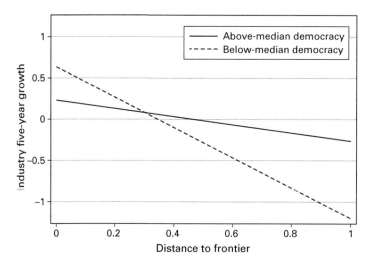

Figure I.8
Industry growth and distance to frontier (below- and above-median-democracy countries)

period). We see that industry growth is less negatively correlated with proximity to the frontier for more democratic countries (the continuous line) than for nondemocratic countries (the broken line). In other words, being nondemocratic appears to be more detrimental to growth in more advanced countries. Does this result reflect a positive effect of democracy on growth in more advanced countries? And if it does, what underlies this positive effect? And does this mean that countries will always end up becoming democratic once they reach a high level of development?

I.4   Four Growth Paradigms

To explain the preceding facts and puzzles, we shall build upon four leading growth paradigms, which we detail in part I of the book.

I.4.1   The Neoclassical Growth Model

The primary reference in growth economics is the neoclassical paradigm. The success of this model owes first to its parsimony; the growth process is described by only two equations: (1) a production equation that expresses the current flow of output goods as a function of the current stocks of capital and labor:

$$Y = AK^\alpha L^{1-\alpha}$$

where A is a productivity parameter and where $\alpha < 1$ so that production involves decreasing returns to capital, and (2) a law of motion that shows how capital accumulation depends on investment (equal to aggregate savings) and capital depreciation:

$$\dot{K} = sY - \delta K$$

where sY denotes aggregate savings and δK denotes aggregate depreciation of capital.

What also makes this model the benchmark for growth analysis is, paradoxically, its implication that, in the long run, economic growth does not depend on economic conditions. In particular, economic policy cannot affect a country's long-run growth rate. Specifically, per capita GDP Y/L cannot grow in the long run unless we assume that productivity A also grows over time, which Solow (1956) refers to as "technical progress." As we will see in chapter 1, the problem is that in this neoclassical model, technical progress cannot be explained or even rationalized. To analyze policies for growth, one needs a theoretical framework in which productivity growth is endogenous, that is, dependent upon characteristics of the economic environment. That framework must account for long-term technological progress and productivity growth, without which decreasing returns to capital and labor would eventually choke off all growth.

I.4.2   The AK Model

The first version of endogenous growth theory is the so-called AK theory. AK models do not make an explicit distinction between capital accumulation and technological progress. In effect they just lump together the physical and human capital whose accumulation is studied by neoclassical theory with the intellectual capital that is accumulated when technological progress is made. When this aggregate of different kinds of capital is accumulated, there is no reason to think that diminishing returns will drag its marginal product down to zero, because part of that accumulation is the very technological progress needed to counteract diminishing returns. According to the AK paradigm, the way to sustain high growth rates is to save a large fraction of GDP, some of which will find its way into financing a higher rate of technological progress and will thus result in faster growth.

Formally, the AK model is the neoclassical model without diminishing returns. The theory starts with an aggregate production function that is linear homogeneous in the stock of capital:

$$Y = AK$$

with A a constant. If capital accumulates according to the same equation

$$\dot{K} = sY - \delta K$$

as before, then the economy's long-run (and short-run) growth rate is simply

$$g = \frac{\dot{K}}{K} = sA - \delta$$

which is increasing in the saving rate s.

AK theory presents a "one-size-fits-all" view of the growth process. It applies equally to advanced countries that have already accumulated capital and to countries that are far behind. Like the neoclassical model, it postulates a growth process that is independent of developments in the rest of the world, except insofar as international trade changes the conditions for capital accumulation. Yet it is a useful tool for many purposes when the distinction between innovation and accumulation is of secondary importance.

We present the AK model in chapter 2, where we show how it can be used to analyze terms-of-trade effects in the context of an open economy. In later chapters we use the model when analyzing the transition from a Malthusian economy to an economy with positive long-run growth, when analyzing the relationship between financial constraints, wealth inequality and growth, when discussing the relationship between volatility, risk, and growth, and when looking at the interplay between growth and culture.

I.4.3 The Product-Variety Model

The second wave of endogenous growth theory consists of "innovation-based" growth models, which themselves belong to two parallel branches. One branch is the product-variety model of Romer (1990), in which innovation causes productivity growth by creating new, but not necessarily improved, varieties of products. This paradigm grew out of the new theory of international trade and emphasizes the role of technology spillovers.

It starts from a Dixit and Stiglitz (1977) production function of the form

$$Y_t = \sum_0^{N_t} K_{it}^{\alpha} di$$

in which there are N_t different varieties of intermediate product, each produced using K_{it} units of capital. By symmetry, the aggregate capital stock K_t will be divided up evenly among the N_t existing varieties, with the result that we can reexpress the production function as

$$Y_t = N_t^{1-\alpha} K_t^{\alpha}$$

According to this function, the degree of product variety N_t is the economy's aggregate productivity parameter, and its growth rate is the economy's long-run growth rate of per capita output. More product variety raises the economy's production potential because it allows a given capital stock to be spread over a larger number of uses, each of which exhibits diminishing returns. Thus, increased product variety is what sustains growth in this mode. New varieties, that is, new innovations, themselves result from R&D investments by researchers–entrepreneurs who are motivated by the prospect of (perpetual) monopoly rents if they successfully innovate.

Note that here there is just one kind of innovation, which always results in the same kind of new product.

Also, this model predicts no important role for exit and turnover; indeed, increased exit can do nothing but reduce the economy's GDP, by reducing the variety variable N_t that uniquely determines aggregate productivity. Thus there is no role for "creative destruction," the driving force in the Schumpeterian growth paradigm.

Yet the product-variety model, which we present in chapter 3, can be used in various contexts where competition and turnover considerations are not so important. For example, we use it when analyzing the source of persistent productivity differences across countries in chapter 8, or when analyzing the relationship between risk, diversification, and growth in chapter 14.

I.4.4   The Schumpeterian Model

The fourth and final paradigm[1] is the other branch of innovation-based theory, developed in Aghion and Howitt (1992)[2] and subsequently elaborated in Aghion and Howitt (1998a). This paradigm grew out of modern industrial organization theory and is commonly referred to as *Schumpeterian* growth theory because it focuses on quality-improving innovations that render old products obsolete and

---

1. The semiendogenous model of Jones (1995b), in which long-run economic growth depends uniquely on the rate of population growth, might be thought of as a fourth paradigm. However, this model has little to say about growth policy, since it predicts that long-run growth is independent of any policy that does not affect population growth.

2. An early attempt at providing a Schumpeterian approach to endogenous growth theory was by Segerstrom, Anant, and Dinopoulos (1990).

hence involves the force that Schumpeter called *creative destruction*. We present it in chapter 4 and then use it and extend it in the subsequent chapters of the book.

Schumpeterian theory begins with a production function specified at the industry level:

$$Y_{it} = A_{it}^{1-\alpha} K_{it}^{\alpha}, \quad 0 < \alpha < 1$$

where A_{it} is a productivity parameter attached to the most recent technology used in industry i at time t. In this equation, K_{it} represents the flow of a unique intermediate product used in this sector, each unit of which is produced one-for-one by final output or, in the most complete version of the model, by capital. Aggregate output is just the sum of the industry-specific outputs Y_{it}.

Each intermediate product is produced and sold exclusively by the most recent innovator. A successful innovator in sector i improves the technology parameter A_{it} and is thus able to displace the previous product in that sector, until it is displaced in turn by the next innovator. Thus a first implication of the Schumpeterian paradigm is that *faster growth generally implies a higher rate of firm turnover, because this process of creative destruction generates entry of new innovators and exit of former innovators.*

Although the theory focuses on individual industries and explicitly analyzes the microeconomics of industrial competition, the assumption that all industries are ex ante identical gives it a simple aggregate structure. In particular, it is easily shown that aggregate output depends on the aggregate capital stock K_t according to the Cobb-Douglas aggregate per-worker production function:

$$Y_t = A_t^{1-\alpha} K_t^{\alpha}$$

where the labor-augmenting productivity factor A_t is just the unweighted sum of the sector-specific A_{it}'s. As in neoclassical theory, the economy's long-run growth rate is given by the growth rate of A_t, which here depends endogenously on the economy-wide rate of innovation.

There are two main inputs to innovation, namely, the private expenditures made by the prospective innovator and the stock of innovations that have already been made by past innovators. The latter input constitutes the publicly available stock of knowledge to which current innovators are hoping to add. The theory is flexible in modeling the contribution of past innovations. It encompasses the case of an innovation that leapfrogs the best technology available before the innovation, resulting in a new technology parameter A_{it} in the innovating sector i, which is some multiple γ of its preexisting value. And it also encompasses the case of an innovation that catches up to a global technology frontier $\overline{A}_t$, which we typically take to represent the stock of global technological knowledge available to innovators in all sectors of all countries. In the former case the country is making a leading-edge innovation that builds on and improves the leading-edge technology in its industry. In the latter case the innovation is just implementing (or imitating) technologies that have been developed elsewhere.

For example, consider a country in which in any sector leading-edge innovations take place at the frequency μ_n and implementation innovations (or imitations) take place at the frequency μ_m. Then the change in the economy's aggregate productivity parameter A_t will be

$$A_{t+1} - A_t = \mu_n \left(\gamma - 1 \right) A_t + \mu_m \left(\overline{A}_t - A_t \right)$$

and hence the growth rate will be

$$g_t = \frac{A_{t+1} - A_t}{A_t} = \mu_n \left(\gamma - 1 \right) + \mu_m \left(a_t^{-1} - 1 \right) \tag{I.1}$$

where

$$a_t = A_t / \overline{A}_t$$

is an inverse measure of "distance to the frontier."

Thus, by taking into account that innovations can interact with each other in different ways in different countries, Schumpeterian theory provides a framework in which the growth effects of various policies are highly context-dependent. In particular, the Schumpeterian apparatus is well suited to analyze *how a country's growth performance will vary with its proximity to the technological frontier a_t, to what extent the country will tend to converge to that frontier, and what kinds of policy changes are needed to sustain convergence as the country approaches the frontier.*

We could take as given the critical innovation frequencies μ_m and μ_n that determine a country's growth path as given, just as neoclassical theory often takes the critical saving rate s as given. However, Schumpeterian theory derives these innovation frequencies endogenously from the profit-maximization problem facing a prospective innovator, just as the Ramsey model endogenizes s by deriving it from household utility maximization. This maximization problem and its solution will typically depend upon institutional characteristics of the economy such as property right protection, the financial system, . . . and also upon government policy; moreover, the equilibrium intensity and mix of innovation will often depend upon institutions and policies in a way that varies with the country's distance to the technological frontier a.

Equation (I.1) incorporates Gerschenkron's (1962) "advantage of backwardness," in the sense that the further the country is behind the global technology frontier (i.e., the smaller is a_t) the faster it will grow, given the frequency of implementation innovations. As in Gerschenkron's analysis, the advantage arises from the fact that implementation innovations allow the country to make larger quality improvements the further it has fallen behind the frontier. As we shall see, this is just one of the ways in which distance to the frontier can affect a country's growth performance.

In addition, growth equations like (I.1) make it quite natural to capture Gerschenkron's idea of "appropriate institutions."[3] Suppose indeed that the institutions that favor implementation innovations (that is, that lead to firms emphasizing μ_m at the expense of μ_n) are not the same as those that favor leading-edge innovations (that is, that encourage firms to focus on μ_n): then, far from the frontier a country will maximize growth by favoring institutions that facilitate implementation; however, as it catches up with the technological frontier, to sustain a high growth rate the country will have to shift from implementation-enhancing institutions to innovation-enhancing institutions as the relative importance of μ_n for growth is also increasing. As we will see in chapter 11, failure to operate such a shift can prevent a country from catching up with the frontier level of GDP per capita.

---

3. See Acemoglu, Aghion, and Zilibotti (2006) for a formalization of this idea.

I BASIC PARADIGMS OF GROWTH THEORY

1 Neoclassical Growth Theory

1.1 Introduction

The starting point for any study of economic growth is the neoclassical growth model, which emphasizes the role of capital accumulation. This model, first constructed by Solow (1956) and Swan (1956), shows how economic policy can raise an economy's growth rate by inducing people to save more. But the model also predicts that such an increase in growth cannot last indefinitely. In the long run, the country's growth rate will revert to the rate of technological progress, which neoclassical theory takes as being independent of economic forces, or *exogenous*. Underlying this pessimistic long-run result is the principle of diminishing marginal productivity, which puts an upper limit to how much output a person can produce simply by working with more and more capital, given the state of technology.

We have a more optimistic view of the contribution that economic policy can make to long-run growth, because we believe that the rate of technological progress is determined by forces that are internal to the economic system. Specifically, technological progress depends on the process of innovation, which is one of the most important channels through which business firms compete in a market economy, and the incentive to innovate depends very much on policies with respect to competition, intellectual property, international trade, and much else. But the neoclassical model is still a useful one, because its analysis of how capital accumulation affects national income, real wages, and real interest rates for any given state of technology is just as valid when technology is endogenous as when it is exogenous. Indeed, neoclassical theory can be seen as a special case of the theory we develop in this book, the special limiting case in which the marginal productivity of efforts to innovate has fallen to zero. A good way to learn a theory is to start with a simple and instructive special case. Accordingly, this first chapter is devoted to an account of the neoclassical growth model.

1.2 The Solow-Swan Model

Consider an economy with a given supply of labor and a given state of technological knowledge, both of which we suppose initially to be constant over time. Suppose labor works with an aggregate capital stock[1] K. The maximum amount

---

1. Of course, K is an aggregate index of the different capital goods and should be interpreted broadly so as to include human as well as physical capital.

of output Y that can be produced depends on K according to an aggregate production function

$$Y = F(K)$$

We assume that all capital and labor are fully and efficiently employed, so $F(K)$ is not only what can be produced but also what will be produced.

A crucial property of the aggregate production function is that there are diminishing returns to the accumulation of capital. If you continue to equip people with more of the same capital goods without inventing new uses for the capital, then a point will be reached eventually where the extra capital goods become redundant except as spare parts in the event of multiple equipment failure, and where therefore the marginal product of capital is negligible. This idea is captured formally by assuming the marginal product of capital to be positive but strictly decreasing in the stock of capital:

$$F'(K) > 0 \quad \text{and} \quad F''(K) < 0 \quad \text{for all } K \tag{1.1}$$

and imposing the *Inada conditions*:[2]

$$\lim_{K \to \infty} F'(K) = 0 \quad \text{and} \quad \lim_{K \to 0} F'(K) = \infty \tag{1.2}$$

Because we are assuming away population growth and technological change, the only remaining force that can drive growth is capital accumulation. Output will grow if and only if the capital stock increases. Assume that people save a constant fraction s of their gross income[3] Y, and that the constant fraction δ of the capital stock disappears each year as a result of depreciation. Because the rate at which new capital accumulates equals the aggregate flow of savings[4] sY and the rate at which old capital wears out is δK. therefore the net rate of increase of the capital stock per unit of time (i.e., net investment) is

$$I = sY - \delta K \tag{1.3}$$

Assume that time is continuous. Then net investment is the derivative of K with respect to time, which we write using dot notation as $\dot{K}$. So, using the

2. The second condition in equation (1.2) is a regularity condition made for convenience. Specifically, as we will indicate, it ensures the existence of a nondegenerate stationary state in the model.

3. We are assuming no taxes, so that national income and output are identical.

4. Recall that with no taxes, no government expenditures, and no international trade, savings and investment are identical. That is, savings and investment are just two different words for the flow of income spent on investment goods rather than on consumption goods.

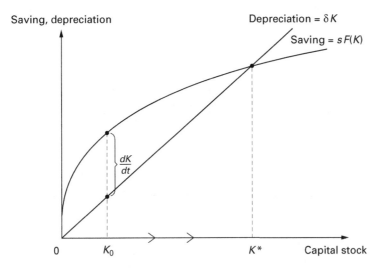

Figure 1.1

aggregate production function to substitute for Y in equation (1.3), we have

$$\dot{K} = sF(K) - \delta K \tag{1.4}$$

Equation (1.4) is the fundamental differential equation of neoclassical growth theory. It indicates how the rate of increase in the capital stock at any date is determined by the amount of capital already in existence at that date. Together with the historically given initial stock of capital, equation (1.4) determines the entire future time path of capital. The time path of output is then determined by substituting this path of capital into the aggregate production function.

Figure 1.1 shows how the fundamental equation (1.4) works. The depreciation line shows how the flow of depreciation depends on the stock of capital. It goes through the origin, with a slope equal to the depreciation rate δ. The savings curve shows how the gross flow of new investment depends on the stock of capital. Because the marginal product $F'(K)$ is positive but diminishes as K increases, therefore the savings curve has a positive but diminishing slope.

Given any stock of capital, such as K_0 in figure 1.1, the rate of increase of that stock is the vertical distance between the savings curve and the depreciation line. Thus whenever the savings curve lies above the depreciation line, as it does when $K = K_0$ in figure 1.1, the capital stock will be increasing. Moreover, it will continue to increase monotonically, and it will converge in the long run to K^*, the capital stock at which the two schedules intersect. Thus K^* is a unique, stable, stationary state of the economy.[5]

The economic logic of this dynamic analysis is straightforward. When capital is scarce it is very productive, so national income will be large in relation to the capital stock, and this fact will induce people to save more than enough to offset the wear and tear on existing capital. Thus the capital stock K will rise, and hence national income $F(K)$ will rise. But *because of diminishing marginal productivity*, national income will not grow as fast as the capital stock, with the result that savings will not grow as fast as depreciation. Eventually depreciation will catch up with savings; at that point the capital stock will stop rising, and growth in national income will therefore come to an end.

Therefore, any attempt to boost growth by encouraging people to save more will ultimately fail. An increase in the saving rate s will *temporarily* raise the rate of capital accumulation, by shifting the savings curve up in figure 1.1, hence raising the gap between it and the depreciation line, but it will have no *long-run* effect on the growth rate, which is doomed to fall back to zero. The increase in s will, however, cause an increase in the long-run *levels* of output and capital as a result of the temporary burst of growth in K; that is, the new intersection point defining K^* will have shifted to the right.

Likewise, an increase in the depreciation rate δ will produce a temporary reduction in growth by shifting the depreciation line up, hence creating a negative gap between the savings curve and the depreciation line. But again the change in the country's growth rate will not last indefinitely. As K approaches its new lower level, the growth rate will rise back up to zero. The levels of output and capital will be permanently lower as a result of this increase in δ; that is, the new intersection point defining K^* will have shifted to the left.

1.2.1 Population Growth

The same pessimistic conclusion regarding long-run growth follows even with a growing population. To see this point, we make explicit that output depends not just on capital but also on labor, by writing the production function as

---

5. Technically, there is another steady state at $K = 0$, where national income is zero and both savings and depreciation are zero. But this degenerate steady state is unstable; as long as the initial stock K_0 is positive, then K will approach the positive steady state K^*.

Note how we use the Inada conditions (1.2). The second one guarantees that, starting from the origin, the saving curve at first rises above the depreciation line. The first one guarantees that eventually the slope of the saving curve will fall below that of the depreciation line. Together these imply that as K increases, the saving curve must eventually cross the depreciation line from above, as it does at K^*.

$$Y = F(K, L)$$

Suppose that this production function is concave,[6] implying that the marginal product of capital is again a diminishing function of K, holding L constant. Suppose also that the aggregate production function exhibits constant returns to scale; that is, F is homogeneous of degree one in both arguments:

$$F(\lambda K, \lambda L) = \lambda F(K, L) \quad \text{for all } \lambda, K, L > 0 \tag{1.5}$$

This formula makes sense under our assumption that the state of technology is given, for if capital and labor were both to double, then the extra workers could use the extra capital to replicate what was done before, thus resulting in twice the output.

Suppose that everyone in the economy always supplies one unit of labor per unit of time, and that there is perpetual full employment. Thus the labor input L is also the population, which we suppose grows at the constant exponential rate n per year.

With constant returns to scale, output per person $y \equiv Y/L$ will depend on the capital stock per person $k \equiv K/L$. That is, equation (1.5) implies that, in the special case where $\lambda = 1/L$,

$$Y/L = F(K, L)/L = F(K/L, 1)$$

so

$$y = f(k) \tag{1.6}$$

where f is the per capita production function:

$$f(k) = F(k, 1)$$

indicating what each person can produce using his or her share of the aggregate capital stock. In the Cobb-Douglas case

$$Y = K^{\alpha} L^{1-\alpha}, \quad 0 < \alpha < 1$$

the per capita production function can be written as

$$y = f(k) = k^{\alpha}$$

---

6. Concavity of a production function is a multidimensional version of diminishing returns. Formally, F is concave if $\dfrac{\partial^2 F}{\partial K^2} < 0$, $\dfrac{\partial^2 F}{\partial L^2} < 0$, and $\dfrac{\partial^2 F}{\partial K^2} \dfrac{\partial^2 F}{\partial L^2} \geq \left(\dfrac{\partial^2 F}{\partial K \partial L} \right)^2$.

The rate at which new saving raises k is the rate of saving per person, sy. The rate at which depreciation causes k to fall is the amount of depreciation per person δk. In addition, population growth will cause k to fall at the annual rate nk (each additional person reduces the amount of capital per person, given the aggregate amount K). The net rate of increase in k is the resultant of these three forces, which by equation (1.6) is[7]

$$\dot{k} = sf(k) - (n + \delta)k \tag{1.7}$$

Note that the differential equation (1.7) governing the capital-labor ratio is almost the same as the fundamental equation (1.4) governing the capital stock in the previous section, except that the depreciation rate is now augmented by the population growth rate and the per capita production function f has replaced the aggregate function F. Also, the per capita function f will have the same shape as the aggregate function F,[8] so the per capita savings curve $sf(k)$ in figure 1.2 will look just like the savings curve in figure 1.1.

As figure 1.2 shows, diminishing returns will again impose an upper limit to capital per person. That is, eventually a point will be reached where all of people's saving is needed to compensate for depreciation and population growth. This point is the *steady-state*[9] value k^*, defined by the condition

7. More formally, it follows from basic calculus that

$$\dot{k} = \dot{K}/L - \dot{L}K/L^2$$

Since L grows at the constant exponential rate n, we have $\dot{L}/L = n$; hence,

$$\dot{k} = \dot{K}/L - nk$$

As in the previous section, we have

$$\dot{K} = sY - \delta K$$

so

$$\dot{K}/L = sy - \delta k$$

and

$$\dot{k} = sy - (n + \delta)k$$

Equation (1.7) follows from this and the per capita production function (1.6).

8. Since $f(k) = F(k, 1)$, therefore $f'(k) = \dfrac{\partial}{\partial k} F(k, 1)$ which is decreasing in k because of the assumption that F is concave.

9. The aggregate capital stock is not stationary, but growing at the same steady rate as the work force.

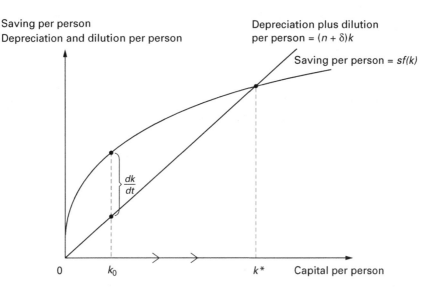

Figure 1.2

$$sf(k) = (n + \delta)k$$

While the capital stock per person converges to k^*, the level of output per person will converge to the corresponding steady-state value $y^* = f(k^*)$. In this steady-state equilibrium, output and the capital stock will both continue to grow, but only at the rate of population growth. Thus growth as measured by the rate of increase in output *per person* will cease in the long run.

1.2.2 Exogenous Technological Change

It follows that the only way to explain the persistent long-run growth in output per person that we have observed in advanced economies since the industrial revolution is through technological change that continually offsets the dampening effect of diminishing returns. How this might work can be seen by supposing that there is a productivity parameter A in the aggregate production function that reflects the current state of technological knowledge, and that this productivity parameter grows at the constant exponential rate g. The exogenous value of g is assumed to reflect progress in science.

Thus, suppose that the aggregate production function has the Cobb-Douglas form

$$Y = (AL)^{1-\alpha} K^{\alpha} \tag{1.8}$$

This way of writing the production function makes technological progress equivalent to an increase in the "effective" supply of labor AL, which grows not at the rate of population growth n but at the rate of growth of population plus the growth rate of productivity[10] $n + g$.

Formally, the only difference from the model of the previous section is that we have everywhere replaced the labor input L by the number of "efficiency units" of labor AL. We can now find a steady state in terms of capital per efficiency unit:

$$\kappa = \frac{K}{AL}$$

and output per efficiency unit, which we can write, using equation (1.8) as

$$\varphi = \frac{Y}{AL} = \kappa^{\alpha}$$

The rate at which new saving raises κ is the rate of saving per efficiency unit sy. The rate at which depreciation causes κ to fall is the amount of depreciation per person $\delta\kappa$. In addition, growth in the number of efficiency units, at the rate $n + g$, causes κ to fall at the annual rate $(n + g)\kappa$. As before, the net rate of increase in κ is the resultant of these three forces:

$$\dot{\kappa} = s\kappa^{\alpha} - (n + g + \delta)\kappa \tag{1.9}$$

which is almost identical to equation (1.7) of the previous section with a change in notation from k to κ, except that the growth rate n of labor input has now been replaced by the growth rate $n + g$ of the number of "efficiency units" of labor. As before, κ will approach a unique steady-state value κ^* in the long run, while φ approaches its steady state $\varphi^* = (\kappa^*)^{\alpha}$.

Although output per efficiency unit does not grow in the long run, the same is no longer true of output per person:

---

10. That A enters the aggregate production function multiplicatively with L is in most cases a very special assumption, amounting to what is sometimes referred to as "Harrod neutrality" or "purely labor-augmenting technical change." There is no good reason why technological change should always take this form; it just leads to tractable steady-state results. In the present Cobb-Douglas framework, however, the assumption of Harrod neutrality is innocuous. That is, because all factors enter multiplicatively in a Cobb-Douglas production function, it would make no observable difference if A multiplied L, K, or both.

$$Y/L = A\varphi = A\kappa^{\alpha}$$

whose growth rate can be expressed as

$$G = \dot{A}/A + \alpha\dot{\kappa}/\kappa = g + \alpha\dot{\kappa}/\kappa$$

In the long run, when κ approaches κ^*, the time derivative $\dot{\kappa}$ approaches zero, so the growth rate G approaches the exogenous rate of technological change g:

$$G \rightarrow g \quad \text{as} \quad t \rightarrow \infty$$

But in the short run, as before, the growth rate can rise above g temporarily as a result of an increase in the saving rate s, which raises the rate of increase in the capital stock per efficiency unit κ according to the fundamental differential equation (1.9).

Intuitively, the growth rate of output per person does not fall to zero because as capital accumulates, the tendency for the output/capital ratio to fall because of diminishing returns to capital is continually offset by technological progress. The economy approaches a steady state in which the two conflicting forces of diminishing returns and technological progress exactly offset each other and the output/capital ratio is constant. Although the *height* of the steady-state growth path will be determined by such parameters as the saving rate s, the depreciation rate δ, and the rate of population growth n, the only parameter affecting the *growth rate* is the exogenous rate of technological progress g.

1.2.3 Conditional Convergence

One of the main questions that growth economics addresses is whether poor countries are likely to catch up with rich ones. If so, we say there is *cross-country convergence*. The neoclassical model answers this question with a qualified yes. That is, suppose country 1 has a lower per capita GDP than country 2. Then the theory predicts that this difference in per capita GDPs will tend to disappear over time if the two countries share the same technology (as defined by the production function F and the path A_t of efficiency units per person) and the same fundamental determinants of capital accumulation (the saving rate s, the depreciation rate δ, and the population growth rate n), but not otherwise. This prediction is known as *conditional convergence*, because it says that convergence is conditional on having the same technology and fundamental variables.

The reason why the model implies conditional convergence is simple. If two countries have the same fundamentals and share the same technology, then they will each be converging to the same steady state, and therefore they will be converging to each other. Otherwise they will generally be converging to different steady states and therefore not to each other.

More specifically, suppose the steady-state level of GDP per efficiency unit of labor is $\varphi_1^* = y_{1t}/A_{1t}$ in country 1 and $\varphi_2^* = y_{2t}/A_{2t}$ in country 2, where y_{it} and A_{it} are, respectively, GDP per person and efficiency units per worker in country i along the country's long-run growth path. If the two countries have the same technology and the same fundamental determinants, then $A_{1t} = A_{2t}$ and $\varphi_1^* = \varphi_2^*$, so their long-run levels of GDP per person will be same: $y_{1t} = y_{2t}$. But if they have different technologies and fundamentals, then there is no reason why their long-run levels of GDP per person should be the same.

The empirical literature on convergence has tested a somewhat stronger version of conditional convergence, namely, that there should be convergence conditional on countries having the same fundamental determinants (s, n, δ) of capital accumulation. This version has been suggested by proponents of the neoclassical model who believe that as a working hypothesis we should assume that all countries share the same technology, so all that remains to guarantee convergence is that countries have the same steady state φ^*. These economists believe that cross-country technology differences are not important because science and technology are global resources available to all countries; they claim that what really separates countries economically is capital accumulation, not technology.

Empirical tests of conditional convergence focus on whether poor countries tend to grow faster than rich ones, after controlling for the fundamental determinants of capital accumulation. As you can see in figure 1.2, a country that starts further behind the steady state k^* will have a faster rate of capital accumulation, and hence a large growth rate of per capita GDP. Of course, this comparison only works for two countries with the same steady states; if a rich country also had a higher k^*, then it might be further behind its steady state than the poor country, and therefore might be growing faster than the poor one.

Authors in this empirical literature often estimate equations of the form

$$\frac{1}{T} \cdot \log \frac{y_{t+T}}{y_t} = \beta_0 + \beta_1 \log y_t + \beta_2 X_t + u_t$$

where X_t is a vector of variables (such as s, δ, and n) that control for the determinants of steady-state output per person. The left-hand side of this equation is the growth rate of the economy measured over an interval of T years. Thus the equation says that growth rates can vary from country to country either because of differences in the parameters determining their steady states (captured in the term $\beta_2 X_t$) or because of differences in initial positions (captured in the term $\beta_1 \log y_t$). An estimated value of $\beta_1 < 0$ is taken as evidence for conditional convergence.

1.2.3.1 Convergence in Growth Rates

Sometimes economists speak of cross-country convergence in terms of the growth rate of per capita GDP rather than its level. We say there is convergence in growth rates if there is a tendency for cross-country differences in growth rates to vanish over time. This form of convergence does not imply that the standard of living of poor countries will catch up to that of rich countries, but that the growth rate in slow-growing countries will catch up with that of faster-growing countries.

The neoclassical model has a stronger prediction with respect to convergence in growth rates than the conditional convergence prediction we have just seen in levels. Specifically, the model implies that there should be convergence in growth rates between all countries that share the same technology. That is, the long-run growth rate in each country is its rate of technological progress, so if they always share the same technology, they will share the same rate of technological progress and hence will share the same long-run growth rate. Indeed, those neoclassical proponents who believe that all countries do indeed share the same technology predict absolute convergence in growth rates—that all countries, with no exceptions, are converging to the same long-run growth rate.

1.3   Extension: The Cass-Koopmans-Ramsey Model[11]*

1.3.1 No Technological Progress

As simple hypotheses go, the assumption of fixed saving rate is not a bad approximation to reality. But many writers believe that the subtleties of the permanent-income and life-cycle savings hypotheses should be taken into account, on the

---

11.* This section contains slightly more advanced material. The details can be skipped by less advanced readers, who should, however, look at the Euler equation (1.19) and the discussion following it. This equation will occasionally be used in chapters 2 and 3, and then again in chapter 16, but nowhere else.

grounds that people save with a view to smoothing their consumption over their lifetimes, taking into account their preferences for consumption at different dates and the rate of return that they can anticipate if they sacrifice current consumption in order to save for the future.

The rest of this chapter is devoted to showing how the neoclassical model can be extended along these lines, to take into account peoples' motives for consumption smoothing. The model we present originates in the seminal contribution of Ramsey (1928), as elaborated by Cass (1965) and Koopmans (1965). This model too predicts that economic policies can affect growth only in the short run, and that in the long run the growth rate of per capita income will always revert to the exogenously given rate of technological progress. Once again the reason is the diminishing marginal productivity of capital.

Suppose accordingly that we model saving as if it were decided by a representative household. Time is discrete: $t = 0, 1, \ldots, T$. At each date the household derives utility from its current consumption; specifically, if it is currently consuming at the rate c, then its current flow of utility is given by the utility function $u(c)$. Assume that marginal utility is positive and decreasing:

$$u'(c) > 0 \quad \text{and} \quad u''(c) < 0 \qquad \text{for all } c > 0$$

To simplify the problem, assume that marginal utility becomes infinite as consumption approaches zero:

$$\lim_{c \to 0} u'(c) = \infty \tag{1.10}$$

The household is farsighted, in the sense that it cares about not just current utility but also expected future utilities. But it is also impatient, in the sense that it cares more about the flow of utility expected in the near future than the flow expected much later. Specifically, when evaluating any lifetime plan for consumption $\{c_t\}_0^T$, it uses a weighted sum of utilities:

$$W = \sum_0^T \beta^t u(c_t), \qquad 0 < \beta < 1$$

The household's impatience is implicit in the fact that the weight β^t assigned to the utility expected at date t declines with t. The geometric rate of decline is a constant β that we call the household's *discount factor*.

We abstract once again from population growth by assuming a constant labor force: $L = 1$. The technological possibilities of the representative household are again given by a production function $F(K)$ with a positive but diminishing marginal product (condition 1.1) and satisfying the Inada conditions (1.2), where K is the amount of capital held by the representative household.

Suppose for simplicity that instead of selling its labor services and renting its capital to business firms, the household does its own production.[12] The household then has to decide how much to consume at each date versus how much to put aside for capital accumulation that will provide for future consumption. The basic constraint that it faces at each date is that the growth in its capital stock K will equal the flow of new output $F(K)$ minus the amount it consumes c and minus the amount that disappears because of depreciation δK. That is,

$$K_{t+1} = K_t + F(K_t) - c_t - \delta K_t \tag{1.11}$$

The household chooses the sequence of consumption and capital $\{c_t, K_{t+1}\}_0^T$ that maximizes its lifetime utility W subject to equation (1.11) every period, taking the initial capital stock K_0 as given, and subject to the condition that the amount of capital K_{T+1} left over at the end of the planning horizon cannot be negative.[13]

As with any constrained optimization problem, the solution is derived by forming the Lagrangian expression

$$\mathcal{L} = \sum_0^T \beta^t u(c_t) + \sum_0^T \mu_{t+1} \left[K_t + F(K_t) - c_t - \delta K_t - K_{t+1} \right]$$

where the μ's are undetermined Lagrange multipliers. Each μ_t can be interpreted as the *shadow value* of a unit of capital in period t—that is, the discounted marginal utility from having more K_t. The partial derivative of $\mathcal{L}$ with respect to each of the choice variables except K_{T+1} must equal zero:

---

12. Equivalently we could have assumed that the markets for labor and capital are perfectly competitive, that they clear at each date, and that people have perfect foresight of all future prices. These assumptions can be made because under constant returns to scale (in capital and labor) the size of firms is indeterminate. The economy can produce exactly as much in aggregate with each household employing its own capital and labor as if they all worked for a few big firms that also employed all the capital, provided that there are frictionless markets in which the firms can buy labor and capital from the households.

13. Notice that we have ignored the nonnegativity constraint for each variable except K_{T+1}. We can do so because there would be an infinite marginal gain from raising each of these variables above zero. That is, the Inada conditions (1.2) imply that with zero capital there would be an infinite marginal product, and the similar condition (1.10) implies that with zero consumption there would be infinite marginal utility. But since K_{T+1} will not enter any production function, it will not generate any gain at all if we raise it above zero. So if we ignored the nonnegativity constraint on K_{T+1} the household would gladly choose to "die broke," which would make no sense in this context because capital cannot be negative.

$$\frac{\partial \mathcal{L}}{\partial c_t} = \beta^t u'(c_t) - \mu_{t+1} = 0, \qquad\qquad t = 0, 1, \ldots T$$

$$\frac{\partial \mathcal{L}}{\partial K_t} = \mu_{t+1}\left[1 + F'(K_t) - \delta\right] - \mu_t = 0, \qquad t = 1, 2, \ldots T$$

The necessary first-order condition with respect to K_{T+1} must take into account the possibility that the derivative of $\mathcal{L}$ could be negative if we are at a corner solution with $K_{T+1} = 0$. That is, we have the Kuhn-Tucker necessary conditions:

$$\frac{\partial \mathcal{L}}{\partial K_{T+1}} = -\mu_{T+1} \le 0, \quad K_{T+1} \ge 0, \quad \mu_{T+1} K_{T+1} = 0$$

Define the *current* shadow values λ_t as

$$\lambda_t = \beta^{-(t-1)}\mu_t$$

Then the preceding first-order conditions imply

$$u'(c_t) - \lambda_{t+1} = 0 \qquad t = 0, 1, \ldots T \tag{1.12}$$

$$\beta\left[1 + F'(K_t) - \delta\right] - \lambda_t / \lambda_{t+1} = 0, \qquad t = 1, 2, \ldots T \tag{1.13}$$

$$\beta^T \lambda_{T+1} K_{T+1} = 0 \tag{1.14}$$

Condition (1.12) states that the marginal utility of consumption must always equal the shadow value λ_{t+1} of a unit of capital next period. This relation holds because, according to the constraint (1.11), each unit of consumption costs one unit of capital next period, and hence optimality requires that these alternatives have the same marginal value.

Condition (1.13) is the Euler equation. Suppose we define the marginal rate of return $r(K)$ as the extra net output that the household could get from a marginal unit of capital:

$$r(K) \equiv \frac{\partial}{\partial K}\left[F(K) - \delta K\right] = F'(K) - \delta$$

Then the Euler equation can be rewritten using equation (1.12) as

$$1 + r(K_{t+1}) = \frac{u'(c_t)}{\beta u'(c_{t+1})}, \qquad t = 0, 1, \ldots T-1 \tag{1.15}$$

which is a familiar condition for optimal consumption smoothing over time, namely, that the marginal rate of substitution between consumption this period and next must equal the marginal rate of transformation $1 + r(K_{t+1})$.

Condition (1.14) is the *transversality* condition, which states that either the terminal capital stock must be zero or it must be valueless ($\lambda_{T+1} = 0$). That is, you must not plan to die leaving anything valuable unconsumed.

1.3.1.1 Continuous Time, Infinite Horizon[14]

To understand how consumption and the capital stock evolve over time, it is helpful to take the limit as the time period shrinks to zero and as the planning horizon becomes infinitely long. First, express the discount factor β as

$$\beta = \frac{1}{1+\rho}$$

where $\rho > 0$ is the household's subjective discount rate, or *rate of time preference*. Next, when the time period is short, we can approximate first-order differences by derivatives. Thus we can write, by approximation,[15]

$$u'(c_{t+1}) - u'(c_t) = u''(c_t)\dot{c}_t$$

where

$$\dot{c}_t = dc_t/dt$$

Dividing through by $u'(c_t)$, we can rewrite the preceding equation as

$$\frac{u'(c_{t+1})}{u'(c_t)} = \frac{u''(c_t)}{u'(c_t)}\dot{c}_t + 1$$

The Euler equation (1.15) then becomes

$$\frac{1}{\beta(1+r)} = \frac{1+\rho}{1+r} = \frac{u''(c_t)}{u'(c_t)}\dot{c}_t + 1$$

---

14. For an alternative treatment using the Hamiltonian method, see appendix 1B.

15. Indeed we have

$$\lim_{dt \to 0} \frac{u'(c_{t+dt}) - u'(c_t)}{dt} = u''(c_t)\dot{c}_t$$

But when the time period is short the rate of time preference ρ and the rate of return r will be small, so we have[16]

$$\frac{1+\rho}{1+r} \simeq 1+\rho-r$$

Therefore, the continuous-time approximation of the Euler equation is

$$\frac{u''(c_t)}{u'(c_t)}\dot{c}_t = \rho - r \tag{1.16}$$

1.3.1.2   The Canonical Euler Equation

Whenever we shall apply this Euler formula in the next chapter, we will do it in the special *isoelastic* case:

$$u(c) = \frac{c^{1-\varepsilon}-1}{1-\varepsilon} \tag{1.17}$$

where $\varepsilon > 0$.[17] In this case, individuals have the same elasticity of substitution $1/\varepsilon$ between present and future consumption[18] no matter the level of consumption. This is the key parameter defining the household's desire to smooth consumption over time, and in this class of utility functions that desire is independent of the level of consumption.

Using the fact that in this case

$$u'(c) = c^{-\varepsilon}; \quad u''(c) = -\varepsilon c^{-(\varepsilon+1)}$$

---

16. This can be seen as a first-order Taylor-series approximation to the function $G(\rho, r) = \dfrac{1+\rho}{1+r}$ around the point $(\rho, r) = (0, 0)$. That is, $G(\rho, r) \simeq G(0, 0) + \rho G_1(0, 0) + r G_2(0, 0) = 1 + \rho - r$, where G_i is the partial derivative of G with respect to its ith argument.

17. Note that as $\varepsilon \to 1$, $\dfrac{c^{1-\varepsilon}-1}{1-\varepsilon} \to \ln(c)$.

18. The elasticity of substitution between c_t and c_{t+1} is an inverse measure of the sensitivity of the marginal rate of substitution $u'(c_{t+1})/u'(c_t)$ to a change in the consumption ratio c_{t+1}/c_t. The greater the elasticity of substitution the more you would have to change the consumption ratio in response to a change in the rate of return r in order to restore the equilibrium condition (1.15). Formally the elasticity is

$$\eta = -\left\{ \frac{c_{t+1}/c_t}{u'(c_{t+1})/u'(c_t)} \frac{d[u'(c_{t+1})/u'(c_t)]}{d(c_{t+1}/c_t)} \right\}^{-1}$$

In this case we have $u'(c) = c^{-\varepsilon}$ so $\eta = 1/\varepsilon$.

the preceding Euler equation becomes

$$-\varepsilon \dot{c}_t / c_t = \rho - r \tag{1.18}$$

or equivalently, if c_t is growing at the rate g

$$r = \rho + \varepsilon g \tag{1.19}$$

This is the canonical form of the Euler equation one finds in all graduate textbooks. The intuition behind it is simple. We can interpret r as an interest rate. That is, if the representative household saves one unit today, then capital will be higher by the amount $1 + r$ next period. Likewise the household could "borrow" one unit, by consuming it today, which would cause capital to be lower by $1 + r$ next period. Equation (1.19) tells us what the equilibrium rate of interest must be in a steady state[19] where the representative household's consumption and capital are growing at the rate g.

Consider first the case where g equals zero. Then in a steady state the representative household must have a constant capital stock. So it must be neither borrowing nor saving. But this household is impatient ($\beta < 1$), so if there were no cost of borrowing it would prefer to borrow. Therefore, the rate of interest, which is the cost of borrowing, must be high enough to persuade the household not to borrow. According to equation (1.19) that steady-state interest rate is the rate of time preference ρ.

Suppose now that g is positive. Then in a steady state the representative household must be saving each period by enough to make its capital stock grow at the rate g. It takes a bigger interest rate to persuade the household to save than it does just to persuade it not to borrow. Specifically, equation (1.19) shows us that for every percentage point rise in the growth rate g, the equilibrium interest rate must rise by ε percentage points.

The Euler equation serves two purposes in growth theory. In the neoclassical model it shows us how the steady-state level of capital depends on the rate of technological progress g, which we do in the next section. The other purpose of the Euler equation is to show how the growth rate depends on the rate of time preference in theories of endogenous growth; we do so in chapter 3 where we analyze Romer's model of endogenous technical change.

1.3.2 Exogenous Technological Change

It is possible to add technological progress to the Cass-Koopmans-Ramsey model, just as we did with the Solow-Swan model, and thereby make growth sustainable

---

19. Appendix 1A shows that the economy will indeed converge to its steady state.

in the long run. Technological progress is typically added by supposing, as in equation (1.8), that the aggregate production function can be written as $F(K, AL)$, where F exhibits constant returns to scale and where A is an exogenous productivity parameter that grows at the constant exponential rate $g > 0$. As before, the parameter A can be interpreted as the number of "efficiency units" per unit of labor. Because we are assuming for simplicity that $L = 1$, we can write the aggregate production function more economically as $F(K, A)$.

The model is exactly the same as in the case of no technological progress, except that the constant quantity of labor input has been replaced by the growing number of efficiency units A. This change allows the stock of capital to grow indefinitely without driving the marginal product below the rate of time preference, because the effect of diminishing returns is now offset by the continual rise in productivity.

To characterize the equilibrium growth path, assume that instantaneous utility is given by the isoelastic function (1.17). Then, from equation (1.18), we know that

$$\dot{c}/c = (r - \rho)/\varepsilon$$

where

$$r = F_1(K, A) - \delta$$

is the equilibrium net rate of return on capital, with the marginal product of capital now being the partial derivative F_1.

The assumption that F exhibits constant returns implies that the marginal product F_1, depends only on the ratio[20] K/A. Therefore, K and A can both grow at the exogenous rate g without driving the marginal product below the rate of time preference ρ. A steady state will thus exist with positive growth if the ratio K/A satisfies

$$g = (1/\varepsilon)\left[F_1(K, A) - \delta - \rho \right]$$

20. Setting $\lambda = 1/A$ in the definition (1.5) of constant returns to scale, we have

$$F(K, A) = AF(K/A, 1)$$

Differentiating both sides with respect to K we have:

$$F_1(K, A) = F_1(K/A, 1)$$

which shows that the marginal product of capital (the left-hand side) is a function of the ratio K/A.

In this steady state,[21] capital, consumption, and output all grow at the exogenous rate g. The growth path will be optimal if and only if the following modified transversality condition[22] also holds:

$$\rho + (\varepsilon - 1)g > 0$$

1.4   Conclusion

The main lesson to take from the neoclassical model is that, in the long run, economic growth (that is, growth in per capita GDP) is driven by technological change. Without technological change an economy can perhaps grow for a while by accumulating capital, but eventually that growth will be choked off by the diminishing marginal product of capital. With technological change, however, growth can be sustained, and indeed the economy will converge to a steady state in which the rate of economic growth is exactly equal to the rate of (Harrod-neutral) technological progress.

The main limitation of the neoclassical model is that it provides no account of the rate of technological progress, which it takes as given by some unspecified process that generates scientific discovery and technological diffusion. So although the model provides a concise account of a country's growth path (the time path of GDP per person) and shows how that path can be raised or lowered by forces such as thrift and fertility, it offers no economic explanation for persistent cross-country differences in growth, other than to say that some countries must have a faster rate of technological progress than others. This limitation will be addressed by the various endogenous growth models that we present in the following chapters, in all of which the rate of technological progress will be shown to depend on economic forces.

1.5   Literature Notes

The pioneering articles were published almost simultaneously by Solow (1956) and Swan (1956), and present the neoclassical growth model with exogenous saving rates. The neoclassical growth models with endogenous saving rate were subsequently developed in the seminal papers of Cass (1965) and Koopmans (1965).

21. Because $\dot{K} = gK$ in the steady state, consumption is given by the law of motion: $gK = F(K, A) - \delta K - c$.

22. This condition is necessary and sufficient for the transversality condition (1.26) to hold in the steady state that we have just described. Although it imposes a direct restriction on the set of allowable parameter values, it is not nearly as arbitrary as it might seem. On the contrary, it is a necessary condition for there to be a finite upper bound to lifetime utility.

The neoclassical framework provided the benchmark for many subsequent extensions and applications developed over the last decades. In particular, (1) Sidrauski (1967) develops an extension of the framework that includes money and inflation; (2) Brock and Mirman (1972) analyze the neoclassical model with uncertainty; (3) Blanchard (1985) presents a version of the neoclassical model with finite horizon, analyzing the impact of government spending, debt, and deficits; (4) Barro (1990) studies more generally the implications of government spending in the model; (5) probably the best known extension of the neoclassical model is the paper by Mankiw, Romer, and Weil (1992), who include human capital as a third factor of production to reconcile the neoclassical model with existing evidence on convergence rates; (6) Caselli and Ventura (2000) allow for various forms of household heterogeneity within the Cass-Koopmans-Ramsey model (Stiglitz 1969 had previously developed a model with heterogeneous agents but exogenous saving functions); and (7) following Laibson's (1997) insights on hyperbolic time discounting, Barro (1999a) analyzes the neoclassical model with nonconstant time-preference rates.

For a synthetic presentation of the neoclassical model, we refer our readers to the excellent handbook survey by Jones and Manuelli (2005).

Appendix 1A: Steady State and Convergence in the Cass-Koopmans-Ramsey Model

Using equation (1.12) and the definition of $r(K)$, we can re-express the continuous-time Euler equation (1.16) as

$$\dot{\lambda} = \lambda(\rho - r) = \lambda\left[\rho - F'(K) + \delta\right] \tag{1.20}$$

Next, using the same approximation devices as before, the constraint (1.11) can be written in continuous time as

$$\dot{K} = F(K) - c(\lambda) - \delta K \tag{1.21}$$

where $c(\lambda)$ is the level of consumption that makes marginal utility equal to λ. That is, $c(\lambda)$ is the solution to the first-order condition (1.12).

Finally, in the limit as the time horizon T goes to infinity, the transversality condition (1.14) can be written as[23]

$$\lim_{t \to \infty} e^{-\rho t} \lambda K = 0 \tag{1.22}$$

---

23. Note that as the time period shrinks to zero, the discount factor $\beta^{T+1} = (1 + \rho)^{-(T+1)}$ becomes $e^{-\rho(T+1)}$.

which states that in the long run the current value of capital λK cannot grow faster than the rate of time preference ρ.

The stationary state to this growth model is one where both capital K and shadow value λ are constant. According to the Euler equation (1.20) this stationary-state stock of capital K^* will be the solution[24] to the modified golden-rule condition

$$F'(K^*) = \rho + \delta$$

which states that the marginal rate of return $r(K^*) = F'(K^*) - \delta$ in the stationary state should be equal to the household's rate of time preference, as we observed in section 1.3.1.2.

As in the model with a fixed saving rate, the capital stock will converge asymptotically to the stationary state. To see this point, note that equations (1.20) and (1.21) constitute a two-dimensional system of differential equations in the two variables K and λ. History determines an initial condition for one of these variables, namely, the initial stock of capital, while the transversality condition (1.22) determines a terminal condition. Thus there are just enough boundary conditions to determine a unique solution to the dynamic system. The following diagrammatic argument shows that this unique solution will converge asymptotically to the stationary state K^*.

The dynamic system is illustrated by the phase diagram in figure 1.3. According to equation (1.20), the locus of points along which the shadow value is constant ($\dot{\lambda} = 0$) is vertical at the modified golden-rule capital stock K^*. To the right of this locus, λ must be rising because the marginal rate of return has fallen below the rate of time preference. Likewise, $\dot{\lambda} < 0$ to the left of the locus.

According to equation (1.21), the locus of points along which the capital stock is constant ($\dot{K} = 0$) is defined by the condition that consumption equals net national product:

$$c(\lambda) = F(K) - \delta K$$

This locus is represented in figure 1.3 by a negatively sloped curve,[25] because higher K implies a higher net national product, which permits people to consume

---

24. The existence of a unique stationary state is again guaranteed by the strict concavity of F and the Inada conditions (1.2).

25. This discussion assumes that the marginal rate of return $F'(K) - \delta$ is positive. The Inada conditions imply, however, that this will cease to be the case when K has risen above K^* by enough. Once that has happened, the economy will have "overaccumulated" capital, in the sense that the sacrifice of consumption that was needed to raise K to this level will have yielded a *negative* social return. This sort of "dynamic inefficiency" cannot occur in an optimal growth model, although it can in the Solow-Swan model.

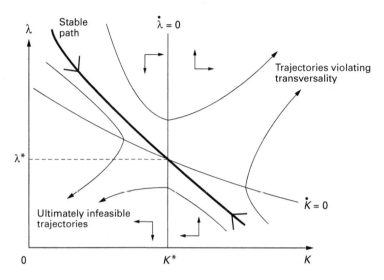

Figure 1.3

more in a steady state, which by diminishing marginal utility requires λ to be lower. Above this locus, consumption will be too low to keep K from growing, so $\dot{K} > 0$. Below it, consumption will be too high to keep K from falling, so $\dot{K} < 0$.

An optimal growth path can never wander into the "northeast" segment of figure 1.3—above the $\dot{K} = 0$ locus and to the right of the $\dot{\lambda} = 0$ locus—for then the product λK would end up growing too fast to satisfy the transversality condition (1.22). People would be postponing consumption forever. Nor can the optimal growth path ever wander into the "southwest" segment in which consumption is rising ($\dot{\lambda} < 0$) and capital falling, because this path would exhaust the capital stock in finite time. There is only one trajectory that avoids both of these forbidden segments. Given any initial K_0, the initial λ_0 must be chosen just right so as to put the economy on this trajectory, usually referred to as the *stable path* or the *saddle path*,[26] which converges to the stationary state K^*.

26. Mathematically the stationary state (λ^*, K^*) is a *saddle point* to the dynamical system, meaning that while it is not locally stable it is reachable by at least some trajectories. Note, however, that steady-state consumption is not maximized at this point (see problem 4).

So, as in the case of a fixed saving rate, the model will exhibit no growth in the long run. A temporary increase in thrift, modeled as a fall in the rate of time preference ρ, would disturb the phase diagram by shifting the stationary state K^* to the right. This shift would cause net investment to increase until it reached the new golden-rule capital stock. But eventually growth would come to an end, and again the reason is the diminishing marginal product of capital. That is, if ever K were to rise above K^*, then the diminishing marginal product of capital would have brought the marginal rate of return below the rate of time preference, and the household would no longer be willing to accumulate more capital.

Appendix 1B: Dynamic Optimization Using the Hamiltonian

Consider a representative infinitely lived individual whose lifetime utility function is

$$W = \int_0^\infty e^{-pt} u\big[c(t)\big] dt$$

where $c(t)$ is the time path of consumption per person, $u(\cdot)$ is an instantaneous utility function exhibiting positive but diminishing marginal utility, and ρ a positive rate of time preference. To simplify the analysis we abstract once again from population growth by assuming a constant labor force: $L = 1$. Then, with continuous market clearing, perfect competition, perfect foresight, and no externalities, the economy will follow an optimal growth path. That is, it will maximize W subject to the constraint that consumption plus investment must equal net national product:

$$\dot{K} = F(K) - \delta K - c \tag{1.23}$$

subject to the historically predetermined value of capital.

Along an optimal growth path, capital should be increasing whenever its net marginal product $F'(K) - \delta$ is greater than the rate of time preference ρ, and decreasing whenever it is less. That is, the rate of time preference can be interpreted as the required rate of return on capital, the rate below which it is not optimal to continue equipping workers with as much capital. This together with the first Inada condition (1.2) implies that growth cannot be sustained indefinitely. For doing so would require capital to grow without limit, which would eventually drive the net marginal product of capital below the rate of time preference.

To see this point more formally,[27] recall that from the theory of optimal control, the level of consumption at each point of time must maximize the Hamiltonian:

$$H = u(c) + \lambda \left[F(K) - \delta K - c \right]$$

where λ is the shadow value of investment, evaluated in current utils. According to equation (1.23) the term in square brackets is net investment. Thus the Hamiltonian is analogous to the familiar concept of net national product—consumption plus net investment—the only difference being that the Hamiltonian measures both consumption and net investment in units of utility rather than units of goods.

A necessary first-order condition for maximizing the Hamiltonian is

$$\frac{\partial H}{\partial c} = 0$$

or equivalently that the marginal utility of consumption equals the shadow value of investment:

$$u'(c) = \lambda \tag{1.24}$$

The shadow value λ is itself determined as the present value of the stream of extra utils that would be created by a marginal unit of capital. Equivalently[28] we can define it in terms of the Euler equation:

$$\dot{\lambda} = \rho\lambda - \frac{\partial H}{\partial K}$$

or equivalently

$$\rho\lambda = \lambda \left(F'(K) - \delta \right) + \dot{\lambda} \tag{1.25}$$

Finally, the following transversality condition must hold:

27. For the mathematical details of optimal growth theory, see Arrow and Kurz (1970). A brief summary of the mathematics of intertemporal optimization in continuous time is provided in Aghion and Howitt (1998a), appendix to chapter 1.

28. As in standard consumer theory, if we start on an optimal path, then the marginal benefit of having an extra unit of net national product is independent of how that marginal unit is allocated between consumption and investment. Suppose, therefore, that all the extra NNP resulting from a marginal unit of capital is always exactly consumed. Then the increment to the capital stock will be permanent, and the marginal value will be

$$\lambda(t) = \int_t^\infty e^{-\rho(\tau - t)} u'\left[c(\tau)\right]\left\{F'\left[K(\tau)\right] - \delta\right\} d\tau$$

By routine calculus, this is equivalent to the pair of conditions (1.25) and (1.26) provided that the optimality condition (1.24) can be invoked to replace the marginal utility at each date in the integral. The transversality condition is needed in order to ensure that the integral converges.

$$\lim_{t \to \infty} e^{-\rho t} \lambda K = 0 \tag{1.26}$$

The Euler equation (1.25) can be interpreted as an equilibrium asset-pricing condition in a world where the numéraire is current utils and everyone is risk-neutral. The right-hand side of equation (1.25) shows the incremental flow of income, including capital gain, that can rationally be anticipated by an individual who holds an incremental unit of K.[29] The ratio of this income flow to the "asset price" λ must equal the "competitive rate of interest" ρ. The transversality condition (1.26) is the condition that rules out the kind of inefficiency involved in accumulating capital forever without consuming it.

Substituting for $\lambda = u'(c)$ in equation (1.25) in turn delivers the Euler equation, namely,

$$\frac{u''(c)}{u'(c)} \dot{c} = \rho - \left[F'(K) - \delta \right]$$

Problems

1. Present the main assumption of the Solow-Swan model. What type of convergence is predicted by the model? What is the long-run effect of short-run growth-enhancing policies (such as an increase in the saving rate)?

2. **Conditional convergence in the Solow model**

This problem illustrates algebraically the concept of conditional convergence, using a Cobb-Douglas production function. Assume that output per capita can be written as $y = Ak^\alpha$ and that population grows at rate n, the depreciation rate is δ, and there is no technical progress.

a. Using the steady-state condition in the chapter, express the saving rate as a function of the per capita steady-state level of capital, $k*$.

b. Using the dynamic equation for capital accumulation of capital, express the growth rate of capital, $\dot{k}/k$, as a function $k/k*$. Interpret the result.

3. **Land in the Solow model**

Assume a production function that takes a Cobb-Douglas form in capital K, labor L, and land C:

$$Y = A e^{gt} K^\alpha L^\beta C^\lambda$$

where $A > 0$, $g > 0$ (rate of technological progress), $\alpha > 0$, $\beta > 0$, $\lambda > 0$, and $\alpha + \beta + \lambda = 1$. The amount of land, C, is fixed.

Labor grows at the constant rate $n > 0$, capital depreciates at rate $\delta > 0$, and the saving rate is exogenously given at the level of s.

---

29. That is, the extra K will raise the flow of output by an amount equal to the net marginal product $F'(K) - \delta$, each unit of which has a utility value of λ, and it will also allow the holder to benefit from the increase in the utility value of the unit (or suffer the loss if negative) at the rate $\dot{\lambda}$.

Define $\kappa \equiv K/Y$, the capital-output ratio.

a. Write down the growth rates of capital stock and output as functions of κ.

b. Using the results from item 3a, write down the growth rate of the capital-output ratio as a function of κ.

c. Defining steady state as a situation in which κ is constant, compute the steady-state value of κ.

d. Compute the steady-state growth rate of output. Is it positive?

e. Compute the steady-state growth rate of output per capita. Is it positive? Explain how this value depends on the growth rate of technological progress g and the presence of land.

4. The Golden Rule of capital accumulation and dynamic inefficiency in the Solow model

Consider the Solow model presented in the chapter.

a. Assuming the economy is in steady state (at per capita capital level k^*), and for given levels of the parameters A, n, δ, s, and g, write down the level of per capita consumption as a function of k^*.

b. For what level of k^* is per capita consumption in steady state maximized? This condition is called the *golden rule of capital accumulation.*

c. Rewrite the preceding condition as a function of the saving rate, instead of per capita capital stock.

d. Explain why an economy that is saving more than the rate implied by the golden rule is *dynamically inefficient*; that is, its per capita consumption at all points in time could be increased by reducing the saving rate.

5. Stone-Geary preferences (based on Barro and Sala-i-Martin 1995a)

Consider the Cass-Koopmans-Ramsey model presented in the chapter, with the following formulation for households' instantaneous utility function (called Stone-Geary preferences):

$$u(c) = \frac{(c - \overline{c})^{1-\varepsilon} - 1}{1 - \varepsilon}$$

where $\overline{c} \geq 0$ represents the subsistence level of per capita consumption.

a. What is the intertemporal elasticity of substitution for the new form of the utility function? For $\overline{c} > 0$, how does the elasticity change as c increases?

b. Consider the Euler equation with the rate of consumption growth on the right-hand side, as seen in the chapter. How would this equation change under the Stone-Geary formulation of preferences?

c. How would the growth rate of consumption change as $\overline{c}$ increases? Provide some intuition for this result.

6. Measuring the speed of convergence in the Solow model

Consider the capital growth rate equation for a Cobb-Douglas aggregate production function, $\dot{k}/k = sk^{-(1-\alpha)} - (n + g + \delta)$.

a. Compute the speed of convergence $\beta \equiv -\partial(\dot{k}/k)/\partial\log(k)$, that is, by how much the capital growth rate declines as the capital stock increases in a proportional sense.

b. How does an increase in α affect β?

c. How does β evolve over time? Compute the speed of convergence in steady state β^*.

d. By log-linearizing the capital growth equation in the neighborhood of the steady state, show that $\dot{k}/k \cong -\beta^*[\log(k/k^*)]$, where k^* is the steady-state level of per capita capital.

2 The AK Model

2.1 Introduction

The neoclassical model presented in the previous chapter takes the rate of technological change as being determined exogenously, by noneconomic forces. There is good reason, however, to believe that technological change depends on economic decisions, because it comes from industrial innovations made by profit-seeking firms and depends on the funding of science, the accumulation of human capital, and other such economic activities. Technology is thus an endogenous variable, determined within the economic system. Growth theories should take this endogeneity into account, especially since the rate of technological progress is what determines the long-run growth rate.

Incorporating endogenous technology into growth theory forces us to deal with the difficult phenomenon of increasing returns to scale. More specifically, people must be given an incentive to improve technology. But because the aggregate production function F exhibits constant returns in K and L alone, Euler's theorem tells us that it will take all of the economy's output to pay capital and labor their marginal products in producing final output, leaving nothing over to pay for the resources used in improving technology.[1] Thus a theory of endogenous technology cannot be based on the usual theory of competitive equilibrium, which requires that all factors be paid their marginal products.

Arrow's (1962) solution to this problem was to suppose that technological progress is an unintended consequence of producing new capital goods, a phenomenon dubbed "learning by doing." Learning by doing was assumed to be purely external to the firms responsible for it. That is, if technological progress

---

1. Euler's theorem states that if F is homogeneous of degree 1 in K and L (the definition of constant returns), then

$$F_1(K,L)K + F_2(K,L)L = F(K,L) \tag{E}$$

where F_i is the partial derivative with respect to the ith argument. The marginal products of K and L are F_1 and F_2, respectively. So if K and L are paid their marginal products, then the left-hand side is the total payment to capital (price F_1 times quantity K) plus the total payment to labor, and the equation states that these payments add up to total output.

To verify Euler's theorem take the equation

$$F(\lambda K, \lambda L) = \lambda F(K,L) \tag{C}$$

that defines homogeneity of degree one, and differentiate both sides with respect to λ at the point $\lambda = 1$. Since equation (C) must hold for all $\lambda > 0$, therefore the two derivatives must be equal, implying equation (E).

depends on the aggregate production of capital and firms are all very small, then they can all be assumed to take the rate of technological progress as being given independently of their own production of capital goods. So each firm maximizes profit by paying K and L their marginal products, without offering any additional payment for their contribution to technological progress.

Learning by doing formed the basis of the first model of endogenous growth theory, which is known as the AK model. The AK model assumes that when people accumulate capital, learning by doing generates technological progress that tends to raise the marginal product of capital, thus offsetting the tendency for the marginal product to diminish when technology is unchanged. The model results in a production function of the form $Y = AK$, in which the marginal product of capital is equal to the constant A.

The AK model predicts that a country's long-run growth rate will depend on economic factors such as thrift and the efficiency of resource allocation. In subsequent chapters we will develop alternative models of endogenous growth that emphasize not thrift and efficiency but creativity and innovation, which we see as the main driving forces behind economic growth. But given its historical place as the first endogenous growth model, the AK paradigm is an important part of any economist's tool kit. Accordingly we devote this chapter to developing the AK model and to summarizing the empirical debate that took place in the 1990s between its proponents and proponents of the neoclassical model of Solow and Swan.

2.1.1 The Harrod-Domar Model

An early precursor of the AK model was the Harrod-Domar model,[2] which assumes that the aggregate production function has fixed technological coefficients:

$$Y = F(K, L) = \min\{AK, BL\}$$

where A and B are the fixed coefficients. Under this technology, producing a unit of output requires $1/A$ units of capital and $1/B$ units of labor; if either input falls short of this minimum requirement, there is no way to compensate by substituting the other input.

With a fixed-coefficient technology, there will either be surplus capital or surplus labor in the economy, depending on whether the historically given supply of capital is more or less than (B/A) times the exogenous supply of labor. When

---

2. See Harrod (1939) and Domar (1946).

$AK < BL$, which is the case that Harrod and Domar emphasize, capital is the limiting factor. Firms will produce the amount

$$Y = AK$$

and hire the amount $(1/B)Y = (1/B)AK < L$ of labor.

Now, with a fixed saving rate, we know that the capital stock will grow according to the same equation as in the neoclassical model:

$$\dot{K} = sY - \delta K \tag{2.1}$$

These last two equations imply

$$\dot{K} = sAK - \delta K$$

so that the growth rate of capital will be

$$g = \dot{K}/K = sA - \delta$$

Because output is strictly proportional to capital, g will also be the rate of growth of output. It follows immediately that the growth rate of output is increasing in the saving rate s.

The problem with the Harrod-Domar model is that it cannot account for the sustained growth in output per person that has taken place in the world economy since the Industrial Revolution. To see this point, let n be the rate of population growth. Then the growth rate of output per person is $g - n$. But if this is positive, then so is the growth rate of capital per person K/L, since K also grows at the rate g. Eventually a point will be reached where capital is no longer the limiting factor in the production function. That is, K/L will eventually exceed the limit B/A above which labor becomes the limiting factor. From then on we will instead have $Y = BL$, implying that Y will grow at the same rate as L; that is, output per person Y/L will cease to grow.

2.2 A Neoclassical Version of Harrod-Domar

2.2.1 Basic Setup

The first AK model that could account for sustained growth in per capita output was that of M. Frankel (1962), who was motivated by the challenge of constructing a model that would combine the virtues of the Solow-Swan and Harrod-Domar models. As in Solow-Swan, this model would display perfect competition, substitutable factors (with Cobb-Douglas production technologies), and full employment. As in Harrod-Domar, the model would generate a long-run growth rate that depends on the saving rate.

Frankel built his model on the foundation of learning by doing. He recognized that because individual firms contribute to the accumulation of technological knowledge when they accumulate capital,[3] the AK structure of the Harrod-Domar model does not require fixed coefficients. Instead, he assumed that each firm $j \in \{1, 2, \ldots, N\}$ has a production function of the form

$$y_j = \bar{A} k_j^\alpha L_j^{1-\alpha}$$

where k_j and L_j are the firm's own employment of capital and labor, and $\bar{A}$ is (aggregate) productivity. Aggregate productivity in turn depends upon the total amount of capital that has been accumulated by all firms, namely,

$$\bar{A} = A_0 \cdot \left(\sum_{j=1}^{N} k_j \right)^\eta$$

where η is a positive exponent that reflects the extent of the knowledge externalities generated among firms.

For simplicity assume that

$$L_j = 1 \quad \text{for all } j;$$

let

$$K = \sum_{j=1}^{N} k_j$$

denote the aggregate capital stock; and let

$$Y = \sum_{j=1}^{N} y_j$$

denote the aggregate output flow.

Since all firms face the same technology and the same factor prices, they will hire factors in the same proportions, so that

$$k_j = K/N \quad \text{for all } j$$

---

3. He called it "development" rather than "knowledge."

This expression in turn implies that in equilibrium

$$\bar{A} = A_0 K^\eta$$

Hence individual outputs are all equal to

$$y_j = A_0 K^\eta (K/N)^\alpha$$

and therefore aggregate output is

$$Y = N A_0 K^\eta (K/N)^\alpha$$

which can be written as

$$Y = A K^{\alpha+\eta} \tag{2.2}$$

where $A = A_0 N^{1-a}$.

The model is then closed by assuming a constant saving rate, which generates the same capital accumulation equation (2.1) as in Solow-Swan and Harrod-Domar. Using the output equation (2.2) to substitute for Y in this equation we have

$$\dot{K} = s A K^{\alpha+\eta} - \delta K$$

so the growth rate of the capital stock is

$$g_K = \dot{K}/K = s A K^{\alpha+\eta-1} - \delta \tag{2.3}$$

2.2.2   Three Cases

We now analyze the dynamic path of the economy defined by equation (2.3). Three cases must be considered.

1. $\alpha + \eta < 1$

In this case the extent of knowledge spillovers η is not sufficiently strong to counteract the effect $1 - \alpha$ of decreasing returns to individual capital accumulation, and the long-run growth rate is zero. The case produces the same aggregate dynamics as the Solow-Swan model with no technological progress and no population growth, which we analyzed in the previous chapter. That is, according to equation (2.3) there is a steady-state capital stock at which the growth rate g_K of capital is zero, namely,

$$K^* = (sA/\delta)^{1/(1-\alpha-\eta)} \tag{2.4}$$

If K were to rise above K^*, the growth rate would turn negative, since in this case equation (2.3) makes g_K a decreasing function of K. Thus K would fall back to its steady state, at which the growth rate of capital is zero and therefore the growth rate of output (2.2) is zero.

2. $\alpha + \eta > 1$

In this case learning externalities are so strong that the aggregate economy experiences an ever-increasing growth rate. That is, again equation (2.4) defines a unique steady-state capital stock but it is no longer stable, because g_K is now an increasing function of K, so that if K were to rise above K^* it would keep on rising, at an ever-increasing rate. This is known as the *explosive growth* case.

3. $\alpha + \eta = 1$

In this knife-edge case, learning externalities exactly compensate decreasing returns to individual capital accumulation, so that the aggregate production function becomes an AK function, namely,

$$Y = AK$$

Thus the aggregate growth rate becomes

$$g = \dot{K}/K = sA - \delta$$

which is nothing but the Harrod-Domar growth rate, now obtained as the long-run growth rate in a model with substitutable factors and full market clearing. In other words, as capital increases, output increases in proportion, even though there is continual full employment of labor and even though there is substitutability in the aggregate production function, because knowledge automatically increases by just the right amount. Unlike in the Harrod-Domar model, here an increase in the saving propensity s will increase the growth rate permanently even though output per person is growing at a positive rate (namely, $g - n = g$).

2.3   An AK Model with Intertemporal Utility Maximization

Romer (1986)[4] developed a Ramsey version of the AK model, in which the constant saving rate is replaced by intertemporal utility maximization by a represen-

---

4. Romer actually laid out more than an AK model, inasmuch as his approach allowed for general production and utility functions and assumed that there were strictly *increasing* social returns to capital. What we present here is the limiting special case that many followers have extracted from Romer's analysis, in which there are constant social returns to capital and an isoelastic utility function.

tative individual, again with the assumption that individuals do not internalize the externalities associated with the growth of knowledge.

2.3.1   The Setup

Romer assumed a production function with externalities of the same sort as considered previously and focused on the case in which the labor supply per firm was equal to unity and the rate of capital depreciation was zero ($\delta = 0$). Saving is determined by the owner of the representative one-worker firm, whose dynamic optimization problem is to

$$\max \int_0^\infty u\left(c_t\right)e^{-\rho t}dt \quad \text{subject to } \dot{k} = \overline{A}k^\alpha - c$$

where k is the capital stock of the individual firm, $y = \overline{A}k^\alpha$ is its output, $c = c_t$ is the current consumption of its owner-worker, and $\overline{A}$ denotes aggregate productivity that is taken as given by each individual firm.[5]

As in the previous section, aggregate productivity depends upon the aggregate capital stock, namely,

$$\overline{A} = A_0 K^\eta$$

where

$$K = \sum_1^N k_j$$

Assuming a constant intertemporal elasticity of substitution as in the previous chapter, namely, $u\left(c\right) = \dfrac{c^{1-\varepsilon} - 1}{1 - \varepsilon}$, one obtains the Euler condition[6]

$$-\varepsilon\dot{c}/c = \rho - \alpha\overline{A}k^{\alpha-1}$$

Having rational expectations, individuals correctly anticipate that all firms will employ the same capital in equilibrium (given that these firms are all identical), so

$$K = Nk$$

---

5. This maximization problem is the same as that of the Cass-Koopmans-Ramsey model analyzed in the previous chapter, but in the limiting case where the length of the time period has shrunk to zero, so time has become continuous.

6. This Euler condition follows from our analysis of the Ramsey model in the previous chapter, but in this case the net private marginal product of capital is $F_1(k,A) - \delta = \alpha\overline{A}k^{\alpha-1} - 0 = \alpha\overline{A}k^{\alpha-1}$.

and therefore the preceding Euler condition can be written as

$$-\varepsilon\dot{c}/c = \rho - \alpha A_0 N^\eta k^{\alpha+\eta-1} \tag{2.5}$$

2.3.2 Long-Run Growth

Aggregate output Y is given by the same equation (2.2) as in the Frankel model, because

$$Y = Ny = NA_0 K^\eta (K/N)^\alpha = AK^{\alpha+\eta}$$

Again there are three cases to consider depending on the exponent $\alpha + \eta$.

1. $\alpha + \eta < 1$

In the case of decreasing returns, again growth will vanish asymptotically as in the neoclassical model without technological progress. To see this point, assume, on the contrary, that the growth rate is bounded above zero. The following argument shows that this assumption leads to a contradiction. Positive growth implies that the capital stock k will converge to infinity over time, implying that the right-hand side of equation (2.5) must converge to ρ, since the exponent $\alpha + \eta - 1$ is negative, and in turn implying that the growth rate $\dot{c}/c$ will become negative, a result which contradicts our assumption of positive growth.

2. $\alpha + \eta > 1$

In the case of increasing returns to capital, then, as in the Frankel model, there will be explosive growth. This can be seen using the Euler equation (2.5). Specifically, if growth is positive in the long run, then the capital stock k converges to infinity over time. This result, together with the fact that $\alpha + \eta > 1$, implies that the right-hand side of equation (2.5) converges to negative infinity, which in turn implies that the growth rate $\dot{c}/c$ must converge to infinity.

3. $\alpha + \eta = 1$

In the AK case where there are constant social returns to capital, then, as in the Frankel model, the economy will sustain a strictly positive but finite growth rate g, in which diminishing private returns to capital are just offset by the external improvements in technology $\overline{A}$ that they bring about. More precisely, in a steady state, consumption and output will grow at the same rate, so in this case (2.5) implies

$$g = \dot{c}/c = \left(\alpha A_0 N^\eta - \rho\right)/\varepsilon$$

In particular, we see that the higher the discount rate ρ (that is, the lower the propensity to save), or the lower the intertemporal elasticity of substitution measured by $1/\varepsilon$, the lower will be the steady-state growth rate g.

2.3.3   Welfare

So far we have just reproduced the results already generated by the model with a constant saving rate. However, moving to a Ramsey model where savings behavior results from explicit intertemporal utility maximization allows us to also conduct a welfare analysis. In particular one can show that, because individuals and individual firms do not internalize the effect of individual capital accumulation on knowledge $\bar{A}$ when optimizing on c and k, the equilibrium growth rate $g = (\alpha A_0 N^\eta - \rho)/\varepsilon$ is less than the socially optimal rate of growth. More formally, the social planner who internalizes the knowledge externalities induced by individual capital accumulation would solve the dynamic program

$$\max \int_0^\infty e^{-\rho t} u\left(c_t\right) dt \quad \text{subject to } \dot{k} = A_0 \left(Nk\right)^\eta k^\alpha - c$$

That is, he would internalize the fact that $\bar{A} = A_0(Nk)^\eta$ when choosing k. When $u(c) = \dfrac{c^{1-\varepsilon} - 1}{1 - \varepsilon}$, we obtain the Euler equation

$$-\varepsilon \dot{c}/c = \rho - \left(\alpha + \eta\right) A_0 N^\eta k^{\alpha + \eta - 1}$$

With constant social returns to capital ($\alpha + \eta = 1$), this yields the socially optimal rate of growth

$$g^* = \left(N^\eta A_0 - \rho\right)\big/\varepsilon > g = \left(\alpha N^\eta A_0 - \rho\right)\big/\varepsilon$$

2.3.4   Concluding Remarks

First, although growth has been endogenized, it relies entirely on *external* (and therefore unremunerated) accumulation of knowledge. Introducing rewards to technological progress, as we shall do in the following chapters, adds a new dimension of complexity, because it moves us away from a world of perfect competition into a world of imperfect competition among large individual firms.

Second, in the case where $\alpha + \eta = 1$, cross-country variations in parameters such as α and ρ will result in permanent differences in rates of economic growth. Thus the simple *AK* approach does *not* predict conditional convergence in income per capita; the cross-section distribution of income should instead exhibit both absolute and conditional divergence. We shall return to this issue in the next sections of the chapter.

2.4   The Debate between Neoclassical and AK Advocates, in a Nutshell

In this section, we briefly reflect on a now closed debate between advocates of the neoclassical approach and those of the AK model. A first argument in favor of the AK approach is that it can account for the persistently positive growth rates of per capita GDP that we observe in most countries worldwide, whereas the neoclassical model cannot explain it.

However, advocates of the neoclassical model can argue that the AK model cannot explain cross-country or cross-regional convergence. Two main types of convergence appear in the discussions about growth across regions or countries. *Absolute convergence* takes place when poorer areas grow faster than richer ones whatever their respective characteristics. However, as we already saw in the previous chapter, there is *conditional convergence* when a country (or a region) grows faster if it is farther below its own steady state; or equivalently, if we take two countries or regions with identical savings rates, depreciation rates, and aggregate production technologies, the country that begins with lower output per capita has a higher growth rate than the country that begins with higher output per capita. This latter form of convergence is definitely the weaker.

Now consider two regions within a country (for example, the United States) or two countries that share the same underlying characteristics (in particular the same saving rate and the same depreciation rate of capital). On the one hand, under constant returns in the aggregate production function, as in AK models, per capita GDP in a country or region with lower initial capital stock will never converge to that of countries with higher initial capital stock, even in the weak sense of conditional convergence, simply because these two countries will always grow at the same rate independently of their amounts of accumulated capital. On the other hand, with diminishing returns to capital, the level of income per capita should converge toward its steady-state value, with the speed of convergence increasing in the distance to the steady state. In other words, lower initial values of income per capita should generate higher transitional growth rates, once the determinants of the steady state are controlled for. Figure 2.1, drawn from Barro and Sala-i-Martin (1995b) shows a clear conditional convergence pattern among U.S. states. This, in turn, questions the AK approach.

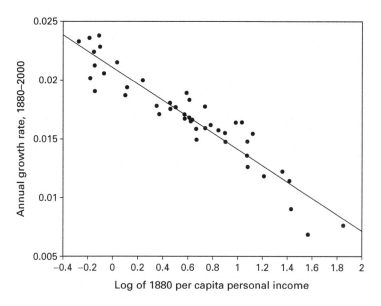

Figure 2.1
Convergence of personal income across U.S. states

Turning to the evidence on convergence of countries, we find that in some countries (in particular China and the Asian tigers, namely, Singapore, Hong Kong, Taiwan, and Korea) per capita GDP manages to converge toward per capita GDP levels in industrialized countries. This finding again may indicate that the Solow-Swan model, with its emphasis on diminishing returns to capital and transitional dynamics, is closer to the truth than the AK model. However, what the neoclassical framework cannot account for is the fact that while some countries appear to converge toward the world technology frontier, other countries (for example, in Africa) diverge from it. In chapter 7 we will show how this phenomenon, commonly referred to as *club convergence*, can be explained using an innovation-based model of endogenous growth, the Schumpeterian growth model. But before we present this new framework and compare it to the AK and neoclassical models, let us briefly see how the AK advocates have tried to argue their case against the proponents of the neoclassical model.

A first counterargument by AK advocates involves the issue of returns to capital and the estimation of the elasticity of output with respect to physical capital. Early empirical work on endogenous-growth models centered on this question. In particular, Romer (1987) carries out the following text. Suppose first that the consumption good is produced according to a Cobb-Douglas production function as in the simplest version of the Solow-Swan model:

$$Y = K^\alpha (AL)^{1-\alpha}, \quad 0 < \alpha < 1$$

Under perfect competition in the market for final goods, and given the assumption of constant returns to scale implicit in this Cobb-Douglas function, the coefficients α and $(1 - \alpha)$ should be equal to the shares of capital and labor in national income, respectively, that is approximately $\frac{1}{3}$ and $\frac{2}{3}$ in the U.S. case. To see why, notice that under perfect competition for final goods, capital and labor are each paid their marginal products. The share of labor in national income is thus equal to

$$\frac{\partial Y}{\partial L} L = (1-\alpha) K^\alpha A^{1-\alpha} L^{-\alpha} \cdot L = (1-\alpha) Y$$

and similarly

$$\frac{\partial Y}{\partial K} K = \alpha K^{\alpha-1} A^{1-\alpha} L^{1-\alpha} \cdot K = \alpha Y$$

Now, using both time series and cross-section data, Romer estimated the true elasticity of final goods output with respect to physical capital to be higher than the value $\frac{1}{3}$ predicted by the Solow-Swan model, and perhaps lying in the range between 0.7 and 1.0. This result in turn appeared to be consistent with the existence of externalities to capital accumulation, as captured by the formalization $A \approx K^\eta$ in the AK model. Such externalities imply that the elasticity of final output with respect to physical capital will be larger than the share of capital income in value added.

A second counterargument involves the speed of convergence predicted by the neoclassical model. First, it is intuitive that the lower α is, that is, the more decreasing returns to capital are, the faster convergence will be over time, since decreasing returns are the source of convergence. And indeed, in the limit case where $\alpha = 1$, that is, in the constant returns case, convergence never happens! This negative correlation between α and the speed of convergence can be formally established (see problem 5 from chapter 1). Now, performing a cross-country regression as specified in section 1.2.3, Mankiw, Romer, and Weil (1992) find that the rate at which countries converge to their steady states is slower than that predicted by a Solow-Swan model with a capital share of one third. The empirically observed speed of convergence suggests a share of broad capital in output of around 0.7–0.8. One explanation may again be the existence of externalities in capital accumulation of the kind emphasized by AK models. However, Mankiw, Romer, and Weil propose an alternative explanation, which boils down to augmenting the Solow-Swan model by including human capital on top of physical capital. They specify the following constant-returns production function:

$$Y = K^{\alpha} H^{\beta} (AL)^{1-\alpha-\beta}$$

Using a simple proxy for the rate of investment in human capital, they argue that this technology is consistent with the cross-country data. Their cross-section regressions indicate that both α and β are about 1/3, suggesting that the AK model is wrong in assuming constant returns to broad capital.

Interestingly, the elasticity of output with respect to the investment ratio becomes equal to $\dfrac{\alpha}{1-\alpha-\beta}$ in the augmented model, instead of $\dfrac{\alpha}{1-\alpha}$. In other words, the presence of human capital accumulation increases the impact of physical investment on the steady-state level of output. Moreover, the Solow-Swan model augmented with human capital can account for a very low rate of convergence to steady states. It is also consistent with evidence on international capital flows; see Barro, Mankiw, and Sala-i-Martín (1995) and Manzocchi and Martin (1996). Yet the constant-returns specification of Mankiw, Romer, and Weil delivers the same long-run growth predictions as the basic Solow-Swan model.

Overall, empirical evidence regarding returns to capital tends to discriminate in favor of decreasing returns, and hence in favor of the neoclassical growth model. Mankiw, Romer, and Weil claim that the neoclassical growth model is correct not only in assuming diminishing returns, but also in suggesting that efficiency grows at the same rate across countries.

True, their augmented model suffers from the same basic problem as the original Solow model, namely, that it cannot explain sustained long-run growth. But here the line of defense is to say that the model can still explain growth on the transition path to the steady state, and that such transition may last for many years so that the data would not allow us to tell apart transitional growth from steady-state growth.

However, another criticism to the augmented neoclassical model came from Benhabib and Spiegel (1994). Their point is that the neoclassical and

Mankiw-Romer-Weil models all predict that growth can increase only as a result of a higher rate of factor accumulation. However, based on cross-country panel data, they argue that the countries that accumulated human capital most quickly between 1965 and 1985 have not grown accordingly, and more importantly, they show that long-run growth appears to be related to the initial *level* of human capital. This finding in turn suggests that, when trying to explain the historical experience of developing countries, one should turn to models in which technology differs across countries and in which human capital stock promotes technological catch-up and/or innovation. We will return to this topic in chapter 13.

Overall, if the AK model appears to be dominated by the neoclassical model, one must still come to grip with the fact that growth appears to be sustained over time, and also positively correlated with variables such as human capital stocks. Building new endogenous growth models that account for those facts, as well as convergence, will be a main challenge of the theories developed in the next chapters.

2.5   An Open-Economy AK Model with Convergence

In this section we present a recent attempt at saving the AK model from the criticism that it cannot explain convergence. This attempt, developed by Acemoglu and Ventura (2002), henceforth AV, links to international trade and the notion of terms of trade. The idea is to show that, if we take into account that countries are tied together by international trade, even AK models can exhibit convergence in growth rates. They can do so because in an open economy the parameter A will depend on the country's terms of trade. If it keeps growing faster than the rest of the world, the supply of its goods on world markets will keep growing relative to the supply of foreign goods, which will drive down their relative price. The terms of trade will fall, lowering A and therefore lowering the country's growth rate until it converges with the growth rate of the rest of the world. In such a world each country will look like an AK model for given terms of trade, and yet it will converge, not because of a diminishing physical marginal product of capital but because of a diminishing value of the marginal product of capital. The argument is clever and logically tight, even though one may object to it on empirical grounds.

Here we present in stages a simplified version of the AV model, with constant savings rates. First we study a closed economy with two sectors—a final sector and an intermediate sector. Next we assume that production in the final sector requires as input not just the domestically produced intermediate product but also a foreign intermediate product, under the assumption that the relative price of that foreign product (the inverse of this country's terms of trade) is given. This produces a similar version of the AK model, one in which A depends positively on the terms of trade. Finally we close the model off by supposing that the foreign country is just like the domestic country but possibly with a different saving rate. In this last model the terms of trade will depend inversely on this country's capital stock relative to the foreign country's.

2.5.1 A Two-Sector Closed Economy

The final good Y and the intermediate good X are both produced under perfect competition. The final good is produced with capital K and intermediates according to

$$Y = K^\alpha X^{1-\alpha} \tag{2.6}$$

and the intermediate is produced with the final good one for one.

Let the final good Y be the numéraire. Then the unit price of good Y is equal to one, and this is also the unit cost of producing the intermediate good. Since markets are perfectly competitive, the price of intermediate good X is equal to its unit cost; thus it is also equal to one. Given these assumptions, the demand for the intermediate good X is determined by profit maximization in the final sector. That is, the optimal X maximizes final-sector profits:

$$\Pi = K^\alpha X^{1-\alpha} - X$$

The first-order condition for this problem is

$$(1-\alpha) K^\alpha X^{-\alpha} = 1$$

or equivalently

$$X = (1-\alpha)^{1/\alpha} K$$

Substituting back into equation (2.6) we obtain

$$Y = (1-\alpha)^{\frac{1-\alpha}{\alpha}} K$$

So even though the production function (2.6) has a diminishing marginal product of capital, we still have an AK model, with $Y = AK$, where the marginal product of capital A is a constant given by

$$A = (1-\alpha)^{\frac{1-\alpha}{\alpha}}$$

The reason is that the production technology for the final good has constant returns with respect to K and X, both of which are produced with K.

Now, let us assume a constant saving rate so that we can close the model with the same capital accumulation equation as in the Solow model, namely,[7]

$$\dot{K} = sY - \delta K$$

Then, as in the Frankel model analyzed in section 2.2, the country's growth rate depends positively on its saving rate according to

$$g = \dot{K}/K = sA - \delta = s(1-\alpha)^{\frac{1-\alpha}{\alpha}} - \delta$$

2.5.2 Opening up the Economy with Fixed Terms of Trade

Now suppose that producing the Y good requires not just X but also a foreign-produced intermediate product X_f, according to the production function

$$Y = K^\alpha X^{\frac{1-\alpha}{2}} \left(X_f\right)^{\frac{1-\alpha}{2}}$$

Both X and X_f are tradable goods; however, capital is not tradable.

As before, since it takes one unit of final good to produce one unit of X, and since the market for X is perfectly competitive, the price of X is unity. Suppose the price p_f of the foreign good is given. Then domestic producers of Y will choose X and X_f to solve the problem

$$\max_{X, X_f} \left\{ K^\alpha X^{\frac{1-\alpha}{2}} \left(X_f\right)^{\frac{1-\alpha}{2}} - X - p_f X_f \right\}$$

---

7. This is not quite the same as in the neoclassical model because Y is not the country's GDP, just its production of the final good, some of which is used as an input to the intermediate sector. However, Y is proportional to GDP because

GDP = Value added in final sector + Value added in intermediate sector
$$= (Y - X) + 0$$
$$= (1-\alpha)^{\frac{1-\alpha}{\alpha}} K - (1-\alpha)^{\frac{1}{\alpha}} K$$
$$= \alpha (1-\alpha)^{\frac{1-\alpha}{\alpha}} K = \alpha Y$$

so the parameter s is actually the country's saving rate, as conventionally defined, multiplied by the constant α.

which yields

$$X = \left(\frac{1-\alpha}{2}\right) Y \tag{2.7}$$

$$p_f X_f = \left(\frac{1-\alpha}{2}\right) Y \tag{2.8}$$

Substituting back into the production function yields

$$Y = \left(\frac{1-\alpha}{2}\right)^{\frac{1-\alpha}{\alpha}} \left(p_f\right)^{-\frac{1-\alpha}{2\alpha}} K \tag{2.9}$$

So again we have an AK model, with $Y = AK$, where now the constant marginal product of capital A depends negatively on the relative price of foreign goods (that is, positively on the country's terms of trade, which are just $1/p_f$):

$$A = \left(\frac{1-\alpha}{2}\right)^{\frac{1-\alpha}{\alpha}} \left(p_f\right)^{-\frac{1-\alpha}{2\alpha}}$$

The reason is that, as p_f goes up, the domestic country needs to spend more on the imported inputs that are combined with capital, thus lowering the amount of income it can generate from an extra unit of capital.

It follows that the growth rate depends not just on saving but also on the terms of trade:

$$g = \dot{K}/K = sA - \delta = s\left(\frac{1-\alpha}{2}\right)^{\frac{1-\alpha}{\alpha}} \left(p_f\right)^{-\frac{1-\alpha}{2\alpha}} - \delta \tag{2.10}$$

Now assume that the domestic country can only export good X in exchange for good X_f, and suppose that "initially" the domestic growth rate exceeds the world growth rate. Then the foreign demand for the country's exported good X will not grow as fast as the country's demand for X_f, implying that the relative price of the foreign good p_f must increase so as to preserve trade balance. This increase in turn will tend to bring the domestic country's growth rate down to the world level. To see how this process might work in more detail, in the next subsection we will suppose that the rest of the world consists of a single country that behaves just like the domestic country.

2.5.3 Closing the Model with a Two-Country Analysis*

Suppose that the rest of the world consists of a single country, just like the domestic country, except possibly with a different saving rate s_f. This foreign country will produce its final good using the same technology as used in the domestic country, so that its output of final product and its use of its own intermediate product and this country's will be determined as before except that from the foreign country's point of view the price of imported intermediate products is $1/p_f$ instead of p_f.

Proceeding as before, we see that the foreign country will import the amount F_X of the domestic country's intermediate good, where F_X is given by

$$\left(1/p_f\right)F_X = \left(\frac{1-\alpha}{2}\right)Y_f$$

which is the same as equation (2.8) except that Y has been replaced by the foreign production Y_f and p_f by $1/p_f$.

By analogy to equation (2.9) we have

$$Y_f = \left(\frac{1-\alpha}{2}\right)^{\frac{1-\alpha}{\alpha}} \left(p_f\right)^{\frac{1-\alpha}{2\alpha}} K_f$$

where K_f is the foreign capital stock.[8] From these last two equations

$$F_X = \left(\frac{1-\alpha}{2}\right)^{\frac{1}{\alpha}} \left(p_f\right)^{\frac{1+\alpha}{2\alpha}} K_f$$

But F_X is not just the foreign country's imports; it is also the domestic country's exports. And trade balance imposes that this figure in turn be equal to the value (in domestic goods) of the domestic country's imports, namely, $p_f X_f$, because exports are what we use to buy imports. So from equations (2.8) and (2.9) we have

$$F_X = \left(\frac{1-\alpha}{2}\right)^{\frac{1}{\alpha}} \left(p_f\right)^{-\frac{1-\alpha}{2\alpha}} K$$

---

* Although section 2.5.3 does not involve advanced mathematics, it does involve several lengthy derivations that some readers may wish to avoid.

8. Note that the exponent of p_f in this equation is the negative of the exponent of p_f in the analogous domestic equation (2.9). This is the case because the price of the other country's intermediate product is p_f for the domestic country but $1/p_f$ for the foreign country.

By equating the right-hand sides of these last two equations, we can solve for the equilibrium relative price of foreign goods:

$$p_f = k_R^\alpha$$

where k_R is the relative capital stock:

$$k_R = \frac{K}{K_f}$$

If the domestic capital stock grows faster than the foreign stock, k_R will rise, so will the relative price p_f of foreign intermediates, and hence the domestic growth rate will fall. This decrease will stabilize k_R. More formally, we have, from the domestic growth equation (2.10),

$$\dot{K}/K = s\left(\frac{1-\alpha}{2}\right)^{\frac{1-\alpha}{\alpha}} \left(p_f\right)^{-\frac{1-\alpha}{2\alpha}} - \delta = s\left(\frac{1-\alpha}{2}\right)^{\frac{1-\alpha}{\alpha}} k_R^{-\frac{1-\alpha}{2}} - \delta$$

and, from the analogous foreign growth equation,[9]

$$\dot{K}_f/K_f = s_f\left(\frac{1-\alpha}{2}\right)^{\frac{1-\alpha}{\alpha}} \left(p_f\right)^{\frac{1-\alpha}{2\alpha}} - \delta = s_f\left(\frac{1-\alpha}{2}\right)^{\frac{1-\alpha}{\alpha}} k_R^{\frac{1-\alpha}{2}} - \delta$$

Since the growth rate of the relative stock k_R is just the differential growth rate $\dot{K}/K - \dot{K}_f/K_f$, these last two equations imply

$$\dot{k}_R/k_R = \left(\frac{1-\alpha}{2}\right)^{\frac{1-\alpha}{\alpha}} \left[sk_R^{-\frac{1-\alpha}{2}} - s_f k_R^{\frac{1-\alpha}{2}} \right]$$

This is a stable ordinary differential equation with the unique steady state

$$k_R^* = \left(\frac{s}{s_f}\right)^{\frac{1}{1-\alpha}}$$

The steady state is asymptotically stable because the right-hand side of the differential equation is decreasing in k_R. So the growth rate of k_R will approach zero,

9. Again, the coefficient of p_f in one equation is the negative of the coefficient in the other, because the price of the other country's intermediate is p_f for the domestic country but $1/p_f$ for the foreign country. Hence the coefficient of k_R in one equation is also the negative of the coefficient in the other.

implying that the growth rates of K and K_f will approach each other—convergence.

2.5.4 Concluding Comment

We have now seen how the AV model delivers convergence through international trade and its effects on capital accumulation. Faster growth in the domestic economy increases the price of the imported intermediate good, thus resulting in a deterioration of the country's terms of trade, which in turn reduces the rate of capital accumulation. Unfortunately, the model is not fully consistent with empirical evidence. In particular, the prediction that growth reduces a country's terms of trade is counterfactual. So although the AV model is an instructive extension of AK theory to the case of an open economy, in the end it too cannot account for the evidence on cross-country convergence.

2.6 Conclusion

In the previous chapter we saw that the neoclassical model provides the standard for parsimoniously modeling growth and convergence. However, the model leaves the rate of technological change exogenous and hence unexplained; therefore, it cannot explain sustained long-run growth. In this chapter we have shown that the AK model can explain long-run growth using the same basic assumptions as the neoclassical model but adding knowledge externalities among firms that accumulate physical capital. However, the AK model does not provide a convincing explanation for convergence.

In our view the underlying source of the difficulties faced by the AK model is that it does not make an explicit distinction between capital accumulation and technological progress. In effect it just lumps together the physical and human capital whose accumulation is studied by neoclassical theory with the intellectual capital that is accumulated when technological progress is made. So starting with the next chapter we will focus mainly on innovation-based models that make explicit the distinction between capital accumulation and technological progress. Innovation-based models do a better job of fitting the data with respect to long-run growth and convergence, and they also generate a rich set of predictions on the determinants of growth across firms and industries, in contrast with the high level of aggregation in neoclassical and AK models.

2.7   Literature Notes

The first AK models go back to Harrod (1939) and Domar (1946), who assume an aggregate production function with fixed coefficients. Frankel (1962) develops the first AK model with substitutable factors and knowledge externalities, with the purpose of reconciling the positive long-run growth result of Harrod-Domar with the factor-substitutability and market-clearing features of the neoclassical model. The Frankel model has a constant saving rate as in Solow (1956), whereas Romer (1986) develops an AK model with intertemporal consumer maximization. The idea that productivity could increase as the result of learning-by-doing externalities was most forcefully pushed forward by Arrow (1962).

Lucas (1988) developed an AK model where the creation and transmission of knowledge occur through human capital accumulation. Rebelo (1991) uses AK models to explain how heterogeneity in growth experiences can be the result of cross-country differences in government policy. King and Rebelo (1990) use the AK model to analyze the effect of fiscal policy on growth. Jones, Manuelli, and Stacchetti (2000) again use the AK framework to analyze the effect of macroeconomic volatility on growth. And Acemoglu and Ventura (2002) use the AK model to analyze the effects of terms of trade on growth.

For a comprehensive account of the AK growth literature, we again refer the readers to the handbook survey by Jones and Manuelli (2005).

Problems

1. Derive the expression for the neoclassical and AK models and contrast their main results with respect to convergence and long-run growth. Based on the evidence presented in the chapter, do you think one of the frameworks finds more support from the data?

2. **Endogenous growth with transitional dynamics**

Consider the following production function for the economy: $Y = AK + BK^{\alpha}L^{1-\alpha}$, where $A > 0$, $B > 0$, and $0 < \alpha < 1$. Assume depreciation at rate δ, population growth at rate n, and a constant saving rate s.

a. Does this production function satisfy the neoclassical properties from section 2.2?

b. Show, by writing down the growth rate of per capita capital stock as a function of per capita capital stock, that this specification allows for transitional dynamics.

c. Assuming $sA > n + \delta$, what is the growth rate of per capita capital when $k \to \infty$?

3. *__Justification for the AK model: Human capital__

Consider a simple model of human capital in which production is given by $Y_t = K_t^{1-\alpha}\left(A_t L_t\right)^{\alpha}$ and A is a measure of the efficiency of labor, such that the productive capacity of the stock of labor, or level of human capital, is $H = AL$. Then $Y_t = K_t^{1-\alpha} H_t^\alpha$. A proportion s_k of income is invested in physical capital, and a proportion s_h in human capital. The depreciation rates are respectively δ_k and δ_h. The population does not grow.

a. Find the equilibrium physical capital to human capital ratio, using the condition that both investments must yield the same return.

b. Show that the production function can be written as an AK function, and find the growth rate.

4. Justification for the AK model: Government expenditure (based on Barro, 1990)

This problem has two purposes. First, it provides a justification for the presence of constant returns in the aggregate production function. Second, it introduces a major mechanism through which the government can affect the output level and its rate of growth. The crucial assumption is that government expenditures affect the productivity of privately owned factors. A possible interpretation of this production function is that γ represents the infrastructure provided by the government. The better the roads are, the more efficient capital and labor will be.

The saving rate is endogenously determined as in Cass-Koopmans-Ramsey with a CES utility function. Output per capita depends on public expenditure on a public good γ, as well as on capital. That is,

$$y_t = Ak_t^{1-\alpha}\gamma_t^\alpha \quad \text{where } 0 < \alpha < 1$$

Public expenditure is financed by a proportional tax on income τ. The government cannot borrow; hence it must always have a balanced budget.

a. Find the dynamic equation for consumption in a competitive economy. What does it depend on?

b. Show that, in equilibrium, output is given by an AK production function. That is, that it can be expressed as being proportional to the stock of capital.

c. How can the government maximize growth in a competitive economy? What happens when there are no taxes? What happens when $\tau = 1$?

d. Is the competitive equilibrium socially optimal? Why?

3 Product Variety

3.1 Introduction

The inability of the AK paradigm to produce a convincing model of long run growth and convergence motivated a second wave of endogenous growth theory, consisting of innovation-based growth models, which themselves belong to two parallel branches. One branch is the product-variety model of Romer (1990), according to which innovation causes productivity growth by creating new, but not necessarily improved, varieties of products.

The other branch of innovation-based theory, developed by Aghion and Howitt (1992), grew out of modern industrial organization theory and is commonly referred to as Schumpeterian growth theory, because it focuses on quality-improving innovations that render old products obsolete and hence involves the force that Schumpeter called creative destruction.

This chapter presents Romer's product-variety model. The next chapter will develop the Schumpeterian version of endogenous growth theory. Section 3.2.1 presents a simple product-variety model in which final output is used as R&D input. Section 3.2.2 presents a variant in which labor is used as R&D input. Section 3.3 confronts the model with empirical evidence.

3.2 Endogenizing Technological Change

The model we present in this section builds on the idea that productivity growth comes from an expanding variety of specialized intermediate products. Product variety expands gradually because discovering how to produce a larger range of products takes real resources, including time. The model formalizes an old idea that goes back to A. A. Young (1928), namely, that growth is induced and sustained by increased specialization.

For each new product there is a sunk cost of product innovation that must be incurred just once, when the product is first introduced, and never again. The sunk costs can be thought of as costs of research, an activity that results in innovations that add to the stock of technological knowledge. In this case, technological knowledge consists of a list of blueprints, each one describing how to produce a different product, and every innovation adds one more blueprint to the list.

What makes this approach different from an AK model is not just the sunk cost of product development, but also the fact that fixed costs make product markets monopolistically competitive rather than perfectly competitive. Imperfect competition creates positive profits, and these profits act as a reward for the creation of new products. This process is important because it allows the economy to overcome the problem created by Euler's theorem, which we discussed in the previous chapter; that is, the problem that under perfect competition all of output would go to those who supplied K and L, with nothing left over to compensate those who provide the technological knowledge underlying A.

3.2.1   A Simple Variant of the Product-Variety Model

There is a fixed number L of people, each of whom lives forever and has a constant flow of one unit of labor that can be used in manufacturing. For simplicity we suppose that no one has a demand for leisure time, so each person offers her one unit of labor for sale inelastically (that is, no matter what the wage rate). Her utility each period depends only on consumption, according to the same isoelastic function that we presented in connection with the Cass-Koopmans-Ramsey model in chapter 1:

$$u(c) = \frac{c^{1-\varepsilon}}{1-\varepsilon}, \quad \varepsilon > 0$$

and she discounts utility using a constant rate of time preference ρ. As we saw in chapter 1, this means that in steady state the growth rate g and the interest rate r must obey the Euler equation, which can be written as

$$g = \frac{r-\rho}{\varepsilon} \tag{3.1}$$

Final output is produced under perfect competition, using labor and a range of intermediate inputs, indexed by i in the interval $[0, M_t]$, where M_t is our measure of product variety. The final-good production function at each date t is

$$Y_t = L^{1-\alpha} \int_0^{M_t} x_i^\alpha \, di \tag{3.2}$$

where Y_t is output, and each x_i is the amount of intermediate product i used as input. Labor input is always equal to the fixed supply L. The coefficient α lies between zero and one.[1]

---

1. We attach a time subscript t to M_t and Y_t because product variety and final-good production will be growing over time in a steady state. However, we leave the time subscript off x_i because, as we will see, the output of each intermediate product will be constant over time.

Each intermediate product is produced using the final good as input, one for one. That is, each unit of intermediate product i produced requires the input of one unit of final good.

According to equation (3.2), product variety enhances overall productivity in the economy. To see how this relationship works, let X_t be the total amount of final good used in producing intermediate products. According to the one-for-one technology, X_t must equal total intermediate output:

$$X_t = \int_0^{M_t} x_i di$$

Now suppose that each intermediate product is produced in the same amount x. (This will indeed be the case in equilibrium, as we will see shortly.) Then $x = X_t/M_t$. Substituting this into the production function (3.2) yields

$$Y_t = L^{1-\alpha} \int_0^{M_t} \left(X_t/M_t \right)^{\alpha} di = M_t^{1-\alpha} L^{1-\alpha} X_t^{\alpha} \tag{3.3}$$

which is increasing in M_t given the factor inputs L and X_t:

$$\partial Y_t/\partial M_t = (1-\alpha) Y_t/M_t > 0$$

The final good is used for consumption and investment (in producing blueprints). Its only other use is in producing intermediate products. So the economy's gross domestic product (GDP) is final output Y_t minus the amount used in intermediate production:

$$GDP_t = Y_t - X_t \tag{3.4}$$

Each intermediate product is monopolized by the person who created it. The monopolist seeks to maximize the flow of profit at each date, measured in units of final good:

$$\Pi_i = p_i x_i - x_i$$

where p_i is the price in units of final good. That is, her revenue is price times quantity, and her cost is equal to her output, given the one-for-one technology.

Since the price of an input to a perfectly competitive industry is the value of its marginal product, therefore we have[2]

---

2. Strictly speaking, the derivative $\partial Y_t/\partial x_i$ makes no mathematical sense, because a change in a single x_i would have no measurable effect on the integral in equation (3.2). But it does make economic

$$p_i = \partial Y_t / \partial x_i = \alpha L^{1-\alpha} x_i^{\alpha-1} \qquad (3.5)$$

Therefore the monopolist's profit depends on her output according to

$$\Pi_i = \alpha L^{1-\alpha} x_i^{\alpha} - x_i$$

She will choose x_i so as to maximize this expression, which implies the first-order condition

$$\partial \Pi_i / \partial x_i = \alpha^2 L^{1-\alpha} x_i^{\alpha-1} - 1 = 0$$

It follows that the equilibrium quantity will be the same constant in every sector i:

$$x = L\alpha^{\frac{2}{1-\alpha}} \qquad (3.6)$$

and so will the equilibrium profit flow:[3]

$$\Pi = \frac{1-\alpha}{\alpha} L\alpha^{\frac{2}{1-\alpha}} \qquad (3.7)$$

Substituting $X_t = M_t x$ into the production relation (3.3) and then again into the definition (3.4), we see that final-good output and the economy's GDP will both be proportional to the degree of product variety:

$$Y_t = M_t L^{1-\alpha} x^{\alpha}$$

---

sense, because our assumption that there is a continuum of intermediate products is itself just an approximation. What we are really saying is that output depends on the sum of contributions from a large discrete number M of intermediate products, each of which makes a small contribution:

$$Y_t = L^{1-\alpha} \sum_1^M x_i^{\alpha} \qquad (Y)$$

and we are approximating this production function by assuming a continuum of products. The derivative of the production function (Y) is indeed given by expression (3.5).

3. By definition

$$\Pi_i = (p_i - 1) x_i$$

Using equation (3.5) to substitute for p_i and then equation (3.6) to substitute for x_i we get

$$\Pi_i = \left[\alpha L^{1-\alpha} \left(L\alpha^{\frac{2}{1-\alpha}} \right)^{\alpha-1} - 1 \right] L\alpha^{\frac{2}{1-\alpha}}$$

Expression (3.7) follows directly from this because the term in square brackets equals $\dfrac{1-\alpha}{\alpha}$.

$$GDP_t = M_t \left(L^{1-\alpha} x^\alpha - x \right)$$

Therefore, the growth rate of GDP will be the proportional growth rate of product variety:

$$g = \frac{1}{M_t} \frac{dM_t}{dt}$$

Product variety grows at a rate that depends on the amount R_t of final output that is used in research. That is, the output of research each period is the flow of new blueprints, each of which allows a new product to be developed. So we have

$$dM_t / dt = \lambda R_t$$

where λ is a (positive) parameter indicating the productivity of the research sector.

Assume that the research sector of the economy is perfectly competitive, with free entry. Then the flow of profit in the research sector must be zero. Each blueprint is worth Π/r to its inventor, which is the present value of the profit flow Π discounted at the market interest rate r. Hence the flow of profit in research is

$$(\Pi/r)\lambda R_t - R_t$$

which is just the flow of revenue (output λR_t time price Π/r) minus cost R_t. For this to be zero we need a rate of interest that satisfies the "research-arbitrage equation":

$$r = \lambda \Pi$$

That is, the rate of interest must equal the flow of profit that an entrepreneur can receive per unit invested in research.

Substituting from the research-arbitrage equation into the Euler equation (3.1) we have

$$g = \frac{\lambda \Pi - \rho}{\varepsilon}$$

Substituting expression (3.7) for Π in this equation yields the following expression for the equilibrium growth rate as a function of the primitive parameters of the model:

$$g = \frac{\lambda \dfrac{1-\alpha}{\alpha} L \alpha^{\frac{2}{1-\alpha}} - \rho}{\varepsilon}$$

We immediately see that growth increases with the productivity of research as measured by the parameter λ and with the size of the economy as measured by labor supply L, and decreases with the rate of time preference ρ.

The prediction that g should increase with L was first seen as a virtue of the model, suggesting that larger countries or larger free-trade zones should grow faster. However, C. Jones (1995b) pointed out that this prediction is counterfactual, to the extent that the number of researchers has substantially increased in the United States over the period since 1950, whereas the growth rate has remained on average at 2 percent over the same period. We shall come back to this debate on "scale effects" in more detail in chapter 4.

3.2.2   The Romer Model with Labor as R&D Input

The original Romer model supposed that labor was the only R&D input.[4] To see how the model works under this alternative assumption, we now suppose that labor can be used either in manufacturing the final good (L_1) or alternatively in research (L_2). Labor used in these two activities must add up to the total labor supply L, which we again assume to be a given constant. So

$$L = L_1 + L_2$$

We restrict attention to steady states in which L_1 and L_2 are both constant.

Final output is produced by labor and intermediates according to the same production function as before:

$$Y_t = L_1^{1-\alpha} \int_0^{M_t} x_i^\alpha di \tag{3.8}$$

where the labor input is now L_1 instead of the total labor supply L. The price of each intermediate product is again its marginal product in the final sector:

$$p = \alpha L_1^{1-\alpha} x^{\alpha-1}$$

---

4. Actually, Romer interpreted the R&D input as "human capital," but since he took its total supply as given, this difference is purely terminological. Romer also supposed that intermediate products were produced by capital, which for simplicity we ignore in this presentation. We defer the integration of endogenous technical change and capital accumulation until chapter 5, and we note here that nothing of importance is lost by ignoring capital accumulation in the Romer model.

Each intermediate product is again produced one for one with final output, so the profit flow to each intermediate monopolist is given by

$$\Pi = \max_{x} \{px - x\}$$
$$= \max_{x} \{\alpha L_1^{1-\alpha} x^\alpha - x\}$$

which implies the profit-maximizing quantity

$$x = L_1 \alpha^{\frac{2}{1-\alpha}} \tag{3.9}$$

and the equilibrium profit flow[5]

$$\Pi = \frac{1-\alpha}{\alpha} L_1 \alpha^{\frac{2}{1-\alpha}} \tag{3.10}$$

The measure of product variety M_t now grows at a rate that depends upon the amount L_2 of labor devoted to research, according to

$$dM_t/dt = \lambda M_t L_2$$

This equation reflects the existence of spillovers in research activities; that is, all researchers can make use of the accumulated knowledge M_t embodied in existing designs. Note that there are *two* major sources of increasing returns in this model: specialization or product differentiation and research spillovers.

The flow of profit in research is now

$$(\Pi/r)\lambda M_t L_2 - w_t L_2$$

where w_t is the equilibrium wage rate that must be paid to researchers. Setting this flow equal to zero yields the research-arbitrage equation for this version of the model:

$$r = \lambda M_t \Pi/w_t$$

which again states that the rate of interest must equal the flow of profit that the entrepreneur can receive from investing one unit of final good into research—that is, from using the services of $(1/w_t)$ units of research labor and thereby producing $\lambda M_t(1/w_t)$ blueprints each worth Π per period.

---

5. Equations (3.9) and (3.10) are the same as equations (3.6) and (3.7), except with L_1 in the place of L. The former can be derived from the first-order condition of profit maximization using the same logic as in the previous section, and the latter can be derived using the logic of footnote 3.

To make use of this research-arbitrage equation we need to solve for the equilibrium wage rate w_t. Since the final sector is perfectly competitive, w_t equals the marginal product of labor, which can be calculated as follows. Since each intermediate sector produces the same constant output x, the production function (3.8) implies that

$$Y_t = L_1^{1-\alpha} M_t x^\alpha \tag{3.11}$$

Therefore

$$w_t = \frac{\partial Y_t}{\partial L_1} = (1-\alpha) L_1^{-\alpha} M_t x^\alpha$$

which can be written, using expression (3.9), as

$$w_t = (1-\alpha) \alpha^{\frac{2\alpha}{1-\alpha}} M_t \tag{3.12}$$

So the research-arbitrage equation can be rewritten using equation (3.10) to substitute for Π and using equation (3.12) to substitute for w_t, as

$$r = \alpha \lambda L_1$$

Since

$$g = \frac{1}{M_t} \frac{dM_t}{dt} = \lambda L_2 = \lambda (L - L_1)$$

we have

$$r = \alpha (\lambda L - g)$$

Substituting this expression for r into the Euler equation (3.1) yields

$$g = \frac{\alpha \lambda L - \rho}{\alpha + \varepsilon}$$

So again, growth increases with the productivity of research activities λ and with the size of the economy as measured by total labor supply L, and decreases with the rate of time preference ρ. Furthermore, both because intermediate firms do not internalize their contribution to the division of labor (i.e., to product diversity) and because researchers do not internalize research spillovers, the preceding equilibrium growth rate is always *less* than the social optimum.[6]

---

6. Benassy (1998) shows, however, that with a slightly more general form of the product-variety model, the equilibrium growth rate could exceed the optimal rate.

3.3 From Theory to Evidence

3.3.1 Estimating the Effect of Variety on Productivity

A recent paper by Broda, Greenfield, and Weinstein (2006), henceforth BGW, exploits trade data to test for the effects of product variety on productivity levels and growth. If we believe in the mechanism described previously, trade should raise productivity because producers gain access to new imported varieties of inputs (the level effect); moreover, trade and the resulting increase in input variety should reduce the cost of innovation and thus result in more variety creation in the future (the growth effect). Also, the impact of increased product variety on productivity should depend upon the elasticity of substitution among different varieties of a good, and/or upon shifts in expenditures shares among new, remaining, and disappearing goods. In particular, increasing the number of varieties should not have much of an effect on productivity if new varieties are close substitutes for existing varieties or if the share of new varieties is small relative to existing ones.

BGW analyze bilateral trade flows between 73 countries over the period 1994–2003. Using import data in the six-digit Harmonized System (HS) product categories, they compute elasticities of substitution and supply for about 200 import sectors in each country. They consider the production function

$$Y_t = \left(A_t L_t\right)^{1-\alpha} \left(\sum_1^{M_t} x_{it}^{\upsilon}\right)^{\alpha/\upsilon}$$

where $\alpha \in (0, 1)$ is one minus the share of labor in output and $\upsilon \in (0, 1)$ measures the elasticity of substitution between varieties of input goods x_{it}, with a higher υ corresponding to more substitutable inputs.

If we focus on equilibria where all input goods are used with the same intensity x_t, the preceding equation becomes

$$Y_t = \left(A_t L_t\right)^{1-\alpha} M_t^{\alpha/\upsilon} x_t^{\alpha}$$

If each input is produced one for one with capital, then

$$Y_t = \left(A_t L_t\right)^{1-\alpha} M_t^{(1-\upsilon)\alpha/\upsilon} K_t^{\alpha}$$

where $K_t = M_t x_t$ is the aggregate capital stock. Taking logs, we obtain

$$\ln Y_t = (1-\alpha)\left(\ln A_t + \ln L_t\right) + \alpha \ln K_t + (1-\upsilon)\alpha/\upsilon \ln M_t$$

Differentiating both sides with respect to time, we obtain

$$\frac{\dot{Y}_t}{Y_t} = \left(1-\alpha\right)\frac{\dot{L}_t}{L_t} + \alpha\frac{\dot{K}_t}{K_t} + \hat{B}_t$$

where

$$\hat{B}_t = \left(1-\alpha\right)\frac{\dot{A}_t}{A_t} + \left(1-\upsilon\right)\alpha/\upsilon\frac{\dot{M}_t}{M_t}$$

is total factor productivity (TFP) growth, also known as the Solow residual.[7] This measure of TFP growth has two components: a product-variety component captured by the term in $\dot{M}_t/M_t$ and a quality component embodied in the term in $\dot{A}_t/A_t$. BGW are primarily interested in the contribution of variety to total productivity growth.

According to the preceding equation, a lower υ (that is, a lower degree of substitutability between inputs) or a higher share of the intermediate goods α should result in a higher impact of increased variety on TFP.

BGW estimate elasticities separately for each good and importing country and then regress per capita GDP on these elasticities. They find no strong relationship between income per capita and the elasticity of substitution across countries. The typical (median) country experienced a net increase in varieties of 7.1 percent over 10 years in the typical (median) sector, which is about 0.7 percent per year. BGW then show that the growth in new varieties over the period 1994–2003 increased productivity by 0.13 percent per year for the typical country in the sample.

The relationship between variety and productivity is even lower for developed countries: "Most of the productivity growth in many of the largest countries cannot be accounted for by new imports" (BGW, 21). In particular the United States has the second-smallest gain among developed countries from imported variety. BGW summarize their findings as follows:

The median developed country's productivity growth was about 2 percent per year, but the median contribution of imported variety growth to productivity was only 0.1 percent per year, suggesting that for the typical developed country, new imported varieties are only a small part of the story behind their productivity growth. The impact of new varieties on developing countries is substantially higher. The typical developing country saw its productivity rise by 0.13 to 0.17 percent per year (depending on the sample) due to new imported varieties. (BGW, 22)

7. TFP and the Solow residual will be explained in more detail in chapter 5.

One might argue that BGW underestimate the effects of variety in more developed countries. In particular, their approach does not take into account inputs that are not imported, and these are likely to be more numerous in developed countries. Nevertheless, the effects of variety on productivity and on productivity growth appear to be relatively small, even in less developed economics.

3.3.2   The Importance of Exit in the Growth Process

An important limitation of the product-variety model is that it assumes away obsolescence of old intermediate inputs. Indeed, if old intermediate inputs were to disappear over time, the variety term in the preceding Solow residual would go down, and thus so would the economy's per capita GDP.

In ongoing work with Pol Antras and Susanne Prantl, we have combined UK establishment-level panel data with the input-output table to estimate the effect on TFP growth arising from growth in high-quality input in upstream industries, and also from exit of obsolete input-producing firms in upstream industries. Specifically, we take a panel of 23,886 annual observations on more than 5,000 plants in 180 four-digit industries between 1987 and 1993, together with the 1984 UK input-output table, to estimate an equation of the form

$$g_{ijt} = \beta_0 + \beta_1 \text{Entry}_{jt-1} + \beta_2 \text{Exit}_{jt-1} + \beta_3 Z_{ijt-1} + \text{Est}_i + \text{Ind}_j + \text{Yr}_t + u_{ijt}$$

where g_{ijt} is the productivity growth rate of firm i in industry j. The first regressor Entry_{jt-1} is the entry measure, calculated as the increase in the fraction of input to the production of good j which is provided by foreign firms (foreign firms are more likely to account for entry that takes place at frontier technological level). The second regressor Exit_{jt-1} is our measure of exit of obsolete upstream input-producing firms: we use the fraction of employment accounted for by upstream exiting firms, thereby putting more weight on large exiting firms than on small ones. Establishment (Est_i), industry (Ind_j), and year (Yr_t) effects are included, along with the other controls in Z_{ijt-1} including a measure of the plant's market share.

The result of this estimation is a significant positive effect of both upstream quality improvement and upstream input-production exit. These results are robust to taking potential endogeneity into account by applying an instrumental variable approach, using instruments similar to those of Aghion, Blundell, and colleagues (2006). The effects are particularly strong for plants that use more intermediate inputs—that is, plants with a share of intermediate product use above the sample median. Altogether, the results we find are consistent with the view that quality-improving innovation is an important source of growth. The results, however, are not consistent with the horizontal innovation model, in which there should be nothing special about the entry of foreign firms, and according to which the exit of upstream firms should if anything reduce growth by reducing the variety of inputs being used in the industry.

Comin and Mulani (2007) have produced additional evidence to the effect that exit as well as entry is important to the growth process. Using a sample of U.S. firms, they show that, according to two measures of turnover in industry leadership that they construct, turnover is positively related to earlier R&D. Again, this finding is evidence of a creative-destruction element in the innovation process that one would not expect to find if the primary channel through which innovation affected economic growth was increasing product variety. Indeed, the product-variety theory has little to say at all about how productivity varies across firms in an industry, let alone how the productivity ranking would change over time.

In addition to these results, Fogel, Morck, and Yeung (2008) have produced evidence to the effect that innovation is linked to the turnover of dominant firms. Using data on large corporate sectors in 44 different countries over the 1975–96 period, they find that economies whose top 1975 corporations declined more grow faster than other countries with the same initial per capita GDP, level of education, and capital stock. Again, this evidence of an association between growth and enterprise turnover has no counterpart in the horizontal-innovation theory.

In order to formalize the notion of (technical or product) obsolescence, one needs to move away from *horizontal* models of product development à la Dixit and Stiglitz (1977) into *vertical* models of quality improvements, as we will do in the next chapter.

3.4   Conclusion

In this chapter we have presented the product-variety model of endogenous growth. In this model, growth is driven by innovations that lead to the introduction of new (input) varieties. Productivity growth is driven both by the increased specialization of labor that works with an increasing number of intermediate inputs and by the research spillovers whereby each new innovator benefits from the whole existing stock of innovations. Ideas are nonrival, which means they can be freely used by new innovators in their own research activities. And they are excludable in the sense that each new innovation is rewarded by monopoly rents. It is the prospect of these rents that motivates research activities aimed at discovering new varieties.

A limitation of this model is that it does not capture the role of exit or turnover in the growth process, which Schumpeter refers to as creative destruction. Indeed, exit is detrimental to growth in this model as it reduces input specialization. Yet recent empirical work points at a strong correlation between productivity growth and exit or turnover of firms and inputs. In the next chapter we present an alternative model of endogenous technical change, where exit and creative destruction feature prominently.

3.5   Literature Notes

Romer (1987) developed a precursory model of growth with expanding variety, where growth is sustained in the long run by the fact that output is produced with an expanding set of inputs, which in turn prevents aggregate capital from running into decreasing returns. The improved division of labor over time is itself made possible by output growth, which makes it possible to pay the fixed costs of producing an ever-expanding set of inputs. Romer used the framework of monopolistic competition introduced by Dixit and Stiglitz (1977) and extended by Ethier (1982). Romer (1990) completes the description of the product-variety model by introducing an R&D sector that generates blueprints for new inputs as a result of voluntary profit-motivated horizontal innovations. Technological change was thereby endogenized.

The framework has been extended in several directions, and we refer the reader to the excellent *Handbook of Economic Growth* chapter by Gancia and Zilibotti (Aghion and Durlauf 2005). Grossman and Helpman (1991a, chapter 3) present a didactic treatment of a framework with expansion of consumer products that enter the utility function (as in Spence 1976) instead of intermediate products entering the production function. Rivera-Batiz and Romer (1991) and Grossman and Helpman (1991b) have used the framework to analyze the effects of market integration on growth. More recently, the idea of directed technological change was integrated by Acemoglu and Zilibotti (2001) into a framework of growth with expanding variety, to analyze implications of the skill-technology complementarity for the persistence of productivity differences across countries.

C. Jones (1995b) challenges the model for generating scale effects for which he could not find any evidence based on U.S. time series (see chapter 4). In contrast, Kremer (1993b) argued that the hypothesis of a positive relation between world per capita growth and world population (or the world aggregate output) might be correct over very long periods of time.

Problems

1. What is the "engine" of growth in the product variety model? Explain. Compare it to the element driving endogenous growth in the AK framework. What does this comparison imply in terms of pro-growth policy design in both settings?

2. **"Labor-or-intermediates" model**

Consider a variant of the Romer model from section 3.2.2. Assume that labor is not used in final good production, but is used as the unique input in the intermediate goods production. Assume the final good production function is given by

$$Y_t = \int_0^{M_t} x_{i,t}^\alpha di$$

Also, suppose that $1/M_t$ units of labor are required to produce one unit of any intermediate good. As in the model presented in the chapter, suppose $dM_t/dt = \lambda M_t L_2$, where L_2 is labor allocated to R&D. Define $L_x \equiv L - L_2$ as the amount of labor allocated to production of intermediates.

a. What is the equilibrium level of intermediate good production?

b. What is the equilibrium price of a unit of any intermediate good?

c. Looking at a balanced-growth equilibrium in which wages and technology grow at the same rate, compute the maximal profit for intermediate producers.

d. Write down the research arbitrage condition.

e. Compute the equilibrium growth rate of the economy.

3. ***Economic integration and trade (based on Rivera-Batiz and Romer 1991 and Gancia and Zilibotti 2005)**

Consider the Romer model with labor as the unique R&D input from section 3.2.2. We have seen that the economy's equilibrium growth rate of output was given by $g = \dfrac{\alpha\lambda L - \rho}{\alpha + \varepsilon}$.
Now, suppose two identical countries with fixed labor endowment $L = L^*$ (the star denotes the economy originally foreign).

a. If the two countries merge and become a unique economy, what will be its growth rate of output?

We will now look at what happens when, instead, trade is introduced between the two economies. Suppose that, before trade starts, $M_0 = M_0^*$ (time zero denotes the moment trade starts). Suppose, in addition, that the two economies produce, before trade, disjoint subsets of intermediate goods (specialization). When trade is introduced, each monopolist can therefore sell its product in two markets. Finally, assume that the production function of varieties depends only on the degree of domestic varieties.

b. Compute the equilibrium profits and wages after trade is introduced.

c. Write down the research arbitrage condition after trade is introduced. Compare it to the one in the closed economy case. Discuss the result.

d. Now, assume $M_0 < M_0^*$. Suppose that trade is introduced and that exchange equalizes wages and interest rates across countries. What is the innovation flow in the home country?

e. Write down the research arbitrage condition for the foreign country. What will happen in the long run?

f. Can we talk about specialization of the two economies here? Discuss.

4. **Innovation, imitation, and product cycles (based on Helpman 1993 and Gancia and Zilibotti 2005)**

Consider a two-region model of labor only used for intermediate goods production (as in problem 2). The aggregate final food production function is $Y_t = \int_0^{M_t} x_{i,t}^{\alpha} di$, and intermediates are manufactured with $1/M_t$ units of labor in both regions. Assume that R&D, producing new goods, is performed in the North only and that costless imitation takes place in the South at a constant rate i. Once a good is copied in the South, it is produced by competitive firms. Therefore, at every point in time, there is a range M_t^N of goods produced by monopolists in the North and a range M_t^S of goods that have been copied and are produced in the South by competitive firms. The rate of introduction of new goods is $\gamma = (dM_t/d_t)/M_t$, and $M_t = M_t^N + M_t^S$. Since imitation is instantaneous and occurs at rate i, we have that $\left(dM_t^S/dt\right)/M_t^S = iM_t^N$. Finally, assume, as in problem 3, that innovation requires labor, that is, $dM_t/d_t = \lambda M_t L_2$, where L_2 is labor allocated to R&D in the North.

a. Show that in a steady state in which the ratio M_t^N/M_t^S is constant the following conditions must hold: $\dfrac{M^N}{M} = \dfrac{\gamma}{\gamma + i}$ and $\dfrac{M^S}{M} = \dfrac{i}{\gamma + i}$.

b. What is the price (p_t^N) charged by Northern intermediate firms before imitation takes place? What is the price (p_t^S) charged by Southern firms producing imitated goods?

c. Show that the labor market-clearing condition for the North can be written as $A_t^N x/A_t + \gamma/\lambda = L$.

d. Using the fact that profits per product are a fraction $(1 - \alpha)$ of total revenue in the North $p^N x$, show that profits in the North can be written as $\pi^N = \dfrac{1-\alpha}{\alpha} \dfrac{w_t^N}{A_t^N} \left(L^N - \dfrac{\gamma}{\lambda} \right)$.

e. Write down the research arbitrage condition for innovators in the North. (Hint: Because there could be imitation, the effective discount rate for innovators is now $r + m$). Show that it can be written as $\dfrac{1-\alpha}{\alpha} \left(\lambda L^N - \gamma \right) \dfrac{\gamma + m}{\gamma} = r + m$.

f. Suppose $r > \gamma$. What is the impact of a reduction in m (e.g., as the result of a tightening of intellectual property rights) on the profitability of innovation and on growth? What happens if $r < \gamma$? Give an intuition for the results. (Hint: Take a log linear approximation of the condition in item e.)

g. Using the condition found in item 4a and the one in item 4e, write down the effect of a reduction of m in the share of goods manufactured in the North.

5. *Social optimum in the Romer (1990) model**

Consider the model from section 3.2.2. Now, instead of looking at the market equilibrium, we focus on the socially optimal allocation, from a social planner with one-period horizon. The planner seeks to maximize $GDP_t = L_1^{1-\alpha} \int_0^{M_t} x_i^{\alpha} di - \int_0^{M_t} x_i$.

a. Solve for the social planner's allocation of intermediate input. Compare it to the market equilibrium level. Explain your results.

b. What is the social planner's allocation of labor to R&D activities?

c. Compare the efficient growth rate of the economy given by the social planner's maximization problem to the market equilibrium growth rate. Interpret your findings.

4   The Schumpeterian Model

4.1   Introduction

This chapter develops an alternative model of endogenous growth, in which growth is generated by a random sequence of quality-improving (or "vertical") innovations. The model grew out of modern industrial organization theory,[1] which portrays innovation as an important dimension of industrial competition. It is called Schumpeterian because it embodies the force that Schumpeter (1942) called "creative destruction"; that is, the innovations that drive growth by creating new technologies also destroy the results of previous innovations by making them obsolete.

Section 4.2 presents a simple one-sector Schumpeterian model, in which it is always the same product that is improved by innovation. This one-sector model contains the essential ideas of the Schumpeterian approach. For most empirical purposes, however, the one-sector model is too simple. Accordingly, section 4.3 develops a multisector Schumpeterian model, in which many different products are improved by innovation each year. Section 4.4 shows how allowing a mixture of horizontal and vertical innovations can shed new light on the "scale effect" discussed in the previous chapter.

4.2   A One-Sector Model

4.2.1   The Basics

There is a sequence of discrete time periods $t = 1, 2, \ldots$ In each period there is a fixed number L of individuals, each of whom lives for just that period and is endowed with one unit of labor services, which she supplies inelastically. Her utility depends only on her consumption and she is risk-neutral, so she has the single objective of maximizing expected consumption.

People consume only one good, called the "final" good, which is produced by perfectly competitive firms using two inputs—labor and a single intermediate product—according to the Cobb-Douglas production function[2]

$$Y_t = (A_t L)^{1-\alpha} x_t^{\alpha} \tag{4.1}$$

---

1. See Tirole (1988).

2. By working through problem 2 of this chapter the reader can verify that nothing of substance is implied by the fact that A_t and L are raised to the same power in equation (4.1).

where Y_t is output of the final good in period t, A_t is a parameter that reflects the productivity of the intermediate input in that period, and x_t is the amount of intermediate product used. The coefficient α lies between zero and one. The economy's entire labor supply L is used in final-good production. As in the neo-classical model, we refer to the product A_tL as the economy's effective labor supply.

The intermediate product is produced by a monopolist each period, using the final good as all input, one for one. That is, for each unit of intermediate product, the monopolist must use one unit of final good as input. Final output that is not used for intermediate production is available for consumption and research, and it constitutes the economy's gross domestic product (GDP):[3]

$$GDP_t = Y_t - x_t \tag{4.2}$$

4.2.2 Production and Profits

Growth results from innovations that raise the productivity parameter A_t by improving the quality of the intermediate product. Before analyzing the process that generates innovations, this section describes what happens in each period once A_t has been determined, and shows that in equilibrium the intermediate monopolist's profit and the economy's GDP are both proportional to the effective labor supply A_tL.

The monopolist at t maximizes expected consumption by maximizing her profit Π_t, measured in units of the final good:

$$\Pi_t = p_t x_t - x_t$$

where p_t is the price of the intermediate product relative to the final good. That is, her revenue is price times quantity $p_t x_t$, and her cost is her input of final good, which must equal her output x_t.

Recall that the equilibrium price of a factor of production used in a perfectly competitive industry equals the value of its marginal product. Thus the monopo-

---

3. Recall the national accounting identity:

$GDP \equiv \text{Consumption} + \text{Investment} + \text{Government purchases} + \text{Net exports}$

Our model economy has no foreign sector, no government spending, and no investment in physical or human capital. However, we do have investment in intellectual capital, in the form of research. So we have

$GDP \equiv \text{Consumption} + \text{Investment}$

Hence equation (4.2).

list's price will be the marginal product of her intermediate product in the final sector, which according to the production function (4.1) is

$$p_t = \partial Y_t / \partial x_t = \alpha (A_t L)^{1-\alpha} x_t^{\alpha-1} \tag{4.3}$$

Therefore, the monopolist chooses the quantity x_t that maximizes

$$\Pi_t = \alpha (A_t L)^{1-\alpha} x_t^{\alpha} - x_t \tag{4.4}$$

which implies an equilibrium quantity[4]

$$x_t = \alpha^{\frac{2}{1-\alpha}} A_t L \tag{4.5}$$

and an equilibrium profit

$$\Pi_t = \pi A_t L, \qquad \pi \equiv (1-\alpha)\alpha^{\frac{1+\alpha}{1-\alpha}} \tag{4.6}$$

that are both proportional to the effective labor supply $A_t L$.

Substituting from equation (4.5) into the production function (4.1) and the GDP equation (4.2), we see that final output and the economy's GDP will also be proportional to $A_t L$:

$$Y_t = \alpha^{\frac{2\alpha}{1-\alpha}} A_t L$$

$$GDP_t = \alpha^{\frac{2\alpha}{1-\alpha}} (1-\alpha^2) A_t L \tag{4.7}$$

4.2.3 Innovation

In each period there is one person (the "entrepreneur") who has an opportunity to attempt an innovation. If she succeeds, the innovation will create a new version of the intermediate product, which is more productive than previous versions. Specifically, the productivity of the intermediate good in use will go from last period's value A_{t-1} up to $A_t = \gamma A_{t-1}$, where $\gamma > 1$. If she fails, then there will be

---

4. The first-order condition for the maximization problem is

$$\alpha^2 (A_t L)^{1-\alpha} x_t^{\alpha-1} - 1 = 0$$

from which equation (4.5) follows directly. Substituting from equation (4.5) into equation (4.4) yields equation (4.6).

no innovation at t and the intermediate product will be the same one that was used in $t-1$, so $A_t = A_{t-1}$.

In order to innovate, the entrepreneur must conduct research, a costly activity that uses the final good as its only input. As indicated earlier, research is uncertain, for it may fail to generate any innovation. But the more the entrepreneur spends on research, the more likely she is to innovate. Specifically, the probability μ_t that an innovation occurs in any period t depends positively on the amount R_t of final good spent on research, according to the innovation function

$$\mu_t = \phi(R_t/A_t^*)$$

where $A_t^* = \gamma A_{t-1}$ is the productivity of the new intermediate product that will result if the research succeeds. The reason why the probability of innovation depends inversely on A_t^* is that as technology advances it becomes more complex and thus harder to improve upon. So it is not the absolute amount of research expenditure R_t that matters for success but the productivity-adjusted expenditure R_t/A_t^*, which we denote by n_t.

For concreteness, assume that the innovation function takes the Cobb-Douglas form

$$\phi(n) = \lambda n^\sigma \tag{4.8}$$

where λ is a parameter that reflects the productivity of the research sector and the elasticity σ lies between zero and one. Thus the marginal product of (productivity-adjusted) research in generating innovations is positive but decreasing:

$$\phi'(n) = \sigma \lambda n^{\sigma-1} > 0 \quad \text{and} \quad \phi''(n) = \sigma(\sigma-1)\lambda n^{\sigma-2} < 0$$

4.2.4   Research Arbitrage

If the entrepreneur at t successfully innovates, she will become the intermediate monopolist in that period, because she will be able to produce a better product than anyone else. Otherwise, the monopoly will pass to someone else chosen at random who is able to produce last period's product.

Thus the reward to a successful innovator is the profit Π_t^* that she will earn as a result. Since she succeeds with probability $\phi(n_t)$, her expected reward is

$$\phi(n_t)\Pi_t^*$$

But the research will cost her R_t whether she succeeds or not; so her net benefit from research is

$$\phi(R_t/A_t^*)\Pi_t^* - R_t$$

The entrepreneur will choose the research expenditure R_t that maximizes this net benefit, which implies that R_t must satisfy the first-order condition

$$\phi'(R_t/A_t^*)\Pi_t^*/A_t^* - 1 = 0$$

which we can write, using equation (4.6), as the "research arbitrage" equation:

$$\phi'(n_t)\pi L = 1 \tag{R}$$

The right-hand side of equation (R) is the marginal cost of research. The left-hand side is the marginal benefit of research—the incremental probability of innovation times the value of a successful innovation. The marginal benefit is decreasing in n_t because the marginal product of the innovation function ϕ is decreasing in n_t. Any parameter change that raises the marginal benefit schedule or lowers the marginal cost will increase the equilibrium research intensity n_t.

The research arbitrage equation implies that the productivity-adjusted level of research n_t will be a constant n, and hence the probability of innovation μ_t will also be a constant $\mu = \phi(n)$. Under the Cobb-Douglas innovation function (4.8) we have

$$n = (\sigma\lambda\pi L)^{\frac{1}{1-\sigma}}$$

and[5]

$$\mu = \lambda^{\frac{1}{1-\sigma}}(\sigma\pi L)^{\frac{\sigma}{1-\sigma}} \tag{4.9}$$

4.2.5   Growth

The rate of economic growth is the proportional growth rate of per capita GDP (GDP_t/L), which according to equation (4.7) is also the proportional growth rate of the productivity parameter A_t:

$$g_t = \frac{A_t - A_{t-1}}{A_{t-1}}$$

---

5. We assume λ and π are small enough that $\mu < 1$.

It follows that growth will be random. In each period, with probability μ the entrepreneur will innovate, resulting in $g_t = \dfrac{\gamma A_{t-1} - A_{t-1}}{A_{t-1}} = \gamma - 1$; and with probability $1 - \mu$ she will fail, resulting in $g_t = \dfrac{A_{t-1} - A_{t-1}}{A_{t-1}} = 0$. The growth rate will be governed by this probability distribution every period, so by the law of large numbers the mean of the distribution

$$g = E(g_t) = \mu \cdot (\gamma - 1)$$

will also be the economy's long-run average growth rate.

To interpret this formula, note that μ is not just the probability of an innovation each period but also the long-run frequency of innovations—that is, the fraction of periods in which an innovation will occur. Also, $\gamma - 1$ is the proportional increase in productivity resulting from each innovation. Thus the formula expresses a simple but important result of Schumpeterian growth theory:

PROPOSITION 1   In the long run, the economy's average growth rate equals the frequency of innovations times the size of innovations.

Using equation (4.9) to replace μ in the preceding formula, we see that the average growth rate is

$$g = \lambda^{\frac{1}{1-\sigma}} (\sigma \pi L)^{\frac{\sigma}{1-\sigma}} (\gamma - 1) \tag{G}$$

4.2.6   A Variant with Nondrastic Innovations

Up to this point we have implicitly assumed that the intermediate monopolist can charge any price to the final good producers without fearing entry by a potential competitor. In industrial organization theory this assumption is called the *drastic innovation* case (see Tirole, 1988).

Suppose, however, that there is a competitive fringe of firms able to produce a "knockoff" product that is perfectly substitutable for the monopolist's intermediate product but costs $\chi > 1$ units of final output to produce. Then the incumbent monopolist cannot charge more than χ in equilibrium, since otherwise the competitive fringe could profitably undercut her price. Thus we have the limit-price constraint:

$$p_t \leq \chi$$

When $\chi > 1/\alpha$, this limit price constraint is not binding because the price chosen by the monopolist in the absence of a competitive fringe is[6] $1/\alpha$. This is the drastic innovation case analyzed previously.

In this section we consider the nondrastic innovation case, where $\chi < 1/\alpha$ and hence the limit-price constraint is binding. Since the monopolist's price is still the marginal product of the intermediate product, it must still obey equation (4.3), so substituting $p_t = \chi$ into equation (4.3) yields the equilibrium quantity

$$x_t = (\alpha/\chi)^{\frac{1}{1-\alpha}} A_t L$$

The monopolist's equilibrium profit is thus

$$\Pi_t = p_t x_t - x_t = \pi A_t L, \qquad \pi = (\chi - 1)(\alpha/\chi)^{\frac{1}{1-\alpha}}$$

where now the profit parameter π is an increasing function[7] of the competitive fringe's cost χ.

Other than this change, the economy functions just as in the drastic case. In particular, the research intensity n is still governed by the research arbitrage equation (R) and the average growth rate is still determined by equation (G), except that the parameter π in both of these equations is now an increasing function of the competitive fringe's cost parameter χ.

4.2.7   Comparative Statics

According to the growth equation (G), our analysis yields the following comparative-statics implications for the average growth rate g:

1. Growth increases with the productivity of innovations λ. This result points to the importance of education, and particularly higher education, as a growth-

---

6. Substituting from equation (4.5) into equation (4.3) yields $p = 1/\alpha$.

7. That is,

$$\frac{d}{d\chi}\left((\chi-1)\Big/\chi^{\frac{1}{1-\alpha}}\right)$$

$$= \chi^{-\frac{1}{1-\alpha}} + (\chi-1)\frac{d}{d\chi}\left(\chi^{-\frac{1}{1-\alpha}}\right)$$

$$= \chi^{-\frac{1}{1-\alpha}}\left(1 - \frac{1-\chi^{-1}}{1-\alpha}\right)$$

which is greater than zero in the nondrastic case because $\chi^{-1} > \alpha$.

enhancing device. Countries that invest more in higher education will achieve a higher productivity of research, and will also reduce the opportunity cost of research by increasing the aggregate supply of skilled labor.

2. Growth increases with the size of innovations, as measured by the productivity improvement factor γ. This result follows directly from Proposition 1, together with the result (4.9) that shows that the frequency of innovation is independent of γ. The result in turn points to a feature that will become important when we discuss cross-country convergence. A country that lags behind the world technology frontier has what Gerschenkron (1962) called an advantage of backwardness. That is, the further it lags behind the frontier, the bigger the productivity improvement it will get if it can implement the frontier technology when it innovates, and hence the faster it can grow.

3. Growth increases with the degree of property-rights protection, as measured by χ. That is, a higher χ may reflect stronger patent protection, which increases the cost of imitating the current technology in the intermediate sector. Thus it should lead to more intense research, as it raises the profit that accrues to a successful innovator. This in turn should result in higher growth.

4. Growth decreases with the degree of product market competition. That is, a lower χ may reflect an increased ability of other firms to compete against the incumbent monopolist, which lowers the value of a successful innovation. This prediction is at odds with most recent empirical studies, starting with the work of Nickell (1996) and Blundell, Griffith, and Van Reenen (1999). Chapter 12 will revisit the relationship between competition and growth.

5. An increase in the size of population should also bring about an increase in growth by raising the supply of labor L. This "scale effect" was also seen in the product-variety model of the previous chapter, and it has been challenged in the literature. In section 4.4 we will see how this questionable comparative-statics result can be eliminated by considering a model with both horizontal and vertical innovations.

4.3   A Multisector Model

4.3.1   Production and Profit

In this section we allow for multiple innovating sectors in the economy. Suppose there is not one intermediate product but a continuum, indexed on the interval [0, 1]. The final-good production function is now

$$Y_t = L^{1-\alpha} \int_0^1 A_{it}^{1-\alpha} x_{it}^{\alpha} di \tag{4.10}$$

where each x_{it} is the flow of intermediate product i used at t, and the productivity parameter A_{it} reflects the quality of that product. In any period the productivity parameters will vary across intermediate products because of the randomness of the innovation process.

According to equation (4.10), the final output produced by each intermediate product is determined by the production function

$$Y_{it} = \left(A_{it} L\right)^{1-\alpha} x_{it}^{\alpha} \tag{4.11}$$

which is identical to the production function (4.1) of the one-sector model.

Each intermediate product has its own monopoly, and its price equals its marginal product in the final sector, which according to equation (4.11) is

$$p_{it} = \partial Y_{it} / \partial x_{it} = \alpha \left(A_{it} L\right)^{1-\alpha} x_{it}^{\alpha-1}$$

Therefore, the monopolist in sector i chooses the quantity x_{it} that maximizes her profit:

$$\Pi_{it} = p_{it} x_{it} - x_{it} = \alpha \left(A_{it} L\right)^{1-\alpha} x_{it}^{\alpha} - x_{it} \tag{4.12}$$

which implies an equilibrium quantity:[8]

$$x_{it} = \alpha^{\frac{2}{1-\alpha}} A_{it} L \tag{4.13}$$

and an equilibrium profit:

$$\Pi_{it} = \pi A_{it} L \tag{4.14}$$

where the parameter π is the same as in the analogous equation (4.6) of the one-sector model.

The aggregate behavior of the economy depends on the aggregate productivity parameter

---

8. The first-order condition for the maximization problem is

$$\alpha^2 \left(A_{it} L\right)^{1-\alpha} x_{it}^{\alpha-1} - 1 = 0$$

from which equation (4.13) follows directly. Substituting from equation (4.13) into equation (4.12) yields equation (4.14).

$$A_t = \int_0^1 A_{it}\, di$$

which is just the unweighted numerical average of all the individual productivity parameters. In particular, final output and GDP in this multisector economy are determined by exactly the same equations as in the one-sector economy of the previous section, but with A_t now being this average, instead of being the productivity parameter of the economy's only intermediate product.

More specifically, using equation (4.13) to substitute for each x_{it} in the production function (4.10) yields the same formula as before for final output:

$$Y_t = \alpha^{\frac{2\alpha}{1-\alpha}} A_t L$$

As before, the economy's GDP equals the output of final good Y_t minus the amount used up in producing each of the intermediate products. Since each intermediate product is produced one for one using final output,

$$GDP_t = Y_t - \int_0^1 x_{it}\, di$$

Using equation (4.13) to substitute for each x_{it} in this integral and combining it with the preceding formula for Y_t yields

$$GDP_t = \alpha^{\frac{2\alpha}{1-\alpha}}\left(1 - \alpha^2\right) A_t L$$

which is identical to equation (4.7). So again the economy's GDP is proportional to its effective labor supply $A_t L$.

4.3.2   Innovation and Research Arbitrage

Innovation in each sector takes place exactly as in the one-sector model. Specifically, there is a single entrepreneur in each sector who spends final output in research and innovates with probability $\phi(n_{it}) = \lambda n_{it}^\sigma$, where now n_{it} is the research expenditure in sector i relative to the target productivity in sector i:

$$n_{it} = R_{it}/A_{it}^*$$

where $A_{it}^* = \gamma A_{i,t-1}$ is the productivity parameter if she succeeds.

The entrepreneur chooses the research expenditure R_{it} that maximizes her net benefit:

$$\phi(R_{it}/A_{it}^*)\Pi_{it}^* - R_{it}$$

where Π_{it}^* is her profit if she succeeds. Therefore R_{it} must satisfy the first-order condition

$$\phi'(R_{it}/A_t^*)\Pi_t^*/A_t^* - 1 = 0$$

which we can write, using equation (4.14), as the research arbitrage equation

$$\phi'(n_{it})\pi L = 1 \tag{R}$$

This is exactly the same as the research arbitrage equation in the one-sector model, so it solves for the same constant productivity-adjusted research and frequency of innovation:

$$n = (\sigma\lambda\pi L)^{\frac{1}{1-\sigma}} \quad \text{and} \quad \mu = \lambda^{\frac{1}{1-\sigma}}(\sigma\pi L)^{\frac{\sigma}{1-\sigma}}$$

One important feature of this model is that the probability of innovation μ is the same in all sectors, no matter what the starting level of productivity $A_{i,t-1}$. This might seem surprising, because the reward $\Pi_{it}^* = \pi\gamma A_{i,t-1}L$ to a successful innovation is higher in more advanced sectors. But this advantage is just offset by the fact that the cost of innovating at any given rate is also correspondingly higher because what matters is research expenditure relative to the target productivity level $\gamma A_{i,t-1}$. As we will see, this feature allows a simple characterization of the aggregate growth rate in the economy.

4.3.3 Growth

Since per capita GDP is again proportional to the aggregate productivity parameter A_t, therefore the economy's growth rate is again the proportional growth rate of A_t:

$$g_t = \frac{A_t - A_{t-1}}{A_{t-1}} \tag{4.15}$$

In this case, however, the aggregate growth rate is no longer random, because bad luck in some sectors will be offset by good luck in others.

In each sector i we have

$$A_{it} = \begin{cases} \gamma A_{i,t-1} & \text{with probability } \mu \\ A_{i,t-1} & \text{with probability } 1-\mu \end{cases} \tag{4.16}$$

By the law of large numbers we know that the fraction of sectors that innovate each period will be μ. Therefore, the economy-wide average A_t can be expressed as μ times the average A_{it} among sectors that innovated at t plus $(1 - \mu)$ times the average among sectors that did not:

$$A_t = \mu A_{1t} + (1 - \mu) A_{2t}$$

Now the average A_{2t} among sectors that did not innovate at t is just last period's economy-wide average A_{t-1}, because these sectors are drawn at random from the economy and each of them has the same productivity parameter as last period. By the same logic, the average A_{1t} among sectors that did innovate is just γ times the average of these same firms' productivity parameters last period—that is, γA_{t-1}. So we have

$$A_t = \mu \gamma A_{t-1} + (1 - \mu) A_{t-1}$$

It follows from this and equation (4.15) that the growth rate each period will equal the constant

$$g = \mu \cdot (\gamma - 1)$$

which is the same as the long-run average growth rate of the one-sector model. Substituting equation (4.9) into this formula produces the same expression (G) as before, implying the same comparative-statics results as before.

4.4   Scale Effects*

Both the innovation-based growth theories we have seen so far, the product-variety model with just horizontal innovations and the Schumpeterian model with just vertical innovations, predict that increased population leads to increased growth. This prediction is implied because increased population raises the size of the market that can be captured by a successful entrepreneur and also because it raises the supply of potential researchers.

This prediction has been challenged, however, on empirical grounds. In particular, C. Jones (1995b) has pointed out that the number of scientists and engineers engaged in R&D has grown almost ninefold since 1953 with no significant trend increase in productivity growth. The present section shows how the counterfactual scale effect can be eliminated from the theory by allowing for both horizontal and vertical innovations.

The way to deal with this problem in Schumpeterian theory is to incorporate A. Young's (1998) insight that as population grows, proliferation of product

---

* The analysis in this section is rather terse, and can be skipped on first reading.

varieties reduces the effectiveness of research aimed at quality improvement by causing it to be spread more thinly over a larger number of different sectors, thus dissipating the effect on the overall rate of productivity growth.

So the first thing we need to do is assume a final-good production function that allows for a variable number of intermediate products:

$$Y_t = (L/M)^{1-\alpha} \int_0^M A_{it}^{1-\alpha} x_{it}^\alpha di \qquad (4.17)$$

which is the same production function (4.10) as before except that now the intermediate products are indexed over the interval [0, M] instead of [0, 1]. Thus M is our measure of product variety.

This production function is the same as the one assumed in the product-variety model of the previous chapter, except that (1) each product has its own unique productivity parameter A_{it} instead of having $A_{it} = 1$ for all products, and (2) we assume that what matters is not the absolute input L of labor but the input per product L/M. Thus the contribution of each intermediate product to final output is now

$$Y_{it} = A_{it}^{1-\alpha} x_{it}^\alpha (L/M)^{1-\alpha}$$

which indicates that as the number of intermediate products goes up, there will be less labor to work with each one, so each will contribute less to final output unless the quality A_{it} or the quantity x_{it} is increased.[9]

The next thing we have to do is model the process by which product variety increases. The simplest scheme is to suppose that each person has a probability ψ of inventing a new intermediate product, with no expenditure at all on research. Suppose also that the exogenous fraction ε of products disappears each year. If population is constant, then each year the length M_t of the list of intermediate products will change by the amount

$$\psi L - \varepsilon M_t$$

and will eventually stabilize[10] at a steady-state value

---

9. The production function is a special case of the one that Benassy (1998) showed does not necessarily yield a positive productivity effect of product variety.

10. That is, the difference equation

$$M_{t+1} = M_t + \psi L - \varepsilon M_t$$

starting at M_0 has the unique solution

$$M_t = (\psi/\varepsilon)L + (1-\varepsilon)^t [M_0 - (\psi/\varepsilon)L]$$

which converges to $(\psi/\varepsilon)L$ as $t \to \infty$ because $(1 - \varepsilon)$ is between zero and one.

$$M = (\psi/\varepsilon)L$$

which is proportional to population. So if population were to increase permanently, the number of products would eventually grow in proportion.

Thus in the long run the final-good production function will be

$$Y_t = (\varepsilon/\psi)^{1-\alpha} \int_0^M A_{it}^{1-\alpha} x_{it}^{\alpha} \, di$$

and the contribution of each intermediate product to final output will be

$$Y_{it} = (\varepsilon/\psi)^{1-\alpha} A_{it}^{1-\alpha} x_{it}^{\alpha}$$

which does not depend at all on the size of the economy.

Proceeding as before we see that the price of each intermediate product will be its marginal product in the final sector:

$$p_{it} = \partial Y_{it}/\partial x_{it} = \alpha (\varepsilon/\psi)^{1-\alpha} A_{it}^{1-\alpha} x_{it}^{\alpha-1} \tag{4.18}$$

Therefore, the monopolist in sector i chooses the quantity x_{it} that maximizes her profit

$$\Pi_{it} = p_{it} x_{it} - x_{it} = \alpha (\varepsilon/\psi)^{1-\alpha} A_{it}^{1-\alpha} x_{it}^{\alpha} - x_{it}$$

which implies an equilibrium quantity

$$x_{it} = \alpha^{\frac{2}{1-\alpha}} (\varepsilon/\psi) A_{it}$$

and an equilibrium profit

$$\Pi_{it} = \pi (\varepsilon/\psi) A_{it}$$

where the parameter π is the same as in the analogous equation (4.6) of the one-sector model.

According to these equations, both the monopolist's equilibrium quantity and equilibrium profit are independent of the scale of the economy as measured by population L, because her demand function (4.18) is independent of L. As a result, the net benefit to research will be independent of scale, and so will the equilibrium intensity of research, the frequency of innovation, and the economy's growth rate. More specifically, the net benefit will be

$$\phi(n_{it})\Pi_{it}^* - R_{it} = \left[\phi(n_{it})\pi(\varepsilon/\psi) - n_{it}\right] A_{it}^*$$

which is maximized by n_{it} satisfying the research arbitrage equation

$$\phi'(n_{it})\pi(\varepsilon/\psi)=1$$

which can be solved for a constant n that depends positively on the equilibrium amount of labor per product (ε/ψ) but is independent of scale. Therefore, the frequency of innovation $\mu = \phi(n)$ and the growth rate $g = \mu \cdot (\gamma - 1)$ are also independent of scale.

4.5   Conclusion

It may be useful to contrast again the Schumpeterian growth paradigm to the two alternative models of endogenous growth analyzed previously. The first was the AK model of chapter 2, according to which knowledge accumulation is a serendipitous by-product of capital accumulation. Here thrift and capital accumulation were the keys to growth, not creativity and innovation. The second endogenous growth model was the product-variety model of chapter 3, in which innovation causes productivity growth by creating new, but not necessarily improved, varieties of products.

Compared to the AK model, both the Schumpeterian model and the product-variety model have the advantage of presenting an explicit analysis of the innovation process underlying long-run growth. Compared to the product-variety model, the Schumpeterian model assigns an important role to exit and turnover of firms and workers, which, as we argued at the end of the previous chapter, is consistent with an increasing number of recent studies demonstrating that labor and product market mobility are key elements of a growth-enhancing policy near the technological frontier.[11]

This is not to say that the Schumpeterian model is free of problems. We have already discussed the problem of the scale effect of increased population on growth, but we have also argued that this difficulty can be resolved within the Schumpeterian paradigm. Another difficulty with the model as presented so far is the absence of capital, which growth-accounting exercises (Jorgenson 1995; A. Young 1995) have shown to be quite important. Chapter 5 will show how to

---

11. As we will see in subsequent chapters, the Schumpeterian model also has the advantage of allowing for entrepreneurs to make the choice between implementation and frontier innovation, and for this choice to vary with distance to the frontier, something that does not fit easily into the product-variety model. This allows the Schumpeterian model to generate context-specific policy implications and comparative-statics predictions, dependent particularly on a country's distance to the frontier.

introduce capital into the analysis in such a way as to make it consistent with these exercises. Another problem with the theory is the assumption of perfect financial markets; in reality, R&D firms rely very much on capital markets, which seem to work much better in some countries than in others. The issue of financial constraints will be dealt with in chapter 6. Another issue is convergence, which we examine in chapter 7, where we will show that the model implies a form of club-convergence consistent with the evidence of Durlauf and Johnson (1995) and Quah (1993, 1997); the key is that in Schumpeterian theory convergence occurs through productivity, by means of a process of technology transfer, as well as through capital accumulation. Finally, as indicated previously, the implication of the first-generation of Schumpeterian models to the effect that more product market competition is harmful to growth runs counter to much evidence. We address this issue in chapter 12, where we will show that various other effects can be found in more sophisticated versions of the theory, which imply a more complicated relationship between competition and growth, one that finds considerable support in the data.

4.6   Literature Notes

The earliest attempts at providing a Schumpeterian approach to endogenous growth theory were by Segerstrom, Anant, and Dinopoulos (1990), who modeled sustained growth as arising from a succession of product improvements in a fixed number of sectors, but with no uncertainty in the innovation process, and Corriveau (1991), who produced a discrete-time model with uncertainty about cost-reducing process innovations. What we present here is a simplified version of the model we laid out in Aghion and Howitt (1988, 1992), using modeling techniques from industrial organization theory (Tirole 1988, chap. 10, and Reinganum 1989). Grossman and Helpman (1991a, 1991b) built on this framework to analyze the relationship between trade and growth, and between growth and the product cycle.

On the scale-effect debate, C. Jones (1995b) has developed a "semiendogenous" model in which the scale effect is dissipated by the diminishing returns to ideas in research, with the implication that population growth is the only long-run determinant of economic growth. The approach was further developed by Kortum (1997) and Segerstrom (1998). Our alternative "fully endogenous" approach was developed by several Schumpeterian endogenous models without scale effects; in particular, see Howitt (1999), Aghion and Howitt (1998a, chap. 12),

Dinopoulos and Thompson (1998), and Peretto (1998). See also the recent contribution of Dinopoulos and Syropoulos (2006) which argues that efforts to build increasing barriers to entry are what dissipate the scale effect. Segerstrom (2000) and C. Jones (2005) point out that small changes in the assumptions of the fully endogenous model can result in drastic changes in its conclusions with respect to scale effects. However, Ha and Howitt (2006) use U.S. data to compare the two main varieties of R&D-based growth models without scale effects, and conclude that the Schumpeterian model without scale effects is more consistent with the long-run trends in R&D and TFP than semiendogenous growth theory. Other texts, such as Laincz and Peretto (2004) and Ulku (2005), point in the same direction, using U.S. data as well.

Problems

1. Both the product-variety and the Schumpeterian models predict scale effects, namely, that a larger population (a larger population of researchers) would predict faster growth. How would you empirically test this prediction?

2. **A variant of the basic Schumpeterian model**

Consider the basic one-sector model from section 4.2. The difference here is simply that final-good production is given by $Y_t = A_t^\psi L^{1-\alpha} x_t^\alpha$, where $0 < \psi \le 1$. Write down intermediate-good monopolists' profits, the research arbitrage condition, and the growth rate of ouput in the economy.

3. **Welfare analysis in the basic Schumpeterian model**

Consider again the model from section 4.2. Now, instead of looking at the market equilibrium, we focus on the socially optimal allocation, from a social planner with one-period horizon. The planner seeks to maximize $GDP_t = (AL)^{1-\alpha} x^\alpha - x$.

a. Solve for the social planner's allocation of intermediate input. Compare it to the market equilibrium value. Explain your results.

b. What is the social planner's adjusted level of innovation expenditures n?

c. Compare the efficient growth rate of the economy given by the social planner's maximization problem to the market equilibrium growth rate. Explain why it could be greater and why it could be lower than the market equilibrium one.

d. Compare your results to the ones in problem 5 from chapter 3.

4. **Semiendogenous growth and scale effects (based on Jones, 1995b)**

Consider a generalized Romer (1990) model from chapter 3 with the following innovation technology: $\dot{A} = \delta L_2 A^\phi$, where $\phi < 1$ and L_2 is the amount of labor devoted to R&D activities. Assume that total labor increases at rate n and $\dot{L}/L = n$, and define $g \equiv \dot{A}/A$.

a. Explain why in balanced-growth path (BGP), $L_2 = \lambda L$, where $\lambda \in (0,1)$ is a constant.

b. Looking at the steady state, where $\dot{g}/g = 0$, compute g.

c. Is there still some type of scale effect in this model? How would you test the predictions of this model in the data?

5. The continuous-time version of the Schumpeterian model, I

The next two problems will guide the reader through the continuous-time version of the Schumpeterian model.

Assume individuals have linear intertemporal preferences: $u(y) = \int_0^\infty y_\tau e^{-r\tau} d\tau$, where r is the rate of time preference, also equal to the interest rate. There are L individuals in the economy, and each individual is endowed with one unit flow of labor, so L is also equal to the aggregate flow of labor supply.

Output of the consumption good is produced at any time using an intermediate good according to

$$y = Ax^\alpha$$

where $0 < \alpha < 1$ and x denotes the flow of intermediate good used in final good production.

Innovations consist of the invention of a new variety of intermediate good that replaces the old one, and whose use raises the technology parameter A by the constant factor $\gamma > 1$.

The economy's fixed stock of labor L has two competing uses. It can produce the intermediate good one for one, and it can be used in research.

a. Assuming labor-market clearing at any period, write the labor-market clearing condition that must hold at each period, with x representing the amount of labor used in manufacturing and n the amount ol labor used in research.

When the amount n is used in research, innovations arrive randomly with a Poisson arrival rate λn, where $\lambda > 0$ is a parameter indicating the productivity of the research technology. The firm that succeeds in innovating can monopolize the intermediate sector until replaced by the next innovator.

Also, output, profits, and wages are all multiplied by γ each time a new innovation occurs.

b. Derive and explain why the amount of labor devoted to research is determined by the following arbitrage condition (where w_t is the wage rate before innovation $t + 1$ and V_{t+1} is the value of innovation $t + 1$):

$$w_t = \lambda V_{t+1}$$

This arbitrage equation governs the dynamics of the economy over its successive innovations. Together with the labor-market equation, it constitutes the backbone of the model.

The value V_{t+1} is determined by the following asset equation:

$$rV_{t+1} = \pi_{t+1} - \lambda n_{t+1} V_{t+1}$$

c. Interpret the different terms of the preceding asset equation.

6. The continuous-time version of the Schumpeterian model, II

In this problem, the reader will derive the equilibrium level of R&D and the steady-state growth rate in the continuous-time Schumpeterian model.

a. Using the intermediate good producers optimization problem to choose x, show that equilibrium profits for intermediate good producers are

$$\pi_t = \frac{1-\alpha}{\alpha} w_t x$$

b. Using the labor market-clearing condition and your result from the previous item, show that the research arbitrage condition can be rewritten as

$$1 = \lambda \frac{\gamma \dfrac{1-\alpha}{\alpha}(L-n)}{r + \lambda n}$$

This allows us to write the steady-state equilibrium R&D, $\hat{n}$, as a function of the parameters of the economy.

In a steady state, the flow of consumption good (or final output) produced during the time-interval between the tth and the $(t+1)$st innovation is

$$y_t = A_t \hat{x}^\alpha = A_t (L - \hat{n})^\alpha$$

Also,

$$y_{t+1} = \gamma y_t$$

c. Take the log of y_t. By how much is this value increased every time an innovation occurs?

d. Show that the average growth rate of the economy in steady state is $g = \lambda \hat{n} \ln \gamma$. (Hint: Take a unit-time interval, say between τ and $\tau + 1$, and note that $\ln y(\tau + 1) = \ln y(\tau) + (\ln \gamma) \varepsilon(\tau)$, where $\varepsilon(\tau)$ is the number of innovations between τ and $\tau + 1$. Use the properties of the Poisson distribution to compute $E[\ln y(\tau + 1) - \ln y(\tau)]$).

e. What are the effects on the growth rate of the economy and on $\hat{n}$ of (i) an increase in the size of the labor market L; (ii) a reduction of the interest rate r; (iii) a decrease in the degree of market competition α; (iv) an increase in the size of innovation γ and/or in the productivity of R&D λ?

5 Capital, Innovation, and Growth Accounting

5.1 Introduction

Neoclassical theory and AK theory focus on capital accumulation, whereas the product-variety and Schumpeterian theories focus on innovations that raise productivity. One way to judge the competing theories is to ask how much of growth is attributable to the accumulation of physical and human capital, and how much is the result of productivity growth. The question can be studied using *growth accounting*, a method first invented by Solow (1957). This chapter shows how growth accounting works.

Economists who have conducted growth accounting exercises in many economies (for example, Jorgenson 1995) have concluded that a lot of economic growth is accounted for by capital accumulation. These findings raise a number of issues that we also deal with in this chapter. For one thing, the results of growth accounting are very sensitive to the way capital is measured. We will discuss some cases in which there is reason to believe that capital is systematically mismeasured. One of these cases concerns the claim by Alwyn Young (1995) that most of the extraordinary growth performance of Singapore, Hong Kong, Taiwan, and South Korea can be explained by factor accumulation, not technological progress. Hsieh (2002) argues that these results are no longer true once one corrects for the overestimates of capital accumulation in the data.

Another issue raised by growth accounting has to do with the difference between accounting relationships and causal relationships. We will show in this chapter that even though there is evidence that somewhere between 30 and 70 percent of the growth of output per worker in OECD countries can be "accounted for" by capital accumulation, nevertheless these results are consistent with the neoclassical model which implies that in the long run *all* the growth in output per worker is caused by technological progress.

In this chapter we also show how capital can be introduced into the Schumpeterian model that we are using as a main workhorse model throughout the book. The result is a hybrid model in which capital accumulation takes place as in the neoclassical model but productivity growth arises endogenously as in the Schumpeterian model. The hybrid model is consistent with the empirical evidence on growth accounting, as is the neoclassical model. But the causal explanation that it provides for economic growth is quite different from that of the neoclassical model.

5.2   Measuring the Growth of Total Factor Productivity

When people mention productivity, often what they are referring to is *labor productivity*, which is output per worker: $y = Y/L$. But this particular measure of productivity confounds the effects of capital accumulation and technological progress, both of which can raise output per worker. To see this point, suppose that output depends on capital and labor according to the familiar Cobb-Douglas production function:

$$Y = BK^\alpha L^{1-\alpha} \tag{5.1}$$

where the parameter B reflects the state of technology. Dividing both sides by L, we see that output per worker equals

$$y = Bk^\alpha \tag{5.2}$$

where $k = K/L$ is the capital stock per worker. According to equation (5.2), labor productivity y depends positively on the technology parameter B but also on the capital stock per worker k.

A better measure of productivity is the parameter B. This parameter tells us not just how productive labor is, but also how productively the economy uses all the factors of production. For this reason, B is called *total factor productivity*, or just TFP.

Our measure of economic growth is the growth rate G of output per person. Under the simplifying assumption that the population and labor force grow at the same rate, G is also the growth rate of output per worker. So from equation (5.2) we can express the growth rate as[1]

$$G = \dot{B}/B + \alpha \dot{k}/k \tag{5.3}$$

According to equation (5.3), the growth rate is the sum of two components: the rate of TFP growth ($\dot{B}/B$) and the "capital-deepening" component ($\alpha \dot{k}/k$). The first one measures the direct effect of technological progress, and the second measures

1. Taking natural logs of both sides of equation (5.2) we get

$\ln y = \ln B + \alpha \ln k$

Differentiating both sides with respect to time we get

$\dot{y}/y = \dot{B}/B + \alpha \dot{k}/k$

which is the same as equation (5.3) because $G = \dot{y}/y$ by definition.

the effect of capital accumulation. The purpose of growth accounting is to determine the relative size of these two components.

If all the variables in equation (5.3) could be observed directly, then growth accounting would be very simple. However, this is not the case. For almost all countries we have time-series data on output, capital, and labor, which allow us to observe G and $\dot{k}/k$, but there are no direct measures of B and α. Growth accounting deals with this problem in two steps. The first step is to estimate α using data on factor prices, and the second step is to estimate TFP growth ($\dot{B}/B$) using a *residual* method. These two steps work as follows.

First, we must make the assumption that the market for capital is perfectly competitive. Under that assumption, the rental price of capital r should equal the marginal product of capital. Differentiating the right-hand side of equation (5.1) to compute the marginal product of capital, we then get[2]

$$r = \alpha Y / K$$

which we can rewrite as

$$\alpha = rK / Y$$

That is, α equals the share of capital income (the price r times the quantity K) in national income (Y). This share can be computed from directly observed data once we observe the factor price r.

To conduct the second step of growth accounting we just rewrite the growth equation (5.3) as

$$\dot{B}/B = G - \alpha \dot{k}/k$$

which says that the rate of TFP growth ($\dot{B}/B$) is the residual left over after we subtract the capital-deepening term from the observed growth rate G. Once we have estimated α using factor prices, we can measure everything on the right-hand side. This measure of TFP growth is known as the *Solow residual*.

5.2.1   Empirical Results

From the national accounts it appears that wage and salaries account for about 70 percent of national income in the United States. In other countries the number is roughly the same. So to a first-order approximation the share of capital is about 0.3, and to get a rough estimate of TFP growth we can set α equal to 0.3. Using

2. That is, $r = \partial Y/\partial K = \alpha BK^{\alpha-1}L^{1-\alpha} = \alpha BK^{\alpha}L^{1-\alpha}/K = \alpha Y/K$.

this value of α and measures of capital stocks constructed from the Penn World Tables (Heston et al. 2002), we can break down the average growth rate from 1960 to 2000 of all OECD countries. The results are shown[3] in table 5.1. The first column is the average growth rate G of output per worker over this 40-year period. The second column shows the corresponding TFP growth rate estimated over that period, and the third column is the other (capital-deepening) component of growth. The fourth and fifth columns indicate the percentage of growth that is accounted for by TFP growth and capital deepening, respectively. As this table indicates, TFP growth accounts for about two-thirds of economic growth in OECD countries, while capital deepening accounts for one third.

Economists such as Jorgenson (1995) have conducted more detailed and disaggregated growth-accounting exercises on a number of OECD countries, in which they estimate the contribution of human as well as physical capital. They tend to come up with a smaller contribution of TFP growth and a correspondingly larger contribution of capital deepening (both physical and human capital deepening) than indicated in table 5.1. In the United States, for example, over the period from 1948 to 1986, Jorgenson and Fraumeni (1992) estimate a TFP growth rate of 0.50 percent, which is about 30 percent of the average growth rate of output per hour of labor input instead of the roughly 58 percent reported for the United States in table 5.1.[4]

The main reason why these disaggregated estimates produce a smaller contribution of TFP growth than reported in table 5.1 is that the residual constructed in the disaggregated estimates comes from subtracting not only a physical-capital-deepening component but also a human-capital-deepening component. Since the middle of the 20th century, all OECD countries have experienced a large increase in the level of educational attainment of the average worker, that is, a large increase in human capital per person. When the contribution of this human capital deepening is also subtracted, we are clearly going to be left with a smaller residual than if we just subtract the contribution of physical capital deepening. But whichever way we compute TFP growth it seems that capital

---

3. We thank Professor Diego Comin of the Harvard Business School for his help in compiling the capital stock estimates underlying this table.

4. Their table 5 indicates that on average output grew at a 2.93 percent rate and that labor input (hours times quality) grew at a 2.20 percent rate. It also indicates that 58.1 percent of the contribution of labor input came from hours, implying an average growth rate in hours of $(.581 \cdot 2.20 =) 1.28$ percent and an average growth rate in output per hour worked of $(2.93 - 1.28 =) 1.65$ percent. Their estimate of the residual was 0.50 percent, which is 30.3 percent of the growth rate of output per hour worked.

Table 5.1
Growth Accounting in OECD Countries: 1960–2000

Country	Growth Rate	TFP Growth	Capital Deepening	TFP Share	Capital Share
Australia	1.67	1.26	0.41	0.75	0.25
Austria	2.99	2.03	0.96	0.68	0.32
Belgium	2.58	1.74	0.84	0.67	0.33
Canada	1.57	0.95	0.63	0.60	0.40
Denmark	1.87	1.32	0.55	0.70	0.30
Finland	2.72	2.03	0.69	0.75	0.25
France	2.50	1.54	0.95	0.62	0.38
Germany	3.09	1.96	1.12	0.64	0.36
Greece	1.93	1.66	0.27	0.86	0.14
Iceland	4.02	2.33	1.69	0.58	0.42
Ireland	2.93	2.26	0.67	0.77	0.23
Italy	4.04	2.10	1.94	0.52	0.48
Japan	3.28	2.73	0.56	0.83	0.17
Netherlands	1.74	1.25	0.49	0.72	0.28
New Zealand	0.61	0.45	0.16	0.74	0.26
Norway	2.36	1.70	0.66	0.72	0.28
Portugal	3.42	2.06	1.36	0.60	0.40
Spain	3.22	1.79	1.44	0.55	0.45
Sweden	1.68	1.24	0.44	0.74	0.26
Switzerland	0.98	0.69	0.29	0.70	0.30
United Kingdom	1.90	1.31	0.58	0.69	0.31
United States	1.89	1.09	0.80	0.58	0.42
Average	2.41	1.61	0.80	0.68	0.32

accumulation and technological progress each account for a substantial share of productivity growth—somewhere between 30 and 70 percent each depending on the details of the estimation.

5.3 Some Problems with Growth Accounting

5.3.1 Problems in Measuring Capital, and the Tyranny of Numbers

One problem with growth accounting is that technological progress is often embodied in new capital goods, a fact which makes it hard to separate the influence of capital accumulation from the influence of innovation. When output rises, is it because we have employed more capital goods or because we have employed better ones? Economists such as Gordon (1990) and Cummins and Violante (2002) have shown that the relative price of capital goods has fallen dramatically for many decades. In many cases this decrease has occurred not because we are able to produce more units of the same capital goods with any given factor inputs but because we are able to produce a higher quality of capital goods than before, so that the price of a "quality-adjusted" unit of capital has fallen. For example, it costs about the same as 10 years ago to produce one laptop computer, but you get much more computer for that price than you did 10 years ago. But by how much has the real price fallen? That is a difficult question to answer, and national income accountants, having been trained to distrust subjective manipulation of the data, probably adjust too little to satisfy growth economists.

To some extent this problem affects not so much the aggregate productivity numbers as how that productivity is allocated across sectors. Griliches (1994) has argued, for example, that the aircraft industry, which conducts a lot of research and development (R&D), has exhibited relatively little TFP growth while the airline industry, which does almost no R&D, has exhibited a lot of TFP growth. If we were properly to adjust for the improved quality of modern aircraft, which fly more safely and more quietly, using less fuel and causing less pollution than before, then we would see that the aircraft industry was more productive than the TFP numbers indicate. But at the same time we would see that productivity has not really grown so much in the airline industry, where we have been under-estimating the increase in their quality-adjusted input of aircraft. More generally, making the proper quality adjustment would raise our estimate of TFP growth in upstream industries but lower it in downstream industries. In aggregate, however, these two effects tend to wash out.

A bigger measurement problem for aggregate TFP occurs when a country's national accounts systematically overestimate the increase in capital taking place each year. Pritchett (2000) argues that such overestimating happens in many countries because of government inefficiency and corruption. Funds are appropri-ated for the stated purpose of building public works, and the amount is recorded as having all been spent on investment in (public) physical capital. But in fact much of it gets diverted into the pockets of politicians, bureaucrats, and their friends instead of being spent on capital. Since we do not have reliable estimates of what fraction was really spent on capital and what fraction was diverted, we do not really know how much capital accumulation took place. We just know that it was less than reported. As a result it is hard to know what to make of TFP numbers in many countries, especially those with high corruption rates.

A similar problem is reported by Hsieh (2002), who has challenged Alwyn Young's (1995) claim that the Eastern "Tigers" (Singapore, Hong Kong, Taiwan, and South Korea) accomplished most of their remarkable growth performance through capital accumulation and the improved efficiency of resource allocation, not through technological progress. Hsieh argues that this finding does not stand up when we take into account some serious overreporting of the growth in capital in these countries.

According to Young's estimates, GDP per capita grew in Hong Kong by 5.7 percent a year over 1966–92. Over 1966–90, Singapore's GDP per capita grew by 6.8 percent a year, South Korea's also by 6.8 percent, and Taiwan's by 6.7 percent. Growth in GDP per worker was between one and two percentage points less, reflecting large increases in labor force participation, but even the per-worker growth rates are very high in comparison to other countries.

Young adjusts for changes in the size and mix of the labor force, including improvements in the educational attainment of workers, to arrive at estimates of the Solow residual. For the same time periods as before, he finds that TFP growth rates were 2.3 percent a year for Hong Kong, 0.2 percent for Singapore, 1.7 percent for South Korea, and 2.6 percent for Taiwan. He argues that these figures are not exceptional by the standards of the OECD or several large developing countries.

Hsieh argues, however, that there is clearly a discrepancy between these numbers and observed factor prices, especially in Singapore. His estimates of the rate of return to capital, drawn from observed rates of returns on various financial instruments, are roughly constant over the period from the early 1960s through 1990, even though the capital stock rose 2.8 percent per year faster than GDP. As we saw in the neoclassical model, technological progress is needed in order to prevent diminishing marginal productivity from reducing the rate of return to capital when such dramatic capital deepening is taking place. The fact that the rate of return has not fallen, then, seems to contradict Young's finding of negligible TFP growth. The obvious explanation for this apparent contradiction, Hsieh suggests, is that the government statistics used in growth accounting have systematically overstated the growth in the capital stock. Hsieh argues that such overstatements are particularly likely in the case of owner-occupied housing in Singapore.

Hsieh also argues that instead of estimating TFP growth using the Solow residual method we should use the "dual" method, which consists of estimating the increase in TFP by a weighted average of the increase in factor prices. That is, if there were no TFP growth, then the marginal products of labor and capital could not both rise at the same time. Instead, either the marginal product of labor could rise while the marginal product of capital falls, a process that would take place if the capital labor ratio k were to rise, or the reverse could take place if k were to fall. Using this fact one can estimate TFP growth as the growth in total factor income that would have come about if factor prices had changed as they did but there had been no change in K or L. By this method he finds that in two out of the four Tiger cases TFP growth was approximately the same as when computed by the Solow residual, but that in the cases of Taiwan and Singapore the dual method produces substantially higher estimates. In the case of Singapore he estimates annual TFP growth of 2.2 percent per year using the dual method versus 0.2 percent per year using the Solow residual.

5.3.2 Accounting versus Causation

When interpreting the results of growth accounting, it is important to keep in mind that an accounting relationship is not the same thing as a causal relationship. Even though capital deepening might *account* for as much as 70 percent of the observed growth of output per worker in some OECD countries, it might still be that all of the growth is *caused* by technological progress. Consider, for example, the case in which the aggregate production function is

$$Y = A^{1-\alpha} L^{1-\alpha} K^{\alpha}$$

as in the neoclassical model, where technological progress is exogenous.[5] As we saw in chapter 1, A is the number of efficiency units per worker, and its growth rate is the rate of labor-augmenting technological progress.

Comparing this to equation (5.1), we see that it implies total factor productivity equal to

$$B = A^{1-\alpha}$$

which implies a rate of TFP growth equal to $1 - \alpha$ times the rate of labor-augmenting technological progress:

$$\dot{B}/B = (1-\alpha)\dot{A}/A$$

Now, as we have seen, in the long run the neoclassical model implies that the growth rate of output per worker in the long run will be the rate of labor-augmenting technological progress $\dot{A}/A$:

$$\dot{A}/A = \dot{y}/y$$

In that sense, long-run economic growth is caused entirely by technological progress in the neoclassical model, and yet the model is consistent with the decomposition reported in table 5.1, because it says that the rate of TFP growth is

5. And also, as we shall see later in this chapter, in the Schumpeterian framework once capital has been introduced.

$$\dot{B}/B = (1-\alpha)\,\dot{y}/y$$

Given the evidence that α is about 0.3, this last equation implies that TFP growth is about 70 percent of the rate of economic growth, which is consistent with the evidence in table 5.1.

Of course, once we take into account the accumulation of human as well as physical capital, then the estimated rate of TFP growth falls to about 30 percent of economic growth. But that is just what we would get from the preceding model if we interpreted K not as physical capital but as a broad aggregate that also includes human capital, in which case α should be interpreted not as the share of physical capital in national income but the share of all capital in national income. Simple calculations such as the one reported by Mankiw, Romer, and Weil (1992) suggest that this share ought to be about two-thirds of national income, in which case the preceding models would again be consistent with the growth-accounting evidence, since it would imply a rate of TFP growth of about one-third the rate of economic growth, even though again the model would imply that in the long run the cause of economic growth is entirely technological progress.

To see what is going on here, recall that the capital-deepening component of growth accounting measures the growth rate that would have been observed if the capital-labor ratio had grown at its observed rate but there had been no technological progress. The problem is that if there had been no technological progress, then the capital-labor ratio would not have grown as much. For example, in the neoclassical model we saw that technological progress is needed in order to prevent diminishing returns from eventually choking off all growth in the capital-labor ratio. In that sense technological progress is the underlying cause of both the components of economic growth—not just of TFP growth but also of capital deepening. What we really want to know in order to understand and possibly control the growth process is not how much economic growth we would get under the implausible scenario of no technological progress and continual capital deepening but rather how much economic growth we would get if we were to encourage more saving, or more R&D, or more education, or more competition, and so on. These causal questions can only be answered by constructing and testing economic theories. All growth accounting can do is help us to organize the facts to be explained by these theories.

5.4   Capital Accumulation and Innovation

In this section we develop a hybrid neoclassical/Schumpeterian model that includes both endogenous capital accumulation and endogenous technological progress in one model. As we shall see, it provides a causal explanation of long-run economic growth that is the same as that of the simpler Schumpeterian model without capital, except that there is now an additional explanatory variable that can affect the growth rate, namely, the saving rate. The model provides a more complete explanation of growth-accounting results than does the neoclassical model because it endogenizes both of the forces underlying growth, whereas the neoclassical model endogenizes only one of them.

5.4.1   The Basics

As in the multisectoral model of the previous chapter, there are three kinds of goods: a final good, labor, and a continuum of specialized intermediate products. But now we assume that the final good is storable, in the form of capital, and the intermediate goods are produced with capital. In other words, we can interpret the intermediate products as the services of specialized capital goods, like computers and automobiles.

There is a constant population of L individuals, each endowed with one unit of skilled labor that she supplies inelastically. The final good is produced under perfect competition according to the production function

$$Y_t = L^{1-\alpha} \int_0^1 A_{it}^{1-\alpha} x_{it}^{\alpha} di, \qquad 0 < \alpha < 1 \tag{5.4}$$

where each x_{it} is the flow of intermediate input i. For simplicity, we set $L = 1$.

Each intermediate input is produced according to the production function

$$x_{it} = K_{it}$$

where K_{it} is the amount of capital used as input. So the local monopolist's cost is now $r_t K_{it} = r_t x_{it}$. Her price is again the marginal product

$$p_{it} = \partial Y_t / \partial x_{it} = \alpha A_{it}^{1-\alpha} x_{it}^{\alpha-1}$$

She will choose x_{it} to maximize her profit

$$\Pi_{it} = \alpha A_{it}^{1-\alpha} x_{it}^{\alpha} - r_t x_{it} \tag{5.5}$$

where r_t is the rental rate of capital, which implies the quantity[6]

$$x_{it} = \left(\alpha^2 / r_t \right)^{\frac{1}{1-\alpha}} A_{it} \tag{5.6}$$

---

6. Equation (5.6) follows directly from the first-order condition

$$\partial \Pi_{it} / \partial x_{it} = \alpha^2 A_{it}^{1-\alpha} x_{it}^{\alpha-1} - r_t = 0$$

The rental rate is determined in the market for capital, where the supply is the historically predetermined capital stock K_t and the demand is the sum of all sectors' demands $\int_0^1 K_{it}\,di = \int_0^1 x_{it}\,di$. Using equation (5.6), we can write the equilibrium condition as

$$K_t = \int_0^1 \left(\alpha^2/r_t\right)^{\frac{1}{1-\alpha}} A_{it}\,di = \left(\alpha^2/r_t\right)^{\frac{1}{1-\alpha}} A_t \tag{5.7}$$

where $A_t = \int_0^1 A_{it}\,di$ is again the average productivity parameter. Let

$$\kappa_t = K_t/A_t$$

denote the aggregate capital stock per effective worker (recall that $L = 1$). Then equation (5.7) solves for

$$r_t = \alpha^2 \kappa_t^{\alpha-1} \tag{5.8}$$

so the equilibrium rental rate is a decreasing function of the capital stock per effective worker. Comparing equations (5.6) and (5.7) we see that

$$x_{it} = A_{it}\left(K_t/A_t\right) = A_{it}\kappa_t \tag{5.9}$$

Substituting from equations (5.8) and (5.9) into equation (5.5), we see that

$$\Pi_{it} = \tilde{\pi}\left(\kappa_t\right)A_{it} \tag{5.10}$$

where the productivity-adjusted profit function

$$\tilde{\pi}\left(\kappa_t\right) = \alpha(1-\alpha)\kappa_t^{\alpha}$$

is increasing in the capital stock per effective worker κ_t, because an increase in κ_t reduces the monopolist's per-unit cost of production, which is r_t. This dependency of profits on the capital stock per effective worker plays an important role in the workings of the model.

Using equation (5.9) to substitute for each x_{it}, we can rewrite equation (5.4) as

$$Y_t = \int_0^1 A_{it}\kappa_t^{\alpha}\,di = A_t\kappa_t^{\alpha} \tag{5.11}$$

which is the production function used in the neoclassical model. In particular, the average productivity parameter A_t is labor-augmenting productivity.[7]

---

7. In this analysis Y_t is not just the aggregate production of the final good but also the economy's GDP, because it equals consumption plus investment, the latter consisting of research plus the production of new capital goods.

5.4.2   Innovation and Growth

In every period t there is an entrepreneur in each sector i who can possibly innovate. If successful, she will become the local monopolist next period, with a productivity parameter $A_{it} = \gamma A_{i,t-1}$, where $\gamma > 1$. Her probability of success is $\mu_t = \phi(n_t) = \lambda n_t^\sigma$, where $n_t = R_{it}/A_{it}^*$ and $A_{it}^* = \gamma A_{i,t-1}$ is the target productivity level. So she will choose her research expenditure R_{it} to maximize her net benefit

$$\phi\left(R_{it}/A_{it}^*\right)\Pi_{it}^* - R_{it}$$

where Π_{it}^* is her profit if she succeeds. The first-order condition is

$$\phi'\left(R_{it}/A_{it}^*\right)\Pi_{it}^*/A_{it}^* - 1 = 0$$

which we can write, using equation (5.10) as the research arbitrage equation,

$$\phi'\left(n_t\right)\tilde{\pi}\left(\kappa_t\right) = 1 \tag{R}$$

Thus the productivity-adjusted level of research n_t is an increasing function of the capital stock per effective worker κ_t because, as we have seen, an increase in κ_t increases the monopoly profit that constitutes the reward for innovation. Since, as before, the productivity growth rate g_t is the frequency of innovations $\phi(n_t)$ times the size $(\gamma - 1)$, therefore productivity growth is also an increasing function of the capital stock per effective worker:[8]

$$g_t = \tilde{g}\left(\kappa_t\right), \qquad \tilde{g}' > 0$$

As in the neoclassical model, there is a fixed saving rate s and a fixed depreciation rate δ, so the aggregate capital stock K_t will evolve according to

$$K_{t+1} - K_t = sY_t - \delta K_t \tag{5.12}$$

which states that net investment equals gross investment sY_t minus depreciation δK_t.

5.4.3   Steady-State Capital and Growth

The appendix to this chapter shows that the growth rate g_t and the capital-stock per effective worker κ_t will converge over time to steady-state values g and κ, as defined by

---

8. More specifically, we can solve equation (R) for $n_t = \left[\sigma\lambda\tilde{\pi}(\kappa_t)\right]^{\frac{1}{1-\sigma}}$ and $\mu_t = \lambda\left[\sigma\lambda\tilde{\pi}(\kappa_t)\right]^{\frac{\sigma}{1-\sigma}}$, so we have $\tilde{g}(\kappa_t) = (\gamma-1)\lambda\left[\sigma\lambda\tilde{\pi}(\kappa_t)\right]^{\frac{\sigma}{1-\sigma}}$.

$$g = \tilde{g}(\kappa) \tag{5.13}$$

and

$$s\kappa^{\alpha-1} = g + \delta \tag{5.14}$$

The last equation is identical to the condition defining the steady-state capital stock per effective worker in the neoclassical model with a Cobb-Douglas production function, and it has the same interpretation. That is, in steady state the growth rate of K_t must equal the growth rate g of labor-augmenting productivity. The actual growth rate of capital is saving per unit of capital $sY/K = sA^{1-\alpha}K^{\alpha}/K = s\kappa^{\alpha-1}$ minus the rate of depreciation δ. Equation (5.14) thus equalizes the actual and required growth rates of capital.

The two equations (5.13) and (5.14) are represented, respectively, by the curves RR and KK in figure 5.1. The "research" equation RR is upward sloping because, as we have noted, an increase in the capital stock per effective worker raises the incentive to innovate and hence spurs productivity growth. The "capital" curve KK is downward sloping because according to equation (5.14) the capital stock per effective worker is a decreasing function of the growth rate.

On one hand, any parameter change that disturbs the research equation (5.13) will shift the RR curve, causing κ and g to move in opposite directions. Thus an

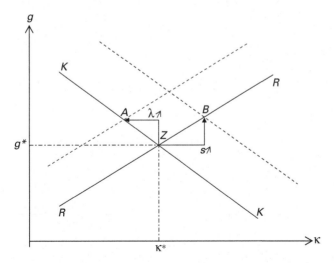

Figure 5.1

increase in the size of innovations γ or the efficiency of research λ will shift RR up. This shift will raise long-run growth, as in the Schumpeterian model of chapter 4, but it will also reduce the long-run capital stock per effective worker.

On the other hand, any parameter change that disturbs the capital equation (5.14) will shift the KK curve, causing κ and g to move in the same direction. Thus an increase in the saving rate s or a decrease in the depreciation rate δ will raise the long-run stock of capital per worker, as in the neoclassical model, but it will also raise the long-run growth rate because, as we have already emphasized, the rise in κ will strengthen the incentive to do productivity-enhancing research.

5.4.4   Implications for Growth Accounting

Like the neoclassical model, the preceding hybrid model implies that in the long run the economy's growth rate will equal the rate of labor-augmenting technological progress g. But this equality does not mean that economic growth is caused by nothing other than technological progress, because g is now endogenous, so we cannot meaningfully speak of it as causing anything.

An analogy from supply and demand theory might help. That theory implies that the quantity that people trade must equal the amount supplied. But this equivalence does not mean that trading volume is caused by nothing other than supply, because the quantity supplied is itself an endogenous variable. We know that the amount traded generally depends on the conditions underlying both supply and demand, although there is one exception to this rule, namely, the case of a vertical supply curve, where supply is completely inelastic, in which case a change in supply is the only thing that can change the equilibrium quantity traded.

Likewise in growth theory, in general the long-run growth rate will be influenced by conditions underlying the research arbitrage equation that governs innovation, but also by the conditions underlying the steady-state capital equation. One exception would be the case in which the RR curve was perfectly horizontal, where the rate of technological progress did not respond to capital accumulation, in which case innovation would be the only force governing the long-run growth rate. This is the case of neoclassical growth theory.

So, for example, when the incentives to perform R&D change, the change will result in a higher g, which we can meaningfully attribute to the force of innovation, since it was the innovation side of the economy that was altered. In this case the hybrid model agrees with the Solow model. But changes in the saving rate s

will displace the *KK* curve in figure 5.1 to the right, again causing *g* to go up, and in this case the change is attributable to capital accumulation, since it was a change in thrift not a change in innovation that caused the shift.

In both of these cases a growth accountant will ultimately conclude that the fraction α of the change in growth was accounted for by capital deepening and $1 - \alpha$ by TFP growth, as implied by the Cobb-Douglas production function (5.11), as we explained in section 5.3.2. Yet in one case it was all caused by innovation, and in the other case it was all caused by capital accumulation.

As these examples illustrate, in order to estimate the extent to which growth is caused by either of these two forces, we need to identify the causal factors that shift the two curves, estimate by how much they shift the curve, estimate the slopes of the curves, and then measure the amount by which the causal factors have changed over the time period in question. One of the main objects of the rest of this book will be to identify the causal factors that shift curves like these, and to survey some of the evidence that would allow us to say what factors have been primarily responsible for economic growth at different times and in different countries.

5.5   Conclusion

In this chapter, we have reflected upon the debates and controversies raised by recent studies on growth accounting. In particular, we have questioned A. Young's (1995) claim that most of the Asian growth was due to factor accumulation, not innovation. We have stressed the importance of measurement issues, in particular that arising from the fact that technological progress is also embodied in new capital goods. More generally, we have questioned the use of accounting relationships for establishing causal relationships between GDP growth and the contributions of factor accumulation and technical progress. And we have argued that moving from an accounting to a causal relationship is a particularly delicate step in the context of a Schumpeterian model augmented with capital accumulation, where the capital stock and the innovation rate are jointly determined and influence each other.

5.6   Literature Notes

The method of growth accounting was first introduced by Solow (1957) and later developed in Kendrick (1961) and especially by Denison (1962). Jorgenson and Griliches (1967) extended and refined the analysis by considering changes in the quality of capital and labor, and by building a "dual approach" to growth accounting in which the Solow residual is calculated using the growth rates of factor prices instead of factor quantities. This idea was also exploited more recently by Hsieh (2002), who applied it to the study of East Asian countries and refuted previous findings by A. Young (1995).

Griliches (1973) outlined a research program in which R&D spending is emphasized as a main determinant of the TFP growth rate. This approach was implemented in a number of analyses for firms and industries in the United States (such as Griliches and Lichtenberg 1984 and Griliches 1988) and was used by Coe and Helpman (1995) on aggregate data for OECD countries to analyze the knowledge spillovers induced by trade.

More recent works, such as Knight, Loayza, and Villanueva (1993), Islam (1995), and Caselli, Esquivel, and Lefort (1996), used panel data techniques in growth accounting and concluded that a large fraction of the cross-country income variance remains unexplained. King and Levine (1994), Klenow and Rodriguez-Clare (1997), Prescott (1998), and Hall and Jones (1999) addressed this issue using a calibration approach instead and concluded that large efficiency differences across countries need to be assumed in order to explain the data.

We refer our readers to the excellent *Handbook of Economic Growth* surveys by Caselli (2005) and Jorgenson (2005) on growth accounting and cross-country income differences.

Appendix: Transitional Dynamics

The dynamic evolution of aggregate capital K_t and productivity A_t are governed by

$$K_{t+1} = sA_t^{1-\alpha}K_t^\alpha + (1-\delta)K_t$$
$$A_{t+1} = \left[1 + \tilde{g}\left(K_{t+1}/A_{t+1}\right)\right]A_t$$

The first equation follows directly from equations (5.12) and (5.11), and the second one is the productivity-growth equation.

As in the neoclassical model, we can write this as one single difference equation in the capital stock per effective worker $\kappa_t = K_t/A_t$. Dividing each side of the first equation by the corresponding side of the second, and then rearranging, yields

$$\kappa_{t+1}\left[1 + \tilde{g}\left(\kappa_{t+1}\right)\right] = s\kappa_t^\alpha + (1-\delta)\kappa_t \qquad (5.15)$$

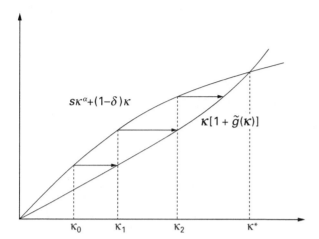

Figure 5.2

The two sides of equation (5.15) are represented by the curves in figure 5.2. The left-hand side is an increasing function of κ whose slope is everywhere increasing and greater than one. The right-hand side is also an increasing function whose slope is infinite at $\kappa = 0$ and then falls monotonically to $1 - \delta$, which is less than one. Therefore, there is a unique positive value κ^* of the capital stock per effective worker where the two curves intersect. This value constitutes the model's steady state.

Moreover, κ^* is a stable steady state. For suppose, as illustrated in figure 5.2, that we started at some level $\kappa_0 < \kappa^*$. Then, according to equation (5.15), κ_1 is the value at which the height of the curve representing the left-hand side equals the height at κ_0 of the curve representing the right-hand side. Likewise, we could find κ_{t+1} given κ_t for each period t. Over time, as figure 5.2 makes clear, κ_t would converge to κ^*, just as in the neoclassical model.

Problems

1. Present and explain some issues with growth-accounting exercises—namely, (a) the separation between technological progress and new capital goods; (b) measurement problems for capital and labor, and (c) accounting versus causation. Do you think that it is possible to empirically determine the actual causal impact of capital deepening on growth (namely, disentangling it from the effect of technological progress)?

2. Growth accounting in the presence of taxes

Suppose that the aggregate production function is $Y = BF(K, L)$. Markets for capital and labor are perfectly competitive and determine the wage w and the capital rental rate r. We are trying to decompose output growth $\dfrac{\dot{Y}}{Y}$ into TFP growth $\dfrac{\dot{B}}{B}$, capital deepening, and growth of the working population, under different tax schemes.

a. Show that output growth is $\dfrac{\dot{Y}}{Y} = \dfrac{\dot{B}}{B} + \dfrac{BF_K K}{Y}\dfrac{\dot{K}}{K} + \dfrac{BF_L L}{Y}\dfrac{\dot{L}}{L} = \dfrac{\dot{B}}{B} + s_K \dfrac{\dot{K}}{K} + s_L \dfrac{\dot{L}}{L}$. Interpret s_K and s_L. How can we estimate TFP growth empirically?

b. Assume firms issue equities to finance their capital purchases, and r is the required rate of return on equities. Earnings, net of wages, are taxed at rate t_1. Write F_K and F_L as a function of factor prices and the tax rate, and derive the decomposition of $\dfrac{\dot{Y}}{Y}$. Is the preceding strategy still valid? What empirical measures of s_K and s_L should we use to estimate TFP growth accurately?

c. Assume there is a tax t_2 on firms' total output (and $t_1 = 0$). Answer the same questions as in part b.

d. Assume the tax rates on value added by capital and labor differ: firms pay a tax rate t_K on capital payments rK and t_L on the wage bill wL. The average tax rate, weighted by shares in total victor income, is $t = \dfrac{rK}{(1-t)Y}t_K + \dfrac{wL}{(1-t)Y}t_L$. Answer the same questions as in part b.

3. Effects of policy changes on capital accumulation and innovation

Consider the model of section 5.4. We want to estimate the impact of different policy measures on the long-run levels of capital per effective worker m and the long-run productivity growth rate g. For each of the following cases, rewrite the research arbitrage condition and the equations of the curves RR and KK in figure 5.1, and explain how the steady-state values of m and g compare to the baseline model.

a. R&D is subsidized at rate s; that is, the effective cost for the researcher of investing one unit of the final good in R&D becomes $1 - s$.

b. Antitrust laws are toughened, so that there is a probability p each period that the innovator will lose his monopoly power and realize zero profits even when no new innovation occurs in the sector. The probability of a successful innovation remains λn_{it} per period.

c. An investment tax credit of rate t is eliminated. For this question we also assume that the savings rate is a function of the interest rate and the tax credit: $s = s(r + t)$, $s' > 0$.

4. "Dual method" and estimates of the Solow residual (based on A. Young 1995 and Hsieh 2002)

This problem contrasts Young's and Hsieh's methods for estimating TFP growth. They rely, respectively, on growth in the stocks of capital and labor and on growth in factor prices. The purpose of this exercise is to disentangle the contributions of factor accumulation and TFP in the postwar growth of the East Asian "Tigers." We consider a generic aggregate production function with capital and labor, which earn returns W and R. We assume factor payments exhaust output: $Y = RK + WL$.

a. Show that the growth rate of output is given by

$$\frac{\dot{Y}}{Y} = s_K\left(\frac{\dot{K}}{K} + \frac{\dot{R}}{R}\right) + s_L\left(\frac{\dot{L}}{L} + \frac{\dot{W}}{W}\right)$$

where $s_K \equiv \dfrac{RK}{Y}$ and $s_L \equiv \dfrac{WL}{Y}$ are the share of capital and labor in total income. (Hint: Note that $\dfrac{\dot{Y}}{Y} = \dfrac{d\ln Y}{dt}$.) What is the Solow residual equal to?

b. A. Young (1995) uses the following data on the postwar growth of the East Asian "Tigers":

	Annual Growth Rate of:			
	Period	Output	Capital	Labor	Labor Share
Hong Kong	1966–91	7.3	8.0	3.2	0.628
Singapore	1966–90	8.7	11.5	5.7	0.509
South Korea	1966–90	10.3	13.7	6.4	0.703
Taiwan	1966–90	9.4	12.3	4.9	0.743

With the standard growth accounting method, calculate the contribution of physical and human capital accumulation to average growth in each country over this period. What are the implied average rates of TFP growth?

c. For the same countries and periods, Hsieh (2002) provides the following data on factor prices:

	Annual Growth Rate of:			
	Period	Interest Rate	Wages	Labor Share
Hong Kong	1966–91	−1.1	4.1	0.628
Singapore	1968–90	1.6	2.7	0.511
South Korea	1966–90	−4.0	4.4	0.703
Taiwan	1966–90	−0.4	5.3	0.739

Using the dual method, compute an alternative estimate of TFP growth for each country. For which countries is there a significant gap between the dual estimate and the Solow residual? What might explain this discrepancy?

5. **Quality of capital (based on Caselli and Wilson, 2004)**

Consider an economy in which final output is produced with N intermediate inputs, according to the technology

$$Y = B \left[\sum_{i=1}^{N} (x_i)^\gamma \right]^{1/\gamma}$$

where B represents "disembodied" total factor productivity (TFP) and $\gamma < 1$. Intermediate goods are produced with capital and labor: $x_i = A_i L_i^{1-\alpha} K_i^{\alpha}$, $0 < \alpha < 1$. The key feature of the model is that A_i and K_i are product specific; in particular, the efficiency level varies across intermediates for identical levels of capital and labor inputs. Labor is homogeneous and mobile within countries. Intermediate-good producers are price takers in the factor markets and therefore consider the wage W and the rental rate of capital R as given. Aggregate endowments of capital and labor are given by $K = \sum_{i=1}^{N} K_i$ and $L = \sum_{i=1}^{N} L$.

a. Derive the demand function for intermediate good x_i. Using this demand function, write the conditions for the intermediate producer's optimal demand of labor and capital, L_i and K_i.

b. Show that the capital-labor ratio is equal in all intermediate sectors and that $\dfrac{K_i}{K} = \dfrac{L_i}{L}$ for all i.

c. Let ξ_i be the share of sector i capital in the country's total capital stock: $\xi_i \equiv \dfrac{K_i}{K}$. Show that the labor share of sector i can be written

$$\frac{L_i}{L} = \frac{\left(A_i \xi_j^\alpha\right)^{\frac{\gamma}{1-\gamma(1-\alpha)}}}{\sum\limits_{j=1}^{N}\left[\left(A_i \xi_j^\alpha\right)^{\frac{\gamma}{1-\gamma(1-\alpha)}}\right]}$$

d. Using the result of the previous question, find the value of ξ_i as a function of the A_j. (Hint: Conjecture $\xi_i = \dfrac{A_i^\delta}{\sum\limits_{j=1}^{N}\left(A_j^\delta\right)}$ and solve for δ.)

e. Obtain an expression for per capita output y in terms of $k \equiv \dfrac{K}{L}$, B, A_i, and ξ_i.

f. Caselli and Wilson find that rich countries typically have higher shares of R&D-intensive capital goods. In the present model, this finding means that a higher proportion of their capital stocks is concentrated in sectors with high "embodied" total factor productivity A_i. What does it imply about the contribution of the quality of capital to cross-country productivity differences? If we conduct a growth-accounting exercise using cross-country data on aggregate capital stocks per worker k, how might capital composition effects affect the estimated TFP contribution to growth?

6. *Cross-country income differences in a Schumpeterian growth model (based on Howitt 2000)

Consider an economy with the final-good production function $Y_t = \int_0^1 A_{it} x_{it}^\alpha di$. Intermediates are produced by monopolists with the technology $x_{it} = \dfrac{K_{it}}{A_{it}}$ at cost $(r_t + \delta)A_{it}x_{it}$. Capital accumulation takes place according to the neoclassical equation $\dot{K}_t = sY_t - \delta K_t$, where $K_t = \int_0^1 K_{it} di$ is the aggregate capital stock and s is the exogenous savings rate. The world is characterized by a technology frontier $\bar{A}_t$ that grows exogenously at rate g. At each instant, when N_{it} units of the final good are invested in R&D, an innovation occurs in sector i with probability λn_{it}, where $n_{it} \equiv \dfrac{N_{it}}{\bar{A}_t}$. Upon innovating, the productivity of sector i, A_{it}, is raised to the "leading-edge" technology $\bar{A}_t$.

a. Noting that the monopolists' decisions are symmetrical, what are the final ouput Y_t, the monopoly profit π_t, and the interest rate r_t for given levels of the capital stock and aggregate productivity?

b. Write the research arbitrage equation. Assuming the conditions for $n_t > 0$ are satisfied, solve for the equilibrium value of R&D investment.

c. Define the economy's average distance to the frontier technology as $a_t = \dfrac{A_t}{\bar{A}_t}$. What are the growth rates of a_t and K_t?

d. Derive the steady-state values of a and K given n and g. How do changes in the savings rate, the probability of success of R&D, and the growth rate of the frontier technology affect the steady state?

e. Under which condition does a country conduct no R&D? What, in this case, is its rate of productivity growth? Why can we say this model exhibits "club convergence"?

f. Decompose long-run log output into a productivity component and a capital-deepening component. If we run a cross-sectional regression of log output per capita on the log of the capital stock, what assumption do we need to make for the coefficient to be unbiased? Is this assumption satisfied in the model?

II UNDERSTANDING THE GROWTH PROCESS

6 Finance and Growth

6.1 Introduction

All the basic paradigms that we presented in part I of this book imply that economic growth depends on investment of one sort or another. According to neoclassical and AK theories, what drives growth is investment in physical and human capital. According to product-variety and Schumpeterian theories, what matters is investment in technology, in the form of research. In the hybrid model of the last chapter, investment in capital and technology are both important.

However, none of these theories analyzed the difficulties that a firm might have financing the investments that drive growth. None of them made any mention of the role that banks and other financial intermediaries might have in mitigating such difficulties. This silence is understandable because a basic theoretical paradigm focuses on the fundamental mechanisms of the growth process, whereas finance is like the lubrication that reduces frictions and thereby enables the machinery to function. Presenting each theory without the complicating factor of financial frictions helps us to see the fundamental mechanisms more clearly.

In order to see the role that finance plays in the growth process, however, we need to go beyond these idealized models and take frictions into account. When we do, we see that financial markets and financial intermediaries play an important role, which varies a lot from country to country. For example, people are willing to save more, and hence make more available to investors, in a country with efficient and trustworthy banks than in a country where banks are likely to waste their depositors' wealth through bad loans or even swindles. Banks can also help by risk pooling. That is, by collecting savings from many people and investing them in a large diversified range of projects, a bank allows even small savers to take advantage of the law of large numbers and get a reasonably safe rate of return; the losses on bad projects will tend to be offset by the gains on good projects. In addition, well-functioning banks can channel savings toward the most efficient uses. Finally, and perhaps most importantly, banks can also help to alleviate agency problems by monitoring investors and making sure that they are making productive use of their loans rather than spending them on private consumption or otherwise defrauding the ultimate lenders. Many of these roles are also served by stock markets, private equity firms, and venture capitalists, all of which help to identify, finance, and monitor good investment projects.

In his survey article on finance and growth in the *Handbook of Economic Growth*, Ross Levine (2005, p. 868) summarizes as follows the existing research on this topic: "Taken as a whole, the bulk of existing research suggests that

(1) countries with better functioning banks and markets grow faster; (2) simultaneity bias does not seem to drive these conclusions, and (3) better functioning financial systems ease the external financing constraints that impede firm and industrial expansion, suggesting that this is one mechanism through which financial development matters for growth."

So when seeking a more detailed understanding of the growth process than we find in any of the frictionless paradigms laid out in the previous five chapters, one of the first complicating factors that we should introduce is financial constraints. Accordingly, this chapter begins part II of the book by showing how one might take these constraints into account. The chapter comprises three main parts. First, we introduce financial constraints into the Schumpeterian growth framework and show explicitly how intermediaries that provide external finance to innovators by channeling savings and mitigating agency problems can enhance growth. We provide two alternative models: in the first one, banks provide screening services to identify good projects, and in the second one, banks provide ex post monitoring to make it difficult for the borrower to abscond with borrowed money. Next, we introduce credit constraints in a simple AK model to analyze the relationship between credit constraints, wealth inequality, and growth. Finally, we review some of the voluminous empirical evidence underlying Levine's summary statement of the role of finance in the growth process.

6.2   Innovation and Growth with Financial Constraints

In this section, we introduce financial constraints into the multisector Schumpeterian growth model of chapter 4.

6.2.1   Basic Setup

First we set up a model without financial constraints. The model is almost identical to that of chapter 4, except for two small changes. The first is that individuals now live for two periods instead of one. In the first period of life an individual works in the final-good sector. In the second period she may become an entrepreneur and/or an intermediate monopolist, and if she becomes an entrepreneur she may use the wage earned in the first period to finance research.

The economy has a fixed population L, which we normalize to unity. Everyone is endowed with one unit of labor services in the first period and none in the second, and is risk neutral. There is one final good, produced under perfect competition by labor and a continuum of intermediate inputs according to

$$Y_t = L^{1-\alpha} \int_0^1 A_{it}^{1-\alpha} x_{it}^\alpha di, \qquad 0 < \alpha < 1 \tag{6.1}$$

where x_{it} is the input of the latest version of intermediate good i and A_{it} is the productivity parameter associated with it. The final good is used for consumption, as an input to R&D, and also as an input to the production of intermediate products. At any date t, one old person in each intermediate sector i has an opportunity to innovate in that sector. If successful, she will become the monopolist in sector i for period t; if not, the monopoly will pass to another old person at random.

Here we introduce the second difference from the model of chapter 4. That is, we suppose now that the starting technology in any given sector i at date t does not have the productivity parameter $A_{i,t-1}$ of that sector last period; instead it has the average $A_{t-1} = \int_0^1 A_{i,t-1} di$ across all sectors last period. So an entrepreneur that succeeds in innovating will have the productivity parameter $A_{it} = \gamma A_{t-1}$, where $\gamma > 1$ is the size of innovations, while the monopolist in a noninnovating sector will have $A_{it} = A_{t-1}$.

Let μ be the probability that an innovation occurs in any sector i at time t (in equilibrium, as we shall see, this probability will be constant over time and the same for all sectors). Then a fraction μ of sectors (those who have innovated) will have productivity γA_{t-1} while the remaining fraction $(1 - \mu)$ will have A_{t-1}. The average across all sectors will therefore be

$$A_t = \mu \gamma A_{t-1} + (1 - \mu) A_{t-1}$$

implying that the growth rate of average productivity is

$$g = \frac{A_t - A_{t-1}}{A_{t-1}} = \mu(\gamma - 1) \tag{6.2}$$

In each intermediate sector where an innovation has just occurred, the monopolist is able to produce any amount of the intermediate good one for one with the final good as input. Her price will be the marginal product of her intermediate good:

$$p_{it} = \alpha A_{it}^{1-\alpha} x_{it}^{\alpha-1}$$

As we saw in the previous chapters, profit maximization by the intermediate-good producer in sector i yields the equilibrium profit

$$\Pi_{it} = \pi A_{it}$$

where $\pi \equiv (1-\alpha)\alpha^{\frac{1+\alpha}{1-\alpha}}$; gross output of the final good will be

$$Y_t = \varphi A_t \tag{6.3}$$

where $\varphi = \alpha^{\frac{2\alpha}{1-\alpha}}$; and the economy's GDP will also be proportional to the average productivity parameter A_t; so the rate of economic growth will again equal the productivity growth rate g.

6.2.2   Innovation Technology and Growth without Credit Constraints

For concreteness we assume a special case of the innovation technology specified in the model of chapter 4, where the elasticity parameter σ is equal to $\frac{1}{2}$:

$$\mu = \phi(R_t/A_t^*) = \lambda(R_t/A_t^*)^{1/2}, \qquad \lambda > 0 \tag{6.4}$$

where R_t is the amount of final good spent on R&D in a given sector at time t and $A_t^* = \gamma A_{t-1}$ is the target productivity level. It follows that the R&D cost of innovating with probability μ is equal to

$$R_t = A_t^* \psi \mu^2 / 2 \tag{6.5}$$

where $\psi = 2/\lambda^2$ is a parameter that measures the cost of innovation.

The entrepreneur will again choose the research expenditure R_t so as to maximize her expected payoff. According to equation (6.5), choosing R_t is equivalent to choosing the innovation probability μ. So her profit-maximization problem is to choose the μ that maximizes

$$\mu \pi A_t^* - A_t^* \psi \mu^2 / 2 \tag{6.6}$$

Thus the equilibrium probability of innovation is

$$\mu = \pi/\psi \tag{6.7}$$

From this and equation (6.2), the equilibrium growth rate is

$$g = (\pi/\psi)(\gamma - 1)$$

which is identical to the equilibrium growth rate of the model in chapter 4 when the elasticity parameter σ in the innovation production function is equal to $\frac{1}{2}$.

6.2.3   Credit Constraints: A Model with Ex Ante Screening

Each innovator at date t is a young person with access to the wage income w_{t-1}. Thus to invest R_t in an R&D project she must borrow $L = R_t - w_{t-1}$, which we suppose is strictly positive, from a lender. In the previous section we implicitly assumed that the activity of borrowing did not cost any resources or create any contracting problems that might impede investments. The expected profit (6.6) that was being maximized was the total expected return to be shared by the entrepreneur and her creditor.

In this section we introduce a cost of borrowing. In particular, we suppose (following King and Levine 1993b) that in addition to the entrepreneurs in our model there are other people seeking to finance projects that are in fact not feasible under any circumstances. Then the bank must pay a cost to screen loan applications, since a loan to someone with an infeasible project will not be repaid.

Let θ be the probability that a borrower coming to a bank is capable (has a feasible project), while $1 - \theta$ is the probability that the borrower's project will yield no payoff at all. A bank can determine whether or not a given project is feasible by paying a cost equal to fR_t units of the final good. Then it will require a repayment of fR_t/θ from each feasible project in order to break even,[1] and the combined payoff to an entrepreneur and her bank will be the expected profit of a successful innovation minus the R&D cost and the screening cost:

$$\mu \pi A_t^* - R_t - fR_t/\theta$$

(Note that we are assuming for simplicity, as we did in chapter 4, that the project takes no time, so there is no discounting of the expected return $\mu \pi A_t^*$.)

Since the R&D cost of innovating with probability μ is given by equation (6.5), the combined payoff can be written as

$$\mu \pi A_t^* - \left(1 + f/\theta\right) A_t^* \psi \mu^2/2$$

which is equal to the expected profit (6.6) in the case of no credit constraints, minus the screening cost. Maximizing this combined payoff results in an equilibrium probability of innovation equal to

$$\mu = \frac{\pi}{\left(1 + f/\theta\right)\psi}$$

From this and equation (6.2), the corresponding equilibrium growth rate is

$$g = \frac{\pi}{\left(1 + f/\theta\right)\psi}(\gamma - 1)$$

---

1. Let P be the repayment from a feasible project. Then the bank's expected profit from screening a project will be

$$\theta P - fR_t$$

because its expected revenue will be the probability θ that the project is feasible times the payment P, whereas the cost will be fR_t with certainty. Therefore, expected profit is zero only if $P = fR_t/\theta$.

Therefore, the higher the screening cost f, the lower will be the frequency of innovations and the lower will be the equilibrium growth rate. Countries with more efficient banks should have a lower f and hence a higher growth rate.

6.2.4   A Model with Ex Post Monitoring and Moral Hazard

Banks do more than screen loan applications. They also monitor the lender's performance during the term of a loan contract to guard against the possibility of fraud. Our second model of credit constraints and growth focuses on ex post monitoring, and is based on Aghion, Banerjee, and Piketty (1999). It introduces the important notion of the *credit multiplier.*

6.2.4.1   Credit Multiplier and R&D Investment

Again, each entrepreneur is a young person with access to the wage income w_{t-1}, who must borrow $L = R_t - w_{t-1}$. Suppose now that what makes it difficult to borrow is that the borrower might default. A bank will monitor the borrower, thereby making it costly for the borrower to default, but not impossible. Specifically, by paying a cost hR_t, where $0 < h < 1$, the entrepreneur can hide the result of a successful innovation and thereby avoid repaying. The cost parameter h is an indicator of the bank's effectiveness in monitoring; a well-functioning bank makes fraud very difficult. The cost also reflects the effectiveness of legal institutions in protecting creditors' rights; in a country where courts rarely enforce loan contracts, it is relatively easy to avoid repaying.

The entrepreneur must pay the hiding cost at the beginning of the period, when she decides whether or not to be dishonest. She will be dishonest when it is in her self-interest, namely, when the following incentive-compatibility constraint is violated:

$$hR_t \geq \mu_t(R_t)\Gamma(R_t - w_{t-1}) \tag{6.8}$$

where Γ is the interest factor on the loan and $\mu_t(R_t)$ is the probability of innovating at date t given the R&D investment R_t, as determined by equation (6.4). The right-hand side of equation (6.8) is the expected saving from deciding to be dishonest; that is, by being dishonest you can avoid making the repayment, which is the interest factor Γ times the loan amount, in the event the project succeeds, which happens with probability μ.

The only potential lenders in this overlapping-generation model are other young people, who will lend only if the expected repayment equals the loan amount. Thus, even though there is no time cost to the project, there will be a positive interest factor on the loan, given by the arbitrage condition

$$\mu_t(R_t)\Gamma = 1$$

which states that for every dollar lent out, the expected repayment (Γ with probability μ) must equal one. Using this arbitrage condition to substitute for Γ, we see that the incentive-compatibility condition (6.8) boils down to an upper limit on the entrepreneur's investment:

$$R_t \leq \frac{1}{1-h} w_{t-1} = vw_{t-1} = \hat{R}_t \tag{6.9}$$

The parameter v is commonly referred to as the *credit multiplier.* A higher cost h of hiding innovation revenue implies a larger credit multiplier.

6.2.4.2   Innovation and Growth under Binding Credit Constraint

The constraint (6.9) will be binding if $\hat{R}_t$ is less than the R&D cost of achieving the innovation probability (6.7) that would be undertaken in the absence of financial constraints, given the cost function (6.5):

$$vw_{t-1} < \gamma A_{t-1}\pi^2 / (2\psi) \tag{6.10}$$

The equilibrium wage w_{t-1} is the marginal product of labor, which under the Cobb-Douglas specification in equation (6.1) equals $(1 - \alpha)$ times final output Y_{t-1}, which together with equation (6.3) implies

$$w_{t-1} = \omega A_{t-1}$$

where $\omega = (1 - \alpha)\varphi$.

Thus we can rewrite condition (6.10) as

$$v < \gamma\pi^2 / (2\psi\omega) \tag{6.11}$$

It follows that entrepreneurs are less likely to face a credit constraint when either financial development is higher, as measured by v, or entrepreneurs' initial wealth ω as a fraction of aggregate output is higher. This conclusion follows because a large v implies a large cost of defrauding a creditor, which makes creditors willing to lend more, and a large ω gives entrepreneurs more wealth, which makes them better able to self-finance when creditors are unwilling.

Whenever equation (6.11) holds, the equilibrium growth rate is obtained by substituting the constrained investment $\hat{R}_t = vw_{t-1}$ into the innovation production function (6.4) and then using equation (6.2) and the definition of ψ to arrive at

$$g^h = (\gamma-1)\sqrt{2v\omega/(\gamma\psi)}$$

which is monotonically increasing in financial development as measured by v and in entrepreneur's wealth as measured by ω. Note that g^h does not depend on productivity-adjusted profit π, because, although a higher profit rate would make entrepreneurs want to do more research, it does not affect the incentive-compatibility constraint, and hence does not make lenders willing to finance any more research. Thus it is only when the credit constraint is not binding that higher profitability translates into faster growth.

When equation (6.11) does not hold, then the growth rate is the same as it was in the absence of credit constraints, namely,

$$g = \mu^*(\gamma - 1) = (\pi/\psi)(\gamma - 1)$$

In this case, profitability again matters, but financial development and the wealth of entrepreneurs no longer matters.

6.3   Credit Constraints, Wealth Inequality, and Growth

It is often believed that policies aimed at equalizing the distribution of wealth and income are detrimental to growth, because taxing the wealthy discourages individuals from investing and innovating. But it has been shown by Banerjee and Newman (1993) and Galor and Zeira (1993) that when credit constraints are present, then reducing wealth inequality can actually have a stimulating effect on growth. So one of the important ways in which finance can matter for the growth process is by changing the relationship between inequality and growth. As we will see, this effect can go in either direction, depending on the precise circumstances of the economy.

6.3.1   Diminishing Marginal Product of Capital

Credit markets allow a separation between the ownership of capital and the employment of capital. When there is a diminishing marginal product of capital, growth can be enhanced by spreading the employment of capital equally over many enterprises, which can be accomplished by having those who own little capital borrow from those who own a lot. Credit constraints impede this process, and are thus detrimental to growth. This is the basic idea behind the model of this section, which is similar to the one suggested by Benabou (1996). In this model, credit constraints generate a negative relationship between wealth inequality and growth.

The basic structure of the model is the same as the AK model of Frankel that we studied in chapter 2. There are N individual producers. At the start of period t, individual j owns e_j units of capital, so the aggregate capital stock is $K_t = \sum_1^N e_j$. Each produces final output according to the production function

$$y_j = \overline{A}k_j^\alpha, \qquad 0 < \alpha < 1$$

where k_j is the amount of capital that the individual employs. A person can employ more than he owns by borrowing the difference $k_j - e_j$, or he can employ less than he owns and lend the difference.

Because of knowledge spillovers, the productivity parameter $\overline{A}$ that each producer takes as given depends on the aggregate capital stock according to[2]

$$\overline{A} = A_0 K_t^{1-\alpha}$$

Growth in the capital stock is given by the accumulation equation

$$K_{t+1} - K_t = sY_t - \delta K_t$$

where s is the saving rate, δ is the depreciation rate, and Y_t is aggregate output.

Suppose there is an unequal wealth distribution; that is, e_j varies across individual producers. Then there will be an incentive for individuals with more than the average amount of capital to lend some of their capital to those with less, because of the diminishing marginal product of capital. That is, the amount of production that the lender sacrifices by lending a small amount of capital instead of employing it himself will be less than what the borrower can produce with that loaned capital, because the borrower is starting with a smaller capital stock than the lender. So between them they can produce a larger total as a result of the loan.

Indeed it is easy to see that aggregate output is maximized when each producer employs the same amount of capital. That is, setting $k_j = K_t/N$ for all j maximizes total output

$$Y_t = \overline{A}\sum_1^N k_j^\alpha$$

---

2. In general, the Frankel model specifies $\overline{A} = A_0 K_t^\eta$. Here we consider only the knife-edge AK case where $\eta = 1 - \alpha$.

subject to the adding-up constraint[3]

$$\sum_1^N k_j = K_t \tag{6.12}$$

A simple way to introduce credit constraints is to assume as before that an individual who owns e_j cannot employ more than $\bar{k}_j = \nu e_j$, where $\nu > 1$ is again the credit multiplier. When $\nu = +\infty$, capital markets are perfect and individuals face no borrowing constraint, whereas in the opposite case, where $\nu = 1$, credit simply becomes unavailable. We will concentrate on these two extreme cases in this section.

Consider first the case of perfect capital markets. In this case, there will be a common interest rate r at which people can borrow or lend all the capital they want. An individual's income will be the amount produced minus the cost of borrowing (or plus the interest income from lending):

$$\bar{A} k_j^\alpha - r\left(k_j - e_j\right)$$

The individual will choose to employ the amount that maximizes his income, implying the first-order condition

$$\alpha \bar{A} k_j^{\alpha-1} - r = 0$$

So all producers will produce the same amount

$$k_j = \left(\alpha \bar{A}/r\right)^{\frac{1}{1-\alpha}}$$

which by the adding-up constraint (6.12) implies $k_j = K/N$, exactly as in the Frankel model. So again we will have final output equal to

$$Y_t = \bar{A} N \left(K_t/N\right)^\alpha = A K_t$$

---

3. The Lagrangean for this maximization problem is

$$\mathcal{L} = \bar{A} \sum_1^N k_j^\alpha + \lambda \left(K_t - \sum_1^N k_j\right)$$

and the first-order conditions are

$$\frac{\partial \mathcal{L}}{\partial k_j} = \alpha \bar{A} k_j^{\alpha-1} - \lambda = 0 \quad \text{for all } j$$

which can be rewritten as

$$k_j = \left(\alpha \bar{A}/\lambda\right)^{\frac{1}{1-\alpha}} \quad \text{for all } j$$

which states that all the k_j's should be equal. Under the adding-up constraint (6.12) this equation implies $k_j = K_t/N$ for all j.

where $A = A_0 N^{1-\alpha}$, and the growth rates of capital and output will both equal

$$g = sA - \delta$$

Next, consider the other extreme case, where there is no borrowing at all. With no borrowing, there cannot be any lending either, so each producer will employ nothing more or less than his own capital:

$$k_j = e_j$$

But as we have already seen, this case will result in a smaller total output than if all employed the same amount. Therefore aggregate output will be less than in the case of perfect capital markets:

$$Y_t < AK_t$$

and the growth rate of capital will also be less:

$$g = \frac{sY_t - \delta K_t}{K_t} < sA - \delta$$

If everyone's capital grows at the same rate, then g will also be the growth rate of output,[4] so output will also grow more slowly than in the case of perfect capital markets.

It follows that when capital markets are perfect, policies that redistribute wealth have no direct effect on growth, because the employment of capital is always equalized in the marketplace even if ownership is not. But when credit constraints are so severe as to eliminate borrowing, wealth redistribution that reduces inequality of ownership will raise growth by reducing the inequality of employment.[5]

6.3.2   Productivity Differences

In the previous model all individual producers were equally productive, and it was for that reason that growth was maximized by having them employ equal amounts of capital. In reality there are large productivity differences across individual producers, a fact which implies that growth is enhanced by having unequal employment of capital, with more being employed by the more productive individuals. Credit markets can therefore facilitate the growth process by allowing

---

4. Next period's output will be $Y_{t+1} = A_0\left[(1+g)K_t\right]^{1-\alpha}\sum_1^N\left[(1+g)k_j\right]^\alpha = (1+g)A_0 K_t^{1-\alpha}\sum_1^N k_j^\alpha = (1+g)Y_t$.

5. Indeed it follows from the theorems of Rothschild and Stiglitz (1976) that any mean-preserving reduction in the dispersion of k_j will raise output $Y_t = \bar{A}\sum_1^N k_j^\alpha$ and hence will raise the growth rate $g = s(Y_t/K_t) - \delta$.

the more productive individuals to borrow from the less productive ones. This is the idea behind our second model, which is based on Kunieda (2008). In this model, credit constraints can generate a positive relationship between inequality and growth; indeed, growth is maximized by having all of the capital owned by a single individual—the most efficient one.

The basic structure is the same as in the previous model, except that we consider here the extreme case where there is no diminishing marginal productivity at the individual level: $\alpha = 1$. We also allow the credit multiplier to take on any value $\nu \geq 1$ instead of looking only at the extremes of 1 and $+\infty$ as we did in the previous model.

The production function of each producer j is

$$y_j = \tau_j k_j$$

where the individual productivity parameters τ_j vary across individuals, with

$$\tau_1 > \tau_2 > \cdots > \tau_N$$

The producer will choose to employ the amount k_j that maximizes his profit

$$\tau_j k_j - r\left(k_j - e_j\right) \tag{6.13}$$

subject to the credit constraint

$$k_j \leq \nu e_j$$

The solution to this constrained maximization problem depends on how productive the individual is.

1. If $\tau_j > r$, then profit (6.13) is strictly increasing in the amount employed, so the individual will employ the maximal amount νe_j allowed by the credit constraint.

2. If $\tau_j < r$, then the individual can earn more from lending than producing, so he will employ nothing and lend the amount e_j.

3. If $\tau_j = r$, then profit will be independent of k_j, so the individual will be willing to employ any amount between 0 and the upper limit νe_j.

Equilibrium in the capital market requires total employment to equal the aggregate stock of capital K_t. This is achieved by an equilibrium rate of interest that equals the productivity parameter τ_m of some marginal producer m. All individuals $j < m$ will fall into case 1, and all individuals $j > m$ will fall into case 2. Aggregate employment will equal the marginal producer's employment plus the maximal amount that all those in case 1 can employ, so the equilibrium condition is[6]

---

6. We define $e_0 = 0$ so that the summation in equation (6.14) makes sense when $m = 1$.

$$k_m + v\sum\nolimits_0^{m-1} e_j = K_t \qquad (6.14)$$

Since the marginal producer is in case 3, we need

$$0 \leq k_m \leq v e_m \qquad (6.15)$$

Thus capital-market equilibrium requires[7]

$$\sum\nolimits_0^{m-1} e_j \leq K_t/v \leq \sum\nolimits_0^{m} e_j \qquad (6.16)$$

Condition (6.16) says that employment by those individuals more productive than m cannot exceed K_t and that if m were to employ the maximal amount allowed by the credit constraint, then employment would be at least K_t. The condition determines the identity of the marginal producer m, because there is almost always just one value of m for which it can hold. The exception is the case where $K_t/v = \sum\nolimits_0^{n} e_j$ for some individual n, in which case we could make either n or $n + 1$ the marginal producer.

We can now see what happens when credit constraints become tighter, that is, when the credit multiplier v is reduced. Suppose first that the most productive individual has no spare borrowing capacity, which happens if $K_t/v \geq e_1$ and $m > 1$. In this case, all the producers $j < m$ who are more productive than the marginal producer will have to reduce employment when v falls, while the marginal producer takes up the slack, unless the marginal producer does not have enough wealth to borrow that much extra capital, in which case someone even less productive will become the new marginal producer. By reallocating capital from more productive to less productive individuals, this tightening of credit will reduce total output.

More specifically, total output in this case is

$$Y_t = \tau_m k_m + \sum\nolimits_0^{m-1} \tau_j k_j = \tau_m k_m + v\sum\nolimits_0^{m-1} \tau_j e_j$$

which together with the market-clearing condition (6.14) implies

$$Y_t = \tau_m K_t + v\sum\nolimits_0^{m-1} (\tau_j - \tau_m) e_j$$

so we have

$$\frac{\partial Y_t}{\partial v} = \sum\nolimits_0^{m-1} (\tau_j - \tau_m) e_j > 0$$

since $\tau_j > \tau_m$, for all $j < m$.

---

7. To derive equation (6.16), use equation (6.14) to substitute for k_m in equation (6.15), then divide all three expressions in the resulting pair of inequalities by v and add $\sum\nolimits_0^{m-1} e_j$ to all of them.

Next consider the case where $K_t/v < e_1$. In this case the credit constraint is loose enough that all capital will be employed by the most productive individual, so output will be the maximum possible amount:

$$Y^{\max} = \tau_1 K_t$$

In either case, as in the previous model, the growth rate will be

$$g = s\left(Y_t/K_t\right) - \delta$$

so a reduction in the credit multiplier will reduce growth by reducing Y_t, except in the case where the most productive individual has spare borrowing capacity, in which case $g = s\tau_1 - \delta$, which is independent of the credit multiplier.

Note that this model can produce a positive relationship between growth and inequality, in the sense that when credit constraints are very tight the economy will grow faster if all of the capital is owned by individual 1 than if everyone owned the same amount K_t/N, because in the latter case borrowing constraints would prevent all of the capital from being employed most productively, whereas in the former case they would not.

This conclusion does not mean, however, that any increase in inequality would raise growth, for what matters is not just that ownership be concentrated but that it be concentrated in the hands of the most talented individuals. So a reduction of inequality that took wealth from rich but not very talented individuals and redistributed it to poor but talented individuals would result in an increase in growth, just as in the previous model.

6.4   The Empirical Findings: Levine's Survey, in a Nutshell

Most of the empirical literature on finance and growth has been concerned with cross-country or panel regressions of the form

$$g_i = \beta_0 + \beta_1 \text{Findev}_i + \beta_2 X_i + u_i$$

where g_i is the average growth rate in country i during the period or subperiod, Findev_i is the country's level of financial development (either at the beginning of the period or averaged over the period), X_i is a vector of controls (policy variables, education, political stability, initial income per capita, etc), and u_i is a noise term.

As explained in Levine's survey, empirical papers on finance and growth differ in terms of: (1) whether they look at cross-country data (like King and Levine

1993a and subsequent work by Levine and coauthors), or at cross-industry data like Rajan and Zingales (1998) or at cross-regional data like Guiso, Sapienza, and Zingales (2002), or at firm-level data like Demirgüç-Kunt and Maksimovic (1998); (2) how Findev$_i$ is measured: by the ratio of bank credit to GDP, or by indicators of stock market development, or if it is also interacted as in Rajan and Zingales (1998) with a measure of external financial dependence of the industry; (3) whether one looks at cross-section or at panel data; and (4) whether or not one instruments for financial development.

6.4.1   Cross-Country

King and Levine (1993a)[8] consider a broader sample of 77 countries over the period 1960 to 1989. They regress average growth of per capita GDP or average growth in TFP on financial development and a number of control variables, as specified in the preceding equation. The controls include initial income per capita, education measures, indexes of political stability, and policy indicators. Financial development is measured in three possible ways: (1) the ratio between the liquid liabilities of the financial system and GDP; (2) the ratio of commercial bank credit to bank credit plus central bank's domestic assets (this measure performs generally more poorly than the others); and (3) the ratio of credit to private enterprises to GDP. Each of these measures is averaged over the period 1960–89. King and Levine's cross-country regression shows a large and significant correlation between productivity growth and the preceding measures of financial development measured as specified earlier.

To make sure they capture the causal relationship from finance to growth and not the reverse, King and Levine repeat the same regression exercise but using initial 1960 values of financial depth instead of their average over the whole period. This regression also shows a positive and significant correlation between financial development and growth, which now suggests that "financial development in 1960 is a good predictor of economic growth over the next 30 years."

Subsequently, Levine and Zervos (1998) concentrate on the nature of financial sectors, especially the importance of stock market development and stock market

---

8. Levine (2005) attributes the first empirical analysis on finance and growth to Goldsmith (1969). Goldsmith uses cross-country data over the period 1860–1963 to regress average growth on financial development as measured by the size of the financial intermediary sector (measured by the value of its assets) over GDP, and finds a positive correlation between financial development and output growth. As explained by Levine, this study has its limits: no controls in the regression, no instrumentation to address potential causality issues, the left-hand-side variable is output growth instead of productivity growth, and the sample consists of 35 countries only. It is these limitations that King and Levine address in their seminal work in 1993.

"liquidity." In particular, Levine and Zervos consider what they call the "turnover ratio," namely, the total value of currently traded shares over the total value of listed shares; and based on a cross-country regression involving 42 countries over the period 1976–93, they find that both the initial level of bank credit *and* the initial level of this turnover ratio in 1976 show a positive and significant correlation with average productivity growth over the period 1976–93.

One may object to the measures of financial development used by Levine and his coauthors; however, this is the best that can be done while remaining at cross-country level.

A more serious objection is causality: what tells us that these positive correlations do not reflect either the fact that financial development occurs in prediction of forthcoming growth or the fact that a third variable, call it institutional development (e.g, measured by property-rights protection), causes both higher growth and higher financial development. To address this endogeneity problem, Levine (1998, 1999) and Levine, Loayza, and Beck (2000) use the legal origins indicators of La Porta and colleagues (1998) as instruments for financial development. Thus the regression exercise now involves a first stage where financial development is regressed over dummy variables for Anglo-Saxon, French, and German legal origins (against Scandinavian legal origins), respectively, and a second-stage regression where average productivity growth is regressed over predicted financial development as derived from the first-stage regression and the same control variables as before. In particular, Levine, Loayza, and Beck (2000) obtain a strongly positive and significant correlation between predicted financial development and average productivity growth over the period 1960–95.

Levine, Loayza, and Beck (2000) go even further by performing panel cross-country regressions in which the period 1960–95 is subdivided in five-year subperiods and where, for each five-year subperiod, average productivity growth over the subperiod is regressed over current and past financial development, controlling for country fixed effects. And again, they find positive and significant correlations between (current and lagged) financial development and average productivity growth during the subperiod.

Because they move from cross-country to cross-regional analysis within a country (Italy), Guiso, Sapienza, and Zingales (2002) can construct more precise measures of financial development and show that financial development as they measure it is an important determinant of cross-regional convergence. More specifically, GSZ construct their measure of regional financial development by estimating a linear probability model in which they regress the probability that individuals be denied access to credit (they obtain information about individual access to credit from a survey conducted by the Bank of Italy, which also provides information on the region to which each individual belongs) over regional dummies and a set of control variables. The coefficients on the regional dummies are the measures of regional financial development, which GSZ instrument using the regional composition of banking branches in 1936.[9]

6.4.2 Cross-Industry

The pioneering attempt at getting at a more microeconomic level by looking at cross-industry comparisons across countries is by Rajan and Zingales (1998). Their insight is that growth in industries that rely more heavily on external finance should benefit more from higher financial development than growth in industries that do not rely so much on external finance. The problem is to identify industries that are more prone to rely on external finance than other industries.

Rajan and Zingales regress average growth of value added of industry k in country i over (1) country and industry dummies; (2) the share of industry k in total manufacturing in country i; and (3) the interaction between financial development (measured by stock market capitalization plus domestic credit over GDP) in country i and industry k's dependence upon external finance (measured by the fraction of capital costs not financed internally in that same industry in the United States). The underlying idea is that firms are not financially constrained in the United States, so that this measure of external dependence can be thought of as being independent from financial development and as depending instead upon technological factors only. Rajan and Zingales do not include financial development independently, as this approach would create collinearity with the country dummies.

Using a sample of 36 industries in 42 countries, Rajan and Zingales find an interaction coefficient between external dependence and their measure of financial development, which is positive and highly significant at the 1 percent level, thereby providing strong evidence to the effect that higher financial development enhances growth in those industries that rely more heavily on external finance. Figure 6.1 summarizes their main findings.

Building upon the Rajan-Zingales methodology, Beck and colleagues (2004) use cross-country/cross-industry data to look at the effect on productivity growth of the interaction between financial development and the average size of firms in the corresponding industry in the United States (again relying on the implicit

9. The year 1936 corresponds to the enactment of a law restricting subsequent entry into the banking sector.

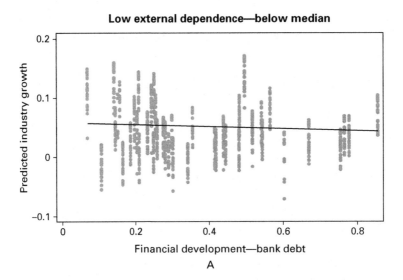

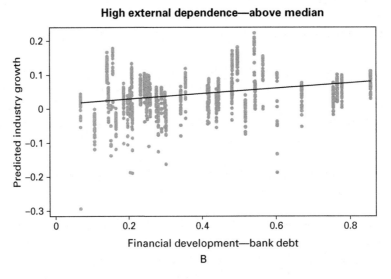

Figure 6.1
External financial dependence and industry growth

assumption that only technological factors, not financial market frictions, determine this average size in the United States). They find that higher financial development enhances growth in those industries that comprise a higher fraction of small firms. This result is consistent with previous work by Bernanke, Gertler, and Gilchrist (1999) suggesting that smaller firms face tighter credit constraints than large firms.

6.5   Conclusion

In this chapter we have introduced financial constraints into the Schumpeterian growth framework and confronted the prediction that growth should increase with financial development using existing empirical evidence from cross-country and cross-industry data. We have also discussed the relationship between wealth inequality and growth in an economy with credit constraints.

In the next chapter we will go one step further and show that by interacting a country's level of financial development with its level of technological development, one can account for observed convergence and divergence patterns. In chapter 14 we will again bring financial constraints into the picture, but this time to analyze the interplay between macroeconomic volatility and growth, and the potentially growth-enhancing role of countercyclical fiscal policies.

6.6   Literature Notes

The pioneering authors to point out the importance of the relationship between finance and growth include Bagehot (1873), Schumpeter (1912), Gurley and Shaw (1955), Goldsmith (1969), and McKinnon (1973).

Ever since, much has been done to improve our understanding of the issue, on both theoretical and empirical grounds. On the theory side, it has been emphasized that financial intermediaries, markets, or contracts can (1) help produce and process information and improve resource allocation (Boyd and Prescott 1986), (2) allocate capital in a more efficient way by producing better information on firms and funding more promising firms (Greenwood and Jovanovic 1990), (3) enhance the rate of technological innovation by identifying entrepreneurs with the best chances of successfully starting new productive processes (King and Levine 1993b), (4) boost corporate governance and therefore influence growth (Bencivenga and Smith 1993), (5) facilitate the trading, hedging, and pooling of risk with positive implications for growth (Acemoglu and Zilibotti 1997),

(6) promote the accumulation of physical and human capital in economies with wealth inequality and credit constraints and thereby accelerate economic growth (Banerjee and Newman 1993; Galor and Zeira 1993; Aghion and Bolton 1997; Piketty 1997), and (7) lower transaction costs and promote greater specialization, innovation, and growth (Greenwood and Smith 1996).

Our formulation of the credit multiplier closely follows Bernanke and Gertler (1989).

On the empirical side, following pioneering work by Goldsmith (1969), the first seminal contribution is by King and Levine (1993a), who used cross-country data to analyze whether financial development predicts long-run economic growth, capital accumulation, and productivity growth. The second seminal contribution is the paper by Rajan and Zingales (1998) that explored multicountry sectoral-level data and the extent to which corresponding sectors depend upon external finance in the United States, to produce regressions that control for country fixed effects and truly capture the causality from financial development to growth (i.e., that address the issue of the endogeneity of financial development). Demirgüç-Kunt and Maksimovic (1998) used a similar methodology to analyze the relationship between growth and finance at the firm level. Levine and Zervos (1998) add measures of stock market development and study the relationship between these latter measures and economic growth. Several econometric techniques have been recently used to get more precise measures of the role of the financial sector on economic growth, such as panel data (Levine, Loayza, and Beck 2000; Rousseau and Wachtel 2000) and time-series analysis (Rousseau and Wachtel 1998; Arestis, Demetriades, and Luintel 2001). Case studies have also been undertaken, such as Jayaratne and Strahan (1996), who examine individual states of the United States, and Guiso, Sapienza, and Zingales (2002), for individual regions of Italy.

A complete and extensive survey on the topic of this chapter can be found in Levine (2005).

Problems

1. Present different channels whereby financial development can foster growth. Levine, Loayza, and Beck (2000) use the legal origins indicators of La Porta and colleagues (1998) as instruments for financial development in cross-country regressions. Explain intuitively how legal origins (i.e., the type of legal system adopted by a country) can affect subsequent financial development.

2. **Causal effect of financial development on economic growth**

As discussed in the empirical section, though there exists a correlation between measures of financial development and economic growth, it is very difficult to establish causality. To address this endogeneity problem, Levine (1998, 1999) and Levine, Loayza, and Beck (2000) use the legal origins indicators of La Porta and colleagues (1998) as instruments for financial development. That is, the regression exercise involves a first stage where financial development is regressed over dummy variables for Anglo-Saxon, French and, German legal origins (against Scandinavian legal origins), respectively, and a second-stage regression where average productivity growth is regressed over predicted financial development as derived from the first-stage regression and the same control variables as were used in the basic regression exercise.

Do you think legal origins is a good instrument to establish causality between financial development and growth? Discuss.

Can you think of any innovative ways to find exogenous variation in financial development (either across country or within country) to test the hypothesis that financial development has a causal effect on economic growth?

3. Liquidation value and R&D

Consider the model with ex ante screening presented in the beginning of the chapter. In the basic case, when the capable innovator is unsuccessful, the project yields a payoff of zero. Instead, now consider a case in which, when the capable innovator is unsuccessful, the project yields an expected payoff of γN_t, for $\gamma < 1$. This payoff can be interpreted as a liquidation value of the unsuccessful project. Assume that the liquidation value is completely observable by the bank when the project fails, and thus the innovator cannot run away with it.

Then the combined payoff to the capable innovator and her bank will be the expected profit of a successful innovation plus the expected liquidation value of an unsuccessful innovation minus the R&D cost minus the screening cost

$$\mu \delta A_{t-1} + (1-\mu)\gamma N_t - f\frac{N_t}{\phi}$$

a. Solve for the equilibrium probability of innovation and the optimal growth rate.

b. Show that the bank's lending is greater if the liquidation value is greater.

4. *Income distribution and human capital

The economy lasts for two periods. In period 1, an individual works for wage w, consumes c, saves s, and decides the level of education investment on behalf of his child, e. He dies at the end of the period. Utility of household i is given by

$$U_i = \alpha \log c_i + (1-\alpha)\log b_i \quad \text{where } 0 < \alpha < 1$$

in which b_i is the consumption of the child. The innate abilities of children vary across households, and therefore the cost of education varies across households. Assume that the cost of education for household i is $\theta_i e_i$. In the second period, individuals receive a wage $w(e)$. Based on the Mincerian regression, assume that $w'(e) > 0$ and $w''(e) < 0$. Assume that households can lend at interest rate r and borrow at interest rate R. The rate of borrowing and lending may differ based on contractual frictions present in the economy.

a. Consider the case in which the credit-market frictions are absent and therefore $R = r$. Characterize the household's decision problem. Show that the choice of education is independent of the form of the utility function.

b. Now introduce a case in which, owing to contractual problems, no one is willing to lend money to the households. That is, the households can lend at r, but cannot borrow going from period 1 to period 2 (or $R = +\infty$). Show that the education and consumption decisions are no longer separable.

c. Discuss how the results in parts a and b differ based on (i) the relative weight the household places on its children's consumption as measured by α; (ii) the initial level of income as measured by w_i.

7 Technology Transfer and Cross-Country Convergence

7.1 Introduction

The history of cross-country income differences exhibits mixed patterns of convergence and divergence. The most striking pattern over the long run is the "great divergence"—Pritchett (1997) estimates that the proportional gap in living standards between the richest and poorest countries grew more than fivefold from 1870 to 1990. More recent evidence (after 1960) points to convergence—the results of Barro and Sala-i-Martin (1992a), Mankiw, Romer, and Weil (1992), and Evans (1996) seem to imply that most countries are converging to parallel growth paths. But many poor countries are continuing to diverge—the proportional gap in per capita income between Mayer-Foulkes's (2002) richest and poorest convergence groups grew by a factor of 2.6 between 1960 and 1995, and the proportional gap between Maddison's (2001) richest and poorest groups grew by a factor of 1.75 between 1950 and 1998.

Thus it seems that there has been "club convergence" since the mid-20th century. Most rich and middle-income countries belong to the convergence club, the group with a common long-run growth rate, whereas many poor countries have been excluded from that club and have strictly lower long-run growth rates.

Club convergence poses a problem for neoclassical theory, which implies absolute convergence in growth rates and thus implies that all countries should be members of the same club. It also poses a problem for AK theory, which implies independent growth rates, suggesting that there should be no convergence club at all. However, it does not pose a problem for Schumpeterian theory. The main purpose of this chapter is to show how Schumpeterian theory can account for club convergence by taking into account the important phenomenon of "technology transfer" and the related idea of "distance to the frontier."

We start with Gerschenkron's (1962) observation that a country far from the world technology frontier has a certain "advantage of backwardness," because it can grow rapidly simply by adopting technologies that have already been developed in more advanced countries. We model that advantage by supposing that in every country the technology that a successful innovator gets to implement embodies ideas from around the world, so "technology transfer" takes place from other countries whenever an innovation takes place.

Technology transfer will stabilize the gap between rich and poor countries, thus allowing the poor countries to grow as fast as the rich, but only if the poor countries devote resources to innovation, because innovation is the process through which technology is transferred. If a country fails to innovate, then it will stagnate while the rest of the world continues to advance. The convergence club will consist of the countries that continue to innovate.

The reason why innovation is necessary for technology transfer to take place is that technological knowledge is often tacit and circumstantially specific.[1] It cannot simply be copied and transplanted costlessly to another country. Instead, the receiving country must invest resources in order to master the technology and adapt it to local conditions. This investment may not look like the frontier R&D that takes place in leading industrial countries, but analytically it has all the same characteristics as R&D—it is a costly activity that builds on the ideas of others to create something new in a particular environment.[2] Although implementing a foreign technology may be easier than inventing an entirely new one, this is a difference in degree, not in kind.

7.2 A Model of Club Convergence

7.2.1 Basics

The model is the same as the multisectoral Schumpeterian model of chapter 4, except for the specification of the innovation technology. Time is discrete. Individuals live for one period and have linear preferences in consumption. There is one final good, which is produced by labor and intermediate products according to

$$Y_t = L^{1-\alpha} \int_0^1 A_{it}^{1-\alpha} x_{it}^{\alpha} di, \qquad 0 < \alpha < 1$$

where x_{it} is the input of intermediate product i and A_{it} is its productivity parameter. We set $L = 1$.

The final good is produced under perfect competition, so the price of each intermediate good equals its marginal product:

$$p_{it} = \alpha A_{it}^{1-\alpha} x_{it}^{\alpha-1}$$

As in previous chapters, each intermediate good i is produced one for one by a monopolist, using the final good as input. The monopolist will choose x_{it} to maximize her profit

1. See Arrow (1969) and Evenson and Westphal (1995).

2. Cohen and Levinthal (1989) and Griffith, Redding, and Van Reenan (2004) have also argued that R&D by the receiving country is a necessary input to technology transfer.

$$\Pi_{it} = p_{it}x_{it} - x_{it} = \alpha A_{it}^{1-\alpha} x_{it}^{\alpha} - x_{it}$$

which gives the equilibrium quantity

$$x_{it} = \alpha^{\frac{2}{1-\alpha}} A_{it}$$

and profit

$$\Pi_{it} = \pi A_{it}^{*}$$

where $\pi = (1-\alpha)\alpha^{\frac{1+\alpha}{1-\alpha}}$ is the same constant as before.

The probability of success μ of the potential innovator in each sector is again an increasing function $\phi(n)$ of her productivity-adjusted research expenditure $n = R_{it}/A_{it}^{*}$, where R_{it} is her R&D expenditure and A_{it}^{*} her target productivity level. As in the previous chapter, she chooses the probability μ to maximize her expected payoff

$$\mu\Pi_{it} - R_{it} = \left[\mu\pi - \tilde{n}(\mu)\right]A_{it}^{*} \tag{7.1}$$

where $\tilde{n}(\mu)$ is her productivity-adjusted R&D cost—the value of n such that $\phi(n) = \mu$.

7.2.2 Innovation

At this point we make a small but important departure from the basic Schumpeterian model. In that basic model we assumed an innovation production function in which the marginal product of research $\phi'(n)$ becomes infinite when no research is done.[3] This assumption is equivalent to assuming that the marginal cost $\tilde{n}'(\mu)$ is zero when $\mu = 0$. For example, in the previous chapter the innovation cost function was $\tilde{n}(\mu) = \psi\mu^2/2$, which has $\tilde{n}'(0) = 0$. This feature helps to simplify the analysis in the same way that the Inada conditions help to simplify the neoclassical model, namely, by ruling out corner solutions. More specifically, it means that some research will always be done, no matter how small the productivity-adjusted profit π, because otherwise there would be a positive marginal gain and a zero marginal cost.

For understanding club convergence it is important to drop this simplifying assumption, so as to allow for the possibility that some countries might do no research. Accordingly we now assume that

$$\tilde{n}(\mu) = \eta\mu + \psi\mu^2/2 \tag{7.2}$$

---

3. That is, with $\phi(n) = \lambda n^{\sigma}$ we have $\phi'(n) = \sigma\lambda n^{\sigma-1}$, which approaches ∞ as $n \to 0$ because $\sigma < 1$.

where both parameters η and ψ are strictly positive.[4] The marginal cost is now

$$\tilde{n}'(\mu) = \eta + \psi\mu$$

which is strictly positive even when $\mu = 0$. In addition, we assume

$$\eta + \psi < \pi$$

which will guarantee that the equilibrium innovation probability is less than one.

With this new form of the innovation cost function, there are two cases to consider:

Case 1   If

$$\eta < \pi$$

then the reward to an innovation is large enough (relative to the cost) that producers will innovate at a positive rate. That is, the first-order condition for maximizing equation (7.1) is

$$\tilde{n}'(\mu) = \pi$$

whose solution is

$$\mu = (\pi - \eta)/\psi > 0$$

Case 2   If

$$\pi \le \eta$$

then the conditions are so unfavorable to innovation in this country that producers will not innovate. That is, the first-order condition for maximizing equation (7.1) has no positive solution, so the maximization problem is solved by setting $\mu = 0$.

7.2.3   Productivity and Distance to Frontier

Assume that a successful innovator in any sector gets to implement a technology with a productivity parameter equal to a level $\bar{A}_t$, which represents the world

---

4. This implies that the innovation production function has the form

$$\phi(n) = \lambda\left(\sqrt{n + \mathcal{H}^2} - \mathcal{H}\right) \tag{I}$$

where $\lambda = (2/\psi)^{1/2}$ and $\mathcal{H} = \eta(2\psi)^{-1/2}$. The function λn^σ that we were using before also has the form (I) when $\sigma = 1/2$, in which case we have $\mathcal{H} = \eta = 0$.

technology frontier and which grows at a rate g determined outside the country. So each productivity parameter A_{it} will evolve according to

$$A_{it} = \begin{cases} \overline{A}_t & \text{with probability } \mu \\ A_{i,t-1} & \text{with probability } 1-\mu \end{cases}$$

The fact that a successful innovator gets to implement $\overline{A}_t$ is a manifestation of the kind of technology transfer that Keller (2002) calls "active"; that is, domestic R&D makes use of ideas developed elsewhere in the world.[5]

It follows that the country's average productivity parameter $A_t = \int_0^1 A_{it} di$ will evolve according to

$$A_t = \mu \overline{A}_t + (1-\mu) A_{t-1} \tag{7.3}$$

That is, in the fraction μ of sectors that innovate productivity is $\overline{A}_t$, whereas in the remaining fraction productivity is the same as in period $t - 1$.

The country's distance to the world technology frontier is measured inversely by the ratio of its average productivity parameter to the global frontier parameter:

$$a_t = A_t / \overline{A}_t$$

We call the ratio a_t the country's "proximity" to the frontier. Dividing both sides of equation (7.3) by $\overline{A}_t$, we see that a_t will evolve according to

$$a_t = \mu + \frac{1-\mu}{1+g} a_{t-1} \tag{7.4}$$

There is a unique steady-state proximity a^*, which is defined by setting $a_t = a_{t+1}$ in equation (7.4):

$$a^* = \frac{(1+g)\mu}{g+\mu} \tag{7.5}$$

---

5. Aghion, Howitt, and Mayer-Foulkes (2005) explore the more general case:

$$A_{it} = \begin{cases} b\overline{A}_t + (1-b)A_{i,t-1} & \text{with probability } \mu \\ A_{i,t-1} & \text{with probability } 1-\mu \end{cases}$$

where b is a real number between 0 and 1.

Moreover, this is a stable steady state because the coefficient of a_{t-1} in equation (7.4) lies between zero and one.[6] Therefore, $a*$ will be the country's long-run proximity to the frontier.

7.2.4 Convergence and Divergence

The first result from this model is as follows:

Result 1   All countries with $\pi > \eta$ will grow at the same rate in the long run.

In other words, all countries that innovate at a positive rate will converge to the same growth rate. The reason for this convergence result is that, because of technology transfer, the further behind the frontier a country is initially, the bigger the average size of its innovations:

$$\overline{\gamma} - 1 = \overline{A}_t / A_{t-1} - 1 = (1+g)/a_{t-1} - 1$$

Because the country's growth rate is just the frequency times the size of innovations,[7]

$$g_t = \mu(\overline{\gamma} - 1)$$

Therefore, the further behind the frontier the country is, the higher its growth rate will be. This fact limits how far behind the frontier a country can fall, because

---

6. Subtracting $a*$ from both sides of equation (7.4) and using the fact that $\mu - a* = -\dfrac{1-\mu}{1+g} a*$ yields

$$a_t - a* = \frac{1-\mu}{1+g}(a_{t-1} - a*)$$

Starting with an initial proximity a_0 and iterating on this formula shows that

$$a_t - a* = \left(\frac{1-\mu}{1+g}\right)^t (a_0 - a*)$$

which approaches zero as $t \to \infty$.

7. To see this point, note that, by definition,

$$g_t = \frac{A_t}{A_{t-1}} - 1 = (1+g)\left(\frac{a_t}{a_{t-1}}\right) - 1$$

Using equation (7.4) to replace a_t in this formula yields

$$g_t = (1+g)\left(\frac{\mu}{a_{t-1}} + \frac{1-\mu}{1+g}\right) - 1 = \mu\left(\frac{1+g}{a_{t-1}} - 1\right) = \mu(\overline{\gamma} - 1)$$

eventually it will get so far behind that its growth rate will be just as large as the growth rate of the frontier, at which point the gap will stop increasing.

Formally, we get the result because in this case $\mu > 0$ (case 1), so the country's steady-state proximity (7.5) will be strictly positive. In turn, in the long run, A_t will be proportional to $\overline{A}_t$:

$$A_t = a^*\overline{A}_t > 0$$

Therefore, the long-run growth rate will be the growth rate g of the world productivity frontier:

$$\frac{A_{t+1}}{A_t} = \frac{a^*\overline{A}_{t+1}}{a^*\overline{A}_t} = \frac{\overline{A}_{t+1}}{\overline{A}_t} = 1 + g$$

However, we also have the following results:

Result 2   All countries with $\pi \leq \eta$ will stagnate in the long run.

That is, countries with poor macroeconomic conditions, legal environment, education system, or credit markets will not innovate in equilibrium, and therefore they will not benefit from technology transfer, but will instead stagnate. Formally, for these countries the fact that $\mu = 0$ means that their equilibrium proximity to the frontier a^* is zero.

Together these two results help to explain the facts about club convergence discussed in the introduction (section 7.1). That is, there is one group of countries that are converging to parallel growth paths (i.e., with identical long-run growth rates) and another group of countries that are falling further and further behind.

Notice that even countries that are converging to parallel growth paths are not necessarily converging in levels. That is, one country's steady-state proximity to the frontier (7.5) can differ from another's if they have different values of the critical parameters π, η, and ψ.

Result 3   For countries with $\pi > \eta$, a^* is increasing in π and decreasing in η and ψ.

Intuitively, if a country improves its education system, for example (thereby reducing the cost parameters η and ψ), it will start to grow faster for a while. As it approaches closer to the frontier, the fact that its size of innovations is getting smaller will bring its growth rate back to g, but the end result will be that it is now permanently closer to the frontier. This result helps us to account for the fact that there are systematic and persistent differences across countries in the level of productivity. That is, convergence in levels is not absolute but conditional. In our model, two countries will end up with the same productivity levels in the long run if they have the same parameter values, but not otherwise.

Finally, the following result is derived from equation (7.5):

Result 4   For countries $\pi > \eta$, a^* is decreasing in g.

That is, a speedup of the global frontier will result in a spreading out of the cross-country productivity distribution. Howitt and Mayer-Foulkes (2005) have used this result to shed light on the "great divergence" discussed in section 7.1. Their argument is that some time around or after the Industrial Revolution there was a speedup in world technology growth associated with the spread of scientific methodology and its application to industrial R&D. Countries that did not take part directly in this change (those whose parameter values remained the same) eventually benefited from technology transfer at an increased rate, but only after they fell further behind. In the long run they were able to grow at the new higher rate but only because their increasing distance to the frontier raised the size of innovations in those countries.

Elsewhere (Aghion and Howitt 2006) we have also used this result to help explain why the gap between Europe and the United States stopped closing some time in the 1970s or 1980s and started rising again. Our argument was that from the end of World War II until some time in the 1970s or 1980s, Europe was catching up to the frontier, but that during the 1990s there was an acceleration of productivity growth in the United States, associated with the revolution in information technology, which caused the frontier growth rate to increase. Because for the most part this wave of frontier innovations did not initiate in Europe, it could not produce a higher European growth rate until Europe had fallen further behind the frontier.

7.3   Credit Constraints as a Source of Divergence*

The preceding framework can be further developed by assuming that while the size of innovations increases with the distance to the technological frontier (because of technology transfer), the frequency of innovations depends upon the ratio between the distance to the technological frontier and the current stock of skilled workers. Howitt and Mayer-Foulkes (2005) show that this enriched framework can explain not only why some countries converge while others stagnate

*This section is more difficult than average and can be skipped.

but also why even countries with a positive long-run growth rate may diverge. Benhabib and Spiegel (2005) develop a similar account of divergence and show the importance of human capital in the process.

In this section we instead explore credit constraints as a reason why the frequency of innovations might fall when a country falls further behind the frontier. We develop a model, based on Aghion, Howitt, and Mayer-Foulkes (2005), that combines elements of the previous section's model and the previous chapter's Schumpeterian model of financial constraints.

7.3.1 Theory

We modify the model of the previous section by supposing that research aimed at making an innovation in t must be done at period $t - 1$. If we assume perfectly functioning financial markets, then nothing happens to the model. But as we already saw in chapter 6, when credit markets are imperfect, an entrepreneur may face a borrowing constraint that limits her investment to a fixed multiple v of her accumulated net wealth. As in chapter 6, this credit multiplier comes from the possibility that the entrepreneur might defraud her creditor. The multiplier will be bigger in countries where it is more costly to get away with fraud.

We assume a two-period overlapping-generations structure in which the accumulated net wealth of an entrepreneur at t is her wage income w_{t-1} from last period. So she cannot spend more than $v w_{t-1}$ in research. Since the cost of innovating at any rate μ is $\tilde{n}(\mu)A_{it}^*$ and the target productivity parameter A_{it}^* is the frontier $\bar{A}_t$, her probability of innovation cannot exceed $\bar{\mu}_t$, where

$$\tilde{n}\left(\bar{\mu}_t\right)\bar{A}_t = v w_{t-1} \tag{7.6}$$

The wage rate w_{t-1} is the marginal product of labor, which, as we saw in the last chapter, is proportional to A_{t-1}:

$$w_{t-1} = \omega A_{t-1}$$

So dividing equation (7.6) by $\bar{A}_t$ and using the fact that $\bar{A}_t$ grows at rate g, we can re-express equation (7.6) in terms of our proximity variable:

$$\tilde{n}\left(\bar{\mu}_t\right) = \bar{\omega} v\, a_{t-1} \tag{7.7}$$

where $\bar{\omega} = \omega/(1 + g)$. Equation (7.7) determines $\bar{\mu}_t$ as an increasing function of the credit multiplier v and of lagged proximity a_{t-1}. Using the specification (7.2), we can rewrite it as[8]

---

8. As explained in footnote 4, ϕ is the innovation production function implied by the cost function $\tilde{n}$.

$$\bar{\mu}_t = \phi(\bar{\omega}va_{t-1}) = \frac{\sqrt{2\psi\bar{\omega}va_{t-1} + \eta^2} - \eta}{\psi}$$

which is increasing in both v and a_{t-1}, and equal to zero for $v = 0$ or $a_{t-1} = 0$.

Suppose that in the absence of credit constraints the equilibrium innovation rate $\mu = (\pi - \eta)/\psi$ would be strictly positive (case 1 of the previous section). The credit constraint will be binding on R&D investment if $\phi(\bar{\omega}va_{t-1})$ is less than μ, in which case we must replace μ by $\phi(\bar{\omega}va_{t-1})$ in the equation (7.4) governing the evolution of proximity, which yields the constrained evolution equation

$$a_t = \phi(\bar{\omega}va_{t-1}) + \frac{1 - \phi(\bar{\omega}va_{t-1})}{1 + g} a_{t-1} \equiv H(a_{t-1}) \tag{7.8}$$

where

$$H' > 0, \quad H'' < 0, \quad H(0) = 0, \quad \text{and} \quad H(1) < 1$$

Figure 7.1 shows the case in which the credit multiplier is large enough that $H'(0) > 1$. Differentiation of equation (7.8) shows that this is the case in which

$$v\phi'(0) > g/\omega \tag{7.9}$$

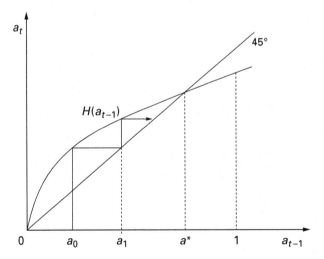

Figure 7.1

In this case, the country will converge to a positive steady state a^*. So, as in the previous section, it will be part of the convergence club with a long-run growth rate equal to g. Moreover, its steady-state proximity is increasing in the credit multiplier v, because an increase in v would shift the H function upward.

But if the credit multiplier is not large enough to satisfy equation (7.9), then $H'(0) \leq 1$ and the country will converge to a degenerate steady state with $a = 0$, as shown in figure 7.2. In this latter case the country's growth rate will fall not to zero but to a rate g^h somewhere between 0 and g, a rate that depends positively on the credit multiplier v.[9]

Thus the lower is a country's level of financial development, the more likely it is to diverge from the global technology frontier. This conclusion follows because a low level of financial development creates a disadvantage of backwardness that can outweigh Gerschenkron's advantage. That is, the further behind the frontier the country falls, the less any entrepreneur will be able to invest in R&D relative to what is needed to maintain any given frequency of innovation, and hence the further it will continue to fall behind for lack of innovation. This is less of a problem in more financially developed countries, where creditors are better protected against fraudulent default and hence are more willing to provide entrepreneurs with the finance needed to keep pace with the frontier.

7.3.2 Evidence

Aghion, Howitt, and Mayer-Foulkes (2005; AHM) test this effect of financial development on convergence by running the following cross-country growth regression:

---

9. More specifically, as in footnote 7,

$$1 + g^h = (1+g)\frac{a_t}{a_{t-1}}$$

A first-order Taylor-series expansion of equation (7.8) shows that when a_{t-1} is close to zero we have

$$a_t \approx a_{t-1}H'(0)$$

Therefore,

$$1 + g^h \approx (1+g)H'(0)$$

which is less than $1 + g$ if $H'(0) < 1$. Moreover, from equation (7.8) we have

$$H'(0) = \bar{\omega}v\phi'(0) + 1/(1+g)$$

which implies that $1 + g^h$ is increasing in the credit multiplier v.

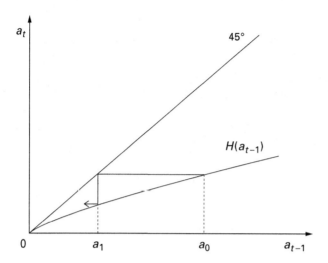

Figure 7.2

$$g_i - g_1 = \beta_0 + \beta_f F_i + \beta_y \cdot (y_i - y_1) + \beta_{fy} \cdot F_i \cdot (y_i - y_1) + \beta_x X_i + \varepsilon_i \qquad (7.10)$$

where g_i denotes the average growth rate of per capita GDP in country i over the period 1960–95, F_i the country's average level of financial development, y_i the initial (1960) log of per capita GDP, X_i a set of other regressors, and ε_i a disturbance term with mean zero. Country 1 is the technology leader, which they take to be the United States.

Define $\hat{y}_i \equiv y_i - y_1$, country i's initial relative per capita GDP. Under the assumption that $\beta_y + \beta_{fy} F_i \neq 0$, we can rewrite equation (7.10) as

$$g_i - g_1 = \lambda_i \cdot \left(\hat{y}_i - \hat{y}_i^* \right)$$

where the steady-state value $\hat{y}_i^*$ is defined by setting the right-hand side of equation (7.10) to zero:

$$\hat{y}_t^* = -\frac{\beta_0 + \beta_f F_i + \beta_x X_i + \varepsilon_i}{\beta_y + \beta_{fy} F_i}$$

and λ_i is a country-specific convergence parameter:

$$\lambda_i = \beta_y + \beta_{fy} F_i$$

that depends on financial development.

A country can converge to the frontier growth rate if and only if the growth rate of its relative per capita GDP depends negatively on the initial value $\hat{y}_i$, that is, if and only if the convergence parameter λ_i is negative. Thus the likelihood of convergence will increase with financial development, as implied by the preceding theory, if and only if

$$\beta_{fy} < 0$$

The results of running this regression using a sample of 71 countries are shown in table 7.1, which indicates that the interaction coefficient β_{fy} is indeed significantly negative for a variety of different measures of financial development and a variety of different conditioning sets X. The estimation is by instrumental variables, using a country's legal origins[10] and its legal origins interacted with the initial GDP gap $(y_i - y_1)$ as instruments for F_i and $F_i(y_i - y_1)$. The data, estimation methods, and choice of conditioning sets X are all taken directly from Levine, Loayza, and Beck (2000), who found a strongly positive and robust effect of financial intermediation on short-run growth in a regression identical to equation (7.10) but without the crucial interaction term $F_i(y_i - y_1)$ that allows convergence to depend upon the level of financial development.

AHM show that the results of table 7.1 are surprisingly robust to different estimation techniques, to discarding outliers, and to including possible interaction effects between the initial GDP gap and other right-hand-side variables.

7.4   Conclusion

We have seen that once technology transfer is taken into account, a country's long-run growth rate may no longer depend on the parameters of that country, because as long as the country remains in the convergence club its growth rate will be the global rate of technological progress, which may be unaffected by local conditions. All the domestic parameter changes that would have changed the country's growth rate in the absence of technology transfer will now change its relative productivity level.

Thus for convergence club members the Schumpeterian model looks much like the neoclassical model with an exogenous long-run growth rate, where policy changes also have only level effects. The difference is that in the Schumpeterian

---

10. See La Porta and colleagues (1998) for a detailed explanation of legal origins and their relevance as an instrument for financial development.

Table 7.1
Growth, Financial Development, and Initial GDP Gap

Financial Development (F) Conditioning Set (X)	Private Credit			Liquid Liabilities			Bank Assets			Commercial-Central Bank		
	Empty	Policy^a	Full^b	Empty	Policy^a	Full^b	Empty	Policy^a	Full^b	Empty	Policy^a	Full^b
Coefficient estimates												
β_f	-0.015	-0.013	-0.016	-0.029	-0.030	-0.027	-0.019	-0.020	-0.022	0.000	0.031	0.013
	(-0.93)	(-0.68)	(-0.78)	(-1.04)	(-0.99)	(-0.90)	(-1.07)	(-1.03)	(-1.12)	(0.00)	(0.17)	(0.07)
β_y	1.507***	1.193*	1.131	2.648***	2.388**	2.384**	1.891***	1.335*	1.365	7.166	5.279	5.645
	(3.14)	(1.86)	(1.49)	(3.12)	(2.39)	(2.11)	(3.57)	(1.93)	(1.66)	(1.04)	(0.73)	(0.72)
β_{fy}	-0.061***	-0.063***	-0.063***	-0.076***	-0.077***	-0.073***	-0.081***	-0.081***	-0.081***	-0.110	-0.100	-0.102
	(-5.35)	(-5.10)	(-4.62)	(-3.68)	(-3.81)	(-3.55)	(-5.07)	(-4.85)	(-4.46)	(-1.29)	(-1.18)	(-1.14)
Instrument test p-values												
1st-stage F-test: F	0.0000	0.0014	0.0024	0.0044	0.0032	0.0042	0.0000	0.0000	0.0000	0.2654	0.2180	0.1704
1st-stage F-test: $F(y-y_i)$	0.0000	0.0000	0.0000	0.0690	0.0078	0.0088	0.0010	0.0003	0.0011	0.5160	0.2743	0.2962
1st-stage F-test: $L(y-y_i)$	0.0000	0.0000	0.0001	0.0003	0.0002	0.0022	0.0000	0.0000	0.0000	0.2329	0.2315	0.4516
Sargan test	0.5372	0.7255	0.5573	0.2217	0.3952	0.3627	0.8486	0.8816	0.8279	0.9661	0.8861	0.9223
C-test for $L(y-y_i)$	0.3773	0.7013	0.4654	0.2700	0.3549	0.2799	0.9940	0.9642	0.8424	0.9482	0.7680	0.8240
C-test for $(y-y_i)$	0.6475	0.7790	0.7781	0.6240	0.6341	0.6226	0.7699	0.9944	0.9784	0.9700	0.9818	0.9320
Sample size	71	63	63	71	63	63	71	63	63	71	63	63

The dependent variable $g - g_1$ is the average growth rate of per capita real GDP relative to the United States, 1960–95; F is average financial development 1960–95 using four alternative measures; and $y - y_1$ is the log of per capita GDP in 1960 relative to the United States.

a. The policy conditioning set includes average years of schooling in 1960, government size, inflation, black market premium, and openness to trade.

b. The full conditioning set includes the policy set plus indicators of revolutions and coups, political assassinations, and ethnic diversity.

Estimation is by IV using L (legal origins) and $L(y - y_1)$ as instruments for F and $F(y - y_1)$. The numbers in parentheses are t-statistics. Significance at the 1%, 5%, and 10% level is denoted by ***, **, and *, respectively.

model, policy affects the level of productivity, not just the level of physical or human capital per person.

The Schumpeterian approach also helps to account for who belongs to the convergence club and what the growth rate will be for nonmember countries. Moreover, one can easily modify the model so as to endogenize the common growth rate of the club members, by assuming that the world technology frontier grows at a rate that depends positively on the innovation rates μ_j in all countries j. For example,

$$g = \sum_1^n \beta_j \mu_j$$

where the coefficient β_j measures the extent to which innovations in country j add to the world's stock of technological knowledge. With this formulation, the common growth rate of leading countries depends on conditions with respect to the costs and benefits of innovation in all the countries undertaking leading-edge R&D.

7.5   Literature Notes

Convergence is one of the most studied topics in the growth literature. A first approach explains convergence as a result of decreasing returns in physical or human capital accumulation. This is the neoclassical approach pioneered by Solow (1956) and subsequently developed by Mankiw, Romer, and Weil (1992) and Barro and Sala-i-Martin (1991, 1995a).

In particular Barro and Sala-i-Martin (1991) have stressed the distinction between absolute convergence (poor countries tend to grow faster per capita than rich ones) and conditional convergence (an economy grows faster the further it is from its own steady-state value). Another important distinction made by Barro and Sala-i-Martin (1992a) is between (1) the fact that growth rates of poor countries are lower than those of their rich counterparts (which they call β-divergence) and (2) the increasing dispersion of income per capita across countries over time (which they call σ-divergence).

More recent studies have analyzed the effect of convergence on the world distribution of income. Thus Pritchett (1997) estimates a large increase in the proportional gap in living standards between the richest and poorest countries between 1870 and 1990 (which he refers to as "divergence, big time"). Sala-i-Martin (2006) gets different results when looking at a more recent time period (1970 to 2000) and claims that there was an overall reduction in global income inequality (which he refers to as "convergence, period").

Based again upon the neoclassical framework, several empirical studies have tried to estimate the speed of convergence using panel data techniques, based on cross-country data, such as Islam (1995) and Caselli, Esquivel, and Lefort (1996), and regional data (Canova and Marcet 1995).

A second approach explains convergence as resulting primarily from cross-country knowledge spillovers. The most natural formulation of this approach uses the Schumpeterian framework, in particular Howitt (2000), who explains club convergence; Howitt and Mayer-Foulkes (2005), who explain convergence and divergence; Keller (2004), who links spillovers and geographical proximity; and more recently Eaton and Kortum (2001), who link convergence with spillovers and trade. The role of credit constraints as a source of divergence is analyzed by Aghion, Howitt, and Mayer-Foulkes (2005).

Evidence on the club-convergence and "twin-peaks" phenomena can be found in the work of Quah (1993, 1996, 1997), Durlauf and Johnson (1995), and Mayer-Foulkes (2002).

Problems

1. Contrast the factors driving convergence in the Schumpeterian and AK models. Describe intuitively how the Schumpeterian approach can explain "club convergence."

2. **Convergence concepts**

Suppose the world consists of five countries whose outputs are given by

$$Y_1 = Ae^{gt}$$
$$Y_2 = \left(A + \frac{B}{1+t}\right)e^{gt}$$
$$Y_3 = Be^{\left(k + \frac{1}{1+t^2}\right)t}$$
$$Y_4 = Ae^{\left(g + \frac{1}{1+t}\right)t}$$
$$Y_5 = \left(B + e^{-lt}\right)e^{kt}$$

where A, B, k, and g are all positive and $l > g$.

a. Which countries converge to the same growth rates as $t \to \infty$?

b. Which countries converge to the same growth paths as $t \to \infty$?

c. A model exhibits conditional convergence if countries with the same underlying parameters always converge to the same growth paths regardless of the initial conditions. Does the model in section 7.2 exhibit conditional convergence?

3. **Alternative diffusion technologies, part 1**

Consider a model identical to the one that is given in section 7.2, except that the R&D investment equation is given by

$$N_t = c(\mu)\bar{A}_t$$
$$= \alpha\left(e^{\beta\mu} - 1\right)\bar{A}_t$$

where $\alpha, \beta > 0$.

a. Write down the maximization problem of an innovator at time t.

b. Solve for the equilibrium probability of innovation μ.

c. Give a condition on α, β, and π that guarantees a positive innovation rate in equilibrium.

d. Solve for the steady-state proximity to frontier, a*. How does a* depend on α and β?

4. *Alternative diffusion technologies, part 2

Consider the model in section 7.2, but with the following innovation technology:

$$A_{it} = \begin{cases} (1+g)A_{t-1} & \text{with probability } \mu_{it} \\ A_{it-1} & \text{with probability } 1 - \mu_{it} \end{cases}$$

$$N_{it} = c(\mu_{it})a_{t-1}$$
$$= \left(\eta\mu_{it} + \delta\frac{\mu_{it}^2}{2}\right)a_{t-1}^2\bar{A}_t$$

where $\bar{A}_t = (1 + g)\bar{A}_{t-1}$ as before.

In this economy the size and the cost of innovations both depend on the economy's current technology level.

a. Write down the maximization problem of an innovator in sector i at time t.

b. Noting from part a that the equilibrium probability of innovation must be constant across sectors, solve for the equilibrium probability of innovation μ_t.

c. Show that the proximity to frontier a_t satisfies the following difference equation:

$$a_t = \frac{1+\mu_t g}{1+g}a_{t-1}$$

d. What is the steady-state proximity to frontier, a*, in this economy?

e. Give intuition for why the proximity to frontier converges to this steady state.

f. Suppose that the R&D investment equation was given by

$$N_{it} = \left(\eta\mu_{it} + \delta\frac{\mu_{it}^2}{2}\right)a_{t-1}\bar{A}_t.$$

How will the proximity to frontier evolve in this case?

5. Skilled-labor-based technology transfer (based on Howitt and Mayer-Foulkes 2005)

Suppose R&D requires skilled labor. Specifically, let the probability of innovation in sector i at time t, μ_{it}, be given by

$$\mu_{it} = \frac{S_{it}^\eta Z_{it}^{1-\eta}}{\bar{A}_t}, \qquad 0 < \eta < 1$$

where S_{it} is the skill level of the innovator and Z_{it} is the amount of final good invested in R&D in sector i. The remainder of the model is the same as in section 7.2.

a. Show that an innovator with skill level S_{it} chooses her R&D investment such that

$$\mu_{it} = \frac{S_{it}}{\bar{A}_t} \left[(1 - \eta)\pi \right]^{\frac{1-\eta}{\eta}}$$

b. Assume that the skill level of innovators in a country is proportional to the country's average productivity the previous period: $S_{it} = \xi A_{t-1}$. Derive a difference equation governing a_t.

c. Solve for the steady-state growth rate g^* and proximity to frontier a^*. How do the steady-state solutions depend on the quality-of-education parameter ξ?

6. *Stochastic technology transfer (based on Eaton and Kortum 2002 and Melitz 2003)

Consider the following variant of the model presented in section 7.2. There is one potential innovator per sector per period. To innovate, the entrepreneur must pay a fixed cost δ. Her productivity A_{it} is then drawn from a uniform distribution on $[A_{it-1}, \bar{A}_t]$.

a. Show that the innovator will choose to pay the fixed cost if and only if $\delta \leq \frac{\pi}{2}\left(\bar{A}_t + A_{it-1}\right)$.

b. What restriction on δ ensures innovation when A_{it} is drawn from a uniform distribution on $[0, \bar{A}_t]$?

c. Show that if δ satisfies the restriction from part b, then

$$Ea_{it} = \frac{1}{2}\left(1 + \frac{a_{it-1}^2}{(1+g)^2}\right)$$

d. Suppose δ satisfies the restriction from part b in every sector. Use the law of large numbers to argue that

$$a_t = \frac{1}{2}\left(1 + \frac{a_{t-1}^2}{(1+g)^2}\right)$$

Find the steady-state proximity to frontier a*, assuming that the innovator always pays the fixed cost.

e. Suppose $\delta = \xi \bar{A}_t$. Show that the innovator pays the fixed cost if and only if $a_{it-1} \leq \hat{a}$, where

$$\hat{a} = \sqrt{\left(1 - \frac{2\xi}{\pi}\right)(1+g)}$$

f. Describe the dynamics governing proximity to the frontier in the case $\hat{a} > a^*$ and in the case $\hat{a} < a^*$, where a* is the steady-state proximity to frontier derived in part d. (Hint: You may find it useful to plot Ea_{it} as a function of a_{it-1}.)

8 Market Size and Directed Technical Change

8.1 Introduction

In all the innovation-based growth models we have seen so far, innovations take place with the same average frequency in all intermediate sectors. In reality, however, some sectors are persistently more innovative than others. A major reason for this difference among sectors has to do with their size. Other things equal, it is more profitable to innovate in a larger sector because a successful innovator has a larger market there. As a result, technical change tends to be directed more toward larger sectors than smaller ones.

The present chapter explores the "market-size" effect on the direction of technical change and draws out some of its economic implications. It is based on a series of papers by Acemoglu with different coauthors, and it is organized as follows. We begin in section 8.2 with an important microeconomic example, namely, the pharmaceutical industry, where innovations are systematically directed toward drugs that are used by wealthier customers. Section 8.3 shows how the market-size effect can help to explain the recent upsurge in wage inequality in developed countries. Section 8.4 shows how the same market-size effect can help account for cross-country productivity differences, using an explanation that is different from the one presented in the previous chapter.

8.2 Market Size in Drugs

8.2.1 Theory

Consider a small open economy in discrete time. The economy is populated by one-period-lived individuals. Each period, there are two kinds (or groups) of individuals, indexed by $j \in \{1,2\}$. There are three goods in the economy: a basic good that everyone needs to consume and two types of drugs, also indexed by $j \in \{1,2\}$. Each drug is produced one for one using the basic good. Group j only cares for drug j. Let A_{jt} denote the quality of drug j at date t, and x_{jt} the quantity of drug j produced at date t.

An individual i who belongs to group j derives utility from consuming the final good and the drug, according to

$$U_{it} = \left(c_{it}\right)^{1-\alpha} \left(A_{jt} x_{ijt}\right)^{\alpha}$$

where c_{it} is individual i's consumption of the basic good and x_{ijt} is her consumption of drug j, at date t.

Let y_{it} denote individual i's income at date t, and let p_{jt} denote the price of drug j at date t, both measured in units of final good. Utility maximization under the budget constraint

$$c_{it} + p_{jt}x_{ijt} \leq y_{it}$$

implies that the individual will always spend the fraction α of her income on the drug:[1]

$$x_{ijt} = \alpha \frac{y_{it}}{p_{jt}} \tag{8.1}$$

Summing over all individuals in group j yields the total demand for drug j

$$x_{jt} = \alpha \frac{Y_{jt}}{p_{jt}} \tag{8.2}$$

where

$$Y_{jt} = \sum_{i \in \text{group } j} y_{it}$$

Drug producers may invest in R&D targeted at a particular drug in hopes of capturing the market from potential competitors. Each innovation in drug j increases its quality A_j by a multiplicative factor $\gamma > 1$. It takes

$$R_{jt} = \psi_j \mu_{jt}^2 / 2$$

units of basic good invested in R&D targeted at drug j at date t to generate an innovation with probability μ_{jt}, where $\psi_j > 0$ is an inverse measure of the productivity of the innovation technology in drug j.

Since the demand curve (8.2) is unit-elastic, a successful innovator will charge the maximum price that avoids competition by the next-best version of the same

---

1. To see this point, note that maximizing U_{it} is equivalent to maximizing

$$\ln U_{it} = (1 - \alpha)\ln c_{it} + \alpha \ln A_{jt} x_{ijt}$$

Substituting for c_{it} using the budget constraint, we get

$$\ln U_{it} = (1 - \alpha)\ln(y_{it} - p_{jt}x_{ijt}) + \alpha(\ln A_{jt} + \ln x_{ijt})$$

The first-order condition for maximizing $\ln U_{it}$ is therefore

$$-\frac{1 - \alpha}{y_{it} - p_{jt}x_{ijt}} p_{jt} + \frac{\alpha}{x_{ijt}} = 0$$

which is equivalent to equation (8.1).

drug.[2] Assume that every innovation is copied after one period. Then the maximum price the successful innovator could charge is γ, since this is the cost at which the competitive fringe could produce and sell a quantity γ of the next-best version that yields the same benefit as one unit of the innovator's new version. Therefore, the profit from innovating in drug j at date t is

$$\Pi_{jt} = \left(p_{jt} - 1 \right) \frac{\alpha Y_{jt}}{p_{jt}} = \left(\frac{\gamma - 1}{\gamma} \right) \alpha Y_{jt}$$

The equilibrium flow of innovations in drug j results from the maximization by a potential innovator of her expected payoff:

$$\max_{\mu_{jt}} \left\{ \mu_{jt} \left(\frac{\gamma - 1}{\gamma} \right) \alpha Y_{jt} - \psi_j \mu_{jt}^2 / 2 \right\}$$

which yields

$$\mu_{jt} = \left(\frac{\gamma - 1}{\gamma} \right) \alpha Y_{jt} / \psi_j$$

In particular, the higher the relative market size for drug j, as measured by Y_{jt}, or the higher the productivity of R&D on drug j, as measured inversely by ψ_j, the higher the flow of innovations in that drug at date t.

8.2.2 Evidence

In their empirical analysis, Acemoglu and Linn (2004) estimate an equation of the form

$$E\left[N_{ct} \mid Z_c, X_{ct} \right] = \exp \left(\beta_1 \ln M_{ct} + \beta_2 X_{ct} + Z_c + u_t \right)$$

where N_{ct} is the flow of new drug approvals by the Food and Drug Administration (FDA), M_{ct} denotes the potential market size, X_{ct} is a vector of controls, and Z_c controls for drug-category fixed effects.

To deal with potential endogeneity problems, the authors explore the exogenous component of market size associated with demographic trends. More specifically, they consider

---

2. That is, the successful innovator's profit will be

$$\Pi_j = p_j x_j - x_j = \alpha Y_j - \alpha \frac{Y_j}{p_j}$$

which is maximized by choosing the highest possible price p_j.

Table 8.1
Effect of Changes in Market Size on New Drug Approvals

	[1]	[2]	[3]	[4]
Panel A: QML for Poisson model, dep var is count of drug approvals				
Market size	6.15	6.84	−2.22	
	[1.23]	[4.87]	[4.12]	
Lag market size		−0.61		
		[3.81]		
Lead market size			10.16	7.57
			[4.28]	[1.99]
Panel B: QML for Poisson model, dep var is count of nongeneric drug approvals				
Market size	3.82	6.72	2.91	
	[1.15]	[7.63]	[5.31]	
Lag market size		−2.49		
		[5.97]		
Lead market size			−1.77	1.73
			[6.94]	[2.02]
Panel C: QML for Poisson model, dep var is count of new molecular entities				
Market size	3.54	5.79	−1.38	
	[1.19]	[6.66]	[5.16]	
Lag market size		−1.99		
		[5.28]		
Lead market size			7.35	5.75
			[5.11]	[2.37]
Panel D: QML for Poisson model, dep var is count of generic drug approvals				
Market size	11.81	8.55	1.28	
	[3.30]	[6.85]	[7.17]	
Lag market size		3.12		
		[5.94]		
Lead market size			13.24	14.65
			[8.66]	[3.71]
Number of observations	198	198	165	165

$$M_{ct} = \sum_a z_{ca} i_{at}$$

where i_{at} is the income of individuals in age group a at time t in the United States, and z_{ca} is the average expenditure share on drugs of category c in the total income of individuals of age a (this does not change much over time).

The demographic data come from the Current Population Survey,[3] 1965–2000. The variable i_{at} is computed for five-year age bracket groups for 0–5 to 90 years and older. Drug categories obey the FDA classification (there are 20 major drug categories, divided into 159 subcategories). Data on drug use (z_{ca}) come from the Medical Expenditure Panel Survey, which covers US households over the period 1996–98. This survey includes age and income data for each household member, for a total of 28,000 individuals, and it provides information on the list of prescription drugs used by each person and the amount she spends on each drug. One can then compute drug expenditure and use by each age bracket, and divide this number by income or population to construct an income-based or population-based measure of z_{ca}.

Table 8.1 summarizes the main findings. It shows a positive and significant value of $\hat{\beta}_1$ ($\hat{\beta}_1 = 6.15$; standard error 1.23, thus significant at the 1% level). This in turn points to a significant effect of market size on innovation flow for each category of drug.

8.3 Wage Inequality

The first application of the notions of market size and directed technical change was Acemoglu's (1998) explanation of the upsurge of wage inequality since the early 1980s in several developed countries. Acemoglu was particularly concerned with the following puzzle concerning the evolution of wage inequality between educational groups: the wage ratio between college graduates and high-school graduates rose substantially in countries like the United States and the United Kingdom between the early 1980s and the mid-1990s even while the relative supply of college-educated workers increased. In the United States, for example, Autor, Krueger, and Katz (1998) show that the ratio of "college-equivalents" (defined as the number of workers with a college degree plus 0.5 of the number of workers with some college education) to "noncollege equivalents" (defined as the complementary set of workers) increased at an average rate of 3.05 percent

3. Available at www.census.gov/cps/.

between 1970 and 1995, up from an average rate of 2.35 percent between 1940 and 1970. In the meantime, the ratio between the average weekly wages of college and high school graduates went up by more than 25 percent during the period 1970–95, after having fallen by 0.11 percent a year on average during the previous period.[4]

8.3.1 The Debate

Various attempts have been made at explaining the observed upsurge in educational wage inequality—in particular, trade liberalization, deunionization, and skill-biased technical change (SBTC).

The trade explanation is fairly straightforward and directly inspired by the standard Heckscher-Ohlin theory of international trade: in a nutshell, a globalization boom should drive up the demand for skilled labor in the developed countries, where skilled labor is cheap relative to developing countries, and it should drive down the relative demand for unskilled labor, which is relatively expensive in developed countries.

Unfortunately, trade liberalization is not supported by the evidence. First, as argued by Krugman and others, how could trade liberalization have such a big impact on wage inequality in a country like the United States where trade with non-OECD countries represents no more than 2 percent of GDP? Second, this explanation would imply a fall in prices of less skill-intensive goods relative to prices of more skill-intensive goods in developed countries, but empirical studies find little evidence of this in either the United States or Europe during the 1980s. A third implication of the trade explanation is that labor should be reallocated from low-skill to high-skill industries, or from those sectors in developed countries that are most exposed to international competition to the other sectors. However, Berman, Bound, and Griliches (1994) for the United States and Machin (1996) for the United Kingdom found that only a minor part of the shift away from manual/blue-collar workers to nonmanual/white collars was due to between-industry changes, the remaining 70 or 80 percent being entirely attributable to

---

4. A second puzzle is that wage inequality has also increased sharply *within* educational and age groups: in particular, Machin (1996) finds that the *residual* standard deviation in hourly earnings has increased by 23 percent in the United Kingdom and by 14 percent in the United States over the period between 1979 and 1993; equally intriguing is the fact that the rise in within-group wage inequality started to occur *before* the rise in between-group inequality and accounts for a substantial fraction of the overall increase in income inequality (Katz and Autor 1999); the final part of this puzzle is that the increase in within-group inequality has mainly affected the *temporary* component of income whereas the increase in between-group inequality has mainly affected the *permanent* component of income (Blundell and Preston 1999). This second puzzle is addressed in chapter 9.

within-industry shifts. Finally, the Heckscher-Ohlin theory would predict that the ratio of skilled to unskilled employment should have gone down in skill-intensive industries in developed economies, a prediction which again was not borne out.

To the extent that unionization is often positively correlated with wage compression,[5] some economists also perceived deunionization[6] as an important source of the observed increase in wage inequality.[7] However, the attempt to attribute the increase in wage inequality to deunionization failed largely on the basis of the following "timing" considerations: on the one hand, in the United Kingdom the rise in wage inequality started in the mid-1970s while union density kept increasing until 1980; on the other hand, in the United States deunionization began in the 1950s at a time when wage inequality was relatively stable.[8]

Meanwhile, a number of empirical studies have pointed to a significant impact of skill-biased technical change on the evolution of wage inequality. For example, using R&D expenditures and computer purchases as measures of technical progress, Berman, Bound, and Griliches (1994) found that these two factors could account for as much as 70 percent of the move away from production to nonproduction labor over the period 1979–87. Murphy and Welch (1992) find that the share of college labor has increased substantially in all sectors since the mid-1970s, a finding which, together with the observed increase in the college premium, provides further evidence of skill-biased technical change. More recently, based on the data reported in Autor, Krueger, and Katz (1998), Acemoglu (2002) estimates that the relative productivity of college graduates has increased from 0.157 in 1980 to 0.470 in 1990 (whereas this relative productivity had risen at a lower rate prior to the early 1980s).

Why did we observe a sharp increase in the college premium in countries like the United States shortly after the relative supply of skilled labor also increased? The existing literature provides two main answers to this puzzle: on the one hand,

5. For example, R. Freeman (1993) showed that the standard deviation of within-firm log wages in the United States was 25 percent lower in unionized firms compared to nonunionized firms.

6. For example, according to Machin (1997), in the United Kingdom union density among male workers fell from 54 percent in 1980 to 38 percent in 1990; in the United States the percentage of private sector workers that are unionized fell from 24 percent in 1980 to less than 12 percent in 1990.

7. For example, Card (1996) and Fortin and Lemieux (1997).

8. While deunionization (organizational change) and trade liberalization do not fully explain the recent evolution in wage inequality, nevertheless we believe that these factors can become more significant when analyzed in relation to skill-biased technical change (see, for example, Acemoglu, Aghion, and Violante 2001 on deunionization and SBTC and Garcia-Peñalosa and Koebel 1998 and Acemoglu 1998 on trade liberalization and SBTC).

Katz and Murphy (1992) argue that the sharp increase in the college premium during the 1980s was the combined result of (1) secular skill-biased technical change at a constant pace over the past 50 years and (2) the temporary fall in the college premium caused by the baby-boom-driven increase in the relative supply of skilled labor in the early 1970s; before moving back to its secular path, the college premium was bound to increase at an accelerated rate. The alternative view is that there has been an acceleration in skill-biased technical change since the 1970s. The first convincing piece of evidence in this respect was provided by Krusell and colleagues (2000): based on an aggregate production function in which physical equipment is more substitutable to unskilled labor than to skilled labor,[9] they argue that the observed acceleration in the decline of the relative price of production-equipment goods since the mid-1970s[10] could account for most of the variation in the college premium over the past 25 years. In other words, the rise in the college premium could largely be attributed to an increase in the rate of (capital-embodied) skill-biased technical progress. This argument, however, does not fully answer our first puzzle; in particular, we still need to understand what would have caused the acceleration in SBTC measured by Krusell and colleagues (2000); second, we also need to reconcile this hypothesis and the evidence on the price of (quality-adjusted) equipment goods with the fact that the recent upsurge in productivity growth follows a long period of slower productivity growth.

8.3.2   The Market-Size Explanation

The following model is adapted from Acemoglu (1998, 2002). The basic idea has two parts. The first part is the same as the scale effect that we saw in Chapter 4. That is, if you can invent improved versions of an intermediate product that is used by a particular kind of labor (either skilled or unskilled) then, other things equal, there is more profit to be earned by improving a product that is used by the more abundant kind of labor. So as people become more highly educated, and skilled labor therefore becomes more abundant, technological progress becomes increasingly directed towards products that are used by skilled people.

The second part of market-size explanation is that technological progress in products that are used by a particular kind of labor raises the equilibrium wage rate of that kind of labor, by raising its marginal product. Therefore, when increas-

---

9. See also Stokey (1996), who analyzes the implications of capital-skill complementarity for trade, using a similar modeling approach.

10. See Gordon (1990).

ing education causes innovations to be directed more towards skilled labor it also raises the relative wage of skilled workers.

8.3.2.1 Basics

Final output consists of two distinct final goods: a skill-intensive good X_s and a labor-intensive good X_u, both produced under perfect competition. The skill-intensive good is produced using *skilled* labor L_s and a continuum of specialized intermediate products (x_{is}), while the labor-intensive good is produced using *unskilled* labor L_u and a different continuum of specialized intermediate inputs (x_{iu}), according to

$$X_s = \int_0^1 A_{is} x_{is}^\alpha di \cdot L_s^{1-\alpha} \qquad X_u = \int_0^1 A_{iu} x_{iu}^\alpha di \cdot L_u^{1-\alpha}$$

where $0 < \alpha < 1$ and the As are productivity parameters.

Assume that the local monopolist in each intermediate sector can produce one unit at no cost, but cannot produce any more than one unit at any cost. So in equilibrium we will have $x_{is} = x_{iu} = 1$, which allows us to rewrite the final output production functions as

$$X_s = A_s L_s^{1-\alpha} \qquad X_u = A_u L_u^{1-\alpha} \tag{8.3}$$

where $A_s = \int A_{is} di$ and $A_u = \int A_{iu} di$ are the average productivity parameters.

Equilibrium in the competitive final markets implies that the wage rate of each type of labor must equal the value of its marginal product:

$$w_s = P_s(1-\alpha)X_s/L_s \qquad w_u = P_u(1-\alpha)X_u/L_u \tag{8.4}$$

where P_s and P_u are the two final-good prices.

8.3.2.2 Immediate Effect of Relative Supply on the Skill Premium

The skill premium is defined as the relative wage w_s/w_u of skilled labor, which according to equation (8.4) can be expressed as

$$\frac{w_s}{w_u} = \left(\frac{P_s X_s}{P_u X_u}\right)\left(\frac{L_s}{L_u}\right)^{-1} \tag{8.5}$$

In equilibrium, the relative price P_s/P_u must equal the marginal rate of substitution in demand between the two goods, which we suppose depends on the relative quantity X_s/X_u according to

$$\frac{P_s}{P_u} = \left(\frac{X_s}{X_u}\right)^{-\upsilon}, \quad \upsilon > 0$$

where υ is an inverse measure of substitutability between the two goods. Therefore

$$\frac{P_s X_s}{P_u X_u} = \left(\frac{X_s}{X_u} \right)^{1-\upsilon} \tag{8.6}$$

From equations (8.3), (8.5) and (8.6) we can express the skill premium as

$$\frac{w_s}{w_u} = \left(\frac{A_s}{A_u} \right)^{1-\upsilon} \left(\frac{L_s}{L_u} \right)^{-1+(1-\alpha)(1-\upsilon)} \tag{8.7}$$

According to equation (8.7), an increase in education levels that raises the relative supply of skilled labor will always reduce the skill premium by making skilled labor less scarce.[11]

However, as time passes there will be an indirect, "market-size" effect of a change in relative supply that arises because the change may induce a reallocation of R&D towards or away from the skill-intensive intermediate inputs, thus affecting the relative productivity parameter A_s/A_u in equation (8.7).

8.3.2.3   The Market-Size Effect on Relative Productivity

To see how this market-size effect works, consider first the situation of the local monopolist in one of the skill-intensive intermediate sectors. Since she produces just one unit and has no cost, her profit will equal her sales revenue, which is also equal to the price of her product:

$$\Pi_{is} = p_{is} x_{is} = p_{is}$$

Equilibrium in the skill-intensive final good market requires that the price p_{is} be equal to the value of the marginal product of x_{is}, from which we get

$$\Pi_{is} = P_s \frac{\partial X_s}{\partial x_{is}} = \alpha P_s A_{is} L_s^{1-\alpha}$$

Each period the unique entrepreneur in the sector has an opportunity to become the monopolist if she innovates, thus raising productivity by the factor $\gamma > 1$. The probability of innovation is $\phi(n_s)$, where $n_s = R_{is}/A_{is}^*$ is her productivity-adjusted R&D expenditure and A_{is}^* is her target productivity level, $\phi' > 0$ and $\phi'' < 0$.

---

11. Note that, since $0 < \alpha < 1$ and $\upsilon > 0$, therefore the coefficient $-1 + (1 - \alpha)(1 - \upsilon)$ is always negative.

The entrepreneur chooses n_s so as to maximize the expected payoff

$$\phi(n_s)\Pi_{is} - A_{is}^* n_s = A_{is}^* \left[\phi(n_s)\alpha P_s L_s^{1-\alpha} - n_s \right]$$

The first-order condition for this maximization problem is

$$\phi'(n_s)\alpha P_s L_s^{1-\alpha} = 1$$

which we can rewrite, using the production function (8.3), as

$$\phi'(n_s)\alpha \frac{P_s X_s}{A_s} = 1 \tag{8.8}$$

The same analysis applies to each of the labor-intensive intermediate sectors, where productivity-adjusted research n_u must satisfy the identical equation:

$$\phi'(n_u)\alpha \frac{P_u X_u}{A_u} = 1 \tag{8.9}$$

The growth rate of each A_{is} will be $(\gamma - 1)$ with probability $\phi(n_s)$ and zero with probability $1 - \phi(n_s)$, so the expected growth rate of each A_{is} will be

$$g_s = (\gamma - 1)\phi(n_s)$$

which by the law of large numbers is also the actual growth rate of the aggregate productivity parameter A_s. By the same reasoning, the growth rate of average productivity A_u in the labor-intensive sector will be

$$g_u = (\gamma - 1)\phi(n_u)$$

In the long run the economy will approach a steady state in which the relative productivity A_s/A_u is constant, which requires $g_s = g_u$, and hence $n_s = n_u$. It then follows from equations (8.8) and (8.9) that in a steady state relative productivity must equal relative expenditure

$$\frac{A_s}{A_u} = \frac{P_s X_s}{P_u X_u}$$

Substituting for the right-hand side using equation (8.6) and then substituting for the relative quantity X_s/X_u using equation (8.3), we arrive at the steady-state condition

$$\frac{A_s}{A_u} = \left[\frac{A_s}{A_u} \frac{L_s^{1-\alpha}}{L_u^{1-\alpha}} \right]^{1-\upsilon}$$

which solves for the equilibrium relative productivity

$$\frac{A_s}{A_u} = \left(\frac{L_s^{1-\alpha}}{L_u^{1-\alpha}} \right)^{\frac{1-\upsilon}{\upsilon}} \tag{8.10}$$

So if the two final goods are close enough substitutes ($\upsilon < 1$) then an increase in the relative supply of skilled labor will have the long-run effect of raising the relative productivity of skill-intensive inputs. If this effect is large enough then, according to equation (8.7) it will override the negative direct effect, so that the overall effect of an increase in education will be to raise the long-run skill premium. Indeed it will be large enough if the two final goods are very close substitutes because as $\upsilon \to 0$ the exponent of L_s/L_u in equation (8.10) approaches infinity.

8.3.2.4   The Long-Run Equilibrium Skill Premium

So one possible explanation for a rising skill premium is that it was caused by the rise in the relative supply of skilled labor. This market-size explanation is quite appealing, especially because it appears to fit the evidence of a wage premium first decreasing (during the early 1970s) and then sharply increasing (starting in the late 1970s), following the increase in relative skilled labor supply in the late 1960s. This result is precisely what the preceding model predicts, since the negative direct effect is what one would observe in the short run. However, this explanation raises two issues that we will discuss briefly.

Issue 1   *Historical Perspective*   Although the preceding story can account for the dynamic pattern followed by the skill premium in the United States after the "baby boom" increase in skilled-labor supply in the early 1970s, it does not explain why the rise in wage inequality occurred around this time in contrast with other historical episodes in which similar increases in the supply of educated labor have not been followed by any noticeable increase in wage inequality. For example, in the paper "The Returns to Skill across the Twentieth Century in the United States," Goldin and Katz (1999) show that in spite of a substantial increase in the relative supply of educated labor between 1900 and 1920 following the "high school movement," the wage ratio between white collars and blue collars fell continuously during the first half of the century and especially during the 1920s and the 1940s. Moreover, while mentioning a "strong association between changes in the use of purchase in electricity and shifts in employment toward more educated labor" (p. 25), Goldin and Katz report no sharp widening of the wage distribution prior to the 1970s. Obviously, any explanation of the recent patterns in wage inequality really needs to integrate the distinguishing features of the past 20 years from previous episodes if it is to be taken as comprehensive. This observation does not invalidate the importance of market-size and labor-supply effects, but it does suggest that any explanation that would rely primarily upon these effects may not be fully satisfactory from a historical point of view. However, Acemoglu (2002) convincingly argues that models of directed technical change can be useful in understanding the rise of the factory system in the 19th century, in relation to the increased supply of unskilled labor induced by the migration of rural populations to cities.

Issue 2 *Market-Size Effect* and *Productivity Slowdown*   In a highly influential paper, Jones (1995a) points out that although OECD countries have experienced substantial increases in the average duration of schooling and in R&D levels during the past 50 years, there has been no apparent payoff in terms of faster growth: if anything, measured productivity growth has slowed, especially between the mid-1970s and the early 1980s.[12] These findings appear to be at odds with R&D-based models of growth that predict that the innovation rate should significantly increase when the supply of skilled L_s increases. The market-size model is actually more subtle in the sense that it predicts a change in the direction—not the speed—of technological change. Yet the growth rate as derived from the preceding model should still increase following a (discontinuous) increase in relative skilled-labor supply, which is still at variance with Jones-style evidence, at least up until the mid-1990s. To reconcile the market-size explanation with this evidence, Acemoglu (2000) invokes the existence of decreasing returns in R&D aimed at skill-biased technical progress. Now, while individual researchers might experience decreasing returns in their R&D activities, it is not clear why the *whole* economy should: the exception would be if individual innovations were more like secondary discoveries induced by an economy-wide

---

12. For example, the annual growth rate in the United States has declined by 1.8 percent on average since the 1970s. The decline has been most pronounced in the service sector, and more generally the productivity slowdown appears to be mainly attributable to a decline in *disembodied* productivity growth. Indeed, since the early 1970s the rate of *embodied* technical progress has accelerated (see McHugh and Lane 1987; Greenwood and Yorukoglu 1997; Hornstein and Krusell 1996; and Comin 2000), and the bulk of this acceleration, e.g., as measured by the decline in the quality-adjusted price of equipment goods, appears to be attributable to computers and other information-processing goods. This contrast, again, points to the important role played by the new information technologies and their diffusion during the past 20 years.

fundamental breakthrough, which becomes more and more incremental over time. We shall come back to these issues in chapter 9.

8.4 Appropriate Technology and Productivity Differences*

Acemoglu and Zilibotti (2001) used a directed technical change model to explain the persistence of productivity differences between North and South, even though no institutional barriers to the adoption of technologies discovered in the North exist in the South. Suppose technological innovation takes place in the North and that the South does not enforce property rights on innovations imported from the North. Then, innovators in the North can only extract rents from selling new technologies in the northern market. It follows that innovation will not respond to market size and skill endowment in the South, but only to those in the North, which in turn implies that the dynamics of relative productivities in skilled- and unskilled-intensive sectors (i.e., A_s/A_u in the previous section) will only be determined by skill endowments in the North. Thus it will generally be inappropriate for the South, with the result that output per worker is higher in the South than in the North, even though both regions have access to the same technological opportunities.

More formally, consider the following variant of the directed technical change model, with horizontal innovations. This section closely follows Gancia and Zilibotti (2005). Consider a world divided into North and South.

8.4.1 Basic Setup

Time is continuous and at each period the North produces a continuum of measure one of variety goods, under perfect competition. Variety goods are indexed by $i \in [0,1]$, and together they give rise to a composite final output

$$Y = \exp\left(\int_0^1 \log y_i \, di\right),$$

which is taken as numeraire.

Each variety good i is produced using skilled labor, unskilled labor, and intermediate input used by each type of labor. Namely, intermediate inputs (L,v) with v in the interval $[0,A_L]$ are used by unskilled workers only, whereas intermediate inputs (H,v) with v in the interval $[0,A_H]$ are used by skilled workers only.

---

*This is a difficult section that may be skipped by the novice reader.

Overall, the production technology for producing variety i, is assumed to be:

$$y_i = \left[(1-i)l_i\right]^{1-\alpha} \int_0^{A_L} x_{L,\upsilon,i}^{\alpha} d\upsilon + \left[ih_i\right]^{1-\alpha} \int_0^{A_H} x_{H,\upsilon,i}^{\alpha} d\upsilon, \tag{8.11}$$

where l_i and h_i are the amounts of unskilled and skilled labor employed in sector i, and $x_{z,\upsilon,i}$ is the amount of intermediate input υ used in that sector.

Note that sectors differ in productivities, $(1 - i)$ for the unskilled technology and i for the skilled technology, so that unskilled labor has a comparative advantage in sectors with a low index, whereas skilled labor has a comparative advantage in sectors with a high index.

Producers of good i take the price of their product, P_i, the prices of intermediate inputs ($p_{L,\upsilon}$, $p_{H,\upsilon}$) and wages (w_L, w_H) as given. Profit maximization leads to the following demands for intermediate inputs:

$$x_{L,\upsilon,i} = (1-i)l_i\left[\alpha P_i/p_{L,\upsilon}\right]^{1/(1-\alpha)} \quad \text{and} \quad x_{H,\upsilon,i} = ih_i\left[\alpha P_i/p_{H,\upsilon}\right]^{1/(1-\alpha)}. \tag{8.12}$$

Intermediate good sectors are monopolistic, and producing one unit of any intermediate input requires spending α^2 units of the numéraire good.

8.4.2   Equilibrium Output and Profits

Profit maximization by intermediate monopolists leads to the equilibrium price $p = \alpha$. This, together with equations (8.11) and (8.12), yields the equilibrium output of variety i:

$$y_i = P_i^{\alpha/(1-\alpha)}\left[A_L(1-i)l_i + A_H ih_i\right]. \tag{8.13}$$

In equilibrium, all sectors whose index i is below some threshold level J will use unskilled labor only, whereas the remaining sectors will employ skilled labor. Equilibrium profits of the intermediate monopolist producing unskilled and skilled inputs are, respectively, given by

$$\pi_{L,\upsilon} \equiv \pi_L = (1-\alpha)\alpha\int_0^{J} P_i^{1/(1-\alpha)}(1-i)l_i di \quad \text{and}$$

$$\pi_{H,\upsilon} \equiv \pi_H = (1-\alpha)\alpha\int_J^{1} P_i^{1/(1-\alpha)}ih_i di \tag{8.14}$$

Finally, given the Cobb-Douglas specification in equation (8.11), the wage bill in each sector is equal to $(1 - \alpha)$ times the output of the sector, namely:

$$w_L = (1-\alpha)P_i^{1/(1-\alpha)}A_L(1-i), \text{ for } i \le J \tag{8.15}$$

$$w_H = (1-\alpha)P_i^{1/(1-\alpha)}A_H i, \text{ for } i > J \tag{8.16}$$

Defining $P_L \equiv P_0$, $P_H \equiv P_1$ and dividing equations (8.15) and (8.16) by their counterparts in sectors 0 and 1, we obtain

$$P_i = P_L(1-i)^{-(1-\alpha)}, \text{ for } i \leq J$$

$$P_i = P_H i^{-(1-\alpha)}, \text{ for } i > J$$

Now, to maximize Y, expenditures across goods must be equalized, thus

$$P_i y_i = P_H y_1 = P_L y_0$$

This, together with the full employment of skilled and unskilled labor, implies that labor is evenly distributed among sectors, that is

$$l_i = L/J, h_i = H/(1-J)$$

Finally, in the cut-off sector $i = J$, the skilled and unskilled technologies are equally profitable:

$$P_L(1-J)^{-(1-\alpha)} = P_H J^{-(1-\alpha)}$$

Together, the preceding equations imply:

$$\frac{J}{1-J} = \left(\frac{P_H}{P_L}\right)^{1/(1-\alpha)} = \left(\frac{A_H}{A_L}\frac{H}{L}\right)^{-1/2} \tag{8.17}$$

The higher the relative endowment of skill (H/L) and the skill-bias of technology (A_H/A_L), the larger the fraction of sectors using the skill-intensive technology ($1 - J$).

Finally, integrating $P_i y_i$ over $[0,1]$, using equations (8.13) and (8.17), and the fact that the consumption aggregate is the numéraire (so that $\exp\left[\int_0^1 \ln P_i di\right] = 1$), we can re-express aggregate output as

$$Y = \exp(-1)\left[(A_L L)^{1/2} + (A_H H)^{1/2}\right]^2 \tag{8.18}$$

8.4.3   Skill-Biased Technical Change

In the preceding subsection we took the technology parameters A_H and A_L as given. Now, we endogenize them by looking at innovation incentives and the resulting equilibrium skill-bias of technology, (A_H/A_L). Assume that to increase A_L or A_H by one unit (that is, the cost of inventing an additional "unskilled" or an additional "skilled" intermediate input) costs μ units of the numéraire. Inventing a new "skilled" input yields instantaneous profits equal to

$$\pi_H = \alpha(1-\alpha) P_H^{1/(1-\alpha)} H \tag{8.19}$$

Similarly, inventing a new "unskilled" input yields instantaneous profits equal to

$$\pi_L = \alpha(1-\alpha) P_L^{1/(1-\alpha)} L$$

Now, balanced growth requires that the innovation intensity be the same on both types of inputs, which in turn requires that

$$\pi_L = \pi_H$$

Balanced growth also implies that A_H and A_L grow at the same rate, so that the ratio A_H/A_L remains constant over time as well as the cut-off index J, and the prices P_L and P_H.

Plugging $\pi_L = \pi_H$ into equation (8.19) and using equation (8.17), we get

$$\frac{A_H}{A_L} = \frac{1-J}{J} = \frac{H}{L} \tag{8.20}$$

8.4.4   Explaining Cross-Country Productivity Differences

So far, our analysis was focused on the case of one country, the North. Consider now a second country, the South. The South is identical to the North, except that skilled labor is more scarce in the South than in the North, namely

$$H^S/L^S < H/L$$

Now, let us assume that intellectual property rights are not enforced in the South and that there is no trade between North and South. This in turn implies that intermediate producers in the North cannot sell goods or copyrights to the South, so that they can only collect rents from the South on their innovations. On the other hand, producers in the South can copy the new technologies invented in the North at a small but positive cost, so that they will choose to simply imitate the technologies invented in the North instead of investing in innovation.

But then the North and the South will end up using the same technologies, with

$$A_H/A_L = H/L$$

that is, the skill-bias is entirely determined by the factor endowment of the North, which in turn follows from the fact that the North is the only market for (northern) innovations.

Apart from that, the equilibrium output in the South is similar as the preceding expression (8.18) for the equilibrium output in the North, except that we must replace the skilled and unskilled labor endowments H and L in the North by H^S and L^S for the South:

$$Y^S = \exp(-1)\left[\left(A_L L^S\right)^{1/2} + \left(A_H H^S\right)^{1/2}\right]^2$$

We are now ready to answer the following questions: Are technologies appropriate for the skill endowment of the countries where they are developed? What happens to aggregate productivity if they are used in a different economic environment?

It is easy to show that expression Y is maximized for $A_H/A_L = H/L$. This is nothing but the previous condition (8.20). In other words, the equilibrium skill-bias A_H/A_L is optimally adapted to the northern skill composition H/L. However, the equilibrium skill bias ignores the relative factor endowments in the South, so that the new technologies developed in the North are inappropriate for the needs of the South. It follows that output per capita, $Y/(L + H)$ is greater in the North than in the South.

This productivity difference is the result of a technology-skill mismatch, and it can help explain the existence of substantial differences in TFP even across countries that have access to the same technology. Acemoglu and Zilibotti (2001) argue that this mismatch can account for one third to one half of the total factor productivity gap between the United States and developing countries. The idea that the choice of appropriate technology depends on factor endowments also features in the analysis of Caselli and Coleman (2006).

8.5   Conclusion

In this model we have explored the idea that innovative firms may decide on how to allocate their R&D efforts across several sectors of the economy, and that their equilibrium decisions will ultimately depend upon both the relative efficiency of R&D investments across the various sectors and the relative size of rents that can be generated by innovating in each sector. The latter in turn depend upon the relative incomes of the potential consumers of the various goods or on the size of the labor force whose productivity can be enhanced by innovating in each particular sector. We provided evidence that market-size effects were at work in the drug industry, and we analyzed implications of the market-size approach for wage inequality and the nonconvergence between South and North.

8.6   Literature Notes

The theory presented in this chapter is based on a series of recent papers by Daron Acemoglu and coauthors. Yet the idea of biased technological change goes back to an earlier literature. Hicks (1932) had already suggested that technological progress would economize on the more expensive factor.

Related to Hicks's idea, the late 1950s and early 1960s saw the emergence of an "induced innovation" literature. In particular, Nelson (1959) discussed the composition of research spending and the amount spent on what he called "basic" research. Arrow (1962) studied the optimality of the resource allocation for inventions from the viewpoint of welfare economics. Kennedy (1964) introduced the idea of "innovation possibilities frontier" that takes into account the trade-off between different types of innovation.

Kennedy (1964) also discussed the issue of relative factor share in the economy and its relation with induced innovations, concluding that these latter would push the economy to an equilibrium with constant relative-factor share. Such points were addressed by Samuelson (1965) and Drandakis and Phelps (1965), among others.

Fellner (1961) studied the factor-saving aspect of inventions and argued that competitive firms would lean toward a relative labor-saving invention only if they would expect wages to rise faster than capital-good rentals. Habakkuk (1962) asserted that labor scarcity, by increasing wages, would induce firms to search for labor-saving inventions, spurring technological progress.

Atkinson and Stiglitz (1969) analyzed the idea that technological progress could improve one technique of production but not other techniques of producing the same product, under their concept of "localized" technical progress.

Because of its lack of strong microfoundations, interest in this literature faded away until the late 1990s when the models analyzed in this chapter were first published. These microfounded models of directed technical change feature the existence of market-size effects (absent in most of the earlier literature mentioned previously, with the exception of works such as Schmookler 1966) and were mostly developed by Acemoglu and coauthors.

The main applications of the framework have been (1) to skill-biased technical change and wage inequality (Acemoglu 1998 and Kiley 1999); (2) to international trade inducing skill-biased technical change (Acemoglu 2003a); (3) to explaining the constancy of factor shares (Acemoglu 2003b); and (4) to explaining the persistence of productivity differences across countries that have equal access to new technologies (Acemoglu and Zilibotti 2001).

Acemoglu (2002) presented a theoretical synthesis of the framework, and we also refer the reader to the *Handbook of Economic Growth* survey by Gancia and Zilibotti (2005, sec. 4).

Problems

1. Explain how taking into account market-size effects and directed technical change might shed light on why there is less incentive to develop vaccines for diseases that are more common in poorer countries. Explain why market-size effects can explain the recent surge in wage inequality.

2. **Product variety and directed technological change**

Consider a mass 1 of identical consumers with preference given by the utility function

$$U = \int_0^\infty e^{-\delta t} \frac{C^{1-\theta}-1}{1-\theta} dt$$

where $C(t) = \left(C_s^\rho + C_u^\rho\right)^{\frac{1}{\rho}}$ is a consumption aggregator over two final goods produced according to

$$Y_s = \int_0^{N_s} x_{i,s}^\alpha L_s^{1-\alpha} di$$
$$Y_u = \int_0^{N_u} x_{i,u}^\alpha L_u^{1-\alpha} di$$

where $x_{i,v}$ is the i intermediate input used in the sector intensive in L_v, and N_v is the number of varieties in this sector. The markets for final goods are perfect, but the producers of intermediate goods are monopolists. It costs one unit of final good to produce one intermediate good. By spending Z units of final good, an entrant faces a probability $\lambda_v Z$ of discovering a new intermediate good in the sector intensive in L_v. There is free entry into research. We will normalize prices such that it costs 1 to get

$$C(t) = 1; \text{ so } \left(p_s^{\frac{\rho}{\rho-1}} + p_u^{\frac{\rho}{\rho-1}} \right)^{\frac{\rho-1}{\rho}} = 1.$$

a. Compute the profit for an intermediate good as a function of p_v, the price of Y_v.

b. Compute the price ratio between the two final goods; derive the wage premium as a function of N_s and N_u. Show that the elasticity of substitution between the two factors is given by

$$\sigma = \frac{1-\alpha\rho}{1-\rho}.$$

c. We now focus on the steady state. State the research-arbitrage equation. Compute the value of a firm as a function of the profit and the interest rate. Taking the ratio for the two sectors, define price and a market-size effects. Then find the ratio $\dfrac{N_s}{N_u}$ as a function of $\dfrac{L_s}{L_u}$.

d. When is an increase in the supply of skilled labor going to increase the wage premium? Compare with the quality-ladder case.

e. Express the Euler equation. Compute the growth rate of the economy.

3. ****Endogenous factors supply**

Consider the model presented in section 8.3. This problem will make endogenous the endowment of skilled and unskilled workers. Time is discrete, and there is a continuum of agents (of mass 1). Instead of living for one period, an agent may die with probability $1 - \delta$ each period. A mass δ of new agents are born each period. When agent z is born, he is unskilled; he can choose to start working immediately or to acquire education in order to become skilled. If he decides to get educated, he won't be able to work for $T(z)$ periods (note that the agent knows how long it is going to take him to get educated), where $T(z)$ is distributed according to a distribution $Q(T)$, such that $q(t) > 0$ for any $t \geq 0$ (Q is the cumulative distribution function and q is the probability distribution function). We consider an economy in steady state where the skill premium and a remain constant, and we assume that if someone is indifferent he will choose to become educated.

There is no friction in the financial market, and a person born at s has the following lifetime expected utility:

$$E(U) = \sum_{t=0} \delta^t c_z(t+s)$$

An innovation increases the productivity of an intermediate good A_i by a factor γ and happens with probability n^β if someone invests n in R&D. Contrary to the benchmark model we assume that the monopoly right is given until a new innovation is made.

a. Show that the interest rate is given by $r = \dfrac{1}{1+\delta}$ and that wages increase at the growth rate of the economy g.

b. Show that there is a stationary cutoff value $\bar{T}$ above which people won't get educated.

c. Compute the threshold as a function of the skill premium, rate of interest, and growth rate in the economy (you can forget the integer constraint on $\bar{T}$).

d. Show that the relative supply is given by

$$\frac{L_s}{L_u} = \frac{Q(\bar{T})}{1 - Q(\bar{T})}$$

e. Show that the present value of the monopoly right (from the following period) on the intermediate good i is

$$V_i = \frac{\pi_i}{1 + r + \left(\dfrac{g}{\gamma - 1}\right)^\beta}$$

f. Compute the research-arbitrage equation; show that the following relation still holds:

$$\omega = \lambda^{\frac{\rho^2 (1-\alpha)^2}{(1-\rho)(1-\alpha\rho)} + \frac{\rho - 1}{1 - \alpha\rho}}$$

g. Give an equation that fully characterizes $\bar{T}$ as a function of the parameters of the economy (you can use the expression of the growth rate in problem 2). Explain why it is possible to get several equilibria. What is the intuition? Will growth necessarily be the same in these equilibria?

4. *Knowledge spillovers

Consider the following variation of the model presented in section 8.3. Innovation now requires the hiring of scientists that are in fixed supply (S). Moreover, instead of having one entrepreneur each period who has the possibility of displacing the monopolist, there is now free entry in the innovation sector (we will consider that the probability that there is more than one innovation per period is 0— think that the time interval this time is very short). A local entrepreneur in the unskilled sector who hires s_{iu} scientists will innovate successfully with probability $\eta_u \dfrac{A_s^{\frac{1-\delta}{2}} A_u^{\frac{1+\delta}{2}}}{A_{iu}} s_{iu}$, $0 < \delta \leq 1$. If he succeeds, he will be the monopolist for good iu next period, using a technology $A_{iu}(t+1) = \gamma A_{iu}(t)$. (And similarly a local entrepreneur in the skilled sector who hires s_{is} scientists will innovate with probability $\eta_s \dfrac{A_u^{\frac{1-\delta}{2}} A_s^{\frac{1+\delta}{2}}}{A_{is}} s_{is}$.)

Note that sections 8.3.2.1, 8.3.2.2, and 8.3.2.3 still apply in this context.

a. Explain what the functional form $\dfrac{A_s^{\frac{1-\delta}{2}} A_u^{\frac{1+\delta}{2}}}{A_{iu}}$ means.

b. State the free-entry condition in R&D and the scientists' market-clearing condition.

c. Prove that the growth rate of A_u is given by

$$\frac{A_u^{t+1} - A_u^t}{A_u^t} = (\gamma - 1)\eta_u \left(\frac{A_s^t}{A_u^t}\right)^{\frac{1-\delta}{2}} S_u$$

d. Compute the skill premium and the growth rate of the economy in steady state.

e. When is the skill premium going to increase if the relative supply of skilled workers in the population increases? Compare with the baseline model (look at what happens when $\delta = 0$); provide an intuition to explain the departure from the baseline model. Typically economists would agree that $\rho > 0$, but there is some debate on how large it is. Explain why this model may help to explain better than the baseline model the historical increase in the skill premium if ρ is not very large.

5. **Skilled labor as the input for R&D**

We consider a model similar to the one introduced in section 8.3; however, this time R&D requires hiring skilled labor instead of using a final good. Moreover, instead of having one entrepreneur each period who has the possibility of displacing the monopolist, there is now free entry in the innovation sector (the probability that there is more than one innovation per period is 0). A local entrepreneur in the unskilled sector who hires h_{iu} units of skilled labor will successfully innovate with probability $\eta \dfrac{A_s^{1/2} A_u^{1/2}}{A_{iu}} h_{iu}$ ($A_s^{1/2} A_u^{1/2}$ represents knowledge spillover). If he succeeds he will be the monopolist for good iu next period, using a technology $A_{iu}(t+1) = \gamma A_{iu}(t)$. (And similarly a local entrepreneur in the skilled sector who hires h_{is} units of skilled labor will innovate with probability $\eta \dfrac{A_s^{1/2} A_u^{1/2}}{A_{is}} h_{is}$.)

a. State the free-entry condition in R&D.

b. Prove that the growth rate of A_u is given by

$$\frac{A_u^{t+1} - A_u^t}{A_u^t} = (\gamma - 1)\eta \left(\frac{A_s^t}{A_u^t}\right)^{1/2} H_u$$

where H_u is the total amount of skilled labor used in the R&D of the unskilled sector

c. Prove that in a steady state where a is constant, the following relations still hold:

$$\omega = a^{\frac{\rho(1-\alpha)}{1-\alpha\rho}} \lambda^{\frac{\rho-1}{1-\alpha\rho}}$$

$$a = \lambda^{\frac{\rho(1-\alpha)}{1-\rho}}$$

provided that we redefine λ conveniently.

d. Find, λ (assume that the supply of skilled labor is large enough so that your computation makes sense). Find the growth rate and the wage premium. What is the effect of an increase in the supply of skilled labor on the wage premium? And on the growth rate? Comment.

6. **Appropriate technology and growth (based on Basu and Weil 1998)**

Here, technologies are specific to particular combinations of inputs.

First suppose a one-country world where output per worker is given by

$$Y = A(K, t)K^\alpha$$

where $A(K,t)$ is the level of technology for capital-labor ratio K at time t.

Suppose there exists a maximal level of technology for each value of K given by $A^*(K) = BK^{1-\alpha}$. (There is a limit for the development of new technologies for any capital-labor ratio.) Assume also that $A^{*\prime}(K) > 0$. Finally, define $k \equiv \ln(K)$.

Let us assume that when a country produces at a log capital-labor ratio k, learning by doing uniformly improves the level of all technologies using a capital-labor ratio in a symmetric neighborhood around k. In particular, suppose that the level of technology at capital-labor ratio j improves according to the following:

$$\frac{dA(j, t)}{dt} = \beta\left[A^*(j) - A(j, t)\right] \quad \text{if } k - \gamma < j < k + \gamma$$
$$= 0 \qquad\qquad\qquad \text{otherwise}$$

where $A^*(j)$ is the highest level of technology attainable at capital-labor ratio j.

Finally, assume there exists $x > k_0$ such that $A(j,0) > 0$ for all $j > x$ and $A(k_0,0) > 0$. (This simply means that at the beginning of time, there was no technology available for high enough levels of capital-labor ratios.) Define $R = A(K,t)/A^*(K)$ as the ratio of used technology to its maximal level.

a. Show that output per worker can be rewritten as $Y = RBK$.

We now look at the steady state of this economy, in which k grows at a constant rate g and $R = R^*$ is constant.

b. Show that in steady state $R^* = (1 - e^{-\beta\gamma/g})$. What is the sign of $\partial R^*/\partial g$? Is there any "penalty" for fast growth in this setting? Provide intuition for your finding. (Hint: Solve the ordinary differential equation for $A(k,t)$ using $e^{\beta x}$ as the integrating factor.)

Now, assume a constant saving rate s so that $\dot{K} = sY - \delta K$.

c. Show that in steady state $g = sR^*B - \delta$. Show graphically that the steady-state level of technology ratio R^* is unique and that it does not depend on initial conditions.

Assume now that the world is composed of two countries and that technology flows freely between them, as well as local learning-by-doing spillovers:

$$\frac{dA(j, t)}{dt} = \beta\left[A^*(j) - A(j, t)\right]\sum_{i=1}^{2}\mathbf{1}\{k_i - \gamma < j < k_i + \gamma\}$$

where $\mathbf{1}\{\}$ is the indicator function and i designates the country. This simply means that when the countries are within the same neighborhood of capital-labor ratios, technology can be simultaneously improved by spillovers from both countries.

Let us look at the case in which the two countries end up in a steady state where they both grow at the same rate g. Let s_1 and s_2 be the saving rates for the two countries, and R^*_1 and R^*_2 the steady-state technology ratios, and assume, without loss of generality, that $s_1 > s_2$.

d. Show that if both countries grow at rate g in steady state and $s_1 > s$, then $R^*_1 < R^*_2$. Explain how this result implies that country 1 has a higher level of capital per worker than country 2 at all times. Let d be the steady-state difference between the leader country's log capital-labor ratio k_1 and the follower's k_2.

e. Using reasoning analogous to item b, derive the steady-state ratios $R^*_1 = 1 - e^{-\beta(2\gamma-d)/g}$ and $R^*_2 = 1 - e^{-\beta(2\gamma+d)/g}$. Explain why the two countries will grow at the same steady-state rate g only if $d < \gamma$.

9 General-Purpose Technologies

9.1 Introduction

What causes long-term accelerations and slowdowns in economic growth, and underlies the long swings sometimes referred to as Kondratieff cycles? In particular, what caused American growth in GDP and productivity to accelerate starting in the mid-1990s? The most popular explanation relies on the notion of general-purpose technologies (GPTs).

Bresnahan and Trajtenberg (1995) define a GPT as a technological innovation that affects production and/or innovation in many sectors of an economy. Well-known examples in economic history include the steam engine, electricity, the laser, turbo reactors, and more recently the information-technology (IT) revolution. Three fundamental features characterize most GPTs. First, their pervasiveness: GPTs are used in most sectors of an economy and thereby generate palpable macroeconomic effects. Second, their scope for improvement: GPTs tend to underperform upon being introduced; only later do they fully deliver their potential productivity growth. Third, innovation spanning: GPTs make it easier to invent new products and processes—that is, to generate new secondary innovations.

The following figures, drawn from Jorgenson (2005), show how the input contribution of IT to U.S. average GDP growth (figure 9.1) and the contribution of IT as a whole to total-factor-productivity growth (figure 9.2) increased substantially from the period 1989–95 to the period 1995–2002.

The next figures, drawn from Jovanovic and Rousseau (2005), illustrate the progressiveness and pervasiveness in the diffusion of GPTs (figure 9.3 and 9.4) and how technological revolutions such as electrification and IT translated into a subsequent surge in innovations measured by patenting flow (figure 9.5).

Jovanovic and Rousseau also emphasize four important economy-wide consequences of the arrival and diffusion of new GPTs. First, an aggregate productivity slowdown: the diffusion of a new GPT requires complementary inputs and learning, which may draw resources from normal production activities and may contribute to future productivity in a way that cannot be captured easily by current statistical indicators. Second, an increase in the skill premium as more skilled labor is required to diffuse a new GPT to all the sectors of the economy. Third, an increase in the flow of firm entry and exit as the GPT generates quality-improving innovations, and therefore creative destruction, in numerous sectors. Fourth, a decline in stock market prices, which mirrors the initial productivity slowdown generated by the new GPT.

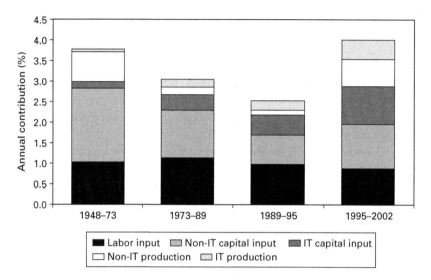

Figure 9.1
Sources of GDP growth

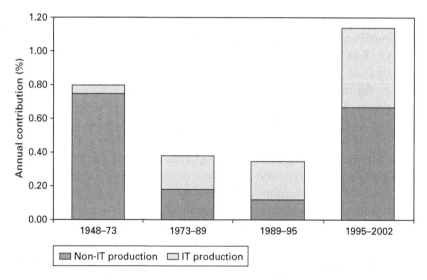

Figure 9.2
Contribution of IT to TFP growth

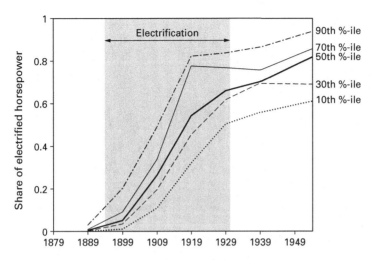

Figure 9.3
Shares of electrified horsepower by manufacturing sectors in percentiles, 1890–1954

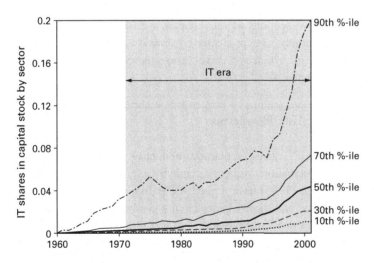

Figure 9.4
Shares of IT equipment and software in the capital stock by sector in percentiles, 1960–2001

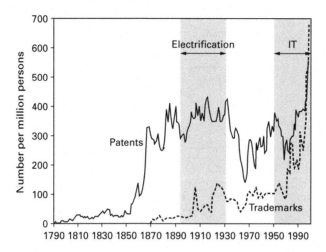

Figure 9.5
Patents issued on inventions and trademarks registered in the United States per million persons, 1790–2000

In the next two sections of this chapter, we focus on the first two aspects, respectively—namely, the productivity slowdown and the increase in wage inequality, both of which we revisit using the Schumpeterian growth model developed in chapter 4.

9.2   Explaining Productivity Slowdowns

Although each GPT raises output and productivity in the long run, it can also cause cyclical fluctuations while the economy adjusts to it. As David (1990) and Lipsey and Bekar (1995) have argued, GPTs like the steam engine, the electric dynamo, the laser, and the computer require costly restructuring and adjustment to take place, and there is no reason to expect this process to proceed smoothly over time. Thus, contrary to the predictions of real-business-cycle theory, the initial effect of a "positive technology shock" may not be to raise output, productivity, and employment but to reduce them.

9.2.1   General-Purpose Technologies in the Neoclassical Model

To get a preliminary sense of the potential magnitude of the downturn or slow-down that might initially be caused by the arrival of a new GPT, consider the following variant of the neoclassical model, where the new GPT can reduce growth by inducing obsolescence of existing capital:

$$\dot{k} = sBk^\alpha - (\delta + n + g + \beta)k$$

where

1. $k = \dfrac{K}{Le^{gt}}$ and $y = \dfrac{Y}{Le^{gt}} = Bk^\alpha$ denote, respectively, the capital stock and aggregate output, both per efficiency unit of labor;

2. s is the saving rate;

3. the parameters δ, n, g, and β denote, respectively, the rate of capital depreciation, the rate of population growth, the (exogenous) rate of labor-augmenting technological progress, and the rate of capital obsolescence.

Obsolescence works just like physical depreciation in reducing $\dot{k}$ because it causes capital to be scrapped. Moreover, the faster the rate of innovation, the faster the rate of obsolescence, because capital used by firms whose products are replaced by an innovation will be scrapped. Accordingly, we assume that both g and β are proportional to the innovation rate μ:

$$\beta = \mu(1 - \eta)$$

and

$$g = \mu\sigma$$

where η is the scrap value of each unit of obsolete capital and σ denotes the size of innovations (in the basic Schumpeterian framework of chapter 4, $\sigma = \gamma - 1$). The growth rate of output per person is thus given by

$$G = \dot{y}/y + g = \alpha\dot{k}/k + g \tag{9.1}$$
$$= \alpha\left[sBk^{\alpha-1} - \delta - n\right] + \left[(1-\alpha)\sigma - \alpha(1-\eta)\right]\mu$$

Now consider the following thought experiment. Starting from a steady state with $G = g$, suppose the discovery of a new GPT raises the innovation rate μ. The immediate effect on the growth rate G is obtained by differentiating equation (9.1):

$$\frac{\partial G}{\partial \mu} = (1-\alpha)\sigma - \alpha(1-\eta) = \sigma(1 - \alpha - \alpha\beta/g)$$

Taking $\alpha = 2/3$ as in Mankiw, Romer, and Weil (1992), $\beta = 0.04$ as in Caballero and Jaffe (1993), and $g = 0.02$ from U.S. data, we thus obtain an elasticity of growth with respect to μ equal to

$$\frac{\mu}{g}\frac{\partial G}{\partial \mu} = \frac{1}{\sigma}\frac{\partial G}{\partial \mu} = 1 - \alpha - \alpha\beta/g = -1$$

So, for example, a 10 percent increase in μ, which would raise long-run growth by 10 percent (from 2 percent per year to 2.2 percent per year) will on impact *reduce* growth by 10 percent (from 2 percent to 1.8 percent). Furthermore, using equation (9.1) with the calibration ($\alpha = {}^2/_3$, $\beta = 0.04$, $g = 0.02$, $\delta = 0.02$, $n = 0.01$), one can show that it will take about two decades for the growth rate to rise back up to 2 percent and more than half a century for aggregate output to catch up with the time path it would have followed had the new GPT (and the resulting shock to μ) not arrived.[1] This example illustrates the potential magnitude of the macroeconomic impact of major technological change for reasonable parameter values.

9.2.2   Schumpeterian Waves

An alternative explanation for slowdowns has been developed by Helpman and Trajtenberg (1998a) using the Schumpeterian apparatus where R&D resources can alternatively be used in production. The basic idea of this model is that GPTs do not come ready to use off the shelf. Instead, each GPT requires an entirely new set of intermediate goods before it can be implemented. The discovery and development of these intermediate goods is a costly activity, and the economy must wait until some critical mass of intermediate components has been accumulated before it is profitable for firms to switch from the previous GPT. During the period between the discovery of a new GPT and its ultimate implementation, national income will fall as resources are taken out of production and put into R&D activities aimed at the discovery of new intermediate input components.

9.2.2.1   The Schumpeterian Model with Labor as R&D Input

As a useful first step toward a Helpman-Trajtenberg-type model, consider the following variant of the basic Schumpeterian model of chapter 4, where labor is used as R&D input. The final good is produced with a single intermediate product according to

---

1. For similar results in a Schumpeterian endogenous growth framework, see Howitt (1998).

$$Y_t = A_t x^\alpha, \qquad 0 < \alpha < 1$$

The intermediate good x is produced one for one with labor, so x also denotes the labor used in manufacturing the intermediate input.

Labor can also be used in research, to produce innovations. Specifically, an innovation arrives each period with probability λn, where n is the aggregate amount of research labor. A new innovation multiplies the productivity parameter A_t by $\gamma > 1$, so $A_{t+1} = \gamma A_t$ if an innovation occurs at $t + 1$. The labor-market clearing condition is

$$L = n + x$$

which says that the aggregate labor supply L each period equals the sum of labor demands in research and manufacturing.

Each period, the entrepreneur with an opportunity to innovate will want to maximize the expected payoff

$$\lambda n \Pi_{t+1} - w_t n$$

That is, she has to pay the going wage rate w_t for each unit of research labor, and with probability λn she will succeed and will therefore be able to monopolize the intermediate sector next period, earning the profit Π_{t+1}. The first-order condition for maximizing this expected payoff with respect to n is the research-arbitrage equation

$$w_t = \lambda \Pi_{t+1}$$

To compute the equilibrium profit Π_{t+1}, note that the successful innovator will be able to charge a price equal to the marginal product:

$$p_{t+1} = \frac{\partial Y_{t+1}}{\partial x} = \alpha A_{t+1} x^{\alpha-1}$$

so that

$$\Pi_{t+1} = \max_x \left\{ \alpha A_{t+1} x^{\alpha-1} x - w_{t+1} x \right\}$$

The first-order condition for this maximization is

$$A_{t+1} \alpha^2 x^{\alpha-1} = w_{t+1}$$

The demand for manufacturing labor is thus

$$x = \tilde{x}(\omega_{t+1}) = \alpha^{\frac{2}{1-\alpha}} \omega_{t+1}^{\frac{1}{\alpha-1}}$$

where $\omega_t = w_t/A_t$ is the productivity-adjusted wage rate. So the equilibrium profit is

$$\Pi_{t+1} = A_{t+1}\tilde{\pi}(\omega_{t+1})$$

where

$$\tilde{\pi}(\omega) = (1-\alpha)\alpha^{\frac{1+\alpha}{1-\alpha}}\omega^{\frac{\alpha}{\alpha-1}}$$

is decreasing in ω.

In steady state the allocation of labor between research and manufacturing remains constant over time, and so does the productivity-adjusted wage rate ω. Using the fact that $A_{t+1} = \gamma A_t$ if the entrepreneur succeeds, and dividing through by A_t, the research arbitrage equation becomes

$$\omega = \lambda\gamma\tilde{\pi}(\omega)$$

which pins down the equilibrium-adjusted wage ω. The labor-market-clearing condition

$$L = n + \tilde{x}(\omega)$$

then determines the equilibrium research employment, and the average growth rate is

$$g = \lambda n(\gamma - 1)$$

That is, with probability λn output grows by the proportional amount $\gamma - 1$.

Note that this is a one-sector economy where each innovation corresponds by definition to a major technological change (i.e., to the arrival of a new GPT), and thus where growth is uneven (figure 9.6) with the time path of output being a random step function.

But although it is uneven, the time path of aggregate output as depicted in the figure does not involve any slump. Accounting for the existence of slumps requires an extension of the basic Schumpeterian model, which brings us to the Helpman-Trajtenberg model.

9.2.2.2   The Helpman-Trajtenberg Model

As before, there are L workers who can engage either in production of existing intermediate goods or in research aimed at discovering new intermediate goods. Again, each intermediate good is linked to a particular GPT. We follow Helpman and Trajtenberg in supposing that before any of the intermediate goods associated

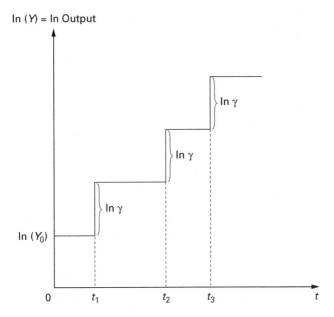

Figure 9.6

with a GPT can be used profitably in the final-goods sector, some minimal number of them must be available. We lose nothing essential by supposing that this minimal number is one. Once the good has been invented, its discoverer profits from a patent on its exclusive use in production, exactly as in the basic Schumpeterian model reviewed earlier.

Thus the difference between this model and our basic model is that now the discovery of a new generation of intermediate goods comes in two stages. First a new GPT must come, and then the intermediate good must be invented that implements that GPT. Neither can come before the other. You need to see the GPT before knowing what sort of good will implement it, and people need to see the previous GPT in action before anyone can think of a new one. For simplicity we assume that no one directs R&D toward the discovery of a new GPT. Instead, the discovery arrives as a serendipitous by-product of learning by doing with the previous one.

The economy will pass through a sequence of cycles, each having two phases, as indicated in figure 9.7. GPT_i arrives at time t_i. At that time the economy enters phase 1 of the ith cycle. During phase 1, the amount n of labor is devoted to research. Phase 2 begins at time $t_i + \Delta_i$ when this research discovers an

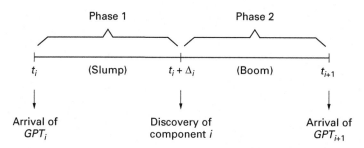

Figure 9.7

intermediate good to implement GPT_i. During phase 2 all labor is allocated to manufacturing until GPT_{i+1} arrives, at which time the next cycle begins. Over the cycle, output is equal to $A_{t_i} F(L - n)$ during phase 1 and $A_{t_i+\Delta} F(L) = \gamma A_{t_i} F(L)$ during phase 2. Thus the drawing of labor out of manufacturing and into research causes output to fall each time a GPT is discovered, by an amount equal to $A_{t_i}[F(L) - F(L - n)]$.

A steady-state equilibrium is one in which people choose to do the same amount of research each time the economy is in phase 1; that is, n is constant from one GPT to the next. As before, we can solve for the equilibrium value of n using a research-arbitrage equation and a labor-market-equilibrium curve. Let ω_j be the wage when the economy is in phase j, divided by the productivity parameter A of the GPT currently in use. In a steady state this productivity-adjusted wage must be independent of which GPT is currently in use.

Because research is conducted in phase 1 but pays off when the economy enters into phase 2 with a productivity parameter raised by the factor γ, the following research-arbitrage condition must hold in order for there to be a positive level of research in the economy

$$\omega_1 = \lambda \gamma \tilde{\pi}(\omega_2)$$

Because no one does research in phase 2, we know that the value of ω_2 is determined independently of research, by the market-clearing condition $L = \tilde{x}(\omega_2)$. Thus we can take this value as given and regard the preceding research-arbitrage condition as determining ω_1. The value of n is then determined, as in the previous subsection, by the labor-market equation

$$L = n + \tilde{x}(\omega_1)$$

The average growth rate will be the frequency of innovations times the size $\gamma - 1$, for exactly the same reason as in the basic model. The frequency, however, is determined a little differently than before because the economy must pass through two phases. An innovation is implemented each time a full cycle is completed. The frequency with which this implementation occurs is the inverse of the expected length of a complete cycle. This in turn is just the expected length[2] of phase 1 plus the expected length of phase 2:

$$1/\lambda n + 1/\mu = \frac{\mu + \lambda n}{\mu \lambda n}$$

Thus the growth rate will be

$$g = (\gamma - 1)\frac{\mu \lambda n}{\mu + \lambda n}$$

which is positively affected by anything that raises research.

The size of the slump $\ln[F(L)] - \ln[F(L - n)]$ that occurs when each GPT arrives is also an increasing function of n, and hence it will tend to be positively correlated with the average growth rate.

One further property of this cycle worth mentioning is that, as Helpman and Trajtenberg point out, the wage rate will rise when the economy goes into a slump. That is, because there is no research in phase 2, the normalized wage must be low enough to provide employment for all L workers in the manufacturing sector, whereas with the arrival of the new GPT the wage must rise to induce manufacturers to release workers into research. This brings us directly to the next section on wage inequality.

We conclude this section with one final remark. In the preceding model, the discovery of a new GPT leads initially to a fall in output. In reality, however, what we observe looks more like a slowdown but still with positive growth. The most obvious way to reconcile the theory with this observation is to extend the model by assuming that the economy consists not of one sector but of many, and

---

2. The length Δ of phase 1 is a random variable that is distributed geometrically with parameter λn; that is,

$$\text{Prob}(\Delta = i) = \lambda n (1 - \lambda n)^{i-1}, \qquad i = 1, 2, \ldots$$

Since the expected value of a geometrically distributed random variable is the inverse of the parameter, therefore the expected length of phase 1 is $1/\lambda n$. Likewise, the length of phase 2 is geometrically distributed with parameter μ, so its expected length is $1/\mu$.

that each sector experiments with the new GPT. Following the discovery of the GPT, some sectors will discover the complementary input that suits them before other sectors, and the accelerated growth of the former will compensate for the output fall of the latter. So the aggregate growth rate may dip for a while before finally taking off, but it will not necessarily turn negative.[3]

9.3   GPT and Wage Inequality

In this section we develop an explanation for increased wage inequality between and within educational groups, which is based on the notion of GPT. We argue that this explanation is consistent with the observed dynamic pattern of the wage premium in the United States and the United Kingdom since 1970, and that it does a better job than the market-size theory at dealing with the following two issues raised in chapter 8.

Issue 1 *Labor Market History*   Unlike in the recent period, the increase in supply of educated labor associated with the high school movement of the 1920s did not result in a comparable increase in the skill premium (see Goldin and Katz 1998).

Issue 2 *Productivity Slowdown*   The market-size explanation cannot account for the concurrence of the rise in skill premium with a productivity slowdown from the mid-1980s until the mid-1990s in the United States.

In addition, we will argue that the GPT explanation is consistent with (1) the increase in within-group inequality affecting primarily the temporary component of income (Blundell and Preston 1999) and (2) the observed increase in the experience premium.

9.3.1   Explaining the Increase in the Skill Premium

Figure 9.8, also drawn from Jovanovic and Rousseau (2005), shows that although the skill premium fell during the latter years of electrification, it rose with the IT wave after 1978.

In this subsection we show how the Helpman-Trajtenberg model of the previous section can account for the rise in the skill premium during the IT revolution.[4]

---

3. In Aghion and Howitt (1998a, chap. 8) we develop such a model, and argue that the diffusion of a new GPT to the whole economy will typically follow a logistic pattern over time.

4. In section 9.4 we argue that a GPT explanation is also consistent with the early-20th-century drop in the skill premium.

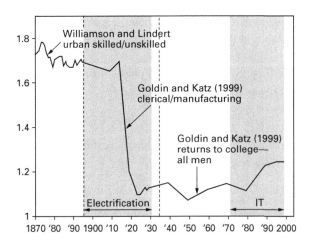

Figure 9.8
The skill premium

We modify that model by assuming that there are two types of labor. Educated labor can work in both research and manufacturing, whereas uneducated labor can only work in manufacturing. Let L^s and L^u denote the supply of educated (skilled) and uneducated (unskilled) labor, let ω_1^s and ω_1^u denote their respective productivity-adjusted wages in phase 1 of the cycle (when research activities on complementary inputs actually take place), and let ω_2 denote the productivity-adjusted wage of labor in phase 2 (when new GPTs have not yet appeared and therefore labor is entirely allocated to manufacturing).

If in equilibrium the labor market is segmented in phase 1, with all skilled labor being employed in research while unskilled workers are employed in manufacturing, we have the labor-market-clearing conditions

$$L^s = n$$

$$L^u = \tilde{x}\left(\omega_1^u\right)$$

and

$$L^s + L^u = \tilde{x}\left(\omega_2\right)$$

and the research-arbitrage condition

$$\omega_1^s = \lambda\gamma\tilde{\pi}\left(\omega_2\right)$$

which expresses the wage of skilled labor as being equal to the expected value of investing (skilled) labor in R&D for discovering complementary inputs to the new GPT.

The labor market will be truly segmented in phase 1 if and only if ω_1^s defined by this research-arbitrage condition satisfies

$$\omega_1^s > \omega_1^u$$

which in turn requires that L^s not be too large. Otherwise the labor market remains unsegmented, with $n < L^s$,

$$\omega_1^s = \omega_1^u$$

in equilibrium. In the former case, the arrival of a new GPT raises the skill premium (from 0 to $\omega_1^s/\omega_1^u - 1$) at the same time as it produces a productivity slowdown because labor is driven out of production.

9.3.2 Explaining the Increase in Within-Group Inequality

Perhaps the most intriguing feature of the upsurge in wage inequality is that it took place to a large extent within control groups, no matter how narrowly those groups are identified (e.g., in terms of experience, education, gender, industry, occupation).

Measurement problems provide an obvious first explanation for this puzzle. For example, a PhD from a top economics department should be valued more than a PhD from a lesser place, even though both PhDs may involve the same number of years "in school." Similarly, different jobs may involve different learning-by-doing and/or training opportunities, thereby leading to wage differences among workers with the same level of seniority. But even when controlling for measurement problems, a substantial amount of residual wage inequality remains to be explained.

Another explanation[5] is that skill-biased technical change enhanced not only the demand for observed skills as described earlier but also the demand for unobserved skills or abilities. Although theoretically appealing, this explanation is at odds with econometric work (Blundell and Preston 1999) showing that the within-group component of wage inequality in the United States and United Kingdom is mainly transitory, whereas the between-group component accounts for most of the observed

---

5. See Acemoglu (1998), Heckman, Lochner, and Taber (1998), Galor and Moav (2000), and Rubinstein and Tsiddon (1999) for models of within-group inequality based on differences in innate ability.

increase in the variance of permanent income. The explanation based on un-observed innate abilities also fails to explain why the rise in within-group inequality has been accompanied by a corresponding rise in individual wage instability (see Gottschalk and Moffitt 1994). In the remaining part of this section, we argue that the diffusion of a new technological paradigm can affect the evolution of within-group wage inequality in a way that is consistent with these facts.

9.3.2.1   GPT and the Adaptability Premium

Building on recent work by Violante (2002), Aghion, Howitt, and Violante (2002) argue that the diffusion of a new GPT raises within-group wage inequality pri-marily because the rise in the speed of embodied technical progress associated with the diffusion of the new GPT increases the market premium to those workers who adapt quickly to the leading-edge technology.

In terms of the preceding model, let us again assume that all workers have the same level of education but that once a new GPT has been discovered, only a fraction α of the total labor force can adapt quickly enough to the new technology so that they can work on looking for a new component that complements the GPT. The other workers that did not successfully adapt have no alternative but to work in manufacturing. Let ω_1^{Adapt} denote the productivity-adjusted wage rate of adaptable workers in phase 1 of the cycle, whereas ω_1 denotes the wage of nonadaptable workers. Labor market clearing implies

$$\alpha L = n$$

$$(1-\alpha)L = \tilde{x}(\omega_1)$$

and

$$L = \tilde{x}(\omega_2)$$

whereas research arbitrage for adaptable workers in phase 1 implies

$$\omega_1^{\text{Adapt}} = \lambda\gamma\tilde{\pi}(\omega_2)$$

Assume α is small enough to generate a positive adaptability premium:

$$\omega_1^{\text{Adapt}} > \omega_1$$

Up to this point in our argument we have just repeated the analysis of the previous section, replacing skilled and unskilled workers with adaptable and nonadaptable workers. A GPT raises the adaptability premium just the same way as it raises the skill premium. But there are two important differences between skill and adaptability. The first is that whereas we can measure a worker's skill level, albeit imperfectly, using years of schooling, we have no way of measuring a worker's adaptability. This inability means that no matter how we group workers in terms of observable characteristics, there will still be within-group variability in wages because of unobserved differences in adaptability.

The second difference between skill and adaptability is that to the extent that skill is associated with education, it is a persistent characteristic of a worker, especially a prime-age worker. Adaptability is not necessarily a persistent characteristic; it may be largely a matter of luck. Some people can catch on to one particular new technology but not to others. It is this random element of adaptability that makes our GPT-based explanation of within-group inequality consistent with rising wage instability.

To be more specific, take the extreme case in which each time a new technology arrives every worker has the same probability α of being adaptable to that new technology, regardless of whether he was or was not adaptable to any past technology. In that case, the variance of each worker's prospective wage prior to the arrival of a new GPT is equal to[6]

$$V = \alpha (1 - \alpha) \left(\omega_1^{\text{Adapt}} - \omega_1 \right)^2$$

which is increasing in γ and λ.

Thus the approach based on the notion of GPT can shed light not only on the observed evolution of the college premium (preceding subsection) but also on the increase in residual wage inequality. Furthermore, it does so in a way that can be made consistent with at least two puzzling facts: first, to the extent that residual wage inequality has to do with the stochastic nature of workers' adaptability to the newest vintage more than with innate ability, the rise in within-group inequality induced by the diffusion of a new GPT should primarily affect the transitory component of income, in line with the empirical work of Blundell and Preston (1999); second, the increase in residual wage inequality should be mirrored by a rise in individual lifetime wage instability as documented by Gottschalk and Moffitt (1994).

9.3.2.2 GPT and the Experience Premium

Another puzzle is that the return to experience has increased at the same time as the skill premium. Aghion, Howitt, and Violante (2002) again appeal to a GPT

---

6. Recall that if a random variable is equal to x_0 with probability p and x_1 with probability $1 - p$, then its variance is $p(1 - p) (x_1 - x_0)^2$. In this case, $p = \alpha$, $x_0 = \omega_1^{\text{Adapt}}$, and $x_1 = \omega_1$.

argument to explain this fact. Their explanation is that the pervasiveness of a GPT means that past experience can be more easily transferred by an adaptable worker who moves from one sector to another. This factor in turn increases the ex ante value of experience, that is, the experience premium.

More formally, using the summary presentation by Hornstein, Krusell, and Violante (2005), consider an overlapping-generations model with two-period-lived individuals. Each cohort of individuals, of measure one, works throughout its two periods of life. Technological progress produces innovations that multiply productivity by the factor $\gamma > 1$. In each period there are only two sectors, a new sector and an old sector. We denote the new sector by its age, namely 0, and similarly we denote the old sector by 1. Output in each sector i is

$$Y_i = A_i h_i^{1-\alpha}$$

where A_i is productivity and h_i is the effective labor input in sector i. We have

$$A_0 / A_1 = \gamma$$

Adaptability Constraint

All young workers can immediately adapt to the new technology and thus work in sector 0, each providing one unit of labor input; however, only a fraction σ of old workers can relocate to the new technology.

Learning Parameter

An old worker that does not relocate can provide $1 + \eta$ units of labor to sector 1, where the parameter η reflects on-the-job learning in what was the leading-edge sector when the worker was young.

Transferability Parameter

An individual who worked in the leading-edge last period and is moving to the new leading-edge this period can transfer some of the knowledge she acquired on the previous leading-edge. That is, every such worker can supply $1 + \tau\eta$ units of labor input to the new sector, where the transferability parameter τ measures the generality of the technology.

We thus have

$$h_0 = 1 + \sigma(1 + \tau\eta)$$
$$h_1 = (1 - \sigma)(1 + \eta)$$

That is, the labor input supplied to the new sector is the unit input from the unit mass of young workers plus the $1 + \tau\eta$ supplied by each of the σ adaptable old workers, while the labor input supplied to the old sector is the $1 + \eta$ supplied by each of the $1 - \sigma$ nonadaptable workers.

Assuming perfect competition, all wages equal their marginal products:

$$\omega_i = \frac{\partial Y_i}{\partial h_i}$$

where ω_i is the wage per unit of labor input in sector i. Thus

$$\frac{\omega_1}{\omega_0} = \gamma^{-1}\left(\frac{h_0}{h_1}\right)^\alpha = \gamma^{-1}\left(\frac{1+\sigma(1+\tau\eta)}{(1-\sigma)(1+\eta)}\right)^\alpha$$

The average wage of an old worker will be

$$\sigma(1+\tau n)\omega_0 + (1-\sigma)(1+\eta)\omega_1$$

because the fraction σ will earn ω_0 for each of their $1 + \tau\eta$ units of labor input supplied to sector 0 while the fraction $1 - \sigma$ earn ω_1 for each of their $1 + \eta$ units in sector 1. Since all young workers earn ω_0, the equilibrium experience premium, defined as the average wage of old workers relative to the average wage of young workers, is given by

$$x = \sigma(1+\tau\eta) + (1-\sigma)(1+\eta)\omega_1/\omega_0$$

which in turn is unambiguously increasing in τ. So the arrival of a new GPT, which increases the parameter τ of generality or transferability, will raise the experience premium of adaptable workers (first term on the right-hand side); it also has the indirect effect of raising the experience premium of nonadaptable workers, because by increasing the total supply of adaptable labor it reduces the wage of young workers.

9.4   Conclusion

In this chapter we have developed very simple models to capture the notion of general-purpose technologies and to analyze why the arrival of a new GPT can generate a productivity slowdown and at the same time an increase in between-group and within-group wage inequality as well as a surge in the experience premium. We can compare the analysis of wage inequality based on GPT to the alternative explanation based on market size and directed technical change that we developed in chapter 8. The advantage of the GPT explanation is fourfold. First, whereas the market-size explanation cannot explain the fall in the skill premium in the 1920s, when there was a rise in the relative supply of skills, the GPT explanation is consistent with this fact, since the 1920s was a period in which the GPT of electrification was entering the mature stage in which the wave of innovations was dying out and the technology was becoming more user-friendly, thereby generating less of a premium on skills needed to use it. Second, as we have seen, the GPT explanation is consistent with the productivity slow-down that took place when the skill premium started to rise in the 1970s. Third, the GPT explanation also accounts for the fact that the rise in within-group inequality starting in the last quarter of the 20th century mainly affected transitory income. And fourth, the GPT story provides an explanation for the observed rise in the experience premium.

9.5   Literature Notes

Although formal analysis of GPTs was not developed before 1992, the idea that long-run cycles may result from technological change goes back to Kondratieff (1925). For more recent evidence on long swings and Schumpeterian waves of innovation see Gordon (1999).

Many economic historians have studied episodes of major technological change. Here we refer the reader to the enlightening studies of Von Tunzelmann (1978) on the steam engine, David (1990) on the parallel between "the computer and the dynamo," and Lipsey and Bekar (1995) on "enabling technologies." Authors such as Freeman, Clark, and Soete (1982) and Freeman and Perez (1988) analyzed the notion of "technoeconomic paradigm," which, as Lipsey, Bekar, and Carlaw (1998) point out, is much broader than a GPT, as it refers to a systematic relationship among products, processes, and the organizations and institutions that coordinate economic activity.

Mokyr (1990) distinguishes between "micro inventions" (improving existing technologies and responding to economic incentives) and "macro inventions" (usually unrelated to incentives, emerging from radically new ideas, without obvious precedent) . These latter inventions are quite similar to new GPTs: both prevent growth from coming to a halt, both involve widespread complementarities, and both provide ground for supporting micro inventions. Lipsey, Bekar, and Carlaw (2005) provide a sweeping history of technological change based on the fundamental notion of the GPT.

The first theoretical analysis of GPTs was by Bresnahan and Trajtenberg (1995), who coined the phrase "general-purpose technology" and defined it as having three main features: pervasiveness, technological dynamism, and innovational complementarities. They argued that technologies have a treelike structure, with a few prime movers located at the top and all other technologies radiating out from them. Helpman and Trajtenberg (1998a, 1998b) extended the Bresnahan-Trajtenberg model by turning it into the first general-equilibrium GPT growth model. Aghion and Howitt (1998b) developed a Schumpeterian model of GPTs to explain the slowdowns and increase in wage inequality that follow the arrival of a new GPT. Schumpeterian waves of innovation also feature in the work of Jovanovic and Rob (1990) and Cheng and Dinopoulos (1992), where each fundamental innovation is followed by a sequence of increasingly more incremental innovations.

A main reference on GPTs is the book edited by Helpman (1998), which presents the main models and also applications to topics such as the effect of GPTs on factor markets (Harris's chapter), the rise in obsolescence of capital as a consequence of faster technological progress (Howitt's chapter), and the effects of GPTs on incentives for vertical integration (Bresnahan and Gambardella's chapter).

We also refer our readers to three chapters in the *Handbook of Economic Growth* (Aghion and Durlauf, 2005): (1) the chapter by Jovanovic and Rousseau on GPTs, which studies two of the most important examples in U.S. modern history, namely, electricity and information technology, especially regarding their dynamic effects on productivity and the skill premium; (2) the chapter by Hornstein, Krusell, and Violante, which discusses the impact of GPTs on wage inequality between and within educational groups; and (3) the chapter by Jorgenson, which analyzes the IT revolution in the light of growth accounting.

Problems

1. Explain intuitively how the arrival of a new GPT can generate a productivity slowdown and at the same time an increase in between-group and within-group wage inequality as well as a surge in the experience premium. Compare and contrast the analysis of wage inequality based on GPT to the alternative explanation based on market size and directed technical change developed in chapter 8.

2. ***Moore's law and learning by doing**

(This problem is adapted from Jovanovic and Rousseau 2002; it studies in a very stylized model the potential impact of a sector where costs decrease sharply—following Moore's law—as is the case in the IT sector.)

A final good is produced according to $Y = AL^{1-\alpha}K^{\alpha} = ALk^{\alpha}\left(k = \dfrac{K}{L}\right)$, where L is the labor force growing at a rate n, and K is a capital good. In this stylized model, the only capital is IT goods that (nonrealistically) do not depreciate and that benefit from knowledge spillover, so that the cost of production follows Moore's law: producing one additional unit of capital requires $\frac{1}{q} = \left(\frac{K}{B}\right)^{-\beta}$ units of final good. The two sectors are perfectly competitive, and firms do not internalize the spillover (so they take q as given). The final good is taken to be the numéraire.

Consumers have the following utility:

$$U = \int_0^\infty e^{-\rho t} c_t \, dt$$

a. What is the price of capital p? Prove that

$$\alpha A k^{\alpha-1} = rp - \frac{dp}{dt}$$

where r is the rate of interest.

b. Show that in steady state, $g_c = \frac{\alpha\beta}{1-\alpha-\beta} n$.

c. Let $z = \frac{K^{1-\alpha-\beta}}{L^{1-\alpha}}$. Show that $\dot{z} = -az + b$, where a and b are two constants to be determined. Solve for the transition path of K. Comment on the effect of α and β on the speed of convergence.

d. We introduce a second capital good X such that $Y = AL^{1-\alpha-\gamma}K^\alpha X^\gamma = ALk^\alpha x^\gamma$. The good X is produced one for one with the final good and depreciates at the rate δ. Show that the previous analysis is still valid as long as A is replaced by $A^* = \left(A\frac{\gamma}{r+\delta}\right)^{\frac{\gamma}{1-\gamma}}$ and α is replaced by $\alpha^* = \frac{\alpha}{1-\gamma}$.

3. **Endogenizing the growth rate

(In this exercise we extend the model presented in section 9.2.2.2 by endogenizing the growth rate and the slump in production.)

We consider a setup similar to the one presented in section 9.2.2.2. Time is discrete, and there is a unit mass of risk-neutral consumers (with discount rate β). A final good is produced according to $Y = A^{1-\alpha}x^\alpha L^{1-\alpha}$, where x is an intermediary input produced by a monopoly with one unit of final good. A is the quality of the intermediary input, and L is the amount of labor force working in the final-good sector. When a new intermediary input is invented, its quality is $\gamma > 1$ times the quality of the previous one (we assume that innovation is drastic).

In phase o, a GPT has just been invented, but the economy still uses the old technology (and so the old intermediary good), and research is conducted to discover the specific technology to implement the new GPT in the intermediate-good sector by the R&D departments of potential competitors to the current monopolist. If a competitor succeeds, he becomes the new monopolist, and the economy enters phase n; he succeeds with probability $\lambda_o n_o$ where n_o is the amount of labor hired in research by this company. The value λ_o is sufficiently small that the probability that two competitors will discover the new intermediate input simultaneously is negligible.

In phase n, the specific input has been invented, so the new technology is used. A new GPT may arrive at a Poisson rate μ.

We consider a steady-state equilibrium in the sense that $z_i = \frac{Z_{it}}{A_t}$ is constant (where Z can be consumption, wages, profits, or the value of a firm; $i = o$; n denotes which phase is the current one; and A_t is the technology used).

a. Prove that the normalized value of a firm v_i (not including the dividend of the current period) can be written as

$$v_o = \frac{(1-\alpha)\alpha^{\frac{1+\alpha}{1-\alpha}}(1-n_o)}{r + \lambda_o n_o}$$

$$v_n = \frac{(1-\alpha)\alpha^{\frac{1+\alpha}{1-\alpha}}}{r + \mu}\left(\frac{\mu(1-n_o)}{r+\lambda_o n_o} + 1\right)$$

where r is the interest rate.

b. Express the research-arbitrage equation.

c. Find n_o. Under what conditions on the parameters do your computations make sense? What are the effects of an increase of the rate of arrival of a GPT on the research of the appropriate intermediate good?

d. Show that the expected growth rate is given by

$$g_{co} = \lambda_1 n_1\left(\gamma\frac{1}{1-n_1} - 1\right)$$
$$g_{c2} = -\mu n_1$$

What is the average growth rate? Comment.

We now consider that μ is also endogenous. With n_n workers in research in phase n, there is a probability $\lambda_n n_n$ that a new GPT is discovered. However, because it is impossible to get any patent on the discovery of a GPT (as it requires the cooperation of many people), the government has to undertake this "fundamental" research. The only tax policy the government can have is a lump-sum tax (in phase n) on the workers in the final good sector; the only expense is to pay the people working in research in phase n.

e. Express n_o as a function of n_n.

f. Express u_n as a function of n_o, n_n. State the problem that is faced by the government; explain intuitively the trade-offs that it faced. (You should not try to explicitly solve for n_n.)

4. *Diffusion of a GPT in the economy

We consider a setup similar to the one described in section 9.2.2.2. The population is of size L, and there is monopolistic competition on a continuum of intermediate goods that are used to produce the final good according to $Y = \left(\int_0^1 A(i)^\alpha x(i)^\alpha di\right)^{1/\alpha}$, where $x(i)$ is the amount of intermediate good i.

Time is continuous. We will consider the arrival of a single GPT: initially for every sector $A(i) = 1$, two further innovations are required before a sector can use the new technology and get $A(i) = \gamma > 1$. First a template on which to experiment must be invented (which is the specificity of this model compared to the one described in section 9.2.2.2), then the intermediate good specific to this sector. We denote by n_1 the number of sectors in the second phase (when the first template has been discovered, but not the specific intermediate good, so that the productivity is still 1) and by n_2 the number of sectors in the third phase (when the specific good has been invented and the productivity is γ). When a sector is in the first phase, discovering the template is an exogenous process with a flow probability $\lambda_0 + \varphi(n_2)$, and the term $\varphi(n_2)$ increases with n_2 and illustrates the fact that a sector can copy the template of the sectors that already went through the last step, which will be easier when there are more of them. To invent the specific intermediate good, a sector (currently in phase 2) must employ N units of labor in R&D, and the specific intermediate good will then be invented with the flow probability λ (note that N is fixed here and we assume that all firms in phase 2 will find it profitable to invest in R&D).

a. Find the differential equations satisfied by n_1 and n_2:

$$\dot{n}_1 = \left[\lambda_0 + \varphi(n_2)\right](1 - n_1 - n_2) - \lambda_1 n_1$$

$$\dot{n}_2 = \lambda_1 n_1$$

b. Show that the production of a good in phase 0 or 1 is given by

$$x_i = \left(\frac{\alpha}{w}\right)^{\frac{1}{1-\alpha}} Y$$

and for a good in phase 2

$$x_i = \left(\frac{\alpha \gamma^\alpha}{w}\right)^{\frac{1}{1-\alpha}} Y$$

where w is the real wage.

c. Solve for w as a function of Y, n_1, and n_2.

d. Prove that aggregate output is given by

$$Y = (L - n_1 N)\left[1 + \left(\gamma^{\frac{\alpha}{1-\alpha}} - 1\right)n_2\right]^{\frac{1-\alpha}{\alpha}}$$

e. Explain intuitively why it is possible to get a delayed slump and how φ will affect this slump. Does this model give any interesting insight in addition to that of the baseline model on the impact of the discovery of the microchip on productivity in the economy?

5. **GPT and inequality

(This exercise follows Aghion, Howitt, and Violante 2002; it is a more detailed version of section 9.3.2.2.)

The setup is similar to the one described in section 9.3.2.2. People live and work for two periods (each generation has a mass of one), and there is a unique final good, which can be produced by different sectors (which can be understood as technology here). A sector lasts for only two periods, and there are two sectors at each period: a new sector (denoted by 0) and an old one (denoted by 1). Technological progress takes a labor-augmenting form: each time a new sector arises, it improves the productivity of the old one by a factor $(1 + \gamma)$ so that the productivity in sector 1 and 0 are related by $A_t^0 = (1 + \gamma)A_t^1 = A_t = (1 + \gamma)^t$. Note that the sector that is denoted as 0 this period will become sector 1 next period.

The labor market functions as in the model described in section 9.3.2.2. Young workers can work in any sector and provide one unit of effective labor; old workers can provide $1 + \eta$ units of effective labor (there is learning by doing) if they keep working with the same technology. If they work with the next technology they will provide $1 + \tau\eta$ if they can adapt but only 1 unit of effective labor if they cannot (a worker can adapt with a probability σ). They provide only 1 unit of labor to a more distant technology.

The difference with the chapter is that here we introduce physical capital. It is assumed to be sector and technology specific, so that it lasts for two periods with no depreciation between the two periods. However, owners of old capital can retool it so that it is used for one period only in the new sector (at the cost that only a fraction κ of the retooled capital can be used). Hence the production technologies in the two sectors are given by

$$Y_t^0 = K_t^\alpha \left(A_t x_t^0\right)^{1-\alpha} + (\kappa D_t)^\alpha \left(A_t \bar{x}_t^0\right)^{1-\alpha}$$

$$Y_t^1 = \left(K_{t-1} - D_t\right)^{\alpha}\left(A_{t-1}x_t^1\right)^{1-\alpha}$$

where K_t is capital installed at time t, D_t is the amount of old capital retooled, x_t^0 is the amount of effective labor used in sector 0 with newly installed capital, $\bar{x}_t^0$ is the amount of effective labor used in sector 0 with retooled capital, and x_t^1 is the amount of effective labor used in sector 1.

a. Explain in what sense an innovation with high κ and τ could be called a GPT.

b. Justify the following table:

	Sector 0	Sector 1
Wage of young worker	w_t^0	w_t^1
Wage of old worker coming from the previous sector 0	$(1 + \tau\eta)w_t^0$	$(1 + \eta)w_t^1$
Wage of old worker coming from the previous sector I	w_t^0	$(1 + \tau\eta)w_t^1$

c. Acquiring some capital at time t, a firm can use it for two periods, only in the new sector for the first period, but it may find it profitable to use it in both sectors in the second period. The only costs are the cost of the initial acquisition, the retooling cost, and labor costs. Profits are discounted at the rate $1 + r$.

For the rest of the problem, we focus on a steady-state equilibrium where the normalized variables $k = \dfrac{K_t}{A_t}$, $d = \dfrac{D_t}{A_t}$, $\omega^0 = \dfrac{w_t^0}{A_t}$, $\omega^1 = \dfrac{w_t^1}{A_t}$, and x_t^0, $\bar{x}_{t+1}^0$ and x_{t+1}^1 are constant. Solve for the firm problem in this case. In particular, show that

$$\frac{\omega^0}{\omega^1} = (1+\gamma)\max\left\{\left(\frac{x^0}{x^1}\right)^{-\alpha}, \kappa^{\frac{\alpha}{1-\alpha}}\right\}$$

d. Assuming that workers will try to maximize the expected value of their income (an old worker discovers if he can adapt at the beginning of his second period), and assuming that $(1 + \tau\eta)\omega^0 > (1 + \eta)\omega^1$, find the effective labor supply.

e. Prove that a steady-state equilibrium exists with

$$\frac{\omega^0}{\omega^1} = (1+\gamma)\max\left\{\left(\frac{(1-\sigma)(1+\eta)}{1+\sigma(1+\tau\eta)}\right)^{\alpha}, \kappa^{\frac{\alpha}{1-\alpha}}\right\}$$

f. Define experience inequality as the average wage of old workers divided by the wage of young workers, within-group inequality as the wage of adaptable old workers divided by the wage of nonadaptable workers, and overall inequality as the highest wage in the economy divided by the lowest wage. Comment on the effect of a GPT phase (with high τ and high κ) on these ratios. Provide the economic intuition.

10 Stages of Growth

10.1 Introduction

Countries tend to go through various stages of growth, in which the rate of growth, the sectoral composition of growth, and also the main driving forces of growth change. This chapter studies how growth evolves from one stage to another, in three different dimensions. First we study the transition from Malthusian stagnation to modern economic growth, associated with the Industrial Revolution. Next we study the transition from growth based on capital accumulation to more innovation-based growth. Finally, we study the transition from manufacturing to a service economy that has been taking place for the past century in leading economies.

10.2 From Stagnation to Growth

Sustained long-term economic growth at a positive rate is a fairly recent phenomenon in human history, most of it having occurred in the last 200 years. According to Maddison's (2001) estimates, per capita GDP in the world economy was no higher in the year 1000 than in the year 1, and only 53 percent higher in 1820 than in 1000, implying an average annual growth rate of only one-nineteenth of 1 percent over the latter 820-year period. Some time around 1820, the world growth rate started to rise, averaging just over one-half of 1 percent per year from 1820 to 1870, and peaking during what Maddison calls the "golden age," the period from 1950 to 1973, when it averaged 2.93 percent per year. By 2000 world per capita GDP had risen to more than $8^{1}/_{2}$ times its 1820 value.

There is now a substantial literature on *unified growth theory*, which attempts to build a growth model that applies not only to the modern era of sustained growth but also to the much longer period before the Industrial Revolution, when growth was negligible. A comprehensive survey of this literature can be found in Galor (2005). The following account is built on Hansen and Prescott (2002) and Ashraf and Galor (2008).

10.2.1 Malthusian Stagnation

10.2.1.1 Population and Per Capita Income

The basic ideas of unified growth theory come from Malthus (1798), who argued that long-run growth in living standards was impossible. The problem, according to Malthus, came from population growth and diminishing returns to labor.

Specifically, if per capita income were to rise substantially, then people would survive longer and have larger families, which would raise the population. But as population rose, per capita income would fall because more people would be working with a fixed amount of land. In the end, per capita income would fall back to where it was in the first place.

To see how this works in greater detail, consider an economy that is entirely agrarian, where aggregate output Y is just the output Y_a produced in agriculture using labor L_a and land X, according to the production function

$$Y_a = AX^\beta L_a^{1-\beta}, \qquad 0 < \beta < 1 \tag{10.1}$$

where for now we take the productivity parameter A as given. For simplicity of notation, suppose that $X = 1$. Suppose that everyone in the population supplies one unit of labor, so L_a is equal to the population size L. Then per capita income will be

$$y = Y/L = AL^{-\beta} \tag{10.2}$$

which goes up when productivity A increases but falls when population L increases.

The reason why population growth reduces per capita income is diminishing returns. That is, although the production function (10.1) exhibits constant returns to scale, in the sense that an equiproportional increase in both factors, land and labor, would have a proportional effect on output, leaving per capita income y unchanged, nevertheless an increase in population will have a less than proportional effect on output, because land is a fixed factor that cannot be increased along with labor.

Now, suppose that higher standards of living translate into a higher rate of population growth. More specifically, the growth rate of population depends on per capita income according to the function n:

$$\dot{L}/L = n(y) \tag{10.3}$$

where

$$n'(y) > 0$$

Suppose also that population growth has a fixed upper limit $n^{\max} > 0$ and that when people are poor enough it becomes negative:

$$n(y) \to n^{\max} > 0 \quad \text{as} \quad y \to \infty \quad \text{and}$$

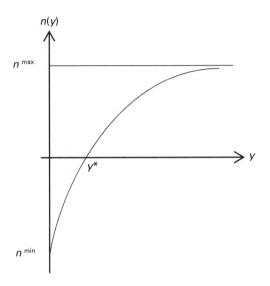

Figure 10.1
Population growth as an increasing function of per capita income

$$n(y) \to n^{\min} < 0 \quad \text{as} \quad y \to 0$$

Then, as figure 10.1 shows, there will be a unique level y^* of income per capita at which population growth is just equal to zero:

$$n(y^*) = 0 \qquad (10.4)$$

Using equation (10.2) to substitute for y in the population-growth equation (10.3) yields

$$\dot{L}/L = n\left(AL^{-\beta}\right)$$

Given the level A of productivity and some initial level L_0 of population, this differential equation can be solved for the entire future time path of population. It implies that there is a unique steady-state level of population L^* such that population growth will equal zero:

$$n\left(A(L^*)^{-\beta}\right) = 0 \qquad (10.5)$$

Combining equations (10.4) and (10.5) we see that

$$L^* = \left(A/y^*\right)^{1/\beta} \qquad (10.6)$$

Population will stabilize at the level L^* in the long run, no matter where it starts. That is, if initially L were to exceed L^*, then per capita income $y = AL^{-\beta}$ would be less than y^* and therefore L would fall back toward L^*. As long as $L > L^*$, the same force would be at work, so that L would in fact converge to L^* from above. By the same reasoning, if L were to start below L^*, then it would converge to L^* from below.

Now the fact that population converges to L^* in the long run implies that per capita income, which depends on population according to equation (10.2), will converge to the corresponding value y^*. In other words, per capita income will ultimately stagnate, not growing beyond the level y^*.

10.2.1.2   The Effects of a Productivity Increase

The Malthusian stagnation result was demonstrated on the assumption of a given level of total factor productivity. Could productivity growth save people from stagnation? As it turns out this is not so easy.

Level Increase

Consider first the case of a once-over increase in productivity to the new level $A' > A$. If the economy were initially at its steady-state level with

$$L = L^* = \left(A/y^*\right)^{1/\beta}$$

and

$$Y/L = y^*$$

then the productivity increase would at first raise per capita income, from y^* to

$$A'L^{-\beta} > AL^{-\beta} = y^*$$

But this short-run increase in per capita income would start the Malthusian process at work again. Because per capita income is now above the level y^*, the population will start to rise, and this increase will start to bring per capita income back down again. This process will continue until per capita income has fallen back to the level that just eliminates population growth—that is, until it has fallen back to its initial level y^*.

Note that although the increase in productivity will have no lasting effect on income per capita, it will have a lasting effect on the size of population. Indeed, it is because of this lasting effect on population size that there is no lasting effect on per capita income. More formally, equation (10.6) indicates that the steady-state population size L^* is an increasing function of productivity. Galor (2005) reviews a great deal of historical evidence confirming this prediction of Malthusian theory, evidence that more technologically advanced countries and regions, as well as those with a higher quality of land, did not have a much higher standard of living but did have a much higher population density, as compared to those with less advanced technology and inferior land quality.

Steady Productivity Growth

The analysis has so far taken the productivity parameter as being an exogenous constant, perhaps subject to occasional increases but not steady growth. However, there was considerable growth in the world's stock of technological knowledge prior to the Industrial Revolution, not as a result of large-scale organized R&D of the sort we are familiar with in advanced countries nowadays but as the result of a combination of the cumulative buildup of lessons learned from experience, creative experimentation by scholars, the need to deal with environmental crises, and the natural human propensity to tinker with things. It is generally agreed, however, that technological progress was a slow process in the Malthusian era. Although there were probably periods in which great discoveries were made (fire, the wheel, the windmill, . . .), there were also long periods of relative technological stagnation.

Suppose we take this factor into account by allowing for some steady exogenous drift in the productivity parameter A. Then our conclusions would be not quite as pessimistic as under Malthusian theory but almost. Specifically, suppose that

$$\dot{A}/A = g, \quad \text{a positive constant}$$

Then according to equation (10.2) the growth rate of per capita income will be[1]

$$\dot{y}/y = \dot{A}/A - \beta\dot{L}/L = g - \beta n(y) \tag{10.7}$$

This is a stable differential equation that now converges not to y^* but to a somewhat higher level $\tilde{y}$, the level that satisfies the stationary condition

$$n(\tilde{y}) = g/\beta \tag{10.8}$$

---

1. It follows immediately from equation (10.2) that

$$\ln y = \ln A - \beta \ln L$$

Taking derivatives of both sides of this equation with respect to time produces equation (10.7).

If g is close to zero, then $\tilde{y}$ will be close to the level y^* of Malthusian theory. As long as[2] $g < \beta n^{\max}$, which undoubtedly was true for almost all of human history, technological progress will still not produce sustained growth in per capita income. Instead, it will just affect the level at which stagnation occurs.

10.2.2   The Transition to Growth

10.2.2.1   Agriculture and Manufacturing

The long period of stagnation ended around the time of the Industrial Revolution, when some countries started reallocating resources away from agriculture and toward manufacturing. To see how this shift might happen, suppose that there is a latent manufacturing technology which has not yet been economically viable, but which, as we shall see, will become viable once technology has progressed enough.

Manufacturing output Y_m is produced by labor alone, according to

$$Y_m = AL_m \tag{10.9}$$

The productivity parameter A is assumed for simplicity to be the same as in agriculture. Total output is now

$$Y = Y_a + Y_m$$

and the two sectors will compete for the given labor supply L

$$L_a + L_m = L \tag{10.10}$$

The two production functions (10.9) and (10.1) are the same except that one uses land while the other does not. So whether the manufacturing technology is used or not will depend on how much land there is relative to labor. When population is very small, there is a lot of land for each person to work with, so no one will produce using the manufacturing technology because it does not take advantage of this abundant factor. But if population were to rise beyond a critical level, then it would be profitable to activate the manufacturing technology in order to escape the land constraint.

10.2.2.2   Wages and Industrialization

To see how this process works, suppose the economy is in a Malthusian equilibrium with a rate of technological progress g, which we can suppose is very close

---

2. If $g > \beta n^{\max}$, then population growth will not be able to undo the effect of productivity increases, because equation (10.7) indicates that the growth rate of per capita income cannot fall below $g - \beta n^{\max} > 0$.

to zero, so per capita income has stagnated at the level $\tilde{y}$. According to equation (10.8), population will be growing at the rate g/β. The real wage rate will equal the marginal product of labor

$$\tilde{w} = (1 - \beta)AL^{-\beta} = (1 - \beta)\tilde{y}$$

which will be constant over time.

Someone wanting to hire labor to produce output using the manufacturing technology would earn a profit equal to

$$\Pi_m = Y_m - \tilde{w}L_m = (A - \tilde{w})L_m$$

So as long as the stock of knowledge is relatively low, A will be less than $\tilde{w}$, and it will not be profitable to use the manufacturing technology. But if A continues to grow, then at some point it will surpass $\tilde{w}$, which remains constant in the Malthusian equilibrium. At this point it becomes profitable to activate the manufacturing sector, and industrialization begins.

Once manufacturing has started, free entry guarantees that the profit rate Π_m will be zero, so the wage rate will equal the productivity parameter

$$w = A$$

The agricultural sector will also have to pay that wage, so its profit (excluding the rent to the fixed factor land) will be

$$\Pi_a = AL_a^{1-\beta} - wL_a = A\left(L_a^{1-\beta} - L_a\right)$$

Employment in the agricultural sector L_a will then be chosen to maximize profit, and the first-order condition determining this profit-maximizing choice is

$$\frac{\partial \Pi_a}{\partial L_a} = A\left[(1 - \beta)L_a^{-\beta} - 1\right] = 0$$

which solves for the constant value

$$L_a = (1 - \beta)^{1/\beta}$$

From this point on, while agricultural labor remains constant, manufacturing labor will equal

$$L_m = L - L_a$$

which will continue to rise over time, since L_a is constant and the total labor supply L will continue to grow, starting at the Malthusian rate $n(\tilde{y})$.

10.2.2.3 Sustainable Growth

Not only will population continue to grow, but it will accelerate, and the rate of economic growth $\dot{y}/y$ will rise from its previous rate of zero to a new steady-state value equal to the rate of technological progress g. To see how this process works, notice that income per capita is now

$$y = Y/L = A(L - L_a)/L + AL_a^{1-\beta}/L$$

Over time the agricultural share will approach zero, since L_a is constant and L becomes infinitely large. Income per capita will thus become approximately equal to A and therefore will grow without bound, approaching the growth rate g of productivity. And the population growth rate will approach its upper limit $n^{\max}$.

This transition from stagnation to growth takes place because the gradual accretion of knowledge has allowed people to escape from the limitations of land, especially from the diminishing marginal returns to labor applied to fixed land which kept wages and per capita income from taking off. Once freed from land, people are no longer subject to diminishing returns, and there is nothing to choke off growth in per capita income.

10.2.3 Commentary

The preceding analysis focuses on industrialization as the key to making the transition from stagnation to growth. Other theories focus on human capital accumulation. For example, Galor and Weil (2000) construct an overlapping-generations model in which people derive utility from consumption and from the quantity and quality of children, where "quality" means the amount of human capital invested in the child.

In their model, the rate of technological progress is assumed to depend on the size of population, through a scale effect, and on the amount of human capital per person. The scale effect triggers the escape from Malthusian stagnation by gradually raising the rate of technological progress. At first the resulting increase in productivity growth leads to a population explosion, but at some point there is a *demographic transition* that brings population growth under control without per capita income having to fall. This demographic transition comes from a tilting of the quality-quantity trade-off; that is, a faster rate of technological progress raises the rate of return to human capital investment because human capital is most valuable during periods of rapid technological change.[3] People respond to

---

3. See our discussion of the Nelson and Phelps (1966) view of human capital in chapter 13.

the increased skill premium by substituting more investment in quality for increased quantity of children.

The Galor-Weil theory has the advantage of predicting not only the Industrial Revolution but also the demographic revolution that took place around the same time; population growth did indeed start to fall. However, Mokyr and Voth (2006) have questioned this line of analysis on the grounds that there is little evidence that Europe was in a Malthusian trap in 1700. Population and per capita income had been rising together in many regions even though Malthusian theory implies that a rise in population should depress per capita income. Likewise, the population in England was roughly constant between 1700 and 1750, long before the Industrial Revolution that was supposed to have been triggered by the scale effect of a large population. Nor can historians find evidence of the skill premium that the human capital theory predicts should have induced the tilting of the quality-quantity trade-off that caused the demographic transition.

Mokyr and Voth suggest alternative factors that might have kept output from taking off before the Industrial Revolution. One is the development of a scientific culture among a critical mass of craftsmen and business people, the factor stressed by Howitt and Mayer-Foulkes (2005). Another is the set of institutions that protect property rights. Suppose, for example, that anyone could steal another person's capital at a cost of σ. Then no one would accumulate capital beyond the level $K = \sigma$ because to do so would result in losing everything to a thief. In an AK model, that limit on capital accumulation would bring growth to an end until some institutional change raised the cost σ of stealing someone else's property.

The evidence will probably never settle the dispute among these competing theories of the transition from stagnation to growth. For, as Mokyr and Voth admit, there was only one Industrial Revolution, and one data point is just not enough. As a result, the Mokyr-Voth critique of Malthusian theories is not decisive, especially when we take into account that there is two-way causation between population and income, and that there may be long lags involved in these causal relationships. For example, the fact that population and per capita income were rising simultaneously in many regions of Europe before the Industrial Revolution might have been the joint effect of a gradual improvement in technology; perhaps the rise in per capita income would have been reversed eventually if the Industrial Revolution had not taken place.

10.3   From Capital Accumulation to Innovation

When growth first starts, it is driven by capital accumulation, which accommodates the gradual increase in knowledge without being subject to the diminishing returns that accrue to land. But then innovation takes over more and more. Figure 10.2 from Ha and Howitt (2006) shows that over the second half of the 20th century the contribution of capital accumulation (physical and human) to growth of per capita income has fallen from about one percentage point per year to about one half. This finding has important consequences for the current debate over the sources of growth (see chapter 5). As time passes, it seems that growth is becoming more and more knowledge based, driven less by the accumulation of human and physical capital and more by innovation. This section, drawn mainly from Ha (2002), analyzes the reasons for this particular transformation.

10.3.1   Human Capital Accumulation

Human capital accumulation in the form of education cannot contribute indefinitely to growth because, unlike physical capital, it is embodied in people, and people are mortal. When they die, so does their human capital. Consider, for example, a stationary population in which people devote the fraction u of their time to education. Over time the education of young people will raise years of

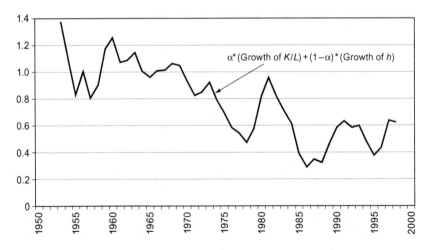

Figure 10.2
U.S. factor accumulation rate, 1950–2000 (Ha and Howitt 2006)

schooling per person s at the rate u. But if the fraction δ of people per year die, and those who die have on average s years of schooling, then these deaths will reduce s at the rate δs. The net effect of education and death is to make average years of schooling change at the rate

$$\dot{s} = u - \delta s$$

which means that average years of schooling will go to a steady-state value (where $\dot{s} = 0$) of

$$s^* = u/\delta$$

According to Mincer (1974), human capital per person h can be represented as an exponentially increasing function of years of schooling

$$h = e^{\theta s}$$

which means that human capital per person will approach a steady-state level

$$h^* = e^{\theta u/\delta}$$

Increasing the fraction of time spent on education will raise this steady-state level of human capital per person, but it cannot result in a permanent increase in the growth rate of human capital per person. Therefore, at some point the direct contribution of human capital accumulation to economic growth must come to an end.

This is not to say, however, that human capital eventually ceases to be important for economic growth. On the contrary, because R&D is a human-capital-intensive activity, therefore as growth becomes more and more dependent on innovation, it also becomes more and more dependent on the level (and quality!) of educational attainment per person.

10.3.2 Physical Capital Accumulation

In contrast to human capital, there is no limit to how much physical capital a person can accumulate. Yet even physical capital accumulation is becoming less important than innovation as a source of growth. To understand this trend we reproduce the hybrid neoclassical-Schumpeterian model that includes both capital accumulation and innovation, which we developed in chapter 5, and we analyze its dynamic evolution.

The basic idea of this analysis is that as an economy develops following industrialization, it goes through a process of "capital deepening," in which the emergent capital-intensive manufacturing technology becomes equipped. As we saw in chapter 5, a higher productivity-adjusted capital stock creates a scale effect that encourages more innovation, because a successful innovator gets a bigger reward in a wealthier economy. But as in the neoclassical model, the higher productivity-adjusted capital stock lowers the marginal product of capital, which weakens the impact of capital accumulation on growth. So over time the contribution of capital accumulation to growth decreases while the contribution of innovation increases.

10.3.2.1   The Hybrid Model

The final good in this hybrid model is produced under perfect competition according to the production function

$$Y_t = L^{1-\alpha} \int_0^1 A_{it}^{1-\alpha} x_{it}^{\alpha} di, \qquad 0 < \alpha < 1$$

where each x_{it} is the flow of intermediate input i. For simplicity, we set $L = 1$. Each intermediate input is produced according to the production function

$$x_{it} = K_{it}$$

where K_{it} is the amount of capital used as input. In equilibrium, each sector will produce at a level x_{it} that is proportional to the productivity parameter A_{it}. When we put these equilibrium values into the production function, we get a neoclassical aggregate production function of the form

$$Y_t = \left(A_t L\right)^{1-\alpha} K_t^{\alpha}$$

where K_t is the aggregate capital stock and the labor-augmenting productivity variable A_t is just the average across all sectors of the individual productivity parameters: $A_t = \int_0^1 A_{it} di$.

As we saw in chapter 5, there are three fundamental equations driving the economy. First, there is the neoclassical law of motion for the capital stock:

$$K_{t+1} - K_t = sY_t - \delta K_t \tag{K}$$

where s is the saving rate and δ is the depreciation rate.

Next, there is the productivity-growth equation:

$$\frac{A_{t+1} - A_t}{A_t} = g_t = (\gamma - 1)\phi(n_t) \tag{G}$$

where γ is the size of innovations, n_t is the productivity-adjusted research expenditure in each sector, and $\phi(n_t)$ is the innovation rate.

The final equation is the research-arbitrage condition:

$$\phi'(n_t)\tilde{\pi}(\kappa_t) = 1 \tag{R}$$

where $\kappa_t = K_t/A_t$ is the productivity-adjusted capital stock and $\tilde{\pi}(\kappa_t)$ is each monopolist's productivity-adjusted profit, which is increasing in κ_t. The research-arbitrage equation makes n_t an increasing function of κ_t, so the productivity-growth rate determined by equation (G) is also an increasing function of κ_t.

Each period, given the historically predetermined value of κ_t, the research-arbitrage equation (R) determines the research intensity n_t; then K_t and A_t change according to equations (K) and (G), which then determine κ_{t+1}; and the process is repeated next period, ad infinitum.

The steady state of the model is a situation in which all three variables g, n, and κ are constant over time. The steady-state conditions are

$$g = (\gamma - 1)\phi(n)$$

$$\phi'(n)\tilde{\pi}(\kappa) = 1$$

$$s\kappa^{\alpha-1} = \delta + g$$

The first two are just steady-state versions of equations (G) and (R), while the last one is the familiar neoclassical condition that requires the growth rate of capital per efficiency unit of labor (that is, the growth rate of κ) to be constant.

Now consider an economy that is at an early stage of growth, with an adjusted capital stock κ_0 far below its steady-state value. In that economy, capital accumulation is very rapid while productivity growth is slow. But as κ_t rises up to its steady-state value, the contribution of capital accumulation to growth will slow down while innovation and productivity growth speed up.

More specifically, we can write the aggregate production function as

$$Y_t = A_t\kappa_t^{\alpha}$$

so if G_t is the growth rate of output, then we can express the growth factor $1 + G_t$ as the product of two factors:

$$1 + G_t = \frac{Y_{t+1}}{Y_t} = \left(\frac{A_{t+1}}{A_t}\right)\left(\frac{\kappa_{t+1}}{\kappa_t}\right)^{\alpha}$$

where the first factor represents the contribution of innovation and productivity growth, while the second factor represents the contribution of capital deepening. Over time, as κ_t approaches its steady state, the second factor falls to unity, as in the neoclassical model, so that in the steady state, capital deepening contributes nothing to growth. And as this is happening, the first factor will be increasing over time because

$$\frac{A_{t+1}}{A_t} = 1 + g_t = 1 + (\gamma - 1)\phi(n_t)$$

and, as we have seen, n_t increases as κ_t rises to its steady-state value. Thus in the steady state, innovation and productivity growth contribute even more to economic growth, both absolutely and relative to capital accumulation, than they did in the earlier stages of growth.

10.4   From Manufacturing to Services

Another dramatic structural change that takes place in an advanced economy is the shift from manufacturing to services. This trend predates the outsourcing movement that many have blamed for the loss of manufacturing jobs in the United States, and it has taken place to a similar extent in all advanced economies, not just the United States. This fact suggests that there is something more fundamental at work than U.S. trade policies. This section shows how we can account for the movement using a model of nonbalanced growth developed by Acemoglu and Guerrieri (2006).

The key feature of services sectors that we focus on is that they are not as capital intensive as manufacturing sectors. To simplify the analysis, we make the extreme assumption that whereas manufacturing requires both labor and capital, services require only labor. Specifically, the output of the manufacturing sector is

$$Y_M = AK^\alpha L_M^{1-\alpha}$$

and the output of the service sector is[4]

$$Y_S = AL_S$$

where K is the economy's capital stock; and the labor inputs must add up to the population L:

$$L_M + L_S = L$$

---

4. Note that we are not assuming differential technological progress in the two sectors as was done, for example, by Baumol (1967). Although it may be true that productivity growth is slower in services, it is very hard to know for certain whether it is or not given the difficulty of measuring the output of services.

We also assume that final output is produced using services and manufactures according to a production function in which they are complementary inputs. Indeed, we make the extreme assumption that services and manufactures must be combined in fixed proportions:

$$Y = \min\{Y_M, Y_S\}$$

Then given the stock of capital K, the level of productivity A, and the size of the labor force L, labor will be allocated across the two sectors in such a way as to result in equal output:

$$K^\alpha L_M^{1-\alpha} = (L - L_M)$$

Define the economy-wide capital-labor ratio as

$$k = K/L$$

and the manufacturing share of employment as

$$\lambda = L_M/L$$

Then we have

$$k^\alpha \lambda^{1-\alpha} = 1 - \lambda$$

Denote by

$$\tilde{\lambda}(k)$$

the solution to this equation. As the economy accumulates more capital per worker, the manufacturing share of employment falls:

$$d\tilde{\lambda}/dk < 0$$

Indeed, as the capital-labor ratio goes to infinity, manufacturing employment falls to zero:

$$\lim_{k \to \infty} \tilde{\lambda}(k) = 0$$

Aggregate output can then be written as

$$Y = AL\left[1 - \tilde{\lambda}(k)\right]$$

Suppose again that saving is a fixed proportion of output. Then,

$$\dot{K} = sAL\left[1 - \tilde{\lambda}(k)\right] - \delta K$$

from which we have

$$\dot{k} = sA\left[1 - \tilde{\lambda}(k)\right] - (\delta + n)k$$

Assume that the long-run growth rate g of A is positive. Then in the long run k will indeed rise without bound, manufacturing share of employment will fall to zero, and per capita income will approach

$$Y/L = AL\left[1 - \tilde{\lambda}(\infty)\right]/L = A$$

which grows at the rate g.

10.5   Conclusion

In this chapter we first presented the Malthusian model where agricultural output is produced with labor and a fixed factor, and where labor supply (population) in turn evolves over time at a rate that depends upon the current level of output per capita. Population increases if current per capita GDP is high, and it decreases if current per capita GDP is low. We saw that this model predicts long-term stagnation, with per capita GDP converging to the steady-state level at which population does not increase or decrease. Then we added an AK manufacturing technology to this model, and we saw that when the knowledge parameter becomes sufficiently high, people start moving from agriculture to manufacturing, at which point the economy escapes from stagnation.

In the subsequent sections, we modeled the transition from capital accumulation to innovation, and then the transition from manufacturing to services. One important limitation of these models, which makes them all appear somewhat mechanical, is that they do not capture the idea that the transition from one production mode to another may require the introduction of new institutions: new ways of regulating or deregulating markets, new financial systems, new ways of organizing firms. Private incentives to move from old to new institutions will typically not coincide with the socially optimal or growth-maximizing paths. This important issue of institutional transition will be taken up in chapter 11.

10.6   Literature Notes

Primary references on the transition process from Malthusian stagnation to growth are the papers by Galor and Weil (2000), Hansen and Prescott (2002), and Ashraf and Galor (2008).

While Galor and Weil emphasize demographic transition as a key feature of the Industrial Revolution, Mokyr and Voth (2006) stress the importance of both the development of a scientific culture among a critical mass of craftsmen and business people, and the setting up of institutions that protect property rights.

The transition from capital accumulation to innovation has been analyzed by Ha (2002). And the transition from manufacturing to services is modeled by Acemoglu and Guerrieri (2006).

For exhaustive references and comprehensive accounts of the literature and debates on the subject, we refer the reader to the *Handbook of Economic Growth* surveys by Galor (2005) and Mokyr (2005).

Problems

1. Present the mechanisms that related population growth and income per capita in the Malthusian model and how they imply long-run stagnation of income per capita. Can technological progress produce sustained growth in per capita income in the setting? Explain.

2. ***Skilled labor and manufacturing**

Consider the following version of the economy studied in sections 10.2.1 and 10.2.2.

The number of births per period is $B = b(y)L$ where y is per capita income, L is population, $b'(y) > 0$, $b(y) \to \bar{b}$ as $y \to \infty$, and $b(y) \to 0$ as $y \to 0$.

Each person has a probability $d > 0$ of dying per period.

Output is produced using the agricultural technology

$$Y^A = A(t)L^{1-\beta}, \qquad \beta \in (0,1)$$

where A is a productivity parameter with exogenous growth rate g.

a. Solve for the steady state of this economy assuming $g > \beta(\bar{b} - d)$. Is it stable? Why is the assumption necessary? How does faster productivity growth affect the steady state?

b. Now suppose there is also a manufacturing technology:

$$Y^M = A(t)S$$

where S is the skilled labor supply. Each agent chooses at birth whether to become a skilled worker and work in manufacturing or an unskilled worker and work in agriculture. To become skilled an agent must pay a fixed cost F. Suppose the economy faces an exogenously given constant interest rate r.

Explain why no agents born at time t will choose to become skilled if

$$\int_t^\infty w^M(\tau)e^{-(r+\lambda)(\tau-t)}d\tau - F < \int_t^\infty w^A(\tau)e^{-(r+\lambda)(\tau-t)}d\tau$$

where w^M is the manufacturing wage and w^A is the wage in agriculture.

c. Assume $g = 0$. Find a condition on A under which all agents will choose to work in agriculture.

d. Does there exist a level of A such that all agents will choose to become skilled?

3. **Property rights**

Suppose each agent has access to an AK production technology, $Y_j = AK_j$, where Y is output, K is capital, A is an economy-wide productivity parameter, with growth rate λ, and j indexes agents.

Suppose, $\dot{K}_j = Y_j - C_j - \delta K_j - G$, where C is consumption and G is government expenditure per capita.

Assume that any agent can expropriate any other agent's capital at cost σ.

a. What will the equilibrium values and growth rates of K_j and C_j be?

b. Now suppose that σ depends on the level of government expenditure; for instance, it could be a measure of the extent of property rights or law enforcement. Assume $\sigma = \sqrt{G}$. What level of G will a benevolent government choose?

c. Assuming the existence of a benevolent government, what are the steady state growth rates of K_j and C_j?

4. **Physical capital and innovation**

Consider an economy similar to that in section 10.3.2 except that the final good is produced using physical capital, in addition to labor and intermediate inputs, according to

$$Y_t = \int_0^1 x_{it}^\alpha K_t^\beta A_{it}^{1-\alpha-\beta} L^{1-\alpha-\beta} di \qquad 0 < \alpha, \beta < 1$$

where x is intermediate input use, K is capital use, and A measures the quality of the intermediate input. The final good is used on a one-for-one basis for consumption, physical-capital investment, and intermediate-input production. Intermediate inputs are produced by monopolists. To invent an intermediate of quality $A_{it} = \gamma A_{it-1}$ with probability μ_t an entrepreneur must spend

$$N_{it} = \gamma A_{it-1} \left(\frac{\mu_t^2}{2} + \delta \mu_t \right)$$

As usual we normalize the total labor force to one.

a. Taking the amount of capital used in final-good production as given, solve for x_{it} and the monopolist's profits π_{it} in equilibrium.

b. Show that the equilibrium probability of innovation in sector i is

$$\mu_{it} = \lambda \left(\frac{K_t}{A_{it}} \right)^{\frac{\beta}{1-\alpha}} - \delta$$

where λ is a constant you should determine. How does the capital stock affect the growth rate? Will the duality of intermediate inputs tend to converge over time?

c. Suppose the economy faces an exogenously determined capital rental rate r. Show that

$$\frac{r}{\beta} = \int_0^1 \alpha^{\frac{2\alpha}{1-\alpha}} \left(\frac{A_{it}}{k_t} \right)^{\frac{1-\alpha-\beta}{1-\alpha}} di$$

d. Solve for μ_t in a symmetric equilibrium in which $A_{it} = A_t \forall i$.

e. Suggest modeling techniques that could be used to make r endogenous.

5. *Agricultural productivity and industrialization (based on Matsuyama 1992)

This question considers the relationship between agricultural productivity and industrialization.

Suppose there are two sectors, agriculture and manufacturing, and a single factor of production, labor. Output in manufacturing is given by

$$Y^M(t) = A(t)\left[L^M(t)\right]^\alpha$$

while output in agriculture is given by

$$Y^A(t) = B\left[L^A(t)\right]^\beta$$

where $\alpha, \beta \in (0, 1)$ and manufacturing productivity A may vary over time. Suppose the total labor force is constant and normalized to one and that the labor market is competitive.

a. Solve for $L^M(t)$ and $L^A(t)$ as a function of $A(t)$ and the relative price of the manufacturing good $p(t)$.

b. Suppose intratemporal consumption preferences are defined over the consumption aggregate

$$C(t) = \left[C^A(t) - \overline{C}\right]^\eta \left[C^M(t)\right]^{1-\eta}$$

where $\eta \in (0, 1)$ and $\overline{C} > 0$. Show that this implies

$$(1-\eta)\left[C^A(t) - \overline{C}\right] = \eta p(t) C^M(t)$$

c. Use market clearing and the preceding results to show

$$\frac{\overline{C}}{B} = \left[1 - L^M(t)\right]^\beta - \frac{\eta}{1-\eta}\frac{\beta}{\alpha}\left[1 - L^M(t)\right]^{\beta-1} L^M(t)$$

d. Explain why there must be a unique solution for $L^M(t)$.

e. How does the proportion of labor allocated to manufacturing change as agricultural productivity increases?

f. Suppose $\dot{A}(t) = Y^M(t)$. Solve for the growth rate of $C(t)$, and discuss how it depends on agricultural productivity. Provide some intuition for this result.

6. ****Nonbalanced growth (based on Kongsamut, Rebelo, and Xie 2001)**

Consider an economy with three sectors—agriculture (A), manufacturing (M), and services (S). At time t, output in the three sectors is given by

$$A_t = B_A L_t^A X_t$$
$$M_t = B_M L_t^M X_t$$
$$S_t = B_S L_t^S X_t$$

where L^J denotes labor allocated to sector $J = A, M, S$, and X is a productivity parameter with exogenous growth rate g. The total labor force is constant and is normalized to one, and all goods are produced under perfect competition.

A representative consumer has preferences such that at time t she seeks to maximize

$$U_t = \left(A_t - \overline{A}\right)^\beta M_t^\gamma \left(S_t + \overline{S}\right)^\theta$$

where $\overline{A} > 0$, $\overline{S} > 0$, and $\beta + \gamma + \theta = 1$.

a. Use labor market clearing to solve for the equilibrium prices of agriculture p_A and services p_S relative to manufacturing.

b. Use consumer optimization to show

$$\frac{p_A\left(A_t - \bar{A}\right)}{\beta} = \frac{M_t}{\gamma} = \frac{p_S\left(S_t + \bar{S}\right)}{\theta}$$

c. Define a balanced growth path as an equilibrium in which the growth rates of A_t, M_t, and S_t are constant and equal. Show that such an equilibrium does not exist.

d. Define a generalized balanced growth path as an equilibrium in which the growth rates of M_t and $p_A A_t + p_S S_t$ are constant. Show that such an equilibrium exists if and only if $B_S \bar{A} = B_A \bar{S}$.

e. Solve for $\dot{L}_t^A$, $\dot{L}_t^M$, and $\dot{L}_t^S$ in equilibrium. Discuss.

11 Institutions and Nonconvergence Traps[1]

11.1 Introduction

Do institutions matter for growth? A common prediction of the growth models
with endogenous innovation in the preceding chapters is that they do! For example,
the analysis in chapters 3 and 4 would suggest that long-run growth would be best
enhanced by some combination of good property-rights protection (to protect the
rents of innovators against imitation) and a good education system (to increase the
efficiency of R&D activities and the supply of skilled manufacturing labor). Our
discussion of convergence clubs in chapter 7 predicts that the same policies or
institutions would also increase a country's ability to join the convergence club.

That institutions should influence economic development had already been convincingly argued by economic historians, in particular by Douglas North (see North
and Thomas 1973; North 1990) and subsequently by Engerman and Sokoloff (1997,
2000). Thus, North and Thomas explain how the institutional changes brought about
by trade and commercial activities led to the Glorious Revolution in 17th-century
England. And North (1990) argues that the development of sedimentary agriculture
followed the Neolithic revolution, which introduced communal property rights.

North (1990) defines institutions as the "rules or constraints on individual
behavior" which in turn may be either formal (political constitutions, electoral
rules, formal constraints on the executive, . . .) or informal (culture, social
norms, . . .). Greif (1994, 2006) extends the notion of institution so that it encompasses not only the rules of the game as in North, but more generally all forms
of economic organizations and finally the set of beliefs that shape the interaction
between economic agents.

Two research teams over the past 10 years have made pathbreaking contributions showing the importance of institutions for economic development using
historical cross-country data. A first team (see La Porta et al. 1998, 1999; Djankov
et al. 2003; Glaeser et al. 2004) has emphasized legal origins as a determinant of
institutions such as investors' rights, debt collection systems, or entry regulations.
A second team (see Acemoglu, Johnson, and Robinson 2001, 2002; Acemoglu
and Johnson 2005) has focused on colonial origins as a determinant of a country's
institutions. These two lines of research have spurred heated debates, which we
shall reflect upon in section 11.2.

Should we recommend the same institutions to all countries? The endogenous
growth models developed in previous chapters suggest we should. In particular,
they call for better property-rights protection and higher education investment

---

1. This chapter was jointly written with Erik Meyersson.

in all countries under all latitudes. However, in *Economic Backwardness in Historical Perspective*, Gerschenkron (1962) argues that relatively backward economies could more rapidly catch up with more advanced countries by introducing "appropriate institutions" that are growth-enhancing at an early stage of development but may cease to be so at a later stage.

Thus countries like Japan or Korea managed to achieve very high growth rates from 1945 up until the 1990s with institutional arrangements involving long-term relationships between firms and banks, the predominance of large conglomerates, and strong government intervention through export promotion and subsidized loans to the enterprise sector. These policies in turn depart significantly from the more market-based and laissez-faire institutional model pioneered by the United States and currently advocated for all countries as part of the so-called Washington consensus.

In section 11.3 we reconcile new growth theories with Gerschenkron's views, thereby addressing the concern that growth theory can only deliver universal, one-size-fits-all policy prescriptions (legal reforms to enforce property rights, investment climate favorable to entrepreneurship, education, macrostability, . . .) to maximize the growth prospects of a country or sector, and does not apprehend structural transformations in the process of convergence. More specifically, we analyze some general implications of the notion of "distance-dependent" appropriate institutions, by which we mean institutions that are growth enhancing only for countries at a certain stage of technological development. Technological development in turn is measured by a country's current productivity divided by current frontier productivity (the variable a in chapter 7). In particular, we show how the failure to adapt institutions to technological development may generate nonconvergence traps whereby a country's average productivity (or per capita GDP) remains bounded away from frontier levels. The section is organized as follows: Section 11.3.1 provides empirical evidence to motivate the notion of appropriate institution. Section 11.3.2 then develops a simple model of appropriate institutions and growth, and illustrates the notion of nonconvergence traps for countries that fail to adapt their institutions and policies as they develop.

11.2   Do Institutions Matter?

In this section[2] we briefly discuss two main attempts at showing a causal relationship between economic institutions (property-rights protection, investors' protection, . . .) and economic performance measured by the aggregate income or

---

2. We encourage the student to look at the appendix at the back of the book before reading this section.

the average growth rate of a country. The first attempt emphasizes differences in legal codes across countries. The second attempt emphasizes differences in colonial histories, in particular in the extent to which European settlers managed to adapt to local conditions, as measured by their mortality rates in the various colonization areas.

11.2.1 Legal Origins

The main idea underlying the paper "Law and Finance" by La Porta and colleagues (1998), along with its various extensions, is that differences in legal codes and organizations should influence growth-enhancing institutions such as contractual enforcement, investor protection, and entry regulations. In particular this approach stresses the differences between the French civil law code and the English common law code. The former, more centralized, relies on detailed written codes that have to be strictly followed by all judges. The latter, more decentralized, relies on broader legal principles and legal experience (so-called jurisprudence), which can be more freely interpreted by judges. The presumption is that common law systems provide a more flexible environment for firms and entrepreneurs and that such systems facilitate financing and investment by inducing more efficient and speedy debt recovery processes.

La Porta and colleagues (1998) use a sample of 49 countries to show that investors' rights and contractual enforcement are highest in countries under common law, intermediate in countries under German or Scandinavian civil law, and lowest in countries under French civil law.

Similarly, La Porta and colleagues (1999) show that countries with common law systems are also countries with better business regulations and better property-rights protection. More recently, Djankov and colleagues (2003) have used data from 109 countries to show that countries under French civil law systems show longer delays for dispute resolution (the authors refer to this as procedural formalism) and consequently lower efficiency when it comes to evicting nonpaying tenants or collecting a bounced check. Thus it is no surprise that countries under French civil law tend to have a lower degree of financial development than countries under common law systems. This correlation, pointed out by Levine, Loayza, and Beck (2000), made it possible to use legal origins as an instrument for financial development when analyzing the role of financial development in growth and convergence in chapter 7.

Finally, Djankov and colleagues (2002) showed that countries with French and German civil law systems show more regulations on product and labor markets than their common law counterparts, where entry regulations are measured by the number of procedures entrepreneurs have to go through when creating a new firm.

A main limitation of this approach is that it remains cross-sectional, and in particular does not control for country or region fixed effects. Another problem with this approach is that it does not explain why France, which initiated the civil law system, performs much better than its colonial transplants. In fact, France itself performs rather well in all the above regressions. This brings us to the second approach based on colonial origins.

11.2.2   Colonial Origins

In their paper "The Colonial Origins of Comparative Development," Acemoglu, Johnson, and Robinson (2001), henceforth AJR, found a clever instrument for economic institutions in colonized countries, namely, the mortality rate of European settlers in these countries. Their idea is that (1) European colonizers could decide the extent to which they truly wish to settle in the new colony and build institutions rather than just extract resources; (2) this decision depends upon how well colonizers could adapt to the local climate and geography, which in turn is reflected in mortality rates of European bishops, sailors, and soldiers from local illnesses; and (3) institutions created during the colonization period persist after independence.

In other words, in colonies where they could truly settle, Europeans would try to replicate their own institutions, whereas colonies where they do not settle would be primarily used as extractive states, with little investment in institutions, in particular to protect property rights. Europeans would thus typically choose to settle in colonies where the disease risk was lower. And mortality rates, recorded by soldiers, bishops, and sailors between the 17th and the 19th centuries, should reflect that risk.

More precisely, AJR perform a two-stage least-square regression.[3] They regress per capita GDP not on expropriation risk, but on its "exogenous" component (predicted by settlers' mortality). Table 11.1 shows the results from this two-stage regression procedure. The second-stage regression is shown at the top of the table; the first stage is shown at the bottom. The first two columns show the OLS regression of per capita GDP in 1995 on expropriation not instrumented by settler mortality (column 2 includes only the sample of former colonies). The next columns show the regression using settler mortality as instrument for expropriation risk. This

---

3. See the appendix.

Table 11.1
Institutions and Income Per Capita 1960–2000

	(1) OLS	(2) OLS (Sample of Former Colonies)	(3) 2SLS	(4) 2SLS (Controlling for Schooling)
			Panel A. Second-stage regressions	
Expropriation risk	0.293***	0.375***	0.663**	1.908
	(0.053)	(0.063)	(0.288)	(3.848)
Years of schooling				−0.551
				(1.539)
Observations	118	63	63	60
Adj. *R*-squared	0.64	0.73		
Instrumented variable			Expr. risk	Expr. risk
Instrument			Log settler mortality	Log settler mortality
			Panel B. First-stage regressions	
Log settler mortality			−0.402**	−0.099
			(0.199)	(0.228)
R-squared			0.371	0.542
Observations			63	60

Dependent variable is log GDP per capita.

table suggests, first, that expropriation risk is highly positively correlated with economic performance in 1995 and, second, that settler mortality is a strong instrument for expropriation risk.[4,5]

However, as shown in column 4, the correlation between expropriation risk and per capita log GDP loses significance when we control for years of schooling. In fact, using the same data as AJR, one can look at what happens when one performs the symmetric exercise where (1) settler mortality is used as an instrument for schooling in the first-stage regression, and (2) income is regressed over schooling instrumented by settler mortality and over expropriation risk not instrumented. Table 11.2 summarizes the findings. As we see in column (2), settler mortality is a good instrument for schooling (first-stage regression results) and income or growth is significantly correlated with schooling but no longer with expropriation risk (second-stage regression results).

4. See the appendix.

5. AJR establish similar results when the left-hand side variable in the second-stage regression is the average growth rate of per capita GDP between 1960 and 2000.

Table 11.2
Alternative Specifications: Institutions and Income Per Capita

	(1) 2SLS (Controlling for Initial Income)	(2) 2SLS (Instrumenting for Schooling)	(3a) 2SLS (Instrumenting for Schooling and Institutions)	(3b)
	Panel A. Second-stage regressions			
Expropriation risk	0.410* (0.212)	0.083 (0.102)	0.386 (0.790)	
Years of schooling		0.346*** (0.111)	0.214 (0.458)	
Log GDP per capita in 1960	0.641*** (0.237)			
Observations	57	60	59	
Instrumented variable	Expr. risk	Schooling	Expr. risk, schooling	
Instruments	Log settler mortality	Log settler mortality	(i) Log settler mortality, (ii) Pop. density in 1500	
	Panel B. First-stage regressions			
			(a) Expr. risk	(b) Schooling
Log settler mortality	−0.309 (0.191)	−0.624*** (0.227)	−0.335 (0.238)	−0.738*** (0.208)
Log population density in 1500			−0.274** (0.106)	−0.395** (0.168)
R-squared	0.517	0.732	0.447	0.700
F-test, excl. instruments (p-value)			6.03 (0.004)	10.79 (0.000)
Observations	57	60	59	59

Dependent variable is log GDP per capita.

So where do we stand at the end? One interpretation, advocated by Glaeser and colleagues (2004), is that the main contribution of colonial settlers was to build physical and human capital, not so much institutions. The other interpretation, which has our preference, is that schooling *is* an institution as much as property-rights protection and entry regulations. At least one thing this discussion suggests is that more can be learned by (1) looking directly at more specific institutions and (2) moving from cross-country to more disaggregated data. This point will come out again when analyzing the relationship between growth and various policy determinants in part III.

11.3   Appropriate Institutions and Nonconvergence Traps

11.3.1   Some Motivating Facts

Using a cross-country panel of more than 100 countries over the 1960–2000 period, Acemoglu, Aghion, and Zilibotti (2006), henceforth AAZ, regress the average growth rate on a country's distance to the U.S. frontier (measured by the ratio of GDP per capita in that country to per capita GDP in the United States) at the beginning of the period. Then, splitting the sample of countries into two groups corresponding to countries that are more open than the median and to countries that are less open than the median, AAZ show that average growth decreases more rapidly as a country approaches the world frontier when openness is low. To measure openness, one can use imports plus exports divided by aggregate GDP. But this measure suffers from obvious endogeneity problems: in particular, exports and imports are likely to be influenced by domestic growth. To deal with this endogeneity problem, Frankel and Romer (1999) construct a more exogenous measure of openness that relies on exogenous characteristics such as land area, common borders, geographical distance, and population, and it is this measure that we use to measure openness in figure 11.1.

Figures 11.1A and 11.1B show the cross-sectional regressions: here, average growth over the whole 1960–2000 period is regressed over the country's distance to the world technology frontier in 1965 for less open and more open countries, respectively. As in previous chapters, a country's distance to the frontier is measured by the ratio between the log of this country's level of per capita GDP and the maximum of the logs of per capita GDP across all countries (which in fact corresponds to the log of per capita GDP in the United States).

Figures 11.1C and 11.1D show the results of panel regressions where we decompose the period 1960–2000 in five-year subperiods, and then for each subperiod we regress average growth over the period on distance to frontier at the beginning of the subperiod for less open and more open countries, respectively. These latter regressions control for country fixed effects. In both cross-sectional and panel regressions we see that while a low degree of openness does not appear to be detrimental to growth in countries far below the world frontier, it becomes increasingly detrimental to growth as the country approaches the frontier.

AAZ repeat the same exercise using entry costs faced by new firms instead of openness. Entry costs in turn are measured by the number of days to create a new firm in the various countries (see Djankov et al. 2002). Here, the country sample is split between countries with high barriers relative to the median and countries

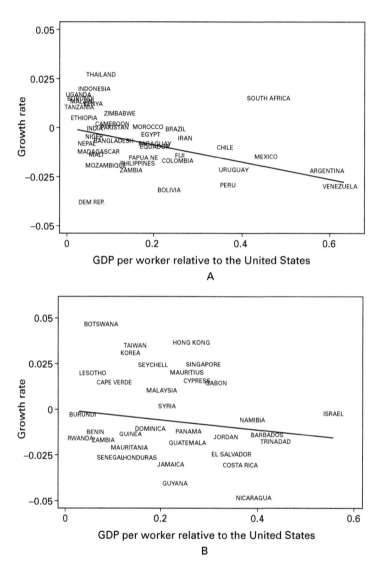

Figure 11.1
Growth and distance to frontier for more and less open countries: *A* and *C*, Closed economies; *B* and *D*, Open economies; *C* and *D*, Fixed effects

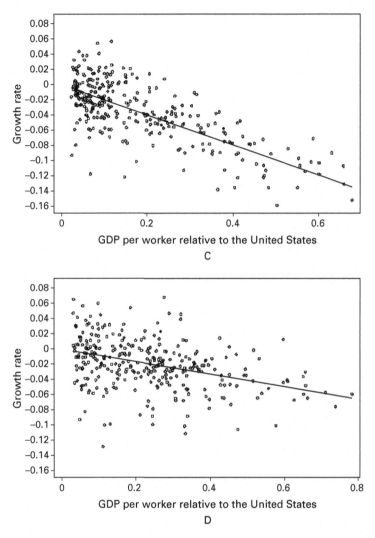

Figure 11.1
Continued

with low barriers relative to the median. Figures 11.2A and 11.2B show the cross-sectional regressions, for high and low barrier countries, respectively, whereas figures 11.2C and 11.2D show the panel regressions for the same two subgroups of countries. Both types of regressions show that while high entry barriers do not appear to be detrimental to growth in countries far below the world frontier, they become increasingly detrimental to growth as the country approaches the frontier.

These two empirical exercises point to the importance of interacting institutions with level of development in growth regressions: openness is particularly growth enhancing in countries that are closer to the technological frontier; entry is more growth enhancing in countries or sectors that are closer to the technological frontier; in chapter 13 we will see that higher (in particular, graduate) education tends to be more growth enhancing in countries or in U.S. states that are closer to the technological frontier, whereas primary and secondary (possibly undergraduate) education tends to be more growth enhancing in countries or in U.S. states that are farther below the frontier.

In the next section we model the notion of appropriate growth institution, and then we analyze the possibility that a country may remain stuck with institutions that might have been growth enhancing at earlier stages of development but that prevent fast growth as the country moves closer to the world technology frontier.

11.3.2   A Simple Model of Distance to Frontier and Appropriate Institutions

11.3.2.1   The Setup

The following setup combines the innovation model in chapter 4 with the convergence model in chapter 7. In each country, a unique final good, which also serves as numéraire, is produced competitively using a continuum of intermediate inputs according to

$$Y_t = \int_0^1 A_{it}^{1-\alpha} x_{it}^{\alpha} di \tag{11.1}$$

where A_{it} is the productivity in sector i at time t, x_{it} is the flow of intermediate good i used in general good production again at time t and $\alpha \in [0, 1]$.

As in chapter 4 (nondrastic innovation case), ex post each intermediate good producer has a constant marginal cost equal to 1 and faces a competitive fringe of imitators that force her to charge a limit price $p_{it} = \chi > 1$. Consequently, equilibrium monopoly profits (gross of the fixed cost) in sector i at date t are simply given by

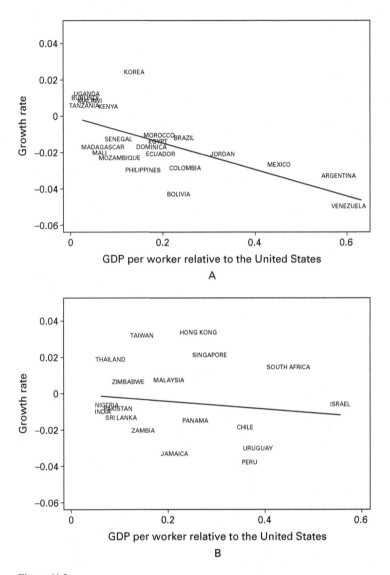

Figure 11.2
Growth and distance to frontier for high- and low-barrier countries: *A* and *C*, High barriers; *B* and *D*, Low barriers; *C* and *D*, Fixed effects

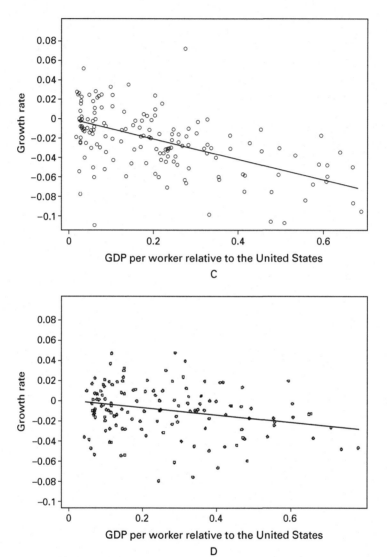

Figure 11.2
Continued

$$\pi_{it} = \pi A_{it}$$

where $\pi \equiv (\chi - 1)(\alpha/\chi)^{\frac{1}{1-\alpha}}$

Again let

$$A_t \equiv \int_0^1 A_{it}\, di$$

denote the average productivity in the country at date t, and let $\bar{A}_t$ denote the productivity at the world frontier. We take this frontier productivity to grow at the constant rate g from one period to the next, that is,

$$\bar{A}_t = (1 + g)\bar{A}_{t-1}$$

Let $a_t = A_t/\bar{A}_t$ denote the country's proximity to the world technology frontier, our inverse measure of the country's distance to the technological frontier at date t.

A main departure from the convergence model in chapter 7 lies in the equation for productivity growth.

11.3.2.2 Two Sources of Productivity Growth

Intermediate firms have two ways to generate productivity growth: (1) they can imitate existing world frontier technologies; (2) they can innovate upon the previous local technology.

More specifically, we assume

$$A_{it} = \eta \bar{A}_{t-1} + \gamma A_{t-1}$$

where $\eta \bar{A}_{t-1}$ and γA_{t-1} refer to the imitation and innovation components of productivity growth, respectively. Imitations use the existing frontier technology at the end of period $(t - 1)$, and thus they multiply $\bar{A}_{t-1}$; whereas innovations build on the knowledge stock of the country, and therefore they multiply A_{t-1}. In other words, this extended model combines the Schumpeterian model of chapter 4 where an innovating sector multiplies its previous productivity by a factor $\gamma > 1$ with the convergence model of chapter 7 where an innovating sector catches up with the technology frontier.

Integrating over all sectors of the economy, we have

$$A_t = \eta \bar{A}_{t-1} + \gamma A_{t-1} \tag{11.2}$$

Dividing both sides of equation (11.2) by $\bar{A}_t$ and using the fact that

$$\bar{A}_t = (1 + g)\bar{A}_{t-1}$$

we immediately obtain the following linear relationship between the country's distance to frontier a_t at date t and the distance to frontier a_{t-1} at date $t - 1$:[6]

$$a_t = \frac{1}{1+g}\left(\eta + \gamma a_{t-1}\right) \tag{11.3}$$

This equation clearly shows that the relative importance of innovation (γ) for productivity growth increases as the country moves closer to the world technological frontier, (that is, as a_{t-1} moves closer to 1); whereas imitation (η) is more important when the country is further below the frontier, (that is, when a_{t-1} is closer to zero).

11.3.2.3   Growth-Maximizing Strategy

The preceding equation immediately generates a theory of "appropriate growth institutions": suppose that imitation and innovation activities do not require the same institutions. For example, the imitation parameter η depends upon institutions that encourage on-the-job training and experience acquisition by providing job tenure guarantees to firm managers (or to entrepreneurs in their relationship with shareholders).[7] However, frontier innovation γ requires a better selection of talents, which in turn is favored by institutions that allow shareholders to dismiss managers who underperform on a particular activity.[8] Then, far below the technological frontier, a country will grow faster if it adopts *imitation-enhancing* (or *experience-enhancing*) institutions, whereas closer to the frontier growth will be maximized if the country switches to *innovation-enhancing* institutions or policies.

More formally, let $\eta \in \{\underline{\eta}, \bar{\eta}\}$ and $\gamma \in \{\underline{\gamma}, \bar{\gamma}\}$, where $\underline{\eta} < \bar{\eta}$ and $\underline{\gamma} < \bar{\gamma}$. Moreover, suppose that an *experience-enhancing* policy ($R = 1$) generates $\{\bar{\eta}, \underline{\gamma}\}$,

---

6. To see this point, note that

$$\frac{A_t}{\bar{A}_t} = \eta\frac{\bar{A}_{t-1}}{\bar{A}_t} + \gamma\frac{A_{t-1}}{\bar{A}_t}$$

$$= \eta\frac{1}{1+g} + \gamma\frac{A_{t-1}}{\bar{A}_{t-1}}\frac{\bar{A}_{t-1}}{\bar{A}_t}$$

$$= \eta\frac{1}{1+g} + \gamma a_{t-1}\frac{1}{1+g}$$

7. More generally, imitation activities will tend to be enhanced by long-term investments within (large) existing firms, which in turn may benefit from long-term bank finance and/or subsidized credit as in Japan or Korea since the end of World War II.

8. More generally, innovation activities will often require initiative, risk taking, the selection of good projects and talents, and the weeding out of those that turn out not to be profitable or operational.

in other words, is better for imitation but worse for frontier innovation; however, an *innovation-enhancing* policy ($R = 0$) generates $\{\eta, \overline{\gamma}\}$, in other words, is better at producing frontier innovation but relatively worse at facilitating imitation.

For simplicity, we shall assume that

$$1 + g = \underline{\eta} + \overline{\gamma}$$

so that, by equation (11.3), a country that pursues an innovation-based strategy and lies exactly on the technological frontier will grow exactly at rate g. In other words, this assumption endogenizes the frontier growth rate as stemming from innovation-based growth.

The productivity growth equation (11.3) becomes

$$a_t = \frac{1}{1+g}\left(\overline{\eta} + \underline{\gamma} a_{t-1}\right) \tag{11.4}$$

under experience-enhancing institutions, and

$$a_t = \frac{1}{1+g}\left(\underline{\eta} + \overline{\gamma} a_{t-1}\right) \tag{11.5}$$

under innovation-enhancing institutions. The two relationships are depicted by the two lines $R = 1$ and $R = 0$ in figure 11.3. The figure clearly shows that experience-enhancing institutions achieve higher growth (that is, higher level of a_t for given a_{t-1})[9] for low values of a_{t-1} but lower growth for high values of a_{t-1}.

The cutoff point $\hat{a}$ at which the two lines intersect is simply calculated by equating the right-hand sides of the two preceding equations, which in turn yields

$$\hat{a} = \frac{\overline{\eta} - \underline{\eta}}{\overline{\gamma} - \underline{\gamma}}$$

Thus it is growth maximizing that countries with $a_{t-1} < \hat{a}$ adopt an experience-enhancing strategy, whereas countries with $a_{t-1} > \hat{a}$ switch to an innovation-enhancing strategy. Moreover, a country that follows this growth-maximizing

9. The domestic growth rate at date t is equal to

$$\frac{A_t}{A_{t-1}} = \frac{a_t \overline{A}_t}{a_{t-1} \overline{A}_{t-1}} = \frac{a_t}{a_{t-1}}(1+g)$$

This rate is thus maximized whenever a_t is maximized for given a_{t-1}.

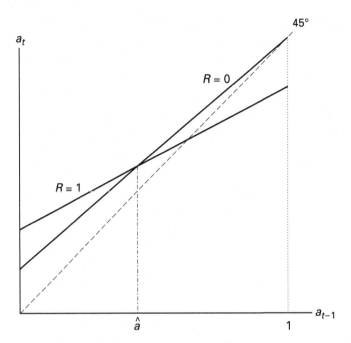

Figure 11.3

plan will always achieve a growth rate higher than g, and it will also ultimately converge to the world technology frontier, that is, $a_t = 1$.

Two important questions arise at this point. First, will institutions actually change when they should; in other words, how do equilibrium institutions at various stages of development compare with the growth-maximizing institutions? Second, what happens if institutions do not change early enough as a country develops? These are the questions we address in the remaining part of the chapter.

11.3.2.4   Decentralized Equilibrium

So far, we have treated (η, γ) directly as (aggregate) institutional variables. In reality, however, the average levels of η and γ result from decentralized decisions made by economic agents that operate in a particular institutional environment.

In this section, we consider the decentralized interactions between firm owners and firm managers. Firm owners can decide whether or not to keep old managers that turn out to be "untalented" for one more period on the job. Keeping existing managers on the job enhances experience but is detrimental to innovation: that is, it increases η, but reduces γ at the firm level. Ultimately, as we shall see later, firm owners' decisions whether or not to maintain old untalented managers on the job will depend on the underlying institutional environment (in particular on firing and hiring costs). In other words, a given set of institutional parameters will correspond to equilibrium average levels of η and γ across firms in the economy. These levels will generally differ from the growth-maximizing policy analyzed previously.

More formally, suppose that intermediate firms are run by managers who live for two periods and are employed by firm owners who also live for two periods and maximize profits. Each period, the current manager is paid a fixed share μ of the firm's profits. And at the beginning of each period, the manager can improve the firm's productivity both by imitating the frontier technology and by innovating upon the local technology:

$$A_{it} = \eta(i, t)\,\overline{A}_{t-1} + \gamma(i, t)\,A_{t-1}$$

where $\eta(i, t)$ and $\gamma(i, t)$ denote the manager's imitation and innovation intensities on firm i at time t.

There are two types of managers: talented and untalented. All young managers imitate with the same intensity $\eta(i, t) = \eta$, and all old managers can imitate with intensity $\eta(i, t) = \eta + \varepsilon$, where ε measures the old manager's *experience* acquired on the job. However, only the talented managers can innovate, with intensity $\gamma(i, t) = \gamma$, whereas $\gamma(i, t) = 0$ for untalented managers. There is a fraction λ of talented managers in the economy, and a manager's talent is publicly revealed only after one period of work.

The institutional aspect we shall consider here is the extent to which unsuccessful managers are shut down or instead renewed by the firm owner whenever they are revealed to be untalented after one period on the job. Refinancing old managers allows the firm's owner to take advantage of the experience and also the retained earnings of these managers. However, keeping old (untalented) managers may prevent the firm's owner from having the possibility of selecting potentially more talented young managers; this inability to recruit talent in turn stifles innovation. Thus, here, the experience-enhancing strategy means that firms maintain their managers, whereas the innovation-enhancing strategy means that firms replace old untalented managers by new managers.

More formally, assuming that managers are ready to use all their retained earnings to maintain their jobs, the firm's owner will choose to renew an old untalented manager whenever

$$(1-\mu)(\eta+\varepsilon)\pi\overline{A}_{t-1}+\mu\pi\overline{A}_{t-2}\geq(1-\mu)(\eta+\lambda\gamma a_{t-1})\pi\overline{A}_{t-1}-\kappa\overline{A}_{t-1}$$

where: (1) $(1-\mu)$ is the residual share of profits that is left to the firm's owner, since the fraction μ of profits accrues to the manager; (2) $(\eta+\varepsilon)\pi\overline{A}_{t-1}$ is the profit generated by an old untalented manager, whereas $\pi(\eta+\lambda\gamma a_{t-1})\overline{A}_{t-1}$ is the expected profit generated by a new manager, with the term $\lambda\gamma a_{t-1}$ being the expected innovation gain (in productivity-adjusted terms) from hiring a new manager; (3) $\mu\pi\overline{A}_{t-2}$ is the retained earning of the old manager, which she can use to bribe the firm's owner to maintain herself on the job; and (4) $\kappa\overline{A}_{t-1}$ is the cost of hiring a new manager.

Using the fact that

$$\overline{A}_{t-1}=\overline{A}_{t-2}(1+g)$$

and dividing through by $\overline{A}_{t-1}$, the preceding condition becomes

$$a_{t-1}\leq a_r=\frac{(1-\mu)\varepsilon+\dfrac{\mu}{1+g}+\dfrac{\kappa}{\pi}}{(1-\mu)\lambda\gamma}$$

Thus the private benefits of renewing old unsuccessful entrepreneurs outweigh the costs whenever $a_{t-1}<a_r$, that is, whenever the country is sufficiently far below the frontier that the corresponding benefit in terms of a higher scope for investment and imitation outweighs the cost in terms of forgone selection of new talented entrepreneurs.

11.3.2.5   Equilibrium Dynamics and Nonconvergence Traps

First, note that the experience-enhancing strategy that consists of renewing old untalented managers yields average imitation and innovation intensities:

$$\overline{\eta}=\eta+\frac{1}{2}\varepsilon;\qquad \underline{\gamma}=\frac{1}{2}\lambda\gamma$$

The first equality results from the fact that only half of the firms have old managers (which here are always kept on the job); the second equality results from the fact that only the young firms hire a new manager, who in turn has probability λ of being talented and therefore innovative.

Similarly, the innovation-enhancing strategy yields average imitation and innovation intensities equal to

$$\underline{\eta}=\eta+\frac{1}{2}\lambda\varepsilon;\qquad \overline{\gamma}=\lambda\gamma\left[1+\frac{1}{2}(1-\lambda)\right]$$

The first equality results from the fact that half of the firms have old experienced managers, and they keep them with probability λ. The second equality results from the fact that in young firms managers are talented with probability λ, whereas in a fraction λ of old firms the incumbent manager is revealed to be talented and therefore is kept on the job, whereas in a fraction $(1 - \lambda)$ of old firms the incumbent manager is replaced by a new manager who will be talented with probability λ.[9]

One can immediately verify that indeed $\underline{\eta} < \bar{\eta}$ and $\underline{\gamma} < \bar{\gamma}$, and let us again assume that

$$1 + g = \underline{\eta} + \bar{\gamma}$$

The growth-maximizing switching point $\hat{a}$ from imitation-based to innovation-based strategy is still equal to

$$\hat{\alpha} = \frac{\bar{\eta} - \underline{\eta}}{\bar{\gamma} - \underline{\gamma}}$$

Now, the comparison between $\hat{a}$ and a_r leads to four types of equilibria:

1. *Growth-maximizing equilibrium*   Suppose that markets and managers can solve their agency problems and can internalize pecuniary and nonpecuniary externalities and also dynamic knowledge externalities. Then the equilibrium will coincide with the growth-maximizing plan described earlier and represented by the upper envelope of the two lines in figure 11.3. That is

$$\hat{a} = a_r$$

In this case, the economy will always converge to the frontier, and if it started from $a_0 < \hat{a}$, it will experience a structural transformation from its initial experience-enhancing strategy to subsequent innovation-enhancing strategy as a_{t-1} crosses the cutoff level $\hat{a}$.

2. *Underinvestment equilibrium and infant-industry argument*   Underinvestment equilibrium corresponds to equilibrium policies of the form

9. Thus

$$\bar{\gamma} = \frac{1}{2}\lambda\gamma + \frac{1}{2}\left[\lambda\gamma + (1 - \lambda)\lambda\gamma\right]$$

which yields

$$\bar{\gamma} = \lambda\gamma\left[1 + \frac{1}{2}(1 - \lambda)\right]$$

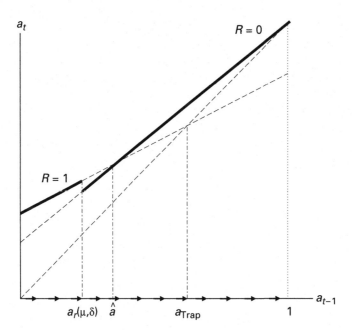

Figure 11.4

$$R_t = \begin{cases} 1 & \text{if } a_{t-1} < a_r \\ 0 & \text{if } a_{t-1} \geq a_r \end{cases}$$

where $a_r < \hat{a}$. Figure 11.4 depicts this type of equilibrium, which we refer to as underinvestment equilibrium because for $a \in (a_r, \hat{a})$ the economy could reach higher rates of growth by investing in managerial experience, that is, by choosing $R = 1$ instead of $R = 0$. In particular, this is the case when the fraction of talented managers λ is high and the fraction of profits μ managers can appropriate is low. When μ is small, entrepreneurs/managers only get limited cash from their current production activities, which in turn limits the amount of the collateral they could put up to convince shareholders to keep them on the job next period. Note, however, that inappropriate institutions are only temporary in this case, as such economies will always pass the threshold $\hat{a}$ above which $R = 0$ becomes the growth-maximizing strategy. Moreover, they will still converge to the frontier productivity $a_t = 1$.

To move toward the growth-maximizing equilibrium outcome, the government may choose to subsidize investment in managerial experience or to increase the hiring cost π.

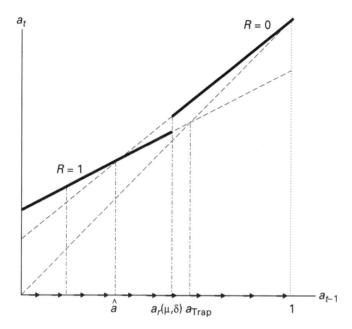

Figure 11.5

3. *Sclerotic equilibrium*   Sclerotic equilibrium corresponds to the case where

$$R_t = \begin{cases} 1 & \text{if } a_{t-1} < a_r \\ 0 & \text{if } a_{t-1} \geq a_r \end{cases}$$

with $a_r > \hat{a}$. Figure 11.5 depicts an equilibrium of this sort in which the economy maintains an experience-enhancing strategy $R = 1$ which has become inappropriate for $a_{t-1} \in (\hat{a}, a_r)$. Note that under the configuration shown in figure 11.5, this does not prevent the country from eventually shifting to the innovation-based strategy as a_{t-1} increases, or from eventually converging to the frontier productivity level. A sclerotic equilibrium is more likely to occur when μ is high so that entrepreneurs-managers obtain enough cash from current production activities to bargain their way in for the next period.

4. *Nonconvergence trap equilibrium*   This equilibrium is just an extreme form of sclerotic equilibrium, in which the equilibrium switching point a_r is not only greater than $\hat{a}$, but also greater than the intersection a_{Trap} between the line $R = 1$ and the 45° line, namely,

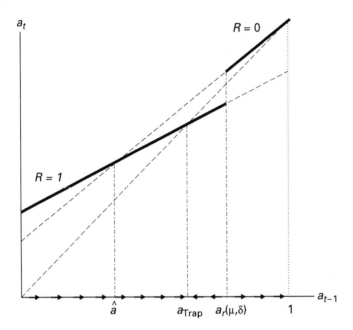

Figure 11.6

$$a_{\text{Trap}} = \frac{\overline{\eta}}{1 + g - \underline{\gamma}}$$

Figure 11.6 depicts such an equilibrium. In this case, transition to the innovation-enhancing strategy is delayed so much that it never occurs. Not only is growth reduced for $a_{t-1} > \hat{a}$, but more importantly the economy is pushed into a nonconvergence trap: the economy fails to converge to the frontier productivity, as its proximity to frontier a_{t-1} never goes beyond $a_{\text{Trap}} < 1$. And here is the danger of preventing competition or subsidizing incumbent managers for too long in a country's development process: such policies may condemn the economy to nonconvergence.

11.4 Conclusion

In this chapter we first discussed attempts at showing a causal effect of institutions on the level or growth of per capita GDP. These approaches consist in instrumenting for economic institutions in cross-country regressions, using legal origins or colonial origins as instruments. Both approaches yield interesting results, yet our discussion would call for more detailed analyses of institutions and growth where (1) institutions should be decomposed into more specific components and (2) regressions should be performed at a more disaggregated level, in particular using cross-industry and/or cross-firm panel data.

In the second part of the chapter we argued that different institutional arrangements may be growth maximizing at different stages of technological development. We showed different ways in which the equilibrium strategy may differ from the growth-maximizing one and explained why maintaining imitation-enhancing strategies for too long may generate nonconvergence traps.

These latter findings in turn raise an interesting question: why not have institutions that are themselves distance-contingent? For example, the government could decide to subsidize investment in experience or increase hiring costs for $a_{t-1} < \hat{a}$, so that $R = 1$ would be chosen in equilibrium by private entrepreneurs when $a_{t-1} < \hat{a}$, but at the same time to eliminate subsidies and to increase competition for $a_{t-1} > \hat{a}$, so that $R = 0$ would be chosen in equilibrium by private agents when $a_{t-1} > \hat{a}$. A main problem with such a contingent strategy is that it is not renegotiation-proof. In particular, suppose that incumbent firms can lobby to influence the choice of institution by governments. Then the following type of inefficient equilibrium sequence could result from this type of distance-contingent strategy: (1) initially, the government adopts an investment-based strategy (subsidizing investment or increasing hiring costs) as the country is far below the frontier ($a_0 < \hat{a}$); (2) as a result, incumbent firms realize high profits; (3) incumbent firms use these profits to bribe the government into maintaining the investment-based strategy even after $a_{t-1} > \hat{a}$; and (4) as a result, $a_r \gg \hat{a}$, with the economy getting into a nonconvergence trap if $a_r > a_{\text{Trap}}$.

The nonconvergence trap and its interactions with political economy and vested interests may reflect the experience of Latin American countries such as Brazil, Mexico, and Peru over the past half century. Import-substitution and protectionist policies helped these countries grow fast until the mid-1970s. However, the same policies generated stagnation thereafter, and these Latin American countries came to be leapfrogged by more flexible economies in Southeast Asia, for example, Hong Kong.

Figure 11.7 reports panel growth regressions of productivity growth over the proximity to the U.S. frontier productivity (measured by per capita GDP of the domestic country relative to U.S. per capita GDP) for Brazil, Argentina, Mexico, and Colombia, where the period 1960–2000 is subdivided into five-year

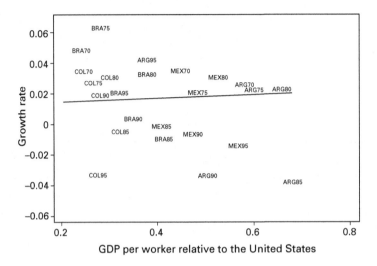

Figure 11.7

subperiods. The continuous line represents growth across all non-OECD countries for different proximities to the U.S. frontier. In particular, we see that when their per capita GDP relative to the United States was below 40 percent, then the four Latin American countries were doing better than the world average at corresponding proximity levels, whereas above 40 percent they are doing worse than the world average. This result in turn points to the persistence of inappropriate institutions. Figure 11.8 shows that the same result carries over to the whole Latin American sample.

Finally, the model in this chapter is also relevant to the case of Korea and Japan. In Japan, the Ministry of International Trade and Industry regulated competition by controlling foreign currency allocations and import licenses and by directing industrial policy, and it also subsidized investment by large firm-bank consortia, the so-called *keiretsu*. In Korea, the government provided subsidized loans, antiunion legislation, and preferential treatment to large family-run conglomerates, the so-called *chaebols*. These investment-based strategies helped foster growth, up to the mid-1980s in Japan and up to the financial crisis of 1998 in Korea. In Korea the financial crisis and the resulting weakening of *chaebols* (several of which went bankrupt) opened the way to subsequent structural reforms, which in turn put Korea back on a high growth path. Structural reforms took longer to occur in Japan, but now seem to be finally happening.

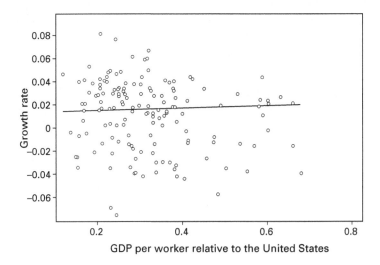

Figure 11.8

11.5   Literature Notes

The pioneering work explaining the influence of institutions on economic development through history is by North (e.g., see North and Thomas 1973; North 1990). North's (1990) concept of institution as "the rules of the game in a society" was later broadened by Greif (e.g., see Greif 2006) to include both forms of economic organizations and beliefs that shape human interaction.

We saw that two lines of empirical analysis became particularly influential. The first one emphasizes the role of "legal origins," that is, how differences in legal codes and organization tended to affect subsequent development of countries through their impact on the efficiency of institutions such as contractual enforcement or property-rights protection. Main papers here include La Porta and colleagues (1998, 1999), Djankov and colleagues (2002), and Glaeser and colleagues (2004).

Another approach considered instead the role of "colonial origins." Pioneering work by Engerman and Sokoloff (1997) stressed the importance of factor endowments (specifically the suitability of crops for plantation and the density of indigenous populations) to explain the observed income divergence within the Americas. However, the most influential papers along this line of research are AJR (2001, 2002), which use settlers' mortality as an instrument for expropriation risk. The idea is that the initial conditions faced by colonizers should affect the objectives they pursue in the new colonies (for example, extraction versus settlement). These objectives, in turn, should affect current institutions in the corresponding countries.

More recently, AJR (2005) emphasized the interaction between European countries' access to Atlantic trade and their premodern institutions to explain the divergence within Europe right before the Industrial Revolution took place. Nunn (2008) assesses the long-term economic impact of Africa's slave trades within that continent. Banerjee and Iyer (2005) focus on a single country, India, evaluating the long-run effects of different land tenure systems set up by the British in that nation.

The *Handbook of Economic Growth* chapter by AJR (2005) presents a complete summary of the framework they have used to study the impact of institutions and the empirical evidence they have gathered on the topic.

The primary reference on the issue of appropriate institutions is Gerschenkron's (1962). In this celebrated essay the author argues that relatively backward economies, such as Germany, France, and Russia during the 19th century, adopted particular policies and arrangements that were growth enhancing given their early stage of development but could cease to be so at a later stage of development. The author also pointed out that some "noncompetitive" arrangements, including long-term relationships between firms and banks, large firms, and state intervention, could make it easier for middle-income countries to catch up to more advanced economies.

Recent empirical work has tested the extent to which growth-enhancing policies or institutions may vary with a country's or sector's level of development as measured by the distance between its own productivity and the corresponding frontier productivity. Thus, using data from the OECD sectoral database, Griffith, Redding, and Van Reenen (2003) constructed a measure of distance to frontier for each industry in each country and year, and found evidence consistent with the observation that R&D and innovation become more important as an economy approaches the world technology frontier: they found a statistically highly significant negative relationship between distance to frontier and R&D intensity.

Acemoglu, Johnson, and Mitton (2003) found evidence that industry-level and aggregate concentration is greater in poorer countries (more distant from the frontier). These results are consistent with the idea that market selection is less important there, whereas firms tend to be larger in countries farther below the technological frontier.

Related works that also build on Gerschenkron's insight include Stiglitz (1995) and Hausmann and Rodrik (2003), both of which call for greater government intervention in less developed countries where market failures tend to be more intense than in more advanced market economies. However, Shleifer and Vishny (1999) have stressed the greater scope for government failure in less developed nations, where checks on governments are typically weaker.

The first systematic attempt at modeling the notion of appropriate institutions and the notion of institutional trap is the paper by Acemoglu, Aghion, and Zilibotti (2006). This approach has been subsequently extended or applied to analyze various aspects of growth policy design. Here, we refer the reader to Aghion and Howitt's (2006) survey article on "appropriate growth policy."

Problems

1. It has long been known that countries that have poor economic growth also have bad "institutions." A substantial challenge for empirical research has been to identify a causal link between institutions and economic growth. To solve this identification problem, we need to find exogenous variation in institutions. The following exogenous variations in institutions have been proposed to support the hypothesis that "bad institutions" cause poor economic growth: (1) distance from the equator as a proxy for European influence (by Hall and Jones 1999); (2) difference in legal codes and organizations as determined (by La Porta et al. 1998, 1999); (3) mortality rates faced by potential colonial settlers as a proxy for institutional development during the era of colonization in the post-1500 world (by AJR 2005). Discuss the plausibility of each of these as a good instrument for institutions. Can you think of any innovative ways to find exogenous variation in institutions to test the hypothesis that institutions have a causal effect on economic growth?

2. **Mechanism for institutional persistence**

The model and empirical evidence presented in this chapter raise an important question: Why do governments not choose institutions and policies that favor the investment-based strategy when the country is in its early stages of development and then switch to policies supporting innovation and selection as the country approaches the frontier? Acemoglu, Aghion, and Zilibotti (2006) argue that the answer lies in the political economy of government intervention. Policies that favor the investment-based strategy create and enrich their own supporters. When economic power buys political power. it becomes difficult to reverse policies that have an economically and politically powerful constituency. Consequently, societies may remain trapped with "inappropriate institutions" and relatively backward technologies.

How can you test this claim using micro evidence? Acemoglu, Aghion, and Zilibotti (2006) discuss the example of South Korea: they suggest that close links between government officials and the *chaebols* had turned into major obstacles to progress and that convergence and growth came to an end during the Asian crisis. If the Asian crisis served as an exogenous negative shock to the political power of the economically powerful constituency in South Korea, what evidence would you look for to verify the hypothesis presented here? If you had access to all possible sources of data, what would be your empirical strategy to identify the causal effect of a change in the "appropriateness of institutions" on economic growth?

3. **Institutions-versus-geography debate**

Most poor countries are located in the tropics. Sachs (2001) interprets this evidence to mean that geography is one of the fundamental causes of underdevelopment. Geography matters because disease environments and agricultural productivity are directly dependent on geographic conditions. For example, countries that are most exposed to widespread malaria tend to lie between the tropics.

AJR (2001), however, argue that the underdevelopment of tropical countries can be traced to historical colonial institutions. They argue that countries in which the European settlers faced greater mortality are the countries in which they chose not to settle and instead adopted "extractive institutions." However, in countries in which they faced lower mortality they chose to settle and therefore adopted good rule of law.

Discuss the plausibility of the two hypotheses. What evidence would you provide to support or refute the two hypotheses?

III GROWTH POLICY

12 Fostering Competition and Entry

12.1 Introduction

Is product market competition good or bad for growth? Innovation-based models (see chapters 3 and 4) seem to provide an unambiguous answer to this question: namely, market competition is bad for growth, the reason being that competition reduces the monopoly rents that induce firms to innovate. By the same token, more intense imitation discourages technological innovations and growth. Hence the importance of preserving intellectual property rights through an adequate system of (international) patent protection.

Unfortunately, the prediction that competition is bad for growth turns out to be highly counterfactual. Indeed, empirical work (e.g., Nickell 1996; Blundell, Griffith, and Van Reenen 1995) points to a *positive* correlation between *product market competition* (as measured either by the number of competitors in the same industry or by the inverse of a market share or profitability index) and *productivity growth* within a firm or industry. This evidence, in turn, appears to be more consistent with the view (e.g., Porter 1990) that product market competition is good for growth because it *forces* firms to innovate in order to survive.

How can we reconcile the evidence with the theory? When does competition foster or discourage innovation? Section 12.2 will focus on the relationship between competition among incumbent firms and innovation. There, we replace the assumption made earlier—that incumbent innovators are automatically leapfrogged by their rivals—by a more *gradualist ("step-by-step")* technological progress assumption. This in turn will generate an inverted-U relationship between competition and productivity growth.

Section 12.3 will analyze the relationship between entry and innovation, showing that incumbent firms respond differently to an increased entry threat depending on their initial distance from the technological frontier in the corresponding industry. It will also consider how entry interacts with labor market regulation, showing how the positive effects of increased entry on productivity growth are reduced by proworker regulations.

12.2 From Leapfrogging to Step-by-Step Technological Progress

Based on Aghion, Harris, and Vickers (1997) and Aghion and colleagues (2001), in this section we shall replace the leapfrogging assumption in the Schumpeterian model (with incumbent innovators being systemically overtaken by outside researchers) with a less radical step-by-step assumption. That is, a firm that is currently m steps behind the technological leader in its industry must catch up with the leader before becoming a leader itself. This step-by-step assumption can be rationalized by supposing that an innovator acquires tacit knowledge that cannot be duplicated by a rival without engaging in its own R&D to catch up. Once it has caught up, we suppose that no patent protects the former leader from Bertrand competition.

This change leads to a richer analysis of the interplay between product market competition, innovation, and growth by allowing firms in an industry to be *neck and neck*. A higher degree of product market competition, by making life more difficult for neck-and-neck firms, will encourage them to innovate in order to acquire a significant lead over their rivals.

12.2.1   Basic Environment

More formally, suppose that time is discrete and that there is a unit mass of identical consumers. Each of them lives for one period and supplies a unit of labor inelastically. Moreover, her utility depends upon the amounts consumed from a continuum of sectors:

$$u_t = \int_0^1 \ln x_{jt} dj$$

in which each x_j is the sum of two goods produced by duopolists in sector j:

$$x_j = x_{Aj} + x_{Bj}$$

The logarithmic structure of this utility function implies that in equilibrium individuals spend the same amount on each basket x_j.[1] We normalize this common amount to unity by using current expenditure as the numéraire for the prices p_{Aj} and p_{Bj} at each date. Thus the representative household chooses each x_{Aj} and x_{Bj} to maximize $x_{Aj} + x_{Bj}$ subject to the budget constraint $p_{Aj}x_{Aj} + p_{Bj}x_{Bj} = 1$; that is, the household will devote the entire unit expenditure to the less expensive of the two goods.

---

1. That is, the representative consumer will choose the x_j's to maximize $u = \int_0^1 \ln x_j dj$ subject to the budget constraint $\int_0^1 p_j x_j dj = E$. The first-order condition is

$$\partial u / \partial x_j = 1/x_j = \lambda p_j \quad \text{for all } j$$

where λ is a Lagrange multiplier. Together with the budget constraint, this first-order condition implies

$$p_j x_j = 1/\lambda = E \quad \text{for all } j$$

12.2.2   Technology and Innovation

Each firm produces using labor as the only input, according to a constant-returns production function, and takes the wage rate as given. Thus the unit costs of production c_A and c_B of the two firms in an industry are independent of the quantities produced. Now, let k_i denote the technology level of duopoly firm i in some industry j; that is, one unit of labor currently employed by firm i generates an output flow equal to

$$A_i = \gamma^{k_i}, \qquad i = A, B$$

where $\gamma > 1$ is a parameter that measures the size of a leading-edge innovation. Equivalently, it takes γ^{-k_i} units of labor for firm i to produce one unit of output.

For expositional simplicity, we assume that knowledge spillovers between the two firms in any intermediate industry are such that neither firm can get more than one technological level ahead of the other. That is, if a firm already one step ahead innovates, the lagging firm will automatically learn to copy the leader's previous technology and thereby remain only one step behind. Thus, at any point in time, there will be two kinds of intermediate sectors in the economy: (1) *level* or *neck-and-neck* sectors where both firms are at technological par with one another and (2) *unlevel* sectors, where one firm (the *leader*) lies one step ahead of its competitor (the *laggard* or *follower*) in the same industry.[2]

By spending the R&D cost $\psi(n) = n^2/2$ in units of expenditure, a leader (or frontier) firm moves one technological step ahead, with probability n. We call n the "innovation rate" or "R&D intensity" of the firm. We assume that a follower firm can move one step ahead with probability h, even if it spends nothing on R&D, by copying the leader's technology. Thus $n^2/2$ is the R&D cost of a follower firm moving ahead with probability $n + h$. Let n_0 denote the R&D intensity of each firm in a neck-and-neck industry, and let n_{-1} denote the R&D intensity of a follower firm in an unlevel industry. If n_1 denotes the R&D intensity of the leader in an unlevel industry, note that $n_1 = 0$, since our assumption of automatic catch-up means that a leader cannot gain any further advantage by innovating.

12.2.3   Equilibrium Profits and Competition in Level and Unlevel Sectors

We can now determine the equilibrium profits of firms in each type of sector and link them with product market competition. Consider first an unlevel sector where

2. Aghion and colleagues (2001) analyze the more general case where there is no limit to how far ahead the leader can get. However, unlike in this chapter, that paper provides no closed-form solution for the equilibrium R&D levels and the steady-state industry structure.

the leader's unit cost is c. She is constrained to setting a price $p_1 \leq \gamma c$ because γc is the rival's unit cost, so at any higher price the rival could profitably undercut her price and steal all her business. Thus the leader's profit will be

$$\pi_1 = p_1 x_1 - c x_1$$

Since the leader is able to capture the whole market, her revenue will be the total consumer expenditure on that sector, which we have normalized to unity:

$$p_1 x_1 = 1$$

She will therefore choose x_1 to

$$\max\{1 - c x_1\}$$
$$\text{subject to} \quad p_1 = \frac{1}{x_1} \leq \gamma c$$

In other words, she will choose the maximal feasible price: $p_1 = \gamma c$, because at any lower price her revenue $p_1 x_1$ would be the same, but her cost $c x_1 = c / p_1$ would be higher. So her equilibrium profit will be

$$\pi_1 = 1 - c x_1 = 1 - c / p_1 = 1 - \gamma^{-1}$$

The laggard in the unlevel sector will be priced out of the market and hence will earn a zero profit:

$$\pi_{-1} = 0$$

Consider now a level sector. If the two firms engaged in open price competition with no collusion, the equilibrium price would fall to the unit cost c of each firm, resulting in zero profit. At the other extreme, if the two firms colluded so effectively as to maximize their joint profits and shared the proceeds, then they would together act like the leader in an unlevel sector, each setting $p = \gamma c$ (we assume that any third firm could compete using the previous best technology, just like the laggard in an unlevel sector) and each earning a profit equal to $\pi_1/2$.

So in a level sector both firms have an incentive to collude. Accordingly, we model the degree of product market competition inversely by the degree to which the two firms in a neck-and-neck industry are able to collude. (They do not collude when the industry is unlevel because the leader has no interest in sharing her profit.) Specifically, we assume that the profit of a neck-and-neck firm is

$$\pi_0 = (1 - \Delta)\pi_1, \qquad \frac{1}{2} \leq \Delta \leq 1$$

and we parameterize product market competition by Δ, that is, one minus the fraction of a leader's profits that the level firm can attain through collusion. Note that Δ is also the incremental profit of an innovator in a neck-and-neck industry, normalized by the leader's profit.

We next analyze how the equilibrium research intensities n_0 and n_{-1} of neck-and-neck and backward firms, and consequently the aggregate innovation rate, vary with our measure of competition Δ.

12.2.4 The Schumpeterian and "Escape-Competition" Effects

In each level sector, each firm chooses its innovation intensity n_0 so as to maximize its expected profit level. Suppose for simplicity that the firm looks only one period ahead. Suppose also that only one of the two neck-and-neck firms has the opportunity to innovate. Then the potential innovator's expected profit not including R&D cost will be π_1 with probability n_0 and π_0 with probability $1 - n_0$. So n_0 will be chosen so as to maximize the expected profit net of R&D cost:

$$n_0 \pi_1 + \left(1 - n_0\right)\pi_0 - n_0^2/2$$

resulting in

$$n_0 = \pi_1 - \pi_0$$

or, in terms of our measure of competition Δ,

$$n_0 = \Delta \pi_1 \tag{12.1}$$

In each unlevel sector, the laggard chooses its innovation intensity n_{-1} so as to maximize its expected profit net of R&D cost:

$$\left(n_{-1} + h\right)\pi_0 - n_{-1}^2/2$$

resulting in

$$n_{-1} = \pi_0 = \left(1 - \Delta\right)\pi_1 \tag{12.2}$$

So we see that the effect of competition on innovation depends on the situation. In unlevel sectors, equation (12.2) reveals the standard Schumpeterian effect that results from reducing the rents that can be captured by a follower who succeeds in catching up with its rival by innovating. In such sectors an increase in competition, as measured by Δ, will discourage innovation.

But in level sectors, equation (12.1) indicates a positive effect of competition on innovation. This occurs because of what we call an *escape-competition* effect;

that is, more competition induces neck-and-neck firms to innovate in order to escape from a situation in which competition constrains profits.

On average, an increase in product market competition will have an ambiguous effect on growth. It induces faster productivity growth in currently neck-and-neck sectors and slower growth in currently unlevel sectors. The overall effect on growth will thus depend on the (steady-state) fraction of level versus unlevel sectors. But this steady-state fraction is itself endogenous, since it depends upon equilibrium R&D intensities in both types of sectors. We proceed to show under which condition this overall effect is an inverted U, and at the same time we will derive additional predictions for further empirical testing.

12.2.5   Composition Effect and the Inverted U

In a steady state, the fraction of sectors μ_1 that are unlevel is constant, as is the fraction $\mu_0 = 1 - \mu_1$ of sectors that are level. The fraction of unlevel sectors that become leveled each period will be $n_{-1} + h$, so the sectors moving from unlevel to level represent the fraction $(n_{-1} + h)\mu_1$ of all sectors. Likewise, the fraction of all sectors moving in the opposite direction is $n_0\mu_0$, since one of the two firms innovates with probability n_0. In steady state, the fraction of firms moving in one direction must equal the fraction moving in the other direction:

$$(n_{-1} + h)\mu_1 = n_0(1 - \mu_1)$$

which can be solved for the steady-state fraction of unlevel sectors:

$$\mu_1 = \frac{n_0}{n_{-1} + h + n_0} \tag{12.3}$$

This implies that the aggregate flow of innovations in all sectors is[3]

$$I = \frac{2(n_{-1} + h)n_0}{n_{-1} + h + n_0}$$

Substituting in this equation for the R&D intensities n_0 and n_{-1} using equations (12.1) and (12.2) yields

$$I = \frac{2\left[(1 - \Delta)\pi_1 + h\right]\Delta\pi_1}{\pi_1 + h}$$

---

3. I is the sum of the two flows: $(n_{-1} + h)\mu_1 + n_0(1 - \mu_1)$. But since the two flows are equal, $I = 2(n_{-1} + h)\mu_1$. Substituting for μ_1 using equation (12.3) yields $I = \dfrac{2(n_{-1} + h)n_0}{n_{-1} + h + n_0}$.

Therefore, the effect of competition on innovation is measured by the derivative

$$\frac{dI}{d\Delta} = \frac{2\pi_1}{\pi_1 + h}\Big[(1 - 2\Delta)\pi_1 + h\Big]$$

which is positive when there is the least amount of competition (at $\Delta = \frac{1}{2}$) and diminishes as competition increases (since $\frac{d^2I}{d\Delta^2} < 0$). Whether or not the effect eventually turns negative depends on the size of the help factor h. Specifically, the effect will be negative when there is the greatest amount of competition (at $\Delta = 1$) if and only if $h < \pi_1$. In summary, we have the following proposition:

PROPOSITION 1   If $h < \pi_1$, then aggregate innovation I follows an inverted-U pattern: it increases with competition Δ for small enough values of Δ and decreases for large enough Δ. When $h \geq \pi_1$, then innovation always increases with competition but at a decreasing rate.

The inverted-U shape results from a "composition effect" whereby a change in competition changes the steady-state fraction of sectors that are in the level state, where the escape-competition effect dominates, versus the unlevel state, where the Schumpeterian effect dominates. At one extreme, when there is not much product market competition, there is not much incentive for neck-and-neck firms to innovate, and therefore the overall innovation rate will be highest when the sector is unlevel. Thus the industry will be quick to leave the unlevel state (which it does as soon as the laggard innovates) and slow to leave the level state (which will not happen until one of the neck-and-neck firms innovates). As a result, the industry will spend most of the time in the level state, where the escape-competition effect dominates (n_0 is increasing in Δ). In other words, if the degree of competition is very low to begin with, an increase in competition should result in a faster average innovation rate.

At the other extreme, when competition is initially very high, there is little incentive for the laggard in an unlevel state to innovate. Thus the industry will be slow to leave the unlevel state. Meanwhile, the large incremental profit $\pi_1 - \pi_0$ gives firms in the level state a relatively large incentive to innovate, so that the industry will be relatively quick to leave the level state. As a result, the industry will spend most of the time in the unlevel state where the Schumpeterian effect is the dominant effect. In other words, if the degree of competition is very high to begin with, an increase in competition should result in a slower average innovation rate.

12.2.6 Empirical Evidence

Aghion, Bloom, and colleagues (2005) test these predictions using a firm-level panel data set of UK firms listed on the London Stock Exchange between 1970 and 1994. Competition measures are computed using firm-level accounting data, and innovation output, measured by citation-weighted patenting, is derived using the National Bureau of Economic Research (NBER) patents database.[4]

Competition is measured by the Lerner Index (LI), or price cost margin. LI is itself defined by operating profits net of depreciation and of the financial cost of capital[5] divided by sales,

$$LI = \frac{\text{Operating profit} - \text{Financial cost}}{\text{Sales}}$$

averaged across firms within the industry.

Aghion, Bloom, and colleagues (2005) then proceed to estimate the equation

$$E\left[p_{jt} \middle| c_{jt}, x_{jt}\right] = e^{\left\{g\left(c_{jt}\right) + x'_{jt}\beta\right\}}$$

where p_{jt} is the patenting measure, c_{jt} is the competition measure for industry j at date t, and x_{jt} represents a complete set of time and industry dummy variables. Figure 12.1 summarizes the findings.

The figure shows that if we restrict the set of industries to those above the median degree of neck-and-neckness, the upward-sloping part of the inverted-U relationship between competition and innovation is steeper than if we consider the whole sample of industries.

12.3 Entry

Until now, competition policy in Europe has emphasized competition among incumbent firms, while paying insufficient attention to entry. Entry, as well as exit and turnover of firms, is more important in the United States than in Europe.

---

4. See Hall, Jaffe, and Trajtenberg (2000). The NBER database contains the patents taken out in the U.S. patent office, which is where innovations are effectively patented internationally, dated by the time of application.

5. The capital stock is measured using the perpetual inventory method. The inverted-U shape is robust to excluding this financial cost from the Lerner measure, principally because it is relatively small and constant over time.

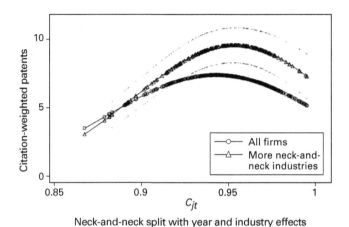

Figure 12.1
Innovation and product market competition: the neck-and-neck split

For example, 50 percent of new pharmaceutical products are introduced by firms that are less than 10 years old in the United States, versus only 10 percent in Europe. Similarly, 12 percent of the largest U.S. firms by market capitalization at the end of the 1990s had been founded less than 20 years before, against only 4 percent in Europe, and the difference between U.S. and European turnover rates is much bigger if one considers the top 500 firms.

That the higher entry costs and lower degree of turnover in Europe compared to the United States are an important part of the explanation for the relatively disappointing European growth performance over the past decade has been shown in empirical work by Nicoletti and Scarpetta (2003). In this section we extend the Schumpeterian model from chapter 4 to analyze the effects of entry on innovation and growth. We then provide evidence that is consistent with the predictions of the augmented model.

Unlike what other endogenous growth models would predict, entry, exit, and turnover all have a positive effect on innovation and productivity growth, not only in the economy as a whole but also within incumbent firms. The idea here is that increased entry, along with increased threat of entry, enhances innovation and productivity growth, not just because these are the direct result of quality-improving innovations by new entrants, but also because the threat of being driven out by a potential entrant gives incumbent firms an incentive to innovate in order to escape entry, through an effect that works much like the escape-competition effect described previously. This "escape-entry" effect is particularly strong for firms close to the world technology frontier. For firms further behind the frontier, the dominant effect of entry threat is a "discouragement" effect that works much like the Schumpeterian appropriability effect described earlier.

12.3.1   Environment

Here we use again our workhorse multisector model in discrete time. All agents live for one period. In each period t a final good (henceforth the numéraire) is produced in each state by a competitive sector using a continuum of intermediate inputs, according to the technology

$$Y_t = \int_0^1 A_{it}^{1-\alpha} x_{it}^{\alpha} di$$

where x_{it} denotes the quantity of the intermediate input produced in sector i at date t, A_{it} is the productivity parameter associated with the latest version of intermediate product i, and $\alpha \in (0, 1)$. The final good, which we take to be the numéraire, is used in turn for consumption, as an input to R&D, and also as an input to the production of intermediate products.

In each intermediate sector i only one firm (a monopolist) is active in each period. Thus the variable i refers both to an intermediate sector (industry) and to the intermediate firm that is active in that sector. Like any other agent in the economy, intermediate producers live for one period only, and property rights over intermediate firms are transmitted within dynasties. Intermediate firms choose how much to produce in order to maximize profits, taking into account that the price at which they sell their intermediate good to the final sector is equal to the marginal productivity of that good. As we saw in chapter 4, the equilibrium profit for each intermediate firm takes the form

$$\pi_{it} = \pi A_{it} \tag{12.4}$$

where

$$\pi = \left(\frac{1-\alpha}{\alpha}\right) \alpha^{\frac{2}{1-\alpha}}$$

12.3.2   Technology and Entry

Let $\bar{A}_t$ denote the new frontier productivity at date t and assume that

$$\bar{A}_t = (1+g)\bar{A}_{t-1}$$

with $1 + g = \gamma > 1$. We shall again emphasize the distinction already made in the previous section between sectors in which the incumbent producer is "neck-and-neck" with the frontier and those in which the incumbent firm is far below the frontier.

At date t an intermediate firm can either be close to frontier, with productivity level $A_{it-1} = \bar{A}_{t-1}$ (type-1 sector i), or far below the frontier, with productivity level $A_{it-1} = \bar{A}_{t-2}$ (type-2 sector i).

Before they produce and generate profits, firms can innovate to increase their productivity. Each innovation increases the firm's productivity by the factor γ. For innovation to be successful with probability z, a type-j intermediate firm with $j \in \{1, 2\}$ at date t must invest

$$c_{it} = cz^2 \bar{A}_{it-j} / 2$$

Intermediate firms are subject to an entry threat from foreign producers. Let p denote the probability that an entrant shows up. Liberalization corresponds to an increase in p. Foreign entrants at date t are assumed to operate with the end-of-period frontier productivity $\bar{A}_t$.

If the foreign firm manages to enter and competes with a local firm that has a lower productivity, it takes over the market and becomes the new incumbent firm in the sector. If it competes with a local firm that has the same productivity, however, Bertrand competition drives the profits of both the local and the foreign firm to zero. Now, suppose that potential entrants observe the postinnovation technology of the incumbent firm before deciding whether or not to enter. Then the foreign firm will find it profitable to enter only if the local firm has a postinnovation productivity level lower than the frontier. However, the foreign firm will never enter in period t if the local firm has achieved the frontier productivity level $\bar{A}_t$. Therefore, the probability of actual entry in any intermediate sector i is equal to zero when the local firm i was initially close to the frontier and has successfully innovated, and it is equal to p otherwise.

12.3.3 Equilibrium Innovation Investments

Using equation (12.4) together with the preceding innovation technology, we can analyze the innovation decisions made by intermediate firms that are close and the decisions of firms that are far below the frontier. Consider first firms that are initially far below the frontier at date t. If they choose to innovate with probability z, then their profit, not including the cost of innovation, will be $\pi \bar{A}_{t-1}$ with probability $(1 - p)z$, which is the probability that they innovate and no entry occurs; and it will be $\pi \bar{A}_{t-2}$ with probability $(1 - p)(1 - z)$, the probability of no innovation and no entry. If entry occurs they earn no profit. Therefore, their expected profit, including the cost of innovation, will be

$$(1-p)z\pi\overline{A}_{t-1}+(1-p)(1-z)\pi\overline{A}_{t-2}-cz^2\overline{A}_{t-2}/2$$

They will choose the probability z that maximizes this expression; the first-order condition of this maximization problem yields the probability

$$z_2 = (1-p)(\gamma-1)(\pi/c) \tag{12.5}$$

Next consider firms that are initially close to the frontier. Their expected profit will be $\pi\overline{A}_t$ if they innovate (with probability z) and $\pi\overline{A}_{t-1}$ if they fail to innovate and no entry occurs [with probability $(1 - p)(1 - z)$], so they will choose their probability of innovation so as to maximize

$$z\pi\overline{A}_t+(1-p)(1-z)\pi\overline{A}_{t-1}-cz^2\overline{A}_{t-1}/2$$

so that

$$z_1 = (\gamma-1+p)(\pi/c) \tag{12.6}$$

We interpret an increase in the threat of product entry p as a liberalization reform. Straightforward differentiation of equilibrium innovation intensities with respect to p yields

$$\frac{\partial z_1}{\partial p}=\pi/c>0; \qquad \frac{\partial z_2}{\partial p}=-\pi(\gamma-1)/c<0$$

In other words, *increasing the threat of product entry (e.g., through trade liberalization) encourages innovation in advanced firms and discourages it in backward firms.* The intuition for these comparative statics is immediate. The higher the threat of entry, the more instrumental innovations will be in helping incumbent firms already close to the technological frontier to retain the local market. However, firms that are already far behind the frontier have no chance to win over a potential entrant. Thus, in that case, a higher threat of entry will only lower the expected net gain from innovation, thereby reducing ex ante incentives to invest in innovation.

12.3.4   The Effect of Labor Market Regulations

Next, consider the effects of changes in labor market regulations. A proemployer change in regulation will raise the profit parameter π, so the qualitative effect on investments will be given by the derivatives

$$\partial z_1 / \partial \pi = (\gamma - 1 + p) / c > 0; \qquad \partial z_2 / \partial \pi = (1 - p) g / c > 0$$

Hence, *proemployer labor market regulations encourage innovation in all firms.*

However, if we look at the cross-partial derivatives with respect to reform p and labor regulation π, we get

$$\frac{\partial^2 z_1}{\partial \pi \partial p} = 1/c > 0; \qquad \frac{\partial^2 z_2}{\partial \pi \partial p} = -g/c < 0$$

Thus *a more proemployer labor regulation—that is, a higher π—increases the positive impact of entry on innovation investments in type-1 industries.*

12.3.5 Main Theoretical Predictions

Let us summarize our two main findings:

1. Liberalization (as measured by an increase in the threat of entry) encourages innovation in industries that are close to the frontier and discourages innovation in industries that are far from it. Productivity, output, and profits should thus be raised by more in industries and firms that are initially more advanced.

2. Proworker labor market regulations discourage innovation and growth in all industries, and the negative effect increases with liberalization.

12.3.6 Evidence on the Growth Effects of Entry

These theoretical predictions have been corroborated by a variety of empirical findings. First, Aghion, Blundell, Griffith, Howitt, and Prantl (2006), henceforth ABGHP, investigate the effects of entry threat on TFP growth of UK manufacturing establishments, using panel data with over 32,000 annual observations of firms in 166 different four-digit industries over the 1980–93 period. They estimate the equation

$$Y_{ijt} = \alpha + \beta E_{jt} + \gamma d_{it} + \delta E_{jt} * d_{it} + \eta_i + \tau_t + \varepsilon_{ijt} \tag{12.7}$$

where Y_{ijt} is TFP growth in firm i, industry j, and year t; η and τ are fixed establishment and year effects; E_{jt} is the industry entry rate, measured by the change in the share of UK industry employment in foreign-owned plants; and d_{it} is the firm's proximity to the world technological frontier in the corresponding industry, measured by the log of the ratio between that firm and the frontier-level labor productivity.

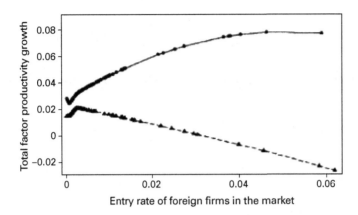

Figure 12.2
Entry, TFP growth, and distance to frontier

Figure 12.2 summarizes the findings. The upper line depicts how productivity growth responds to increased entry for firms that are more-than-median close to the technology frontier in the corresponding sector. The lower line shows the productivity growth response to entry in firms that are more-than-median distant from the technology frontier in their sector. As we can see, the first group of firms react positively to increased entry, whereas the latter group reacts negatively.

12.3.7   Evidence on the Effects of (De)Regulating Entry

Evidence that the effect of regulatory policy depends on a country's circumstances is provided by Aghion, Burgess, Redding, and Zilibotti (2006), hereafter ABRZ, who study the effects of delicensing entry in India over the period from 1980 to 1997, during which there were two major waves of delicensing whose timing varied across states in industries. Using an annual panel with roughly 24,000 observations on 85 industries, 16 states, and 18 years, they show that although delicensing had no discernible effect on overall entry, it did increase the dispersion of output levels across establishments in the delicensed state-industries. Thus it seems that the effects of regulatory liberalization depend upon specific industry characteristics. ABRZ focused on one specific characteristic, namely, the restrictiveness of labor market regulation. They estimated an equation of the form

$$\ln\left(y_{ist}\right) = \alpha + \beta \cdot \text{Delicense}_{ist} + \gamma \cdot \text{Lreg}_{st} + \delta \cdot \text{Delicense}_{sit} * \text{Lreg}_{st}$$
$$+\eta_{is} + \tau_t + \varepsilon_{ijt} \tag{12.8}$$

where y_{ist} is real output, Delicense is a dummy that switches when the state-industry is delicensed, and Lreg$_{st}$ is a measure of the degree of proworker regulation. Although the coefficient β was statistically insignificant, the interaction coefficient δ was highly significantly negative, indicating that one of the characteristics of an industry that makes it grow faster as a result of deregulation is the absence of restrictive labor market regulation. This finding suggests a complementarity between different kinds of regulatory policy that needs to be taken into account when designing progrowth policies. Relaxation of entry barriers may not succeed in promoting growth if not accompanied by other changes that are favorable to business development.

That the overall effect β of delicensing should be negligible is consistent with the preceding theoretical model. Indeed, this model says that the marginal effect of entry threat on average incumbent innovation or productivity growth will be positive only if the threat already exceeds some threshold level. In fact, Aghion, Blundell, and colleagues (2004) find that the effect of (foreign) entry on average productivity growth among incumbent firms is positive in the United Kingdom. That the effect is higher in the United Kingdom than in India is explained easily in the model by the fact that entry is more open in the United Kingdom than in India, together with the fact that a higher fraction of UK sectors are close to their world frontier.

Generally speaking, the message is again that the reaction to the threat of entry posed by liberalization is different for "advanced" and "backward" state-industries in the same sector. Removing barriers to entry incentivizes competitive advanced state-industries to invest in new production and management practices but may have the opposite effect on "backward" state-industries that have little chance of competing in the new environment.

12.4 Conclusion

What have we learned from our analysis in this chapter? First, we have seen that empirical evidence supports the prediction of an inverted-U relationship between competition and innovation. Second, the evidence also supports the prediction that entry and delicensing have a more positive effect on growth in sectors or countries that are closer to the technological frontier, but have a less positive effect on sectors or countries that lie far below the frontier. These findings can be explained through suitable extensions of the Schumpeterian model. At the same time, they question the other models of endogenous growth. First, AK models make no prediction on the relationship between competition and growth, since they assume perfect competition from the start. The product-variety model predicts a negative effect of competition (which in that model corresponds to a higher degree of substitutability α between intermediate inputs) on innovation and growth, as a higher α results in lower rents to reward new product innovators. It also suggests that entry should always be growth enhancing to the extent that it leads to higher product variety.

The findings in this chapter have important policy implications. First, they go directly against the belief that existing national or European "champions" are best placed to innovate at the frontier or that these should be put in charge of selecting new research projects for public funding. Disregarding entry was no big deal during the 30 years immediately after World War II when European industries were still far behind their counterparts in the United States; however, now that Europe has come closer to the world technology frontier, it needs to open up its markets in order to foster growth. Another implication is that domestic-economy competition and entry policies should be accompanied by complementary policies aimed at helping workers and capital reallocate from the laggard sectors that suffer from such policies to the more advanced sectors that benefit from these same policies. A last implication concerns the relationship between growth and democracy: as we shall argue in chapter 17, democracy facilitates entry. This in turn may explain the finding that democracy is more positively correlated with growth in more advanced sectors and countries.

12.5   Literature Notes

The relationship between competition and innovation/entry has first been extensively analyzed by standard IO theory. Here we refer the reader to Tirole (1988). The idea that innovation should decline with competition, as more competition reduces the monopoly rents that reward successful innovators, has been most forcefully formulated by Dasgupta and Stiglitz (1980), but this idea also underlies the spatial competition model of Salop (1977) and the symmetric product differentiation model of Dixit and Stiglitz (1977). The same effect features in the first generation of Schumpeterian growth models, in particular Aghion and Howitt (1992), Grossman and Helpman (1991a), and Caballero and Jaffe (1993).

Some empirical studies have found a positive correlation between monopoly power and innovations (see, for example, Crépon, Duguet, and Mairesse 1998); however, most recent empirical studies, in particular Geroski (1995), Nickell

(1996), and Blundell, Griffith, and Van Reenen (1999), point to a positive correlation between product market competition and innovative output.

Some early analyses pointed instead at the existence of an inverted-U relationship between product market competition and innovation, starting with Scherer (1967)—however, without explaining why and without testing the robustness of this empirical findiing.

A first theoretical attempt at extending the Schumpeterian model in order to generate the possibility of a positive correlation between competition and innovation was by Aghion, Dewatripont, and Rey (1999), who built on previous work by Hart (1983) and Schmidt (1997) showing that competition could act as an incentive scheme in firms with "satisficing" managers.

Aghion, Harris, and Vickers (1997) and then Aghion, Harris, and colleagues (2001) introduced step-by-step innovations into the Schumpeterian framework, thereby generating an inverted-U relationship between competition and innovation. The inverted-U relationship was subsequently tested on a UK firm-level panel by Aghion and colleagues (2005).

The first empirical analysis of the relationship between entry, innovation, and growth is by Nicoletti and Scarpetta (2003) using cross-country data from the OECD. Subsequently, Aghion and colleagues (2004; 2006) introduced entry into the Schumpeterian framework, with predictions on the interplay between distance to frontier, entry, and innovation, which they confronted to UK firm-level panel data.

For an extensive analysis of the relationship between competition, innovation, and growth, we refer the reader to Aghion and Griffith (2005).

Problems

1. Present one argument for why product market competition promotes growth and one argument predicting the opposite effect. Looking at the inverted-U prediction of the relationship between competition and growth presented in the chapter, explain intuitively the "escape-competition effect" and the "Schumpeterian effect." What does this imply in terms of growth-promoting policy?

2. **More on the inverted-U pattern (based on Aghion, Bloom, et al. 2005)**
This exercise extends a bit the model presented in section 12.2.
We consider the setup of section 12.2.

a. Explain why the expected technological gap is given by μ_1; show that it increases with competition.

b. Compute the optimal degree of competition; comment on the effect of γ and h.

c. In their empirical study Aghion, Bloom, and colleagues use the following measure of competition:

$$c = 1 - \text{Average lerner index}$$

Compute this empirical measure in this theoretical setup. Comment.

3. *Cournot versus Bertrand competition, I (based on Aghion, Harris, and Vickers 1997)

This problem uses a setup similar to the one presented in section 12.2 and compares the impact of Cournot and Bertrand competition.

There is a representative consumer with preference defined as

$$U = \int_0^\infty \left\{ \ln \left[C(t) \right] - L(t) \right\} e^{-rt} dt$$

where L is the labor supply (perfectly elastic then) and $C(t)$ is a consumption index defined as $\ln \left[C(t) \right] = \int_0^1 \ln \left[q_i(t) \right] di$ where q_i is the number of goods consumed from the industry $i \in [0, 1]$. In each industry i there is a duopoly. One firm x in industry i can produce one unit of consumption good i using $\gamma^{-k_i^x}$ ($\gamma > 1$) units of labor where k_i^x is the technological level achieved by firm x in sector i. As in the chapter, we assume that the technological gap between two firms cannot be greater than one step and that a firm innovates with a Poisson rate z by employing $\frac{z^2}{2}$ units of labor; in addition, if it is one step behind, there is a Poisson rate of h that it innovates by mere spillover (and if the gap is wider, the Poisson rate to innovate by spillover is infinite). We index by 1 the leader in a sector when it is unleveled (and by -1 the laggard) and by 0 the two firms in leveled sectors.

The wage is normalized at 1, and we focus on a steady state. Also, note that contrary to the model presented in the chapter we do not assume that in the level case only one firm can innovate (but the probability that both do innovate is negligible).

a. Show that the consumer spends $p_i q_i = 1$ on each good.

b. Assuming that the flow of profits only depends on the gap in the sector, show that

$$z_1 = 0$$

$$z_{-1} = \sqrt{(r+h)^2 + (z_0)^2 + 2(a+b)} - \sqrt{(r+h)^2 + 2a}$$

$$z_0 = -s + \sqrt{(r+h)^2 + 2a}$$

where z_l denotes the investment undertaken by a firm in position l, $a = \pi_1 - \pi_0$, and $b = \pi_0 - \pi$. If $a \geq b$, when does a firm undertake more investment?

c. Compute the share of leveled sectors λ.

4. *Cournot versus Bertrand competition, II

This problem is a continuation of the previous one.

a. Show that the growth rate of consumption is given by $g = 2\lambda z_0 \ln(\gamma)$. To do so,

i. Denoting by γ_0 the proportional increase in the aggregate consumption index when a firm in a level sector innovates and by γ_1 the proportional increase in aggregate output when a firm in an unlevel sector innovates, prove (mathematically or heuristically) that

$$g = \frac{d \ln \left[C(t) \right]}{dt} = 2\lambda z_0 \ln(\gamma_0) + (1 - \lambda)(z_{-1} + h) \ln(\gamma_1)$$

ii. Explain why $\gamma_0 \gamma_1 = \gamma$.

iii. Conclude.

b. We consider now the cases of Bertrand (indexed by B) and Cournot (indexed by C) competition. Prove that in this case the flow of profit in a sector is in fact independent of the level of the technology. Show that

$$a_B = \frac{\gamma - 1}{\gamma}$$

$$b_B = 0$$

$$a_C = \frac{(\gamma - 1)(3\gamma + 1)}{4(1 + \gamma)^2}$$

$$b_C = \frac{(\gamma - 1)(3 + \gamma)}{4(1 + \gamma)^2}$$

Note that $a_B > a_C + b_C$.

c. Then show that when $h = r = 0$,

$$\frac{g_B}{g_C} = \left(\frac{1 + \sqrt{\dfrac{7\gamma + 1}{3\gamma + 1}}}{1 + \sqrt{2}} \right)^2 \sqrt{\frac{3\gamma + 1}{4\gamma}}$$

Is Cournot or Bertrand competition better for growth? Explain.

5. **Patent race and Stackelberg competition (based on Etro 2004)**

This problem compares the effect of Stackelberg competition versus Cournot competition on who is going to undertake research.

We consider a market where a monopolist gets a flow of profits π. The monopolist and n competitors can engage in research to discover a new patent with value $V > \pi$ (innovation is drastic, so that the discovery of the new patent kills the market for the old version). Time is continuous, and if a firm engages a flow z of resources in research, it faces a Poisson rate of success of z_i^ε ($0 < \varepsilon < 1$). There is a fixed cost in entering the patent race of $F < V$.

a. Show that the incumbent solves

$$\max_{\tilde{z}} \left\{ \frac{\tilde{z}^\varepsilon V + \pi - \tilde{z}}{r + \sum_{j=1}^{n} z_j^\varepsilon + \tilde{z}} - F \quad \text{if } \tilde{z} > 0, \qquad \frac{\tilde{z}^\varepsilon V + \pi}{r + \sum_{j=1}^{n} z_j^\varepsilon} \quad \text{if } \tilde{z} = 0 \right\}$$

and the entrant i solves

$$\max_{z_i} \left\{ \frac{z_i^\varepsilon V - z_i}{r + \sum_{j=1}^{n} z_j^\varepsilon + \tilde{z}} - F \quad \text{if } z_i > 0, \qquad 0 \quad \text{if } z_i = 0 \right\}$$

b. We consider the case of a Cournot Nash equilibrium.

i. For a fixed n, show that the incumbent undertakes less research than an entrant, and that if n is large enough, the incumbent does not undertake any research.

ii. Under free entry, what is the effect of a decrease in the fixed cost F? (We assume that V is large enough so that there is a large number of entrants, and you can consider it as a real in writing the free entry condition.) Comment.

c. We now consider the case of Stackelberg competition; that is, the monopolist can choose its level of investment before the other firms (and then take their reaction into account).

i. Explain why Stackelberg competition looks natural in this setup.

ii. For a fixed n, show that an entrant chooses to invest more if the incumbent invests more and that the incumbent invests less than an entrant. Compare the aggregate rate of innovation under Cournot and Stackelberg competition.

d. Still in the Sackelberg setup, but with free entry,

i. Prove that the entrant invests $z = \left[\varepsilon (V - F) \right]^{\frac{1}{1-\varepsilon}}$. Comment.

ii. Prove that the aggregate amount of research by entrants decreases with the amount of investment undertaken by the incumbent.

iii. Prove that the incumbent will invest $\tilde{z} = (\varepsilon V)^{\frac{1}{1-\varepsilon}}$, compare it with the investment of the entrant, and compare it with the Nash equilibrium case.

iv. What is the effect of a decrease in the fixed cost on the aggregate amount of R&D?

13 Investing in Education

13.1 Introduction

Does education matter for growth? Which kind of education investment matters most? How best to allocate public funds between primary, secondary, and tertiary education? These are questions that preoccupy governments. For example, they feature prominently in the so-called Lisbon Agenda set by countries in the European Union as part of an effort to reduce the growth gap between the European Union and the United States. A first look at the United States versus the European Union in 1999–2000 shows that 37.3 percent of the U.S. population aged 25–64 had completed a higher education degree, against only 23.8 percent of the EU population. This educational attainment comparison is mirrored by that on tertiary education expenditure, with the United States devoting 3 percent of its GDP to tertiary education versus only 1.4 percent in the European Union. Is this European deficit in tertiary education investment a big deal for growth?

In this chapter, we look at what existing growth models have to say on this type of question. A first class of models emphasizes capital accumulation. Within that class, the neoclassical reference is Mankiw, Romer, and Weil (1992), henceforth MRW, and the AK reference is the celebrated article by Lucas (1988). Both papers emphasize *human capital accumulation* as a source of growth. MRW is an augmented version of the Solow model with human capital as an additional accumulating factor of production, and in particular human capital accumulation slows down the convergence to the steady state by counteracting the effects of decreasing returns to physical capital accumulation. In Lucas, human capital accumulates at a speed proportional to the existing stock of human capital, which in turn leads to a positive long-run growth rate. Whether on the transition path to the steady state (in MRW) or in steady state (in Lucas), the rate of growth depends upon the rate of accumulation of human capital, not upon the stock of human capital.

A second approach, which goes back to the seminal contribution by Nelson and Phelps (1966) and the subsequent empirical work by Benhabib and Spiegel (1994), describes growth as being driven by the *stock* of human capital, which in turn affects a country's ability to innovate or to catch up with more advanced countries.[1] By linking the stock of human capital (measured either by the flow of

1. Barro and Sala-i-Martín (1995a, chap. 13) also used a large sample of countries during the time period 1965–85 to regress the average growth rate on several macroeconomic variables, including educational attainment and public spending on education as a fraction of GDP. Their main findings are (1) that educational attainment (measured by average years of schooling) is significantly

education spending or by school attainment) to the process of technological change, this approach helps answer questions, for example, on how to maximize growth through a proper design of education spending policy.

However, this second approach raises a number of empirical problems. First, the correlation between growth and education ceases to be significant once we restrict the analysis to OECD countries or when we control for country fixed effects. Second, the positive correlation between education—measured by stocks—and growth found in the overall country samples may reflect reverse causalities from growth to education. In this chapter we present potential solutions to these problems. In particular, we argue that significant correlations between education spending and growth can be restored even if we restrict the analysis to OECD countries by (1) decomposing total education spending or attainment into different types or levels (for example, between primary/secondary and tertiary education, or between pregraduate and postgraduate education) and (2) interacting the different types of education spending or attainment with a country's or region's distance to the technology frontier, adapting the appropriate institution idea introduced in chapter 11.

The chapter is organized as follows. Section 13.2 summarizes the growth models based on human capital accumulation. Section 13.3 presents the Nelson-Phelps approach and discusses its limits. Section 13.4 extends the Nelson-Phelps framework by embedding it into a model of appropriate education systems, and then addresses the empirical questions raised by previous regression exercises.

13.2   The Capital Accumulation Approach

13.2.1   Back to Mankiw, Romer, and Weil

13.2.1.1   The Model

To refresh memories, it might be useful to start the chapter by reminding ourselves of the Mankiw, Romer, and Weil (1992) model. What the model does is simply to extend the Solow model by introducing human capital on top of physical capital and raw labor as a third factor of production:

---

correlated with subsequent growth (with a correlation coefficient at around 0.05), although if we decompose the aggregate measure of educational attainment, the impact of primary education remains largely insignificant, and (2) that public spending on education also has a significantly positive effect on growth: a 1.5 percent increase of the ratio of public education spending to GDP during the period 1965–75 would have raised the average growth rate during the same period by 0.3 percent per year.

$$Y = AK^{\alpha}H^{\beta}L^{1-\alpha-\beta}$$

where human capital H *may* also accumulate over time.

Even if H does not accumulate, differences in schooling across countries now partly account for differences in GDP per capita across countries. Taking $L = \bar{L} = 1$, so that GDP is equal to GDP per capita, let us consider two countries, i and j, that have the same steady-state capital/output ratio: $K_i^{ss}/Y_i^{ss} = K_j^{ss}/Y_j^{ss}$. The ratio of country i's steady-state level of output to country j's is given by

$$\frac{Y_i^{ss}}{Y_j^{ss}} = \left(\frac{AH_i^{\beta}}{AH_j^{\beta}} \right)^{\frac{1}{1-\alpha}}$$

so that the difference in GDP per capita across the two countries is entirely explained in this case by differences in schooling.

Now, suppose that human capital does accumulate as physical capital does. Then, the complete model with physical and human capital accumulation boils down the following system of three equations:

$$Y_t = AK_t^{\alpha}H_t^{\beta}$$

$$\frac{dK_t}{dt} = s_k Y_t - \delta K_t$$

$$\frac{dH_t}{dt} = s_h Y_t - \delta H_t$$

Dividing the last two equations by K_t and H_t, respectively, we obtain the steady-state values:

$$K^* = \left(A \frac{s_k^{1-\beta} s_h^{\beta}}{\delta} \right)^{\frac{1}{1-\alpha-\beta}}$$

$$H^* = \left(A \frac{s_k^{\beta} s_h^{1-\beta}}{\delta} \right)^{\frac{1}{1-\alpha-\beta}}$$

and

$$Y^* = \left(A \frac{s_k^{\alpha} s_h^{\beta}}{\delta^{\alpha+\beta}} \right)^{\frac{1}{1-\alpha-\beta}}$$

Thus, as with the Solow model, no long-run growth of per capita GDP is predicted by the MRW model, which again follows from decreasing returns, now to physical *and to human* capital accumulation. However, the MRW model also implies that a government policy that would maintain a positive rate of human capital accumulation would also guarantee a positive long-run rate of growth. For example, suppose that

$$H_t = e^{mt}$$

where $m > 0$. Then the economy will grow at a long-run rate of $m\beta$.

In MRW, human capital accumulation slows down the convergence to the steady state by counteracting the effects of decreasing returns to physical capital accumulation. In the Lucas model we shall present in the next subsection, the assumption that human capital accumulates at a speed proportional to the existing stock of human capital leads to a positive long-run growth rate, even in the absence of human capital accumulation by the government.

13.2.1.2   Development Accounting[2]

The MRW model predicts a positive relationship between per capita GDP and physical and human capital intensities. It can thus be used to analyze the determinants of cross-country differences in per capita GDP, in other words, to perform "development accounting." Thus, for example, if we assume that the aggregate production function takes the form

$$Y = K^\alpha H^\beta (AL)^{1-\alpha-\beta}$$

where L grows at rate n and A grows at rate g, and physical and human capital depreciate at the same rate δ, then we have

$$Y/L = A(K/Y)^{\frac{\alpha}{1-\alpha-\beta}}(H/Y)^{\frac{\beta}{1-\alpha-\beta}} = AX$$

The physical capital intensity is computed in steady state, using the fact that in steady state we have

$$K/Y = \frac{I_K/Y}{\delta+n+g}$$

where I_K/Y is the physical investment intensity, and

$$H/Y = \frac{I_H/Y}{\delta+n+g}$$

---

2. Here we closely follow Banerjee and Duflo (2005).

where I_H/Y is the human capital investment intensity.

MRW use the ratio

$$\frac{cov\left[\log Y/L, \log X\right]}{var\left[\log Y/L\right]}$$

where cov[log Y/L, log X] is the covariance between log Y/L and log X across countries, and var[log Y/L] is the variance of log Y/L across countries, to measure the fraction of cross-country income differences that can be explained by differences in physical and human capital investment intensities, and they find a ratio of 78 percent.

Subsequent studies by Klenow and Rodriguez-Clare (1997) and by Caselli (2005) have extended this development accounting framework, in particular by coming up with refined measures for human and physical capital investments and stock.

13.2.1.3 Discussion

A main challenge to the MRW model comes from Benhabib and Spiegel (1994), who simply refuted the role of human capital *accumulation* as a driver of growth. Using cross-country estimates of physical and human capital stocks over the 1965–85 period, they perform the growth-accounting regressions suggested by a neoclassical production function à la MRW, namely,

$$
\begin{aligned}
\ln y_\tau - \ln y_0 &= \ln A_\tau - \ln A_0 \\
&+ \alpha\left(\ln K_\tau - \ln K_0\right) \\
&+ \beta\left(\ln L_\tau - \ln L_0\right) \\
&+ \gamma\left(\ln H_\tau - \ln H_0\right) \\
&+ \ln \varepsilon_t - \ln \varepsilon_0
\end{aligned}
$$

where ε_τ is the error term. They find that γ is insignificant. This finding in turn implies that log differences in human capital over time have no effect on log differences in income. In other words, human capital accumulation does not matter for growth. See figure 13.1.

Why then did MRW find significant effects of schooling on per capita GDP levels (which imply that the rate of growth of schooling should have a significant effect on the growth rate of per capita GDP)? Benhabib and Spiegel's answer is that MRW use school enrollment as a proxy for average level of human capital, which in turn assumes that the economy is already . . . in a steady state!

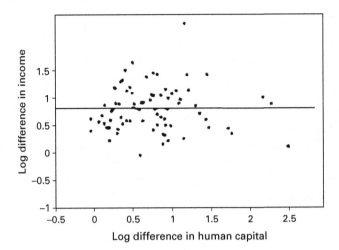

Figure 13.1
Income versus human capital (Benhabib and Spiegel 1994)

Krueger and Lindahl (2001), however, disagree with Benhabib and Spiegel: using panel data over 110 countries between 1960 and 1990, choosing the number of years in education instead of the logarithm of that number to measure human capital,[3] and correcting for measurement errors, they find significant correlations between growth and both the stocks and accumulation rates of human capital. However, these correlations become insignificant once the cross-country sample is restricted to OECD countries.

13.2.2 Lucas

Inspired by Becker's (1964) theory of human capital, Lucas (1988) considers an economy populated by (infinitely lived) individuals who choose at each date how

---

3. This change was in turn motivated by the so-called Mincerian approach to human capital, whereby the value of one more year in schooling is measured by the wage increase that is forgone by the individual who chooses to study during that year instead of working. This amounts to measuring the value of a human capital stock by the log of the current wage rate earned by an individual. And that log was shown by Mincer to be positively correlated with the number of years spent at school by the individual, after estimating an equation of the form

$$\ln w = a_0 + a_1 n$$

The Mincerian approach can itself be criticized, however, for (1) assuming perfectly competitive labor markets, (2) ignoring the role of schools as selection devices, and (3) ignoring interpersonal and intertemporal knowledge externalities.

to allocate their time between current production and skill acquisition (or schooling), where skill acquisition increases productivity in future periods. Thus, if H denotes the current *human capital* stock of the representative agent and u denotes the fraction of his or her time currently allocated to production, then the two basic equations of the Lucas model are

$$y = k^{\beta}(uH)^{1-\beta} \tag{13.1}$$

which describes the way human capital affects current production (k denotes the physical capital stock, which evolves over time according to the same differential equation as in the Solow or Ramsey model, namely, $\dot{k} = y - c$, where c is current consumption), and

$$\dot{H} = \delta H(1-u), \qquad \delta > 0 \tag{13.2}$$

which spells out how current schooling time $(1 - u)$ affects the accumulation of human capital.[4] The reader will have certainly noticed the similarity between equation (13.2) and the differential equation that describes the growth of the leading-edge technology parameter A in chapter 4 or the equation that describes the accumulation of horizontal innovations in the product-variety model of chapter 3. However, in contrast to the nonrival technological knowledge embodied in innovations, human capital acquisition does not necessarily involve externalities (or "spillovers") across individuals of the same generation. Yet the assumption that human capital accumulation involves constant returns to the existing stock of human capital produces a positive growth rate in steady state equal to

$$g = \delta(1-u^*)$$

where u^* is the optimal allocation of individuals' time between production and education.[5] Education effort $(1 - u^*)$ can in turn be shown to depend negatively

---

4. If learning by doing rather than education were the primary source of human capital accumulation, equation (13.2) should be replaced by something like

$$\dot{H} = \delta hu$$

That is, the growth of human capital increases with *production.*

5. That is, u^* maximizes the representative consumer's intertemporal utility

$$\int_0^{\infty} \frac{c_t^{1-\sigma}}{1-\sigma} e^{-\rho t} dt$$

subject to equations (13.1) and (13.2) and $\dot{k} = y - c.$

on the rate of time preference ρ and the coefficient of relative risk aversion σ and positively on the productivity of schooling measured by δ, therefore displaying comparative static properties similar to the steady-state R&D investment in chapters 3 and 4.

The Lucas model is elegant, but at the same time also stylized in its description of the return to education. For example, in this model an individual's returns to education remain constant over his or her whole lifetime, an assumption that is at odds both with the empirical evidence on education and with Becker's theory of human capital. Becker (1964) indeed suggests that returns to education tend to *decrease* over the lifetime of an individual. One easy way to deal with this objection is to reformulate the Lucas model in the context of an overlapping-generations framework where individuals inherit the human capital accumulated by their parents.[6]

For example, consider the following simplified version of the Lucas model, with discrete time and successive generations of two-period-lived individuals. In her first period of life, an individual chooses how to share her time between production and human capital accumulation. Human capital accumulates according to

$$H_2 - H_1 = \delta(1-u)H_1 \tag{13.3}$$

where H_1 (resp. H_2) is the individual's stock of human capital in period 1 (resp. period 2), and u still denotes the fraction of time u spent on production in period 1.

The individual chooses u to

$$\max_u \left\{ \frac{(H_1 u)^{1-\sigma}}{1-\sigma} + \beta \frac{(H_2)^{1-\sigma}}{1-\sigma} \right\}$$

subject to equation (13.3), where β is the discount factor.

The first-order condition for this maximization is simply

$$u^{-\sigma} - \beta\delta \left[1 + \delta(1-u) \right]^{-\sigma} = 0$$

or equivalently

$$u = u^* = \frac{1}{\delta + (\beta\delta)^{\frac{1}{\sigma}}}$$

6. See d'Autume and Michel (1994) for a systematic analysis of the overlapping-generations version of the Lucas model.

which is decreasing in δ and β.

Thus the equilibrium growth rate

$$g = \delta(1 - u^*)$$

is increasing in the productivity of schooling δ and decreasing with the rate of time preference, which itself is inversely measured by β.

13.2.3   Threshold Effects and Low-Development Traps

Consider the following extremely simple overlapping-generations model with human accumulation: there is a continuum of overlapping-generations families, in which each individual lives for two periods. All individuals born at date t inherit the aggregate human capital accumulated by the previous generation of individuals born at date $t - 1$, that is,

$$h_{1,t}^i \equiv h_{1,t} = H_{2,t-1} \tag{13.4}$$

where

$$H_{2,t-1} = \int h_{2,t-1}^i \, di$$

Thus, if for simplicity we assume that individuals of a same generation are identical and of total mass equal to one (so that total population remains constant equal to two), we have

$$h_{1,t} = h_{2,t-1}$$

where $h_{2,t-1}$ is the human capital accumulated by an individual born at date $t - 1$.

Next, we must specify how human capital accumulates during the lifetime of an individual. We shall assume, for all t,

$$h_{2,t} = \left[1 + \gamma(v_{t-1}) \cdot v^{\theta}\right] h_{1,t} \tag{13.5}$$

where v is the fraction of time allocated to education by a young individual born at date t, $\gamma(v_{t-1})$ is a positive number that is nondecreasing in the amount of time v_{t-1} devoted to education by the previous generation, and $\theta < 1$.[7]

The complementary time $1 - v$ is allocated to production activities, and to simplify the argument to the extreme, we will assume that an individual with

---

7. See section 13.3.2 for an alternative model that has multiple development paths but that does not rely on intertemporal threshold externalities, that is, in which $\gamma(v) \equiv \gamma =$ constant.

current human capital endowment h contributes a marginal product equal to h and therefore earns a wage also equal to h.[8] Therefore, an individual born at date t (with initial skills $h_{1,t}$) will choose how much time v to spend in education so as to maximize his or her intertemporal utility of consumption. Assuming linear preferences and letting ρ denote the discount factor, the optimal education time v^* solves the maximization program

$$\max_{v} \left(1-v\right)h_{1,t} + \rho h_{2,t}$$

$$\text{subject to: } h_{2,t} = \left[1 + \gamma\left(v_{t-1}\right) \cdot v^{\theta}\right]h_{1,t} \tag{13.6}$$

A special case occurs when γ is a constant. Then, we obtain the unique solution

$$v^* = \left(\rho\theta\gamma\right)^{\frac{1}{1-\theta}}$$

which in turn corresponds to a unique steady-state growth path, at rate

$$g^* = \frac{h_{2,t}}{h_{2,t-1}} = 1 + \gamma\left(v^*\right)^{\theta} = 1 + \gamma\left(\rho\theta\gamma\right)^{\frac{\theta}{1-\theta}}$$

As in the Lucas model, we see that g^* is an increasing function of the productivity of education measured by γ and a decreasing function of the rate of time preference r (where $\rho = \dfrac{1}{1+r}$).

However, the more interesting case considered by Azariadis and Drazen (1990) occurs when the education technology in equation (13.6) displays positive *threshold externalities*. In particular, suppose that

$$\gamma\left(v_{t-1}\right) = \begin{cases} \underline{\gamma} & \text{if } v_{t-1} \le v_0 \\ \overline{\gamma} & \text{if } v_{t-1} > v_0 \end{cases}$$

where $0 < v_0 < 1$ and $\underline{\gamma} \ll \overline{\gamma}$. Then, if the previous generation has insufficiently invested in education, and therefore $\gamma(v_{t-1}) = \underline{\gamma}$, investing in education tends to become unattractive for the current generation as well; hence the possibility of a low-growth path where all successive generations invest too little in education. This low-growth path, or "low-development trap," can naturally coexist with a high-growth path where all generations invest at least v_0 in education and therefore $\gamma(v_{t-1}) \equiv \overline{\gamma}$ for all t.

---

8. Equivalently, we could assume that all individuals are self-employed and that the self-employment technology is linear, with s working-time units producing $h \cdot s$ units of output, where h denotes the individual's current human capital endowment.

More precisely, a low-growth steady-state equilibrium will involve the stationary educational attainment level $\underline{v}$, where

$$\underline{v} = \arg\max \left(1-v\right)h_{1,t} + \rho\left(1+\underline{\gamma}v^{\theta}\right)h_{1,t}$$

that is, $\underline{v} = \left(\rho\theta\underline{\gamma}\right)^{\frac{1}{1-\theta}}$, with corresponding growth rate

$$\underline{g} = 1+\underline{\gamma}\cdot\underline{v}^{\theta} = 1+\underline{\gamma}\left(\rho\theta\underline{\gamma}\right)^{\frac{\theta}{1-\theta}}$$

Similarly, the high-growth equilibrium will involve the educational attainment level $\bar{v}$, where

$$\bar{v} = \arg\max_{v} \left(1-v\right)h_{1,t} + \rho\left(1+\bar{\gamma}\cdot v^{\theta}\right)h_{1,t}$$

that is, $\bar{v} = \left(\rho\theta\bar{\gamma}\right)^{\frac{1}{1-\theta}}$, with correspondingly high growth rate

$$\bar{g} = 1+\bar{\gamma}\cdot\bar{v}^{\theta} = 1+\bar{\gamma}\left(\rho\theta\bar{\gamma}\right)^{\frac{\theta}{1-\theta}}$$

For these two equilibria to actually coexist, it is necessary and sufficient that $\underline{v} < v_0 < \bar{v}$, a requirement which in turn imposes restrictions on the parameters v_0, ρ, θ, $\underline{\gamma}$ and $\bar{\gamma}$.

In short, the existence of threshold externalities in the education technology case naturally leads to a multiplicity of steady-state growth paths, including a low-development trap where insufficient investment in education in the past discourages further skill acquisition and thereby future growth. Thus Azariadis and Drazen provide a perhaps more natural story than Lucas (1988) for why countries with unequal initial human-capital endowments may keep growing at different rates forever. But they also suggest a role for government intervention in the education sector, namely, to avoid low-development traps and thereby promote high sustained growth.[9]

9. Becker, Murphy, and Tamura (1990) develop a similar model but one in which individuals decide also about "fertility," that is, about how many children they wish to have. Assuming that the returns to human capital investments increase with the human capital stock, the authors show the existence of multiple equilibria. One equilibrium corresponds to a "development trap," with a high rate of population growth but low levels and low growth rates of individual human capital. The other equilibrium instead corresponds to a low rate of population growth but also to high levels and rapid growth of human capital per head. The contrast with the Solow-Swan model is interesting: here, the rate of population growth is negatively correlated with the rate of productivity growth.

13.3 Nelson and Phelps and the Schumpeterian Approach

13.3.1 The Nelson and Phelps Approach

Nelson and Phelps (1966) did not have a model of endogenous growth with endogenous R&D and innovation, but they were already thinking of growth as being generated by productivity-improving adaptations, whose arrival rate would depend upon the stock of human capital. More formally, Nelson and Phelps would picture a world economy in which, in any given country, productivity grows according to an equation of the form

$$\dot{A} = f(H)(\overline{A} - A)$$

where again $\overline{A}$ denotes the frontier technology (itself growing over time at some exogenous rate) and H is the current stock of human capital in the country. A higher stock of human capital would thus foster growth by making it easier for a country to catch up with the frontier technology. Benhabib and Spiegel (1994) tested a slightly augmented version of the Nelson-Phelps model in which human capital not only facilitates the adaptation to more advanced technologies, but also makes it easier to innovate at the frontier, according to a dynamic equation of the form

$$\dot{A} = f(H)(\overline{A} - A) + g(H)\gamma A$$

where the second term captures the innovation component of growth.

Using cross-country regressions of the increase in the log of per capita GDP over the period 1965–85 as a linear function of the sum of logs of human capital stocks over all the years between 1965 and 1985, Benhabib and Spiegel found a significantly positive correlation between H and g. More specifically, Benhabib and Spiegel perform the regression

$$
\begin{aligned}
\ln y_\tau - \ln y_0 = {} & \ln A_\tau - \ln A_0 \\
& + \alpha\left(\ln K_\tau - \ln K_0\right) \\
& + \beta\left(\ln L_\tau - \ln L_0\right) \\
& + \gamma\left(\frac{1}{\tau}\sum_{t=0}^{\tau}\ln H_t\right) \\
& + \ln \varepsilon_\tau - \ln \varepsilon_0
\end{aligned}
$$

and find a positive and significant γ. This in turn implies that human capital stock is positively correlated with output growth. Moreover, Benhabib and Spiegel find

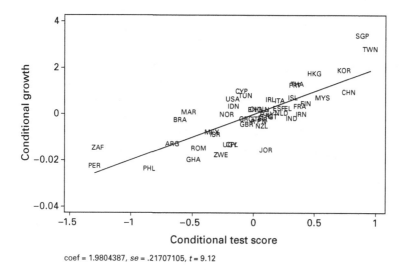

coef = 1.9804387, *se* = .21707105, *t* = 9.12

Figure 13.2
Education quality and economic growth

a larger correlation for countries further below the world technology frontier, which suggests that the catch-up component of growth is the dominant one. Does this approach help us understand the comparison between Europe and the United States?

Unfortunately, Krueger and Lindahl (2001) found that the significance of the correlation between growth and human capital stocks disappears when restricting the regression to OECD countries. One interpretation of that result is that human capital stocks only matter for catching up but not for innovating at the frontier. Another interpretation is that this regression is too aggregate or tells an incomplete story.

A first attempt at moving beyond the Benhabib-Spiegel regression is the one recently pursued by Hanushek and Woessmann (2007)—that it is not so much the amount of spending on education that matters for growth but rather the quality of education. Using test scores to construct an aggregate measure of education quality, Hanushek and Woessmann find a significantly positive correlation between the average growth rate over the period 1960–2000 and the average quality of education over that period, as shown in figure 13.2.

A second attempt, detailed in the following section, is to look at the composition of education spending and to interact it with the country's or region's level of technological development.

13.3.2   Low-Development Traps Caused by the Complementarity between R&D and Education Investments

The following model, inspired by Acemoglu (1997) and Redding (1996), delivers multiple development paths as in the Azariadis-Drazen model, although under more natural assumptions about human-capital accumulation. In particular, the following story does not rely on intertemporal threshold externalities in human-capital accumulation.

There is again a continuum of overlapping generations of individual workers each of whom lives for two periods and has preferences

$$u(c_1, c_2) = c_1 + \rho c_2$$

where ρ is the discount factor. All individuals are born with one unit of human capital ($h_{1,t} \equiv 1$ for all t) and, by investing the fraction v of their working time to education when young, individuals can end up with $h_{2,t} = 1 + \gamma \cdot v^\theta$ units of human capital, where γ is now constant and $0 < \theta < 1$.

There is also a continuum of overlapping generations of entrepreneurs, who can produce only when old according to the linear technology

$$y^i_{j,t+1} = A^i_{t+1} \cdot h_{j,t+1}$$

where (a) A^i_{t+1} denotes entrepreneur i's productivity at date $t + 1$ (which itself depends on whether or not the entrepreneur has innovated the existing leading-edge technology $A_t = \max A^i_t$ available to him or her upon birth at date t; (b) $h_{j,t+1}$ is the human capital of worker j employed by the entrepreneur at date $t + 1$.

The time-path of productivity parameters A^i_t is then governed by the following innovation technology: by investing a nonmonetary cost equal to $\alpha \mu A$, entrepreneurs can increase productivity from A (the current leading edge) to λA with probability μ, where $\lambda > 1$ and $0 < \mu < 1$.

Now assume that individual workers remain self-employed when young, producing output $(1 - v)A$ where $(1 - v)$ is production time and A denotes the current leading-edge technology,[10] and when old are randomly matched with firms from which they earn the fraction β of output surplus.[11] Then the optimal allocation of working time between current production and education will solve the following maximization program:

---

10. The analysis would remain essentially unchanged if A were instead taken to be the average technology.

11. We assume a one-to-one matching process between firms and workers, based on the implicit assumption that firms are capacity constrained and can employ at most one worker.

$$\max_v \left\{ (1-v)A + \beta\rho[\mu\lambda + 1 - \mu](1+\gamma v^\theta)A \right\}$$

This yields the optimal education time

$$v^* = \min\left(1, \left[\beta\rho\theta\gamma(\mu\lambda + 1 - \mu)\right]^{\frac{1}{1-\theta}}\right)$$

which is an increasing function of the probability of innovation μ.

The entrepreneurs, in turn, will choose R&D effort (i.e., μ) to

$$\max_\mu V(\mu) = \left\{ -\mu\alpha A + \rho(1-\beta)(\mu\lambda + 1 - \mu)\cdot(1+\gamma v^\theta)A \right\}$$

Hence

$$\mu^* = \begin{cases} 1 & \text{if } \alpha < \rho(\lambda - 1)(1+\gamma v^\theta)(1-\beta) \\ 0 & \text{otherwise,} \end{cases}$$

thus the more workers invest in education (i.e., the higher v) the more will entrepreneurs invest in R&D.

This strategic complementarity between workers' education decisions and firms' R&D decisions will not surprisingly open the possibility for multiple steady-state growth paths, including a low-development trap. Such a trap will involve $\mu^* = 0$ and therefore $v^* = \underline{v} = (\beta\rho\theta\gamma)^{\frac{1}{1-\theta}}$. For it to exist we simply need

$$\alpha > \rho(1-\beta)(\lambda - 1)\left(1 + \gamma(\beta\rho\theta\gamma)^{\frac{1}{1-\theta}}\right).$$

Conversely, a high-growth equilibrium will involve $\mu^* = 1$ and therefore $v^* = \overline{v} = (\lambda\beta\rho\theta\gamma)^{\frac{1}{1-\theta}}$. In order for a high-growth steady-state path to exist, we need

$$\alpha < \rho(1-\beta)(\lambda - 1)\left(1 + \gamma(\lambda\beta\rho\theta\gamma)^{\frac{1}{1-\theta}}\right).$$

The corresponding growth rates will be $g = \overline{g} = \ln\lambda$ in the high-growth equilibrium and $g = \underline{g} = 0$ in the low-development trap.[12]

Two quick remarks conclude our analysis in this section. First, because of the strategic complementarity between R&D and education, we did not have to introduce threshold externalities in the accumulation of human capital in order to generate multiple equilibria and low-development traps. Second, targeted education

---

12. Had we introduced an intertemporal human capital externality, of the kind assumed in the previous section, namely $y_{1t} = (1 - d)H_{t-1}$, where $H_{t-1} = \int h^i_{2,t-1} di$, the analysis would remain identical except that $\overline{g} = \ln\lambda + \ln(1 - d)(1 + \gamma\cdot\overline{v}^\theta)$ and $\underline{g} = \ln(1 - d)(1 + \gamma\cdot\underline{v}^\theta) \neq 0$. Interestingly, in that case the growth differential $\overline{g} - \underline{g}$ is magnified by the fact that the high-growth equilibrium also displays a higher rate of human capital accumulation.

policies and R&D subsidies appear as substitutable instruments for moving the economy away from a low-development trap. In practice, however, education subsidies may be easier to monitor than R&D subsidies to industries (the scope for diversion and manipulation being presumably larger in the latter case).

13.4   Schumpeter Meets Gerschenkron

Suppose that, as in Benhabib and Spiegel (1994), productivity growth can be generated either by implementing (or imitating) the frontier technology or by innovating on past technologies. As in Benhabib and Spiegel, the relative importance of innovation increases as a country or region moves closer to the technology frontier. However, departing from Benhabib and Spiegel, different types of education spending lie behind implementation and innovation activities. In particular, investment in tertiary education should have a bigger effect on a country's ability to make leading-edge innovations, whereas primary and secondary education are more likely to affect the country's ability to implement existing (frontier) technologies. Then, the closer a country is to the world technology frontier, the more growth enhancing it is for that country to invest in tertiary education. Conversely, the farther below the frontier this country is, the more growth enhancing it is for that country to invest in primary or secondary education. Interestingly, when regressing productivity growth on the various kinds of education spending and their interaction with the country's distance to frontier, we recover significant correlation results even when restraining the regression to OECD countries. In other words, this approach helps address the Krueger-Lindahl irrelevance puzzle.

13.4.1   A Model of Distance to Frontier and the Composition of Education Spending[13]

13.4.1.1   A Toy Model

As in previous chapters, the final good is produced according to

$$y_t = \int_0^1 A_{it}^{1-\alpha} x_{it}^\alpha \, di$$

where the intermediate good x_{it} is itself produced one for one using the final good as input. We know that the equilibrium profit of firm i is equal to

---

13. The analysis in this section is drawn from Vandenbussche, Aghion, and Meghir (2006), henceforth VAM.

$$\pi_{it} = \pi A_{it}$$

where π is a constant.

Following the model of appropriate institutions developed in chapter 11, productivity in firm i evolves according to

$$A_{it} - A_{t-1} = f(u)\overline{A}_{t-1} + g(s)\gamma A_{t-1} \tag{13.7}$$

where $\overline{A}_{t-1}$ is the frontier productivity last period, A_{t-1} is the average productivity in the country last period, u is the number of workers with primary/secondary education (unskilled workers) used in imitation, s is the number of workers with higher education (skilled workers) used in innovation, and f and g are increasing functions of their argument.

Let $a_t = A_t / \overline{A}_t$ denote the country's proximity to the technological frontier at date t, and suppose that the frontier productivity grows at constant rate $\overline{g}$, that is,

$$\overline{A}_t = (1 + \overline{g})\overline{A}_{t-1}$$

The intermediate producer will choose u and s to maximize profits. Dividing through by $\overline{A}_{t-1}$ and dropping time subscripts, the producer's problem simply becomes

$$\max_{u,s} \left\{ \delta\left[f(u) + \gamma g(s) a \right] - w_u u - w_s s \right\}$$

where w_u and w_s denote the wage rates of unskilled and skilled workers, respectively.

Using the fact that all intermediate firms face the same maximization problem and that there is a unit mass of intermediate firms, in equilibrium we necessarily have

$$u = U; \qquad s = S$$

where U is the total supply of lower education and S is the total supply of higher education.

Using equation (13.7), the equilibrium growth rate can then be simply expressed as

$$g^* = \frac{A_{it} - A_{t-1}}{A_{t-1}} = f(U)\frac{1}{a_{t-1}} + g(S)\gamma$$

In particular, looking at the cross derivatives of g^* with respect to U and a, we find

$$\frac{\partial^2 g^*}{\partial a \partial U} = -f'(U)\frac{1}{a^2} < 0$$

In other words, *a marginal increase in the fraction of workers with lower education enhances productivity growth all the less the closer the country is to the world technology frontier.*

Note, however, that the cross derivative

$$\frac{\partial^2 g^*}{\partial a \partial S}$$

is equal to zero. Thus this model is too simple to deliver the symmetric prediction that the closer a country is to the frontier the more growth-enhancing it is to invest more in tertiary education in that country.

13.4.1.2 Cobb-Douglas Growth Technologies

As in the previous subsection, intermediate firms can increase productivity either by imitating frontier technologies or by innovating upon existing technologies in the country. However, imitation and innovation can be performed by both types of workers, even though the elasticity of highly educated labor (skilled labor) is larger for innovation, whereas the elasticity of low-education labor (unskilled labor) is higher in imitation.

More formally, we focus on the following class of productivity-growth functions:

$$A_{it} - A_{t-1} = u_{m,i,t}^{\sigma} s_{m,i,t}^{1-\sigma}\left(\bar{A}_{t-1} - A_{t-1}\right) + \gamma u_{n,i,t}^{\phi} s_{n,i,t}^{1-\phi} A_{t-1} \tag{13.8}$$

where $u_{m,i,t}$ (resp. $s_{m,i,t}$) is the amount of unskilled (resp. skilled) labor used in imitation in sector i at time t, $u_{n,i,t}$ (resp. $s_{n,i,t}$) is the amount of unskilled (resp. skilled) units of labor used by sector i in innovation at time t, σ (resp. ϕ) is the elasticity of unskilled labor in imitation (resp. innovation), and $\gamma > 0$ measures the relative efficiency of innovation compared to imitation in generating productivity growth.

We shall assume the following:

ASSUMPTION 1   The elasticity of skilled labor is higher in innovation than in imitation, and conversely for the elasticity of unskilled labor, that is, $\phi < \sigma$.

Let $w_{u,t}\bar{A}_{t-1}$ (resp. $w_{s,t}\bar{A}_{t-1}$) denote the current price of unskilled (resp. skilled) labor. Then the total labor cost of productivity improvement by intermediate firm i at time t is equal to

$$W_{i,t} = \left[w_{u,t}\left(u_{m,i,t} + u_{n,i,t}\right) + w_{s,t}\left(s_{m,i,t} + s_{n,i,t}\right) \right]\bar{A}_{t-1}$$

Letting $a_t = A_t/\bar{A}_t$ measure again the country's proximity to the technological frontier at date t and letting the frontier technology $\bar{A}_t$ grow at constant rate g, the intermediate producer will solve

$$\max\left\{\pi\left[u_{m,i,t}^{\sigma} s_{m,i,t}^{1-\sigma}\left(1 - a_{t-1}\right) + \gamma u_{n,i,t}^{\phi} s_{n,i,t}^{1-\phi} a_{t-1}\right]\bar{A}_{t-1} - W_{i,t}\right\} \tag{13.9}$$

Using the fact that all intermediate firms face the same maximization problem and that there is a unit mass of intermediate firms, we necessarily have

$$u_{j,i,t} \equiv u_{j,t}; \qquad s_{j,i,t} \equiv s_{j,t} \quad \text{for all } i \text{ and for } j = m, n \tag{13.10}$$

and

$$S = s_{m,t} + s_{n,t}; \qquad U = u_{m,t} + u_{n,t} \tag{13.11}$$

Taking first-order conditions for the maximization problem (13.9), then making use of equations (13.10) and (13.11), and then computing the equilibrium rate of productivity growth

$$g_t = \int_0^1 \frac{A_{it} - A_{t-1}}{A_{t-1}}\, di$$

one can establish the following:

LEMMA 1   Let $\psi = \dfrac{\sigma(1-\phi)}{(1-\sigma)\phi}$. If parameter values are such that the solution to equation (13.9) is interior, then we have

$$\frac{\partial g_t}{\partial a} = \phi(1-\phi)h'(a)h(a)^{-1-\phi}\left[h(a)U - S\right]$$

where

$$h(a) = \left(\frac{(1-\sigma)\psi^{\sigma}(1-a)}{(1-\phi)\gamma a}\right)^{\frac{1}{\sigma-\phi}}$$

This lemma, together with the fact that $h(a)$ is obviously decreasing in a given assumption 1, immediately implies the following:

PROPOSITION 1   Given assumption 1, a marginal increase in higher education investment S enhances productivity growth all the more the closer the country is from the world technology frontier, that is,

$$\frac{\partial^2 g_t}{\partial a \partial S} > 0$$

And a marginal increase in lower education investment U enhances productivity growth all the less the closer the country is from the world technology frontier, that is,

$$\frac{\partial^2 g_t}{\partial a \partial U} < 0$$

The intuition underlying this proposition follows directly from the Rybczynski theorem in international trade. Stated in the context of a two-sector–two-input economy, this theorem says that an increase in the supply of input in the sector that uses that input more intensively should increase "output" in that sector more than proportionally. To transpose this result to the context of our model, consider the effect of an increase in the supply of skilled labor, keeping the supply of unskilled labor fixed and for given a. Given that skilled workers contribute relatively more to productivity growth and profits if employed in innovation rather than in imitation (our assumption 1), the demand for additional skilled labor will tend to be higher in innovation. But then the marginal productivity of unskilled labor should also increase more in innovation than in imitation; hence, a net flow of unskilled workers should also move from imitation into innovation. This in turn will enhance further the marginal productivity of skilled labor in innovation, thereby inducing an ever greater fraction of skilled labor to move to innovation. Now, the closer the country is to the technology frontier (that is, the higher a), the stronger this Rybczynski effect, as a higher a increases the efficiency of both skilled and unskilled labor in innovation relative to imitation. A second, reinforcing, reason is that an increase in the fraction of skilled labor reduces the amount of unskilled labor available in the economy, hence reducing the marginal productivity of skilled labor in imitation, all the more the closer the country is to the frontier.

13.4.1.3   Back to Krueger and Lindahl

Before we confront this prediction with evidence on higher education, distance to frontier, and productivity growth, let us go back to Krueger and Lindahl's irrelevance result, namely, that human capital stocks and growth are no longer significantly correlated when restricting cross-country panel regressions to OECD countries. More specifically, consider two countries, 1 and 2, that have the same total human capital stock and lie at the same distance from the world technology frontier. The only difference is that country 1 is better endowed in highly educated labor whereas country 2 is better endowed in unskilled labor.

Thus

$$H_1 = H_2 = H$$

but

$$H = S_1 + U_1 = U_2 + S_2$$

where

$$S_1 > S_2$$

Which of these two countries grows faster? The answer depends upon these countries' proximity to the world technology frontier. Namely, country 1 will grow faster if the two countries are sufficiently close to frontier, because country 1 is better endowed in what is most important for growth close to the frontier. And country 2 will grow faster if both countries are far from frontier, since country 2 is better endowed in what is more important for growth far below the frontier. Yet the two countries have the same total amount of human capital.

This reasoning just shows that the total stock of human capital is not a sufficient statistic to predict the growth rate of a country. In addition, one needs to know about the composition of human capital in the country and about the country's proximity to the world technology frontier in order to predict the growth rate in that country.

13.4.2   Cross-Country and Cross-U.S.-State Evidence

13.4.2.1   Cross-Country Evidence

Vandenbussche, Aghion, and Meghir (2006) confront the preceding prediction with cross-country panel evidence on higher education, distance to frontier, and productivity growth. Aghion, Bouston, Hoxby, and Vandenbussche (2005), henceforth ABHV, test the theory on cross-U.S.-state data. Each approach has its pros and cons. Cross-U.S.-state analysis uses a much richer data set and also good instruments for higher and lower education spending. However, a serious analysis of the growth impact of education spending across U.S. states must take into account an additional element not considered in previous models, namely, the effects on the migration of skilled labor across states at different levels of technological development. In contrast, cross-country analysis can safely ignore the migration; however, the data are sparse and the instruments for educational spending are weak (consisting mainly of lagged spending). In the remaining part of the section we shall consider the two pieces of empirical analysis in turn.

VAM consider a panel data set of 22 OECD countries over the period 1960–2000, which they subdivide into five-year subperiods. Output and investment data are drawn from Penn World Tables 6.1 (2002) and human capital data from Barro and Lee (2000). The Barro and Lee data indicate the fraction of a country's population that has reached a certain level of schooling at intervals of five years, so they use the fraction that has received some higher education together with their measure of TFP (constructed assuming a constant labor share of 0.65 across country) to perform the following regression:

$$g_{j,t} = \alpha_0 + \alpha_1 \text{Prox}_{j,t-1} + \alpha_2 \text{Fraction}_{j,t} + \alpha_3\left(\text{Prox}_{j,t-1} * \text{Fraction}_{j,t}\right) + v_j + u_{j,t}$$

where $g_{j,t}$ is country j's growth rate over a five-year period, $\text{Prox}_{j,t-1}$ is country j's proximity to the technological frontier at $t-1$ (i.e., 5 years before), $\text{Fraction}_{j,t}$ is the fraction of the working-age population with some higher education, and v_j is a country's fixed effect. The proximity and human capital variables are instrumented with their values at $t-2$, and the equation is estimated in differences to eliminate the fixed effect. The results are shown in table 13.1.

Before controlling for country fixed effects, VAM obtain a statistically significant coefficient for the human capital variable and a statistically significant coefficient for the interaction variable, indicating that indeed higher education matters more as a country gets closer to the frontier. Controlling for country fixed effects removes the significance of the coefficients; however, this significance is restored once countries are regrouped into subregions and country fixed effects are replaced by group fixed effects. This result in turn suggests that cross-country data on only 122 countries are too sparse for significant regression results to survive when we control for country fixed effects.

To see how this result translates in terms of the effect of an additional year of schooling of higher education, they perform the following regression in logs:

$$g_{j,t} = \alpha_0' + \alpha_1' \text{Prox}_{j,t-1}' + \alpha_2' N_{j,t} + \alpha_3'\left(\text{Prox}_{j,t-1} * N_{j,t}\right) + v_j' + u_{j,t}'$$

where this time $\text{Prox}_{j,t-1}'$ is the log of the closeness to the technological frontier and $N_{j,t}$ is the average number of years of higher education of the population. The econometric technique employed is the same as before. Before controlling for country fixed effects, VAM find the coefficient of the number of years to be 0.105 and of little significance, but the coefficient of the interaction variable to be equal to 0.368 and significant. This result again demonstrates that it is more important to expand years of higher education close to the technological frontier.

Table 13.1
TFP Growth Equation (Fractions, Barro and Lee 2000)

	[1]	[2]	[3]	[4]	[5]
Proximity	−0.071 [0.05]	−0.222 [0.161]	−0.16 [0.045]***	−0.05 [1.06]	−0.35 [0.057]***
Fraction	−0.048 [0.084]	0.49 [1.9]	0.125 [0.058]**	1.54 [4.1]	0.386 [0.13]***
Proximity*Fraction			0.78 [0.2]***	−1.88 [11.2]	1.46 [0.35]***
Country dummies	No	Yes	No	Yes	Groups
p-value country dummies				0	
Proximity threshold			−0.16 [0.062]		
Rank test (p value)					7%
Number of observations	122	122	122	122	122

Note: Standard errors in square brackets. Time dummies not reported. In column [5], countries are grouped in the following way: group 1: Belgium, France, Italy, Netherlands; group 2: the four Scandinavian countries, Austria, UK, Switzerland; group 3: Canada, United States; group 4: Australia, New Zealand; group 5: Portugal, Spain; group 6: Greece; group 7: Ireland. Proximity is the log ratio of a country's TFP to the technological frontier's TFP (hence it is a negative number). Proximity threshold indicates the value of proximity above which fraction is growth-enhancing. One, two, and three asterisks indicate significance at the 10, 5, and 1% level, respectively.

13.4.2.2   Cross-U.S.-State Evidence

ABHV test the same theory on cross-U.S.-state data instead of cross-country data. As mentioned previously, one potential problem when moving from cross-country to cross-region data is that educational policy should affect migration flows across regions more than it affects migration flows across countries. Thus a suitable model of education amid growth across regions within the same country ought to include an additional equation describing how migration flow varies, for example, with the wage differential between a particular state and the state currently at the technological frontier. Introducing the possibility of migration reinforces the positive interaction between closeness to the frontier and higher education. Namely, in addition to the Rybczynski effect described earlier, investing in higher education in a state that is far from the technological frontier would contribute all the less to growth in that state because the newly skilled workers would migrate to a more frontier state where productivity and therefore wages are higher.

Any regression with growth on the left-hand side and education on the right-hand side raises an obvious endogeneity problem, best emphasized by Bils and Klenow

(2000). Here, as in the preceding cross-country panel regressions, the endogeneity problem can be stated as follows: If states or countries choose their composition of education spending according to the model, then we should see the composition of educational investments being highly correlated with technology and productivity, and therefore the regressions would say nothing about causality.

However, the great advantage of moving from cross-country to cross-state analysis is that we have access to a natural source of exogenous variation in education investment, namely, political economy considerations that may lead the Congress or other federal authorities to misallocate the funding to higher education across states. For example, because it has a representative on a congressional commission for higher education, a far-from-the-frontier state may end up mistakenly receiving excessive funding for research-related education. Conversely, because of local political economy considerations, a close-to-the-frontier state may end up mistakenly focusing its investment in primary education, neglecting higher education.

In other words, political economy considerations and politicians' ability and incentive to deliver "pork" to their constituencies provide a natural source of instruments that predict states' tendencies to make exogenous "mistakes" when investing in education.

The actual instruments used in ABHV are as follows:

1. For research-university education: whether a state has a congressman on the appropriations committee that allocates funds for research universities but not other types of schools.

2. For "lowbrow" postsecondary education (community colleges, training schools): whether the chairman of the state's education committee represents voters whose children attend one- or two-year postsecondary institutions.

3. For primary and secondary education: whether the overall political balance on the state's supreme court interacts with the state school finance system.

Then, using annual panel data over the period 1970–2000, ABHV perform a two-stage procedure whereby (1) in first-stage regressions, the various kinds of educational spending are regressed over their respective instruments, and (2) the growth rate in each state and year is regressed over the instruments for the various kinds of educational spending, the state's proximity to the frontier, and the interaction between the two, controlling for state and year fixed effects. We refer our readers to ABHV for the detailed regression results, which are summarized in figure 13.3.

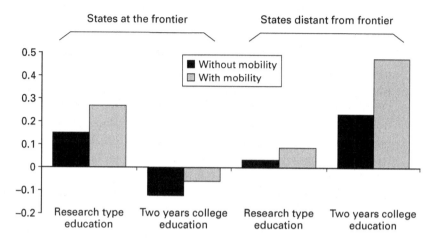

Figure 13.3
Long-term growth effects of $1,000 per person spending on education, U.S. states

First, in contrast to the previous cross-country analysis, here the correlations remain significant even after controlling for state fixed effects without having to regroup the country dummies. Second, these instruments are very strong, with an F-statistic of more than 10 for the joint significance of the two dummies for senator and house representative on the corresponding appropriation committees as determinants of research education spending. For example, every additional representative on the House appropriation committee increases the expenditure on research-type education by $597 per cohort member, which is considerable. Now, turning to the second-stage regressions, ABHV find that an additional $1,000 per person in research education spending raises the state's per-employee growth rate by 0.27 percent if the state is at the frontier (with a close to 1), whereas it raises it by only 0.09 percent if the state is far from the frontier (with a close to 0.3) . More generally, the closer a state gets to the technological frontier, the more growth enhancing it becomes to invest in higher education and the less growth enhancing it becomes to emphasize lower education.

13.5 Conclusion

What have we learned from our analysis in this chapter? First, capital-accumulation-based models predict that cross-country differences in growth rates across countries have to do with differences in rates of human capital accumulation. And these models can be used to perform development accounting or to generate low-development traps. Second, Schumpeterian models that emphasize the interplay between human capital stocks and the innovation process have potential for delivering policy recommendations. Yet, when looking at educational spending as a whole, not much can be said from looking at cross-OECD comparisons. However, once one distinguishes between imitation and frontier innovation and maps these two sources of productivity growth to different segments of the education system, then one can come up with relevant policy recommendations, even for OECD countries or regions. In particular, the theoretical and empirical analyses in the previous section suggest that countries with productivities far from the technological frontier should put more emphasis on primary/secondary education, whereas countries that are closer to the frontier should put more emphasis on tertiary education. Thus, for European countries to put the emphasis on primary/secondary education was fine as long as Europe was technologically far from the United States: at that stage, Europe was relying more on imitation as a main source of growth. But now that Europe has moved closer to the productivity frontier, the potential of imitation is wearing out, and thus it becomes more urgent to invest more in higher education in order to foster innovation. Similarly, the closer a U.S. state is to the current frontier productivity, the more its growth will be enhanced by investing more in research education instead of two-year colleges. More recent work has extended this analysis by looking at growth and the governance of universities. Thus Aghion, Dewatripont, and colleagues (2007) use the same data as in ABHV to show that growth in more advanced states also benefits more from having more autonomous universities, where autonomy is measured either by the fraction of private universities in the state or by an index measuring the extent to which public universities can make decisions (hiring, student recruitment, salaries, . . .) without state interference. They also show that research education funding and autonomy are strategic complements: that is, more research education funding is more growth enhancing in states with more autonomous universities.

13.6   Literature Notes

A first approach to the relationship between education and growth emphasizes the importance of human capital accumulation as a source of economic growth. Within the neoclassical framework, the main reference is Mankiw, Romer, and

Weil (1992). Within the AK framewok, the main reference is Lucas (1988), who was himself directly inspired by Becker's (1964) theory of human capital. This paradigmatic framework builds on a model developed by Uzawa (1965) in which existing human capital is the unique input in the education sector.

Several extensions have been suggested to this approach, such as Rebelo (1991), which introduces physical capital into the human-capital-accumulation equation and then looks at the effect of taxation policies on steady-state growth. A shortcoming of the Lucas model was the assumption that an individual's returns to education remain constant over her entire lifetime. Azariadis and Drazen (1990) deal with this objection by reformulating the theory using an overlapping-generations (OLG) model where individuals inherit the human capital accumulated by their parents. Azariadis and Drazen point to the existence of multiple steady-state growth paths, including low-development traps in which insufficient investment in education in the past discourages further skill acquisition and thereby future growth. Glomm and Ravikumar (1992) address the issue of heterogeneous access to human capital across individuals of the same generation, assessing its impact on the dynamics of inequality and growth, as depending on the adopted system of education (public or private). This topic is also analyzed by Benabou (1996). For a systematic analysis of OLG versions of the Lucas model, see d'Autume and Michel (1994).

An early test of the implication of the Lucas model is provided by Romer (1990), who found evidence that the initial level of literacy (but not the change in literacy) predicted output growth. Barro and Sala-i-Martin (1995) also address empirically the relationship between education and growth based on a large sample of countries between 1965 and 1985, finding significantly positive effect of education attainment and public spending on education on subsequent growth. Barro (1997) and Caselli, Esquivel, and Lefort (1996) examine the differential impact of male and female education on growth.

A second approach to the relationship between education and growth goes back to the seminal contribution of Nelson and Phelps (1966), where the stock of human capital affects a country's ability to innovate or catch up with more advanced countries. This approach was extended by Benhabib and Spiegel (1994), where human capital not only facilitates adaptation to more advanced technologies, but also makes it easier to innovate at the frontier. Benhabib and Spiegel then confronted the prediction of a positive relationship between growth and the stock of human capital to cross-country panel data. However, more recent work by Krueger and Lindahl (2001) concludes that the significance of the correlation between growth and human capital stocks disappears when restricting the regression to OECD countries, leading one to think that education only matters for catching up but not for innovating at the frontier.

Vandenbussche, Aghion, and Meghir (2006) and Aghion, Boustan, and colleagues (2005) build on the idea of appropriate institutions (see chapter 11) to analyze the relationship between growth and the composition of human capital, under the assumption that human capital does not affect innovation and implementation uniformly: primary/secondary education tends to produce imitators, whereas tertiary (especially graduate) education is more likely to produce innovators. The first of these two papers confronts this prediction to cross-OECD-country panel data, whereas the latter paper confronts the same prediction to cross-U.S.-state panel data. For an extensive survey on the topic of this chapter, see Krueger and Lindahl (2001).

Problems

1. Explain how education accumulation fosters growth in the neoclassical and AK models. Describe how education stock might matter instead. Finally, provide some intuition for why the composition of education for promoting growth may change with a country's distance to the world technological frontier.

2. **Human capital accumulation in the neoclassical growth model (based on Mankiw, Romer, and Weil 1992)**

In this problem, we solve Mankiw, Romer, and Weil's augmented version of the Solow growth model. Output is produced using physical capital, human capital, and raw labor with a Cobb-Douglas technology: $Y = AK^\alpha H^\beta L^{1-\alpha-\beta}$ where the level of technology A is assumed to be constant. Human and physical capital depreciate at the same exogenous rate δ. The labor force grows at rate n. Constant fractions of output s_h and s_k are invested in human and physical capital accumulation, respectively.

We also assume $\alpha + \beta < 1$; that is, there are decreasing returns to the accumulation of both forms of capital.

a. Let y, h, and k be the levels of output, human capital, and physical capital per capita: $y \equiv \dfrac{Y}{L}$, $h \equiv \dfrac{H}{L}$, and $k \equiv \dfrac{K}{L}$. What are the growth rates of k and h?

b. Solve for the steady-state values of h, k, and y. Show that

$$y^* = \left(\frac{As_h^\beta s_k^\alpha}{(n+\delta)^{\alpha+\beta}} \right)^{\frac{1}{1-\alpha-\beta}}$$

What are the growth rate of GDP per capita and the growth rate of GDP in the steady state?

c. Assume now that $\alpha + \beta = 1$. What are the growth rates of k and h? Can there be positive long-run growth of GDP per capita?

d. Show that the steady-state log income per capita is

$$\ln\left(y_t\right) = \ln\left(A_t\right) + \frac{\alpha}{1-\alpha-\beta}\ln\left(s_k\right) + \frac{\beta}{1-\alpha-\beta}\ln\left(s_h\right) - \frac{\alpha+\beta}{1-\alpha-\beta}\ln\left(n+\delta\right)$$

while the standard neoclassical growth model yields

$$\ln\left(y_t\right) = \ln\left(A_t\right) + \frac{\alpha}{1-\alpha}\ln\left(s_k\right) - \frac{\alpha}{1-\alpha}\ln\left(n+\delta\right)$$

e. How does the presence of human capital accumulation affect the impact of the savings rate s_k on GDP per capita? The impact of population growth?

3. **Skill acquisition and human capital externalities (based on Lucas 1988)

We consider a version of the Lucas model that allows for externalities in human capital accumulation. Agents are infinitely lived and maximize their lifetime utility. Per-period utility is $u(c) = \frac{c_t^{1-\sigma}}{1-\sigma}$, and the discount rate is ρ.

Each period, they allocate a fraction u of their time to production and $(1-u)$ to the acquisition of human capital. Current production is

$$y = k^\beta\left(uh\right)^{1-\beta}\bar{h}^\gamma$$

where $\bar{h}$ is the average level of human capital in the economy and captures human capital spillovers. Human capital growth takes the form

$$\dot{h}_t = \delta h_t^\xi\left(1-u_t\right), \qquad \delta > 0, \xi > 0$$

a. If $\xi < 1$, can human capital accumulation sustain long-run growth of the economy?

b. Assume for the rest of the problem that skill acquisition has constant returns ($\xi = 1$). Set up the Lagrangian for the representative household's problem. Note that there are two constraints, the evolution of the physical capital stock and the evolution of the human capital stock. Derive the first-order conditions for the choice of c and u and the equations for the change in the shadow prices of human and physical capital.

c. Using the first-order conditions, express the growth rate of consumption as a function of k, h, and u. Note that in equilibrium $\bar{h} = h$.

d. On a balanced growth path, human capital, physical capital, and consumption must grow at constant rates g_h, g_k, and g_c, respectively, and the share of time spent in production u is constant. Show that these growth rates are linked by $g_k = g_c = \left(\frac{1-\beta+\gamma}{1-\beta}\right)g_h$ and $g_h = \delta(1-u)$.

e. Using the first-order conditions and the evolution of the shadow prices of human and physical capital, solve for the growth rate of human capital (note that agents take the average stock of human capital $\bar{h}$ as given). Show that

$$g_c = \frac{1-\beta+\gamma}{\sigma\left(1-\beta+\gamma\right)-\gamma}\left(\delta-\rho\right)$$

f. A social planner internalizes the effect of $\bar{h}$ on output. Does the socially optimal allocation of time between production and skill acquisition differ from the private equilibrium? Using a similar approach to part e, solve for the growth rate of consumption implied by the social planner's choice of u. How does the gap between the socially optimal and the equilibrium growth rates depend on γ?

4. *Growth and the composition of education (based on Aghion, Boustan, and colleagues 2005)

Here we allow both types of workers to be employed in final goods production as well as in imitation and innovation. The final good is produced with the technology

$$y_t = \int_0^1 \left(A_t u_{f,t}^\beta s_{f,t}^{1-\beta} \right)^{1-\alpha} x_{i,t}^\alpha di$$

where u_f and s_f are unskilled and skilled labor in the final goods sector. Monopolists produce intermediate goods $x_{i,t}$ one for one using the final good as input. Their output is $x_{i,t} = \dfrac{\alpha}{1-\alpha} \delta A_t u_{f,t}^\beta s_{f,t}^{1-\beta}$ and their profits $\pi_{i,t} = \delta A_t u_{f,t}^\beta s_{f,t}^{1-\beta}$. The dynamics of productivity are given by

$$A_{t+1} - A_t = u_{m,t}^\sigma s_{m,t}^{1-\sigma} \left(\bar{A}_t - A_t \right) + \gamma u_{n,t}^{1-\sigma} s_{n,t}^\sigma A_t$$

The first component is the improvement in technology driven by imitation, and the second component is driven by innovation. We assume $\sigma > \frac{1}{2}$. Labor market equilibrium requires $s_{f,t} + s_{m,t} + s_{n,t} = S$ and $u_{f,t} + u_{m,t} + u_{n,t} = U$.

a. Given a competitive final-goods sector, what are the unskilled and skilled wages as a function of u_f and s_f?

b. The representative intermediate producer chooses $u_{m,t}$, $u_{n,t}$, $s_{m,t}$, and $s_{n,t}$ to maximize period $t + 1$ profits. Derive the first-order conditions for these labor demands. Dropping time subscripts, show that the skill intensities in imitation and in innovation are given by

$$\frac{s_m}{u_m} = \frac{1-\sigma}{\sigma} \left(\frac{1-a}{\gamma a} \right)^{\frac{1}{2\sigma-1}}$$

$$\frac{s_n}{u_n} = \frac{\sigma}{1-\sigma} \left(\frac{1-a}{\gamma a} \right)^{\frac{1}{2\sigma-1}}$$

where $a \equiv \dfrac{A}{\bar{A}}$ is the proximity of the country to the technological frontier. How do these elasticities depend on a and σ?

c. If the amount of skilled labor $S - s_f$ used in technology improvement increases, how is the allocation of each type of workers between imitation and innovation affected? Do both activities expand? Give an intuitive explanation.

d. Solve for the relative wage of skilled workers and the skill intensity of the final-goods sector. How do they depend on the parameter a?

e. Solve for the equilibrium growth rate of technology as a function of $S - s_f$ and $U - u_f$. How do the relative contributions of skilled and unskilled labor to growth evolve when proximity to the frontier increases?

5. **Human capital and technology diffusion (based on Benhabib and Spiegel 2005)

This is a variation on the Nelson and Phelps model where catch-up parameters may depend on distance to the frontier, reflecting, for instance, the difficulty for less advanced countries of adopting distant, less "appropriate" technologies.

a. First consider the original model of technology diffusion:

$$\dot{A}_t = f(h)\left(\bar{A}_t - A_t \right) + g(h) A_t$$

For simplicity we assume a constant human capital stock. The frontier technology grows at rate $\bar{g} > g(h)$, so that $\bar{A}_t = \bar{A}_0 e^{\bar{g}t}$. Show that

$$A_t = \left(A_0 - \frac{f}{f - g + \bar{g}}\right) e^{(g-f)t} + \left(\frac{f}{f - g + \bar{g}}\right) \bar{A}_0 e^{\bar{g}t}$$

where $f = f(h)$ and $g = g(h)$.

What is $\lim_{t \to \infty} \frac{A_t}{\bar{A}_t}$? Does the country's productivity eventually grow at the same rate as the frontier?

b. Now we allow the rate of technology diffusion to depend on distance to the frontier for each level of human capital stock. As distance to the frontier increases, the catch-up rate may be dampened, in particular, by large differences in factor proportions between the frontier country and the follower that render frontier innovations more difficult to adopt. Productivity grows according to the following equation:

$$\dot{A}_t = f(h)\left(\frac{A_t}{\bar{A}_t}\right)(\bar{A}_t - A_t) + g(h)A_t$$

The other assumptions are unchanged. Show that

$$A_t = \bar{A}_0 e^{\bar{g}t}\left[e^{-(f+g-\bar{g})t}\left(\frac{\bar{A}_0}{A_0} - \frac{f}{f + g - \bar{g}}\right) + \frac{f}{f + g - \bar{g}}\right]^{-1}$$

What is $\lim_{t \to \infty} \frac{A_t}{\bar{A}_t}$ if $f > \bar{g} - g$? if $f < \bar{g} - g$? Interpret.

6. *Low-skill, low-development traps (based on Redding 1996)

In this problem, we examine the possibility of multiple equilibria stemming from strategic complementarities between investment in education and R&D. There is a continuum of overlapping generations of individuals who live for two periods. Workers maximize their lifetime consumption in a linear form $u(c_1, c_2) = c_1 + c_2$. They are born at the beginning of period t with an endowment of human capital $h_{1,t} \equiv 1$. When young, they allocate a fraction u_t of their time to production, earning $u_t A_t$, and the remainder to education. Their human capital when old is then $h_{2,t} = 1 + \gamma(1 - u_t)^\theta$, where $0 < \theta < 1$.

Entrepreneurs choose R&D spending at time t and hire one old worker at time $t + 1$ to produce $y_{t+1} = A_{t+1}h_{t+1}$. The price of the good is normalized to 1. A fraction α of revenues goes to the worker and $1 - \alpha$ to the entrepreneur. The R&D technology is as follows: by incurring a cost $\delta \mu A_t$, an innovation of size λ (such that $A_{t+1} = \lambda A_t$) occurs with probability μ.

a. Set up the workers' maximization problem. What is the optimal fraction of time devoted to education in the first period? How does it change if μ increases?

b. For u given, derive the entrepreneur's choice of R&D spending. Show that it is a threshold decision, that is, $\mu^* = 1$ or $\mu^* = 0$. Why do we say that the model displays strategic complementarity between investment in education and R&D spending?

c. Under what condition does a low-development trap exist, with no productivity growth? What then is the human capital investment u?

d. Under what condition does a steady-state path with positive productivity growth exist? What then is the human capital investment u? What is the rate of growth of technology?

e. Suppose the economy is initially in a zero-growth trap. The government decides to implement a subsidy of s per unit of time spent in education, so that young workers earn $u_t A_t + (1 - u_t)s$. What is the minimum subsidy required to move the economy to the high-growth steady state? How does it depend on δ and γ?

14 Reducing Volatility and Risk

14.1 Introduction

Macroeconomic textbooks generally present the view that there is a perfect dichotomy between (1) macroeconomic policy (budget deficit, taxation, money supply), whose primary aim is to stabilize the economy, and (2) long-run economic growth, which is either taken to be exogenous or assumed to depend only upon structural characteristics of the economy (property-rights enforcement, market structure, market mobility, and so forth). Thus, although common wisdom states that growth requires macroeconomic (or price) stability, conventional macro theory contains no explicit link between macropolicy and long-run growth.

The idea that growth and business cycles should be analyzed separately is deeply rooted in the history of economic thought. For example, the Keynesian multiplier/accelerator (or "oscillator") model analyzed fluctuations of aggregate output around an exogenous trend. Meanwhile, the Harrod-Domar and neoclassical growth models analyzed a long-run deterministic growth path of aggregate output while ignoring business cycle fluctuations. As Kaldor pointed out in the mid-1950s, "As a pure cyclical model, the oscillator model had little resemblance to the cyclical fluctuations in the real world, where successive booms carry production to successively higher levels."[1]

The real business cycle (RBC) literature of the 1980s (e.g., Kydland and Prescott 1982; Long and Plosser 1983), with its emphasis on productivity shocks as a main source of persistent fluctuations, could be seen as a preliminary step toward overcoming the traditional division of macroeconomic theory between trend and cycles. However, based on the same kind of production technologies as in the neoclassical growth literature, the RBC models were unable to account for a trend that was causally related to the business cycle.

One attempt at overcoming the dichotomy between short-run fluctuations and long-run growth came with the AK wave of endogenous growth models. This approach introduced productivity shocks in an AK model à la Romer (1986). We refer the reader to pioneering contributions in the late 1980s by King and Rebelo (1986) and Stadler (1990). The most recent contribution to this line of research is by Jones, Manuelli, and Stachetti (2000), henceforth JMS, which updates the pioneering work of Phelps (1962).

---

1. The same criticism also applies to other versions of the oscillator model (e.g., Hicks 1950) where an exogenous linear trend is superimposed on the original cycle model.

Another wave of volatility and growth models uses the Schumpeterian paradigm. In this approach, the relationship between volatility and growth is governed by research-arbitrage equations. A first attempt at explaining the cyclicality of R&D investments over the business cycle relies on the idea that new ideas are quickly imitated (see Barlevy 2007), so that it is more profitable to innovate in booms when these ideas are most profitable. A second attempt relies on the existence of credit constraints. The idea is that, in the absence of credit constraints, recessions should encourage firms to reorganize, innovate, or reallocate to new markets. Schumpeter himself summarized that view as follows: "[Recessions] are but temporary. They are means to reconstruct each time the economic system on a more efficient plan." However, credit constraints will affect firms' ability to innovate in recessions; typically, in a recession, current earnings are reduced, and therefore so is the firm's ability to borrow in order to innovate. This "Schumpeterian" approach delivers the prediction that the lower the level of financial development, the more negative the correlation between macroeconomic volatility and growth. This in turn suggests that macroeconomic policy may directly affect long-run growth, in particular to the extent that it can either counteract or, at the opposite, amplify the effect of credit constraints on the cyclical composition of firms' investments.

Another attempt at linking volatility and growth is the stochastic growth model by Acemoglu and Zilibotti (1997), henceforth AZ. There, the idea is that each new activity involves a fixed cost, and, therefore, less developed economies can only finance a limited number of activities. Hence the limited scope for risk diversification in these economies, which in turn pushes them to choose inferior but safer technologies. At the same time the fact that less developed economies cannot diversify idiosyncratic risks makes these economies more volatile, and therefore more vulnerable to shocks.

The chapter is organized as follows. Section 14.2 presents the AK approach by JMS and discusses its implications. Section 14.3 uses the Schumpeterian approach to analyze the cyclicality of R&D investments and the prediction that volatility is more detrimental to growth in economies with lower levels of financial development. This section also discusses Schumpeterian models of the cyclicality of R&D that are not based on credit market imperfections. Section 14.4 presents the Acemoglu and Zilibotti model of risk diversification and growth. Section 14.5 concludes by summarizing our main findings in this chapter.

14.2   The AK Approach

The idea here is that macroeconomic volatility may affect long-run growth through its effects on aggregate savings and investment (recall that in the AK framework, growth is entirely driven by capital accumulation). Thus higher volatility will increase the supply of savings if individuals wish to save more for precautionary motives; but higher volatility will tend to reduce the demand for investment by reducing the risk-adjusted rate of return on investment. Phelps (1962) showed that which of these two effects dominates depends upon the representative household's elasticity of intertemporal substitution. JMS (2000) validate Phelps's findings in a modern setting.

14.2.1   The Jones, Manuelli, and Stacchetti Model

We present here a simple overlapping-generations version of the JMS model. Consider an economy populated by a continuum of two-period-lived individuals. Each member of generation t (call her Mrs. t) is born in period t and has an intertemporal utility function:

$$U_t = \frac{\left(c_t^y\right)^{1-\sigma}}{1-\sigma} + \beta \frac{\left(c_{t+1}^o\right)^{1-\sigma}}{1-\sigma}, \qquad 0 < \beta < 1, \quad 0 < \sigma$$

where $c_t^y = c_t$ is Mrs. t's consumption when young, and c_{t+1}^o is her consumption when old; β is the discount factor; and σ is the elasticity of marginal utility, otherwise known as the coefficient of relative risk aversion. Alternatively, $e = 1/\sigma$ is the intertemporal elasticity of substitution. The size of each generation is constant and normalized to equal unity. The economy comprises only one good, which can be consumed or used as capital.

At any date t, the economy's aggregate output depends on k_t, the amount of capital saved in period $t - 1$, according to the stochastic AK technology

$$y_t = u_t k_t$$

where u_t, is an aggregate productivity shock, independently and identically distributed with

$$Eu_t = A > 1$$

Each period's output is divided between the young and the old in fixed proportions, with the fraction γ going to the old.[2] Thus the old will consume γy_t. The young will consume c_t, and their savings will be k_{t+1}, the amount of capital used next period; that is,

$$c_t + k_{t+1} = (1 - \gamma) u_t k_t \tag{14.1}$$

When the representative member of generation t is old her consumption will be

$$c_{t+1}^o = \gamma u_{t+1} k_{t+1}$$

so although she can determine k_{t+1} at date t, her consumption when old will be uncertain, depending on the random productivity shock u_{t+1}, which will not be realized until next period. Accordingly, she will choose c_t and k_{t+1} so as to maximize expected utility:

$$E\left\{ \frac{c_t^{1-\sigma}}{1-\sigma} + \beta \frac{\left(\gamma u_{t+1} k_{t+1}\right)^{1-\sigma}}{1-\sigma} \right\}$$

subject to the budget constraint (14.1).

Since the budget constraint says that c_t and k_{t+1} can be traded off one for one, optimality requires that the expected marginal utility of c_t must equal the expected marginal utility of k_{t+1}. That is, the first-order condition for expected utility maximization is

$$c_t^{-\sigma} = \beta \gamma^{1-\sigma} E\left(u_{t+1}^{1-\sigma}\right) k_{t+1}^{-\sigma}$$

Thus the equilibrium ratio of savings to consumption $\varphi = k_{t+1}/c_t$ is invariant over time:

$$\varphi = \left[\beta \gamma^{1-\sigma} E\left(u_{t+1}^{1-\sigma}\right) \right]^{1/\sigma} \tag{14.2}$$

---

2. One way to rationalize this approach is to assume that output depends on capital and labor according to

$$y_t = u_t k_t L^\alpha$$

that only the young can supply labor, that each young person has a fixed labor supply, and that there is a competitive labor market. In this case the wage rate will equal the marginal product

$$w_t = \alpha u_t k_t L^{\alpha-1}$$

so the income $w_t L$ of the young will be the constant fraction α of aggregate output.

and the expected growth rate g in turn depends positively on this ratio, namely,[3]

$$1+g = E\left(\frac{y_{t+1}}{y_t}\right) = E\left(\frac{u_{t+1}k_{t+1}}{y_t}\right) = \frac{\varphi}{\varphi+1} A(1-\gamma) \qquad (14.3)$$

We are now able to address the question, How does the average growth rate g vary with macroeconomic volatility? We represent an increase in volatility by a mean-preserving spread of the distribution of aggregate productivity shocks u_t for all t. According to equations (14.2) and (14.3), this will raise growth if and only if it raises the saving-consumption ratio φ. This in turn will happen if and only if it raises the expression:

$$E\left(u_{t+1}^{1-\sigma}\right)$$

Now from the uncertainty literature we know that if $h(u)$ is concave in u, then any mean-preserving spread of u reduces the expected value $E[h(u)]$; similarly, if $h(u)$ is convex in u, then any mean-preserving spread of u increases the expected value $E[h(u)]$.

Here, the function we are interested in is $h(u) = u^{1-\sigma}$, which is concave if the elasticity of marginal utility σ is less than unity and convex if $\sigma > 1$. Thus the answer to the preceding question depends on whether the intertemporal elasticity of substitution $e = 1/\sigma$ is greater or less than unity. If e is greater than one, then $u^{1-\sigma}$ is concave, and therefore an increase in volatility reduces expected growth. In this case, the dominant effect of volatility is to reduce the risk-adjusted return

3. To get the last equality, recall first that

$$c_t + k_{t+1} = y_t(1-\gamma)$$

$$k_{t+1} = \varphi c_t$$

$$E(u_{t+1}) = A$$

Thus,

$$\begin{aligned}
E\left(\frac{y_{t+1}}{y_t}\right) &= E\left(\frac{u_{t+1}k_{t+1}}{y_t}\right) \\
&= E(u_{t+1})\frac{k_{t+1}}{y_t} \\
&= A\frac{\varphi c_t}{(1+\varphi)c_t/(1-\gamma)} \\
&= A\frac{\varphi}{1+\varphi}(1-\gamma)
\end{aligned}$$

on investment and thereby discourage savings. If instead, as it appears to be in most countries according to aggregate consumption studies, the elasticity of substitution is less than one, then $u^{1-\sigma}$ is convex, and therefore volatility increases expected growth. In this case, the dominant effect of volatility is to increase precautionary savings.

Thus, according to the AK approach, growth should *increase* with volatility for observed values of the intertemporal elasticity of substitution e.

14.2.2   Counterfactuals

A first prediction of the AK approach, derived in the previous subsection, is that volatility and growth should be positively correlated for realistic values of the intertemporal elasticity of substitution parameter. However, the empirical work of Ramey and Ramey (1995), henceforth RR, suggests the opposite. Specifically, RR consider cross-sectional data from 92 countries and regress average growth over aggregate volatility. Annual growth is computed as the log difference of per capita income obtained from the Penn World Tables mark 6.1. Aggregate volatility is measured by the country-specific standard deviation of annual growth over the 1960–92 period. Ramey and Ramey also construct an estimate of the volatility due to exogenous shocks to growth by filtering the time series first. They first find a negative correlation between the standard deviation of per capita annual growth rates and the average growth rate. Second, the correlation between volatility and growth appears to move from negative to negligible once the cross-country regression is restricted to OECD countries. Third, they find that the negative correlation between volatility and growth persists when one controls for average investment over GDP. These findings, summarized in table 14.1, are clearly at odds with existing theories. Yet no attempt has been made to explain them.

A second prediction of the AK approach is that volatility should affect growth only through its effects on total savings, or equivalently, on total investment. However, Aghion, Angeletos, Banerjee, and Manova (2005), henceforth AABM, show that controlling for total investment over GDP reduces the (negative) correlation between volatility and growth (or the positive correlation between good shocks and growth) by only 20 percent and without reducing the significance of these correlation terms.

This finding in turn implies that total investment cannot be the main channel whereby a stabilizing macroeconomic policy may affect growth through affecting the impact of volatility.

Table 14.1
Relationship between Mean Growth and Volatility (Ramey and Ramey 1995)

Independent Variable	92-Country Sample (2,208 Observations)	OECD-Country Sample (888 Observations)
Constant	0.0727	0.158
	(3.72)	(5.73)
Volatility (σ)	−0.211	−0.385
	(−2.61)	(−1.92)
Average investment share of GDP	0.127	0.069
	(7.63)	(2.76)
Average population growth rate	−0.058	0.212
	(−0.38)	(0.70)
Initial human capital	0.00078	0.00014
	(1.18)	(2.00)
Initial per capita GDP	−0.0088	−0.0172
	(−3.61)	(−5.70)
Summary of variance estimates (all variance numbers are multiplied by 1,000)		
Mean variance	3.58	0.99
Lowest-variance country	0.317	0.299
	(Sweden)	(Norway)
Highest-variance country	28.7	2.9
	(Iraq)	(Turkey)
U.S. variance	0.663	0.596
Percentage of countries with variances different from the United States at the 10 percent significance level	65.9	52.2
Log of likelihood function	3,589.40	1,883.80

Note: Numbers in parentheses are *t*-statistics.

Our discussion in this subsection suggests that we need to move out of AK and consider alternative models of endogenous growth.[4]

---

4. Krebs (2003) has a two-sector AK model that produces a negative effect of volatility on growth even with a unitary elasticity of intertemporal substitution. In his model, the main impact of volatility on the representative household is to increase the variance of uninsurable human capital shocks (e.g., spells of unemployment), which leads the household to invest too little in human versus physical capital, taking the economy away from the growth-maximizing von Neumann ray. This is also an effect that depends upon financial development, to the extent that increased financial development brings about more complete risk-sharing arrangements and therefore reduces the extent of underinvestment in human capital. To rule out Krebs's interpretation of the correlation between volatility and growth, we would have to control for investment rates in both human and physical capital, allowing for the composition of investments to matter.

14.3   Short- versus Long-Term Investments

In this section we analyze an alternative route for analyzing the relationship between volatility and growth. This route emphasizes the distinction between short-run capital investments and long-term productivity-enhancing investments. Examples of long-term growth-enhancing investments include R&D, IT equipment, and organizational capital. Macroeconomic volatility will affect firms' choice between these two types of investments, and differently so depending upon the extent to which firms are credit constrained. In particular, this approach can explain why the relationship between volatility and growth is more negative for non-OECD countries than for OECD countries, an important difference between the two being precisely that OECD countries are less credit constrained than non-OECD countries.

14.3.1   The Argument

The theoretical argument in AABM, which we formalize in this section, can be summarized as follows: In the absence of credit constraints, long-run growth-enhancing investments tend to be countercyclical, as they often take place at the expense of directly productive activities. Because the return to the latter is lower in recessions as a result of lower demand for the manufactured good, so will the opportunity cost of long-run productivity-enhancing investments also be lower. Hence there is a possibility of a growth-enhancing effect of recessions.[5]

However, things become quite different when credit market imperfections prevent firms from innovating and reorganizing in recessions: in a recession, current earnings are reduced, and therefore so is the firm's ability to borrow in order to innovate. This reduced ability, in turn, implies that the lower financial development is, the more the anticipation of recessions will discourage R&D investments if these are decided before firms know the realization of the aggregate shock (since firms anticipate that with higher probability their R&D investment will not pay out in the long run, as it will not survive the liquidity shock). Then recessions will have a damaging effect on R&D and growth.

---

5. This "opportunity-cost" argument was first spelled out by R. Hall (1991), who constructed a model where a constant labor force is allocated between production and the creation of organizational capital (in contrast to real business cycle models where the choice of activities is between production and leisure). Subsequent work by Bean (1990), Gali and Hammour (1991), Saint-Paul (1993), and Nickell (1996) looked for empirical evidence supporting the existence of an opportunity-cost effect. Using a VAR estimation method on a cross-OECD panel data set, Saint-Paul (1993) showed that the effect of demand fluctuations on productivity growth was stronger when demand fluctuations are more transitory. More recently, Nickell (1996) found evidence that more reorganization takes place during recessions.

A natural implication of this argument is that macroeconomic policies that stabilize the business cycle should be more growth enhancing in countries and sectors that are more financially constrained. Thus Aghion and Marinescu (2007) use cross-country panel data to argue that countercyclical fiscal policies—that is, fiscal policies that involve higher budget deficits during recessions—are more growth enhancing the lower the country's level of financial development. Aghion and Kharroubi (2007) use the Rajan-Zingales (1998) methodology (see chapter 6) to look at cross-country/cross-industry panel data showing that countercyclical fiscal policies are more growth enhancing in sectors that are both more heavily dependent upon external finance and also located in countries with lower levels of financial development.

14.3.2 Motivating Evidence

That credit constraints affect the relationship between aggregate volatility and growth comes out very clearly in the following regression exercise, done by AABM. Annual growth is computed as the log; difference of per capita income obtained from the Penn World Tables mark 6.1. As in Ramey and Ramey (1995), aggregate volatility is measured by taking the country-specific standard deviation of annual growth over the 1960–95 period. Financial development is measured by the ratio of private credit—that is, the value of loans by financial intermediaries to the private sector—over GDP. Data for 71 countries on five-year interval averages between 1960 and 1995 (1960–64, 1965–69, etc.) were first compiled by Levine, Loyaza, and Beck (2000); an annual dataset was more recently prepared and made available by Levine on his Web page.[6]

Then, building upon Ramey and Ramey who studied the response of long-term growth to volatility and upon Levine, Loayza, and Beck who focused on the direct effects of credit constraints on growth, AABM estimate the basic equation

$$g_i = \alpha_0 + \alpha_1 \cdot y_i + \alpha_2 \cdot \text{Vol}_i + \alpha_3 \cdot \text{Priv}_i + \alpha_4 \cdot \text{Vol}_i * \text{Priv}_i + \beta \cdot X_i + \varepsilon_i$$

where y_i is the initial income in country i, g_i denotes the average rate of productivity growth in country i over the whole period 1960–95, Vol_i is the measure of aggregate volatility, Priv_i is the average measure of financial development over the period 1960–95, X_i is a vector of country-specific controls, and ε_i is the noise term.

6. Private credit is the preferred measure of financial development by Levine, Loyaza, and Beck because it excludes credit granted to the public sector and funds coming from central or development banks. AABM also conduct sensitivity analysis with two alternative measures of credit constraints: liquid liabilities and bank assets.

Table 14.2
Growth, Volatility, and Credit Constraints (Dependent Variable: Average GDP Per Capita Growth, 1960–2000)

	No Investment		With Investment	
	(1)	(2)	(3)	(4)
Initial income	−0.0030	−0.0102	−0.0063	−0.0094
	(−1.51)	(−3.79)***	(−3.78)***	(−3.97)***
Growth volatility	−0.1606	−0.2571	−0.1725	−0.2182
	(−2.35)**	(−2.46)**	(−3.15)***	(−2.37)**
Private credit	0.0144	−0.0045	−0.0042	−0.0154
	(1.20)	(−0.35)	(−0.43)	(−1.33)
Volatility*private credit	0.5204	0.7566	0.4414	0.5755
	(2.23)**	(2.50)**	(2.36)**	(2.14)**
Investment/GDP			0.0015	0.0012
			(7.59)***	(4.45)***
Controls				
Population growth, secondary enrollment	No	Yes	No	Yes
Levine, Loayza, and Beck policy set	No	Yes	No	Yes
F-test (volatility terms)	0.0456	0.0268	0.0082	0.0473
F-test (credit terms)	0.0000	0.0019	0.0026	0.1022
R-squared	0.3558	0.5289	0.5912	0.6444
N	106	73	106	73

Note: All regressors are averages over the 1960–2000 period, except for initial income and secondary school enrollment, which are taken for 1960. Growth volatility is constructed as the standard deviation of annual growth in the 1960–2000 period. The Levine, Loayza, and Beck (2000) policy set of controls includes government size as a share of GDP, inflation, black market premium, and trade openness. Constant term not shown. t-statistics in parenthesis. ***, **, * significant at 1%, 5%, and 10%.

Of particular interest is the interaction term $\alpha_4 \cdot \text{Vol}_i * \text{Priv}_i$, and here the prediction is that α_4 should be positive and significant, whereas α_2 should be negative and significant, so that volatility is negatively correlated with growth in countries with low financial development, but less so when financial development increases.

Table 14.2 presents the results reported in AABM. They find a strong direct negative correlation between volatility and long-term growth and a significant positive coefficient on the interaction term (column 1).

For sufficiently high levels of private credit (which we observe for many OECD countries), these results predict that the overall contribution of volatility to economic growth becomes positive. Moreover, for intermediate levels of private credit, the gross contribution may be close to zero. Regressing long-run growth on volatility alone without accounting for the direct and interacted effects of financial development could thus produce an insignificant coefficient. This possibility may explain why Ramey and Ramey find a strong negative effect of volatility on growth in the full cross section but a nonsignificant one in the OECD sample. In columns 3 and 4, AABM estimate the preceding equation for the OECD countries only and find coefficients similar to the ones we find for the entire sample.

Finally, AABM show that the growth impact of both volatility itself and its interaction with private credit are little affected by the inclusion of investment as a control. Risk arguably affects savings rates and investment, and investments fuel growth. However, controlling for the ratio of investment to GDP reduces the coefficient on volatility by only 20 percent, suggesting that 80 percent of the total effect of volatility on growth goes by way of a channel other than the rate of investment.

These findings question the AK approach. Next we present an approach, directly inspired by second-wave endogenous growth models, that explores the impact of volatility on entrepreneurs' arbitrage between short-term capital and long-term innovative investment.

14.3.3   The AABM Model

Time is discrete and indexed by t. There is a continuum of two-period-lived entrepreneurs, which are all ex ante identical. Entrepreneurs are risk neutral and consume only in the last period of their lives. Each entrepreneur born in period t has initial wealth (or human capital endowment that can generate income using a one-for-one technology) W_t, and this wealth is proportional to the knowledge level T_t, with $w_t = W_t / T_t$ denoting the knowledge-adjusted wealth of an individual upon birth.

14.3.3.1   Aggregate Volatility

Suppose that at each date t, aggregate productivity A_t fluctuates around a benchmark level T_t, which we refer to as the stock of knowledge at date t. We denote by a_t the ratio A_t / T_t; therefore, a low value of a_t corresponds to a bad productivity shock, whereas a high value of a_t corresponds to a good productivity shock. In the absence of aggregate volatility, productivity would coincide with the level of knowledge, namely, $A_t = T_t$. We introduce aggregate volatility in the model by letting

$$\ln A_t = \ln T_t + \ln a_t \tag{14.4}$$

where a_t, represents an exogenous aggregate productivity (or demand) shock in period t.[7]

As in real business cycle (RBC) models, the shock is assumed to follow a random process of the form

$$\ln a_t = \rho \ln a_{t-1} + \varepsilon_t \tag{14.5}$$

where ε_t is normally distributed so that the expectation of the productivity level A_t is equal to the level of knowledge T_t, and where $\rho \in [0, 1)$ measures the persistence of the exogenous aggregate shock. Note that T_t can be interpreted as the "trend" in productivity.

14.3.3.2   Timing and Payoff Functions

In the first period of her life, an entrepreneur must decide on how to allocate her initial wealth endowment between short-run capital investments K_t and long-term R&D investments Z_t. To ensure a balanced-growth path, we assume that, as for initial wealth, the costs of capital and R&D investments are also proportional to current knowledge T_t, and thus denote by $k_t = K_t / T_t$ and $z_t = Z_t / T_t$ the knowledge-adjusted holdings of capital and R&D investments, respectively. Thus the entrepreneur faces the budget constraint

$$k_t + z_t \leq w_t$$

Short-run capital investment at date t generates income

$$\Pi_t = A_t \pi(k_t)$$

at the end of the same period, where the profit function π is increasing and concave. Thus, in the short-run, the entrepreneur produces according to a completely standard production technology with productivity parameter A_t.

Next, long-term R&D investment at date t generates income at date $t + 1$ only in the next period and only if the firm can meet an adjustment cost that arises at the end of period t and whose realization is specific to the firm. We call this an idiosyncratic shock. Why introduce these shocks on top of aggregate volatility? Simply to have a role for credit, with firms that faced a low shock lending to firms that faced a high shock. This adjustment cost amounts to a liquidity shock,

---

7. We assume that ε_t is normally distributed with mean equal to $(-\sigma^2/2)$ and variance equal to σ^2 (so that the expectation of the productivity level A_t is equal to the level of knowledge T_t). The parameters $\rho \in [0, 1)$ and $\sigma > 0$ measure, respectively, the persistence and volatility of the exogenous aggregate shock. Note that T_t can be interpreted as the "trend" in productivity.

the magnitude of which remains unknown until the end of period t. Like all other variables, the adjustment cost is assumed to be proportional to the current knowledge level T_t, and we denote by c_t the knowledge-adjusted adjustment cost of R&D. The realization of this cost is uncertain ex ante when the entrepreneur decides on how to allocate her wealth between short- and long-term investment. Let $F(c)$ denote the cumulative distribution function associated with the probability distribution over c.

The initial R&D investment pays out in period $t + 1$ only if the adjustment cost has been met, in which case the entrepreneur recoups her adjustment cost and in addition realizes the long-term profit in period $t + 1$:

$$\Pi_{t+1} = V_{t+1} q\left(z_t\right)$$

where $q(z_t)$ is the probability that the R&D investment is successful and V_{t+1} is the value of a new innovation (which we will spell out). As in previous chapters, we assume that q is increasing and concave. Thus either the entrepreneur can meet the adjustment cost of R&D, in which case she innovates and recoups the cost, or she cannot meet that cost, and in that case nothing happens in period $t + 1$.

For simplicity, we shall focus on the special case where the value of innovation only depends upon next period's productivity:

$$V_{t+1} = A_{t+1} \tag{14.6}$$

14.3.3.3   Growth Equation

Now we turn our attention to growth and the dynamics of knowledge over time. Suppose that only the R&D investments z_t contribute to long-run growth, with knowledge accumulating over time at a rate proportional to the aggregate rate of innovation in the economy, namely,

$$\ln T_{t+1} - \ln T_t = q\left(z_t\right) f_t \tag{14.7}$$

where f_t denotes the fraction of entrepreneurs who manage to meet their adjustment cost of R&D. Finally, the long-run average growth rate is simply equal to the long-term average, or the expectation over all possible realizations of a_t, of the right-hand side of the equation.

14.3.3.4   Perfect Credit Markets and the Opportunity Cost Effect

In this subsection we assume perfect capital markets, so that $f_t = 1$, since then all entrepreneurs can freely borrow in order to meet their R&D adjustment costs.

Let $v_{t+1} = V_{t+1}/T_t$ denote the knowledge-adjusted final wealth and the knowledge-adjusted value of a new innovation in period $t + 1$. Then equations (14.5) and (14.6) together imply that

$$E_t v_{t+1} = (a_t)^\rho \qquad (14.8)$$

which in turn implies that the returns to R&D investment are less procyclical than the return to capital investments. Namely the ratio

$$\frac{a_t}{E_t v_{t+1}} = \frac{a_t}{(a_t)^\rho} = a_t^{1-\rho} \qquad (14.9)$$

is higher in a boom (when a_t is high) and lower in a slump (when a_t is low). This property holds more generally as long as the productivity shock is less than fully persistent and the value of innovation represents a present value of returns over a horizon extending beyond period t.

In the absence of credit constraint (that is, with perfect credit markets), an entrepreneur will always be able to borrow what is necessary in order to cover her R&D adjustment costs. This fact implies that the R&D investment of an entrepreneur in her first period of life will always pay out next period in the form of future revenues v_{t+1} from innovating. More formally, consider an entrepreneur born at date t. Her final expected knowledge-adjusted wealth at the end of period $t + 1$ is equal to

$$a_t \pi(k_t) + E_t v_{t+1} q(z_t)$$

where the entrepreneur maximizes her final wealth subject to her budget constraint

$$k_t + z_t \le w_t$$

Now, if we concentrate on interior solutions, we obtain the first-order conditions

$$\begin{aligned} a_t \pi'(k_t) &= \lambda \\ q'(z_t) E_t v_{t+1} &= \lambda \end{aligned} \qquad (14.10)$$

where λ is the Lagrange multiplier.

Dividing the first of these conditions by the second and using equation (14.9), we immediately obtain

$$a_t^{1-\rho} \cdot \frac{\pi'(k_t)}{q'(w_t - k_t)} = 1$$

This, together with the concavity of π *and q,* implies that k_t increases with a_t. In other words, k_t is procyclical (that is, higher in booms), whereas z_t is counter-cyclical (that is, higher in slumps).

The intuition for the countercyclicality of R&D investment is straightforward: Suppose there is a good productivity shock, that is, a high realization of a_t at date *t.* Then, it is more profitable to invest in short-run production with such a high productivity level than in long-term R&D that opens access to future production at a probably lower productivity. As a result, R&D investment at date *t* will be relatively low as its opportunity cost in terms of forgone current production is high. Conversely, suppose there is a bad productivity shock at date *t.* Then it becomes more profitable for the entrepreneur to invest in long-term R&D. Hence the countercyclicality of R&D: low R&D investment in a boom, high R&D investment in a slump. The countercyclicality of R&D will in turn mitigate aggregate volatility; that is, it will partly counteract the volatility in a_t.

14.3.3.5   Cyclicality of R&D under Imperfect Credit Markets

Let us augment the preceding model by introducing credit market imperfections. Namely, after the realization of the liquidity cost c_t on the long-term investment at the end of period *t,* the entrepreneur can invest up to μ times her end-of-current-period wealth for the purpose of covering these liquidity needs. Thus her initial long-term investment z_t at the beginning of period *t* will pay out in period $t + 1$ if and only if

$$c_t \le \mu a_t \pi(k_t)$$

Thus the entrepreneur's long-term investment will pay out next period with probability

$$\Pr\left[c_t \le \mu a_t \pi(k_t) \right] \equiv F\left[\mu a_t \pi(k_t) \right]$$

Assume again for simplicity that the knowledge-adjusted value v_{t+1} of innovating at date $t + 1$ is equal to the knowledge-adjusted productivity a_{t+1} at that date. An entrepreneur born at date *t* will now choose her investment profile (k_t, z_t) so as to

$$\max_{k,z}\left\{ a_t \pi(k_t) + E_t a_{t+1} \pi(z_t) F\left[\mu a_t \pi(k_t) \right] \right\}$$

subject to

$$k_t + z_t \le w_t$$

Now we see that a_t appears also in the second term of the maximand, in a way that counteracts the opportunity cost effect pointed out earlier. A lower realization of a_t lowers the probability $F[\mu a_t \pi(k_t)]$ of a productivity-enhancing investment being completed in the next period. This result in turn will tend to make such investment become more procyclical as the credit constraint tightens.

The intuition for why long-term investment becomes more procyclical the tighter the credit constraints, can be explained as follows: Under tight credit constraints, a low realization of current productivity a_t means a low level of profits $a_t \pi(k_t)$ at the end of the current period. But, under tight credit constraints, this in turn implies a low borrowing capacity and therefore a low ability to respond to the liquidity shock c on the long-term investment, and therefore it makes it very unlikely that the long-term investment today at date t will pay out in the future. Anticipating this outcome, an entrepreneur facing a low productivity shock today will shy away from long-term investment; hence the procyclicality of long-term investment under tight credit constraints.

Figures 14.1 and 14.2 show how credit constraints affect the level and procyclicality of long-term investment when $\pi(x) = q(x) = x^\alpha$. Here we assume that the distribution of c is lognormal. We also assume that $\alpha = \dfrac{1}{3}$, and we let μ vary between 1 (no credit) and 5.

Figure 14.1 depicts the equilibrium level of z_t, evaluated at the mean productivity level ($a_t = 1$). Figure 14.2 depicts the equilibrium cyclical elasticity of z_t (also evaluated at $a_t = 1$). In particular, we see that for μ sufficiently small, z_t is

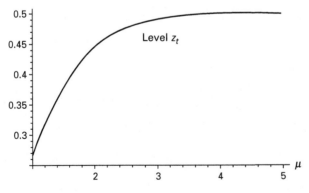

Figure 14.1

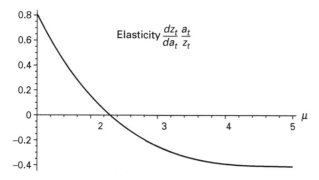

Figure 14.2

increasing in $a_t \left(\dfrac{dz_t}{da_t} > 0 \right)$: In other words, long-term investment becomes procyclical when μ is small and becomes countercyclical for μ sufficiently large.

14.3.3.6   Credit Constraints, Volatility, and Growth

The preceding analysis provides a first explanation for why the correlation between volatility and growth should be more negative with tighter credit constraints, and that explanation holds under very general conditions. Namely, the tighter the credit constraint, the more risky it is to make long-term investments in general, therefore the lower the mean long-term investment over time, and consequently the lower the average growth rate. At the same time, the tighter the credit constraints, the more procyclical R&D investments will be, and therefore the more will the (endogenous) cyclicality of R&D investment reinforce the (exogenous) volatility in a_t. Thus, even before considering the potential causal effects of volatility on growth, the model already predicts a correlation between volatility and growth, which is more negative as credit constraints are tighter. This prediction is robust to considering other functional forms for the production and innovation technologies than the preceding Cobb-Douglas specification.

A second potential explanation for the more negative correlation between volatility and growth in more credit-constrained economies, is causal; namely, higher volatility means deeper recessions and therefore lower investment capacities for firms in recessions. True, higher volatility also means higher output in booms, but presumably there is asymmetry between booms and slumps, in the sense that firms are more credit constrained in the latter than in the former. Thus, while deeper recessions should be expected to have a highly negative effect on R&D investment, a higher boom should have only a small positive effect on such investments.[8] As a result, average R&D and growth should be negatively affected by higher volatility in credit-constrained economies. This reasoning is illustrated by the following example.

Example 1 (AABM) Assume linear production and long-term investment technologies

$$\pi(k) = k; \quad q(z) = \lambda z$$

Suppose also that the long-term growth-enhancing investment is indivisible, equal to some $z_0 \in (0, w)$, that the distribution for the liquidity shock $\tilde{c}$ is uniform over the interval $[0, 1]$, and that, in the absence of volatility, firms could always pay $\tilde{c}$ with their retained earnings from short-run production; more precisely,

$$\bar{a}\pi(k_0) = \bar{a}(w - z_0) \geq 1$$

where $\bar{a}$ is the average productivity shock.

We are interested in the effect of increased macroeconomic volatility (that is, of increased variance of a, denoted by σ) on the expected growth rate

$$g = E_a\left[\lambda z_0 \delta(a)\right]$$

where

$$\delta(a) = \Pr\left[\mu a(w - z_0) \geq \tilde{c}\right]$$

Since the liquidity shock is uniform, we have

$$\delta(a) = \delta(a, \mu) = \min\left[\mu a(w - z_0), 1\right]$$

which is obviously concave in a. Figure 14.3 shows $\delta(a)$ as a function of a. In particular we see that randomizing between two values of a below and above the kink can only reduce the average δ so that volatility is unambiguously detrimental to average growth.

It then immediately follows that the expected growth rate g must decrease when the variance of a increases, and all the more when μ is lower. This result is quite intuitive: more volatility does not improve firms' ability to overcome the liquidity shock in a boom, since firms already do it without volatility. However, it reduces

8. Example 2 provides a counterexample to this story.

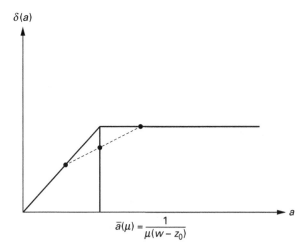

Figure 14.3

the probability that they will overcome the liquidity shock in a slump, and to a larger extent when firms face tighter borrowing constraints. We thus have

$$\frac{\partial g}{\partial \sigma} < 0 \quad \text{and} \quad \frac{\partial^2 g}{\partial \sigma \partial \mu} > 0$$

where σ measures the variance of the aggregate shock.

Moreover, the ex post growth rate

$$\lambda z_0 \delta(a)$$

is increasing and concave in a, but it becomes constant and equal to λz_0 when μ is sufficiently large. Thus growth reacts positively to favorable productivity shocks and at the same time more volatility is detrimental to growth. Now, figure 14.4 depicts $\delta(a) = \delta(a, \mu)$ for two values of μ, namely, μ and $\mu' > \mu$. We see that a negative shock on a has a less detrimental effect for μ' than for μ.

Thus increased access to credit (a higher μ) reduces the sensitivity of growth to productivity shocks and also the extent to which volatility is detrimental to growth (since growth becomes less concave in a).

Unfortunately, these latter findings cannot be generalized to all functional forms for production, innovation, and cost distribution. In particular, one counteracting effect of volatility on growth, not shown by example 1, is that higher volatility also means higher profits in booms, and therefore a possibly higher

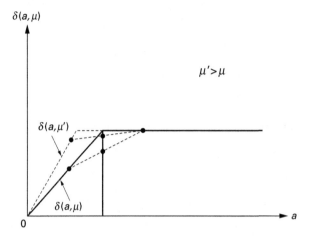

Figure 14.4

ability for firms to innovate during booms. The following example illustrates this "resurrecting effect" of higher volatility.

Example 2 (AABM)   Suppose that

$$c = \begin{cases} \overline{c} & \text{with probability } p \\ 0 & \text{with probability } (1-p) \end{cases}$$

Suppose, as in example 1, that the R&D investment is indivisible and equal to z_0, that

$$\pi(w - z_0) = q(z_0) = 1$$

and that $a_t \in [\underline{a}, \overline{a}]$ with $E(a_t) = 1$.

Then, if $\mu < \overline{c}$, only a fraction of firms will manage to overcome their liquidity shocks in the absence of volatility, that is, if

$$a \equiv 1$$

However, if volatility becomes sufficiently high that $\overline{a} > \dfrac{\overline{c}}{\mu}$, then the occurrence of a boom will allow all firms to overcome their liquidity shocks and thereby innovate.

This "resurrection" effect cannot be first-order; otherwise, we would have observed a positive correlation between volatility and growth in the cross-country regressions, and we did not. And if we restrict attention to functional forms such that the overall correlation between volatility and growth is negative, then the causal effect pointed out in example 1 will dominate.

14.3.4   Confronting the Credit Constraints Story with Evidence

In a recent paper, Barlevy (2007) challenges the view that credit constraints are the main explanation for the observed procyclicality of R&D investments. He looks at the Compustat database, which includes larger firms, but these account for most of R&D expenditures in the United States. What Barlevy finds is that R&D is procyclical even among this subgroup of firms, even though it may be argued that large firms are less credit constrained than small firms (see Bernanke and Gertler, 1989). Barlevy goes further and shows that the reduction in R&D expenditure during recessions is even more pronounced for firms that hold at least $50 million in cash over a year.

Now, Barlevy himself acknowledges that this finding is not enough to invalidate the preceding credit-constraint story. Indeed large firms and/or firms with large cash holdings may well be those that face binding credit constraints, for example, due to the combination of big investment needs and of the intangibility of their assets, and the cash holdings may be precisely the way for such firms to make sure they can overcome liquidity shocks.

In fact, a recent study by Berman, Eymard, Aghion, Askhenazy, and Cette (2007), henceforth BEAAC, uses a French firm-level panel dataset covering 13,000 firms over the period 1980–2000 to test the predictions of AABM. Credit constraints are measured at firm level by a firm's ability to obtain new bank loans, which turns out to depend upon the firm's credit record vis-à-vis its trade creditors. More specifically, firms that fail to repay their trade creditors are put on a blacklist called "Payment Incident," and being included on that list affects firms' ability to access credit in the future. Using the interaction between this firm-level instrument and a variable that reflects the dependence of the firm's industry upon external finance, and controlling for firm size, BEAAC show (1) that R&D spending is more positively correlated with sales in more credit-constrained firms; (2) that higher volatility of sales has an asymmetric effect on R&D investments: these are more harmed in slumps than they are encouraged in booms; and (3) that higher volatility is more harmful to productivity growth in more credit-constrained firms.

14.3.5   An Alternative Explanation for the Procyclicality of R&D

To account for why even firms with deep pockets tend to have procyclical R&D, Barlevy (2007)[9] proposes the following explanation, also developed using the Schumpeterian paradigm: Because firms are afraid of being quickly imitated, they adopt a shortsighted attitude when it comes to innovating. This in turn explains why firms will concentrate their R&D efforts in booms where the gains from innovating are larger.

More formally, consider a simple overlapping-generations model where firms live for two periods. Innovation in the first period gives access to positive profit in the current period and also in the next period provided the innovation is not imitated. Moreover, current productivity-adjusted profits are equal to a_t where $a_t \in \{\underline{a}, \overline{a}\}$, with $\underline{a} < \overline{a}$.

Then, if $c(z)$ denotes the productivity-adjusted cost of innovating with probability z, a firm will choose $z = z(a_t)$ to solve

$$\max_z \left\{ z \left[\varepsilon a_t + (1-q)\delta E(a_{t+1}/a_t) \right] - c(z) \right\}$$

where q is the probability of imitation, $\delta \in (0, 1)$ is the discount factor, ε reflects the extent to which the firm can benefit from the innovation in the short run, and

$$E(a_{t+1}/a_t) = pa_t + (1-p)a_{-t}$$

where a_{-t} is equal to $\overline{a}$ (resp. $\underline{a}$) when $a_t = \underline{a}$(resp. $\overline{a}$).

Now, even if $\varepsilon < 1$ so that it takes time for the firm to fully learn how to implement the innovation, yet for q sufficiently large (high imitation) or for δ sufficiently small (high impatience), we clearly have

$$z(\underline{a}) < z(\overline{a})$$

that is, procyclical R&D investment.

One problem with this explanation is that it relies on the assumption that R&D investments yield immediate results. There is surely truth to the idea that firms target the implementation of innovations strategically over the business cycle (see Shleifer 1986), but still there is a big time gap between R&D investments and innovation results.

---

9. See also Francois and Lloyd-Ellis (2003).

14.4   Risk Diversification, Financial Development, and Growth

Acemoglu and Zilibotti (1997), henceforth AZ, propose an alternative explanation for the Ramey and Ramey (1995) finding that the correlation between volatility and growth is more negative in less (financially) developed economies. The basic idea in AZ is that, because each new activity involves a fixed cost, economies at an early stage of development can only finance a limited number of intermediate industries. This drawback limits the scope for risk diversification in these economies, in turn inducing agents to choose inferior but safer technologies. At the same time the fact that less developed economies cannot diversify idiosyncratic risks makes these economies more volatile than more developed economies.

The development process goes through several stages: first, a period of primitive accumulation where aggregate output is highly volatile; second, a take-off phase where the economy achieves higher financial development with more scope for risk diversification; third, a developed phase with high and steady growth that relies on a high degree of risk diversification. Thus the growth process is slow and volatile at early stages of development, and then speeds up and stabilizes in later stages of development.

14.4.1   Basic Framework

More formally, suppose that time is discrete and that the economy is populated by a continuum of two-period-lived individuals. Total population is constant, and each generation has a unit mass ($L = 1$). Individuals born at date t are assumed to consume only in period $t + 1$,[10] and they face uncertainty over the state of nature to be realized in this next period. There is a continuum of equally likely states of nature $s \in [0, 1]$. Agents have the following (expected) utility function, inducing unit relative risk aversion:

$$E_t U(c_{t+1}) = \int_0^1 \log(c_{t+1}^s) ds \tag{14.11}$$

where c_{t+1}^s is agent's consumption of the final good in period $(t + 1)$ if state s is realized.

10. This assumption is for simplicity. Acemoglu and Zilibotti (1997) assume that agents consume in both periods. It is also possible to study the case of a general constant relative risk aversion (CRRA) utility function.

The production side of the economy is described as follows: The unique final good is produced by the unit mass continuum of individuals using capital and labor, according to the AK technology

$$Y_{s,t} = K_{s,t}^{\alpha} L_t^{1-\alpha} \overline{K}_{s,t}^{1-\alpha}$$

where $\overline{K}_{s,t}$ denotes the aggregate amount of physical capital in the economy in period t and state s. Because we assume a constant population L_t normalized to unity, and all individual firms are identical so that

$$\overline{K}_{s,t} = \int K_{s,t} \cdot di = K_{s,t}$$

in equilibrium, we have $Y_{s,t} = K_{s,t}$.

Capital in turn can be produced in two ways: (1) through a risky but more advanced technology, which uses existing intermediate industries, thereby producing some state-contingent amount of output (x_s): namely, industry i produces positive output only if state $s = i$ occurs; if this industry does not exist in the country, then the risky technology generates zero output in state $s = i$; (2) through a "safe technology" (x_Φ) that generates output no matter the realization of the state of nature. We thus have

$$K_{s,t} = x_{s,t-1} = x_{\Phi,s,t-1} \tag{14.12}$$

Let $A_t \in [0, 1]$ denote the number (mass) of intermediate industries generating state-contingent production at date t. What limits this number to lie below one in less developed economies is that operating each intermediate activity involves a fixed cost. More precisely, it requires a fixed cost equal to

$$M_i = \max\left\{0, \frac{D}{(1-x)}(i-x)\right\}$$

with $x \in (0, 1)$, to operate industry i. Thus industries $i \le x$ have no fixed-cost requirement, whereas in industries $i > x$ the fixed cost increases linearly with the index i.

The intermediate industry i produces capital using the final good, according to the production function

$$x_{i,s} = \begin{cases} RF_i & \text{if } i = s \text{ and } F_i \ge M_i \\ 0 & \text{otherwise} \end{cases}$$

where F_i is the amount of final good input, and $R > 0$ is the rate of return on this technology.

The safe technology is also linear, with

$$x_{\Phi,s} = r\phi, \qquad \forall s \in [0,1]$$

where $r < R$. Thus the safe technology yields a lower rate of return than the risky technology.

All markets are assumed to be competitive, and a firm's output is entirely distributed to the holders of securities in that firm.

When young, agents work in the final-good sector and earn the competitive wage

$$\frac{\partial Y_{s,t}}{\partial L} = w_{s,t} = (1-\alpha)Y_{s,t} = (1-\alpha)K_{s,t}$$

At the end of this period, agents decide in which assets to save this wage revenue. In other words, they make portfolio decisions. They may decide to invest their savings in a set of risky securities ($\{F_i\}_{i \in [0,A_t]}$), consisting of state-contingent claims to the output of the intermediate industries that are currently operational in the country. Or they may invest their savings in the safe technology.

14.4.2 Analysis

Given the risky and safe technologies that we have specified, the i security entitles its owner to a claim to R units of capital in state i (as long as the minimum size constraint is satisfied, which is always the case in equilibrium), and otherwise to nothing. Savings invested in the safe technology give the return rate r in all states of nature.

Since the risky securities yield symmetric returns, it is optimal for the risk-averse agents to hold a symmetric portfolio, with $F_i \equiv F$ for all $i \in [0, A_t]$. We refer to this as a *balanced portfolio*.

If the economy is sufficiently developed that it can finance all contingent intermediate activities, then $A_t = 1$, so that a balanced portfolio of risky securities bears no risk. In this case, since $R > r$, nobody will invest in the safe technology.

If the economy is less developed so that $A_t < 1$, then individuals face a trade-off between risk and rate of return. More formally, the representative young agent at date t solves the optimal portfolio problem

$$\max_{\phi_t, F_t} A_t \log[RF_t + r\phi_t] + (1 - A_t)\log[r\phi_t] \tag{14.13}$$

subject to

$$\phi_t + A_t F_t \leq w_t \tag{14.14}$$

(Note that each individual takes the range of securities offered A_t as given.)

From first-order conditions, we immediately get

$$\phi_t^* = \frac{(1-A_t)R}{R-rA_t} w_t \tag{14.15}$$

$$F_t^* = \begin{cases} F(A_t) \equiv \dfrac{R-r}{R-rA_t} w_t, & \forall i \leq A_t \\ 0 & \forall i > A_t \end{cases} \tag{14.16}$$

The *FF* schedule in figure 14.5 depicts the resulting demand for any available risky asset $F(A_t)$ as a function of the number A_t of intermediate industries that are active. The *FF* schedule is upward sloping, which in turn captures a *complementarity* in the demand for risky assets: the demand for *each asset* grows with the variety of intermediate industries. What happens here is that the more numerous active intermediate activities are, the better risk diversification is. This improvement in turn encourages savers to shift their investments away from the safe asset into high-productivity risky projects. Such complementarity hinges on risk aversion being sufficiently high.[11]

Now we know, given A_t, how much individuals are ready to invest in each activity. The equilibrium measure of active industries A_t^* is then simply determined as the maximum industry index i such that the fixed cost M_i can be financed by the amount of savings $F(A_t)$. In other words, it satisfies the fixed-point condition

$$F(A_t^*) = M_{A_t^*}$$

In figure 14.5, the equilibrium is given by the intersection between the two schedules *FF* and *MM*, where *MM* depicts the $A \rightarrow M_A$ mapping. Intuitively, A_t^* is the largest number of industries for which the fixed-cost requirement can be met, subject to the demand of securities being given by $F(A)$.

As the economy grows, so does wage income and therefore so does the stock of savings over time. In equilibrium, this growth induces an expansion of the number of active intermediate industries A_t^*. Looking at figure 14.5: growth

---

11. Suppose agents were risk averse, but only moderately so. Suppose, in particular, that they were so little risk averse that they would decide not to hold any safe asset in their portfolio. Then, an expansion in the set of risky securities would induce agents to spread their savings (whose total amount is predetermined) over a larger number of assets. In this case, assets would be substitutes rather than complements.

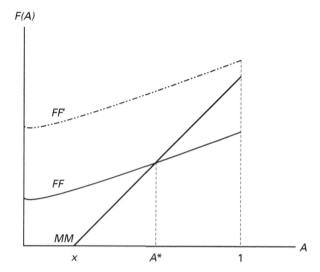

Figure 14.5

induces an upward shift of the *FF* schedule, with the equilibrium thus moving to the right. In other words, growth generates financial development.

When the stock of savings becomes sufficiently large that all intermediate industries become active, the economy is sufficiently rich to afford $A_t^* = 1$, at which point the safe technology is abandoned.

14.4.3 Equilibrium Dynamics

The stochastic equilibrium dynamics of capital can be easily derived from the preceding analysis. Using the fact that

$$w_{s,t} = (1 - \alpha)K_t$$

and that

$$K_{t+1} = Y_{t+1}$$

we have

$$
K_{t+1} =
\begin{cases}
F_B(K_t) = (1 - \alpha)\dfrac{R(1 - A_t^*)}{R - rA_t^*}R_t, & prob.\ 1 - A_t^* \\[4mm]
F_G(K_t) = (1 - \alpha)RK_t, & prob.\ A_t^*
\end{cases}
\tag{14.17}
$$

where $A_t^* = A(K_t) \leq 1$, defined by

$$F(A_t) \equiv \frac{R-r}{R-rA_t}(1-\alpha)K_t = M_{A_t}$$

is the equilibrium mass of intermediate industries given capital stock K_t. The first line in equation (14.17) corresponds to the case of a "bad realization" at time t, such that $s \in (A_t^*, 1]$. In this case, none of the active intermediate industries turned out to pay off at time t, and capital at time $t + 1$ is only given by the return of the safe technology. The second line corresponds to the case of a "good realization" at t, such that $s \in [0, A_t^*]$. In this case, the risky investment paid off at time t, and capital and output are relatively large at time $t + 1$.[12] Note that the probability of a good realization increases with the level of development, since A_t^* increases with K_t.

Figure 14.6 describes the dynamics of capital accumulation. The two schedules depict capital at time $t + 1$ as a function of capital at time t conditional on good news $[F_G(K_t)]$ and bad news $[F_B(K_t)]$. We assume throughout that $(1 - \alpha)R > 1$, so there is positive growth under the positive realization. In the case considered in the figure, at low levels of capital ($K \leq K_L$), growth is positive, even conditional on bad news. In the intermediate range where $K \in [K_L, K_M]$, growth only occurs if news is good, since $F_B(K_t) < K_t < F_G(K_t)$. The threshold K_L is not a steady state; however, it is a point around which the economy will oscillate for awhile. When the initial capital stock is below K_L, the economy necessarily grows toward it. When it is above K_L, capital stock falls back whenever bad news occurs. So, in this region, the economy is still exposed to undiversified risks and experiences fluctuations and setbacks. Finally, for $K \geq K_M$, there are enough savings in the economy to cover the fixed costs for all intermediate activities. In this region, all idiosyncratic risks are removed, and the economy enters a regime of sustained growth.

---

12. In case of a good realization of the state of nature with $s < A_t^*$, individuals obtain payoff on both the safe and the risky technologies, with total payoff equal to

$$P = F(A_t)Rw_t + \phi_t^* r w_t$$

We can reexpress P as

$$P = \left\{ \frac{R-r}{R-rA_t} + \frac{r(1-A_t)}{R-rA_t} \right\} Rw_t$$
$$= Rw_t = R(1-\alpha)K_t$$

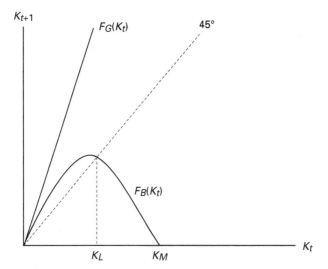

Figure 14.6

14.5   Conclusion

In this chapter we have investigated the relationship between macroeconomic volatility and growth. We have first explored the AK approach, whereby volatility affects growth through its effects on aggregate savings and investment rates. In particular, this approach predicts that whether volatility is positively or negatively correlated with growth hinges primarily upon the intertemporal elasticity of substitution between current and future consumption.

Second, we have looked at the relationship between volatility and growth in the cross-country panel data. The evidence shows a negative correlation between volatility and growth, mostly in less financially developed economies.

We have analyzed two explanations for why volatility should be more negatively correlated with growth in less financially developed economies. The first explanation relies on the idea that R&D investments become more procyclical in more credit-constrained films. This in turn can explain why in countries with lower levels of financial development, not only is average growth slower (as R&D investments are less likely to be completed in the long run), but also macroeconomic volatility is higher as the cyclicality of R&D investments reinforces the volatility of aggregate productivity. The second explanation relies on the idea that less developed economies are less able to diversify risk: this implies both that aggregate output will be more volatile and also that agents will tend to invest more in safe but inferior technologies in order to escape risk.

14.6   Literature Notes

In the traditional post-Keynesian literature, growth and business cycles were analyzed separately. Thus Harrod-Domar's model of long-run growth would have no cycle in it, and Samuelson's oscillator would be detrended.

This dichotomy between trend and cycles was first questioned by the real business cycle literature of the 1980s (see Kydland and Prescott 1982; Long and Plosser 1983). According to the RBC approach, fluctuations are an integral part of the growth process, as both of them result from productivity shocks.

King and Rebelo (1986) and Stadler (1990) were first to analyze the impact of volatility on long-run growth, using AK models. More recently, Jones, Manuelli, and Stachetti (2000) perfected this line of research and updated an idea by Phelps (1962) on how macroeconomic volatility would affect long-run growth through its effects on aggregate savings and investment: the conclusion is that volatility could hurt growth by decreasing total investment. Nevertheless, for reasonable values of the parameters of the model, the correlation between volatility and growth should be positive, as more volatility would induce more precautionary savings.

Cross-country evidence by Ramey and Ramey (1995) suggested, however, that the correlation between growth and macroeconomic volatility is clearly negative. Additional evidence of the detrimental effects of volatility on growth can be found in the work of Bruno (1993) on inflation and growth, and Hausmann and Gavin (1996) for Latin American countries.

First attempts at analyzing the relationship between volatility and growth using the Schumpeterian paradigm include the work of Gali and Hammour (1991), Caballero and Hammour (1994), Bean (1990), and Aghion and Saint-Paul (1998). More recently, Barlevy (2007) and Francois and Lloyd-Ellis (2003) revisited the relationship between growth and cycles, looking at the combined effects of creative destruction and of implementation-cycle types of externalities as in Shleifer (1986). Finally, AABM (2005) introduced credit constraints into the Schumpeterian framework and analyzed how, depending upon how binding the credit constraint is, macroeconomic volatility can affect firms' choice between short-run capital investments and long-term productivity-enhancing investments.

Their framework has been used to analyze the relationship between long-run growth and the choice of exchange-rate regimes (see Aghion, Bacchetta, et al., 2006), and the relationship between growth and the countercyclicality of budgetary policies (Aghion and Marinescu 2007; Aghion and Kharroubi 2007).

Comin and Gertler (2006) provided evidence on the procyclicality of R&D at the medium-term frequencies and the countercyclicality of the relative price of capital. Comin, Gertler, and Santacreu (2008) looked at the connection between long-run growth and short-term fluctuations from the opposite angle. Using a simplified version of Comin and Gertler (2006), they explored the short- and medium-term effects of a shock about the arrival rate of future technologies on output productivity, employment, the relative price of capital, and the stock market.

Finally, the Acemoglu and Zilibotti model developed in section 14.4 has given rise to subsequent contributions, both theoretical and empirical, in particular by Koren and Tenreyro (2007).

A detailed presentation of the main topics of this chapter can be found in Aghion and Banerjee (2005).

Problems

1. Explain intuitively how a lower level of financial development can imply a more negative correlation between macroeconomic volatility and growth.

2. **Short and long-term investment (based on Aghion, Angeletos, and colleagues 2005)**

This problem solves a version of the AABM model. We consider an economy populated by two-period-lived entrepreneurs who allocate their initial wealth w between short-term capital investments k_t and long-term R&D investments z_t, and maximize their expected terminal wealth. Profits in the first period are $\pi_t = a_t k_t^\alpha$, $a \leq 1$. The dynamics of the productivity parameter a_t are given by $a_t = \varepsilon_t a_{t-1}^\rho$, where $0 < \rho < 1$ and $E_{t-1}(\varepsilon_t) = 1$. At the end of the first period, entrepreneurs face an adjustment cost c_t which is distributed normally on [0, 1]. If the cost is met, profits in the second period are $\pi_{t+1} = a_{t+1} z_t^\alpha$; otherwise, profits in the second period are zero. Assume first that markets are complete.

a. Write the entrepreneur's first-order conditions for k_t and z_t. Solve for the optimal ratio of capital expenses to R&D expenses $\dfrac{k_t}{z_t}$. What is its cyclical behavior? Interpret.

Next, assume that credit markets are imperfect. Entrepreneurs can only invest up to μ times their first-period profits to pay for the adjustment cost.

b. What is the probability that the long-term investment will pay off? Show that for a_t large enough—that is, when a sufficiently good shock occurs—credit constraints do not change the optimal composition of investment.

c. Suppose that $a_t < \dfrac{1}{\mu k^*(a_t)}$, where $k^*(a_t)$ *is* the investment in capital under perfect markets. Use the entrepreneur's expected wealth maximization problem to solve for the ratio $\dfrac{k_t}{z_t}$. What is its cyclical behavior? Interpret.

3. *Imitation and procyclical R&D (based on Barlevy 2007)

Consider an overlapping-generations model where a representative firm exists for two periods and hires labor for production (l_t) and R&D (z_t). Its total labor input is constrained to be $l_t + z_t = 1$. When z_t units of labor are employed in R&D. the firm innovates with probability z_t. In addition to the wage bill, which is independent *of* z_t, it incurs a cost *of* c per unit of labor in R&D. If it does not innovate, it realizes profits of $a_t l_t$ in period t and zero in period $t + 1$. If it innovates, it makes a profit *of* $\varepsilon \gamma a_t l_t$ in period t, where $\gamma > \dfrac{1}{\varepsilon}$. There is a probability q that a successful innovation will be imitated, in which case profit at $t + 1$ is driven to zero by competition with the entrant. Otherwise, profit at $t + 1$ is $a_{t+1} l_{t+1} = a_{t+1}$, as there is no R&D in the second period. The discount factor is δ. Productivity can take two values $\{1, \bar{a}\}$, with $\bar{a} > 1$, and follows a process of the form $E_t a_{t+1} = pa_t + (1 - p)_{a-t}$.

We assume c is small, $c < \delta(1 - p)(1 + \bar{a})$.

a. What is the expected total profit over the two periods, as a function *of* z_t, a_t, a_{-t}, and the parameters of the model?

b. Derive the firm's optimal choice of z for the two states of the economy, $z(1)$ and $z(\bar{a})$.

c. If $q = 1$ (absence of patent protection), what is the sign of $z(\bar{a}) - z(1)$? Is R&D procyclical or countercyclical?

d. If $q = 0$ (perfect protection against imitation), what is the sign of $z(\bar{a}) - z(1)$? Is R&D procyclical or countercyclical? How does this expression depend on the parameters δ and p?

4. *Exchange-rate regime, volatility, and productivity growth (based on Aghion, Bacchetta, and colleagues 2006)

This problem examines the impact of exchange-rate volatility on productivity growth under different exchange-rate regimes. We assume that there is a single good produced by a continuum of measure one of two-period-lived firms according to the technology $y_t = A_t \sqrt{l_t}$, where l_t is the labor input. The price level is determined by purchasing power parity. It is equal to the exchange rate after normalizing foreign prices to one: $P_t = S_t$. Under fixed exchange rates, $S_t = \bar{S}$ is a constant. Under flexible exchange rates, S_t fluctuates around its mean $E(S_t) = \bar{S}$. Wages are set in nominal terms one period ahead as $W_t = \omega A_t E(P_t)$.

At the end of period t, firm i faces a liquidity cost $C_t^i = c^i P_t A_t$. The random component c^i has a concave cumulative distribution function F over the interval $[0, \bar{c}]$. In order to meet this cost, firms can borrow up to $\mu - 1$ times their period-t profit (we assume $\mu < 4\omega\bar{c}$). Let q_t be the fraction of firms that survive the shock. At period $t + 1$, these firms innovate and realize value $P_{t+1} A_{t+1} = P_{t+1} \gamma A_t$. We also assume γ is high enough that it is always profitable for a firm to try to overcome the liquidity shock.

a. Given that producers maximize their total wealth over the two periods, derive the demand for labor and profit in period t.

b. Calculate the probability of innovation q_t as a function of S, μ, and ω.

c. What is the expected productivity growth rate of the economy? Is it higher under fixed or flexible exchange rates? What is the growth gap between the two regimes when $\mu \to \infty$?

d. Assume for the rest of the problem that there are stochastic shocks to productivity: $A_t = \bar{A}_t e^{u_t}$, where

$\bar{A}_t = \rho_{t-1}\gamma A_{t-1} + (1 - \rho_{t-1})A_t$, and u_t is a mean-zero shock of variance σ_u^2. What is the modified demand for labor and profit in period t?

e. Suppose interest-rate parity holds (in logs) when exchange rates are flexible: $s_t = E_{t-1}s_t + \ln(1 + i^*) - \ln(1 + i_t) + \eta_t$. Here $s_t = \ln(S_t)$, i and i^* are the domestic and foreign nominal interest rate, and η_t has mean zero and variance σ_η^2 (under fixed exchange rates, we normalize $s_t = 0$). The central bank follows a Taylor rule and sets $\ln(1 + i_t) = \ln(1 + i^*) + \phi_1 s_t + \phi_2 u_t$. Assume there are no bubbles, that is, $\lim_{i \to \infty} E_t s_{t+i} = 0$. Solve for s_t as a function of the monetary and real shocks η_t and u_t.

f. What is the probability of innovation under fixed and flexible exchange rates if $\sigma_u^2 = 0$? if $\sigma_\eta^2 = 0$? Which regime yields the highest growth in each case?

5. **Timing of innovation and timing of adoption (based on Comin and Gertler, 2006)

Suppose a final good is produced with a continuum of intermediate inputs, where the producer of each intermediate good realizes profits $\pi_t = \delta A_t$ per period; A_t follows a process of the form $A_{t+1} = \rho A_t + (1 - \rho)\bar{A} + \varepsilon_{t+1}$, with $0 < \rho < 1$, $\bar{A} > 0$, and $E_t(\varepsilon_{t+1}) = 0$. The development of a new input takes place in two stages. First, each innovator i spends an amount R_t^i of the final good in research, which leads to $\dfrac{\varphi}{(R_t)^\eta}R_t^i$ new innovations. R_t is the average amount of research spending in the economy and captures congestion effects. The innovator can then sell each design in the next period, for the expected price $E_t P_{t+1}$, to an "adopter" who develops it into a marketable good. Second, for each design he has purchased at or before date t, the adopter chooses a level of spending Z_t so that the product becomes usable with a probability $\lambda\sqrt{Z_t}$, $\lambda > 0$. He earns monopoly profits from a successful innovation; hence the value for the adopter of a product that has been developed is $V_t = \pi_t + \beta E_t V_{t+1}$. We assume free entry in both innovation and adoption of technologies. The discount factor is noted β.

a. Using the condition of free entry into innovation, obtain the level of R_t for given expected prices.

b. Find the value W_t of an innovation that has not yet been adopted. as a function of Z_t, $E_t V_{t+1}$, and $E_t W_{t+1}$. Derive the optimal choice of Z_t. What is the equilibrium relationship between P_t and W_t?

c. Solve for the value of a developed product V_t. How does an increase in the aggregate productivity parameter A_t affect V_t and W_t?

d. Are research spending R_t and adoption spending Z_t procyclical or countercyclical? Explain these results intuitively.

15 Liberalizing Trade

15.1 Introduction

In this chapter we examine the consequences for productivity growth and innovation of interaction between countries. We concentrate on international trade in goods, but as we shall see, when we introduce trade in goods, the nature of international flows in knowledge also becomes very important to the results.

One may think of several reasons why trade should increase world income and enhance productivity growth. First, trade openness increases the size of markets that can be appropriated by successful innovators, or it increases the scale of production and therefore the scope for learning-by-doing externalities. This *market-size* effect should be more important for smaller countries that increase market size by a higher proportion when opening up to trade. Thus, when regressing growth over "openness" and its interaction with the size of the domestic economy (for example, as measured by the log of population), one should find that the interaction coefficient between country size and openness is negative. And indeed this is what Alesina, Spolaore, and Wacziarg (2005) find when they regress growth over country openness and size, using cross-country panel data.[1]

Second, trade induces knowledge spillovers from more advanced to less advanced countries and sectors. Thus one should expect the interaction between openness and initial income in the growth regressions to be negative; that is, growth is less enhanced by openness in more advanced countries. To the extent that knowledge tends to flow from richer to poorer countries, it is not surprising that the more advanced a country already is, the less it should benefit from knowledge spillovers inducing trade. This *knowledge spillover* effect has been

---

1. A natural measure of openness would have been imports plus exports over GDP. However, this raises an obvious endogeneity problem: a positive correlation between imports/exports and growth may reflect the fact that a booming country imports and exports more. To deal with this problem, we follow Frankel and Romer (1999) who instrument the value of imports plus exports over GDP using a simple "gravity model" where trade flows depend upon a country's geographical characteristics such as the extent of common borders with neighboring countries, access to the sea, and the size of the country in population and in surface terms. This instrumentation strategy helps make sure that we capture the causal effect of trade openness on growth and not the reverse causality or the effect of third omitted variables that might affect both trade and growth.

analyzed at length by Keller (2004). It also underlies the work of Sachs and Warner (1995).[2]

There is an additional effect of trade on growth that is not captured in the preceding discussion, namely, that trade liberalization tends to enhance product market competition, by allowing foreign producers to compete with domestic producers. This in turn should enhance domestic productivity for at least two reasons. First, it forces the most unproductive firms out of the domestic market. Thus Trefler (2004) shows that trade liberalization in Canada resulted in a 6 percent increase in average productivity. Second, as in chapter 12, it forces domestic firms to innovate in order to escape competition with their new foreign counterparts.

In the following sections we develop a synthetic framework that embodies all these potential effects that trade may have on productivity growth and innovation.[3] In section 15.2 we outline a simple multisector Schumpeterian model of a closed economy, much like the one developed at greater length in chapter 4, which will serve as a reference point for our analysis of an open economy. In section 15.3 we examine the immediate impact of trade on sectoral productivities and the level of national income, by taking two economies of the sort described in section 15.2 and allowing them to trade costlessly with each other. In that section we take productivities in the domestic and foreign sectors as given. In section 15.4 we show how trade affects the innovation process and use this analysis to study the long-run growth effects of trade between the two economies studied in the previous section, but now focusing on endogeneizing productivity and its dynamics in both countries.

Overall the theory shows that there are good reasons for supposing that trade has a positive impact on both the level and the growth rate of a country's national income. However, the analysis in this chapter also points to possible exceptions to this general supposition. In particular, small economies that have the potential for becoming world leaders in some sectors but have not yet realized that potential seem to be the most likely to lose as a result of international trade.

---

2. Additional evidence on trade and research spillovers is provided in an important paper by Coe and Helpman (1995). For each country they construct measures of domestic and foreign R&D capital stocks, where the latter are weighted averages of the domestic stocks of trade partners. They find that foreign R&D appears to have a beneficial effect on domestic productivity and that the effect increases in strength with the degree of openness. Hence, not only are there important spillovers, but there is also some evidence that these are mediated by trade. However, one may argue that even if a correlation is observed between domestic productivity and foreign research, this may simply represent the outcome of common demand or input price shocks. Weighting the contribution of foreign research using data on bilateral trade flows, as in Coe and Helpman, is likely to mitigate this problem but will not overcome it altogether.

3. In chapter 2 we saw yet another potential effect of trade on growth: *a terms-of-trade effect* whereby trade allows small countries to avoid the consequences of decreasing returns to capital accumulation.

15.2   Preliminary: Back to the Multisector Closed-Economy Model

In the next sections we introduce trade into the Schumpeterian model of chapter 4. First we review the closed-economy version of the model, introducing the notion of national income.

15.2.1   Production and National Income

There is a single country in which a unique final good, which also serves as numéraire, is produced competitively using a continuum of intermediate inputs according to

$$Y_t = L^{1-\alpha} \int_0^1 A_{it}^{1-\alpha} x_{it}^{\alpha} \, di, \qquad 0 < \alpha < 1 \tag{15.1}$$

where L is the domestic labor force, assumed to be constant, A_{it} is the quality of intermediate good i at time t, and x_{it} is the flow quantity of intermediate good i being produced and used at time t.

In each intermediate sector there is a monopolist producer who uses the final good as the sole input, with one unit of final good needed to produce each unit of intermediate good. The monopolist's cost of production is therefore equal to the quantity produced x_{it}. The price p_{it} at which she can sell this quantity of intermediate good to the competitive final sector is the marginal product of intermediate good i in the final-good production function (15.1).

As we showed in chapter 4, the monopolist will choose the level of output that maximizes profits, namely,

$$x_{it} = A_{it} L \alpha^{2/(1-\alpha)} \tag{15.2}$$

resulting in the profit level

$$\pi_{it} = \pi A_{it} L \tag{15.3}$$

where $\pi \equiv (1-\alpha)\alpha^{\frac{1+\alpha}{1-\alpha}}$.

The equilibrium level of final output in the economy can be found by substituting the x_{it}'s into equation (15.1), which yields

$$Y_t = \varphi A_t L \tag{15.4}$$

where A_t is the average productivity parameter across all sectors

$$A_t = \int_0^1 A_{it} \, di$$

and $\varphi = \alpha^{\frac{2\alpha}{1-\alpha}}$.[4]

We are interested in the equilibrium level of national income N_t which is not quite the same as final sector output Y_t, because some of the final goods are used up in producing the intermediate products that in turn are used in producing the final output. There are only two forms of income—wage income and profit income. Each of the L workers is employed in the final-goods sector, where he is paid his marginal product. So according to the production function (15.1) total wage income is the fraction $1 - \alpha$ of final output:

$$W_t = L \times \partial Y_t / \partial L = (1-\alpha) Y_t$$

Profits are earned by the local monopolists who sell intermediate products to the final sector. (There are no profits in the final-good sector because that sector is perfectly competitive and operates under constant returns to scale.) Since each monopolist charges a price equal to[5] $1/\alpha$ and has a cost per unit equal to 1, therefore the profit margin $p_{it} - 1$ on each unit sold can be written as $(1 - \alpha)p_{it}$, which means that total profits equal

$$\Pi_t = \int_0^1 (p_{it} - 1) x_{it} dt = (1-\alpha) \int_0^1 p_{it} x_{it} dt$$

And since the price p_{it} is the marginal product of the ith intermediate product, therefore equation (15.1) implies

$$\int_0^1 p_{it} x_{it} dt = \int_0^1 (\partial Y_t / \partial x_{it}) x_{it} dt = \alpha Y_t$$

So from the last two lines we have

$$\Pi_t = (1-\alpha)\alpha Y_t$$

Gathering results, we see that national income is

$$N_t = W_t + \Pi_t = (1-\alpha^2) Y_t \tag{15.5}$$

---

4. To derive this expression for Y_t, substitute the x_{it}'s into equation (15.1) to get

$$Y_t = L^{1-\alpha} \int_0^1 A_{it}^{1-\alpha} \left(A_{it} L \alpha^{2/(1-\alpha)} \right)^\alpha di$$
$$= \left(\alpha^{2/(1-\alpha)} \right)^\alpha L \int_0^1 A_{it}^{1-\alpha} A_{it}^\alpha di$$
$$= \varphi A_t L$$

5. That is, since the final-good market in which the intermediate product is sold is perfectly competitive, therefore its price equals its marginal product:

$$p_{it} = \partial Y_t / \partial x_{it} = \alpha L^{1-\alpha} A_t^{1-\alpha} x_{it}^{\alpha-1}$$

Using equation (15.2) to substitute for x_{it} in this equation yields $p_{it} = 1/\alpha$.

From equations (15.4) and (15.5) we see that national income is strictly proportional to average productivity and to population:

$$N_t = \left(1 - \alpha^2\right)\varphi A_t L \tag{15.6}$$

It follows from this last result that the growth rate of national income is also the growth rate of productivity:

$$\dot{N}_t / N_t = \dot{A}_t / A_t = g_t$$

15.2.2 Innovation

Productivity growth comes from innovations. In each sector at each date there is a unique entrepreneur with the possibility of innovating in that sector. She is the incumbent monopolist, and an innovation would enable her to produce with a productivity (quality) parameter $A_{it} = \gamma A_{i,t-1}$ that is superior to that of the previous monopolist by the factor $\gamma > 1$. Otherwise her productivity parameter stays the same: $A_{it} = A_{i,t-1}$. In order to innovate with any given probability μ she must spend the amount

$$c_{it}(\mu) = (1 - \tau) \cdot \phi(\mu) \cdot A_{i,t-1}$$

of final good in research, where $\tau > 0$ is a subsidy parameter that represents the extent to which national policies encourage innovation, and ϕ is a cost function satisfying

$$\phi(0) = 0$$

and

$$\phi'(\mu) > 0, \quad \phi''(\mu) > 0 \quad \text{for all } \mu > 0$$

Thus the local entrepreneur's expected profit net of research cost is

$$\begin{aligned} V_{it} &= E\pi_{it} - c_{it}(\mu) \\ &= \mu \pi L \gamma A_{i,t-1} + (1 - \mu)\pi L A_{i,t-1} - (1 - \tau)\phi(\mu) A_{i,t-1} \end{aligned}$$

Each local entrepreneur will choose a frequency of innovations $\hat{\mu}$ that maximizes V_{it}. The first-order condition for an interior maximum is $\partial V_{it}/\partial \mu = 0$, which can be expressed as the research-arbitrage equation

$$\phi'(\mu) = \pi L (\gamma - 1)/(1 - \tau) \tag{15.7}$$

If the research environment is favorable enough (i.e., if τ is large enough), or the population large enough, so that

$$\phi'(0) > \pi L(\gamma-1)/(1-\tau)$$

then the unique solution μ to the research-arbitrage equation (15.7) is positive, so in each sector the probability of an innovation is that solution ($\hat{\mu} = \mu$) which is an increasing function of the size of population L and of the policies favoring innovation τ. Otherwise there is no positive solution to the research-arbitrage equation, so the local entrepreneur chooses never to innovate ($\hat{\mu} = 0$).

Since each A_{it} grows at the rate $\gamma - 1$ with probability $\hat{\mu}$, and at the rate 0 with probability $1 - \hat{\mu}$, therefore the expected growth rate of the economy is

$$g = \hat{\mu}(\gamma-1)$$

So we see that countries with a larger population and more favorable innovation conditions will be more likely to grow, and if they grow will grow faster than countries with a smaller population and less favorable innovation conditions.

15.3   Opening Up to Trade, Abstracting from Innovation

Now, let us open trade in goods (both intermediate and final) between the domestic country and the rest of the world, and we first take productivities in all domestic and foreign sectors to be given. Productivity-enhancing innovations are introduced in the next section.

To keep it simple, suppose that there are just two countries, "home" and "foreign," which differ in terms of the size of population and the policies favoring innovation. Suppose that the range of intermediate products in each country is identical, that they produce exactly the same final product, and that there are no transportation costs. Within each intermediate sector the world market can then be monopolized by the producer with the lowest cost. We use asterisks to denote foreign-country variables.

15.3.1   The Experiment

Consider the following conceptual experiment. To begin with, each country does not trade, and hence behaves just like the closed economy described in the previous section. Then at time t we allow countries to trade costlessly with each other. The immediate effect of this opening up is to allow each country to take advantage of greater productive efficiency. In the home country, final-good production will equal

$$Y_t = \int_0^1 Y_{it}\,di = L^{1-\alpha}\int_0^1 \hat{A}_{it}^{1-\alpha} x_{it}^\alpha\,di, \qquad 0 < \alpha < 1 \tag{15.8}$$

where $\hat{A}_{it}$ is the higher of the two initial productivity parameters:

$$\hat{A}_{it} = \max\{A_{it}, A^*_{it}\}$$

Likewise in the foreign country final-good production will equal

$$Y^*_t = \int_0^1 Y^*_{it} di = (L^*)^{1-\alpha} \int_0^1 \hat{A}^{1-\alpha}_{it} (x^*_{it})^\alpha di, \qquad 0 < \alpha < 1 \tag{15.9}$$

The profit of a monopolist will now be higher than it was under autarky, because she can now sell to both countries. Specifically, if she charges the price p_{it}, then final-good producers in each country will buy good i up to the point where its marginal product equals p_{it}:

$$x_{it} = \hat{A}_{it} L \left(p_{it}/\alpha \right)^{\frac{1}{\alpha-1}} \quad \text{and} \quad x^*_{it} = \hat{A}_{it} L^* \left(p_{it}/\alpha \right)^{\frac{1}{\alpha-1}} \tag{15.10}$$

Adding these two equations and rearranging, we see that her price will depend on total sales $X_{it} = x_{it} + x^*_{it}$ according to

$$p_{it} = \alpha (L + L^*)^{1-\alpha} \left(\hat{A}_{it} \right)^{1-\alpha} X^{\alpha-1}_{it} \tag{15.11}$$

which is the same as the demand relationship in the closed economy[6] except that now we have global sales relative to global population instead of local sales relative to local population on the right-hand side. Accordingly, the monopolist's profit π_{it} will equal revenue $p_{it} X_{it}$ minus cost X_{it}:

$$\pi_{it} = p_{it} X_{it} - X_{it} = \alpha \left(\hat{A}_{it} \right)^{1-\alpha} (L + L^*)^{1-\alpha} X^\alpha_{it} - X_{it}$$

As in the case of the closed economy, the monopolist will choose the level of output that maximizes π_{it}, namely,

$$X_{it} = \hat{A}_{it} (L + L^*) \alpha^{2/(1-\alpha)}$$

resulting in the same price

$$p_{it} = 1/\alpha$$

as before and the profit level

$$\pi_{it} = \pi \hat{A}_{it} (L + L^*) \tag{15.12}$$

where once again $\pi \equiv (1-\alpha)\alpha^{\frac{1+\alpha}{1-\alpha}}$

Substituting the prices $p_{it} = 1/\alpha$ into the demand functions (15.10) yields

6. See footnote 5.

$$x_{it} = \hat{A}_{it} L \alpha^{2/(1-\alpha)} \quad \text{and} \quad x_{it}^* = \hat{A}_{it} L^* \alpha^{2/(1-\alpha)}$$

and substituting these into the production functions (15.8) and (15.9), we see that final-good production in the two countries will be proportional to their populations:

$$Y_t = \varphi \hat{A}_t L \quad \text{and} \quad Y_t^* = \varphi \hat{A}_t L^* \tag{15.13}$$

where once again $\varphi = \alpha^{\frac{2\alpha}{1-\alpha}}$ and where $\hat{A}_t$ is the cross-sectoral average of the $\hat{A}_{it}$'s:

$$\hat{A}_t = \int_0^1 \hat{A}_{it} di$$

15.3.2   The Effects of Openness on National Income

Within each country, national income is still equal to the sum of wage income and profit income. As before, wage income in each country is earned in the final sector:

$$W_t = (1-\alpha)Y_t = (1-\alpha)\varphi \hat{A}_t L$$

$$W_t^* = (1-\alpha)Y_t^* = (1-\alpha)\varphi \hat{A}_t L^*$$

Profit income in each country depends on the fraction of the intermediate monopolies that resides in that country. Define

$$\lambda_{it} = \begin{cases} 1 & \text{if } A_{it} > A_{it}^* \\ 0 & \text{otherwise} \end{cases}$$

So λ_{it} is an indicator of whether the monopoly resides in the home country, and $1 - \lambda_{it}$ is an indicator of whether it resides in the foreign country. (For simplicity we assume that there are no sectors in which $A_{it} = A_{it}^*$.) According to equation (15.12), total profits across all sectors monopolized by each country will be

$$\Pi_t = \pi(L+L^*)\int_0^1 \lambda_{it} \hat{A}_{it} di$$

$$\Pi_t^* = \pi(L+L^*)\int_0^1 (1-\lambda_{it}) \hat{A}_{it} di$$

Therefore, national income in the two countries is

$$N_t = (1-\alpha)Y_t + \alpha(1-\alpha)\int_0^1 \lambda_{it}(Y_{it} + Y_{it}^*)di \tag{15.14}$$

$$N_t^* = (1-\alpha)Y_t^* + \alpha(1-\alpha)\int_0^1 (1-\lambda_{it})(Y_{it} + Y_{it}^*)di \tag{15.15}$$

which can be rewritten as

$$N_t = \left[(1-\alpha)\hat{A}_t L + \alpha(1-\alpha)\int_0^1 \lambda_{it}\hat{A}_{it}(L+L^*)di \right]\varphi$$

$$N_t^* = \left[(1-\alpha)\hat{A}_t L^* + \alpha(1-\alpha)\int_0^1 (1-\lambda_{it})\hat{A}_{it}(L+L^*)di \right]\varphi$$

15.3.2.1 The Selection Effect

One way in which international trade can raise a country's national income is through the selection effect of increased competition (see Melitz 2003). That is, firms can buy intermediate products from the most efficient producer. This is bad news for the less efficient producer, who is forced to exit, but it raises aggregate incomes by increasing the overall level of efficiency with which the economy converts labor input into final output (by means of intermediate products).

To see how this effect works in the present model, note that when the world economy is opened up to trade, total world income is the sum of equations (15.14) and (15.15), namely,

$$N_t + N_t^* = (1-\alpha)(Y_t + Y_t^*) + \alpha(1-\alpha)(Y_t + Y_t^*)$$
$$= (1-\alpha^2)\varphi(L\hat{A}_t + L^*\hat{A}_t)$$

whereas when the world economy was closed it was[7]

$$N_t + N_t^* = (1-\alpha^2)\varphi(LA_t + L^*A_t^*)$$

Comparing these two formulas, we see that the total world income has been raised by international trade because the average productivity parameter $\hat{A}_t$ is generally larger than either A_t or A_t^*. That is, in sectors where the home country gets the monopoly we have $\hat{A}_{it} = A_{it}$, while in all other sectors $\hat{A}_{it} > A_{it}$, so the average of all the $\hat{A}_{it}$'s is bigger than the average of all the A_{it}'s. Likewise, it is also bigger than the average of all the A_{it}^*'s.

15.3.2.2 Scale Effect

We saw earlier that smaller countries appear to gain more from openness than larger countries. The present model helps us to see why this statement might be accurate. As we have seen, the home country's national income was

$$N_t = (1-\alpha^2)A_t L\varphi$$

---

7. This is the sum of equation (15.6) for each country.

when it was closed, and then changed to

$$N_t' = \left[(1-\alpha)\hat{A}_t L + \alpha(1-\alpha)\int_0^1 \lambda_{it}\hat{A}_{it}(L+L^*)\,di \right]\varphi$$

We would like to see what the model implies about how the gains from openness depend upon population, holding constant the initial level of technological development. To do so, suppose that the home and foreign countries started at equal levels of technological development. That is, in half of the sectors the home country starts with higher productivity and captures the monopoly, while in the other half the foreign country captures the monopoly, and on average the productivity of the monopolies in either country is the same as the global average, namely, $\hat{A}_t$. In that case the home country's national income after opening up to trade would be

$$N_t' = \left[(1-\alpha)\hat{A}_t L + \alpha(1-\alpha)(1/2)\hat{A}_t(L+L^*) \right]\varphi$$
$$= \left(1-\alpha^2\right)\hat{A}_t L\varphi + \alpha(1-\alpha)(1/2)(L^*-L)\hat{A}_t\varphi$$

so the proportional gain from openness is

$$\frac{N_t'}{N_t} = \frac{\hat{A}_t}{A_t}\left(1 + \frac{\alpha}{2(1+\alpha)}\frac{L^*-L}{L}\right)$$

It follows directly that the smaller the country, as measured by L, the larger the proportional gain. This scale effect works entirely through the profit component of national income. By opening up to international trade, technologically advanced intermediate producers can now sell their products to a larger market. The smaller the market was before opening up, the bigger this gain will be.

15.3.2.3   Backwardness

We also saw that technologically less advanced countries seemed to gain more from openness. To see why this conclusion might be true, let us control for size by supposing that the home and foreign countries are of equal size ($L = L^*$). Then going through the same exercise as before we see that the relative gain from openness is

$$\frac{N_t'}{N_t} = \frac{1}{1+\alpha}\frac{\hat{A}_t}{A_t} + \frac{2\alpha\int_0^1 \lambda_{it}\hat{A}_{it}\,di}{(1+\alpha)A_t}$$

where the first term represents wage income and the second profit income, both relative to pretrade national income.

In this case the effect is not quite as clear-cut as in the case of the scale effect. The reason is that opening up to trade will definitely raise wage income, since workers will be working with more advanced intermediate inputs and hence will be more productive, but it might not raise the home country's profit income. In the extreme case where the home country lags behind the foreign country in every sector, we would find that $\lambda_{it} = 0$ in all sectors i, so the profit component of national income would vanish as a result of openness (i.e., the case in which opening up to trade would make the country a mere assembler of imported components). In that case, the gain in wage income might not be enough to compensate for the loss of profit income.

Nevertheless, even in this extreme case, we can say unambiguously that if the country starts far enough behind the rest of the world, it will definitely gain from international trade, and will gain more in relative terms the further behind it starts. That is, if the initial productivity level A_t of the home country is less than $\hat{A}/(1 + \alpha)$ to begin with, then even the first component in the preceding expression for N_t'/N_t will exceed unity, and the smaller A_t is, the higher it will be.

This analysis of backwardness should warn us, however, that although international trade raises total world income, through the selection effect, there is no guarantee that it will raise national income in every country.

15.4   The Effects of Openness on Innovation and Long-Run Growth

15.4.1   Step-by-Step Innovation

Assume the following step-by-step innovation process in a given sector i. In the country where the monopoly currently resides, the country is on the global technology frontier for sector i, and the local entrepreneur will aim at making a frontier innovation that raises the productivity parameter from $\hat{A}_{it}$ to $\gamma \hat{A}_{it}$. If successful, that country will retain a global monopoly in intermediate product i. In the other country, the local entrepreneur will be trying to catch up with the frontier by implementing the current frontier technology. If she succeeds and the frontier entrepreneur fails to advance the frontier that period, then the lagging country will have caught up, both countries will be on the frontier, and then we can suppose that each entrepreneur will monopolize the market for product i in her own country. But if the frontier entrepreneur does advance the frontier, then the entrepreneur in the lagging country will still remain behind and will earn no profit income.

Over time, the lead in each sector will tend to pass from country to country, as long as the lagging sector is innovating. (Otherwise the leader will remain the country that starts with the lead when trade is opened up.) However, there will be no immediate leapfrogging of one country by the other, because in order to retake the lead a country must first catch up. So in between lead changes there will be a period when the sector is level, or neck and neck, as we saw in chapter 12 when we studied the effect of product market competition on innovation. As in chapter 12, the growth rate of productivity will be determined by the incentives to perform R&D in the different cases (when the country is the sole leader, when it is the laggard, and when the sector is level). So we need to study each case in turn.

15.4.2 Three Cases

Three possibilities must be considered. Either a domestic sector leads over the corresponding sector in the foreign country (case A); or the domestic sector is level (neck and neck) with its counterpart in the foreign country (case B); or the domestic sector lags behind its foreign counterpart (case C).

A. Case A is the case in which the lead in sector i resides in the home country, while the foreign country lags behind. In this case the expected profit of the entrepreneur in the home country, net of R&D costs, is

$$EU_A = \mu_A \gamma (L + L^*) \pi + (1 - \mu_A)[L + (1 - \mu_A^*)L^*]\pi - (1 - \tau)\phi(\mu_A)$$

while the expected profit of the foreign entrepreneur is

$$EU_A^* = \mu_A^*(1 - \mu_A)\pi L^* - (1 - \tau^*)\phi(\mu_A^*)$$

where everything is normalized by the preexisting productivity level. That is, with probability μ_A the home entrepreneur will innovate, thus earning all the global profits in the market at productivity level γ times the preexisting level; if she fails to innovate then she will still earn all domestic profits in the market, at the preexisting profit level, and if the foreign entrepreneur fails to innovate (which occurs with probability $1 - \mu_A^*$) she will also earn all the foreign profits in the market. In any event she must incur the R&D cost $(1 - \tau)\phi(\mu_A)$. Likewise, the foreign entrepreneur will earn all the profits in the foreign market if she innovates and her rival does not, which occurs with probability $\mu_A^*(1 - \mu_A)$.

B. Case B is the case in which the sector is level. In this case the expected profits of the respective entrepreneurs net of R&D costs are

$$EU_B = \{\mu_B[L + (1 - \mu_B^*)L^*]\gamma + (1 - \mu_B)(1 - \mu_B^*)L\}\pi - (1 - \tau)\phi(\mu_B)$$
$$EU_B^* = \{\mu_B^*[L^* + (1 - \mu_B)L]\gamma + (1 - \mu_B^*)(1 - \mu_B)L^*\}\pi - (1 - \tau^*)\phi(\mu_B^*)$$

Thus, for example, the home entrepreneur innovates with probability μ_B, which earns her all the home profits for sure and in addition all the foreign profits if her rival fails to innovate, whereas if both fail to innovate, then she retains all the domestic profits.

C. Case C is the case in which the foreign country starts with the lead. By symmetry with case A the expected profits minus R&D costs are

$$EU_C = \mu_C(1-\mu_C^*)\pi L - (1-\tau)\phi(\mu_C)$$

$$EU_C^* = \mu_C^*\gamma(L+L^*)\pi + (1-\mu_C^*)\left[L^* + (1-\mu_C)L\right]\pi - (1-\tau^*)\phi(\mu_C^*)$$

15.4.3 Equilibrium Innovation and Growth

The research-arbitrage equations that determine the innovation rates in equilibrium are simply obtained by taking the first-order conditions for each of the preceding expressions for expected profit minus R&D cost. Innovation rates in the domestic country thus satisfy

$$(1-\tau)\phi'(\mu_A)/\pi = (\gamma-1)(L+L^*) + \mu_A^*L^*$$

$$(1-\tau)\phi'(\mu_B)/\pi = (\gamma-1)L + \mu_B^*L + (1-\mu_B^*)\gamma L^*$$

$$(1-\tau)\phi'(\mu_C)/\pi = (1-\mu_C^*)L$$

and symmetrically for innovation in the foreign country.[8]

Our conclusions in the remaining part of the section will be derived from comparing the home-country research-arbitrage equations under openness with the closed-economy research-arbitrage equation (15.7), which we reproduce here for convenience:

$$(1-\tau)\phi'(\mu)/\pi = (\gamma-1)L \qquad (15.16)$$

15.4.4 Scale and Escape Entry

Comparing the closed-economy research-arbitrage equation with the one governing μ_A,

---

8. That is,

$$(1-\tau^*)\phi'(\mu_A^*)/\pi = (1-\mu_A)L^*$$

$$(1-\tau^*)\phi'(\mu_B^*)/\pi = (\gamma-1)L^* + \mu_B L^* + (1-\mu_B)\gamma L$$

$$(1-\tau^*)\phi'(\mu_C^*)/\pi = (\gamma-1)(L+L^*) + \mu_C L$$

$$(1-\tau)\phi'(\mu_A)/\pi = (\gamma-1)(L+L^*)+\mu_A^* L^* \tag{15.17}$$

we see that when the home country has the technology lead (case A) it will innovate at a faster rate than when it was a closed economy, because the right-hand side of the leader's research-arbitrage equation (15.17) is larger than the right-hand side of the closed economy counterpart (15.16). This result comes about because of two effects, scale and escape entry.

The scale effect arises because the successful innovator gets enhanced profits from both markets, not just the domestic market, thus giving her a stronger incentive to innovate. It is for this reason that equation (15.17) has the sum of size variables $L + L^*$ where equation (15.16) has just the domestic size variable L.

The escape-entry effect arises because the unsuccessful innovator in the open economy is at risk of losing the foreign market to her foreign rival, a risk that she can avoid by innovating. By contrast, the unsuccessful innovator in the closed economy loses nothing to a foreign rival and thus does not have this extra incentive to innovate. Of course, this is just the same escape-entry effect that we saw in chapter 12. Formally, this effect accounts for the extra term $\mu_A^* L^*$ that appears on the right-hand side of equation (15.17) but not of equation (15.16).

Comparing the closed-economy research-arbitrage equation (15.16) to the one governing the home country's innovation rate in a level sector,

$$(1-\tau)\phi'(\mu_B)/\pi = (\gamma-1)L+\mu_B^* L+(1-\mu_B^*)\gamma L^*$$

we see the same two effects at work. The term $\mu_B^* L$ is the escape-entry effect; by innovating the home entrepreneur can avoid the risk of losing the local market. The term $(1 - \mu_B^*)\gamma L^*$ is the scale effect; by innovating the home entrepreneur can capture (with some probability) the foreign market as well as the domestic market.

It follows that both μ_A and μ_B will be larger than the closed-economy innovation rate μ. The same will be true for the foreign innovation rates μ_C^* and μ_B^*, which will both be larger than the foreign country's innovation rate when it was closed, μ^*.

15.4.5   The Discouragement Effect of Foreign Entry

We saw in chapter 12 that a country behind the world technology frontier may be discouraged from innovating by the threat of entry because even if it innovates it might lose out to a superior entrant. The possibility of a similar effect of trade openness is reflected in the research-arbitrage equation governing the home country's innovation rate when it is the technological laggard:

$$(1-\tau)\phi'(\mu_C)/\pi = (1-\mu_C^*)L$$

If the foreign country's innovation rate is large enough when it has the lead, then the right-hand side of this research-arbitrage equation will be strictly less than that of the closed-economy equation (15.16), so we will have $\mu_C < \mu$. This fact will not have a direct effect on the growth rate (see following), which depends only on the leader's innovation rate μ_C^*. That is, in this state the home country is just catching up, not advancing the global technology frontier. However, as we shall see, a fall in μ_C will nevertheless have an indirect effect on growth by affecting the steady-state fractions of productivity accounted for by the sectors in states A, B, C.

15.4.6 Steady-State Aggregate Growth

In steady state, there will be a constant fraction of sectors in each state, q_A, q_B, and q_C, with $q_A + q_B + q_C = 1$, while aggregate productivity will be

$$\hat{A}_t = q_A \hat{A}_{At} + q_B \hat{A}_{Bt} + q_C \hat{A}_{Ct}$$

where, for example, $\hat{A}_{At}$ is the average productivity level in sectors where the lead resides in the home country. It follows that the growth rate of aggregate productivity (and hence of each country's national income) in steady state will be

$$g = \eta_A g_A + \eta_B g_B + \eta_C g_C \tag{15.18}$$

where for each state $S = A, B, C$, $\eta_s = q_s \hat{A}_{St}/\hat{A}_t$ is the share of aggregate productivity accounted for by sectors in state S in the steady state, and g_s is the expected growth rate of the leading technology $\hat{A}_{St}$ in each sector currently in state S.

Since the η's add up to one, it is implied that the steady-state growth rate of the open economy is a weighted average of the productivity growth rates g_s. These are

$$g_A = (\gamma - 1)\mu_A$$

$$g_B = (\gamma - 1)(\mu_B + \mu_B^* - \mu_B \mu_B^*)$$

$$g_C = (\gamma - 1)\mu_C^*$$

We now consider the effect of trade openness on aggregate growth in two opposite situations: (1) trade liberalization enhances growth in all countries, and (2) trade liberalization reduces growth in one country.

15.4.7 How Trade Can Enhance Growth in All Countries

Suppose first that one country, say the home country, is less innovative than the other, in the sense that its closed-economy innovation rate μ is less than the foreign country's innovation rate when closed μ^*. Suppose also that the discouragement effect of foreign entry is so great that once it is exposed to foreign trade the home country does no research in sectors where it is a laggard. That is, the preceding research-arbitrage equation governing μ_C cannot be satisfied by any positive μ_C, so instead the equilibrium innovation rate of the home country in state C is $\mu_C = 0$. Suppose, however, that all the other innovation rates are positive in all three states.

In this case, what will happen is that the home country will eventually lose the technology lead in all sectors. In the steady state the fraction of sectors in state C will become $q_C = 1$, while $q_A = q_B = 0$. Thus, according to the steady state, all profit income will be earned in the foreign country, and the growth rate of national income in all countries will be

$$g = g_C = (\gamma - 1)\mu_C^*$$

Since μ_C^* is larger than the foreign innovation rate μ^* before opening up to trade, therefore trade will raise the foreign growth rate. Since both countries grow at the same rate in the open economy, and by assumption the foreign country grew faster than the home country before trade, therefore trade will raise the growth rate in the home country as well.

This result illustrates how trade can allow productivity growth even in countries that do not innovate, something that was not possible without foreign trade. For example, as we saw in chapter 7, a country with a low level of financial development might end up stagnating relative to the rest of the world. In the present model, if the policies favoring innovation τ in the home country are perverse enough, then the country will not innovate at all when it is closed, and hence will have a zero growth rate when closed. Yet when it is open to trade it will grow as fast as the most innovative country.

The reason for this effect is what Keller (2004) calls the direct channel of technology transfer. Productivity of workers in the final sector in the noninnovating country can grow despite the lack of domestic innovation because they are able to work with imported intermediate products whose quality continues to grow as a result of foreign innovations. In this sense trade can act as a substitute for innovation in some countries while it acts as a spur to innovation in others.

As another example, suppose that neither country innovates when it is a laggard. Then the fractions q_A and q_B of sectors in which each country has a lead will remain constant over time. If the home country has a smaller innovation rate than the foreign country (i.e., $\mu_A < \mu_C^*$) then average productivity of sectors in state C will grow without bound relative to average productivity of sectors in state A, so in the steady state we will again have $q_C = 1$ and $g = (\gamma - 1)\mu_C^*$. Again both countries will have their growth rates raised by trade.

Finally, in the case where both countries are identical ($L = L^*$ and $\tau = \tau^*$), then by symmetry the growth rate will be

$$
\begin{aligned}
g &= (1 - \eta_B)g_A + \eta_B g_B \\
&= (\gamma - 1)\big[(1 - \eta_B)\mu_A + \eta_B(2\mu_B - \mu_B^2)\big] \\
&= (\gamma - 1)\big[(1 - \eta_B)\mu_A + \eta_B\mu_B\big] + (\gamma - 1)\mu_B(1 - \mu_B)
\end{aligned}
$$

which is larger than the closed-economy growth rate $(\gamma - 1)\mu$ not only because of the scale and escape-entry effects that make μ_A and μ_B both larger than μ, which is why the first term on the right-hand side of this last expression is greater than $(\gamma - 1)\mu$, but also because of a duplication effect. That is, when sectors are level, then there are two possible frontier innovators, so even if one fails to advance the frontier, the other might; this possibility accounts for the second term on the right-hand side of the last line.

15.4.8   How Trade Can Reduce Growth in One Country

The fact that trade raises growth in both countries when either the countries are symmetrical or one country fails to innovate when behind suggests that trade will usually raise growth in both countries. But there can be exceptions. These exceptions, of course, must involve countries that are asymmetrical. For example, consider the case of a small country (home) whose policies used to be very unfavorable to innovation but which has recently undertaken a reform to make the country more innovative. Suppose these policies have been so successful that just before opening up to trade, the home country has a faster growth rate than the foreign country:

$$\mu > \mu^*$$

but the reforms have been so recent that the home country is still behind the foreign country in all sectors. Then immediately after the opening up to trade all monopolies will reside in the foreign country; that is, all sectors will be in case C. Now suppose furthermore that the discouragement effect is large enough that the home country does not innovate when behind ($\mu_C = 0$). Then, as we have seen, all monopolies will remain forever in the foreign country.

This is the case in which, as we saw previously, the home country's level of national income might actually fall when trade is opened up, because the increased efficiency of the selection effect might be outweighed by the loss of profits from the home-country monopolists that are forced out of business by foreign competition. What we can now see is that whether or not national income falls at first, the home country's growth rate from then on may be lower than if it had never opened up to trade.

More specifically, if it had not opened up for trade, then the home country's growth rate would have remained equal to

$$g = (\gamma - 1)\mu$$

whereas under open trade its growth rate will be that of each sector in case C, namely,

$$g' = (\gamma - 1)\mu_C^*$$

So the home country growth rate will be reduced by trade if and only if $\mu_C^* < \mu$. Now we know from our preceding analysis that μ_C^* must exceed the innovation rate that the foreign country would have experienced under autarky:

$$\mu_C^* > \mu^*$$

but this fact does not guarantee that it exceeds the innovation rate that the home country would have experienced under autarky. Indeed if μ_C^* is close enough to μ^*, then it will be strictly less than μ, and the home country's growth rate will indeed be reduced by trade.

This is where our assumption that the home country is small comes into play. For if it is very small relative to the foreign country, then the scale effect of trade on the foreign innovation rate μ_C^* will be small. Since we are assuming that the home country never innovates when behind, therefore there is no escape-entry effect on μ_C^*, so if the home country is small enough, then μ_C^* will indeed be close enough to μ^* that it falls below μ and the home country's growth rate is diminished by trade.

So we have a presumption that if there are instances where trade is bad for growth, they are probably in small countries that start off far behind the global technology frontier. We also have an example of how economic reform needs to be sequenced properly in order to have its desired effect. That is, generally speaking a country's growth prospects are enhanced by liberalizing trade and by removing barriers to innovation. But if these reforms are undertaken simultaneously, then their full benefits might not be realized. Instead, it might be better to remove the barriers to innovation first and then to wait until several domestic industries have become world leaders before removing the barriers to international trade.

15.5   Conclusion

In this chapter we analyzed the effects of opening up to trade on domestic productivities and on innovation incentives. We saw that international trade raises total world income for several reasons. First, it selects the most productive producer in each sector. Second, it allows the most advanced producer in each sector to sell to a larger market. Third, it allows backward sectors to catch up with the technological frontier. Then we turned our attention to trade and innovation. By increasing market size, trade increases the size of ex post rents that accrue to successful innovators, thereby encouraging R&D investments. Moreover, by increasing product market competition, trade encourages innovations aimed at escaping competition by more advanced firms in the domestic economy. However, it may discourage innovation by laggard firms. This discouragement effect in turn introduces the possibility that trade may sometimes reduce growth, in particular in small countries that are far below the world technology frontier. Our analysis in fact suggests that it might be better to remove barriers to innovation prior to fully liberalizing trade in such countries.

A natural next step is to confront the predictions derived in this chapter to the data. In a nutshell, we saw the following:

• Selection effects predict a positive effect of measures of openness on income. In addition, trade will increase the productivity of the final sector everywhere.

• Scale effects predict

  • A negative impact from the interaction of openness and size on income; that is, smaller countries should gain proportionately more from openness than large countries.

  • A negative impact from the interaction of openness and size on growth; that is, smaller countries should gain proportionately more from openness than large countries.

• Backwardness effects predict

• An ambiguous effect from the interaction of openness and distance from the technological frontier on income. As long as the distance is not excessive, the impact should be positive; the greater the distance, the greater the proportionate gain from openness. However, where the distance from the frontier is too great, the impact can be reversed.

• An ambiguous effect from the interaction of openness and distance from the technological frontier on growth. While firms that are the technological leader or that are at level pegging with the technological leader should increase innovation under trade liberalization, firms that lag behind the technological leader may decrease productivity growth if the lag is large enough. The net effect is ambiguous.

Aghion, Fedderke, Howitt, Kularatne, and Viegi (2008), or AFHKV, test for these effects in a middle-income-country context, namely, using South African manufacturing sector data. South Africa is interesting as a natural experiment of gradual liberalization in a country that is sectorally heterogeneous and suffers from significant internal market monopolies. Their results confirm a positive direct impact of trade liberalization on productivity growth. Moreover, the results suggest that the direct effect of liberalization operates through the impact of the liberalization on product market competition and the pricing power of domestic producers. The results also confirm that the greatest positive impact of trade liberalization is on small rather than large domestic sectors; however, no differential impact of the liberalization on sectors that are far from or close to international technological frontiers could be found.

15.6   Literature Notes

The theoretical literature on trade and growth is broad, in contrast to the limited set of empirical papers on the subject. Having already mentioned the main empirical studies in section 15.1, here we concentrate on the theory.

The idea that trade openness should generate both static gains (higher quality or variety of products) and dynamic gains (faster rate of innovation) has been stressed most forcefully by Grossman and Helpman (1989, 1991a, 1991b) and by Rivera-Batiz and Romer (1991). In particular, what induces faster productivity growth following trade liberalization is both (1) that successful innovators have access to larger rents as market size increases and (2) that knowledge spillovers operate across borders. Note that the market-size effect of trade amounts to a scale effect of the kind questioned by C. Jones (1995a and b), which we discussed in chapter 4.

However, extending the Rivera-Batiz and Romer model to the case of two countries with different initial productivity levels, Devereux and Lapham (1994) show that trade openness may inhibit innovation in the initially poorer country.

Helpman (1993) used the expanding-variety model to analyze the interplay between trade and imitation. In his model, R&D and innovation (which here amounts to the introduction of new products) occur in the most developed region referred to as "the North." Then, costless imitation takes place in the South at a constant rate. The interesting result is that tighter intellectual property rights protection does not necessarily enhance growth, unlike what would happen in a closed economy. On the one hand, reducing the scope for imitation increases the expected lifetime of a product, a result which is good for northern innovators' rents. On the other hand, firms in the North spend more time producing, which in turn raises the demand for (skilled) labor, therefore the wage, and therefore the cost of innovation, in the North. This latter effect may sometimes dominate. See Gancia (2003) for an interesting extension of the Helpman model.

Terms-of-trade effects have been mostly analyzed by Ventura (1997) and by Acemoglu and Ventura (2002). In particular, as shown in chapter 2, introducing terms-of-trade effects can restore convergence in a multicountry AK model.

Young (1991) and Grossman and Helpman (1995) have developed models of trade and growth based on learning-by-doing externalities. The main idea in Young (1991) is that opening up to trade may inhibit learning by doing in less developed economies that may then specialize in more traditional production activities where learning-by-doing opportunities have already been exhausted. More generally, Grossman and Helpman (1995) show that whether trade will accelerate or slow down long-run growth in a country relative to autarky depends upon the effect of trade on the country's specialization and also on whether or not learning-by-doing spillovers are international in scope. Moreover, as already stressed by Krugman (1987), trade does not lead to convergence in growth rates of income per capita across countries when learning-by-doing spillovers are national in scope, whereas it does lead to convergence when learning-by-doing spillovers are international in scope.

Finally, the interplay between trade, firm heterogeneity, and average productivity has become a main focus of trade economics following the pioneering work by Melitz (2003). However, this literature does not analyze the impact of trade on innovation by incumbent firms, as we do in this chapter.

Eaton and Kortum (2001) develop a tractable, generalized Ricardian trade model with stochastic technology differences. Trade flows are shaped by the interaction of productivity-based comparative advantage and geographic location, and bilateral trade follows a gravity equation. Since the model is static, the state of technology is exogenously given and there is no role for research and development.

For further references on this subject, we refer the reader to Ventura's (2005) and Alesina, Spolaore, and Wacziarg's (2005) *Handbook of Economic Growth* chapters, and to Helpman (2004).

Problems

1. Explain intuitively the following three reasons why trade openness may increase world income and enhance productivity growth: (a) the market-size effect; (b) the knowledge spillover effect; (c) the product-market-competition effect.

2. **Static effects of trade liberalization**

This question concerns the static effects of opening up to trade, as discussed in section 15.3.
    Let N_t denote national income under autarky and N_t' denote national income under trade.

a. Suppose $A_{it} = a \in [0, 1]$ $\forall_i \in [0, 1]$, and let A_{it}^* be independently uniformly distributed on $[0, 1]$ $\forall_i \in [0, 1]$. Show that

$$\hat{A}_t = \frac{a^2}{2} + \frac{1}{2}$$

b. Evaluate $J = \dfrac{N_t'}{N_t}$.

c. Calculate $\dfrac{\partial J}{\partial L}$ and $\dfrac{\partial J}{\partial a}$. Relate these derivatives to the scale effect and the backwardness effect discussed in sections 15.3.2.2 and 15.3.2.3.

d. Suppose that small countries have higher productivity in fewer sectors. In particular, assume that the home country has higher productivity in a fraction $\dfrac{L}{L+L^*}$ of sectors and that both countries have the same average productivity in sectors in which they have a higher productivity. Does a smaller country gain more from trade under these assumptions?

3. ***Dynamic effects of trade liberalization**

This question concerns the dynamic effects of opening up to trade, as discussed in section 15.4.
Consider two symmetric countries with $L = L^* = 1$ and $\tau = \tau^* = 0$. Suppose further that $\phi(\mu) = \dfrac{\mu^2}{2}$.

a. What is the equilibrium probability of innovation in the two countries under autarky?

b. Suppose now that the two countries start to trade. Solve for μ_A, μ_B, and μ_C. Under what conditions is $\mu_B > \mu_A$? is $\mu_A > \mu_C$? Discuss.

c. Explain why in steady state

$$q_A = \mu_A q_A + (1 - \mu_A)(1 - \mu_C)q_A + \mu_B(1 - \mu_B)q_B$$

Provide similar expressions for q_B and q_C.

d. Using symmetry to set $q_A = q_C$, solve for steady-state q_A and q_B.

4. **Trade and learning by doing.**

Consider a two-country (South and North), two-sector (traditional and modern) model in which labor is the only factor of production.

In the traditional sector the production technology is $Z_t = L_t^T$.

In the modern sector the production technology is $Y_t = A_t L_t^M$.

Modern-sector labor productivity evolves according to $\dot{A}_t = Y_t$; that is, there is learning by doing in the modern sector.

Each country has a representative consumer with preferences $U_t = Z_t^\alpha Y_t^{1-\alpha}$.

There is no savings or investment.

The South has fixed labor supply L_S, and $A_0^S = 1$.

The North has fixed labor supply L_N, and $A_0^N = 1 + \varepsilon$, where $\varepsilon > 0$.

a. Suppose the South is in autarky. Solve for the equilibrium of this economy and show that

$$\frac{\dot{A}_t^S}{A_t^S} = (1-\alpha)L_S$$

b. Now suppose there is free trade between North and South, but that there are no knowledge spillovers across countries.

i. Solve for the equilibrium at $t = 0$ assuming both countries have nonzero production in the modern sector.

ii. Why is $\dfrac{L_S}{L_N} > \dfrac{\alpha}{1-\alpha}(1+\varepsilon)$ a necessary condition for the equilibrium found in part i to exist?

iii. Derive a condition guaranteeing that at $t = 0$ modern-sector labor productivity grows faster in the North than in the South.

iv. Assume the conditions from parts ii and iii both hold. What happens to the location of modern sector production when

$$\frac{A_t^N}{A_t^S} > \frac{L_S}{L_N}\frac{1-\alpha}{\alpha}$$

v. Show that there exists $T > 0$ such that for all $t > T$, $\dfrac{\dot{A}_t^N}{A_t^N} = L^N$.

vi. Deduce that in the long run the equilibrium growth rate of real consumption is the same in both countries. Discuss the importance of the terms of trade in generating this result.

vii. Repeat the question assuming that the elasticity of substitution between traditional and modern goods is greater than one:

$$U_t = \left[\frac{1}{2}Z_t^{\frac{\sigma-1}{\sigma}} + \frac{1}{2}Y_t^{\frac{\sigma-1}{\sigma}}\right]^{\frac{\sigma}{\sigma-1}}, \qquad \sigma > 1$$

Discuss the difference from the results obtained with Cobb-Douglas preferences.

16 Preserving the Environment[1]

16.1 Introduction

A growing number of observers and policy makers have been alerting public opinion to the existence of serious environmental dangers associated with growth. First, growth precipitates the depletion of exhaustible energy resources (coal, oil, . . .). This in turn led some individuals or groups particularly concerned with ecology back in the 1970s (and especially after the oil shock hit the industrialized countries) to argue that zero growth was the only sustainable long-run objective. Second, growth induces a deterioration of the environment, for example, through CO_2 emissions that may eventually gravely damage production and life on earth. The Al Gore movie, *An Inconvenient Truth*, and the Stern Report (2006) on the economic costs of not reducing CO_2 emissions have contributed to turning this issue into a top headline and prompting government heads in the G8 to act quickly on it.

In this chapter, we analyze how new growth theories can integrate the environmental dimension, and in particular how endogenous innovation and directed technical change make it possible to reconcile the sustained growth objective with the constraints imposed by exhaustible resources or the need to maintain the environment.

The chapter is organized as follows. Section 16.2 introduces an exhaustible resource constraint in the AK model. Section 16.3 introduces that constraint in the Schumpeterian growth model. We will see that the one-sector AK model can no longer explain positive long-run growth once we make production dependent on an exhaustible resource, whereas sustainable growth can be restored nevertheless in a world with endogenous innovation. Finally, section 16.4 uses the directed technical change model of chapter 8 to analyze the growth effect of a tax on dirty production activities, as well as how this tax should be chosen so as to maintain the environment in the long run.

16.2 The One-Sector AK Model with an Exhaustible Resource

We consider the following variant of the one-sector AK growth model. Time is continuous, and aggregate output is produced according to the production technology

---

1. This chapter was written with the collaboration of Leonardo Bursztyn.

$$Y = AKR^\phi, \qquad \phi > 0 \tag{16.1}$$

where K is the current aggregate capital stock and R is the current flow of extracted resource. If we denote the current stock of natural resource by S, then we simply have

$$\dot{S} = -R \tag{16.2}$$

Capital accumulates over time as in the Solow or AK model with constant savings rate, according to

$$\dot{K} = sY - \delta K \tag{16.3}$$

where s is the constant savings rate and δ is the constant rate of capital depreciation.

In the absence of an exhaustible resource (that is, with just $Y = AK$), such an economy would grow forever at rate

$$g = \frac{\dot{K}}{K} = sA - \delta$$

However, things change dramatically once the exhaustible resource is introduced. More precisely, we now show that positive growth can no longer be sustained in the long run.

To see this point, note that in the long run the rate of extraction R must fall to zero, since otherwise the stock S would become negative in finite time. But from equations (16.1) and (16.3) we have

$$\frac{\dot{K}}{K} = sAR^\phi - \delta$$

so therefore the growth rate $\dfrac{\dot{K}}{K}$ must converge to $-\delta < 0$, which of course means that the capital stock K must also fall to zero in the long run. Since R and K are both falling to zero, therefore $Y = AKR^\phi$ must also fall to zero in the long run. In other words, not just the growth rate but even the *level* of output will vanish in the long run in this AK model with exhaustible resource.

The reason for this no-growth result can be simply explained as follows: In order to sustain growth in this AK model, it is necessary that the flow of extracted resource R become arbitrarily small as time goes to infinity. Otherwise, the resource stock S and therefore the output flow Y would vanish in finite time. Now, to counteract the effect of R going to zero, that is, to maintain production in spite of saving increasingly on the resource factor, requires technical progress. However, technical progress requires capital accumulation, and therefore an acceleration of resource-consuming production . . . and therefore a more intense use of the exhaustible resource. In other words, this AK economy with exhaustible resources looks like a snake that would eat its own tail in order to survive.

16.3   Schumpeterian Growth with an Exhaustible Resource

In contrast to the one-sector AK model, growth can be sustained in a Schumpeterian world with innovations. The basic idea is that in a such a world one can conceive of technical progress and innovations that are distinct from the accumulation of physical capital, and in particular innovations that are greener (less resource-intensive) than capital accumulation.

More formally, suppose that the economy is populated by a continuum of mass $M = 1$ of one-period-lived individuals, each of whom is endowed with one unit of labor that she can allocate between manufacturing or research activities. Final output is produced according to

$$Y = L^{1-\alpha} A^{1-\alpha} x^{\alpha} R^{\phi} \tag{16.4}$$

where L is the flow of labor employed in production (manufacturing labor), A and x denote the productivity and quantity of intermediate input, respectively, and R again denotes the current flow of extracted resource, so that the stock of natural resources still evolves over time according to

$$\dot{S} = -R$$

Labor can be used either in manufacturing the final good (L) or in research to produce innovations (n); thus labor-market clearing imposes that

$$L + n = 1$$

The intermediate producer uses the final good one for one to produce her intermediate input. Taking the final good as numéraire, and assuming that the final-good sector is competitive, the intermediate producer can sell her intermediate product to the final sector at price

$$p(x) = \frac{\partial Y}{\partial x} = \alpha L^{1-\alpha} A^{1-\alpha} x^{\alpha-1} R^{\phi}$$

She chooses x to maximize profits, solving

$$\pi = \max_{x}\{p(x)x - x\}$$

which yields

$$x = \alpha^{\frac{2}{1-\alpha}} A L R^{\frac{\phi}{1-\alpha}}$$

which, in turn yields (after substituting the x's in the expression for Y)

$$Y = \alpha^{\frac{2\alpha}{1-\alpha}} L A R^{\frac{\phi}{1-\alpha}} \tag{16.5}$$

Now suppose that the government can impose that R decreases over time at an exponential rate, according to

$$\dot{R} = -qR$$

with $q > 0,$[2] so that S remains always positive. Can positive growth still be sustained in that case? Using equation (16.5) and taking logarithmic derivatives, one has

$$\frac{\dot{Y}}{Y} = \frac{\dot{A}}{A} + \phi\frac{\dot{R}}{R} = g_A - \phi q$$

where g_A is the rate of productivity growth.

Now, suppose that productivity growth results from innovations and that innovations result from R&D labor, so that the rate of productivity growth can be expressed as

$$g_A = (\gamma - 1)\lambda n$$

where n is the equilibrium amount of R&D labor, γ is the size of innovations, and λ is an R&D productivity parameter.

Overall, the economy will sustain positive growth in the long run whenever

$$(\gamma - 1)\lambda n > \phi q$$

or

$$n > \frac{\phi q}{(\gamma - 1)\lambda} \tag{16.6}$$

Given the preceding labor-market-clearing condition, this outcome is possible if and only if the right-hand side of equation (16.6) is less than the total available labor supply, which we normalize to unity:

---

2. In the appendix to this chapter we solve for the social planner problem in the case where preferences are isoelastic, and show that the optimal solution involves a constant q.

$$\frac{\phi q}{(\gamma-1)\lambda} < 1$$

for this is the necessary and sufficient condition for there to be enough R&D labor available in order to offset the deleterious effects of resource depletion through innovation. The condition will be satisfied if the productivity of R&D λ or the size of innovation γ are sufficiently large, or if the depletion rate q is sufficiently small.

Thus, in contrast to the one-sector AK model where growth can never be sustained when final production requires the use of an exhaustible resource, growth can be sustained in a Schumpeterian world where innovations save on the use of the resource (whereas technical progress involved a more intensive use of the resource in the AK model).

Note that our analysis in this section has implicitly assumed that innovations are "green," that is, do not exhaust resources or do not degrade the environment. In the next section we remove this restrictive assumption and look at whether governments can sustain growth by taxing the wrong kind of innovations, that is, by appropriately directing technical change.

16.4   Environment and Directed Technical Change

We now move to a world with both clean and dirty innovation activities. On the one hand, dirty activities deplete the stock of environmental capital; on the other hand, environment regenerates at some exogenous rate ω. When the clean and dirty input baskets are perfect substitutes in producing final output, the effect of a tax on dirty production activities will be to encourage innovation in the clean production technologies instead.

16.4.1   Basic Setup

Time t is discrete. Final output each period is

$$Y_t = \begin{cases} Y_{ct} + Y_{dt} & \text{if } S_t > 0 \\ 0 & \text{otherwise} \end{cases} \tag{16.7}$$

where Y_{ct} is output produced by a clean process, Y_{dt} is output produced by a dirty process, and S_t is the environmental stock. According to equation (16.7) no production is possible once S_t has disappeared.

Dirty production causes the environment to deteriorate. Specifically, the change in the environmental stock is

$$S_{t+1} - S_t = -\phi Y_{dt} + \omega S_t \tag{16.8}$$

where the parameter $\phi > 0$ indicates the impact of dirty production and the parameter $\omega \geq 0$ indicates the rate at which the environment can regenerate through natural processes.

Equation (16.8) imposes a speed limit on dirty production. Specifically it implies that Y_{dt} cannot grow faster than ω in the long run. To see how this process works, divide both sides by S_t and you see that the growth rate $(S_{t+1} - S_t)/S_t$ cannot exceed ω. Therefore if Y_{dt} were to grow steadily at the rate $g > \omega$, then the negative term on the right-hand side of equation (16.8) would grow faster than the positive term, so the right-hand side would eventually become negative, at which time S_t would start to fall, eventually resulting in environmental disaster: $S_t \leq 0$.

Suppose the economy starts at date 0 with $S_0 > 0$. We now proceed to examine under what conditions an environmental disaster will occur, how a tax on dirty production might avert the disaster, and how the economy's growth path would be affected by such a tax.

16.4.2   Equilibrium Outputs and Profits

16.4.2.1   Production with a Given Allocation of Labor

Each period, the production functions for final output are

$$Y_c = L_c^{1-\alpha} \int_0^1 A_{ci}^{1-\alpha} x_{ci}^\alpha di \qquad Y_d = L_d^{1-\alpha} \int_0^1 A_{di}^{1-\alpha} x_{di}^\alpha di \tag{16.9}$$

where $0 < \alpha < 1$, L_c and L_d are the amounts of labor allocated to producing clean and dirty output, respectively, the x's are quantities of specialized intermediate inputs, and the A's are the associated productivity parameters. Each specialized input is produced one for one using final output.

Let final output be the numéraire. Then the price of each component of final output is unity. Final output is produced under perfect competition, so the equilibrium price of each specialized input is the value of its marginal product:

$$p_{ci} = \alpha L_c^{1-\alpha} A_{ci}^{1-\alpha} x_{ci}^{\alpha-1} \qquad p_{di} = \alpha L_d^{1-\alpha} A_{di}^{1-\alpha} x_{di}^{\alpha-1}$$

Each specialized input is produced by a monopolist, who chooses her output level by maximizing profit

$$\pi_{ci} = \max_{x_{ci}} \left\{ p_{ci} x_{ci} - x_{ci} \right\} \qquad \pi_{di} = \max_{x_{di}} \left\{ p_{di} x_{di} - x_{di} \right\}$$

which yields the equilibrium quantities

$$x_{ci} = \alpha^{\frac{2}{1-\alpha}} A_{ci} L_c \qquad x_{di} = \alpha^{\frac{2}{1-\alpha}} A_{di} L_d$$

and the equilibrium profits

$$\pi_{ci} = \frac{1-\alpha}{\alpha} x_{ci} \qquad \pi_{di} = \frac{1-\alpha}{\alpha} x_{di}$$

Substituting the equilibrium quantities into equation (16.9), we obtain the expressions

$$Y_c = \alpha^{\frac{2\alpha}{1-\alpha}} A_c L_c \qquad Y_d = \alpha^{\frac{2\alpha}{1-\alpha}} A_d L_d \tag{16.10}$$

where $A_c = \int A_{ci} di$ is the average productivity of the clean intermediate inputs and $A_d = \int A_{di} di$ is the average productivity of the dirty intermediate inputs.

16.4.2.2   The Allocation of Labor between Clean and Dirty Production

The competitive producers of final output take as given the wage rate w. So they will hire labor in each use (clean and dirty) up to the point where its marginal product equals w. From equation (16.9), the two marginal products are

$$\partial Y / \partial L_c = (1-\alpha) Y_c / L_c \qquad \partial Y / \partial L_d = (1-\alpha) Y_d / L_d$$

which can be reexpressed, using equation (16.10), as

$$\partial Y / \partial L_c = (1-\alpha) \alpha^{\frac{2\alpha}{1-\alpha}} A_c \qquad \partial Y / \partial L_d = (1-\alpha) \alpha^{\frac{2\alpha}{1-\alpha}} A_d$$

It follows that the marginal product of labor cannot equal w in both uses, except in the case where $A_c = A_d$. Assuming that this unlikely case does not occur, w will equal the marginal product of labor in the sector with the higher average productivity, and no labor will be allocated to the other sector.[3]

If the clean sector were more productive than the dirty sector ($A_c > A_d$), then no labor would be allocated to the dirty sector ($L_d = 0$), so no dirty output would be produced ($Y_d = 0$). In this case, equation (16.8) implies that S_t would remain positive forever, so environmental deterioration would not be a problem.

In the alternative case, in which the dirty sector is more productive than the clean sector ($A_d > A_c$), only the dirty technology would be used, so according to equation (16.8), an environmental disaster would ensue if dirty output grew faster

---

3. That way producers in both sectors will be hiring the profit-maximizing quantity of labor, which is zero in the sector where the wage exceeds labor's marginal product.

than the environmental regeneration rate ω. We now proceed to examine the effect of a tax of dirty output aimed at averting this disaster.

16.4.3   Taxing Dirty Production

Suppose that $A_d > A_c$ and that the government imposes a tax on dirty production. Specifically, final producers must pay a tax τ on each unit of dirty output produced. Then the after-tax price of dirty output becomes $1 - \tau$.

In the clean sector, for any given allocation of labor L_c, all prices, outputs, and profits will remain the same as before, because the tax does not directly affect that sector.

In the dirty sector, the price of each specialized input will now equal the after-tax value of its marginal product:

$$p_{di} = (1-\tau)\alpha L_d^{1-\alpha}A_{di}^{1-\alpha}x_{di}^{\alpha-1}$$

so each specialized monopolist will choose her output level by maximizing profit

$$\pi_{di} = \max_{x_{di}}\left\{p_{di}x_{di} - x_{di}\right\}$$

which yields the equilibrium quantities

$$x_{di} = (1-\tau)^{\frac{1}{1-\alpha}}\alpha^{\frac{2}{1-\alpha}}A_{di}L_d$$

and the equilibrium profits

$$\pi_{di} = \frac{1-\alpha}{\alpha}x_{di}$$

Substituting the quantities into equation (16.9), we obtain

$$Y_d = (1-\tau)^{\frac{\alpha}{1-\alpha}}\alpha^{\frac{2\alpha}{1-\alpha}}A_dL_d \tag{16.11}$$

The wage rate in this case will be the value of the marginal product of labor. In the clean sector this will still be given by

$$\partial Y/\partial L_c = (1-\alpha)Y_c/L_c = (1-\alpha)\alpha^{\frac{2\alpha}{1-\alpha}}A_c$$

but now in the dirty sector it will be

$$(1-\tau)\partial Y/\partial L_d = (1-\tau)(1-\alpha)Y_d/L_d = (1-\tau)^{\frac{1}{1-\alpha}}(1-\alpha)\alpha^{\frac{2\alpha}{1-\alpha}}A_d$$

Again, production will take place only in the sector where the marginal product of labor has the highest value. So production will remain all dirty if

$$(1-\tau)^{\frac{1}{1-\alpha}} A_d > A_c$$

but otherwise it will switch to being all clean. Accordingly the minimal tax needed to convert the economy to clean production is

$$\tau^{\min} = 1 - \left(A_c / A_d \right)^{1-\alpha} \qquad (16.12)$$

16.4.4   Equilibrium Innovation

Suppose the economy is in a stationary equilibrium with a constant allocation of labor (L_c, L_d) and a constant tax rate τ. If the economy is producing only dirty output, then equation (16.11) implies that the growth rate g of final output will be the growth rate of average productivity across all dirty intermediates $(A_{dt} - A_{d,t-1})/A_{d,t-1}$. Alternatively, if just clean output is produced, then the first part of equation (16.10) implies $g = (A_{ct} - A_{c,t-1})/A_{c,t-1}$. Productivity growth in turn comes from innovations.

In each intermediate sector, each period, there is one potential innovator—the "entrepreneur"—who can hire labor in the hope of inventing a better version of that sector's product that can be put into use next period. Consider a type-j intermediate good, where $j \in \{c, d\}$ indicates clean or dirty. If the entrepreneur last period was successful, then she will be the monopoly producer this period, with a productivity parameter equal to $\gamma A_{j,t-1}$, where $\gamma > 1$ indicates the size of innovations and $A_{j,t-1}$ is last period's average productivity parameter across all type-j intermediates. If the entrepreneur was not successful, then the monopoly this period will be awarded to someone with a productivity parameter equal to $A_{j,t-1}$.

In order to innovate with probability z, an entrepreneur must devote εz units of labor to R&D. She will choose z to maximize her expected discounted profit net of R&D cost:

$$\max_z \left\{ z\beta\pi_{jt} - w_{t-1}\varepsilon z \right\}$$

where β is a discount factor, w_{t-1} is the wage rate, and π_{jt} is the monopoly profit earned if successful. So if she is undertaking R&D, the first-order condition

$$\beta\pi_{jt} = \varepsilon w_{t-1} \qquad (16.13)$$

must hold.

16.4.4.1   Innovation When Only Clean Output Is Produced

Suppose that the economy is producing only clean output. Then the wage rate is the marginal product of labor in clean production:

$$w_{t-1} = (1-\alpha)\alpha^{\frac{2\alpha}{1-\alpha}}A_{c,t-1}$$

and it follows from the results of section 16.4.2.1 that the monopoly profit of a successful innovator of a clean input will be

$$\pi_{ct} = \frac{1-\alpha}{\alpha}x_{ct} = \frac{1-\alpha}{\alpha}\alpha^{\frac{2}{1-\alpha}}\gamma A_{c,t-1}L_c$$

Substituting for w_{t-1} and π_{ct} in equation (16.13) yields

$$L_c = \frac{\varepsilon}{\alpha\beta\gamma}$$

There is a fixed supply of labor, normalized to equal unity. Labor can be used for manufacturing or research. So the labor-market-clearing condition is

$$L_c + \varepsilon z = 1$$

where εz is the R&D labor hired by clean entrepreneurs (no dirty R&D is performed because monopoly profit is zero in the inactive dirty sector). Therefore, the equilibrium probability of innovation in each clean intermediate sector is

$$z = \frac{1}{\varepsilon} - \frac{1}{\alpha\beta\gamma}$$

which we assume to be positive.

16.4.4.2   Innovation When Only Dirty Output Is Produced

Suppose alternatively that only dirty output is produced. Then the wage rate is the value of the marginal product of labor in dirty production:

$$w_{t-1} = (1-\tau)^{\frac{1}{1-\alpha}}(1-\alpha)\alpha^{\frac{2\alpha}{1-\alpha}}A_{d,t-1}$$

and, from the results of section 16.4.3, the profit of a successful innovator is

$$\pi_{dt} = \frac{1-\alpha}{\alpha}x_{dt} = \frac{1-\alpha}{\alpha}(1-\tau)^{\frac{1}{1-\alpha}}\alpha^{\frac{2}{1-\alpha}}\gamma A_{d,t-1}L_d$$

Substituting for w_{t-1} and π_{dt} in equation (16.13) yields

$$L_d = \frac{\varepsilon}{\alpha\beta\gamma}$$

In this case, the labor-market-clearing condition is

$$L_d + \varepsilon z = 1$$

where εz is the R&D labor hired by dirty entrepreneurs. Therefore, the equilibrium probability of innovations will be exactly the same as when the economy is producing only clean output:

$$z = \frac{1}{\varepsilon} - \frac{1}{\alpha\beta\gamma}$$

Notice that the equilibrium probability of innovations does not vary with the tax rate τ, because even though an increase in τ reduces the profit of a successful innovator, it also reduces the wage that must be paid to the R&D workers, in exactly the same proportion.

16.4.5   Growth and the Cost of Taxing Dirty Output

As we have seen, the growth rate of final output will equal the growth rate of average productivity in the active sector:

$$g = g_{A_j} = \frac{A_{jt} - A_{j,t-1}}{A_{j,t-1}}$$

where the active sector j is either c or d depending on whether the tax rate τ is above or below the minimal rate (16.12) needed to encourage clean production.

In either case, in each period t, each entrepreneur in the active sector will innovate with probability z, so by the law of large numbers the fraction z of intermediates in the active sector will have a productivity equal to $\gamma A_{j,t-1}$, while the remaining $1 - z$ will have a productivity equal to $A_{j,t-1}$. Therefore, average productivity in the active sector will be

$$A_{jt} = z\gamma A_{j,t-1} + (1-z)A_{j,t-1}$$

so the growth rate will be

$$g = z(\gamma - 1) = \left(\frac{1}{\varepsilon} - \frac{1}{\alpha\beta\gamma}\right)(\gamma - 1)$$

which is the same whether the economy is producing clean or final output, and which is also independent of the tax rate τ.

It follows that without a tax on dirty production the economy will eventually face an environmental disaster if

$$\left(\frac{1}{\varepsilon} - \frac{1}{\alpha\beta\gamma}\right)(\gamma - 1) > \omega \qquad\qquad (16.14)$$

because without the tax only dirty output will be produced and its growth rate will exceed the speed limit ω for averting disaster.

It also follows that imposing a tax on dirty production does not require any sacrifice of long-run growth, which can proceed at the same rate (16.14) as without the tax. Indeed, the tax raises growth in the very long run by averting the disaster that would have brought growth to a sudden end. The mechanism at work is directed technical change. The tax that discourages dirty innovation also encourages clean innovation, with no effect on the overall rate of innovation.

This does not mean that the tax is entirely costless. On the contrary, according to equation (16.10), switching to clean production would immediately reduce final output by the factor A_d/A_c. Thus, the tax reduces the level of the economy's growth path but not its growth rate.

Finally, our analysis implies that the tax on dirty production need not be permanent. This is because it activates innovation in clean intermediates while stopping innovation in dirty intermediates, causing A_c to grow at the rate shown in equation (16.14) while A_d stagnates. Therefore, A_c eventually becomes larger than A_d. At this point the tax could be eliminated because even without any tax advantage the economy would continue to produce only clean output.

Remark   So far, we have assumed that

$$Y = Y_c + Y_d$$

so that the clean and dirty input baskets Y_c and Y_d are perfect substitutes in final consumption. Now, instead, suppose that

$$Y = \left(Y_c^{1/\varepsilon} + Y_d^{1/\varepsilon}\right)^{\varepsilon}$$

where $\varepsilon < 1$. Would all the preceding conclusions still go through? The answer is no.

More specifically, when the two baskets become sufficiently complementary in final consumption, then inducing innovation on clean inputs will end up increasing the relative price of the dirty basket (which consequently becomes scarcer). But in turn, this result will encourage potential innovators to target the dirty input sectors instead—unless the tax on dirty production is maintained over time. Also, when the two baskets are sufficiently complementary, taxing the dirty basket will also limit the growth rate of final output.

16.4.6   Evidence of Directed Technical Change Effects in the Energy Sector

In an important *American Economic Review* paper published in 2002, Popp uses U.S. patent data from 1970 to 1994 to study the effect of energy prices on energy-efficient innovations.

On the left-hand side of the regression equation, Popp uses patenting to measure innovation. For that purpose, 11 subcategories of patents are identified as being energy savers (6 groups pertaining to energy supply, such as solar energy, and 5 groups relating to energy demand, such as methods of reusing industrial waste heat). All patents granted in the United States between 1970 and 1993 for all those technology groups are being considered. The dependent variables of the innovation regression are the ratios of the number of successful nongovernment U.S. patent applications for technology field i in year t over the total number of successful nongovernment U.S. patent applications for the same year for all pairs (i, t). By using such a dependent variable, Popp can measure the response of innovative effort in the direction of saving energy as a response to changes in energy prices.

On the right-hand side of the regression equation, the following explanatory variables are used: (1) energy prices, from the *State Energy Price and Expenditure Report* (see Popp, 2000), in constant 1987 dollars (both current-period energy prices and lagged energy prices); (2) technology-specific variables (that can help explain individual trends for the 11 groups) and government R&D expenditures, instrumented by lagged federal energy R&D and a dummy for the lagged political party of the president; and (3) the existing stock of knowledge on which inventors can build.[4] Popp constructs two different measures of the knowledge stocks for the innovation regressions: (1) a simple stock of previously granted U.S. patents (no concerns for the "quality" of inventions) and (2) a stock of patents weighted by the productivity estimates (concern for the quality and number of patents). The regression results are shown in table 16.1.

In particular, we see a significant impact from both energy prices and the quality of the stock of knowledge available to the inventor on directed

---

4. Considering this stock as exogenous instead of estimating it (as Popp does) would entail not considering the effects of current research on future research (for instance, the existence of diminishing returns to research that would make future research more difficult).

To construct measures for the stocks of knowledge to inventors from 1970 to 1991, Popp uses data on patent citations (previous patents cited by a new patent that work as an indicator of previous knowledge used by the inventor).

Table 16.1
Induced-Innovation Regression Results (Dependent Variable: Percentage of Total Domestic Patent Applications in Each Technology Group)

Independent Variables	Unweighted Stock of Patents	Weighted Stock of Patents
Constant	−9.015	−7.311
	(−12.362)	(−46.625)
Energy prices	0.028	0.060
	(2.146)	(2.852)
Lagged knowledge stock	0.719	0.838
	(25.612)	(72.323)
Government R&D	0.006	−0.009
	(0.968)	(−1.741)
Truncation error	1.924	−1.203
	(2.445)	(−5.054)
Lambda	0.933	0.829
	(18.905)	(13.662)
Long-run energy elasticity	0.421	0.354
Long-run government R&D elasticity	0.085	−0.052
Median lag	13.81	4.86
Mean lag	9.92	3.71
GMM criterion	86.560	93.421
Number of technology groups	11	11

Notes: The table shows the induced-innovation regression results. Lagged party of the president and lagged government R&D are used as instruments for government R&D. A time trend and lagged values of other exogenous variables are used as instruments for the knowledge stocks. *t*-statistics appear in parentheses below estimates. Data are from 1971–91.

innovations. This provides strong evidence in favor of directed technical change as a response to change in energy prices.[5]

16.4.7   Concluding Remarks

In this section we have discussed the implications of resource or environmental constraints on growth in the context of a model with directed technical change, and we reported evidence for the existence of directed technical change (DTC) in the context of energy costs. A natural question then is: What are the consequences in terms of estimating the costs of environmental regulation when DTC is not considered?

5. More evidence of directed technical change applied to the context of saving energy can be found in Newell, Jaffe, and Stavins (1999). This paper focuses on the air-conditioning industry and gets the following results: between 1960 and 1980 the direction of innovation was essentially toward reducing the price of air conditioners and not toward making them more energy efficient, whereas, as a response to higher energy prices, between 1980 and 1990 there was little change in costs, but the devices became much more energy efficient (especially after energy-efficiency product labeling was required).

Several papers have tried to estimate these consequences and concluded that ignoring DTC overstates the costs of environmental regulation (see Grübler and Messner 1998; Manne and Richels 2004; Messner 1997; Buonanno, Carraro, and Galeotti 2003; Nordhaus 2002; Sue Wing 2003). The measure of the overstatement of costs depends on specific characteristics of the models found in these papers, namely, the possibility of crowding out in R&D toward energy-saving innovations.

As an example, Popp (2004) modifies the standard Nordhaus model of climate change (DICE model) to allow for induced innovation in the energy sector. After some calibration and simulation exercises and allowing for the possibility of crowding out across different kinds of R&D investment, he concludes that ignoring DTC overstates the welfare costs of an optimal tax policy by 9.4 percent in the base case (where partial—50 percent—crowding out is allowed).

16.5   Literature Notes

The importance of the environment has been increasingly acknowledged in both policy-making and academic circles. This is particularly the case for the relationship between economic growth and natural resources.

One focus on the relationship between economic development and the environment has been the study of the so-called environmental Kuznets curve, that is, an inverted-U relationship between levels of country income and indicators of environmental quality (air and water pollution, for instance). The pioneering studies of such relationships were conducted by Grossman and Krueger (1991, 1995), using cross-country analyses with various environmental indicators. Those studies started a whole branch of literature discussing the validity of such reduced-form relationships (for an extensive discussion on the topic, see Dasgupta et al. 2002; Harbaugh, Levinson, and Wilson 2002).

On the relationship between growth and the environment, pioneering work has been done by Nordhaus (1974, 1977), who addressed the consequences of economic growth on the conservation of the environment and ways in which natural resources could put constraints on growth.

More specifically on the issue of climate change, the same author later developed (see, for instance, Nordhaus 1993) a dynamic integrated model of climate change and the economy (the DICE model), which extended the neoclassical Ramsey model with equations representing geophysical relationships (emissions equation, concentrations equation, climate-change equation, climate-damage equation) and their relationships with economic outcomes. The analysis of economic activity and its consequences in terms of climate change has been the subject of a recent and extensive report conducted by Stern (2006).

Still in the exogenous growth framework, Stockey (1998) analyzed pollution in terms of an AK model delivering an inverted-U relationship between per capita income and environmental quality and the result of nonsustainability of long-run growth (nonpositive growth).

Several recent studies have shown that the predictions of exogenous growth models are debatable, especially if one allows for the possibility of (endogenous) directed technical change (DTC). Recent empirical papers have presented evidence of induced technical change, namely, that energy prices affect the choice of the type of innovations (see Popp 2002 for the effect of energy prices on energy-saving innovations and Newell, Jaffe, and Stavins 1999 for the specific case of the air-conditioning industry).

Given the observed existence of directed technical change in energy-saving innovations, many recent papers, such as Grübler and Messner (1998), Manne and Richels (2004), Messner (1997), Buonanno, Carravo, and Galeotti (2003), Nordhaus (2002), and Sue Wing (2003), have attempted to discuss how much the costs of environmental regulation are overestimated when DTC is not considered.

The debate on the appropriate measure of costs of climate change has become an important topic of research in the field, with the acknowledgment of the importance of taking factors such as risk, uncertainty, and discounting into account in the analysis, as pointed out by Weitzman (2007) and Dasgupta (2008).

Appendix: Optimal Schumpeterian Growth with an Exhaustible Resource

In this appendix we solve the problem of a social planner who chooses the optimal research intensity and depletion rate of a natural resource, but then lets firms choose intermediate production to maximize profits. This solution will give us an optimal growth rate and an optimal rate q^* at which to reduce the flow R of the exhaustible resource over time to maximize the intertemporal utility of the representative agent.

Suppose that the representative individual has isoelastic preferences, with instantaneous utility for final-good consumption given by

$$u(c) = \frac{c^{1-\sigma}}{1-\sigma}$$

The social planner will maximize intertemporal consumption

$$\max \int_0^\infty u(c_t) e^{-\rho t} dt$$

subject to the following constraints (we drop subindex t)

1. That final consumption be equal to final output

$$c = L^{1-\alpha} A^{1-\alpha} x^\alpha = (1-n)^{1-\alpha} A^{1-\alpha} x^\alpha$$

where the latter equality results from the labor-resource constraint

$$1 = L + n$$

where n still denotes the amount of research labor.

2. That profit-maximizing firms choose to produce

$$x = \delta ALR^{\frac{\phi}{1-\alpha}} = \delta A(1-n) R^{\frac{\phi}{1-\alpha}}$$

Thus

$$c = \delta(1-n) A R^\varphi \qquad (16.15)$$

where $\varphi = \dfrac{\phi\alpha}{1-\alpha}$.

3. That productivity evolves over time according to

$$\dot{A} = gA = \lambda n(\gamma - 1) A \qquad (16.16)$$

4. That the exhaustible resource be depleted according to

$$\dot{S} = -R \qquad (16.17)$$

where $S \geq 0$.

By analogy with appendix 1B, the Hamiltonian for this problem can be expressed as

$$H = u(c) + \mu_A \lambda n(\gamma - 1) A - \mu_S R$$

where μ_A and μ_S are the multipliers associated with the growth equation (16.16) and the depletion equation (16.17) respectively.

Again by analogy with appendix 1B, the first-order conditions for this dynamic optimization are

$$\frac{\partial H}{\partial n} = 0 \qquad\qquad (16.18)$$

$$\frac{\partial H}{\partial R} = 0 \qquad\qquad (16.19)$$

plus the two Euler conditions

$$\dot{\mu}_A = \rho\mu_A - \frac{\partial H}{\partial A} \qquad\qquad (16.20)$$

$$\dot{\mu}_S = \rho\mu_S. \qquad\qquad (16.21)$$

Now, using (16.15), we can reexpress the first equation as

$$-u'(c)\delta AR^{\varphi} + \mu_A\lambda(\gamma-1)A = 0 \qquad\qquad (16.22)$$

Next, we have

$$\frac{\partial H}{\partial A} = u'(c)\delta(1-n)R^{\varphi} + \mu_A\lambda n(\gamma-1)$$

Using equation (16.22), we simply get

$$\frac{\partial H}{\partial A} = \mu_A\lambda(\gamma-1)$$

so that equation (16.20) can be reexpressed as

$$\frac{\dot{\mu}_A}{\mu_A} = \rho - \lambda(\gamma-1)$$

which we assume to be negative.

However, equation (16.22) and its time derivative yield, respectively,

$$u'(c)\delta R^{\varphi} = \mu_A\lambda(\gamma-1)$$

and

$$u''(c)\dot{c}\delta R^{\varphi} = \dot{\mu}_A\lambda(\gamma-1)$$

so that

$$\frac{\dot{\mu}_A}{\mu_A} = \frac{u''(c)}{u'(c)}\dot{c} = -\sigma\frac{\dot{c}}{c}$$

This in turn gives us the optimal growth rate

$$g = \frac{\dot{c}}{c} = \frac{\lambda(\gamma - 1) - \rho}{\sigma}$$

What is the corresponding rate q^* at which the flow of exhaustible resource R should be reduced over time? Taking the time derivative of equation (16.19) together with equation (16.21), and dividing through by $\delta A(1 - n) \varphi$, yields the condition

$$-\sigma g R + \lambda n(\gamma - 1)R + (\varphi - 1)\dot{R} = \rho R$$

which is in turn equivalent to

$$\dot{R} = q^* R$$

with

$$q^* = \frac{\lambda(\gamma - 1)(1 - n)}{\varphi - 1}$$

Thus optimal growth leads to a well-defined constant rate at which the flow of the natural resource should be reduced over time.

Problems

1. Explain why the AK model can no longer generate long-run growth when production requires the use of an exhaustible resource. Suppose innovations can occur in either a clean or a dirty sector according to the relative profitability of each sector. Then explain why the possibility of endogenous innovation on the clean input implies a lower negative impact on growth of an environmental policy that taxes the use of dirty inputs, compared to a framework in which there is only one type of innovation.

2. ***Optimality in the AK model with an exhaustible resource**

Consider the model from section 16.2. Suppose, as in the appendix to this chapter, that a social planner wants to maximize intertemporal consumption:

$$\max \int_0^\infty \left(\frac{c^{1-\sigma}}{1-\sigma} \right) e^{-\rho t} dt$$

subject to

$$\dot{K} = AKR^\theta - c - \delta K$$

$$\dot{S} = -R$$

Setting up the Hamiltonian for this problem, compute the optimal growth rate of consumption in this economy. Contrast the short-run and long-run effects of an increase in R.

3. *A variant of the directed-technical-change model with R&D externalities between the clean and dirty sectors

Consider a variant of the model from section 16.4. The final-good production function and the equation for the change in environmental stock are the same here as in the chapter and given by

$$Y_t = \begin{cases} Y_{ct} + Y_{dt} & \text{if } S_t > 0 \\ 0 & \text{otherwise} \end{cases}$$

and

$$S_{t+1} - S_t = -\phi Y_{dt} + \omega S_t$$

However, at each period the input baskets Y_c and Y_d are now produced according to

$$Y_c = A_c^{1-\alpha} x_c^{\alpha} \qquad Y_d = A_d^{1-\alpha} x_d^{\alpha}$$

With respect to the innovation side of the economy, innovators may still invest in R&D targeted at a particular type of input. Let $j \in \{c, d\}$ denote the kind of input—clean or dirty—produced in sector i. No matter in which sector they occur, innovations are assumed to increase productivity by the same multiplicative factor $\gamma > 1$. Moreover, R&D efforts in both sectors make use of a common fixed factor, which results in R&D costs for each innovation activity being an increasing function of the total R&D intensity.

More specifically, it costs $A_j[\varepsilon(z_j)^2 + \theta(z_j + z_h)^2]/2$ units of final output spent on R&D targeted at input basket j to generate an innovation on that input with probability z_j, where z_j and z_h denote the R&D intensities on inputs j and $h \neq j$

a. Compute specialized monopolists' profits and the equilibrium values for Y_c, Y_d, and Y.

b. Working on the innovators' problem, find the equilibrium R&D intensities z_c, z_d.

Now, suppose dirty-input monopolists' profits are taxed at rate $\tau > 0$ so that they are reduced to $\pi_d(1 - \tau)$ instead of π_d.

c. What are the new R&D intensities $\hat{z}_c$, $\hat{z}_d$ with the introduction of the tax rate?

d. How does an increase in τ affect the growth rates of A_d and A_c?

4. **Sustainable growth and optimality in the directed-technical-change model with R&D externalities

Consider the model from the previous problem.

a. Show that the dynamic equation for the change in environmental stock can be rewritten as

$$S_t = (1 + \omega)^t \left[S_0 - \phi \sum_{\tau=0}^{t-1} Y_{d\tau} / (1 + \omega)^{\tau+1} \right], \qquad t \geq 1$$

b. Looking at a steady state with $Y_{dt} = Y_{d0}(1 + g_{Ad})^t$, show that the expression in the previous item can be rewritten as

$$S_t = (1 + \omega)^t \left\{ S_0 - \frac{\phi Y_{d0}}{\omega - g_{Ad}} \left[1 - \left(\frac{1 + g_{Ad}}{1 + \omega} \right)^t \right] \right\}$$

c. What is the upper bound for g_{Ad} for growth to be sustainable (i.e., non-negative in steady state)?

d. Argue that another necessary condition for sustainable growth is $\phi Y_{d0} \leq (\omega - g_{Ad})S_0$. Interpret this condition.

Suppose the economy has a government that is interested in maximizing the net present value of consumption minus R&D effort cost and that ignores the R&D externalities between the clean and dirty sectors (i.e., ignores the directed-technical-change effect and acts as if θ were equal to zero). It will choose the steady-state growth rate $g_{Ad} = g$ of the dirty basket to maximize

$$U = \sum_0^\infty \left[\left(\frac{1+g}{1+\rho} \right)^t \left(Y_{d0} - \frac{1}{2}\mu g^2 \right) \right] = \frac{1+\rho}{\rho - g} \left[(\omega - g)(S_0/\phi) - \frac{1}{2}\mu g^2 \right]$$

where $\rho < \omega$ is the social discount rate and

$$\frac{1}{2}\mu g^2$$

is the R&D cost imputed by the government to dirty producers.

e. Using the fact the government acts as if θ were equal to zero, what is μ equal to?

f. Write down the first-order condition for the government's problem and compute the unique feasible solution g^* to it.

g. Intuitively, what should we expect for the growth rate of A_d chosen by a government that takes into account the externalities in R&D compared to the value found in the previous item?

17 Promoting Democracy

17.1 Introduction

Does democracy enhance or hamper economic growth? Recent empirical studies on the subject (see section 17.2) suggest no clear relationship between democracy and growth in cross-country panel regressions once we control for country fixed effects. However, one may think of various channels whereby democracy should affect per capita GDP growth. A first channel is that democracy reduces corruption and thus facilitates entry and exit, which in turn facilitates innovation and technical progress. A second channel is that democracy pushes for more redistribution from rich to poor, and that redistribution in turn affects growth. In section 17.3 we explore the first channel: we introduce political economy considerations into the entry model of chapter 12. And we show that democracy enhances entry, which in turn is more growth-enhancing in more advanced countries and sectors. This prediction of a positive interaction between democracy, entry, and technological development is tested in section 17.4. The second channel is explored in section 17.5. There we present a model by Persson and Tabellini (1994)[1] where the redistribution policy is chosen by the median voter. The more unequal the distribution of wealth, the higher the median voter's demand for redistribution. Redistribution in turn affects growth negatively as it discourages capital accumulation.

17.2 Democracy, Income, and Growth in Existing Regressions

Cross-country regressions by Barro (1999a) point to a positive correlation between income and democracy, that is, richer countries tend to be more democratic. Similarly, Aghion, Alesina, and Trebbi (2004) show that richer countries tend to have less insulated political institutions, where insulation is measured by the extent to which the political system is presidential instead of parliamentary and/or representatives are elected through majority rule rather than through proportional rule.

However, these relationships are between democracy and income, not democracy and growth. Moreover, the emphasis is on the causality from income to democracy, not the causality from democracy to income or income growth.

---

1. A continuous-time variant of that model, developed in parallel by Alesina and Rodrik (1994), is presented in the problem set section to this chapter.

Two recent studies have contributed to lowering our hopes of uncovering any interesting effect of democracy on growth. The first study, by Acemoglu, Johnson, Robinson, and Yared (2008), henceforth AJRY, shows that the positive correlation between democracy and income in cross-country regressions disappears once we move to panel data and control for country fixed effects. The second study, by Mulligan, Gil, and Sala-i-Martin (2004), henceforth MGS, has produced cross-country regressions over the period 1960–90 showing that democracy is uncorrelated with policies such as education spending, pensions and welfare, corporate taxation, openness to trade, and other policies that should affect barriers to entry. In the remaining part of this section we describe these two studies in somewhat greater detail.

17.2.1   Irrelevance Results When Controlling for Country Fixed Effects

Being primarily interested by the causality from income to democracy, and using cross-country panel data over the period 1960–2000, AJRY estimate the regression model

$$d_{it} = \alpha d_{it-1} + \gamma y_{it-1} + X_{it-1}\beta + \mu_t + \delta_i + u_{it}$$

where d_{it} measures democracy in country i at date t,[2] y_{it-1} is country i's per capita GDP in period $t - 1$, X_{it-1} are covariates, μ_t controls for time effects, δ_i controls for country fixed effects, and u_{it} is the error term. Each time period lasts for five years.

AJRY find that the estimate for γ becomes insignificant once we control for country fixed effects. And indeed, figure 17.1, which plots changes in these two measures of democracy as a function of the change in GDP per capita over the period 1970–2003, shows no significant relationship between democracy and income per capita.

17.2.2   No Apparent Correlation between Democracy and Public Policy

Using a cross-section of 142 countries over the whole period 1960–90, Mulligan, Gil, and Sala-i-Martin (2004), MGS, estimate the effect of democracy, measured by the same Polity index as in AJRY, on a whole range of policies: redistribution policies such as government consumption, education spending, and social spending, and policies affecting entry and turnover such as death penalty, military spending, civil liberties, state religion, conscription, and open trade.

2. AJRY use both the *Freedom House* indicator and the *Polity* indicator to measure democracy. The former index is constructed for each country as an aggregate score based on the answers to such questions as "Are there free elections?"; "Are there competitive parties?"; "Does the opposition enjoy power?" The Polity code reflects the openness of the political process and the constraints on government executives. Freedom and Polity scores are computed for each country for each year between 1970 and 2003.

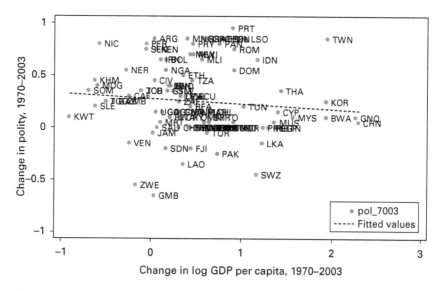

Figure 17.1
Change in democracy (polity) and change in GDP per capita, 1970–2003 (Penn World Tables and Polity IV Database)

None of these policies turns out to be significantly correlated with democracy, except for a negative and significant correlation between democracy and the level of military spending. Thus, if we believe the MGS analysis, democracy should not affect growth in any major way, since it does not affect policies whereby growth could itself be affected.

17.3   Democracy, Entry, and Growth: A Simple Model

The model in this section is inspired from Acemoglu's (2008) paper on oligarchies, from Caselli and Gennaioli's (2006) paper on dynastic management, and, more directly, from Aghion, Alesina, and Trebbi (2008), who blend the political economy considerations in Acemoglu (2008) and Acemoglu, Aghion, and Zilibotti (2006) with an entry model as in chapter 12.[3] In this model, democracy affects growth by constraining politicians' ability to collude with incumbent firms against new potential innovators (entrants).

3. The following entry model is in fact directly borrowed from Aghion, Burgess, Redding, and Zilibotti (2006).

17.3.1 Production and Profits

Time is discrete, and all agents live for one period. There is one final good produced competitively using a continuum of intermediate inputs, indexed from 0
to 1, according to the technology

$$y_t = \int_0^1 A_{it}^{1-\alpha} x_{it}^{\alpha} di$$

where x_{it} is the quantity of intermediate input produced in sector i at date t, A_{it} is
a productivity parameter that measures the quality of the intermediate input i in
producing the final good, and the parameter $\alpha \in (0, 1)$. The final good can be
used either for consumption, or as an input in the process of production of intermediate goods, or for investments in innovation.

In each intermediate sector i, only one firm (a monopolist) is active in each
period, and it produces intermediate input i using final output as input, one for one.
Since the final-good sector is competitive, the intermediate monopolist i sells its
intermediate good to the final-good sector at a price equal to its marginal cost:

$$p_{it} = \alpha \left(A_{it} / x_{it} \right)^{1-\alpha} \tag{17.1}$$

Then, profit maximization yields the choice

$$x_{it} = A_{it} \alpha^{\frac{2}{1-\alpha}}$$

and the equilibrium profit

$$\pi_{it} = \pi A_{it} \tag{17.2}$$

where $\pi \equiv \left(\dfrac{1}{\alpha} - 1 \right) \alpha^{\frac{2}{1-\alpha}}$.

Substituting for x_{it} in the production function for final output, we also get

$$y_t = \varphi A_t \tag{17.3}$$

where

$$A_t = \int_0^1 A_{it} di$$

is the average productivity at date t and φ is a constant.

17.3.2 Entry and Incumbent Innovation

Let p denote the probability that a potential entrant shows up in any intermediate
sector. The government directly chooses this parameter, but it is subject to

influence activities by incumbent firms that want to prevent entry. We consider these influence activities in more detail in the next subsection.

There are only two types of intermediate firms: advanced firms, with frontier productivity $A_{it} = \overline{A}_t$, and backward firms with below-frontier productivity $A_{it} = \frac{1}{\gamma}\overline{A}_t$, where frontier productivity $\overline{A}_t$ grows at a constant rate over time, namely,

$$\overline{A}_t = \gamma \overline{A}_{t-1}$$

with $\gamma > 1$.

We focus on technologically advanced entry; accordingly, each potential entrant arrives at date t with the current leading-edge technology $\overline{A}_t$. An advanced incumbent firm can use its first-mover advantage to block entry and thereby retain its monopoly power. However, if the incumbent firm fails to reach the new technological frontier, and if entry occurs in the corresponding sector, then Bertrand competition will take place between the incumbent and the entrant. As a result of Bertrand competition, the technologically dominated incumbent will be eliminated and replaced by the entrant.

We assume that to innovate at date t an intermediate firm must incur the R&D cost $c_{it}A_{it-1}$ (where A_{it-1} denotes its current productivity), and innovating in turn allows the incumbent firm to multiply its productivity by the factor γ. We assume c_{it} to be random and independently and identically distributed across intermediate sectors, with $c_{it} \in \{0, \overline{c}\}$, and

$$\Pr\left(c_{it} = 0\right) = \Pr\left(c_{it} = \overline{c}\right) = \frac{1}{2}$$

The effect of entry threat (as parametized by p) on incumbent innovation will depend on the marginal benefit that the incumbent expects to receive from an innovation given p.

Consider first an incumbent who was an advanced firm last period. If she innovates, then she will remain a frontier firm this period, and hence will be immune to entry.[4] Her profit will then be equal to $\pi\overline{A}_t$. If she fails to innovate, then with probability p she will be eliminated by entry and earn zero profit, while

---

4. As in chapter 12, we implicitly assume that entry entails a positive sunk cost, and that a potential entrant observes whether the incumbent firm in its target sector has innovated or not, before deciding whether or not to enter. If the incumbent firm managed to innovate and thereby to move to current frontier productivity, then entering would yield zero ex post profit to the entrant. Anticipating this outcome, the potential entrant will decide not to pay the sunk cost of entry.

with probability $1 - p$ she will survive the entry threat (as entry is not occurring) and thereby earn profit $\pi\bar{A}_{t-1}$. Thus an advanced firm with innovation cost c_{it} will innovate whenever

$$\pi\left[\gamma-(1-p)\right] = \pi(\gamma-1+p) > c_{it} \tag{17.4}$$

and then its profit will be

$$\pi_{it} = \left(\pi\gamma - c_{it}\right) A_{it-1} \tag{17.5}$$

In particular, we see from equation (17.4) that an increase in entry threat encourages this incumbent to innovate. Intuitively, a firm close to the frontier responds to increased entry threat by innovating more in order to escape the entry threat.

Next, consider an incumbent who was a backward firm last period, and who will therefore remain behind the frontier even if he manages to innovate, since the frontier will also advance by the factor γ. For this firm, profits will be zero if entry occurs, whether he innovates or not, because he cannot catch up with the frontier. Thus he will innovate whenever

$$\pi(1-p)(\gamma-1) > c_{it} \tag{17.6}$$

in which case his profit will be

$$\pi_{it} = \left[\pi\gamma(1-p) - c_{it}\right] A_{it-1}$$

where the first term is the profit gain from innovation that will be realized with probability $(1 - p)$, the probability that no potential entrant shows up in the corresponding sector. Thus in this case innovation incentives depend negatively on the entry threat p. Intuitively, the firm that starts far behind the frontier is discouraged from innovating as much by an increased entry threat because he is unable to prevent the entrant from destroying the value of his innovation.

We assume that initially the entry rate p is equal to zero, and we make the following assumption (assumption 1):

$$\pi(\gamma-1) < \bar{c}$$

so that, absent any entry threat, no firm with innovation cost equal to $\bar{c}$ ever innovates.

Using these assumptions, one can determine the steady-state fraction of advanced firms conditional upon $p = 0$. Thus, suppose that an advanced firm that successfully innovates at date t starts out in period $t + 1$ as an advanced firm. All other firms start out as backward firms. Moreover, with exogenous probability h, a backward firm at the end of period t is replaced by a new, advanced firm at date $t + 1$. If a_t denotes the fraction of advanced firms at t, then it satisfies the dynamic equation

$$a_{t+1} = z_A a_t + h\left(1 - z_A a_t\right)$$

where

$$z_A = \Pr\left(c = 0\right) = \frac{1}{2}$$

is the probability that an advanced firm innovates if $p = 0$.

In particular the steady-state fraction of advanced firms is simply

$$a^* = \frac{h}{1 - \frac{1}{2}\left(1 - h\right)} = \frac{2h}{1 + h}$$

17.3.3   Politics and the Equilibrium Probability of Entry

Suppose that entry policy p is determined each period by a politician who cares about current consumption but may also respond to bribes. Following Acemoglu, Aghion, and Zilibotti (2006), or AAZ, we assume that the politician's payoff is equal to $H\overline{A}_t$, where $H > 0$, if she chooses the policy that maximizes current output y_t, and to B_t otherwise, where B_t denotes the bribe that the politician may receive from private firms to limit entry. The parameter H reflects the aggregate welfare concerns of politicians, or the effectiveness of checks and balances that the political system imposes on politicians, and we use it as our proxy for democracy.

To compute the equilibrium bribe that incumbent firms are willing to pay to prevent moving from initial entry probability $p_0 = 0$ to $p > 0$, we need to compute the equilibrium payoffs for each type of firm (advanced or backward) and for each cost realization $c_{it} = 0$ or $\overline{c}$ as a function of p.

Consider first an advanced firm. If this firm's innovation cost is zero, then the firm will always innovate, and its postinnovation profit $\pi\gamma$ is independent of the entry probability. However, if the innovation cost is $\overline{c}$, this firm will lose from higher entry threat only if the threat p becomes sufficiently high that condition (17.4) holds. Then, indeed, using expression (17.5) for profits, the firm will lose $A_{it-1} = \overline{A}_t$ times the amount

$$\pi - (\pi\gamma - \overline{c}) = \overline{c} - \pi(\gamma - 1)$$

which is positive by assumption 1. Thus the maximum bribe that advanced firms as a group would be ready to pay to prevent an increase in entry threat from zero to p is given by

$$B_a(p) = \overline{A}_t a^* \left[\overline{c} - \pi(\gamma - 1)\right] \cdot 1_{\left[\pi(\gamma - 1 + p) > \overline{c}\right]}$$

where $1_{\left[\pi(\gamma - 1 + p) > \overline{c}\right]}$ is equal to one whenever equation (17.4) holds and to zero otherwise.

Now, consider a backward (or below-frontier) firm. Such a firm will innovate if and only if $c_{it} = 0$ by assumption 1, no matter the entry probability. And it will lose from a higher threat of entry, whether it innovates or not, just because this reduces its probability of survival. If the firm turns out to have low innovation cost ($c_{it} = 0$), it innovates and therefore loses $A_{it-1} = \dfrac{1}{\gamma}\overline{A}_t$ times the amount

$$\pi\gamma\left[1 - (1 - p)\right] = \pi\gamma p$$

if the entry probability increases from 0 to p. If the firm turns out to have high innovation cost ($c_{it} = \overline{c}$), it will not innovate and therefore loses $A_{it-1} = \dfrac{1}{\gamma}\overline{A}_t$ times the amount

$$\pi\left[1 - (1 - p)\right] = \pi p$$

if the entry probability increases from 0 to p. Since, ex ante, the firm has equal probabilities $\frac{1}{2}$ to have high or low innovation costs, the maximum bribe backward firms as a group are willing to pay to prevent an increase in entry threat from zero to p, is equal to

$$B_b(p) = \frac{1}{\gamma}\overline{A}_t (1 - a^*)\left(\frac{1}{2}\pi\gamma p + \frac{1}{2}\pi p\right)$$

where the first (resp. second) term in the bracket is the expected loss incurred by backward firms with low (resp. high) innovation cost.

Altogether, incumbent firms will successfully prevent the increase in entry threat from zero to p whenever p is greater than p^* such that the politician is just indifferent between accepting and refusing the aggregate bribe in order not to increase the entry threat from zero to that probability, namely,

$$B(p^*) = B_a(p^*) + B_b(p^*) = H\overline{A}_t \tag{17.7}$$

Given that $B(p)$ is strictly increasing in p, equation (17.7) defines the equilibrium entry probability p^* as an increasing function of H. In other words, the higher the level of democracy, the less profitable it is for incumbent firms to bribe the politician in order not to increase the entry threat up to a given level.

17.3.4   Main Prediction

Combining equation (17.7) with expressions (17.4) and (17.6) yields the prediction that an increase in democracy as measured by H will stimulate innovation by advanced firms but not by backward ones. One should thus expect a higher impact of democracy on productivity growth in sectors that are closer to the world technological frontier.

Remark   In this section, we have explored one channel whereby democracy should stimulate greater growth in more advanced sectors; that is, democracy stimulates entry and entry is more growth enhancing in more advanced sectors. Another reason, suggested in recent work by Acemoglu, Aghion, and colleagues (2007), is that democracy (or decentralization—its equivalent within firms) enhances frontier innovation. In contrast, democracy is less instrumental to growth in less advanced sectors where growth relies more on imitation or factor accumulation. In other words, in less advanced sectors when the objective is clearly defined, a firm can operate like an army, which is indeed the case when the firm is in the business of imitating an existing technology. However, when the nature of technological change is not so clearly defined—which is the case when firms enact innovations at the frontier—it may be better to grant freedom to downstream employees or to subcontract research to independent individuals. In the next section, we submit our prediction to cross-country, cross-industry panel data.

17.4   Evidence on the Relationship between Democracy, Growth, and Technological Development

17.4.1   Data and Regression Equation

Departing from previous work on political institutions and growth, Aghion, Alesina, and Trebbi (2008), henceforth AAT, use employment and productivity data at industry level across countries and over time. Their sample includes 28 manufacturing sectors for 180 countries over the period 1964 to 2003.

Democracy is measured using the Polity 4 civil rights and political rights indicators. Distance to the frontier is measured by the log of the value added of a sector divided by the maximum of the log of the same variable in the same sectors across all countries, or by the ratio of the log of GDP per worker in the sector over the maximum of the log of per capita GDP in similar sectors across all countries. AAT take one minus these ratios as proxies for a sector's distance to the technological frontier.

On the left-hand side of the regression equation is the rate of growth of either value added or employment in the industrial sector. On the right-hand side are the measure of democracy (and other measures of civil rights), a measure of the country's or industry's distance from the technological frontier, and an interaction term between the latter two. AAT also add time, country, and industry fixed effects. More formally, if y_{ict} denotes either value added or employment, AAT consider the regression

$$\Delta_s \log y_{ict} = \beta_0 + \beta_1 \text{Distance}_{ict} + \beta_2 \text{Pol}_{ct} + \beta_3 \text{Distance}_{ict} * \text{Pol}_{ct} + u_{ict}$$

where

$$\Delta_s \log y_{ict} = \log y_{i,c,t+s} - \log y_{ict}$$

is the growth rate of value added or employment in the industry, Pol_{ct} is the measure of democracy in the country, Distance_{ict} is the industry's distance to the technological frontier, and

$$u_{ict} = \delta_t + \gamma_c + \lambda_i + \varepsilon_{i,c,t+s}$$

where δ_t, γ_c and λ_i are time, country, and sector fixed effects, respectively, and $\varepsilon_{i,c,t+s}$ is the noise term.

AAT focus on five-year and ten-year growth rates ($s = \{5, 10\}$). They compute rates over nonoverlapping periods, and in particular five-year growth rates are computed over the periods 1975, 1980, 1985, 1990, 1995, and 2000. For the ten-year growth rates they use either the years 1975, 1985, 1995, or the years 1980, 1990, and 2000.[5]

17.4.2   Basic Results

First, AAT confirm the absence of a significant effect of democracy on growth rates for manufacturing in a regression at the country level where one controls

---

5. All the standard errors are robust and clustered at the country or country-industry level when possible, in order to account for general variance-covariance structures at the country-industry level within the panel.

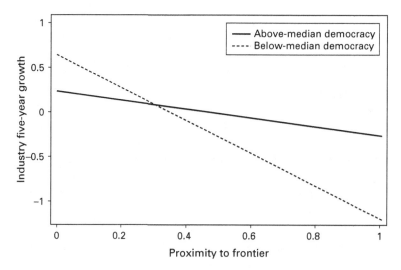

Figure 17.2
Industry growth and proximity to frontier (below- and above-median democracy countries)

for country fixed effects. The same absence of correlation between democracy and growth is obtained when moving from cross-country to cross-country-industry regressions. This first result is consistent with the findings of AJRY and MGS mentioned earlier.

However, the conclusions change dramatically once we introduce the interaction term between democracy and the industry's distance to the technological frontier. Namely, the interaction coefficient is negative and significant. meaning that the closer the industry is to the technology frontier, the more growth-enhancing democracy is for that sector. Figure 17.2 provides an illustration of the results. It plots the rate of value-added growth against a measure of the country's proximity to the technological frontier (namely, the ratio of the country's labor productivity to the frontier labor productivity). The broken line represents countries that are less democratic than the median country (on the democracy scale), whereas the solid line represents countries that are more democratic than the median country. We see that growth in more advanced sectors is enhanced by having those sectors operate in more democratic countries.

The theoretical model in the preceding section suggested that one explanation for the interaction between distance to frontier and democracy could be entry. In fact AAT report evidence that democracies tend to have lower barriers and cost of entry by employing the data from Djankov and colleagues (2002). Perotti and Volpin (2006) also report evidence that democracies favor entry more. The measure of entry barriers in AAT, borrowed from Djankov and colleagues, is the number of bureaucratic procedures needed for a firm to enter the market. This is important for our story because we argue that democracy matters for more advanced sectors of the economy because of the need for more entry and competition in sectors close to the technological frontier where innovation is especially important for growth.

But this is not enough to conclude that entry is truly the reason behind the positive correlation between democracy and growth in more advanced sectors. In addition, one needs to make sure that, once controlling for entry barriers, the effect of democracy and of its interaction with technological development remains significant. Unfortunately, using the Djankov and colleagues' index (the number of procedures needed to start up a new firm) as a proxy for entry does not affect the preceding regression results in any significant way. However, when replacing the number of procedures with the effective level of entry in the sector, measured by the growth rate in the number of establishments, AAT find that the effect of democracy is substantially reduced. This finding suggests that the entry channel at least partly explains why democracy may be conducive to growth in sectors closer to the technological frontier rather than other less advanced sectors. Overall, there is evidence of a differential effect of democracy across sectors and countries at different stages of development.

17.5   Democracy, Inequality, and Growth

In parallel contributions, Persson and Tabellini (1994) and Alesina and Rodrik (1994) analyze the relationship between inequality, democratic voting, and growth. They develop models in which redistribution from rich to poor is detrimental to growth as it discourages capital accumulation. More inequality is then also detrimental to growth because it results in the median voter becoming poorer and therefore demanding more redistribution.

17.5.1   The Model

More formally, consider an economy populated by a continuum of overlapping generations. Each individual lives for two periods. An individual i born at date $t-1$ has intertemporal utility function

$$U\left(c_{t-1}^{i}, d_{t}^{i}\right) = \ln c_{t-1}^{i} + \ln d_{t}^{i}$$

where c_{t-1}^{i} denote individual i's consumption when young (in period $t-1$) and d_{t}^{i} denote the individual's consumption when old (in period t).

Individual i starts out with initial income endowment

$$y_{t-1}^{i} = \left(w + e^{i} \right) k_{t-1} \tag{17.8}$$

where w is an average endowment of basic skills available to all individuals, and e^{i} is an extra skill endowment specific to individual i. Richer individuals have more positive e's, poorer individuals have more negative e's. We assume that the mean value of e^{i} across individuals is equal to zero.

Note the term k_{t-1} on the right hand side of equation (17.8). This term encapsulates an AK externality: all individuals born at date $t-1$ benefit from the general knowledge embodied in the accumulated aggregate capital k_{t-1}.

This initial income is divided between consumption c_{t-1}^{i} and investment k_{t}^{i}:

$$y_{t-1}^{i} = c_{t-1}^{i} + k_{t}^{i} \tag{17.9}$$

Finally, consumption of the old is assumed to be equal to

$$d_{t}^{i} = \left(1 - \theta_{t} \right) k_{t}^{i} + \theta_{t} k_{t} \tag{17.10}$$

where the variable θ_{t} measures the level of redistribution. When $\theta_{t} = 1$, all individuals consume the same amount when old.

The timing of events is the following within each period: (1) at the beginning of period $t-1$ young voters choose the level of redistribution θ_{t} that will apply to them when old; (2) each individual i chooses her investment k_{t}^{i}.

17.5.2   Solving the Model

17.5.2.1   Equilibrium Growth Rate for Given Redistribution Policy

Take first the redistribution policy θ_{t} as given. Individual i will choose her investment k_{t}^{i} to solve

$$\max_{k_{t}^{i}} \left\{ \ln c_{t-1}^{i} + \ln d_{t}^{i} \right\}$$

subject to equations (17.9) and (17.10).

In other words, individual i will choose k_{t}^{i} to

$$\max_{k_{t}^{i}} \left\{ \ln \left[\left(w + e^{i} \right) k_{t-1} - k_{t}^{i} \right] + \ln \left[\left(1 - \theta_{t} \right) k_{t}^{i} + \theta_{t} k_{t} \right] \right\}$$

The first order condition for this maximization is

$$\frac{1}{\left(w + e^{i} \right) k_{t-1} - k_{t}^{i}} = \frac{\left(1 - \theta_{t} \right)}{\left(1 - \theta_{t} \right) k_{t}^{i} + \theta_{t} k_{t}}$$

or equivalently

$$2(1-\theta_t)k_t^i = (1-\theta_t)(w+e^i)k_{t-1} - \theta_t k_t \qquad (17.11)$$

Not surprisingly, the more negative e^i, the lower the investment k_t^i.

Now, using the fact that

$$k_t = \int k_t^i di$$

and integrating equation (17.11) over all individuals i, we obtain

$$2(1-\theta_t)k_t = (1-\theta_t)wk_{t-1} - \theta_t k_t$$

or equivalently

$$(2-\theta_t)k_t = (1-\theta_t)wk_{t-1} \qquad (17.12)$$

The equilibrium growth rate between period $t-1$ and period t is then simply given by

$$g_t = \frac{k_t}{k_{t-1}} - 1 = \frac{(1-\theta_t)w}{2-\theta_t} - 1$$

which is clearly decreasing in the level of redistribution θ_t. The intuition is simply that more redistribution discourages individual capital accumulation.

17.5.2.2   Political Equilibrium and the Effect of Inequality on Growth

So far, we have taken the level of redistribution θ_t as given. Now, we endogenize it as the equilibrium outcome of a median voter game among all individuals. A first step is to analyze the preferred redistribution policy of individual i with initial skills $w + e^i$.

This individual would choose the redistribution level θ_t that maximizes

$$V_t^i(\theta_t) = \max_{k_t^i} \left\{ \ln\left[(w+e^i)k_{t-1} - k_t^i\right] + \ln\left[(1-\theta_t)k_t^i + \theta_t k_t\right] \right\}$$

The optimal θ_t (from the point of view of individual i) satisfies

$$\frac{dV_t^i}{d\theta_t} = 0$$

which, using the envelope theorem and then equation (17.12), implies

$$0 = k_t - k_t^i + \theta_t \frac{\partial k_t}{\partial \theta_t} = k_t - k_t^i - \theta_t \frac{wk_{t-1}}{(2-\theta_t)^2} \qquad (17.13)$$

Because the function

$$\frac{\theta_t}{\left(2-\theta_t\right)^2}$$

is increasing in θ_t, we obtain the redistribution θ_t, which is preferred by individual i, is a decreasing function of k_t^i and therefore a decreasing function of her initial endowment $w + e^i$. In other words, poorer individuals have higher demand for redistribution. The preceding equation also shows that individual preferences over redistribution are single-peaked. This in turn implies that the equilibrium redistribution policy in a majority voting game is the redistribution chosen by the median voter.[6]

Now the more unequal the skill distribution, the more negative the idiosyncratic skill e^m of the median voter, and therefore the higher her demand $\theta(e^m)$ for redistribution. This in turn will result in a lower equilibrium growth rate

$$g = \frac{\left(1-\theta\left(e^m\right)\right)(w)}{2-\theta\left(e^m\right)} - 1$$

17.5.3 Discussion

Persson and Tabellini (1994) test the predictions of this model using postwar data on 56 countries. Regressing growth on income equality in a cross-section of these countries, they find that the better the relative position of the middle quintile of income (which they take to reflect a higher degree of income equality), the higher the average annual growth rate over the period 1960–85. Moreover, this positive correlation between income equality and growth is found to be significant only for democracies, not for nondemocracies.

Using the Gini coefficient as the measure for income inequality, and a somewhat different cross-country sample over the period 1960–85, Alesina and Rodrik (1994) also find a negative correlation between inequality and growth. However, they do not find a significant interaction between the democracy dummy and the Gini coefficient. More recent studies have questioned the robustness of the relationship between inequality and growth, and therefore the robustness of the findings and predictions in this section.[7]

---

6. Here we refer the reader to the classic political economy textbook by Persson and Tabellini (2000).

7. In particular, see Banerjee and Duflo (2003).

17.6   Conclusion

In this chapter we have looked at the causal relationship between democracy and growth. Starting from the negative finding that democracy and growth are uncorrelated in cross-country data, we moved the analysis forward by (1) looking at cross-industry data; (2) interacting democracy with technological development at sectoral level, and (3) looking at the specific role of entry. In particular, we saw that democratic institutions favor growth in sectors of the economy that are more technologically advanced. Then in the second part of the chapter we discussed the relationship between democracy, inequality, and growth.

The fact that growth is increasingly enhanced by democracy as a country becomes more technologically advanced does not imply that countries should automatically move to democracy as they develop. Indeed, as we saw in chapter 11, countries may get stuck with political institutions that become increasingly inappropriate as they move closer to the technological frontier. However, there is an idea, neither precisely formalized by the existing literature nor extensively confronted with data, that economic growth requires the development of an educated middle class that eventually pushes for the transition to democracy. We saw this process at work in South Korea, South Africa, Latin America, and the Soviet bloc. The big exception so far is of course China, but for how much longer?

17.7   Literature Notes

Existing analyses of the relationship between democracy and growth address both the causality from income or growth to democracy or the reversed causation.

Przeworski and Limongi (1993) present a summary of theoretical arguments in the direction of both positive and negative effects of democracy on growth. Then, as we discussed in section 17.5, Persson and Tabellini (1994) suggest that democracy tends to magnify the negative correlation between inequality and growth. In a first attempt at looking at democracy and growth in the data and using cross-country panel regressions (but not controlling for country fixed effects), Barro (1996) points at a nonlinear relationship whereby more democracy enhances growth at low levels of political freedom but reduces growth when a moderate level of freedom has already been achieved.

Looking at the reverse causation from growth to democracy, Barro (1999a) points out that higher levels of income predict increases in democracy (measured by an indicator of electoral rights). Aghion, Alesina, and Trebbi (2004) endogenize the choice of political institutions and show that richer countries tend to have less insulated political systems (i.e., there is a higher degree of expost control over the politician once appointed).

Recent work by Acemoglu, Johnson, Robinson, and Yared (2005) shows that the positive correlation between democracy and income in cross-country regressions disappears once one controls for country fixed effects in cross-country panel regressions. Similarly, Mulligan, Gil, and Sala-i-Martin (2004) show that democracy is uncorrelated with several policy variables that affect growth (such as education spending, pensions and welfare, and openness to trade). However Aghion, Alesina, and Trebbi (2007) show that significant correlations between democracy and growth reappear once we allow for interaction terms between democracy and countries' or industries' levels of technological development.

Regarding the impact of electoral rules (such as presidentialism versus parliamentarianism) on economic outcomes, an extensive treatment can be found in Persson and Tabellini (2003). Finally, we refer the reader to a book edited by Helpman (2008) on *Institutions and Economic Performance*, for frontier work on the subject.

Problems

1. Explain intuitively how democracy can promote innovation and technical progress. Why does democracy affect growth more positively in more advanced countries?

2. *The factor distribution of income and economic growth (based on Alesina and Rodrik 1994)

This problem presents a model related to Persson and Tabellini (1994) presented in the chapter. The main idea is that the saving behavior of capitalists and workers is different, and hence the pattern of ownership of the means of production can affect economic growth.

Consider an economy with two types of individuals, workers and capitalists. Workers supply inelastically one unit of labor, do not save, and consume all their income. The capitalists own all the stock of capital, do not work, consume, and save. Output depends on public expenditure on a public good, γ, as well as on labor and capital (see Barro 1990). That is,

$y = Ak^{\alpha}\gamma^{1-\alpha}l^{1-\alpha}$ where $0 < \alpha < 1$

The labor endowment is constant and normalized to unity.

Public expenditure is financed by a tax on the return to capital, τ. The government cannot borrow; hence it must always have a balanced budget. Tax revenues can be spent on transfers to workers as well as on the provision of γ. Let $\lambda \in [0, 1]$ be the share of government revenue that is transferred to workers. Transfers are then $\lambda \tau \kappa$,

a. Explain why the government budget constraint implies

$$\gamma = (1-\lambda)\tau k$$

The representative capitalist faces the following problem:

$$\max U^k = \int_0^\infty \log c^k e^{-\rho t} dt$$

subject to $\quad \dot{k} = (r-\tau)k - c^k$

where c^k is the capitalist's consumption level. Similarly, denote a worker's consumption by c^l. Her consumption decision problem is then given by

$$\max U^l = \int_0^\infty \log c^l e^{-\rho t} dt$$

subject to $\quad c^l = w + \lambda \tau k$

where w is the wage, which is equal to the marginal product of labor.

The government chooses λ and τ at each point in time to maximize the weighted average of the welfare of the two groups. Let $\beta \in [0, 1]$ be the weight given to workers' welfare, and $(1 - \beta)$ that of capitalists' welfare.

b. Find the dynamic equation for the capitalists' consumption. What are the steady-state rates of growth of capital and of workers' consumption? Express the steady-state rate of growth of the economy in terms of model parameters and the policy instruments only.

c. How does the steady-state rate of growth depend on λ and τ? Find the values of these two policy instruments that maximize the steady-state growth rate.

d. Suppose the government maximizes the welfare of the capitalists (i.e., $\beta = 0$). Which values of λ and τ will it choose?

e. Suppose the government cares also about the welfare of the workers (i.e., $\beta > 0$). Obtain the first-order conditions for welfare maximization. Examine them to see that whenever workers' welfare enters the welfare function, the growth rate is not maximized. Show that if $\beta \geq [(1 - \alpha)A]^{1/\alpha}/\rho$, then the optimal transfers value is $\lambda^{**} = 1 - [(1 - \alpha)A]^{1/\alpha}/\beta\rho$ and the optimal tax rate is $\tau^{**} = \beta\rho$. What are the optimal values of λ and τ if the preceding restriction is not satisfied?

3. *Majority voting, the distribution of factor endowments and economic growth (based on Alesina and Rodrik 1994)

Consider the same economy as in the previous problem, except that now all individuals own some labor and some capital, although in different proportions. Let l^i and k^i denote the amount of labor and of capital owned by agent i. Let k denote the aggregate stock of capital. Then her relative factor endowment is given by

$$\sigma^i = \frac{l^i}{k^i/k} \qquad \sigma^i \in [0, \infty)$$

The tax system is the same as before, except that there are no transfers ($\lambda = 0$). The instantaneous-utility function is logarithmic for all agents. All agents save and borrow at the risk-free interest rate.

a. Show that the rate of growth of individual consumption is the same for all agents.

b. Which is the tax rate that maximizes the growth rate?

c. Which is the tax rate preferred by individual i?

d. If the tax rate is chosen by majority voting, is there a relationship between inequality and growth?

CONCLUSION

18 Looking Ahead: Culture and Development

Let us conclude our journey into the economics of growth by pointing out uncharted territory, at issues that should preoccupy growth economists but have yet remained largely unexplored. Our main focus in this chapter will be on culture and on the relationship between growth, development, and industrial policy. But before we proceed, let us step back and briefly review what we have learned from our discussions in the previous chapters.

18.1 What We Have Learned, in a Nutshell

Part I laid down the main growth paradigms. We first analyzed the benchmark neoclassical growth model and showed why this model can explain cross-country convergence but not long-run growth. Then we moved to the AK model of growth and saw that this model can explain long-run growth but not convergence in the context of a closed economy. Yet this model may explain convergence in the context of an open economy subject to terms-of-trade effects. Then we analyzed the two leading models of growth with endogenous innovation. In the product-variety model, innovations lead to new products and to an improved division of labor between a larger number of intermediate activities. In the Schumpeterian model, innovations lead to better products; thus new innovations displace old inputs. We saw how equilibrium innovation and growth depend upon the basic characteristics of the economy, in particular the extent of property-rights protection, the efficiency of the innovation technology, and the size of the economy. We also discussed the scale-effect criticism and argued that it can be addressed without losing the main features and implications of innovation-based models. Finally, we revisited growth accounting in models with endogenous innovation.

In part II we used the growth paradigms to understand several facts about the growth process. In particular, we tried to explain (1) why some countries converge and others do not; (2) the role of financial development in helping convergence; (3) why wage inequality has increased over the past decades in developed economies while productivity has gone through an initial period of slowdown; (4) why, in the process of development, countries go through different stages of growth (for example, from a Malthusian agricultural economy to an industrial economy that accumulates capital, and then from an accumulating industrial economy to an economy based on innovation and services); and (5) why different institutions tend to be growth enhancing at different stages of development, and why the failure to make the required institutional transitions can generate non-convergence traps.

In part III we looked at growth-enhancing policies in more detail. First, we saw that competition and entry can be growth enhancing in spite of reducing post innovation rents. We showed that competition and entry enhance growth mostly in sectors and countries that are more technologically advanced, whereas they may discourage growth in less advanced sectors. Then we saw that education investments can have large effects on growth, both because they help counteract the effect of diminishing returns on physical capital accumulation and because they enhance technological progress. We saw that the complementary relationship between education and R&D investments can generate multiple equilibria and the existence of low-development traps. We also argued that while primary and secondary education tend to be more growth enhancing in countries or regions that are far below the technological frontier, tertiary education is more growth enhancing in countries or regions that are more technologically advanced. Then we turned to the relationship between volatility and growth. We saw that macroeconomic volatility has two counteracting effects on savings and, therefore, on growth. Then we argued that volatility tends to be more detrimental to growth in countries or sectors that are less financially developed (or, equivalently, that are subject to tighter credit constraints), thereby suggesting that countercyclical macroeconomic policies might be more growth enhancing in such countries or sectors. We also saw that countries with less complete asset markets are more vulnerable to risk, which in turn may prevent them from converging towards higher levels of development. Then we analyzed the effects of trade openness. In particular, we saw that trade openness can enhance growth for at least three reasons: it increases the scale of the economy; it generates knowledge spillovers; and it fosters competition and weeds out the less productive firms. This in turn can explain why trade liberalization tends to be more growth enhancing in smaller countries and/or in more advanced sectors. We then turned our attention to environmental policy, and showed how it can be appropriately designed to encourage clean innovations and thereby guarantee sustainable growth. Finally, we identified several channels whereby democracy can affect growth. A first channel is through the median voter's mechanism. A second channel is through the entry that democracy fosters.

18.2   Culture and Growth

One could view the process of economic growth and the design of growth policy as consisting of several layers. A first layer is that of direct incentives to innovation and capital accumulation: subsidies to capital investment, R&D subsidies, tax credits that encourage innovation, or income tax policies that balance individual incentive considerations with the need to create broad opportunities. A second layer is that of institutions and structural reforms. For example, product and trade liberalization, the structure of educational spending, the organization of financial systems, the design of constitutions, and the allocation of control rights in government and firms. These institutional features affect growth indirectly, in particular through their effects on innovation incentives.

But there is also a third, and perhaps more fundamental, layer of growth: it is that of culture and beliefs. A new literature has been developing over the past five years on the impact of "culture" on economic outcomes. The word "culture" in the economic literature refers to individual and collective beliefs, social norms, and various attributes of individuals' preferences that are somehow influenced by their environment, but typically slow moving.

For example, Easterly and Levine (1997) produce cross-country regressions that show a negative correlation between ethnic heterogeneity and growth. Tabellini (2007) analyzes the impact of culture measured as accumulated human capital. Knack and Keefer (1997) use cross-country data over a sample of 29 market economies to show that mutual trust among individuals is positively correlated with growth and investment over GDP. Zak and Knack (2001) extend this analysis to a larger sample of 41 countries, and figure 18.1 summarizes their main finding.[1] Here, the trust indicator is computed by averaging over two waves of the World Values Survey, and at country level, the individual responses to the question: "... would you say that most people can be trusted or that you need to be very careful in dealing with people?" The individual indicator is equal to zero if the respondent answers "most people can be trusted," and to 1 if she answers "need to be very careful." The explained variable is average annual growth in per capita income. We see on figure 18.1 that this measure of trust is positively correlated with growth, and the empirical analysis shows that this correlation is significant. However, this says nothing about causality between trust and growth (in particular no good instrument is found for trust), and also it says very little about the particular channels whereby trust and growth are related.

A convincing attempt at instrumenting for trust is by Guiso, Sapienza, and Zingales (2005), who show how mutual trust among individuals or across individuals in different countries has an impact on trade and other economic outcomes, and they instrument mutual trust using measures of genetic resemblance.

---

1. The underlying point is that people spend less time monitoring each other and more time producing when mutual trust is higher.

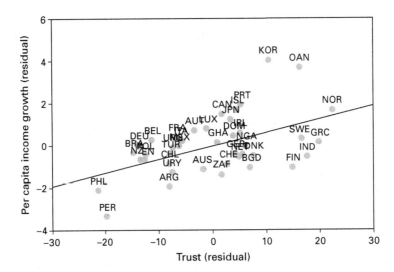

Figure 18.1
Trust and growth (Zak and Knack 2001)

In this section we briefly present two attempts at understanding potential channels whereby culture can have an impact on growth. The first attempt, by Aghion, Algan, Cahuc, and Shleifer (2008), henceforth AACS, links a country's ability to deregulate to the degree of trust and civic education that prevails in that country. The second approach, by Doepke and Zilibotti (2008), henceforth DZ, endogenizes the rate of time preference by making it a choice variable of individuals' parents.

18.2.1   Regulation and Trust

18.2.1.1   An Illustrative Picture

Figure 18.2, from Aghion, Algan, and Cahuc (2008), henceforth AAC, reports cross-country information from the World Values Survey in 1999 on the correlations between the stringency of minimum wage regulations and the extent to which individuals trust each other. The stringency index encompasses the level and rigidity of minimum wage arrangements.[2] In particular, more rigid minimum wage regulations do not allow for variations across ages, occupations, or sectors. As in Zak and Knack (2001), the trust measure is computed by averaging, at

---

2. It is computed as the product of the level of minimum wage and of the extent to which the minimum wage is statutory or is allowed to vary across ages, sectors, or occupations.

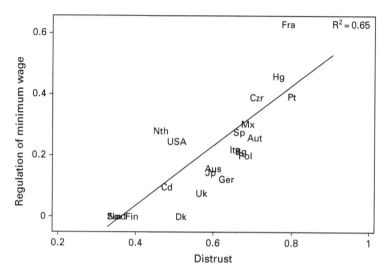

Figure 18.2
Distrust and state regulation of minimum wages (WVS database and AAC)

country level, the individual answers to the question "can most people be trusted." (The only difference is that AAC use three waves of the World Values Survey, not two.) We see a significantly negative correlation between trust and the stringency of the minimum wage regulations, with countries like France lying at the low trust/high regulation end of the spectrum and Sweden and Finland lying at the opposite end, that is, high trust/low regulation. AAC argue that this correlation reflects a two-way causality between regulation and trust in labor markets. Namely, more stringent and/or higher minimum wage regulations discourage decentralized experimentation by workers and employers, which in turn tends to perpetuate the lack of trust between them. Further, distrust between employers and employees induces the median voter to vote for a more stringent minimum wage regulation so as to limit her ex post risk.

AAC extend this logic to other sectors of the economy. More importantly, they try to explain the striking fact that there is a higher demand for regulation in countries where distrust is higher, not only among individuals, but also between individuals and the country's government and other public institutions.

18.2.1.2   A Toy Model

The following model accounts for the positive interplay between beliefs in cooperation and regulation, with a causality running in both directions. On the one hand, when individuals have low trust in the civic behavior of other individuals, they fear negative externalities from other individuals' production activities. Individuals then vote for more stringent regulations that limit the scope of productive activities and thereby protect against the negative externalities. On the other hand, more stringent regulations reduce individuals' incentives to invest in civic education aimed at increasing productivity while reducing the negative externalities on other individuals because the opportunity to directly interact with other individuals in productive activities is reduced by the regulations.

To detail the argument further, consider the following timing of moves. First, individuals choose the level of their investment in civic education. Thus, each individual ends up being either educated or uneducated. Educated individuals share two virtues: they are more productive and they generate lower externalities on other individuals. Uneducated individuals are less productive, generate more negative externalities on other individuals, and are uncivil. Second, given their beliefs as to how many individuals are educated, individuals vote on whether or not to regulate the economy, that is whether or not to forbid productive activities. In this framework, there are two stable equilibria. In the first there is zero investment in education and public authorities forbid productive activities because people are uncivil. The second equilibrium is characterized by positive investment, first in education, and then in civic individuals who allow public authorities to authorize productive activities. The second equilibrium pareto-dominates the first.

More formally, consider an economy with a continuum of identical risk-neutral individuals of mass one. There are two goods in the economy: labor and a numéraire good produced with labor. The timing of events is detailed as follows:

1. Individuals can either invest a fixed amount $i > 0$ to be educated or not invest at all. Educated individuals are able to produce one unit of the numéraire good and do not generate externalities when they produce. Uneducated people produce $y < 1$ and generate a negative externality which costs ℓ to everyone. Education is a private investment. It is assumed that education is observable but not verifiable.

2. People vote to authorize or forbid production. It is assumed that public authorities can forbid production activity at zero cost. It is impossible to forbid the production of the uneducated and to authorize the production of educated people because education is not verifiable.

3. People produce if this is authorized.

For simplicity, we assume that investment has positive private returns if the productive activity is authorized:

$1 - i > y$

and that the social returns of production are negative if people are not educated

$y < \ell$

Now, let α denote the share of educated people as anticipated by each individual. At the voting stage, production is authorized if and only if this maximizes individuals' expected utility, namely whenever

$$\alpha + (1 - \alpha)(y - \ell) > i$$

or equivalently

$$\alpha > \frac{i + \ell - y}{1 + \ell - y} = \bar{\alpha} \qquad (18.1)$$

Moving back to the investment stage, the private returns of (civic) education investment are positive if and only if the productive activity is authorized in the next step. Thus, the best reply of each individual is to invest in education if $\alpha > \bar{\alpha}$ and not to invest if $\alpha < \bar{\alpha}$. This implies that there are two (stable) equilibria. In the first equilibrium, all individuals invest in education ($\alpha = 1$) and it is optimal to authorize the productive activity. In the second equilibrium, nobody invests in education ($\alpha = 0$) and the productive activity is not authorized. The second equilibrium clearly pareto-dominates the first because social welfare amounts to zero in the equilibrium without education and to $1 - i > 0$ in the equilibrium with education.

This line of analysis is potentially important because it suggests that maintaining lower levels of regulation, which in turn have been shown to be growth enhancing, particularly in more advanced sectors and countries, may require investing in mutual trust. The difficulty of course is how to design policies that can durably move a country from a low-trust/high-regulation equilibrium, as we currently see in France or Italy, to a high-trust/low-regulation equilibrium, as currently exemplified by the Scandinavian countries.

18.2.2   Investing in Children's Patience

18.2.2.1   The Argument

Doepke and Zilibotti (2008) propose a neo-weberian theory of culture and growth. The basic idea is that parents can invest in their children's degree of patience, which in turn will affect the children's choice between current consumption and capital accumulation. Investments in children's work ethic and patience respond to economic incentives that depend on the occupation in which a family (or dynasty) is engaged. Some professions require young workers to sacrifice consumption and put in high labor effort, but then offer high rewards later in life. This is typically the case for professions that entail the acquisition of skills over the life cycle, such as artisanry and trade (the most common activities of the preindustrial middle class). Other occupations, such as unskilled labor in agriculture, provide flatter returns over the life cycle. Finally, there are occupations (in particular landowning) that are characterized neither by hard work nor by delayed consumption.

Given these differences between occupations, parents who anticipate their children to be artisans or merchants have a stronger incentive to instill patience in their children, since this will help them endure early sacrifices and enjoy their future success. Over centuries, the preindustrial middle class became the patient class. This attribute became a major advantage once new opportunities for capital accumulation arose with the Industrial Revolution. At that point, the thrifty middle class had a cultural edge that allowed it to exploit the new investment-based technology: this is the "spirit" that the development of capitalism required. Doepke and Zilibotti's theory can thus explain the rise of the bourgeoisie, which possessed a new ethic and a different culture from the landowning elite, and the demise of the aristocracy after the Industrial Revolution.

18.2.2.2 The Doepke-Zilibotti Model

In this section, we present a simplified version of Doepke and Zilibotti (2008) where the only endogenous preference asset is patience, labor supply is exogenous, and there is no occupational choice. We focus on the relationship between patience and physical capital accumulation, that is, the process describing the heyday of the Industrial Revolution, after patience levels had already diverged across social classes during the preindustrial period. The economy is populated by overlapping generations of altruistic people who live for four periods, two as children and two as adults. People work throughout both adult periods (young and old), and their earnings may vary over time as the result of occupational choice (which will be ignored here) and physical investment decisions. Agents consume and make economic decisions only when they are adult. At the beginning of adulthood, every agent gives birth to a single child.

All adults have the same basic preferences. However, patience, that is, the relative weight of old versus young adult consumption in utility, is endogenous. In particular, patience is determined during an agent's childhood as a result of her parent's child-rearing effort (i.e., investment in patience). Once an agent reaches adulthood, preferences no longer change. An adult therefore takes her own preferences as given, but gets to shape her child's tastes. Agents are altruistic toward their children. In addition, their utility depends on consumption and on investment in patience in each of the two adult periods.

The recursive representation of the decision problem of a young adult with patience B and inherited capital stock K is given by the following Bellman equation:

$$V(B, K) = \max_{c_1, c_2, l} \left\{ (1-B)\log(c_1) + B\log(c_2) - l + zV\left[B', (1-\delta)K' \right] \right\} \quad (18.2)$$

where V is the value of being a young adult with inherited capital stock K and inherited patience B; l is the cost of investing in patience; z is the altruism factor; and B' is the children's patience, determined by the law of motion

$$B' = (1-v)B + f(l),$$

where $v \in [0, 1]$, and the function f is continuous, strictly increasing, and weakly concave. Note that patience is modeled like a standard human asset whose intergenerational transmission features some persistence; that is, part of the patience capital is transmitted effortlessly from parents to children through imitation.

The second state variable is physical capital, which we interpret as a family-owned enterprise. Young adults decide how much of their first-period income to consume and how much to invest into the family business. Investments in the business are assumed to be irreversible: agents can consume the output of the investment technology, but the capital stock itself cannot be liquidated and turned into consumption. The capital owned by an old agent is bequeathed—up to depreciation—to her child. We assume that agents cannot borrow.

The capital stock of the family business depreciates at the rate δ. The rate of return on capital is denoted by A. Let $K \geq 0$ denote the bequest of capital received by a young adult. The budget constraints and the irreversibility constraint are given by

$$c_1 + K' = (1 - \delta + A)K \quad (18.3)$$

$$c_2 = AK' \quad (18.4)$$

$$K' \geq (1 - \delta)K \quad (18.5)$$

where c_1 is consumption in period 1, c_2 is consumption in period 2, and K' is the capital stock in period 2. The budget constraint (18.3) corresponds to the first adult period, where total income consists of capital income $(1 - \delta + A)K$. Because of the irreversibility constraint (18.5), consumption cannot exceed current output: $c_1 \leq AK$. In the second-period budget constraint (18.4), the agent earns capital income AK'. Since the capital stock cannot be liquidated, the agent bequeaths the remaining capital $(1 - \delta)K'$ to her child.

18.2.2.3   Solving the Model

Let $k = \dfrac{K'}{K}$. In the Appendix we show that

$$k = \max\left\{1-\delta, \left[(1-z)B+z\right](1-\delta+A)\right\} \tag{18.6}$$

Given any initial condition, patience B and the growth rate of capital k converge to a steady state. As in standard AK models, the growth rate of capital depends on the rate of time preference, but not on K. However, here the rate of time preference is endogenous. Whether agents find it optimal to accumulate capital and patience over time depends on the initial B. In particular, equation (18.6) implies that agents are going to save and invest in capital accumulation only if B is sufficiently large, namely, if

$$B > \hat{B} \equiv \frac{1-\delta}{(1-z)(1-\delta+A)} - \frac{z}{1-z} \tag{18.7}$$

In Doepke and Zilibotti (2008), the initial level of B is determined by the structure of preindustrial occupations, which gave agents engaged in different activities different incentives to accumulate patience. In particular, dynasties of artisans and merchants had converged to a level of B larger than $\hat{B}$, whereas both unskilled laborers and rich landowners had converged to a B lower than $\hat{B}$.

In the preindustrial world, no one accumulated capital, since A was too low, even for the patient artisans and merchants. Then technological change increased the productivity parameter A, making savings and investments attractive to the patient groups. In other words, patience became a key asset—a "spirit of capitalism"—when opportunities of economic advancement through entrepreneurship and investment arose at the outset of the industrial revolution. In an already stratified society, it was members of the patient (and hardworking) middle class who made the most of the new opportunities and ultimately gained economic ascendency over the landed elite.

More generally, Doepke and Zilibotti's theory shows the importance of culture and preferences for growth takeoff and development. Countries whose citizens are for cultural reasons more patient will be better placed to profit from the arrival of new technological opportunities or even institutional reforms that increase the rate of return of capital. For instance, one may argue that Chinese culture is traditionally geared toward patience and future orientedness, but institutions were preventing private capital accumulation and growth before 1979. Then economic reforms removed the constraints, and the country could benefit from the high predisposition to growth of Chinese people. Moreover, growth may be reinforcing people's drive to accumulation because of its effect on parents' investment in children's patience. Yet, under the same initial institutional conditions as China today, other countries with different initial cultures would not grow as fast.

18.3   Growth and Development

Over the past two decades development economists have legitimately questioned existing aggregative growth models, and they have moved instead towards more microeconomic analyses. A first attempt at revisiting growth theory from a development economist's perspective is the *Handbook of Economic Growth* chapter by Banerjee and Duflo (2005), henceforth BD.[3] By pointing out the importance of sectoral reallocations as a main engine of growth, their chapter suggests a way to bridge the gap between growth and development economics, and also to regenerate our thinking on the delicate issue of why and how to design adequate industrial policy.

18.3.1   Growth through the Lens of Development Economics

Banerjee and Duflo start from the same growth puzzle that animates growth economists: why does labor productivity remain low in some countries and high in others? But coming from the world of micro evidence, they come at this question from a very different angle. Whereas a growth theorist might see this as evidence of increasing returns (in the broadest sense of the word) in the aggregate production function or the fact that TFP in the aggregate production function varies at the country level, they are skeptical of the usefulness of the aggregate production function as an intellectual construct. Drawing on micro evidence from developing countries, they argue that the assumptions underlying the construction of the aggregate production function (namely, that the aggregate supplies of all factors are efficiently allocated across their myriad alternative uses in the economy) are so far from the truth as to make the idea of an aggregate production function more or less irrelevant. In particular, they point to micro evidence of very high

3. See Hsieh and Klenow (2007) for the best piece of empirical work in this line of research so far.

marginal rates of return in certain investment opportunities in both physical and human capital coexisting with much lower returns, whereas in the world of the aggregate production function all these marginal returns would have to be more or less equalized.

As an explanation of why these large differences in returns coexist, they point to micro evidence suggesting very substantial market failures in the markets for credit, insurance, and labor, as well as evidence of slow learning about new opportunities and a multitude of behavioral problems, including problems of self-control. These failures, in turn, derive in part from the (poor) quality of formal and informal institutions in many of these countries, but also from specific policy choices that they have made and the distribution of assets (both human and financial) that they start from.

18.3.1.1   The Lucas Argument

Given that they are prepared to give up on aggregation, BD naturally question the reasoning that goes into some of the standard arguments made by growth theorists. For example, take Lucas's (1990) famous argument for why the United States and India must have different levels of TFP. Lucas points out that if the productivity-per-worker gap between United States and India were to be explained entirely by the fact that India has less capital per worker (plus some adjustment for human capital differences), then capital would have to be extremely scarce in India. This explanation would imply, given that both countries' share the standard Cobb-Douglas production function used in growth analysis (with a coefficient of 0.4 on capital), that the marginal product of capital in India would have to be 5 times that in the United States. This figure, he concludes, cannot possibly be right, since it would induce massive capital flows from United States to India. Therefore the United States must have a different production function with, in particular, a higher level of TFP.

More precisely, suppose that in the United States and India the aggregate production function is:

$$Y_j = A_j L_j^{1-\alpha} K_j^{\alpha}$$

with $\alpha = 0.4$, and $j \in \{I, US\}$ denotes the country (India or the United States); and let us compare the rates of return on capital in India and the United States.

Letting

$$y_j = Y_j / L_j$$

denote per capita GDP in country j, and

$$k_j = K_j/L_j$$

denote per capita investment in capital in country j, we have

$$y_j = A_j k_j^\alpha$$

Assuming perfect credit markets in both countries, we then have

$$r_j = \frac{\partial y_j}{\partial k} = \alpha A_j k_j^{\alpha-1} \tag{18.8}$$

where r_j denotes the rate of return on capital, equal to the marginal productivity of capital, in country j.

In 1990 the ratio of per capita GDP levels between the United States and India was

$$y_{US}/y_I = 11$$

Moreover, BD estimate a productivity ratio between the two countries, equal to

$$A_{US}/A_I = 2$$

But then, using the fact that from equation (18.8) we have

$$y_{US}/y_I = \left(r_I/r_{US}\right)^{\frac{\alpha}{1-\alpha}} \left(A_{US}/A_I\right)^{\frac{1}{1-\alpha}}$$

the ratio r_I/r_{US} should be approximately equal to 5. This, together with the fact that the average real stock market return in the United States is at around 9 percent, would suggest a 45 percent rate of return in India. However, if there are individual projects in India that earn more than a 45 percent rate, the average rate of return on capital is much lower.

BD take the view that this whole reasoning is flawed. They point out that a difference in marginal product of capital of that magnitude is actually quite common within the same subeconomy, and there is no evidence that capital automatically flows to equalize returns.

Similarly they question the value of trying to use evidence on convergence (or the lack of it) to say something on the nature of returns to scale in production. Given the lack of equalization of returns across firms, the same production function can generate very different outcomes: two economies with identical technologies may grow very differently depending on whether the marginal unit of capital flows to the more productive firms rather than the less productive firms.

18.3.1.2   Moving Beyond Endogenous Growth Models?

Finally they argue that the available micro evidence is not fully accounted for by existing endogenous growth models. They first consider the AK model where knowledge externalities are generated by aggregate (human) capital accumulation,

$$Y_i = \left(K_H^i \right)^\alpha K_H^\eta$$

where K_H^i is the human capital investment by firm i and K_H is the aggregate human capital stock in the economy. This would explain why average interest rates on capital are lower in poorer countries: being more poorly endowed in aggregate capital, externalities should be lower in these countries. However, externalities should be much larger than estimated in recent empirical studies (for example, Acemoglu and Angrist 2000; Duflo 2004) in order to generate the preceding productivity differential between the United States and India.

Then BD turn their attention to endogenous differences in technology, as generated, for example, by the Schumpeterian models. They calculate that if the gap between rates of return on capital in the United States and India had to be fully explained by differences in productivities in an aggregative model, the ratio of total factor productivities between the United States and India should be at least equal to 2. However, TFP grows at a rate of 1 to 1.5 percent per year in the United States. Even at a rate of 1.5 percent per year, it would take 45 years for U.S. TFP to grow by 200 percent. Or, put in other words, if this was the story we would see India in 2000 using U.S. machines of 1950. However, BD quote a recent report by the McKinsey Global Institute saying that in many Indian industries the best firms use close-to-frontier technologies.

BD are careful not to say that this evidence points toward a wholesale rejection of the endogenous growth models. Yet they feel that these models miss something important—to explain, for example, why some firms or industries have access to the latest technologies but others do not requires moving away from an aggregative growth approach and explicitly introducing cross-firm heterogeneity into the analysis.

In an admittedly speculative section of their paper, BD go on to ask whether it is possible to explain the entire Indo-U.S. productivity gap simply based on firm-level heterogeneity (they do not claim that this is the entire explanation, just ask whether it could be). They start from a model where each firm i produces according to

$$Y = AL^\gamma K^\alpha$$

where $\gamma < 1 - \alpha$. In other words, there are decreasing returns at the firm level. However, firm i has access to at most $K(i)$ units of capital. Profit maximization by firm i implies that the demand for labor for a firm that invests $K(i)$ is equal to

$$L(i) = \left[\frac{A\gamma K(i)^\alpha}{w} \right]^{\frac{1}{1-\gamma}}$$

Labor-market clearing implies that

$$\bar{L} = \int L(i)\, di$$

or equivalently

$$w = A\gamma \left[\frac{\int \left[K(i)^\alpha \right]^{\frac{1}{1-\gamma}} di}{\bar{L}} \right]^{1-\gamma} = \gamma y$$

where y is average output per worker. Now, since $\alpha < 1 - \gamma$, the mapping $\left[K(i)^\alpha \right]^{\frac{1}{1-\gamma}}$ is concave in $K(i)$, and therefore more heterogeneity in $K(i)$ reduces the integral $\int \left[K(i)^\alpha \right]^{\frac{1}{1-\gamma}} di$. Therefore, greater heterogeneity in India could help explain the Indo-U.S. gap.

However, based on some rough calibration to micro data, BD find that the reduction in aggregate per capita output generated by the heterogeneity between small and large firms in India is not sufficient to explain the discrepancy in average rates of return between the United States and India. The main reason it fails is that given the extent of decreasing returns that is consistent with the observed profit shares (which in the model would be equal to $\frac{\alpha}{1-\gamma}$), the extent of heterogeneity that would be required to explain the Indo-U.S. gap is simply not in the data. In particular, the large (and therefore, because of decreasing returns, inefficient) Indian firms would have to be much larger than the largest firms in the United States, which is not what we find in the data.

Finally, BD obtain a better fit between the model and the data by introducing heterogeneous fixed costs leading to heterogeneous productivities. More precisely, they consider a heterogeneous population of firms where each firm i produces according to

$$Y = AL^\gamma \left(K - \bar{K} \right)^\alpha$$

where $\bar{K}$ is the fixed cost required to access technology A, and where again $\alpha + \gamma < 1$. Introducing fixed costs makes it possible that larger firms also have larger marginal products (which seems to fit the Indian case) and that the average product gap between small and large firms be large even if marginal products are similar (which again seems to fit the facts). BD then concentrate on the case where $\bar{K}$ takes three possible values ($\bar{K}_1 < \bar{K}_2 < \bar{K}_3$) corresponding to $A_1 < A_2 < A_3$ and show that in principle it could explain most of the Indo-U.S. gap, without straining credibility too much.

Note that this explanation means that productivity differences matter after all, even though it is by taking into account the existence of cross-firm heterogeneity that we can explain the discrepancy between average and marginal returns. Note that this model does not explain the heterogeneity in productivity levels across firms, and explaining it would presumably bring us back to something closer to the model in chapter 7 on convergence with credit constraints, but with cross-firm heterogeneity instead of cross-country heterogeneity.

One additional factor that may further explain the lower average rates of return in India compared to the United States and the discrepancy between average and marginal returns is the complementarity between small and large firms in the production process in India. The most productive Indian firms could well be almost as productive as their U.S. counterparts. Yet average productivity is more likely to be driven by the lower tail when the production process involves strong complementarities—for example, if the production of a whole range of intermediate components is subcontracted to small inefficient firms (see Kremer (1993a) and Jones 2008).

Overall, taking a development economist's approach, Banerjee and Duflo make us revisit the various growth paradigms, starting from the aggregative neoclassical model and leading us toward a model that appears to be more closely related to the Schumpeterian growth paradigm, but adequately enriched, in particular by fully integrating the heterogeneity across firms and/or sectors.

18.3.2   The Case for Targeted Growth Policy

Over the past decades governments and policy advisers have become suspicious about policies targeted at particular sectors, because such policies allow governments to "pick winners" in a discretionary fashion. But what if one could use market information together with information on the size of externalities to come up with suitable targeted policies? Although this is a research area where essentially everything remains to be done, we would like to provide the reader with two insights that may guide further thinking on this question.

The first insight, suggested by Young (1991), Lucas (1993), and more recently Hausmann and Klinger (2006), is that successful growth stories are ones involving gradual processes whereby neighboring sectors experiment with new technologies one after the other because experimentation involves learning-by-doing externalities across sectors. The second insight, from Kremer (1998), is that governments may use or simulate market mechanisms to determine the amount of R&D subsidies to targeted industries.

18.3.2.1 Learning-by-Doing Externalities and Industrial Policy

The notion that the existing pattern of specialization may limit the evolution of comparative advantage over time has not received much attention in the growth literature so far. In the product variety model analyzed in chapter 3, the current set of inputs displays the same degree of imperfect substitutability with respect to any new input that might be introduced and, therefore, does not make one new input more likely than any other: This property stems directly from the fully symmetric nature of the Dixit-Stiglitz model of product differentiation on which the Romer model is built.

To illustrate the notion of industrial niches in the simplest possible way, consider the following toy example. Individuals each live for one period. There are four *potential* sectors in the economy, which we number from 1 to 4, but only one sector, namely sector 1, is active at date zero. Thus the economy at date 0 can be represented by the 4-tuple

$$\Omega_0 = (1, 0, 0, 0)$$

where the number 1 (resp. 0) in column i refers to the corresponding sector i being currently active (resp. inactive). At date t, a sector that is active produces at the frontier productivity level $\bar{A}_t = (1 + g)^t$. Once activated a sector automatically remains active forever. Aggregate output at date t is

$$Y_t = A_t = N_t \bar{A}_t$$

where N_t is the number of active sectors at date t.

R&D investments activate new sectors, but there is a cost of learning about faraway sectors. Specifically, there is a fixed R&D cost $\gamma(1 + g)^t$ of activating a sector in period t, but this is only possible if (1) the sector is adjacent to an already active sector or (2) the R&D cost $\gamma(1 + g)^{t-1}$ was also incurred in that sector last period.

Consider first the economy under laissez-faire. Being populated by one-period lived individuals, the economy will never invest in a sector that is not adjacent to a sector already active. At best, a local entrepreneur will find it optimal to activate a sector adjacent to an already active sector. This will be the case whenever

$$\gamma < \theta$$

where θ is the fraction of output that can be appropriated by a private innovator. Note, however, if

$$\theta < \gamma$$

private firms will not explore new sectors, even neighboring ones, even though it might be socially optimal to do so.

Going back to the former case, the laissez-faire sequence of active sectors will be

$$\Omega_1 = (1, 1, 0, 0)$$

$$\Omega_2 = (1, 1, 1, 0)$$

$$\Omega_t = (1, 1, 1, 1), \quad t \geq 3$$

Now consider a social planner. The social planner will invest in sector 2 in period 1, whenever the cost $\gamma(1 + g)$ of doing so is less than the net present revenue of activating sector 2, namely

$$\sum_{t=1}^{\infty} \frac{\overline{A}_t}{(1+r)^t} = \frac{1+g}{r-g}$$

that is whenever

$$\gamma < \frac{1}{r-g}$$

For g sufficiently close to r or for γ sufficiently small, this inequality is automatically satisfied, in which case it will also be optimal to invest in sector 3 in period 2 because at that date sector 3 will be adjacent to an already active sector (namely sector 2).

But in addition, when γ is sufficiently small, it will be optimal to invest in sector 4 in period 1, because that will allow sector 4 to be activated in period 2 whereas otherwise it can only be activated in period 3. Investing in period 1 instead of period 2 in sector 4 will yield an additional

$$\bar{A}_2/(1+r)$$

and will cost an additional $\gamma(1 + g)$. So, if γ is small enough, namely if

$$\gamma < \frac{1+g}{1+r},$$

the optimal sequence of active sectors will be

$$\Omega_1 = (1, 1, 0, 0)$$

$$\Omega_2 = (1, 1, 1, 1)$$

$$\Omega_t = (1, 1, 1, 1), \quad t \geq 3$$

The laissez-faire equilibrium is suboptimal here because people do not invest far enough away from already active sectors. In this example, output will be lower than optimal in period 2 ($3\bar{A}_2$ versus $4\bar{A}_2$) because individuals were not farsighted enough to invest in sector 4, which was too far away from already active sectors, in period 1.

Thus this model suggests a role for targeted industrial policy: namely to overcome the potential underinvestment in new sectors.[4] In the model we just developed, investment inertia results from insufficient appropriability. In practice they may also result from the existence of credit constraints or the unavailability of complementary inputs.

The idea that the product space is heterogeneous, with an uneven density of active product lines, and that the current density distribution of active sectors has an impact on the evolution of comparative advantage, is taken to the data by Hausmann and Klinger (2006), henceforth HK. A main finding in HK is that the probability of a country exporting product i in year $t + 1$, is positively and significantly correlated with the country's density around product i in year t.

18.3.2.2   The Kremer Mechanism

Kremer (1998) designed a market-based mechanism for buying out pharmaceutical patents. Kremer's mechanism is based on ex post reward for inducing the

---

4. In particular, if targeted subsidies were to be implemented by a government, we conjecture that such subsidies should be more growth enhancing (1) if they target sectors that are currently inactive but close "input-wise" to already active sectors, and (2) if the country experiences low levels of financial development and/or low labor mobility and/or low levels of education. Part 1 implies that the targeted sectors are likely to benefit from learning-by-doing externalities from existing sectors. Part 2 makes it less likely that market forces would spontaneously take advantage of these externalities.

socially optimal amount of R&D. The basic idea is to make use of the information conveyed by the laissez-faire patent price V in order to fix the optimal price at which the social planner (government) will *repurchase* the innovations to put them in the public domain. Putting innovations in the public domain in turn removes the (static) monopoly distortion created by patents.

Directly inspired by the mechanism-design literature,[5] the Kremer "scheme" can be described as follows:

1. The innovator obtains a patent for his or her innovation.

2. The ("laissez-faire") price of the patent is revealed through an *auction* for the exclusive right to implement the innovation. Suppose that the laissez-faire value V emerges as the equilibrium price in this (say, first-price) auction; that is, $p_0 = V$.

3. With probability $(1 - \varepsilon)$ the government repurchases the innovation from the inventor at a price $p_1 = m \cdot V$ that tries to approximate the social value of innovation V^*. With probability ε, the patent remains in the hands of the winner of the auction. Note that ε needs to be strictly positive in order for private bidders to find it worth their while to come and participate in the auction. However, ε should not be too large in order for innovation incentive to remain socially optimal and also for (static) monopoly distortions to be largely removed. The multiplier $m = \dfrac{p_1}{V}$ should typically be greater than 1. For example, in the case of pharmaceutical innovations, Kremer estimates at about 2 the average value of m.

What makes this proposal attractive in our view is that it does a good job at eliciting information about the value of innovations and also that, insofar as ε remains small, the scheme removes all incentives to engage in (duplicative) imitation activities while at the same time eliminating the (static) monopoly distortions generated by innovations in the absence of imitations.

However, the scheme raises a number of questions. First, how does one *compute the multiplier m*? The value of m will typically depend on parameters such as the productivity of research or the elasticity of substitution between intermediate inputs, which the government is unlikely to know. Second, what guarantees that the equilibrium price that emerges in the auction is actually equal to the *true* value of the innovation under laissez-faire (i.e., to V)? In particular, when ε is

---

5. In particular by the literature on Nash and subgame perfect implementation under *symmetric* information. (Primary references in this literature are Maskin 1999; Moore and Repullo 1986.)

small, will private bidders still have adequate incentive to acquire *information* about V?

Third, what would prevent the innovator from *colluding* with potential bidders in order to (artificially) increase the auction price p_0 far above the true (private) value of the innovation V?[6]

Fourth, is the scheme adapted to the case of multiple *successive* innovations? There are actually several aspects to this question. In particular, how can the government make sure that by putting a first (fundamental) innovation in the public domain "too soon" it will not discourage other researchers from engaging in the development activities that are required in order to give (full) value to that innovation?[7] Another aspect of the same question about successive innovations has to do with the case where subsequent innovations may *substitute for* (rather than complement) the first innovation.[8] For example, what should happen in the case where subsequent innovations, especially when put in the public domain, reduce the (laissez-faire) value of the current innovation?[9]

Overall, Kremer's idea is interesting and important, not least because it suggests that by using the market mechanism at the margin one can come up with policies that take sectoral diversity into account while minimizing the scope for discretionarity.

18.4   Conclusion

In this chapter we have raised two particular themes, culture and sectoral development, that are highly relevant to growth but where a lot more research remains to be done. But there are other important issues for growth economists to look at that either have been barely touched on or simply not addressed at all. For

6. Well aware of this latter problem, the author proposes to use not the winning bid but the third or fourth bid price as the basis for computing the multiplier. But then the concern about information acquisition by private bidders might end up being dramatically reinforced.

7. On the other hand, the proposed mechanism would ensure that potential inventors of subsequent complementary innovations will assume that the earlier good is being sold at marginal cost.

8. In particular, this system may fail to provide adequate incentives for the invention of durable goods. This failure is because the expectation that future substitutes will be placed in the public domain, and hence sold at marginal cost, may reduce current demand for durable patented goods.

9. Here, Kremer suggests that the government repurchase the first innovation at its private value $p_0 = V$ and then later resume the auction process for the overall package of innovations. But this in turn presupposes that the government will know *in advance* whether the first innovation is to be substituted for by subsequent innovations, and that it also knows *how many* successive innovations of this kind are to take place in the future, two heroic assumptions!

example, (1) the impact of financial bubbles and regulations on innovation and growth; (2) the interplay between growth, the design of the tax system, and the composition of government spending; (3) the contribution of basic science and open research to growth.

Another important question relates to the dynamics of institutions and policies. In the previous chapters, we have seen that different institutions and policies tend to be growth enhancing at different stages of development. And in chapter 11 we saw that failure to implement the required institutional reforms may lead a country into a nonconvergence trap. Then what guarantees that institutions and policies will change in a timely fashion? For example, Acemoglu and colleagues (2007) show that firms tend to decentralize more when they become more technologically advanced, and that this evolution towards more decentralization is also growth enhancing. Aghion, Alesina, and Trebbi (2008) show that more advanced countries tend to be more democratic, which again is a growth-enhancing dynamic pattern. However, institutional transition is not automatic. For example, some countries in continental Europe find it difficult to liberalize markets, particularly labor and services markets, or to reform their higher education system. Also, while Latin America and South Africa have managed to democratize, China has not. Will China eventually change its political regime? Will Japan become more open to trade? Will Korea reduce the power of its conglomerate firms?

More generally, what are the main obstacles to institutional change: Vested interests and the existing distribution of economic and/or political power? Beliefs about gains and losses from structural reforms? Is there a role for international incentives in prompting changes? To what extent can wars or economic and financial crises help reduce the power of vested interests? For example, it is argued that the financial crisis of the late 1990s stimulated reforms in Scandinavia and in Southeast Asia by weakening vested interests opposed to such reforms. Similarly, the crisis of 1929 and the two World Wars spurred entrepreneurship and growth in Europe during the postwar period by dramatically reducing the power of rentiers in European countries. It is also argued that the prospect of becoming members of the European Union has prompted structural reforms in Central Europe, and that the prospect of becoming a member of the World Trade Organization may foster democracy in China or Russia. This whole issue of institutional change awaits further investigation.

Appendix: Solving the Doepke-Zilibotti Model

The solution proceeds in two steps.

Step 1 The functional equation (18.2) has a unique fixed point, υ, and υ is separable in the two assets: $\upsilon(B, K) = \dfrac{1}{1-z} \log K + V(B).$[10] Moreover, the function $V(B)$ is convex in B, and the optimal policy functions $l(B)$ and $k(B)$ are continuous and nondecreasing in B, where we define $k \equiv K'/K$. The intuition for the convexity of V highlights the key properties of the model. Two features of the decision problem generate the convexity result. First, patience B enters utility linearly ($B[\log(c_2) - \log(c_1)]$; see equation (18.2). Second, there is a complementarity between patience and the choice of steep consumption profiles (higher saving implies a steeper consumption profile). To gain intuition, consider the decision problem if the consumption profile $\{c_1, c_2\}$ were exogenous and constant. (i.e., saving is fixed). In this case, if we vary B while holding the investment choice l constant over all generations, utility is a linear function of B. The reason is that initial utility is a linear function of present and future patience, and initial patience has a linear effect on future patience by means of the depreciation factor $1 - v$. Moreover, given the fixed income profile, choosing a constant l is optimal: the marginal return to investing in patience in a given period is given by $z\log(c_2/c_1)$, which does not depend on B. Generalizing from this observation, the value function is linear over any range of B such that it is optimal for the

---

10. A sketch of the proof goes as follows. We start by guessing that $\upsilon(B,K) = \dfrac{1}{1-z} \log(K) + V(B)$ and that V is strictly increasing and convex in B. Then, the Bellman equation can be written as

$$\upsilon(B,K) = \frac{1}{1-z}\log(K) + V(B) = \max_{l,k}\Big\{\log(K) + (1-B)\log\big[(1-\delta+A) - k\big] +$$
$$B\log(Ak) - l + \frac{z}{1-z}\Big(\big[\log(K) + \log((1-\delta)k)\big] + zV\big[(1-v)B + f(l)\big]\Big)\Big\}$$

subject to the set of relevant constraints. Subtracting from both sides of the expression $\log(K)$ and substituting in the constraints, we obtain $\upsilon(B,K) = \dfrac{1}{1-z}\log(K) + V(B)$ where

$$V(B) = \max_{\substack{l\in[0,1],\\ k\in[1-\delta,1-\delta+A]}} \Big\{(1-B)\log\big[(1-\delta+A) - k\big] + B\log(Ak)$$
$$+ \frac{z}{1-z}\big[\log((1-\delta)k)\big] - l + zV\big[(1-v)B + f(l)\big]\Big\}$$

current and future members of a dynasty to hold their savings level fixed. However, in general saving does vary with B, so that the consumption profile $\{c_1, c_2\}$ depends on patience. Given that B is the relative weight on utility late in life, it is optimal to choose high saving (and thus a steep lifetime consumption profile) when B is high. As we increase B, the slope of the value function therefore increases. The optimal l increases too, since the marginal benefit of being patient increases with the steepness of the wage profile. Thus the value function is convex.

Step 2   The growth rate of capital satisfies the following equation:

$$k = \max\left\{1-\delta, \left[(1-z)B+z\right](1-\delta+A)\right\} \tag{18.8}$$

To see this, take the first order condition with respect to K' in the maximization (18.2), after substituting for $V(B, K) = \dfrac{1}{1-z}\log K + V(B)$. We get:

$$\frac{1-B}{1-\delta+A-k} = \frac{B}{k} + \frac{z}{1-z}\frac{1}{k}$$

Rearranging terms (i.e., solving for k) and taking into account the irreversibility condition, yields equation (18.8).

Appendix: Basic Elements of Econometrics[1]

In this appendix we provide our readers with a few basic elements to understand the econometric tables of this book. For more details, we refer our readers to Wooldridge (2006) and Stock and Watson (2007).

A.1   The Simple Regression Model[2]

Let x and y be two variables, and suppose we are interested in *explaining y in terms of x,* or, in other words, to estimate how *y varies with changes in x.* For instance, y refers to the average growth rate of GDP in a country over a certain time period, and x refers to some explanatory factor, such as the average level of education in the country over the period. A simple way of writing such a relationship is with the equation

$$y = \beta_0 + \beta_1 x + u \tag{A.1}$$

which we refer to as *a simple linear regression* equation.

The right-hand-side variable x is called the *explanatory* (or *independent*) variable, whereas the left-hand-side variable y is called the *explained* (or *dependent*) variable. The variable u is called the *error term* or *disturbance* factors other than x that affect y.

For given value of u, β_1 is a slope parameter that measures the extent to which a change in x affects y. But to focus on this ceteris paribus effect of x on y, without having to deal with the effects of u, we need a restriction on the relationship between x and u. The restriction is simply to assume that x and u are uncorrelated; namely, if the former varies, then the latter does not, so that we can indeed look at the ceteris paribus effect of changes in x on y.

More formally, we assume that the average value of u does not depend on the value of x, namely,

$$E\left(u|x\right) = E(u) = 0$$

In other words, for any x, the average of the unobservables is the same: this is called the *zero conditional mean assumption.* The value of zero comes from a normalization; indeed, we can always rewrite the model, changing the intercept, so that this average becomes equal to zero.

Using this assumption, together with the linearity of the expectation operator, we have

---

1. This chapter was written making unrestrained use of notes by Leonardo Bursztyn.
2. The first four sections of this appendix draw on chapters 2, 3, and 4 of Wooldridge (2006).

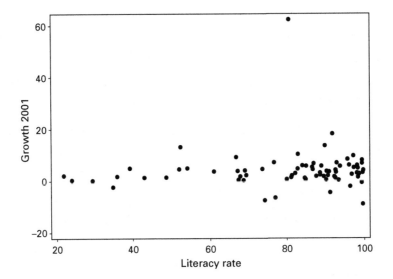

Figure A.1
Education (literacy rate) and growth, 2001 (World Development Indicators)

$$E(y|x) = \bar{y} = \beta_0 + \beta_1 x$$

which means that a one-unit increase in x changes the expected value of y by the amount β_1.

The problem is that we only observe a random sample of countries, and we do not observe the exact values of the coefficients β_0 and β_1 from the overall population of countries. How can we *estimate* these coefficients?

A.2   The Ordinary Least Squares Estimator

Consider a sample of countries indexed by i, each of them with two observable characteristics (say, their growth rate in 2001, y_i, and their education levels x_i, measured by their literacy rate). We can look at the scatter plot in figure A.1.

Remember that we are trying to estimate the coefficients β_0 and β_1 in order to understand how x explains y. Our estimates for these two coefficients will be denoted by $\hat{\beta}_0$ and $\hat{\beta}_1$. For each individual i, we can rewrite the relationship between the two variables as

$$y_i = \hat{\beta}_0 + \hat{\beta}_1 x_i + \hat{u}_i$$

The last term is called the *residual* for individual i. The amount $\hat{y}_i = \hat{\beta}_0 + \hat{\beta}_1 x_i$ is the *predicted* (or fitted) value of y when $x = x_i$ in the sample.

To get the best possible estimates, we want to get the predicted values as close as possible to the true value of the explained variable; in other words, we want to make the residuals as small as possible. Then, why not simply minimize the sum of the residuals over all pairs of observations (x_i, y_i)? The problem is that by doing so we might be canceling out positive and negative residuals. And at the end we may end up getting a low level for the sum even though the level of the residuals is generally high.

Thus, instead, econometricians choose to minimize the *sum of the squared residuals*. The result of this minimization is what we call the ordinary least squares (OLS) estimates for the coefficients of interest.

Note that once we get the estimate $\hat{\beta}_1$, we can easily compute the predicted change in y for any given change in x, namely,

$$\Delta\hat{y} = \hat{\beta}_1 \Delta x$$

We can also give a geometrical interpretation of the OLS estimator. The minimal distance between a vector y representing the dependent variable and a vector x representing the explanatory one is found by use of the orthogonal projection of y onto x, as shown in figure A.2.

How can we assess the "goodness of fit" of the regression, in other words, how well x explains y? We already know that

$$y_i - \hat{y}_i = \hat{u}_i$$

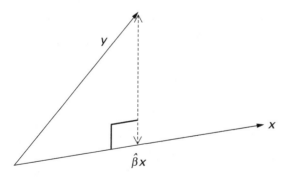

Figure A.2
Geometry of OLS

Let us define the *total sum of squares* $\text{SST} \equiv \sum_{i=1}^{n}(y_i - \bar{y})^2$. That the OLS estimates minimize the sum of squared residuals implies that the vector $(\hat{y}_i - \bar{y})_i$ is orthogonal to the vector $(\hat{u}_i)_i$, so that, by the Pythagorean theorem,

$$\text{SST} = \sum_{i=1}^{n}(\hat{y}_i - \bar{y})^2 + \sum_{i=1}^{n}\hat{u}_i^2$$

The first term on the right-hand side of this equation is the *explained sum of squares* (SSE), and the second term is the *residual sum of squares* (SSR). And SST measures the total sample variation in the dependent variable (how spread out it is in the sample).

The goodness of fit, called the R^2 (or *coefficient of determination*), is then simply defined by

$$R^2 = \text{SSE}/\text{SST}$$

This is simply the ratio of the explained variation compared to the total variation: it is the *fraction of the sample variation in y that is explained by x*. This ratio always lies between 0 and 1 because $\text{SSE} \leq \text{SST}$.

A.3   Multiple Regression Analysis

We can extend the simple regression model by adding explanatory variables on the right-hand side of the regression equation and thus explicitly controlling for many other factors that simultaneously affect the dependent variable.

For example, why assume that education is the only observable factor that affects growth? Competition, property-rights protection, financial development, and others are factors that are also relevant to the growth process.

We thus write

$$y = \beta_0 + \beta_1 x_1 + \beta_2 x_2 + \cdots + \beta_k x_k + u$$

Each β_j tells us about the effect on y of a change in x_j holding fixed all the other explanatory variables and the error term u. To extend the logic of the simple linear regression model, we make the zero-conditional-mean assumption:

$$E(u|x_1, x_2, \ldots, x_k) = 0$$

The OLS method estimates $\hat{\beta}_j$ again by minimizing the sum of the squared residuals $\hat{u}_i$, where

$$\hat{u}_i = y_i - \left[\hat{\beta}_0 + \hat{\beta}_1 x_{1,i} + \hat{\beta}_2 x_{2,i} + \cdots + \hat{\beta}_k x_{k,i} \right]$$

A simple interpretation of $\hat{\beta}_j$ is that it measures the impact of a unit change in x_j on y, namely,

$$\Delta \hat{y} = \hat{\beta}_j \Delta x_j$$

Dummy variables and interaction effects: If the explanatory variable is binary, we can create a *dummy variable* to compute its effect on the dependent variable. For instance, we could be interested in estimating the impact of being male on personal earnings. For that purpose, we create a dummy variable that has value one if the individual is male and zero otherwise. If we run a wage regression on that dummy variable, the interpretation on its coefficient will be exactly the one we are looking for.

Sometimes we might think that the effect of an explanatory variable on the dependent variable varies when the value of another variable changes. For instance, we could think that education matters more for growth the more democratic a country is. In this case, there is an *interaction effect* between education and democracy. The effect of education on growth varies with its degree of democratization. To estimate this effect, we create a variable given by the product of education with the degree of democratization, and we use the notation $*$ to write this product on the right-hand side of the regression equation; for example, we denote the interaction variable by $e * d$ if e denotes education and d denotes democracy. The interpretation of a coefficient of 0.01, for instance, will be that once the level of democratization is increased by one unit, the effect of one more unit of education on growth is increased by 0.01.

A.4 Inference and Hypothesis Testing

In order to test hypotheses about the parameters in the regression model, we need to know the distributions of the estimates $\hat{\beta}_j$. In turn we derive these distributions under the assumption that u is normally distributed in the population (*normality assumption*). Because of suitable properties of the normal distribution, it turns out that this implies that OLS-estimated coefficients will also be normally distributed (for a proof, look at the appendix to chapter 4 in Wooldridge 2006).

Then, even though the true β_j's are unknown, we can "hypothesize" about the value of these parameters and test such hypotheses based on the OLS estimates $\hat{\beta}_j$. Given that the sample estimates have sampling errors, the idea is pretty simple: is the observed estimate of a coefficient consistent with a formulated hypothesis about the true parameter?

For example, based on our sample and estimation, can we reject the hypothesis that the coefficient on a right-hand-side variable, say "competition," is different from zero in the total population of countries? In other words, can our regression tell us that competition indeed affects the predicted growth rate in the overall population of countries? If we can reject such a hypothesis, we say that the estimated coefficient is *significantly different from zero*, or *statistically significant*.

Now, an important result in statistics is that the ratio of an estimated coefficient to its standard error (a measure of the precision of its estimation) has a known distribution: the *t-distribution*. Thus by computing this ratio for a specific $\hat{\beta}_j$ we get the *t-statistic* for $\hat{\beta}_j$, which we denote by $t_{\hat{\beta}_j}$.

Before testing the null hypothesis that $\beta_j = 0$, we need to determine the *significance level* we are willing to work with. Loosely speaking, if we reject the hypothesis that $\beta_j = 0$ at the 5 percent significance level (the most commonly used one) there is a chance of 95 percent that the true parameter is actually different from zero. The lower the significance level at which we reject the hypothesis, the more confident we are that the true parameter is actually different from zero.

Under the hypothesis that $\beta_j = 0$, then, $t_{\hat{\beta}_j}$ has a t-distribution with zero mean. Under the alternative hypothesis that $\beta_j \neq 0$, the expected value of $t_{\hat{\beta}_j}$ is different from zero. Therefore, if the observed value of $t_{\hat{\beta}_j}$ is either sufficiently negative or sufficiently positive, we have evidence against the hypothesis that $\beta_j = 0$.

The rule of thumb that we use to determine the degree of significance of a regression coefficient is that a coefficient is statistically significant whenever its t-statistic (the ratio between its estimated value and its standard error) is greater than 2 or less than −2.

Thus in the following regression, where the standard error for each coefficient is put in parentheses right underneath the coefficient,

$$\widehat{\text{Growth}} = 0.66 + 0.0626 \times \text{Years\_of\_educ} + 0.0025 \times \text{Health}$$
$$\qquad\qquad (0.021) \qquad\qquad\qquad (0.024)$$

$$n = 408, \quad R^2 = 0.32$$

education is significant but health is not.

In many cases, instead of selecting a significance level a priori, we may choose to answer the question. Based on the observed value of the t-statistic, what is the *smallest* significance level at which the null hypothesis would be rejected? This level is known as the *p-value* of the test. For instance, if the p-value is less than 0.05, then null hypothesis is rejected at the 5 percent level. If it is greater than 0.05, it is not rejected at that level. The p-value summarizes the strength or weakness of the empirical evidence against the null hypothesis. The smaller its value, the greater is the strength of the evidence against the null hypothesis. In other words, a small value suggests that the coefficient is indeed statistically different from zero.

Finally, one can test for the hypothesis that *several* coefficients are simultaneously equal to zero. The relevant distribution here is the *F-distribution,* but the underlying logic is the same as before, with a high level of the computed *F-statistic* providing evidence against the null hypothesis that the coefficients are all equal to zero.

A.5   How to Deal with the Endogeneity Problem[3]

We raise the endogeneity problem in several chapters of the book—in particular, the chapter on finance, the chapter on democracy, and the chapter on education.

Remember the *zero conditional mean assumption,* whereby the average value u does not depend on the value of explanatory variables. It turns out that in many cases, this assumption is not satisfied. For example, suppose that the true model is

$$\text{Growth} = \beta_0 + \beta_1 \times \text{Education} + \beta_2 \times \text{Ability} + u$$

where we expect that in reality ability affects growth positively ($\beta_2 > 0$). Whenever the zero-conditional-mean assumption holds for an explanatory variable, we say it is *exogenous.* When this assumption does not hold, we say that the explanatory variable is *endogenous.* For example, the latter case occurs if ability is not fully observable and may be part of the error term u or may be correlated with education.

This first cause for endogeneity is referred to as the *omitted-variable bias.* How can we assess the bias? Suppose that education and ability are positively

3. This section draws on chapter 15 from Wooldridge (2006) and chapter 12 from Stock and Watson (2007).

correlated. In particular, if education is increased, so is ability—for example, as a result of selection by schools. Then, by not considering the effect of ability on growth, we assign an additional effect of education on growth that should have been attributed to ability instead.

Another potential source of endogeneity is the *reverse-causality problem:* namely, the left-hand-side variable may be affecting the level of the right-hand-side variable. For example, countries that grow faster can afford higher spending in education. In that case, we may end up overestimating the causal effect of education on growth (if the effect is positive in both directions).

This problem of reverse causality is quite pervasive. For example, suppose you are trying to assess the impact of slave trades on the economic development of African countries. You estimate

$$\text{GDP\_per\_capita}_i = \beta_0 + \beta_1 \text{Number\_of\_traded\_slaves}_i + u_i$$

for country i. What could possibly go wrong in this regression?

It may be that some countries display bad unobservable features (say, a distant history of wars) which made them poorer, and being poor in turn made these countries more prone to engaging in slave trades. By looking at β_1, we would not be simply measuring the impact of slave trades on economic development.

One way to deal with the endogeneity problem is to use *instrumental variables* (IV). A good instrumental variable is a variable that is correlated with the endogenous variable (*instrument relevance condition*), but not with the error term (*instrument exogeneity*), and we want such a variable to "replace" the original endogenous variable.

It is as if the endogenous variable x had two components: one component that is correlated with u (which causes the endogeneity problem) and a component that is uncorrelated with u. Using an IV amounts to only considering the exogenous component of x. In the previous example, when ability is omitted, education could have as instrument the number of siblings per individual (which affects the average level of education negatively, but is not correlated with ability). And the number of traded slaves could have as instrument the distance of each country to the major port outside of Africa where slaves were shipped to (see Nunn 2008).

In terms of the econometric technique, if the instruments satisfy both conditions, we proceed to the so-called *two-stage least squares* (2SLS) estimation method. The idea is fairly simple: suppose z is an instrument for x. In the *first stage,* we regress

$$x = \gamma_0 + \gamma_1 z + \varepsilon$$

using the OLS method. We thus obtain the part of x that is predicted by z and that is exogenous (since z is exogenous), namely,

$$\hat{x} = \hat{\gamma}_0 + \hat{\gamma}_1 z$$

We then replace x by $\hat{x}$ in the original regression, and run that regression

$$y = \delta_0 + \delta_1 \hat{x} + e$$

again using the OLS method. This is our *second stage*.

How can we check that these two conditions for instrument validity (namely, the relevance and the exogeneity conditions) are indeed satisfied? Here is how we proceed:

1. *Instrument relevance:*   When there is a single endogenous explanatory variable, one way to check for the relevance of the instruments is to test the hypothesis that the coefficients on the instruments for the variable are all zero in the first-stage regression, computing the F-statistic. As a rule of thumb, if the first-stage F-statistic is greater than 10, one should not worry about instrument relevance.

2. *Instrument exogeneity:*   When the number of instruments is equal to the number of endogenous explanatory variables being instrumented for, it is not possible to test the hypothesis that the instruments are exogenous. However, if there are more instruments than the number of endogenous explanatory variables, it is possible to test if the "extra" instruments are exogenous under the assumption that there are enough valid instruments to identify the coefficients of interest. This is called an *overidentifying restrictions test*.[4]

There are different ways of dealing with the endogeneity problem. In chapter 6 we present a paper by Rajan and Zingales (1998) that used cross-industry,

---

4. For example, suppose that we have two instruments (z_1 and z_2) for one endogenous explanatory variable (x). The idea of the test is fairly simple: we assume that one instrument is exogenous, and we test whether, conditional on this assumption, the other instrument is also exogenous. The underlying intuition for this test is the following: we could compute two different 2SLS estimators, one of which would take the first instrument as exogenous, the other estimator taking the second instrument as exogenous. If the second instrument is truly exogenous, the estimator from the second regression should be close to the estimator from the first regression. If the two instruments produce very different estimates, it is reasonable to conclude that one or both of these instruments are not exogenous. More generally, we proceed by getting the 2SLS residuals of the second-stage regression using all instruments and all exogenous variables and then by regressing those residuals on all instruments and exogenous variables. If the instruments are in fact exogenous, then their coefficients in the latter regression should all be zero. This is the hypothesis to be tested. The test statistic is commonly called the *J-statistic*.

cross-country data to assess the extent to which growth in industries that rely more heavily on external finance should benefit more from higher financial development than growth in industries that do not rely so much on external finance. The problem is to identify those industries that are more prone to rely on external finance than other industries. Here is where the endogeneity problem appears. To deal with it, the authors make use, as a control variable, of the interaction between financial development (measured by stock market capitalization plus domestic credit over GDP) in country i and industry k's dependence upon external finance (measured by the fraction of capital costs not financed internally in that same industry in the United States). The underlying idea is that firms are not financially constrained in the United States, so that this measure of external dependence can be thought of as being independent from financial development and to depend instead upon technological factors only.

Using a sample of 36 industries in 42 countries, Rajan and Zingales find an interaction coefficient between external dependence and their measure of financial development, which is positive and highly significant at the 1 percent level, thereby providing strong evidence to the effect that higher financial development enhances growth in industries that rely more heavily on external finance.

A.6 Fixed-Effects Regressions[5]

Consider, for example, the effect of income taxes on labor productivity, comparing different states of the United States. We want to estimate the regression

$$\text{Productivity}_i = \beta_0 + \beta_1 \times \text{Tax}_i + u_i$$

It might well be the case that, in addition to income taxes, other factors that vary across states could be affecting the level of labor productivity. If we observed these factors, we could control for them as additional explanatory variables. If not, we can still do something, if we think these omitted factors are constant over time.

More precisely, we can look at our observations in different periods of time, say from year 1 to year T, so that each observation refers to a specific state in a specific year. When we have observations for the same entities at two or more periods of time, we say we have *panel data*. Going back to our example, we can get over the problem of omitted variables by using what we call a *fixed-effects* regression model. The regression looks like

---

5. This section draws on chapter 10 from Stock and Watson (2007).

$$\text{Productivity}_{it} = \beta_0 + \beta_1 \times \text{Tax}_{it} + \alpha_1 \times \text{State}_1 + \alpha_2 \times \text{State}_2 + \cdots + \alpha_n \times \text{State}_n + u_{it}$$

Here, each State_j is a *dummy* (or binary) variable that is constant over time and has value one if the observation is in state j and value zero if not. These are called state fixed effects, because they vary across states but are the same (fixed) for each state across time.

Equivalently, for each state j, the regression line will be

$$\text{Productivity}_{it} = \beta_0 + \beta_1 \text{Tax}_{it} + \alpha_j$$

In other words, the fixed effects create a different intercept for the regression line corresponding to each state, which captures the omitted variables that are present in each state and that are constant over time. For state j, the intercept will be $\beta_0 + \alpha_j$. The slope coefficient will be the same for all states.

We can also control for fixed effects that are constant across entities but change over time: these are called time fixed effects. The idea is to create dummies that take value one if the observation is at a specific time period and zero otherwise, regardless of the location of the observation.

Sometimes, controlling for too many fixed effects destroys the significance of regression coefficients. This is the case, for example, when we control for country fixed effects in cross-country panel regressions of growth on education.

A.7   Reading a Regression Table

At this stage, the reader should be able to interpret a regression table.

We first present a table based on the paper by Acemoglu, Johnson, and Robinson (2001) described in chapter 17. Table A.1 presents the results from different regressions on the impact of institutions on per capita income. Institutions are measured by expropriation risk and instrumented by the log of settler mortatility. The idea is that in former colonies, wherever the initial disease conditions were particulary deleterious for settlements, colonizers focused their activity on extraction and expropriation activities, thereby generating worse institutions.

Let us focus on columns 1 and 3. The first column reports the OLS estimation (without the use of the proposed instrument). It is found that the quality of institutions (as measured inversely by expropriation risk) positively and significantly affects income per capita (at the 1 percent level). By looking at the third column, we observe that the coefficient on institutions for the 2SLS procedure is still significant (at the 5 percent level) and has a higher magnitude. This result suggests

Table A.1
Institutions and Income Per Capita, 1960–2000

	(1) OLS	(2) OLS (Sample of Former Colonies)	(3) 2SLS	(4) 2SLS (Controlling for Schooling)
			Panel A. Second-stage regressions	
Expropriation risk	0.293***	0.375***	0.663**	1.908
	(0.053)	(0.063)	(0.288)	(3.848)
Years of schooling				−0.551
				(1.539)
Observations	118	63	63	60
Adjusted R-squared	0.64	0.73		
Instrumented variable			Expropriation risk	Expropriation risk
Instrument			Log settler mortality	Log settler mortality
			Panel B. First-stage regressions	
Log settler mortality			−0.402**	−0.099
			(0.199)	(0.228)
R-squared			0.371	0.542
Observations			63	60

Dependent variable is log GDP per capita.
Columns 1–2 are OLS regressions where log GDP per capita is regressed on expropriation risk, latitude, and continent dummies, with column 2 including only the sample of former colonies. Columns 3–4 are 2SLS regressions where log GDP per capita is regressed on the same variables as in columns 1–2, but with expropriation risk instrumented by settler mortality. Column 4 also includes total years of schooling as a control. Robust standard errors in parentheses. *** $p < 0.01$, ** $p < 0.05$, * $p < 0.1$.

that the possible omitted variables in the OLS specification were likely to be biasing down the coefficient. By looking at the first-stage regression results in panel B for column 3, we observe that the proposed instrument (log settler mortality) affects the endogenous variable negatively and significantly (at the 5 percent level), with an adjusted R^2 of 0.371.[6]

Table A.2 is from the paper on financial development and convergence by Aghion, Howitt, and Mayer-Foulkes (2005), or AHM, discussed in chapter 7.

AHM test this effect of financial development on convergence by running the following cross-country growth regression:

$$g_i - g_1 = \beta_0 + \beta_f F_i + \beta_y \cdot (y_i - y_1) + \beta_{fy} \cdot F_i \cdot (y_i - y_1) + \beta_x X_i + \varepsilon_i \tag{A.2}$$

---

6. The adjusted R^2 is computed adjusting the original coefficient of determination by using unbiased estimators of the population variances of the dependent variable and the error term (see chapter 6 in Wooldridge 2006).

Table A.2
Growth, Financial Development, and Initial GDP Gap

Financial Development *(F)*	Private credit		
Conditioning Set *(X)*	Empty	Policy[a]	Full[b]
Coefficient estimates			
β_f	−0.015	−0.013	−0.016
	(−0.93)	(−0.68)	(−0.78)
β_y	1.507***	1.193*	1.131
	(3.14)	(1.86)	(1.49)
β_{fy}	−0.061***	−0.063***	−0.063***
	(−5.35)	(−5.10)	(−4.62)
Instrument test p-values			
First-stage *F*-test: F	0.0000	0.0014	0.0024
First-stage *F*-test: $F(y - y_1)$	0.0000	0.0000	0.0000
First-stage *F*-test: $L(y - y_1)$	0.0000	0.0000	0.0001
Sargan test	0.5372	0.7255	0.5573
C-test for $L(y - y_1)$	0.3773	0.7013	0.4654
C-test for $(y - y_1)$	0.6475	0.7790	0.7781
Sample size	71	63	63

The dependent variable $g - g_1$ is the average growth rate of per capita real GDP relative to the United States, 1960–95. F is average financial development 1960–95 using private credit as its measure and $y - y_1$ is the log of per capita GDP in 1960 relative to the United States.
[a]The policy conditioning set includes average years of schooling in 1960, government size, inflation, black market premium, and openness to trade.
[b]The full conditioning set includes the policy set plus indicators of revolutions and coups, political assassinations, and ethnic diversity. Estimation is by IV using L (legal origins) and $L(y - y_1)$ as instruments for F and $F(y - y_1)$. The numbers in parentheses are *t*-statistics. Significance at the 1%, 5%, and 10% level is denoted by ***, **, and *, respectively.

where g_i denotes the average growth rate of per capita GDP in country i over the period 1960–95, F_i the country's average level of financial development, y_i the initial (1960) log of per capita GDP, X_i a set of other regressors, and ε_i a disturbance term with mean zero. Country 1 is the technology leader, which they take to be the United States. Note that there is an interaction term $F_i \cdot (y_i - y_1)$ that allows one to assess how the effect of financial development on convergence varies with the initial GDP gap with respect to the United States.

The estimation uses the country's legal origins (summarized by three dummy variables) and its legal origins interacted with the initial GDP gap $(y_i - y_1)$, respectively as instruments for F_i and $F_i \cdot (y_i - y_1)$.

We will now interpret this table. We are trying to measure here the effect of financial development on convergence and how it varies according to the initial distance of the country's GDP to the American GDP. In the table, private credit is used as the measure of financial development. The second column controls for "policy" indicators, which include average years of schooling in 1960, government size, inflation, black market premium, and openness to trade. The coefficient β_f is not statistically significant; β_y is significant at the 10 percent level. The interpretation of the latter coefficient is that a higher level of initial GDP compared to the United States would translate into a higher average growth rate over the period also compared to the United States: an increase of one unit in the difference between country i's initial log GDP and the American one increases on average 1.193 percent of the difference in the average growth rate of country i compared to the American one over the period of interest. The coefficient β_{fy} is significant at the 1 percent level and is negative, which means that the likelihood of convergence will increase with financial development.

The table also provides p-values for instrument tests. The F tests for significance all yield highly significant results (p-values below 0.01), providing evidence in favor of the strength of the proposed instruments.

The Sargan and C tests are overidentifying restrictions tests. As mentioned in the section on IV estimation, we would want all the coefficients from the regression of the 2SLS residuals on all instruments and exogenous variables to be statistically insignificant. The high levels of the p-values for those tests indicate that we cannot reject such null hypothesis, which provides evidence that the instruments are not affecting growth through an omitted nonfinancial variable.

References

Abramovitz, M. (1986). "Catching Up, Forging Ahead, and Falling Behind." *Journal of Economic History*, 46, 385–406.

Acemoglu, D. (1997). "Training and Innovation in an Imperfect Labour Market." *Review of Economic Studies*, 64, 445–464.

Acemoglu, D. (1998). "Why Do New Technologies Complement Skills? Directed Technical Change and Wage Inequality." *Quarterly Journal of Economics*, 113, 1055–1090.

Acemoglu, D. (2002). "Technical Change, Inequality, and the Labor Market." *Journal of Economic Literature*, 40, 7–72.

Acemoglu, D. (2003a). "Patterns of Skill Premia." *Review of Economic Studies*, 70, 199–230.

Acemoglu, D. (2003b). "Labor and Capital-Augmenting Technical Change." *Journal of the European Economic Association*, 1, 1–37.

Acemoglu, D. (2008a). *Introduction to Modern Economic Growth.* Forthcoming.

Acemoglu, D. (2008b). "Oligarchic versus Democratic Societies." *Journal of the European Economic Association*, 6, 1–44.

Acemoglu, D., P. Aghion, C. Lelarge, J. Van Reenen, and F. Zilibotti. (2007). "Technology, Information, and the Decentralization of the Firm." *Quarterly Journal of Economics*, 4, 1759–1799.

Acemoglu, D., P. Aghion, and G. L. Violante. (2001). "Deunionization, Technical Change, and Inequality." Carnegie-Rochester Conference Series on Public Policy.

Acemoglu, D., P. Aghion, and F. Zilibotti. (2006). "Distance to Frontier, Selection, and Economic Growth." *Journal of the European Economic Association*, 37–74.

Acemoglu, D., and J. Angrist. (2000). "How Large Are Human Capital Externalities? Evidence from Compulsory Schooling Laws." *NBER Macroannual*, 9–59.

Acemoglu, D., and V. Guerrieri. (2006). "Capital Deepening and Non-Balanced Economic Growth." NBER Working Paper No. 12475.

Acemoglu, D., and S. Johnson. (2005). "Unbundling Institutions." *Journal of Political Economy*, 113, 949–995.

Acemoglu, D., S. Johnson, and T. Mitton. (2003). "Institutions and Market Structure." Mimeo, MIT.

Acemoglu, D., S. Johnson, and J. Robinson. (2005). "Institutions as a Fundamental Cause of Long-Run Growth." In P. Aghion and S. N. Durlauf. (Eds.), *Handbook of Economic Growth.* Amsterdam: Elsevier North-Holland.

Acemoglu, D., S. Johnson, J. Robinson, and P. Yared. (2005). "Income and Democracy." CEPR Discussion Paper No. 5273.

Acemoglu, D., and J. Linn. (2004). "Market Size in Innovation: Theory and Evidence from the Pharmaceutical Industry." *Quarterly Journal of Economics*, 119, 1049–1090.

Acemoglu, D., J. A. Robinson, and S. Johnson. (2001). "The Colonial Origins of Comparative Development: An Empirical Investigation." *American Economic Review*, 91, 1369–1401.

Acemoglu, D., J. A. Robinson, and S. Johnson. (2002). "Reversal of Fortune: Geography and Institutions in the Making of the Modern World Income Distribution." *Quarterly Journal of Economics*, 117, 1231–1294.

Acemoglu, D., J. A. Robinson, and S. Johnson. (2005a). "Institutions as a Fundamental Cause of Long-Run Growth." In P. Aghion and S. N. Durlauf (Eds.). *Handbook of Economic Growth.* Elsevier North-Holland, Amsterdam.

Acemoglu, D., J. A. Robinson, and S. Johnson. (2005b). "The Rise of Europe: Atlantic Trade, Institutional Change and Economic Growth." *American Economic Review*, 95, 546–579.

Acemoglu, D., and J. Ventura. (2002). "The World Income Distribution." *Quarterly Journal of Economics*, 117, 659–694.

Acemoglu, D., and F. Zilibotti. (1997). "Was Prometheus Unbound by Chance? Risk, Diversification, and Growth." *Journal of Political Economy*, 105, 709–775.

Acemoglu, D., and F. Zilibotti. (2001). "Productivity Differences." *Quarterly Journal of Economics*, 116, 563–606.

Aghion, P., A. Alesina, and F. Trebbi. (2004). "Endogenous Political Institutions." *Quarterly Journal of Economics*, 119, 565–611.

Aghion, P., A. Alesina, and F. Trebbi. (2008). "Democracy, Technology, and Growth." In E. Helpman (Ed.). *Institutions and Economic Performance*. Cambridge, MA: Harvard University Press.

Aghion, P., Y. Algan, and P. Cahuc. (2008). "Can Policy Interact with Culture? Minimum Wage and the Quality of Labor Relations." NBER Working Paper No. 14327.

Aghion, P., Y. Algan, P. Cahuc, and A. Shleifer. (2008). "Regulation and Distrust." Mimeo, Harvard University.

Aghion, P., G. M. Angeletos, A. Banerjee, and K. Manova. (2005). "Volatility and Growth: Financial Development and the Cyclical Behavior of the Composition of Investment." Mimeo, Harvard University.

Aghion, P., P. Bacchetta, R. Ranciere, and K. Rogoff. (2006). "Exchange Rate Volatility and Productivity Growth: The Role of Financial Development." CEPR Discussion Paper No. 5629.

Aghion, P., and A. Banerjee. (2005). "Volatility and Growth." Clarendon Lectures in Economics. Oxford, UK: Oxford University Press.

Aghion, P., A. Banerjee, and T. Piketty. (1999). "Dualism and Macroeconomic Volatility." *Quarterly Journal of Economics*, 114, 1359–1397.

Aghion, P., N. Bloom, R. Blundell, R. Griffith, and P. Howitt. (2005). "Competition and Innovation: An Inverted-U Relationship." *Quarterly Journal of Economics*, 120, 701–728.

Aghion, P., R. Blundell, R. Griffith, P. Howitt, and S. Prantl. (2004). "Entry and Productivity Growth: Evidence from Microlevel Panel Data." *Journal of the European Economic Association*, 2, 265–276.

Aghion, P., R. Blundell, R. Griffith, P. Howitt, and S. Prantl. (2006). "The Effects of Entry on Incumbent Innovation and Productivity." CEPR Discussion Paper No. 5323.

Aghion, P., and P. Bolton. (1997). "A Trickle Down Theory of Growth and Development." *Review of Economic Studies*, 64, 151–172.

Aghion, P., L. Boustan, C. Hoxby, and J. Vandenbussche. (2005). "Exploiting States' Mistakes to Identify the Causal Effect of Higher Education on Growth." Mimeo, Harvard University.

Aghion, P., R. Burgess, S. Redding, and F. Zilibotti. (2006). "The Unequal Effects of Liberalization: Evidence from Dismantling the License Raj in India." CEPR Discussion Paper No. 5492.

Aghion, P., M. Dewatripont, C. Hoxby, A. Mas-Colell, and A. Sapir. (2007). "Why Reform Europe's Universities?" Bruegel Policy Brief.

Aghion, P., M. Dewatripont, and P. Rey. (1999). "Competition, Financial Discipline, and Growth." *Review of Economic Studies*, 66, 825–852.

Aghion, P., and S. N. Durlauf (Eds.). (2005). *Handbook of Economic Growth*. Amsterdam: Elsevier North-Holland.

Aghion, P., J. Fedderke, P. Howitt, C. Kulatane, and N. Viegi. (2008). "Testing Creative Destruction in an Opening Economy: The Case of the South African Manufacturing Industries." Mimeo, Harvard University.

Aghion, P., and R. Griffith. (2005). *Competition and Growth: Reconciling Theory and Evidence*. Cambridge, MA: MIT Press.

Aghion, P., C. Harris, P. Howitt, and J. Vickers. (2001). "Competition, Imitation and Growth with Step-by-Step Innovation." *Review of Economic Studies*, 68, 467–492.

Aghion, P., C. Harris, and J. Vickers. (1997). "Competition and Growth with Step-by-Step Innovation: An Example." *European Economic Review, Papers and Proceedings*, 771–782.

Aghion, P., and P. Howitt. (1988). "Growth and Cycles through Creative Destruction." Mimeo, MIT.

Aghion, P., and P. Howitt. (1992). "A Model of Growth through Creative Destruction." *Econometrica*, 60, 323–351.

Aghion, P., and P. Howitt. (1998a). *Endogenous Growth Theory*. Cambridge, MA: MIT Press.

Aghion, P., and P. Howitt. (1998b). "On the Macroeconomic Effects of Major Technological Change." In E. Helpman (Ed.). *General Purpose Technologies and Economic Growth*. Cambridge, MA: MIT Press.

Aghion, P., and P. Howitt. (2006). "Joseph Schumpeter Lecture: Appropriate Growth Policy: A Unifying Framework." *Journal of the European Economic Association*, 4, 269–314.

Aghion, P., P. Howitt, and D. Mayer-Foulkes. (2005). "The Effect of Financial Development on Convergence: Theory and Evidence." *Quarterly Journal of Economics*, 120, 173–222.

Aghion, P., P. Howitt, and G. L. Violante. (2000). "General Purpose Technology and Within-Group Inequality." CEPR Discussion Paper No. 2474.

Aghion, P., P. Howitt, and G. L. Violante. (2002). "General Purpose Technology and Wage Inequality." *Journal of Economic Growth*, 7, 315–345.

Aghion, P., and E. Kharroubi. (2007). "Cyclical Budgetary Policy and Growth: A Sectoral Analysis. Mimeo, Harvard University.

Aghion, P., and I. Marinescu. (2007). "Cyclical Budgetary Policy and Economic Growth: What Do We Learn from OECD Panel Data?" Mimeo, Harvard University.

Aghion, P., and G. Saint-Paul. (1998). "Uncovering Some Causal Relationships between Productivity Growth and the Structure of Economic Fluctuations: A Tentative Survey." *Labour*, 12, 279–303.

Alesina, A., and D. Rodrik. (1994). "Distributive Politics and Economic Growth." *Quarterly Journal of Economics*, 109, 465–490.

Alesina, A., E. Spolaore, and R. Wacziarg. (2005). "Trade, Growth and the Size of Countries." In P. Aghion and S. N. Durlauf (Eds.). *Handbook of Economic Growth*. Amsterdam: Elsevier North-Holland.

Arestis, P., P. O. Demetriades, and K. B. Luintel. (2001). "Financial Development and Economic Growth: The Role of Stock Markets." *Journal of Money, Credit, and Banking*, 33, 16–41.

Arrow, K. J. (1962). "The Economic Implications of Learning by Doing." *Review of Economic Studies*, 29, 155–173.

Arrow, K. J. (1969). "Classificatory Notes on the Production and Transmission of Technological Knowledge." *American Economic Review, Papers and Proceedings*, 59, 29–35.

Arrow, K. J., and M. Kurz. (1970). *Public Investment, the Rate of Return and Optimal Fiscal Policy*. Baltimore: Johns Hopkins University Press.

Ashraf, Q., and O. Galor. (2008). "Malthusian Population Dynamics: Theory and Evidence." Working Papers 2008-6, Brown University, Department of Economics.

Atkinson, A. B., and J. E. Stiglitz. (1969). "A New View of Technological Change." *Economic Journal*, 79, 573–578.

Autor, D., A. Krueger, and L. Katz. (1998). "Computing Inequality: Have Computers Changed the Labor Market?" *Quarterly Journal of Economics*, 113, 1169–1214.

Azariadis, C., and A. Drazen. (1990). "Threshold Externalities in Economic Development." *Quarterly Journal of Economics*, 105, 501–526.

Banerjee, A., and E. Duflo. (2003). "Inequality and Growth: What Can the Data Say? *Journal of Economic Growth*, 8, 267–299.

Banerjee, A., and E. Duflo. (2005). "Growth Theory through the Lens of Development Economics." In P. Aghion and S. N. Durlauf (Eds). *Handbook of Economic Growth.* Amsterdam: Elsevier North-Holland.

Banerjee, A., and L. Iyer. (2005). "History, Institutions, and Economic Performance: The Legacy of Colonial Land Tenure Systems in India." *American Economic Review*, 95, 1190–1213.

Banerjee, A., and A. Newman. (1993). "Occupational Choice and the Process of Development." *Journal of Political Economy*, 101, 274–298.

Barlevy, G. (2007). "On the Cyclicality of Research and Development." *American Economic Review*, 97, 1131–1164.

Barro, R. J. (1990). "Government Spending in a Simple Model of Endogenous Growth." *Journal of Political Economy*, 98, 103–125.

Barro, R. J. (1996). "Democracy and Growth." *Journal of Economic Growth*, 1, 1–27.

Barro, R. J. (1997). *Determinants of Economic Growth: A Cross-Country Empirical Study.* Cambridge, MA: MIT Press.

Barro, R. J. (1999a). "The Determinants of Democracy." *Journal of Political Economy*, 107, S158–S183.

Barro, R. J. (1999b). "Laibson Meets Ramsey in the Neoclassical Growth Model." *Quarterly Journal of Economics*, 114, 1125–1152.

Barro, R. J., and J. W. Lee. (2000). "International Data on Educational Attainment Updates and Implications." NBER Working Paper No. 791.

Barro, R. J., N. G. Mankiw, and X. Sala-i-Martin. (1995). "Capital Mobility in Neoclassical Models of Growth." *American Economic Review*, 85, 103–115.

Barro, R., and X. Sala-i-Martin. (1991). "Convergence across States and Regions." *Brookings Papers on Economic Activity*, 1, 107–182.

Barro, R. J., and X. Sala-i-Martin. (1992a). "Convergence." *Journal of Political Economy* 100, 223–251.

Barro, R. J., and X. Sala-i-Martin. (1992b). "Public Finance in Models of Economic Growth." *Review of Economic Studies*, 59, 645–661.

Barro, R. J., and X. Sala-i-Martin. (1995a). *Economic Growth*. New York: McGraw-Hill.

Barro, R. J., and X. Sala-i-Martin. (1995b). "Technological Diffusion, Convergence and Growth." CEPR Discussion Paper No. 1255.

Barro, R. J., and X. Sala-i-Martin. (1997). "Technological Diffusion, Convergence, and Growth." *Journal of Economic Growth*, 2, 1–27.

Basu, S., and D. N. Weil. (1998). "Appropriate Technology and Growth." *Quarterly Journal of Economics*, 113, 1025–1054.

Baumol, W. (1967). "Macroeconomics of Unbalanced Growth: The Anatomy of Urban Crisis." *American Economic Review*, 57, 415–426.

Baumol, W. (1986). "Productivity Growth, Convergence and Welfare: What the Long Run Shows." *American Economic Review*, 76, 1072–1085.

Baumol, W., J. Blackman, S. A. Batey, and E. N. Wolff. (1989). *Productivity and American Leadership*. Cambridge MA: MIT Press.

Baumol, W., and E. N. Wolff. (1988). "Productivity Growth, Convergence and Welfare: Reply." *American Economic Review*, 78, 1155–1159.

Bean. C. R. (1990). "Endogenous Growth and the Procyclical Behaviour of Productivity." *European Economic Review*, 34, 355–363.

Beck, T., A. Demirgüç-Kunt, L. Laeven, and R. Levine. (2004). "Finance, Firm Size, and Growth." NBER Working Paper No. W10983.

Becker, G. (1964). *Human Capital.* New York: Columbia University Press.

Becker, G., K. Murphy, and R. Tamura. (1990). "Human Capital, Fertility and Economic Growth." *Journal of Political Economy*, 98, part 2, 513–537.

Benabou, R. (1996). "Inequality and Growth." In B. S. Bernanke and J. Rotemberg (Eds.). *NBER Macroeconomics Annual* 11. Cambridge, MA: MIT Press.

Benassy, J.-P. (1998). "Is There Always Too Little Research in Endogenous Growth with Expanding Product Variety?" *European Economic Review*, 42, 61–69.

Bencivenga, V. R., and B. D. Smith. (1993). "Some Consequences of Credit Rationing in an Endogenous Growth Model." *Journal of Economic Dynamics and Control*, 17, 97–122.

Benhabib, J., and M. M. Spiegel. (1994). "The Role of Human Capital in Economic Development: Evidence from Aggregate Cross-Country Data." *Journal of Monetary Economics*, 34, 143–173.

Benhabib, J., and M. M. Spiegel. (2005). "Human Capital and Technology Diffusion." In P. Aghion and S. N. Durlauf (Eds.). *Handbook of Economic Growth.* Amsterdam: Elsevier North-Holland.

Berman, E., J. Bound, and Z. Griliches. (1994). "Changes in the Demand for Skilled Labor within U.S. Manufacturing: Evidence from the Annual Survey of Manufacturers," *Quarterly Journal of Economics*, 109, 367–397.

Berman, N., L. Eymard, P. Aghion, P. Askhenazy, and G. Cette. (2007). "Credit Constraints and the Cyclicality of R&D: Lessons from French Firm-Level Panel Data." Mimeo, Banque de France.

Bernanke, B., and M. Gertler. (1989). "Agency Costs, Net Worth and Business Fluctuations." *American Economic Review*, 79, 14–31.

Bernanke, B., M. Gertler, and S. Gilchrist. (1999). "The Financial Accelerator in a Quantitative Business Cycle Framework." In J. Taylor and M. Woodford (Eds.). *Handbook of Macroeconomics.* Amsterdam: North-Holland.

Bils, M., and P. Klenow. (2000). "Does Schooling Cause Growth?" *American Economic Review*, 90, 1160–1183.

Blanchard, O. (1985). "Debt, Deficits, and Finite Horizons." *Journal of Political Economy*, 93, 223–247.

Blundell, R., R. Griffith, and J. Van Reenen. (1995). "Dynamic Count Data Models of Technological Innovation." *Economic Journal*, 105, 333–344.

Blundell, R., R. Griffith, and J. Van Reenen. (1999). "Market Share, Market Value and Innovation in a Panel of British Manufacturing Firms." *Review of Economic Studies*, 66, 529–554.

Blundell, R., and I. Preston. (1999). "Inequality and Uncertainty: Short-Run Uncertainty and Permanent Inequality in the US and Britain." Mimeo, University College, London.

Boyd, J. H., and E. C. Prescott. (1986). "Financial Intermediary-Coalitions." *Journal of Economic Theory*, 38, 211–232.

Bresnahan, T., and A. Gambardella. (1998). "The Division of Inventive Labor and the Extent of the Market." In E. Helpman (Ed.). *General Purpose Technologies and Economic Growth.* Cambridge, MA: MIT Press.

Bresnahan, T., and M. Trajtenberg. (1995). "General Purpose Technologies: Engines of Growth?" *Journal of Econometrics*, 65, 83–108.

Brock, W., and L. Mirman. (1972). "Optimal Economic Growth under Uncertainty: The Discounted Case." *Journal of Economic Theory*, 4, 497–513.

Broda, C., J. Greenfield, and D. Weinstein. (2006). "From Groundnuts to Globalization: A Structural Estimate of Trade and Growth." NBER Working Paper No. 12512.

Bruno, M. (1993). *Crisis, Stabilization and Economic Reform: Therapy by Consensus.* Oxford, UK: Clarendon Press.

Buonanno, P., C. Carraro, and M. Galeotti. (2003). "Endogenous Induced Technical Change and the Costs of Kyoto." *Resource and Energy Economics*, 25, 11–34.

Caballero, R. J., and M. Hammour. (1994). "The Cleansing Effects of Recessions." *American Economic Review*, 84, 1350–1368.

Caballero, R., and A. Jaffe. (1993). "How High Are the Giants' Shoulders? An Empirical Assessment of Knowledge Spillovers and Creative Destruction in a Model of Economic Growth." *NBER Macroeconomic Annual*, 15–74.

Canova, F., and A. Marcet. (1995). "The Poor Stay Poor: Nonconvergence across Countries and Regions." CEPR Discussion Paper No. 1265.

Card, D. (1996). "The Effects of Unions on the Structure of Wages: A Longitudinal Analysis." *Econometrica*, 64, 957–979.

Caselli, F. (2005). "Accounting for Cross-Country Income Differences." In P. Aghion and S. N. Durlauf (Eds). *Handbook of Economic Growth*. Amsterdam: Elsevier North Holland.

Casselli F., and J. Coleman. (2006). "The World Frontier Technology." *American Economic Review*, 96, 499–522.

Caselli, F., G. Esquivel, and F. Lefort. (1996). "Reopening the Convergence Debate: A New Look at Cross-Country Growth Empirics." *Journal of Economic Growth*, 1, 363–389.

Caselli, F., and N. Gennaioli. (2006). "Dynastic Management." CEP Discussion Paper No. 741.

Caselli, F, and J. Ventura. (2000). "A Representative Consumer Theory of Distribution." *American Economic Review*, 90, 909–926.

Caselli, F., and D. J. Wilson. (2004). "Importing Technology." *Journal of Monetary Economics*, 51, 1–32.

Cass, D. (1965). "Optimum Growth in an Aggregative Model of Capital Accumulation." *Review of Economic Studies*, 32, 233–240.

Cheng, L. K., and E. Dinopoulos. (1992). "Schumpeterian Growth and International Business Cycles." *American Economic Review, Papers and Proceedings*, 82, 409–414.

Coe, D. T., and E. Helpman. (1995). "International R&D Spillovers." *European Economic Review*, 39, 859–887.

Cohen, W. M., and D. A. Levinthal. (1989). "Innovation and Learning: The Two Faces of R&D." *Economic Journal*, 99, 569–596.

Comin, D. (2000). "An Uncertainty-Driven Theory of the Productivity Slowdown: Manufacturing." Mimeo, Harvard University.

Comin, D., and M. Gertler. (2006). "Medium-Term Business Cycles." *American Economic Review*, 96, 523–551.

Comin, D., M. Gertler, and A. M. Santacreu. (2008). "International Medium Term Business Cycles." Mimeo.

Comin, D., and S. Mulani. (2007). "A Theory of Growth and Volatility at the Aggregate and Firm Level." *Proceedings, Federal Reserve Bank of San Francisco*.

Corriveau, L. (1991). "Entrepreneurs, Growth and Cycles." PhD dissertation. University of Western Ontario.

Crépon, B., E. Duguet, and J. Mairesse. (1998). "Research, Innovation, and Productivity: An Econometric Analysis at the Firm Level." NBER Working Paper No. 6696.

Cummins, J. G., and G. L. Violante. (2002) "Investment-Specific Technical Change in the United States (1947–2000): Measurement and Macroeconomic Consequences." *Review of Economic Dynamics*, 5, 243–284.

Dasgupta, S. (2008). "Discounting Climate Change." *Review of Environmental Economics and Policy*, forthcoming.

Dasgupta, S., B. Laplante, H. Wang, and D. Wheeler. (2002). "Confronting the Environmental Kuznets Curve." *Journal of Economic Perspectives*, 16, 147–168.

Dasgupta, P., and J. Stiglitz. (1980). "Industrial Structure and the Nature of Innovative Activity." *Economic Journal*, 90, 266–293.

d'Autume, A., and P. Michel. (1994). "Education et Croissance." *Revue d.Économie Politique*, 104, 457–499.

David, P. A. (1990). "The Dynamo and the Computer: An Historical Perspective on the Modern Productivity Paradox." *American Economic Review*, 80, 355–361.

Deaton, A., and J. Dreze. (2002). "Poverty and Inequality in India: A Reexamination." Working Paper 107, Princeton University.

De Gregorio, J. (1996). "Borrowing Constraints, Human Capital Accumulation, and Growth." *Journal of Monetary Economics*, 37, 49–71.

DeLong, B. (1988). "Productivity Growth, Convergence and Welfare: Comment." *American Economic Review*, 78, 1138–1154.

Demirgüç-Kunt, A., and V. Maksimovic. (1998). "Law, Finance, and Firm Growth." *Journal of Finance*, 53, 2107–2137.

Denison, E. F. (1962). "Sources of Growth in the United States and the Alternatives before Us." Supplement Paper 13. Committee for Economic Development, New York.

Devereux, M., and B. J. Lapham. (1994). "The Stability of Economic Integration and Endogenous Growth." *Quarterly Journal of Economics*, 59, 299–305.

Dinopoulos, E., and C. Syropoulos. (2006). "Rent Protection as a Barrier to Innovation and Growth." *Economic Theory*, 32, 309–332.

Dinopoulos, E., and P. Thompson. (1998). "Schumpeterian Growth without Scale Effects." *Journal of Economic Growth*, 3, 313–335.

Dixit, A. K., and J. E. Stiglitz. (1977). "Monopolistic Competition and Optimum Product Diversity." *American Economic Review*, 67, 297–308.

Djankov, S, R. La Porta, F. Lopez-de-Silanes, and A. Shleifer. (2002). "The Regulation of Entry." *Quarterly Journal of Economics*, 117, 1–37.

Djankov, S., R. La Porta, F. Lopez-de-Silanes, and A. Shleifer. (2003). "Courts." *Quarterly Journal of Economics*, 118, 453–517.

Doepke, M., and F. Zilibotti. (2008). "Occupational Choice and the Spirit of Capitalism." *Quarterly Journal of Economics*, 123, 747–795.

Domar, E. D. (1946). "Capital Expansion, Rate of Growth, and Employment." *Econometrica*, 14, 137–147.

Dowrick. S., and D. Nguyen. (1989). "OECD Comparative Economic Growth, 1950–1985: Catch-up and Convergence." *American Economic Review*, 79, 1010–1030.

Drandakis, E., and E. Phelps. (1965). "A Model of Induced Invention, Growth and Distribution." *Economic Journal*, 76, 823–840.

Duflo, E. (2004). "The Medium Run Consequences of Educational Expansion: Evidence from a Large School Construction Program in Indonesia." *Journal of Development Economics*, 74, 163–197.

Durlauf, S., and P. Johnson. (1995). "Multiple Regimes and Cross-Country Growth Behavior." *Journal of Applied Econometrics*, 10, 365–384.

Easterly, W. (2005). "National Policies and Economic Growth." In P. Aghion and S. N. Durlauf (Eds.). *Handbook of Economic Growth*. Amsterdam: Elsevier North-Holland.

Easterly, W., and R. Levine. (1997). "Africa's Growth Tragedy: Policies and Ethnic Divisions." *Quarterly Journal of Economics*, 112, 1203–1250.

Eaton, J., and S. Kortum. (2001). "Technology, Trade, and Growth: A Unified Framework." *European Economic Review, Papers and Proceedings*, 45, 742–755.

Eaton, J., and S. Kortum. (2002). "Technology, Geography, and Trade." *Econometrica*, 70, 1741–1779.

Engerman, S. L., and K. L. Sokoloff. (1997). "Factor Endowments, Institutions, and Differential Growth Paths among New World Economies." In S. Haber (Ed.). *How Latin America Fell Behind*. Stanford, CA: Stanford University Press.

Engerman, S. L., and K. L. Sokoloff. (2000). "History Lessons: Institutions, Factor Endowments, and the Paths of Development in the New World." *Journal of Economic Perspective*, 14, 217–232.

Ethier, W. J. (1982). "National and International Returns to Scale in the Modern Theory of International Trade." *American Economic Review*, 72, 389–405.

Etro, F. (2004). "Innovation by Leaders." *Economic Journal*, 114, 281–303.

Evans, P. (1996). "Using Cross-Country Variances to Evaluate Growth Theories." *Journal of Economic Dynamics and Control*, 20, 1027–1049.

Evenson, R. E., and L. E. Westphal. (1995). "Technological Change and Technology Strategy." In T. N. Srinivasan and J. Behrman (Eds.). *Handbook of Development Economics*, vol. 3A. Amsterdam: Elsevier.

Fellner, W. (1961). "Two Propositions in the Theory of Induced Innovations." *Economic Journal*, 71, 305–308.

Fogel, K., R. Morck, and B. Yeung. (2008). "Big Business Stability and Economic Growth: Is What's Good for General Motors Good for America?" *Journal of Financial Economics*, forthcoming.

Fortin, N. M., and T. Lemieux. (1997). "Institutional Changes and Rising Wage Inequality: Is There a Linkage?" *Journal of Economic Perspectives*, 11, 75–96.

Francois, P., and H. Lloyd-Ellis. (2003). "Animal Spirits through Creative Destruction." *American Economic Review*, 93, 530–550.

Frankel, J., and D. Romer. (1999). "Does Trade Cause Growth?" *American Economic Review*, 89, 379–399.

Frankel, M. (1962). "The Production Function in Allocation of Growth: A Synthesis." *American Economic Review*, 52, 995–1022.

Freedom House. (2004). *Freedom in the World*. Website and book, Washington DC.

Freeman, C., J. Clark, and L. Soete. (1982). *Unemployment and Technical Innovation: A Study of Long Waves and Economic Development*. London: Francis Pinter.

Freeman, C., and C. Perez. (1988). "Structural Crises of Adjustment, Business Cycles and Investment Behaviour." In G. Dosi et al. (Eds.). *Technical Change and Economic Theory*. London: Francis Pinter.

Freeman, R. B. (1993). "How Much Has Deunionization Contributed to the Rise in Male Earnings Inequality?" In S. Danziger and P. Gottschalk (Eds.). *Uneven Tides: Rising Inequality in America*. New York: Russell Sage Foundation.

Gali, J., and M. Hammour. (1991). "Long-Run Effects of Business Cycles." Papers 540. Columbia University.

Galor, O. (2005). "From Stagnation to Growth: Unified Growth Theory." In P. Aghion and S. N. Durlauf (Eds.). *Handbook of Economic Growth*. Amsterdam: Elsevier North-Holland.

Galor, O., and O. Moav. (2000). "Ability Biased Technological Transition, Wage Inequality within and across Groups, and Economic Growth." *Quarterly Journal of Economics*, 115, 469–497.

Galor, O., and D. N. Weil. (2000). "Population, Technology and Growth: From the Malthusian Regime to the Demographic Transition." *American Economic Review*, 110, 806–828.

Galor, O., and J. Zeira. (1993). "Income Distribution and Macroeconomics." *Review of Economic Studies*, 60, 35–52.

Gancia, G. (2003). "Globalization, Divergence and Stagnation." IIES Seminar Paper 720.

Gancia, G., and F. Zilibotti. (2005). "Horizontal Innovation in the Theory of Growth and Development." In P. Aghion and S. N. Durlauf (Eds.). *Handbook of Economic Growth*. Amsterdam: Elsevier North-Holland.

Garcia-Peñalosa, C., and B. Koebel. (1998). "International Trade, Material Prices and Wages." Mimeo, Nuffield College, Oxford.

Geroski, P. (1995). *Market Structure, Corporate Performance and Innovative Activity*. Oxford, UK: Oxford University Press.

Gerschenkron, A. (1962). *Economic Backwardness in Historical Perspective: A Book of Essays*. Cambridge, MA: Belknap Press of Harvard University Press.

Glaeser, E., R. La Porta, F. Lopez-de-Silanes, and A. Shleifer. (2004). "Do Institutions Cause Growth?" *Journal of Economic Growth*, 9, 271–303.

Glomm, G., and B. Ravikumar. (1992). "Public versus Private Investment in Human Capital Endogenous Growth and Income Inequality." *Journal of Political Economy*, 100, 813–834.

Goldin, C., and L. M. Katz. (1998). "The Origins of Technology-Skill Complementarity." *Quarterly Journal of Economics*, 113, 693–732.

Goldin, C., and L. F. Katz. (1999). "The Returns to Skill across the Twentieth Century in the United States." NBER Working Paper No. 7126.

Goldsmith, R. W. (1969). *Financial Structure and Development*. New Haven, CT: Yale University Press.

Gordon, R. J. (1990). *The Measurement of Durable Goods Prices*. Chigaco: University of Chicago Press.

Gordon, R. J. (1999). "U.S. Economic Growth since 1870: One Big Wave?" *American Economic Review, Papers and Proceedings*, 89, 123–128.

Gottschalk, P., and R. Moffitt. (1994). "The Growth of Earnings Instability in the US Labour Market." *Brookings Papers on Economic Activity*, 2, 217–272.

Greenwood, J., and B. Jovanovic. (1990). "Financial Development, Growth, and the Distribution of Income." *Journal of Political Economy*, 98, 1076–1107.

Greenwood, J., and B. Smith. (1996). "Financial Markets in Development, and the Development of Financial Markets." *Journal of Economic Dynamics and Control*, 21, 145–181.

Greenwood, J., and M. Yorukoglu. (1997). "1974." *Carnegie-Rochester Series on Public Policy*, 46, 49–95.

Greif, A. (1994). "Cultural Beliefs and the Organization of Society: A Historical and Theoretical Reflection on Collectivist and Individualist Societies." *Journal of Political Economy*, 102, 912–950.

Greif, A. (2006). *Institutions and the Path to the Modern Economy*. New York: Cambridge University Press.

Griffith, R., S. Redding, and J. Van Reenan. (2004). "Mapping the Two Faces of R&D: Productivity Growth in a Panel of OECD Industries." *Review of Economics and Statistics*, 86, 883–895.

Griliches, Z. (1973). "Research Expenditures and Growth Accounting." In B. R. Williams (Ed.). *Science and Technology in Economic Growth*. New York: Macmillan.

Griliches, Z. (1979). "Issues on Assessing the Contribution of Research and Development to Productivity Growth." *Bell Journal of Economics*, 10, 92–116.

Griliches, Z. (1988). "Productivity Puzzles and R&D: Another Explanation." *Journal of Economic Perspectives*, 2, 9–21.

Griliches, Z. (1994). "Productivity, R&D, and the Data Constraint." *American Economic Review*, 84, 1–23.

Griliches, Z., and F. Lichtenberg. (1984). "R&D and Productivity Growth at the Industry Level: Is There Still a Relationship?" In Z. Griliches (Ed.). *R&D, Patents, and Productivity*. Chicago: University of Chicago Press.

Grossman, G., and E. Helpman. (1989). "Product Development and International Trade." *Journal of Political Economy*, 97, 1261–1283.

Grossman, G., and E. Helpman. (1991a). *Innovation and Growth in the World Economy*. Cambridge, MA: MIT Press.

Grossman, G. M., and E. Helpman. (1991b). "Quality Ladders in the Theory of Growth." *Review of Economic Studies*, 58, 43–61.

Grossman, G. M., and E. Helpman. (1991c). "Quality Ladders and Product Cycles." *Quarterly Journal of Economics*, 106, 557–586.

Grossman, G. M., and E. Helpman. (1991d). "Trade Knowledge Spillovers and Growth." *European Economic Review*, 35, 517–526.

Grossman, G., and E. Helpman. (1995). "Technology and Trade." In G. Grossman and K. Rogoff (Eds.). *Handbook of International Economics*, vol. 3. Amsterdam: Elsevier.

Grossman, G. M., and A. B. Krueger. (1991). "Environmental Impact of a North American Free Trade Agreement." NBER Working Paper No. 3914.

Grossman, G. M., and A. B. Krueger. (1995). "Economic Growth and the Environment." *Quarterly Journal of Economics*, 110, 353–377.

Grübler, A., and S. Messner. (1998). "Technological Change and the Timing of Mitigation Measures." *Energy Economics*, 20, 495–512.

Guiso, L., P. Sapienza, and L. Zingales. (2002). "Does Local Financial Development Matter?" NBER Working Paper No. 8922.

Guiso, L., P. Sapienza, and L. Zingales. (2005). "Does Culture Affect Economic Outcomes?" *Journal of Economic Perspectives*, 20, 23–48.

Gurley, J. G., and E. S. Shaw. (1955). "Financial Aspects of Economic Development." *American Economic Review*, 45, 515–538.

Ha, J. (2002). "From Factor Accumulation to Innovation: Sustained Economic Growth with Changing Components." Mimeo, Brown University.

Ha, J., and P. Howitt. (2006). "Accounting for Trends in Productivity and R&D: A Schumpeterian Critique of Semi-Endogenous Growth Theory." *Journal of Money, Credit, and Banking*, 39, 733–774.

Habakkuk, H. J. (1962). *American and British Technology in the Nineteenth Century: Search for Labor Saving Inventions*. Cambridge, UK: Cambridge University Press.

Hall, B. H., A. Jaffe, and M. Trajtenberg. (2000). "Market Value and Patent Citations: A First Look." NBER Working Paper No. W7741.

Hall, R. E. (1991). "Recessions as Reorganizations." *NBER Macroeconomics Annual*.

Hall, R. E., and C. I. Jones. (1999). "Why Do Some Countries Produce So Much More Output Per Worker Than Others?" *Quarterly Journal of Economics*, 114, 83–116.

Hansen, G., and E. Prescott. (2002), "Malthus to Solow." *American Economic Review*, 92, 1205–1217.

Hanushek, E. A., and L. Woessmann. (2007). "The Role of Education Quality for Economic Growth." Policy Research Working Paper Series 4122, World Bank.

Harbaugh, B., A. Levinson, and D. Wilson. (2002). "Reexamining the Empirical Evidence for an Environmental Kuznets Curve." *Review of Economics and Statistics*, 84, 541–551.

Harris, R. (1998). "The Internet as a GPT: Factor Market Implications." In E. Helpman (Ed.). *General Purpose Technologies and Economic Growth*. Cambridge, MA: MIT Press.

Harrod, R. F. (1939). "An Essay in Dynamic Theory." *Economic Journal*, 49, 14–33.

Hart, O. (1983). "The Market Mechanism as an Incentive Scheme." *Bell Journal of Economics*, 14, 366–382.

Hauk, E., and M. Saez-Marti. (2002). "On the Cultural Transmission of Corruption." *Journal of Economic Theory*, 107, 311–335.

Hausmann, R., and M. Gavin. (1996). "Securing Stability and Growth in a Shock Prone Region: The Policy Challenge for Latin America." InterAmerican Development Bank Working Paper 315.

Hausmann, R., and B. Klinger. (2006). "Structural Transformation and Patterns of Comparative Advantage in the Product Space." CID Working Paper no. 128, Harvard University.

Hausmann, R., and D. Rodrik. (2003). "Economic Development as Self-Discovery." *Journal of Development Economics*, 72, 603–633.

Hausmann, R., D. Rodrik, and A. Velasco. (2005). "Growth Diagnostics." Mimeo, Harvard University.

Heckman, J. J., L. Lochner, and C. Taber. (1998). "Explaining Rising Wage Inequality: Explorations with a Dynamic General Equilibrium Model of Labor Earnings with Heterogeneous Agents." *Review of Economic Dynamics*, 1, 1–58.

Helpman, E. (1993). "Innovation, Immitation, and Intellectual Property Rights." *Econometrica*, 61, 1247–1280.

Helpman, E. (Ed.). (1998). *General Purpose Technologies and Economic Growth*. Cambridge, MA: MIT Press.

Helpman, E. (2004). *The Mystery of Economic Growth*. Cambridge, MA: Belknap Press of Harvard University Press.

Helpman, E. (Ed.). (2008). *Institutions and Economic Performance*. Cambridge, MA: Harvard University Press.

Helpman, E., and M. Trajtenberg. (1998a). "A Time to Sow and a Time to Reap: Growth Based on General Purpose Technologies." In Helpman, E. (Ed.). *General Purpose Technologies and Economic Growth*. Cambridge, MA: MIT Press.

Helpman, E., and M. Trajtenberg. (1998b). "Diffusion of General Purpose Technologies." In E. Helpman (Ed.). *General Purpose Technologies and Economic Growth*. Cambridge, MA: MIT Press.

Heston, A., R. Summers, and B. Aten. (2002). "Penn World Table Version 6-1." Center for National Comparisons at the University of Pennsylvania (CICUP).

Hicks, J. (1932). *The Theory of Wages*. London: Macmillan.

Hicks, J. R. (1950). *A Contribution to the Theory of the Trade Cycle*. New York: Oxford University Press.

Hornstein, A., and P. Krusell. (1996). "Can Technology Improvements Cause Productivity Slowdowns?" *NBER Macroeconomics Annual*, 11, 209–259.

Hornstein, A., P. Krusell, and G. L. Violante. (2005). "The Effects of Technical Change on Labor Market Inequalities." In P. Aghion and S. N. Durlauf (Eds.). *Handbook of Economic Growth*. Amsterdam: Elsevier North-Holland.

Howitt, P. (1998). "Measurement, Obsolescence, and General Purpose Technologies." In E. Helpman (Ed.). *General Purpose Technologies and Economic Growth*. Cambridge, MA: MIT Press.

Howitt, P. (1999). "Steady Endogenous Growth with Population and R&D Inputs Growing." *Journal of Political Economy*, 107, 715–730.

Howitt, P. (2000). "Endogenous Growth and Cross-Country Income Differences." *American Economic Review*, 90, 829–846.

Howitt, P., and D. Mayer-Foulkes. (2005). "R&D, Implementation and Stagnation: A Schumpeterian Theory of Convergence Clubs." *Journal of Money, Credit and Banking*, 37, 147–177.

Hsieh, C.-T. (2002). "What Explains the Industrial Revolution in East Asia? Evidence from the Factor Markets." *American Economic Review*, 92, 502–526.

Hsieh, C.-T., and P. J. Klenow. (2007). "Misallocation and Manufacturing TFP in China and India." NBER Working Paper No. 13290.

Islam, N. (1995). "Growth Empirics: A Panel Data Approach." *Quarterly Journal of Economics*, 110, 1127–1170.

Jacoby, H. G. (1994). "Borrowing Constraints and Progress through School: Evidence from Peru." *Review of Economics and Statistics*, 76, 151–160.

Jayaratne, J., and P. E. Strahan. (1996). "The Finance-Growth Nexus: Evidence from Bank Branch Deregulation." *Quarterly Journal of Economics*, 111, 639–670.

Jones, C. (1997). "On the Evolution of the World Income Distribution." *Journal of Economic Perspectives*, 11, 19–36.

Jones, C. (1998). *Introduction to Economic Growth*. New York: W.W Norton.

Jones, C. (2008). "Intermediate Goods, Weak Links, and Superstars: A Theory of Economic Development." Mimeo, UC Berkeley.

Jones, C. I. (1995a). "Time Series Tests of Endogenous Growth Models." *Quarterly Journal of Economics*, 110, 495–525.

Jones, C. I. (1995b). "R&D-Based Models of Economic Growth." *Journal of Political Economy*, 103, 759–784.

Jones, C. I. (2005). "Growth and Ideas." In P. Aghion and S. N. Durlauf (Eds.). *Handbook of Economic Growth*. Amsterdam: Elsevier North-Holland.

Jones, C. I. (1999). "Growth: With or without Scale Effects." *American Economic Review*, 89, 139–144.

Jones, L. E., and R. E. Manuelli. (2005). "Neoclassical Models of Endogenous Growth: The Effects of Fiscal Policy, Innovation, and Fluctuations." In P. Aghion and S. N. Durlauf (Eds.). *Handbook of Economic Growth*. Amsterdam: Elsevier North-Holland.

Jones, L., R. Manuelli, and E. Stacchetti. (2000). "Technology and Policy Shocks in Models of Endogenous Growth." Federal Reserve Bank of Minneapolis Working Paper 281.

Jorgenson, D. W. (1995). *Productivity*. Cambridge, MA: MIT Press.

Jorgenson, D. W. (2005). "Accounting for Growth in the Information Age." In P. Aghion and S. N. Durlauf (Eds.). *Handbook of Economic Growth*. Amsterdam: Elsevier North-Holland.

Jorgenson, D. W., and B. M. Fraumeni. (1992). "Investment in Education and US Economic Growth." *Scandinavian Journal of Economics*, 94, 51–70.

Jorgenson, D. W., and Z. Griliches. (1967). "The Explanation of Productivity Change." *Review of Economic Studies* 34, 249–280.

Jovanovic, B., and R. Rob. (1990). "Long Waves and Short Waves: Growth through Intensive and Extensive Search." *Econometrica*, 58, 1391–1409.

Jovanovic, B., and P. L. Rousseau. (2002). "Moore's Law and Learning-by-Doing." *Review of Economic Dynamics*, 5, 356–375.

Jovanovic, B., and P. L. Rousseau. (2005). "General Purpose Technologies." In P. Aghion and S. Durlauf (Eds.). *Handbook of Economic Growth*. Amsterdam: Elsevier North-Holland.

Judd, K. L. (1985). "On the Performance of Patents." *Econometrica*, 53, 567–585.

Katz, L., and D. Autor. (1999). "Changes in the Wage Structure and Earnings Inequality." In Ashenfelter, O. and E. Card (Eds.). *Handbook of Labor Economics*. Amsterdam: Elsevier North-Holland.

Katz, L., and K. Murphy. (1992). "Changes in Relative Wages: Supply and Demand Factors." *Quarterly Journal of Economics*, 105, 35–78.

Keller, W. (2002). "Technology Diffusion and the World Distribution of Income: The Role of Geography, Language, and Trade." University of Texas, unpublished.

Keller, W. (2004). "International Technology Diffusion." *Journal of Economic Literature*, 42, 752–782.

Kendrick, J. W. (1961). *Productivity Trends in the United States*. Princeton, NJ: Princeton University Press.

Kennedy, C. (1964). "Induced Bias in Innovation and the Theory of Distribution." *Economic Journal*, 74, 541–547.

Kiley, M. (1999). "The Supply of Skilled Labor and Skill-Biased Technological Progress." *Economic Journal*, 109, 708–724.

King, R. G., and R. Levine. (1993a). "Finance and Growth: Schumpeter Might Be Right." *Quarterly Journal of Economics*, 108, 717–738.

King, R. G., and R. Levine. (1993b). "Finance, Entrepreneurship, and Growth: Theory and Evidence." *Journal of Monetary Economics*, 32, 513–542.

King, R. G., and R. Levine. (1994). "Capital Fundamentalism, Economic Development, and Economic Growth." *Carnegie-Rochester Conference Series on Public Policy*, 40, 259–292.

King, R. G., and S. Rebelo. (1986). "Business Cycles with Endogenous Growth." Mimeo.

King, R. G., and S. Rebelo. (1990). "Public Policy and Economic Growth: Developing Neoclassical Implications." *Journal of Political Economy*, 98, S126–S150.

Klenow, P. J., and A. Rodriguez-Clare. (1997). "The Neoclassical Revival in Growth Economics: Has It Gone Too Far?" In B. S. Bernanke and J. J. Rotemberg (Eds.). *NBER Macroeconomics Annual, 1997*. Cambridge, MA: MIT Press.

Knack, S., and P. Keefer. (1997). "Does Social Capital Have an Economic Payoff? A Cross-Country Comparison." *Quarterly Journal of Economics*, 112, 1251–1288.

Knight, M., N. Loayza, and D. Villanueva. (1993). "Testing the Neoclassical Theory of Economic Growth." *IMF Staff Papers*, 40, 512–541.

Kondratieff, N. (1925). *The Long Wave Cycle*. New York: Richardson and Snyder.

Kongsamut, P., S. Rebelo, and D. Xie. (2001). "Beyond Balanced Growth." *Review of Economic Studies*, 68, 869–882.

Koopmans, T. C. (1965). "On the Concept of Optimal Economic Growth." In *The Econometric Approach to Development Planning*. Amsterdam: North-Holland.

Koren, M., and S. Tenreyro. (2007). "Volatility and Development." *Quarterly Journal of Economics*, 122, 233–287.

Kortum, S. (1997). "Research, Patenting, and Technological Change." *Econometrica*, 65, 1389–1419.

Krebs, T. (2003). "Growth and Welfare Effects of Business Cycles in Economies with Idiosyncratic Human Capital Risk." *Review of Economic Dynamics*, 6, 846–868.

Kremer, M. (1993a). "The O-Ring Theory of Economic Development." *Quarterly Journal of Economics*, 108, 551–575.

Kremer, M. (1993b). "Population Growth and Technological Change: One Million B.C. to 1990." *Quarterly Journal of Economics*, 108, 681–716.

Kremer, M. (1998). "Patent Buyouts: A Mechanism for Encouraging Innovation." *Quarterly Journal of Economics*, 113, 1137–1167.

Krueger, A., and M. Lindahl. (2001). "Education for Growth: Why and for Whom?" *Journal of Economic Literature*, 39, 1101–1136.

Krugman, P. (1987). "The Narrow Moving Band, the Dutch Disease, and the Competitive Consequences of Mrs. Thatcher: Notes on Trade in the Presence of Dynamic Scale Economies." *Journal of Development Economics*, 27, 41–55.

Krusell, P., L. E. Ohanian, J.-V. Rios-Rull, and G. L. Violante. (2000). "Capital-Skill Complementarity and Inequality: A Macroeconomic Analysis." *Econometrica*, 68, 1029–1053.

Kunieda, T. (2008). Macroeconomics for Credit Market Imperfections and Heterogeneous Agents. PhD dissertation, Brown University.

Kydland, F. E., and E. C. Prescott. (1982). "Time to Build and Aggregate Fluctuations." *Econometrica*, 50, 1345–1370.

Laibson, D. (1997). "Golden Eggs and Hyperbolic Discounting." *Quarterly Journal of Economics*, 112, 443–477.

Laincz, C. A., and P. F. Peretto. (2004). "Scale Effects in Endogenous Growth Theory: An Error of Aggregation, Not Specification." Mimeo.

La Porta, R., F. Lopez-de-Silanes, A. Shleifer, and R. W. Vishny. (1998). "Law and Finance." *Journal of Political Economy*, 106, 1113–1155.

La Porta, R., F. Lopez-de-Silanes, A. Shleifer, and R. W. Vishny. (1999). "The Quality of Government." *Journal of Law, Economics, and Organization*, 15, 222–279.

Levine, R. (1998). "The Legal Environment, Banks, and Long-Run Economic Growth." *Journal of Money, Credit and Banking*, 30, 596–613.

Levine, R. (1999). "Law, Finance, and Economic Growth." *Journal of Financial Intermediation*, 8, 8–35.

Levine, R. (2005). "Finance and Growth: Theory and Evidence." In P. Aghion and S. N. Durlauf (Eds.). *Handbook of Economic Growth*. Amsterdam: Elsevier North-Holland.

Levine, R., N. Loayza, and T. Beck. (2000). "Financial Intermediation and Growth: Causality and Causes." *Journal of Monetary Economics*, 46, 31–77.

Levine, R., and S. Zervos. (1998). "Stock Markets, Banks, and Economic Growth." *American Economic Review*, 88, 537–558.

Lipsey, R., and C. Bekar. (1995). "A Structuralist View of Technical Change and Economic Growth." *Bell Canada Papers on Economic and Public Policy*, 3, 9–75.

Lipsey, R., C. Bekar, and K. Carlaw. (1998). "What Requires Explanation." In E. Helpman (Ed.). *General Purpose Technologies and Economic Growth*. Cambridge, MA: MIT Press.

Lipsey, R., K. Carlaw, and C. Bekar. (2005). *Economic Transformations: General Purpose Technologies and Long-term Economic Growth*. Oxford, UK: Oxford University Press.

Long, J. B., and C. I. Plosser. (1983). "Real Business Cycles." *Journal of Political Economy*, 91, 39–69.

Lucas, R. E., Jr. (1988). "On the Mechanics of Economic Development." *Journal of Monetary Economics*, 22, 3–42.

Lucas, R. E., Jr. (1990). "Why Doesn't Capital Flow from Rich to Poor Countries?" *American Economic Review*, 80, 92–96.

Lucas, R. E., Jr. (1993). "Making a Miracle." *Econometrica*, 61, 251–272.

Machin, S. (1996). "Wage Inequality in the UK." *Oxford Review of Economic Policy*, 12, 47–64.

Machin, S. (1997). "The Decline of Labor Market Institutions and the Rise in Wage Inequality in Britain." *European Economic Review*, 41, 647–657.

Maddison, A. (2001). "The World Economy: A Millennial Perspective." Development Centre Studies. Paris: OECD.

Malthus, T. R. (1798). *An Essay on the Principle of Population.* Printed for J. Johnson, in St. Paul's Church-Yard, London.

Mankiw, N. G., P. Romer, and D. N. Weil. (1992). "A Contribution to the Empirics of Economic Growth." *Quarterly Journal of Economics*, 107, 407–437.

Manne, A. S., and R. G. Richels. (2004). "The Impact of Learning-by-Doing on the Timing and Costs of CO_2 Abatement." *Energy Economics*, 26, 603–619.

Manzocchi, S., and P. Martin. (1996). "Are Capital Flows Consistent with the Neoclassical Growth Model? Evidence from a Cross-Section of Developing Courtries." CEPR Discussion Paper No. 1400.

Marshall, M.G., and K. Jaggers. (2004). "Political Regime Characteristics and Transitions, 1800–2002." Polity IV Project, University of Maryland.

Maskin, E. (1999). "Nash Equilibrium and Welfare Optimality." *Review of Economic Studies*, 66, 23–38.

Matsuyama, K. (1992). "Agricultural Productivity, Comparative Advantage, and Economic Growth." *Journal of Economic Theory*, 58, 317–334.

Mayer-Foulkes, D. (2002). "Global Divergence." Documento de Trabajo del CIDE, SDTE.

McHugh, R., and J. Lane. (1987). "The Age of Capital, the Age of Utilized Capital, and Tests of the Embodiment Hypothesis." *Review of Economics and Statistics*, 69, 362–367.

McKinnon, R. I. (1973). *Money and Capital in Economic Development.* Washington, DC: Brookings Institution.

Melitz, M. (2003). "The Impact of Trade on Intra-industry Reallocations and Aggregate Industry Productivity." *Econometrica*, 71, 1695–1725.

Messner, S. (1997). "Endogenized Technological Learning in an Energy Systems Model." *Journal of Evolutionary Economics*, 7, 291–313.

Miklós, K., and S. Tenreyro. (2007). "Volatility and Development." *Quarterly Journal of Economics*, 122, 243–287.

Mincer, J. (1974). *Schooling, Experience and Earnings.* New York: Columbia University Press (for NBER).

Mokyr, J. (1990). *The Lever of Riches: Technological Creativity and Economic Progess.* Oxford, UK: Oxford University Press.

Mokyr, J. (2005). "Long-Term Economic Growth and the History of Technology." In P. Aghion and S. N. Durlauf (Eds.). *Handbook of Economic Growth.* Amsterdam: Elsevier North-Holland.

Mokyr, J., and H. J. Voth. (2006). "Understanding Growth in Europe, 1700–1870: Theory and Evidence." Dynamics, Economic Growth, and International Trade Conference Papers c011_002.

Moore, J., and R. Repullo. (1986). "Subgame Perfect Implementation." *Econometrica*, 56, 1191–1220.

Mulligan, C., R. Gil, and X. Sala-i-Martin. (2004). "Do Democracies Have Different Public Policies Than Nondemocracies?" *Journal of Economic Perspectives*, 18, 51–74.

Murphy, K., and F. Welch. (1992). "The Structure of Wages." *Quarterly Journal of Economics*, 107, 255–285.

Nelson, R., and E. Phelps. (1966). "Investment in Humans, Technological Diffusion, and Economic Growth." *American Economic Review*, 61, 69–75.

Nelson, R. R. (1959). "The Simple Economics of Basic Scientific Research." *Journal of Political Economy*, 77, 297–306.

Newell, R. G., A. B. Jaffe, and R. N. Stavins. (1999). "The Induced Innovation Hypothesis and Energy-Saving Technological Change." *Quarterly Journal of Economics*, 114, 941–975.

Nickell, S. J. (1996). "Competition and Corporate Performance." *Journal of Political Economy*, 104, 724–746.

Nicoletti, G., and S. Scarpetta. (2003). "Regulation, Productivity, and Growth: OECD Evidence." Policy Research Working Paper Series 2944, World Bank.

Nordhaus, W. D. (1974). "Resources as a Constraint on Growth." *American Economic Review*, 64, 22–26.

Nordhaus, W. D. (1977). "Economic Growth and Climate: The Case of Carbon Dioxide." *American Economic Review*, May.

Nordhaus, W. D. (1993). "Optimal Greenhouse-Gas Reductions and Tax Policy in the DICE Model." *American Economic Review*, 83, 313–317.

Nordhaus, W. D. (2002). "Modeling Induced Innovation in Climate-Change Policy." In A. Grübler, N. Nakicenovic, and W. D. Nordhaus (Eds.). *Technological Change and the Environment*. Washington, DC: Resources for the Future.

North, D. C. (1981). *Structure and Change in Economic History*. New York: W. W. Norton.

North, D. C. (1990). *Institutions, Institutional Change, and Economic Performance*. New York: Cambridge University Press.

North, D. C., and R. P. Thomas. (1973). *The Rise of the Western World: A New Economic History*. Cambridge, UK: Cambridge University Press.

Nunn, N. (2008). "The Long Term Effects of Africa's Slave Trades." *Quarterly Journal of Economics*, 123, 139–176.

Peretto, P. (1998). "Technological Change and Population Growth." *Journal of Economic Growth*, 3, 283–311.

Perotti, E., and E. Volpin. (2006). "Investor Protection and Entry." Mimeo.

Persson, T., and G. Tabellini. (1994). "Is Inequality Harmful for Growth?" *American Economic Review*, 84, 600–621.

Persson, T., and G. Tabellini. (2000). *Political Economics—Explaining Economic Policy*. Cambridge, MA: MIT Press.

Persson, T., and G. Tabellini. (2003). *The Economic Effects of Constitutions*. Cambridge, MA: MIT Press.

Phelps, E. S. (1962). "The Accumulation of Risky Capital: A Sequential Utility Analysis." *Econometrica*, 30, 729–743.

Piketty, T. (1997). "The Dynamics of Wealth Distribution and the Interest Rate with Credit Rationing." *Review of Economic Studies*, 64, 173–189.

Popp, D. (2002). "Induced Innovation and Energy Prices." *American Economic Review*, 92, 160–180.

Popp, D. (2004). "ENTICE: Endogenous Technological Change in the DICE Model of Global Warming." *Journal of Environmental Economics and Management*, 48, 742–768.

Porter, M. (1990). *The Competitive Advantage of Nations*. New York: Free Press.

Prescott, E. (1998). "Needed: A Theory of Total Factor Productivity." *International Economic Review*, 39, 525–551.

Prescott, E. C. (2004). "Why Do Americans Work So Much More Than Europeans?" *Federal Reserve Bank of Minneapolis Quarterly Review*, 28, 2–13.

Pritchett, L. (1997). "Divergence, Big Time." *Journal of Economics Perspectives*, 11, 3–17.

Pritchett, L. (2000). "The Tyranny of Concepts: CUDIE (Cumulated, Depreciated, Investment Effort) Is Not Capital." *Journal of Economic Growth*, 5, 361–384.

Przeworski, A., and F. Limongi. (1993). "Political Regimes and Economic Growth." *Journal of Economic Perspectives*, 7, 51–69.

Quah, D. (1993). "Galton's Fallacy and Tests of the Convergence Hypothesis." *Scandinavian Journal of Economics*, 95, 427–444.

Quah, D. (1997). "Empirics for Growth and Distribution: Polarization, Stratification, and Convergence Clubs." *Journal of Economic Growth*, 2, 27–59.

Quah, D. T. (1996). "Twin Peaks: Growth and Convergence in Models of Distribution Dynamics." *Economic Journal*, 106, 1045–1055.

Rajan, R. G., and L. Zingales. (1998). "Financial Dependence and Growth." *American Economic Review*, 88, 559–586.

Ramey, G., and V. Ramey. (1995). "Cross-Country Evidence on the Link between Volatility and Growth." *American Economic Review*, 85, 1138–1151.

Ramsey, F. (1928). "A Mathematical Theory of Saving." *Economic Journal*, 38, 543–559.

Rebelo, S. (1991). "Long-Run Policy Analysis and Long-Run Growth." *Journal of Political Economy*, 99, 500–521.

Redding, S. (1996). "The Low-Skill, Low-Quality Trap: Strategic Complementarities between Human Capital and R&D." *Economic Journal*, 106, 458–470.

Reinganum, J. F. (1989). "The Timing of Innovation: Research, Development and Diffusion." In R. Schmalensee and R. D. Willig (Eds.). *Handbook of Industrial Organization*, vol. 1. New York: North-Holland.

Rivera-Batiz, L., and P. Romer. (1991). "Economic Integration and Endogenous Growth." *Quarterly Journal of Economics*, 106, 531–555.

Rodrik, D., and A. Subramanian. (2004). "From Hindu Growth to Productivity Surge: The Mystery of the Indian Growth Transition." CEPR Discussion Paper No. 4371.

Romer, P. (1986). "Increasing Returns and Long-Run Growth." *Journal of Political Economy*, 94, 1002–1037.

Romer, P. (1987). "Growth Based on Increasing Returns Due to Specialization." *American Economic Review*, 77, 56–62.

Romer, P. (1990). "Endogenous Technological Change." *Journal of Political Economy*, 98, 71–102.

Rothschild, M., and J. E. Stiglitz. (1976). "Equilibrium in Competitive Insurance Markets: An Essay on the Economics of Imperfect Information." *Quarterly Journal of Economics*, 90, 629–649.

Rousseau, P. L., and P. Wachtel. (1998). "Financial Intermediation and Economic Performance: Historical Evidence from Five Industrial Countries." *Journal of Money, Credit and Banking*, 30, 657–678.

Rousseau, P. L., and P. Wachtel. (2000). "Equity Markets and Growth: Cross-Country Evidence on Timing and Outcomes, 1980–1995." *Journal of Business and Finance*, 24, 1933–1957.

Rubinstein, Y., and D. Tsiddon. (1999). "Coping with Technological Progress: The Role of Ability in Making Inequality So Persistent." Mimeo, Tel Aviv University.

Sachs, J., and A. Warner. (1995). "Economic Reform and the Progress of Global Integration." *Brookings Papers on Economic Activity*, 1, 1–118.

Sachs, J. D. (2001). "Tropical Underdevelopment." NBER Working Paper No. 8933.

Saint-Paul, G. (1993). "Productivity Growth and the Structure of the Business Cycle." *European Economic Review*, 37, 861–883.

Sala-i-Martin, X. (2006). "The World Distribution of Income: Falling Poverty and Convergence, Period." *Quarterly Journal of Economics*, 121, 351–397.

Salop, S. (1977). "The Noisy Monopolist: Imperfect Information, Price Dispersion, and Price Discrimination." *Review of Economic Studies*, 44, 393–406.

Samuelson, P. (1965). "A Theory of Induced Innovations along Kennedy-Weizsacker Lines." *Review of Economics and Statistics*, 47, 444–464.

Scherer, F. (1967). "Market Structure and the Employment of Scientists and Engineers." *American Economic Review*, 57, 524–531.

Schmidt, K. M. (1997). "Managerial Incentives and Product Market Competition." *Review of Economic Studies*, 64, 191–213.

Schmookler, J. (1966). *Invention and Economic Growth*. Cambridge, MA: Harvard Univeristy.

Schumpeter, J. A. (1912). *Theorie der Wirtschaftlichen Entwicklung*. Leipzig: Dunker & Humblot.

Schumpeter, J. A. (1942). *The Theory of Economic Development*, Cambridge, MA: Harvard University Press.

Segerstrom, P. S. (1998). "Endogenous Growth without Scale Effects." *American Economic Review*, 88, 1290–1310.

Segerstrom, P. S. (2000). "The Long-Run Growth Effects of R&D Subsidies." *Journal of Economic Growth*, 5, 277–305.

Segerstrom, P. S., T. Anant, and E. Dinopoulos. (1990). "A Schumpeterian Model of the Product Life Cycle." *American Economic Review*, 80, 1077–1092.

Shleifer, A. (1986). "Implementation Cycles." *Journal of Political Economy*, 94, 1163–1190.

Shleifer, A., and R. Vishny. (1999). *The Grabbing Hand: Government Pathologies and Their Cures.* Cambridge, MA: Harvard University Press.

Sidrauski, M. (1967). "Rational Choice of Patterns of Growth in a Monetary Economy." *American Economic Review*, 57, 534–544.

Solow, R. M. (1956). "A Contribution to the Theory of Economic Growth." *Quarterly Journal of Economics*, 70, 65–94.

Solow, R. (1957). "Technical Change and the Aggregate Production Function." *Review of Economics and Statistics*, 39, 312–320.

Spence, M. (1976). "Product Selection, Fixed Costs, and Monopolistic Competition." *Review of Economic Studies*, 43, 217–235.

Stadler, G. (1990). "Business Cycle Models with Endogenous Technology." *American Economic Review*, 80, 763–778.

Stern, N. (2006). *The Economics of Climate Change: The Stern Review.* Cambridge, UK: Cambridge University Press.

Stiglitz, J. E. (1969). "Distribution of Income and Wealth among Individuals." *Econometrica*, 37, 382–397.

Stiglitz, J. E. (1995). *Whither Socialism?* Cambridge, MA: MIT Press.

Stock, J. H., and M. W. Watson. (2007). *Introduction to Econometrics.* Boston: Addison Wesley Companion, Pearson.

Stockey, N. L. (1998). "Are There Limits to Growth?" *International Economic Review*, 39, 1–31.

Stokey, N. (1996). "Free Trade, Factor Returns, and Factor Accumulation." *Journal of Economic Growth*, 1, 421–447.

Sue Wing, I. (2003). "Induced Technical Change and the Cost of Climate Policy." Technical Report 102, MIT Joint Program on the Science and Policy of Global Change.

Swan, T. W. (1956). "Economic Growth and Capital Accumulation." *Economic Record*, 32, 334–361.

Tabellini, G. (2007). "Culture and Institutions: Economic Development in the Regions of Europe." Mimeo, Bocconi University.

Tirole, J. (1988). *The Theory of Industrial Organization.* Cambridge, MA: MIT Press.

Trefler, D. (2004). "The Long and Short of the Canada-U.S. Free Trade Agreement." *American Economic Review*, 94, 870–895.

Ulku, H. (2005). "An Empirical Analysis of R&D-Based Growth Models." Mimeo, Manchester University.

Uzawa, H. (1965). "Optimal Technical Change in an Aggregative Model of Economic Growth." *International Economic Review*, 6, 18–31.

Vandenbussche, J., P. Aghion, and C. Meghir. (2006). "Growth, Distance to Frontier and Composition of Human Capital." *Journal of Economic Growth*, 11, 97–127.

Ventura, J. (1997). "Growth and Interdependence." *Quarterly Journal of Economics*, 112, 57–84.

Ventura, J. (2005). "A Global View of Economic Growth." In P. Aghion and S. N. Durlauf (Eds.). *Handbook of Economic Growth.* Amsterdam: Elsevier North-Holland.

Violante, G. L. (2002). "Technological Acceleration, Skill Transferability and the Rise in Residual Inequality." *Quarterly Journal of Economics*, 117, 297–338.

Von Tunzelmann, G. N. (1978). *Steam Power and British Industrialization to 1860.* Oxford, UK: Clarendon Press.

Weil, D. (2008). *Economic Growth,* 2nd ed. Boston: Addison Wesley.

Weitzman, M. (2007). "A Review of the Stern Review on the Economics of Climate Change." *Journal of Economic Literature*, 45, 703–724.

Wooldridge, J. (2006). *Introductory Econometrics: A Modern Approach.* South Western College Publishing, Thompson Learning.

Young, A. (1991). "Learning by Doing and the Dynamic Effects of International Trade." *Quarterly Journal of Economics*, 106, 369–405.

Young, A. (1995). "The Tyranny of Numbers: Confronting the Statistical Realities of the East Asian Growth Experience." *Quarterly Journal of Economics*, 110, 641–680.

Young, A. (1998). "Growth without Scale Effects." *Journal of Political Economy*, 106, 41–63.

Young, A. A. (1928). "Increasing Returns and Economic Progress." *Economic Journal*, 38, 527–542.

Zak, P. J., and S. Knack. (2001). "Trust and Growth." *Economic Journal*, 111, 295–321.

Index

Printed in the United States
by Baker & Taylor Publisher Services